DATE DUE

Component Software

The Addison-Wesley Component Software Series

Clemens Szyperski, Series Editor

The Addison-Wesley Component Software Series collects key contributions that help architects, CTOs, project managers, technologists, component developers, component assemblers, and system integrators to embrace and understand the diverse field of component software. Taking its ingredients from the core areas of object technology, software architecture, software process management, and others, component software as a discipline is a unique synthesis. At the intersection of technology and market forces, the series covers the concepts of component software and the business case, tried and tested methods and processes, practical success stories, and lessons learned, current technologies, boundary integration technologies, leading commercial component products, and their backing business modes.

Publications in the series are selected based on both their applicability and their visionary strength, yielding both immediate and long-term value for the reader.

P. Allen, *Realizing eBusiness with Components*

C. Atkinson, *Component-based Product Line Engineering with UML*

J. Cheeseman and J. Daniels, *UML Components: A Simple Process for Specifying Component-based Software*

K. Whitehead, *Component-based Development: Principles and Planning for Business Systems*

Component Software

The Addison-Wesley Component Software Series

Clemens Szyperski, Series Editor

The Addison-Wesley Component Software Series collects key contributions that help architects, CTOs, project managers, technologists, component developers, component assemblers, and system integrators to embrace and understand the diverse field of component software. Taking its ingredients from the core areas of object technology, software architecture, software process management, and others, component software as a discipline is a unique synthesis. At the intersection of technology and market forces, the series covers the concepts of component software and the business case, tried and tested methods and processes, practical success stories, and lessons learned, current technologies, boundary integration technologies, leading commercial component products, and their backing business modes.

Publications in the series are selected based on both their applicability and their visionary strength, yielding both immediate and long-term value for the reader.

P. Allen, *Realizing eBusiness with Components*

C. Atkinson, *Component-based Product Line Engineering with UML*

J. Cheeseman and J. Daniels, *UML Components: A Simple Process for Specifying Component-based Software*

K. Whitehead, *Component-based Development: Principles and Planning for Business Systems*

Component Software

Beyond Object-Oriented Programming

Second Edition

CLEMENS SZYPERSKI

with

DOMINIK GRUNTZ and STEPHAN MURER

ACM Press
New York

An imprint of PEARSON EDUCATION

London · Boston · Indianapolis · New York · Mexico City · Toronto
Sydney · Tokyo · Singapore · Hong Kong · Cape Town · New Delhi
Madrid · Paris · Amsterdam · Munich · Milan · Stockholm

PEARSON EDUCATION LIMITED

Head Office:
Edinburgh Gate
Harlow CM20 2JE
Tel: +44 (0)1279 623623
Fax: +44 (0)1279 431059

London Office:
128 Long Acre
London WC2E 9AN
Tel: +44 (0)20 7447 2000
Fax: +44 (0)20 7447 2170

Website: www.it-minds.com
        www.awprofessional.com

© Pearson Education Limited 1999, 2002

First published in Great Britain 1999
Second edition published in Great Britain in 2002

The right of Clemens Szyperski to be identified as the Author of this Work has been asserted by him in accordance with the Copyright, Designs and Patents Act 1988.

ISBN 0-201-74572-0 2nd edition
(ISBN 0-201-17888-5 1st edition)

British Library Cataloguing in Publication Data
A CIP catalogue record for this book can be obtained from the British Library.

Library of Congress Cataloging in Publication Data
Applied for.

Many of the designations used by manufacturers and sellers to distinguish their products are claimed as trademarks. Pearson Education Limited has made every attempt to supply trademark information about manufacturers and their products mentioned in this book. A list of trademark designations and their owners appears on page xiv.

10 9 8 7 6 5 4 3 2 1

Typeset by Pantek Arts Ltd, Maidstone Kent.
Printed and bound in the United States of America

The Publishers' policy is to use paper manufactured from sustainable forests.

Contents

Component Software

Beyond Object-Oriented Programming

Second Edition

CLEMENS SZYPERSKI

with

DOMINIK GRUNTZ and STEPHAN MURER

ACM Press
New York

An imprint of PEARSON EDUCATION
London · Boston · Indianapolis · New York · Mexico City · Toronto
Sydney · Tokyo · Singapore · Hong Kong · Cape Town · New Delhi
Madrid · Paris · Amsterdam · Munich · Milan · Stockholm

PEARSON EDUCATION LIMITED

Head Office:
Edinburgh Gate
Harlow CM20 2JE
Tel: +44 (0)1279 623623
Fax: +44 (0)1279 431059

London Office:
128 Long Acre
London WC2E 9AN
Tel: +44 (0)20 7447 2000
Fax: +44 (0)20 7447 2170

Website: www.it-minds.com
         www.awprofessional.com

First published in Great Britain 1999
Second edition published in Great Britain in 2002

The right of Clemens Szyperski to be identified as the Author of this Work has been asserted by him in accordance with the Copyright, Designs and Patents Act 1988.

ISBN 0-201-74572-0 2nd edition
(ISBN 0-201-17888-5 1st edition)

British Library Cataloguing in Publication Data
A CIP catalogue record for this book can be obtained from the British Library.

Library of Congress Cataloging in Publication Data
Applied for.

10 9 8 7 6 5 4 3 2 1

Typeset by Pantek Arts Ltd, Maidstone Kent.
Printed and bound in the United States of America

The Publishers' policy is to use paper manufactured from sustainable forests.

Trademark notice

AppleScript, Cyberdog, HyperCard, Macintosh, Mac OS, **NeXT**, **OpenStep**, QuickTime and SANE are trademarks of Apple Computer, Inc., registered in US and other countries.
Tuxedo and WebLogic are registered trademarks of BEA Systems, Inc.
Borland, the Borland Logo, Delphi ™, C++Builder™, Borland® VisiBroker® - RT are trademarks or registered trademarks of Borland Software Corporation in the United States and other countries.
Jbed is a registered trademark of esmertec, inc.
CBToolkit, **CBConnector**, **ComponentBroker**, **DSOM**, PowerPC®, **REXX**, SOM®, VisualAge® and WebSphere® are trademarks of International Business Machines in the United States, other countries, or both.
Orbix, **OrbixCOMet Desktop and OrbixWeb are trademarks of IONA**.
LEGO® is a trademark of the LEGO Group.
Netscape and the Netscape N and Ship's Wheel logos are registered trademarks of Netscape Communications Corporation in the US and other countries. Netscape Communicator and Netscape Navigator are also trademarks of Netscape Communications Corporation and may be registered outside the US.
Authenticode®, ActiveX®, Visual C#™, **COM**, **COM+**, **DCOM**, **OLE**, EXCEL®, **Internet Explorer**, Microsoft® Office, Word®, Microsoft®.NET™, PowerPoint®, Visual Basic®, Visual C++®, Visual J++®, Visual Studio® and Windows® are either registered trademarks or trademarks of Microsoft Corporation in the United States and/or other countries.
BlackBox, Component Pascal, Direct-To-COM and Safer OLE are trademarks of Oberon Microsystems, Inc.
CORBA®, CWM™, IIOP®, MOF™, **OMA**, OMG Interface Definition Language (IDL)™, UML™ and XMI® are either registered trademarks or trademarks of the Object Management Group, Inc. in the United States and/or other countries.
X/Open® and OSF/1® are registered trademarks of The Open Group in the US and other countries.
R/3® is a registered trademark of SAP AG in Germany and in several other countries all over the world.
Sun, Sun Microsystems, the Sun Logo, EJB™, Enterprise JavaBeans™, J2EE™, Java™, JavaBeans™, Java Naming and Directory Interface™, **Java Naming and Discovery Service**, Java™ Servlets, JavaMail™, JavaServer Pages™, JDBC™, JNDI™, JSP™, Java™RMI, and Solaris™ are trademarks or registered trademarks of Sun Microsystems, Inc. in the United States and other countries.
Texas Instruments Composer is a trademark of Texas Instruments.
W3C® and XML are trademarks or registered trademarks of the World Wide Web Consortium, Massachusetts Institute of Technology.

Preface to the second edition

Writing a book is hard work; preparing a new edition of one's own old words is even harder in many ways. My motivation for venturing into this work is the strong and positive feedback and encouragement I received over the past years from so many of my readers. The first edition of this book achieved a level of worldwide recognition well beyond my hopes. Today, the topic area is prominent enough to attract many good authors to write books on the many facets of component software. Some of this work comes to my attention in its early stages, for instance when submitted to a conference where I serve on the program committee. More mature work reaches me in my function as series editor of Addison-Wesley's Component Software Series. Yet, all this is only scratching the tip of the proverbial iceberg: *much* is happening in this field at large. Any fair and complete coverage of this ballooning field is now close to impossible and I make no pretense that this second edition gets close to such coverage. Instead, I hope to include what I perceive as the major trends, both as a continuation from what I described in the first edition and also entirely new developments that have emerged since.

In its first edition, this book has been adopted as primary or recommended reading for many university courses in countries around the globe. Close to my heart is the fact that the first edition was translated into Polish – my family name is Polish – but reading it is entirely beyond my own language skills as I hardly speak two Polish words. Some of these developments are traced on a web page I maintain (there is a link from my homepage at www.research.microsoft. com/~cszypers/). Some of the problems I had reported as open in the first edition have attracted the attention of several researchers, leading to progress on several fronts: this second edition reports on some of the progress made.

Concurrent to these scientific developments, we have seen an explosive development of component software technologies. On the one hand, many technologies did not survive long after I closed the first edition in mid 1997 – OpenDoc and SOM are two visible cases; there are many others. On the other hand, many of the technologies relevant today were not even around back then. For example, Enterprise JavaBeans and Java 2 Enterprise Edition on the Java front, as well as the CORBA Component Model and CORBA 3 had yet to happen. CORBA had yet to embrace Java and J2EE had yet to embrace CORBA. COM+ had just become visible and .NET did not exist back then. XML and UML were just appearing on the radar screen, but hadn't had their over-whelming impact yet. Practically all XML-related standards (XML Schema, XML Namespaces, XPath, XLink, XPointer, XQuery, XSL, XSLT, and others) had yet to be publicized. Web Services and their supporting standards (SOAP, WSDL, UDDI, and so on) were entirely unheard of. Much of the work lead-ing to many of these had, of course, been going on behind the scenes – and for years – but it had been far too early for any useful coverage to be included in a work like this book.

At the time of writing the first edition, it had been painfully clear that for component technologies to go much further, domain-specific standards were an absolute requirement. Much has happened since, especially in connection with XML. Put under pressure by a rapidly tightening need for businesses to form business-to-business chains, and put into agreeable form by the technol-ogy-neutral and thus "harmless" XML approach, domain-specific standards are now mushrooming. Organizations such as BizTalk, DMTF, IETF, OAG, OASIS, OMG, UDDI, W3C, and WS-I rapidly build repositories of XML-based domain standards. Domain-specific organizations in many industries are adding to this gold rush. Clearly, we will soon see too many rather than too few standards in many important domains, which will undoubtedly lead to a shake-out over the coming years. (However, notice that the world seems to have an insatiable hunger for standards!)

In line with many hopeful predictions, yet still not quite as explosive as some had hoped, the market side of software components has also matured signifi-cantly since this book first appeared. There are now several companies, includ-ing ILOG and Rogue Wave Software, deriving most of their revenue from soft-ware components and several others fully focusing on making the market-side work, including ComponentSource and Flashline. The latter companies include warehousing, brokering, and mediation services that bridge supply and demand sides, just as is already well-established practice in the component worlds of other engineering disciplines.

All in all, it is now time for a second edition. The theme, the balanced and critical viewpoint (I hope), overall structure, and emphasis on foundations and principles have not changed. A myriad of detail-level improvements and cor-rections re-establish the link to this quickly evolving field. The most significant additions can be found in Part Three, covering the state-of-the art component technologies. Part Four used to be about the next generation of technologies and problems to tackle. This has now changed and offers, instead, a perspective on components meeting architecture and processes. While this has always been the main theme of the fourth part, it is now possible to draw on rich examples from current technologies rather than on speculation of what might be.

For guidance on how to read this book and on whom it addresses, consult the original preface that I retain in its entirety.

The endless struggle for perfect terminology

What is a software component? As with the first edition, this book has many pages on that fundamental question. It contains three different definitions that adopt different levels of abstraction: a first one is found at the very beginning of the original Preface; a second in Chapter 4; and a final one in Chapter 20. The existence of more than one definition in this book – and quite a few more cited from related work (see Chapter 11) – has led to some turbulence. Krzysztof Czarnecki and Ulrich Eisenecker (2000), in their excellent book *Generative Programming*, went as far as claiming that the term "component" (and thus "software component") cannot be defined – for a brief discussion see section 11.12.

I received a lot of feedback on the first edition that addressed my choice of terminology, telling me that I had overstretched certain terms. I ran into particular trouble with my use of the terms "binary form" and "no persistent state," both of which I claimed a software component had to comply with. This has led to toing and froing on various occasions, but I have ended up defending my original choice of words. Such disputes over words have led to rather productive opinion-forming exchanges over the deeper issues – the one that has run the longest and is my favorite being the "Beyond Objects" series of monthly columns in *Software Development* magazine (www.sdmagazine.com), created by Roger Smith. This series includes contributions by Grady Booch, Cris Kobryn, Bertrand Meyer, Bruce Powel Douglass, Jeff Scanlon, and me; others might chip in as the series evolves. I encourage readers to browse these columns as they are naturally closer to the pulse of time than a book can be.

New terminology in this second edition focuses on two developments – the growing importance of component deployment, and the relationship between components and services. To address the deployment process, I now distinguish deployable components (or just components) from deployed components (and, where important, the latter again from installed components). Component instances are always the result of instantiating an installed component – even if installed on the fly. Services are different from components in that they require a service provider. A service is an instance-level concept – where such instances can be component instances. These instances are "live" and thus require grounding in concrete hardware, software, and organizational infrastructure. The term "service" is unfortunately even more overloaded than the term "component." I did not try to rename the many things called service throughout the book, following the many established usages of this word. Instead, I use the term "web service" when referring to a service that is concretely provided, ultimately by some organization (or individual). This convention isn't strictly accurate, as non-web services can have the same properties, but trying to establish an entirely new term, such as "provided service" seemed worse. (To be even more precise, most concrete discussion in this book is about XML web services – a subset of web services that relies on XML as the fundamental representation format.)

I have tried to improve some terminology over the first edition to minimize misunderstandings. After careful deliberation, I decided to change terms only in two cases. I avoided changes in all other cases to maintain continuity from the first edition and avoid confusion that would be caused by the many references to this book that can be found in the wider literature. (For the same reason, I also decided to leave the top-level chapter structure intact.)

The first change is from old "binary form" to new "executable form." This new term makes it much more obvious that I am after a form for components that is defined relative to some execution engine, whether this is a script interpreter, a JIT compiler, or a processor, and that I am not insisting on the binary format dictated by a particular processor or operating system. This change causes some slight friction when discussing the notions of "COM as a binary standard" and "binary release-to-release compatibility." I retained the use of "binary" in these widely established cases. The new term is also somewhat too specific in that a software component also contains metadata and resources (immutable data), none of which are executable in a strict sense, but then neither are they necessarily binary. (For completeness, a degenerate component might contain nothing but such non-executable items. Other authors have thus opted for "machine interpretable.") Finally, there is a danger that some might interpret executable as meaning "must have a main() entry point," which clearly isn't intended. With terminology it is impossible to win.

The second change is from old "no persistent state" to new "no observable state." This addresses a common confusion, that persistence in the sense of external stable storage is somehow involved here, which wasn't the intention. Another common confusion cannot be addressed by simple terminology change. This is that whenever I say "component" (or, more precisely, "software component") I am not referring to object-like instances, but, rather, to notions that are more stable across time and space, such as classes, modules, or immutable prototype objects. Components are the units of deployment and, often, components contain classes or other means to create regular instances (objects). I am not, in general, worried about stateful objects, but merely exclude stateful components, which amounts to excluding the observable use of global variables (aka static variables). Occasionally it is appropriate to use such variables for caching purposes – thus the restricted exclusion of an observable state only. Much of this confusion has been triggered by the discussion of whether or not to support objects that carry state across transactional session boundaries in systems such as COM+ or EJB (EJB does allow such objects; COM+ does not.) As should be clear by now, such "stateful objects" and the claim that software components have no (observable) state have nothing to do with each other.

Updated statement and time stamp

I completed the second edition in the first half of 2002 – after a lengthy journey of well over a year's duration. I wish to acknowledge that I have added yet another bias to my list of biases – this time by joining Microsoft Research in 1999. While I hope that I succeeded in retaining the balance of my original work, I certainly understand if readers are more skeptical about this than they were before this development. After all, I am now employed by one of the primary parties involved, rather than being an academic observer with a hand in a small Swiss company alone (a role that I happily still retain). However, this book should certainly not be seen as necessarily coinciding with the views of Microsoft. Some may sense that I am overly or prematurely enthusiastic about .NET or web services, but I gave the same benefit of the doubt to then-young Java (JavaBeans, for instance, emerged while I was working on the first edition) and today I am giving it to the CORBA Component Model.

To offset such skepticism, I invited Dominik Gruntz to carefully review and contribute to the core chapter on Java and Stephan Murer to do the same for the core chapter on OMG standards and technologies. Both are long-standing friends who had already helped with their comments on the draft of the first edition. I am most grateful to them both for accepting my invitation and helping me to uphold the spirit of this book into its second edition. I would like to thank Christian Becker, Bill Councill, Scott Crawford, George Heineman, and an anonymous reviewer for reviewing the entire draft and providing many useful comments and suggestions. Hans Jonkers and Ron Kay provided further comments on the basis of the first edition. Alistair Barros drew on his extensive experience and helped with many details regarding EJB servers.

Any remaining mistakes and possibly undue bias are of course mine.

Clemens Szyperski
Redmond, May 2002

Preface

(The following preface remains unedited from the first edition. References to "recent" developments should be seen from a historic perspective in our fast-moving world.)

Software components enable practical reuse of software "parts" and amortization of investments over multiple applications. There are other units of reuse, such as source code libraries, designs, or architectures. Therefore, to be specific, *software components are binary units of independent production, acquisition, and deployment that interact to form a functioning system.* Insisting on independence and binary form is essential to allow for multiple independent vendors and robust integration.

Building new solutions by combining bought and made components improves quality and supports rapid development, leading to a shorter time to market. At the same time, nimble adaptation to changing requirements can be achieved by investing only in key changes of a component-based solution, rather than undertaking a major release change.

For these reasons, component technology is expected by many to be *the* cornerstone of software in the years to come. There exists at least one strong indicator: the number of articles and trivia published on these matters grows exponentially. Software component technology is one of the most sought-after and at the same time least-understood topics in the software field. As early as 1968, Doug McIlroy predicted that mass-produced components would end the so-called software crisis (Naur and Randall, 1969). With component technology just on the verge of success in 1997, this is a 30-year suspense story.

Software components are clearly not just another fad – the use of components is a law of nature in any mature engineering discipline. It is sometimes claimed that software is too flexible to create components; this is not an argument but an indication of immaturity of the discipline. In the first place, component markets have yet to form and thus many components still need to be custom-made. Introduction of component software principles at such an early stage means: preparing for future markets.

Even in a pre-market stage component software offers substantial software engineering benefits. Component software needs modularity of requirements, architectures, designs, and implementations. Component software thus encourages the move from the current huge monolithic systems to modular structures that offer the benefits of enhanced adaptability, scalability, and maintainability. Once a system is modularized into components, there is much less need for major release changes and the resulting "upgrade treadmill" of entire systems.

Once component markets form, component software promises another advantage: multiplication of investment and innovation. Naturally, this multiplier effect, caused by combining bought and custom-made components, can only take effect when a critical mass is reached – that is, a viable market has formed. For components to be multipliers, there needs to be a competitive market that continually pushes the envelope – that is, it continually improves cost–performance ratios. However, creating and sustaining a market is quite a separate problem from mastering component technology. It is this combination of technical and economic factors that is unique to components.

It is indeed the interplay of technology and market strategies that is finally helping components to reach their long-expected role. However, it would be unfair to say that technically this has been possible since the early days of objects. After all, objects have been around for a long time: Simula's objects, for example, date back to 1969. The second driving force behind the current component revolution is a series of technological breakthroughs. One of the earliest was the development at Xerox PARC and at NeXT in the late 1980s. The first approach that successfully created a substantial market came in 1992 with Microsoft's Visual Basic and its components (VBXs). In the enterprise arena, OMG's CORBA 2.0 followed in mid-1995. The growing popularity of distribution and the internet led to very recent developments, including Microsoft's DCOM (distributed component object model) and ActiveX, Sun's Java and its JavaBeans, the Java component standard.

There is one technical issue that turned out to be a major stumbling block on the way to software component technology. The problem is the widespread misconception of what the competing key technologies have to offer and where exactly they differ. In the heat of the debate, few unbiased comparisons are made. It is a technical issue, because it is all about technology and its alleged potential. However, it is just as much a social or societal issue. In many cases, the problems start with a confusion of fundamental terminology. While distribution, objects, and components really are three orthogonal concepts, all combinations of these terms can be found in a confusing variety of usages. For example, distributed objects can be, but do not have to be, based on components – and components can, but do not have to, support objects or distribution.

The early acceptance of new technologies (and adoption of "standards") is often driven by non-technical issues or even "self-fulfilling prophecies." Proper standardization is one way to unify approaches and broaden the basis for component technology. However, standards need to be feasible and practical. As a sanity check, it is helpful if a standard can closely follow an actual and viable implementation of the component approach. What is needed is a demonstration of the workability of the promised component properties, including a demonstration of reasonable performance and resource demands. Also, there need to be at least a few independently developed components that indeed interoperate as promised.

For a good understanding of component software, the required level of detail combined with the required breadth of coverage can become overwhelming. However, important decisions need to be made – decisions that should rest firmly on a deep understanding of the nature of component software. This book is about component software and how it affects engineering, marketing, and deployment of software. It is about the underlying concepts, the currently materializing technologies, and the first stories of success and failure. Finally, it is about people and their involvement in component technology.

This book aims to present a comprehensive and detailed account of most aspects of component software: information that should help to make well-founded decisions; information that provides a starting point for those who then want to dig deeper. In places, the level of detail intentionally goes beyond most introductory texts. However, tiring feature enumerations of current approaches have been avoided. Where relevant, features of the various approaches are drawn together and directly put into perspective. The overall breadth of the material covered in this book reflects that of the topic area; less would be too little.

Today there are three major forces in the component software arena. The Object Management Group, with its CORBA-based standards, entered from a corporate enterprise perspective. Microsoft, with its COM-based standards, entered from a desktop perspective. Finally, Sun, with its Java-based standards, entered from an internet perspective. Clearly, enterprise, desktop, and network solutions will have to converge. All three players try to embrace the other players' strongholds by expansion and by offering bridging solutions. As a result, all three players display "weak spots" that today do not withstand the "sanity check" of working and viable solutions. This book takes a strategic approach by comparing technical strengths and weaknesses of the approaches, their likely directions, and consequences for decision making.

Significant parts of this book are non-technical in nature. Again, this reflects the very nature of components – components develop their full potential only in a component market. The technical and non-technical issues are deeply intertwined and coverage of both is essential. To guide readers through the wide field of component software, this book follows an outside-in, inside-out approach. As a first step, the component market rationale is developed. Then, component technology is presented as a set of technical concepts. On the basis of this foundation, today's still evolving component approaches are put into perspective. Future directions are explained on the grounds of what is currently emerging. Finally, the market thread is picked up again, rounding off the discussions and pointing out likely future developments.

Who should read this book – and how: roadmaps

As wide as the spectrum of this book is so, it is envisioned, are the backgrounds and interests of its expected readers. To support such a variety of readers, the book is written with browsing in mind. Most chapters are relatively self-contained and so can be read in any order, although sequential reading is preferable. Where other material is tightly linked, explicit cross-references are given. For selective "fast forwards," various references to later sections are given to aid skipping to natural points of continuation. Forward references are always of an advisory nature only and can be safely ignored by those reading the book sequentially.

Professionals responsible for a company's software strategy, technology evaluation, or software architecture will find the book useful in its entirety. Reading speed may need to be adjusted according to pre-existing knowledge in the various areas covered in Parts Two and Three. The numerous discussions of relative advantages and disadvantages of methods and approaches are likely to be most useful.

Managers will find the coverage sufficiently general to enable the formation of a solid intuition, but may want to skim over some of the more detailed technical material. In the end, decisions need to be based on many more factors than just the aspects of a particular technology. To this end, the book also helps to put component technology into perspective. A suggested path through this book is Part One; Chapters 4, 8, and 11 of Part Two; Chapters 12 and 17 of Part Three; Part Five.

Developers will appreciate the same intuition-building foundation, but will also find enough detail on which to base technical decisions. In addition, developers facing multiple platforms or multiple component approaches will find the many attempts at concept unification useful. Fair technical comparison of similarities and differences is essential to develop a good understanding of the various tradeoffs involved; terminology wars are not. A suggested path through this book is Parts Two, Three, and Four, supported by Parts One and Five if market orientation is required.

Academics and students on advanced courses will find the book a useful and rich source of material. However, although it could serve as reference reading for various units, it is not a textbook. Those studying units focusing on component technology will benefit the most from reading this book, including coverage of specific component technologies such as Java or ActiveX. If the units are on software engineering, students will also benefit from the information in these pages. Finally, if the units are on advanced or comparative programming languages, students could find this book useful as they may expand to language issues in component technology. A suggested path through this book depends on the needs of the particular subject. Part Two, and in particular Chapter 4, forms a basis; Chapters 5, 6, and 7 can be included for more intensive courses or postgraduate studies. The remaining chapters of Part Two can be included selectively. Part Three offers a rich selection of detailed information on current technology. Part

Four explores current developments. Parts One and Five may be of interest for readers on courses with an organizational or market perspective.

Statement and time stamp

I completed this book in the first half of 1997. In a rapidly emerging and changing field, a certain part of the material is likely to be out of date soon. I tried to avoid covering the obviously volatile too deeply and, instead, aimed at clear accounts of the underlying concepts and approaches. For concreteness, I nevertheless included many technical details. I am a co-founder of Oberon microsystems, Inc., Zurich (founded in 1993), one of the first companies to focus fully on component software. In addition to carefully introducing and comparing the main players, I frequently drew on Oberon microsystems' products for leading-edge examples and comparison. These include the programming language Component Pascal, the BlackBox component framework and builder, and the component-oriented real-time operating system Portos with its development system Denia. The choice of these examples clearly reflects my involvement in their development, as well as my active use of several of these tools in university courses. Despite this personal bias, I aimed at a fair positioning of all the approaches I covered.

This book in its present form would not have been possible without the help of many who were willing to read early drafts and supported me with their scrutiny and richness of comments and ideas. In particular, I would like to thank Cuno Pfister, who reviewed the entire draft, some parts in several revisions, and provided numerous comments and suggestions. Daniel Duffy, Erich Gamma, Robert Griesemer, Stephan Murer, Tobias Murer, Wolfgang Pree, and Paul Roe also commented on the entire draft. Dominik Gruntz, Wolfgang Weck, and Alan Wills provided deep and important comments on selected chapters. Marc Brandis, Bert Fitié, John Gough, and Martin Odersky provided further important comments. Remaining mistakes and oversights are of course mine.

Clemens Szyperski
Brisbane, June 1997

About the author

Clemens Szyperski joined Microsoft Research at its Redmond, Washington, facility in 1999 to continue his work on component software. He is currently also an Adjunct Professor of the Faculty of Information Technology at the Queensland University of Technology (QUT), Brisbane, Australia, where he was previously an Associate Professor. He joined the faculty in 1994 and received tenure in 1997. From 1995 to 1999 he has been director of the Programming Languages and Systems Research Centre at QUT.

From 1992 to 1993 he held a Postdoctoral Fellowship from the International Computer Science Institute (ICSI) at the University of California at Berkeley. At ICSI he worked in the groups of Professor Jerome Feldman (Sather language) and Professor Domenico Ferrari (Tenet communication suite with guaranteed Quality of Service).

In 1992, Clemens received his PhD in Computer Science from the Swiss Federal Institute of Technology (ETH), Zurich, Switzerland, where he designed and implemented the extensible operating system Ethos under the supervision of Professor Niklaus Wirth and Professor Hanspeter Mössenböck. In 1987, he received a degree in Electrical Engineering/Computer Engineering from the Aachen University of Technology (RWTH), Germany. Ever since joining ETH in 1987, his work has been heavily influenced by the work of Professor Wirth and Professor Jürg Gutknecht on the Oberon language and system.

In 1993, he co-founded Oberon microsystems, Inc., developer of BlackBox Component Builder, first marketed in 1994 and one of the first development environments and component frameworks designed specifically for component-oriented programming projects. In 1997, Oberon microsystems released the new component-oriented programming language Component Pascal. He was a key contributor to both BlackBox and Component Pascal. In 2000, Professor John Gough, Dean of Information Technology at QUT, ported Component Pascal to the Microsoft .NET common language runtime.

In 1999, Oberon microsystems spun out a new company, esmertec, inc., that took the hard realtime operating system then called Portos and turned it into JBed, an industry-leading hard realtime operating system for Java in embedded systems.

Clemens has been a consultant to major international corporations. He served as an assessor and reviewer for Australian, Canadian, Irish, and US federal funding agencies and for learned journals across the globe. He served as a member of program and organizing committees of numerous events, including ECOOP, ICSE, and OOPSLA conferences. He has published numerous papers and articles, several books, and frequently presents at international events.

About the contributing authors

Dominik Gruntz is professor for software architecture and design at the Northwestern Switzerland University of Applied Sciences, Aargau, Switzerland. He runs courses on distributed component software and framework design. He is a member of the enterprise computing research group and leads the mobile enterprise project. Dominik also has a lectureship at the Swiss Federal Institute of Technology (ETH) in Zurich.

Dominik has deep knowledge of the Java platform (from J2ME to J2EE) and is a Sun Certified Programmer for the Java 2 Platform. Besides this focus, he is also interested in the .NET platform and currently writing a book on C$^\#$.

From 1995 to 1999, Dominik worked at Oberon microsystems, Inc., where he contributed to the BlackBox Component Framework. At that time he also examined the Microsoft Component Object Model (COM) and taught this technology in industry courses and at conferences.

Dominik has a masters and a Ph.D. in Computer Science from ETH Zurich.

Stephan Murer is the Chief Information Systems Architect of Crédit Suisse Financial Services, a major financial services company based in Zurich. He is responsible for the overall design of all Crédit Suisse information systems. He has been with Crédit Suisse since 1994 as head of Advanced Technologies and project manager IT Strategy, among other positions. Besides his line function, Stephan is also a member of the investment committee of Innoventure, Crédit Suisse's venture capital company, where he helps develop startup companies in Switzerland.

From 1992 to 1994, he was a postdoctoral researcher at the International Computer Science Institute at the University of California in Berkeley. In Berkeley, Stephan worked in Professor Jerome Feldman's group on the Sather programming language and extensions to it for parallel computing.

In 1992, he received his Ph.D. from the Swiss Federal Institute of Technology (ETH) in Zurich. He worked on the ADAM parallel computer architecture, a project conducted at the Laboratory of Computer Engineering and Networks under the supervision of Professor Albert Kündig. In 1988 he received his degree in Computer Science from the ETH Zurich.

About the contributing authors

Dominik Gruntz is professor for software architecture and design at the Northwestern Switzerland University of Applied Sciences, Aargau, Switzerland. He runs courses on distributed component software and framework design. He is a member of the enterprise computing research group and leads the mobile enterprise project. Dominik also has a lectureship at the Swiss Federal Institute of Technology (ETH) in Zurich.

Dominik has deep knowledge of the Java platform (from J2ME to J2EE) and is a Sun Certified Programmer for the Java 2 Platform. Besides this focus, he is also interested in the .NET platform and currently writing a book on C#.

From 1995 to 1999, Dominik worked at Oberon microsystems, Inc., where he contributed to the BlackBox Component Framework. At that time he also examined the Microsoft Component Object Model (COM) and taught this technology in industry courses and at conferences.

Dominik has a masters and a Ph.D. in Computer Science from ETH Zurich.

Stephan Murer is the Chief Information Systems Architect of Crédit Suisse Financial Services, a major financial services company based in Zurich. He is responsible for the overall design of all Crédit Suisse information systems. He has been with Crédit Suisse since 1994 as head of Advanced Technologies and project manager IT Strategy, among other positions. Besides his line function, Stephan is also a member of the investment committee of Innoventure, Crédit Suisse's venture capital company, where he helps develop startup companies in Switzerland.

From 1992 to 1994, he was a postdoctoral researcher at the International Computer Science Institute at the University of California in Berkeley. In Berkeley, Stephan worked in Professor Jerome Feldman's group on the Sather programming language and extensions to it for parallel computing.

In 1992, he received his Ph.D. from the Swiss Federal Institute of Technology (ETH) in Zurich. He worked on the ADAM parallel computer architecture, a project conducted at the Laboratory of Computer Engineering and Networks under the supervision of Professor Albert Kündig. In 1988 he received his degree in Computer Science from the ETH Zurich.

Acknowledgements

We are grateful to the following for permission to reproduce copyright material:

Figures 13.4, 13.6 and 13.7 based on figures from *CORBA 3: Fundamentals and Programming, 2nd Edition* by John Siegel, PhD. Copyright © 2000 Object Management Group. All rights reserved. Reproduced here by permission of Wiley Publishing, Inc.; Figure 14.9 after figure in *Enterprise JavaBeans, 3rd Edition*, O'Reilly and Associates, Inc. (Monson-Haefel, R. 2001).

Extract from Booch, *Software Components with Ada: Structures, Tools and Subsystems*, pg. 7, © 1987, Benjamin/Cummings Publishing Company, Inc. Reprinted by permission of Pearson Education, Inc.; Extract from A plea for graybox components. Workshop on Foundations of Component-Based Systems, Zürich *Technical Report No. 122*, published by Turku Centre for Computer Science, reprinted by permission of the authors (Büchi, M. and Weck, W. 1997); Extracts and abridged extracts from *Generative Programming: Methods, Tools and Applications* by Czarnecki/Eisenecker, © 2000. Reprinted by permission of Pearson Education, Inc., Upper Saddle River, NJ; Extract from *Objects, Components and Frameworks with UML* by D'Souza/Wills, © 1999. Reprinted by permission of Pearson Education, Inc., Upper Saddle River, NJ; Extract and an abridged extract from *Design Patterns: Elements of Reusable Object-Oriented Software* by Gamma et al, © 1995. Reprinted by permission of Pearson Education, Inc., Upper Saddle River, NJ; Extracts from *Component-Based Software Engineering* by Heinemann et al, © 2001. Reprinted by permission of Pearson Education, Inc., Upper Saddle River, NJ; Extracts and an abridged extract from *Business Component Factory* by Peter Herzum and Oliver Sims. Copyright © 1999 Wiley Publishing, Inc. All rights reserved. Reproduced here by permission of Wiley Publishing, Inc.; Extract from *Meta-object Facility (MOF), version 1.3*, Object Management Group, Inc. (OMG 2000); Extracts from *The Essential Distributed Objects Survival Guide* by Robert Orfali, Dan Harkey and Jeri Edwards. Copyright © 1995 Wiley Publishing, Inc. All rights reserved. Reproduced here by permission of Wiley Publishing, Inc.; Extract from *Distributed Objects – Creating the Virtual Mainframe*, Ovum (Ring, K. and Carnelly, P. 1995); Extracts from *Software Engineering with Reusable Components*, Springer-Verlag GmbH and Co. KG (Sametinger, J. 1997); Extract from Component-oriented programming: a refined variation on object-oriented programming in *The Oberon Tribune*, 1(2), December, Oberon Microsystems, Inc. (Szyperksi, C. 1995); Extract from Workshop on Component-Oriented Programming, Summary in *Special Issues in Object-Oriented Programming – ECCOP '96 Workshop Reader* edited by M. Mühlhäuser, dpunkt verlag GmbH (Szyperski, C. and Pfister, C. 1997).

In some instances we have been unable to trace the owners of copyright material, and we would appreciate any information that would enable us to do so.

Motivation – components and markets

Part One covers the motivations and fundamental non-technical underpinnings of component software technology in a market context. Chapter 1 explains what is meant by the terms "software component" and "component software." The important benefits of component software are outlined and the peculiar nature of software is explored to compare component software with component approaches in other engineering disciplines. Finally, some early and recent component success stories are analyzed briefly. Chapter 2 links component technology to markets and shows market development as seen by analysts and statisticians over the years, including some forecasts as to how component technology is expected to develop over the coming years. Chapter 3 covers the notion of standards, which is all-important for any component approach. A brief clarification of terms can be found in the Glossary (at the end of the book).

CHAPTER ONE

Introduction

This chapter defines the term software component and summarizes the key arguments in favor of component software. Components are well established in all other engineering disciplines, but, until the 1990s, were unsuccessful in the world of software. The reasons behind this failure can be linked to the particular nature of software. The chapter concludes with a discussion of the nature of software, its consequences for component software, and lessons learned from successful and unsuccessful approaches.

1.1 Components are for composition

One thing can be stated with certainty: components are for composition. *Nomen est omen*. (Literally, "the name is a sign"; usually interpreted as: one's name predicts one's fate.) Composition enables prefabricated "things" to be reused by rearranging them in ever-new composites. Beyond this trivial observation, much is unclear. Are most current software abstractions not designed for composition as well? What about reusable parts of designs or architectures? Is reuse not the driving factor behind most of these compositional abstractions?

Reuse is a very broad term covering the general concept of a reusable asset. Such assets can be arbitrary descriptions capturing the results of a design effort. Descriptions themselves normally depend on other, more detailed and more specialized descriptions. To become a reusable asset, it is not enough to start with a monolithic design of a complete solution and then partition it into fragments. The likely benefits of doing so are minimal. Instead, descriptions have to be carefully generalized to allow for reuse in a sufficient number of different contexts. Overgeneralization has to be avoided to keep the descriptions nimble and lightweight enough for actual reuse to remain practicable. Descriptions in this sense are sometimes called components (Sametinger, 1997).

This book is not about reuse in general, but about the use of software components. To be specific, for the purposes of this book, software components are executable units of independent production, acquisition, and deployment that can be composed into a functioning system. To enable composition, a software component adheres to a particular component model and targets a particular component platform. (The details will be explored later; also, there are several other attempts at defining this and related concepts; see Chapter 11.) Composite systems composed of software components are called component software. The requirement for independence and executable form rules out many software abstractions, such as type declarations, C macros, C^{++} templates, or Smalltalk blocks. Other abstractions, such as procedures, classes, modules, or even entire applications, could form components, as long as they are in an executable form that remains composable. Indeed, procedural libraries are the oldest example of software components. Insisting on potential independence and executable form is essential in order to allow for multiple independent vendors, independent development, and robust integration. These issues are therefore covered in great detail in this book.

What is the motive for producing, distributing, buying, or using software components? What are the benefits of component software? The simplest answer is that components are the way to go because all other engineering disciplines introduced components as they became mature – and still use them. Shortly after the term software crisis was coined, the solution to the often-cited crisis was also envisioned: software integrated circuits (ICs) (McIlroy, 1968; Cox, 1990)! Since then, for 30 years, people have wondered why this intuitive idea never truly came to fruition.

1.2 Components – custom-made versus standard software

In the following discussions it is assumed that component software technology is available. The question addressed in this section is "What are the benefits of using components?"

Traditional software development can broadly be divided into two camps. At one extreme, a project is developed entirely from scratch, with the help of only programming tools and libraries. At the other extreme, everything is "outsourced" – in other words, standard software is bought and parametrized to provide a solution that is "close enough" to what is needed. Full custom-made software has a significant advantage (when it works): it can be optimally adapted to the user's business model and can take advantage of any in-house proprietary knowledge or practices. Hence, custom-made software can provide the competitive edge in the information age – if it works.

Custom-made software also has severe disadvantages, even if it does work. Production from scratch is a very expensive undertaking. Suboptimal solutions in all but the local areas of expertise are likely. Maintenance and "chasing" of the state-of-the-art, such as incorporating web access, can become a major burden. Interoperability requirements further the burden, with other in-house systems and, more critically, also with business partners and customers. As a result, most large projects fail partially or completely, leading to a substantial risk. Also, in a world of rapidly changing business requirements, custom-made software is often too late – too late to be productive before becoming obsolete.

With all these guaranteed disadvantages in mind, which are offset by only potential advantages, the major trend toward "outsourcing" in the industry is understandable. Production of custom-made software is outsourced under fixed-price contracts to limit the financial risk. To cover the time-to-market risk, there is a strong trend toward using standard software – that is, software that is only slightly adjusted to actual needs. The burden of maintenance, product evolution, and interoperability is left to the vendor of the standard package. What remains is to carry over parametrization and configuration detail when moving to the next release – still a substantial effort, but unavoidable in a world of change.

What, then, is wrong with standard software? Several things. First, standard software may necessitate a greater or lesser reorganization of the business processes affected. Although business process re-engineering can be a very worthwhile undertaking, it should be done for its own sake rather than to make the best of suboptimally fitting standard software. Second, standard software is a standard: competitors have it as well and no competitive edge can possibly be achieved by using it (except by using it extraordinarily well). In any case, this is acceptable only when tight regulations eliminate competitive advantages. Third, as standard software is not under local control, it is not nimble enough to adapt quickly to changing needs.

Here is an example of standard software forcing its footprint on to a large and well-established organization. In 1996, Australia Post decided to use SAP's R/3 integrated solution. With R/3, Australia Post can keep track of each individual transaction, down to the sale of a single stamp. Australia Post is a large organization with a federated structure; each Australian state has its own head office reporting to the central head office.

Traditionally, state head offices reported on the basis of summaries and accounts "in-the-large." For example, detailed sales figures for each branch office were not passed on beyond the state head office. R/3, however, supports only a monotonic hierarchy of access authorizations. It is not possible to grant the national head office access to the accounts in-the-large without also granting access to every individual transaction. This was disturbing news for state head offices as their tradition of relative autonomy in making local decisions was undermined. Indeed, the strictly hierarchical business model enforced by R/3 clashed with the concept of a federated organization that delegates much responsibility and authority to its members – in this case, the state posts. SAP's comment, when asked if this aspect of R/3 could be changed, was: "Our systems implement best practice – why would you want to deviate from that?" The key point is that adoption of a standard solution may force drastic changes on the culture and operation of an organization.

With only two poles available, custom-made software loses out to a great extent. Standard packages create a level playing field and a necessary competitive edge has to come from other areas. Increasingly, software services are seen as something that is necessary simply to survive. Clearly, this is far from ideal when information and information processing have a great effect on most businesses and even define many of the newer ones.

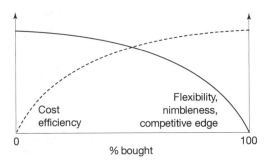

Figure 1.1 Spectrum between make-all and buy-all.

The concept of component software represents a middle path that could solve this problem. Although each bought component is a standardized product, with all the attached advantages, the process of component assembly allows the opportunity for significant customization. It is likely that components of different qualities (level of performance, resource efficiency, robustness, degree of certification, and so on) will be available at different prices. It is thus possible to set individual priorities when assembling based on a fixed budget. In addition, some individual components can be custom-made to suit specific requirements or to foster strategic advantages. Figure 1.1 illustrates some of the tradeoffs brought about by the spectrum of possibilities opened up by component software.

The figure is in no way quantitative, and the actual shape of the two curves is somewhat arbitrary. Intuitively, however, it is clear that non-linear effects will be observed when approaching the extremes. For example, at the left end of the scale, when everything is custom-made, flexibility has no inherent limits, but cost efficiency plummets.

Component software also puts an end to the age-old problem of massive upgrade cycles. Traditional fully integrated solutions required periodic upgrading. Usually this was a painful process of migrating old databases, ensuring upwards compatibility, retraining staff, buying more powerful hardware, and so on. In a component-based solution, evolution replaces revolution, and individual upgrading of components as needed and "out of phase" can allow for much smoother operations. Obviously, this requires a different way of managing services, but the potential gains are immense.

1.3   Inevitability of components

Developing excellent component technology does not suffice to establish a market. The discipline is full of examples of technically superior products that failed to capture sufficiently large markets. Besides technical superiority, a component approach needs critical mass to take off. A component approach gains

critical mass if the offered components are of sufficient variety and quality, there is an obvious benefit of using the components, and the offering is backed by sufficiently strong sources or sufficiently many second sources. Once critical mass is reached in a market segment, use of components in that segment quickly becomes inevitable. A "vortex" forms that pulls in traditional solutions in the area.

Not using available components requires reinvention of solutions. This can only be justified when the made solution is greatly superior to the buyable alternatives. Also, in a competitive market, components will improve in quality much faster than "hand-crafted" solutions. The result is the above-mentioned vortex: it becomes increasingly difficult to escape from using components.

As long as all solutions to problems are created from scratch, growth can be at most linear. As components act as multipliers in a market, growth can become exponential. In other words, a product that utilizes components benefits from the combined productivity and innovation of all component vendors. The component vendors are focused, supply many different customers, and are thus able to perfect their components rapidly. Therefore, even where an organization manages to sustain its proprietary technology, its relative market share will quickly dwindle in a market rapidly dominated by component technology. Avoiding the proximity of a component vortex promises calm waters but also eliminates the impulse that can be gained from the mighty pull of the vortex.

Preparedness for an emerging component market can be the deciding success factor for a company approaching such a vortex. Insistence on proprietary approaches can be catastrophic. Part of being prepared is the adoption of software engineering approaches that are component friendly – that is, they support modularity of requirements, architectures, designs, and implementations. Preparing for components thus leads to substantial advantages as a result of a better software engineering process, even if component markets are still seen as beyond the "planning horizon."

Out of preparedness a more proactive role can be developed. The first organization to create a convincing set of components for a certain market segment can set standards and shape the then emerging market to its own advantage. Instead of waiting for others or claiming that it is unlikely that, in a particular domain, a component market will ever form, stronger organizations may want to take the lead. An interesting example was the move by Sun to make its Solaris operating system "modular" (Wirthman, 1997). Instead of offering a collection of specialized operating systems, Sun factored Solaris into modules that can be combined according to needs (Mauro and McDougall, 2001). In a similar fashion, Microsoft factored Windows CE and provides means to custom-assemble a Windows CE version for a particular device to trim resource consumption and match device capabilities and purpose (Boling, 2001; Wilson and Havewala, 2001). These are first steps. If Sun or Microsoft allowed third-party modules (beyond device drivers), then this could well create a component market supporting the creation of highly customized operating infrastructure for specialized devices and appliances.

1.4   The nature of software and deployable entities

Software components were initially considered to be analogous to hardware components in general and to integrated circuits in particular. Thus, the term software IC became fashionable. Other related notions followed, such as software bus and software backplane (Figure 1.2).

Also popular is the analogy between software components and components of stereo equipment. More far fetched are analogies with the fields of mechanical and civil engineering – gith gears, nuts, and bolts, for example. However, comparisons did not stop at engineering disciplines and continued on into areas as extreme as the world of toys. The Lego block model of object technology was conceived but has also been strongly criticized. These analogies helped to sell the idea of software components by referring to other disciplines and areas in which component technology has been in use for some time and had begun to fulfill its promises.

All the analogies tend to give the impression that the whole world, with the one exception of software technology, is already component oriented! Thus, it ought to be possible – if not straightforward – to follow the analogies and introduce components to software as well. This did not happen for most of the industry, and for good reason. None of the analogies aids understanding of the true nature of software.

Software is different from products in all other engineering disciplines (for a comprehensive analysis, see Messerschmitt and Szyperski, 2002). Rather than delivering a final product, delivery of software means delivering the blueprints for products. Computers can be seen as fully automatic factories that accept such blueprints and instantiate them. Special measures must be taken to prevent repeated instantiation – the normal case is that a computer can instantiate delivered software as often as required. The term software IC and the associated analogy thus fail to capture one of the most distinctive aspects of software as a metaproduct. It is important to remember that it is these metaproducts that are actually deployed when acquiring software. The same holds true for software components.

It is as important to distinguish between software and its instances as it is to distinguish between blueprints and products, between plans and a building, or between beings and their genes (between phenotypes and genotypes). Whereas such lines are clearly drawn in other engineering disciplines, software seems "soft" enough to tolerate a confusion of these matters.

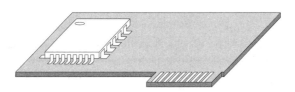

Figure 1.2 The software IC connected to a software bus.

There has been confusion about abstractions and instances since entity–relationship modeling (this was pointed out to the author by Alan Wills). To reintroduce a distinction that should have been in place from the beginning, phrases such as "entity occurrence" and "entity definition" are used. This confusion is even encouraged in the world of object technology. The corresponding distinction between class and object is frequently omitted, although there is occasional clarification of something as an "object instance" or an "object class." The established practice of not distinguishing between objects and classes leads the way, so the large number of nebulous publications on objects is not astonishing. To take an arbitrary example, consider the following astounding quotation (Cheung, 1996, p. 72):

"The port class has 1024 virtual-circuit classes."

The article refers to an object model diagram as defined by the object modeling technique (OMT) (Rumbaugh *et al.*, 1991). A small excerpt of the diagram is shown in Figure 1.3.

What the author meant was: "The port object has 1024 virtual-circuit objects." There is nothing wrong with the cited article. The most likely explanation is that this "glitch" was the result of an attempt by the editor to introduce sharpness of terms and not call everything an object. This sort of mistake is easy to make – OMT object model diagrams describe the static relations of classes, but, when annotations refer to numbers of partners in a relation class, instances (objects) are meant. The UML diagrams and notation used throughout this book are much clearer in that they advocate a clear distinction between objects and classes.

The confusion between objects and classes is closely related to the nature of software. For example, both the plan of a building and the building itself can be modeled as objects. At the same time, the plan is the "class" of the building. There is nothing wrong with this, as long as the two kinds of objects are kept apart. In the world of logic, but also in database theory, this is called stratification – that is, introduction and maintenance of strata or levels of organization. Construction (and breach) of such layers has to be based on deep understanding. Some might argue that this lighthearted way of dealing

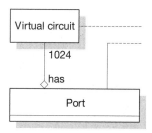

Figure 1.3 OMT object model with quantified "has" relationship. (After Rumbaugh, J., Blaha, M., Lorenson, W., Eddy, F., and Premerlani, W. (1991) *Object-Oriented Modelling and Design.* Prentice Hall, Englewood Cliffs, NJ.)

with object-oriented (OO) terminology had to be expected. After all, "object" is one of the most indefinite and imprecise terms that people could possibly use to name a concept. It seems fairly objective to say that.

To understand why it is so important to differentiate between plans and instances, it is useful to take a brief look at some of the ramifications of delivering plans rather than instances. Plans can be parametrized, applied recursively, scaled, and instantiated any number of times. None of this is possible with actual instances. As, with software, it is the plans that are delivered, instances can be of different shapes by using different parametrizations of the plan. In other words, software is a generic metaproduct that can be used to create entire families of instances.

If analogies to components in other engineering disciplines break down, then what about mathematics? Although defended by some, the purely mathematical approach fails exactly where the engineering analogies help – and vice versa. Mathematics and logic draw their strength from the isolation of aspects, their orthogonal treatment, and their static capturing. These are excellent tools to understand the software concepts of uniformity of resources, arbitrary copying, recursive nesting, parametrization, or configuration. However, mathematical modeling fails to capture the engineering and market aspects of component technology – that is, the need to combine all facets, functional and extra-functional, into one interacting whole, forming a viable product.

In conclusion, software technology is an engineering discipline in its own right, with its own principles and laws. Analogies with other engineering disciplines help us to understand certain requirements, such as those of proper interaction with markets and consideration of complex feature interactions. At the same time, these analogies break down quickly when going into technical detail. Deriving software architecture (component-oriented or not) by analogy with approaches in other disciplines is downright dangerous. The distinguishing properties of software are of a mathematical rather than a physical nature. However, placing emphasis solely on the mathematical underpinning is never enough to carry any engineering discipline. In particular, from a purely formal point of view, there is nothing that could be done with components that could not be done without them. The differences are concepts such as reuse, time to market, quality, and viability. All of these are of a non-mathematical nature – and value. Mathematics is not goal-driven, whereas engineering is: the goal is to create products.

1.5   Components are units of deployment

A software component is what is actually deployed – as an isolatable part of a system – in a component-based approach. Contrary to frequent claims, objects are almost never sold, bought, or deployed. The unit of deployment is something rather more static, such as a class, or, more likely, a set or framework of classes, compiled and linked into some package. Objects that logically form parts of component "instances" are instantiated as needed, based on the classes that have been deployed with a component. Although a component can be a single class, it is more likely to be a collection of classes, sometimes called a module. (Components have further characteristics that distinguish them from modules – details can be found in section 20.3.) Components as a whole are thus not normally instantiated. Also, a component could just as well use some totally different implementation technology, such as pure functions or assembly language, and look not at all object-oriented from the inside (Udell, 1994):

> "Object orientation has failed but component software is succeeding."

If classes are so similar to components, why did object technology not succeed in establishing significant component markets? The answers are manifold. First, the definition of objects is purely technical – briefly, encapsulation of state and behavior, polymorphism, and inheritance. The definition does not include notions of independence or late composition. Although such conditions can be added (Chapter 4, section 4.1), their lack has led to the current situation in which object technology is mostly used to construct monolithic applications.

Second, object technology tends largely to ignore the aspects of economies and markets and their technical consequences. Early proponents of object orientation predicted object markets, places that would offer catalogs full of objects or, more likely, classes, class libraries, and frameworks (Cox, 1990). The opposite has in fact occurred (Nierstrasz, 1991). Today we have only a small number of such sources. Most of them are driven by vendors that provide such semifinished software products to sell something else. The classic Microsoft Foundation Classes (MFC) is a good example. MFC primarily serves as a vehicle to simplify and unify programming for Microsoft's operating systems, component model, and application environments. There is no doubt that the vision of object markets did not happen. On the contrary, most of the few early component success stories were not even object-oriented, although some are object-based. (The relatively successful class libraries and frameworks are not software components in the strict sense used here.)

More recently, and based on true component technologies, successful markets began forming. Companies such as ComponentSource.com or Flashline.com sell thousands of ready-made components, mostly in the COM and Java categories, but VCL (a Delphi/C^{++} Builder technology by Borland) and .NET components are also present. CORBA components, however, are essentially non-existent on these markets. Companies such as ILOG and Rogue Wave Software generate substantial revenues by focusing on the production of components. ILOG approached $80 million in revenues in its fiscal year ending mid 2001. ILOG focuses on C, C^{++}, and Java components for simulation/optimization, visual presentation, and business rule-based applications.

To some extent, the misprediction of object markets is understandable. For a technologist, markets are too easily considered marginal, as something left for others to worry about once the technological problems have been solved. However, components are as much about the potential of technology as they are about technology. The additional investment required to produce components – rather than fully specialized solutions – can only be justified if the return on investment follows.

Typically, a component has to have a sufficiently large number of uses, and therefore clients, for it to be viable. As a rule of thumb, most components need to be used three times before breaking even. That is, two separate, from-scratch development efforts are still cheaper than a single effort to produce a more generic component. Repeated use is the central idea behind the notion of "reuse." For clients to use a component instead of a specialized solution, the component needs to have substantial advantages. One advantage could be technological superiority, but other advantages are more likely to help, such as the first solution to a known open problem, broad support base, brand name, and so on. Obviously, for larger organizations, "markets" could be found in-house – interestingly, most large organizations are now organized into cost centers and selling to internal clients is not much simpler than selling to external clients.

1.6   Lessons learned

Where are the mentioned component success stories? For many years, the most popular has been Microsoft's Visual Basic. Later, successes based on Java, Enterprise JavaBeans (EJB) and COM+ have followed. However, the oldest success stories are all modern operating systems. Applications are coarse-grained components executing in the environment provided by an operating system. Interoperability between such components is as old as the sharing of file systems and common file formats, or the use of pipe-and-filter composition. Other older component examples are relational database engines and transaction-processing monitors. Further, more recent successes, using finer-grained components, are plugin architectures. These have been in widespread use since the introduction of Netscape's Navigator web browsers. One of the first successful plugin architectures was Apple's QuickTime. Plugins (under the name of "extensions") have also been cultivated in the Mac OS, where they originated from "inits," patches to the system software in ROM that are loaded at boot time. DOS terminate-and-stay-resident applications (TSRs) were of comparable nature. Active Server Pages (ASP) and Java Server Pages (JSP) architectures for web servers follow a similar approach, accepting application-specific plugins into the server to provide server-side computations and web page synthesis to service incoming web requests. Finally, modern application and integration servers around J2EE and COM+ / .NET offer refined component models that bring much-needed discipline and opportunities for component use to the complex realm of enterprise applications.

What do all the above examples have in common? In all cases there is an infrastructure providing rich foundational functionality for the addressed domain. Components can be purchased from independent providers and deployed by clients. The components provide services that are substantial enough to make duplication of their development too difficult or not cost-effective. Multiple components from different sources can coexist in the same installation. None of the named systems really shines when it comes to arbitrary combinations of components. In all cases, such combinations can lead to misbehavior. Apparently, for a working component market, it is sufficient that composability is highly likely rather than absolutely guaranteed.

Besides all this, there is another aspect that is often overlooked. In all the successful examples, components exist on a level of abstraction where they directly mean something to the deploying client. With Visual Basic, this is obvious – a control has a direct visual representation, displayable and editable properties, and has meaning that is closely attached to its appearance. With plugins, the client gains some explicable, high-level feature and the plugin itself is a user-installed and configured component.

Most objects have no meaning to clients who are not programmers. Class libraries and frameworks are typical developer tools and require highly trained and qualified programmers for their proper use. It is appropriate that component construction is left to persons of such standing. However, for components to be successful, composition and integration – that is, component assembly must not generally be confined to such a relatively small elite group. Today, there are many more authors of scripts than there are programmers. These customers are more interested in products that are obviously useful, easy to use, and can be safely mixed and matched – they are not in the least interested in whether or not the products are internally object-oriented.

Objects are rarely shaped to allow for mix-and-match composition by a third party – also known as "plug and play." Configuring and integrating an individual object into some given system is not normally possible, so objects cannot be sold independently. Frameworks – the larger units, which are sold – are even worse. Frameworks have traditionally been designed almost to exclude composition. Combining multiple traditional object-oriented frameworks is difficult, to say the least.

Taligent's CommonPoint – the best-known approach that aimed at the construction of many interoperating frameworks – failed to deliver on its promises (although other projects at Taligent did lead to the successful development of new technology). Above all, the approach was overdesigned, aiming for maximum flexibility everywhere, so even the simplest things turned out to be complex. Individual developers were responsible for relatively small parts of the system and thus naturally aimed for *the* solution. The result was an extremely large system for its time. According to a 1995 Ovum report (Ring and Carnelly, 1995), CommonPoint provided over 100 frameworks, covering about 2000 public classes, an equal number of non-public classes and 53000 methods. For comparison, Win32, the Microsoft Windows API, supports roughly 1500 calls. However, the Taligent size has been exceeded by both

Sun's Java and Microsoft's .NET frameworks. The Java 2 Standard Edition, version 1.4, comprises around 2700 classes and interfaces in about 130 packages. The Java 2 Enterprise Edition, v1.3 (which includes the Standard Edition 1.3), comprises around 3900 classes and interfaces (over 5000 when counting CORBA and Apache contributions). The first version of the Microsoft .NET Framework comprises around 4000 classes, interfaces, and types in about 70 assemblies. In comparison to these more recent frameworks, the size of the Taligent effort almost pales, yet it would be fair to observe that these later efforts learned from the Taligent attempt.

Dependencies in such a large system need to be managed carefully. However, the CommonPoint frameworks exposed far too many details and were only weakly layered. In other words, the overall architecture was underdeveloped. For the same reasons, other large industry projects have struggled before, including the major redevelopment effort at Mentor Graphics (Lakos, 1996).

A direct contributor to many of the early fiascos was the chosen implementation language, C^{++}. C^{++} does not directly support a component concept, so management of dependencies becomes difficult. For example, a fundamental mistake made at Taligent when designing CommonPoint was to assume that the C^{++} object model would be an appropriate component model, whereas in reality it is too fragile. Blackbox reuse, as introduced in later parts of the book, was neglected in preference for deep and entangled multiple inheritance hierarchies. Finally, overdesign and the C^{++} template facilities led to massive code bloat.

Merely replacing C^{++} with another, perhaps cleaner, object-oriented programming language does not solve the problem. A component-oriented approach goes much deeper than simply picking the right language. For example, while some fragilities of C^{++} are avoided in the design of Java and even more in the design of $C^{\#}$, it is still close to trivial to miss the boat with these languages. Truly component-oriented languages have yet to arrive and even then they will not solve many of the intrinsic engineering tradeoffs that engineers of software components and component software have to face and address.

A project that struggled for a long time is IBM's SanFrancisco framework, which has changed course and reset sails several times over the past years – moving from C^{++} and CORBA on to Java, and finally to EJB. In its version 2.1 (released in October 2000) the SanFrancisco frameworks counted over 1100 components. In late 2001, IBM stopped SanFrancisco and instead started promoting WebSphere Business Components (WSBC). Then, according to IBM, WSBC was the largest component collection focusing on the server side. WSBC consists of newly designed server-side EJB session and entity components with a focus on financial industries. At least for the part of WSBC that follows the EJB model of strong separation through declared and configurable dependencies, WSBC may now succeed where previous framework approaches failed.

For components to be independently deployable, their granularity and mutual dependencies have to be carefully controlled from the outset. For large systems, it becomes clear that components are a major step forward from objects (classes). This is not to say that objects are to be avoided. On the contrary, object technology, if harnessed carefully, is probably one of the best ways to realize component technology. In particular, the modeling advantages of object technology are certainly of value when constructing a component. On the flip side, modeling of component-based systems is still a largely unsolved problem, although there have been some recent inroads (for example, D'Souza and Wills, 1999, and Cheeseman and Daniels, 2000). UML, for instance, is still ill equipped to model component-based designs, though improvements in this area are one of the major goals for the UML 2.0 definition (still in its early phases in early 2002).

Under the constant pressure of Moore's law, the world of software has been expanding to take advantage of exponentially more powerful hardware resources. The resulting solutions reach into ever more areas of business and society, leading to new requirements, new markets, and new overall dynamics at a rapid pace. Software technology responded with a very dynamic evolution. However, components are hard to establish in a world of extreme dynamics. While much in the world of software needs to continue to progress rapidly, certain aspects need to evolve more gradually at a more controlled pace. These include the foundations of software components, including component models and basic technologies. The significant market advantage that can be gained from having third-party component backing for any platform creates the necessary feedback loop. To grow and sustain any such third-party communities, the major drivers of software technology, such as Sun and Microsoft, need to maneuver carefully. Players focusing on supplying components can only be viable if investments can be amortized (and profits drawn) before the rules change again. The following chapter covers the interaction between technology and markets in more depth.

CHAPTER TWO

Market versus technology

Components are reusable assets. Compared with specific solutions to specific problems, components need to be carefully generalized to enable use in a variety of contexts. Solving a general problem rather than a specific one takes more work. In addition, because of the variety of deployment contexts, the creation of proper documentation, test suites, tutorials, online help texts, and so on is more demanding for components than for a specialized solution. This is especially so when components are to be sold as separate products.

Components are thus viable only if the investment in their creation is returned as a result of their deployment. If components are developed for in-house use, such a return on investment can be indirect via benefits of using components rather than monolithic solutions. Such benefits are typically a reduction in the time to market and increased manageability, maintainability, configurability, flexibility, and so on.

Of course, return on investment can also be sought by selling components. The direct sale of components to deploying customers is one way, but it is not the only one. Another way is the coupling of components and services. For example, while the components may be cheap or free, their effective use may require significant expertise that is offered as a service. Yet another way drops components as a direct income source entirely, and instead leverages the vendor–customer relations built into a component market as a target for highly specific advertising. As with all mature markets, software component industries will eventually converge on a mixed income model.

Part Four, in particular Chapter 26, covers the aspects of component markets in much more detail. For now, it is sufficient to say that software components – as is the case for all components in all areas – need to be understood in terms of the market they are embedded within. Components will exist only where component vendors and component clients join forces in sufficient numbers to reach a "critical mass." Of course, there are also substantial technical problems that need to be addressed and overcome, and Parts Two, Three, and Four cover these. However, the following simple observation may help to put things into perspective:

> **imperfect technology in a working market is sustainable;**
> **perfect technology without any market will vanish.**

For the existence of software components, software component technology needs to meet with proper software component markets. The market cannot exist without, possibly primitive, technology and, equally, the technology cannot be sustained or evolved without a sufficiently strong market. To address a common concern again, for larger organizations or organizations with many similar products, "markets" could be found in-house. However, as stated before, most such organizations are now organized into cost centers, and selling to internal clients is not much simpler than selling to external clients. Obviously, to escape from the vicious circle of component technology and component markets, a techno-economic "bootstrap" is required.

Consider a simple example. (This and the following example follow a suggestion by Alan Wills.) An engineering company, Souped-Up Software Inc., works on a contract basis for many clients in a confined field – say tuning software for engine control. Its clients have varied requirements and traditionally each project started from scratch. Then the company realized that most of its jobs had a lot in common, so it decided to extract and generalize a set of generic components. This effort sat firmly on the experience obtained with the concrete specific projects that it had run before. Thus, the new component set was slim and apt for its purposes – the efficiency of the company increased substantially, quickly amortizing the initial investment in component development. In the meantime, the company opened a subsidiary selling the components to other engineering companies in the same business but serving different regions.

Consider another example. The story of the above company's success reached a startup company, Daft Solutions Ltd. Its engineers knew everything about componentware and decided to start by designing the ultimate component collection before even approaching a single first client. As first projects came in, most of the generic facilities of the component set and even some of the components were not used at all. Also, the solutions it eventually delivered required excessive amounts of processing power and resources. It turned out to be a fatal mistake to generalize before solving some specific problems.

The two flipsides of the component market "coin," markets versus technology, are covered in more detail in the following sections.

2.1 Creating a market

How can markets be created? A full answer to this question is far beyond the scope of this book. Clearly, markets thrive where supply and demand are in balance. A new product can only create a market if its arrival is already awaited – otherwise, the cost of creating demand can be prohibitive.

An elegant way in which to avoid creating markets is to expand established markets carefully. This approach involves taking two steps. The first takes into account that, in a competitive environment, it is necessary to improve offerings to retain the existing customer base and, thus, the existing market. Instead of aiming for revolutionary new products and therefore new markets, a succession of evolutionary refinements is used to "migrate" the existing customer base to better technology. In the second step, this initial customer base helps to support the effort of attracting new customers for the improved product – that is, it helps to expand the market. Microsoft's strategy from Visual Basic to the internet is a good example. In a first step, Visual Basic controls (VBXs) were generalized to OLE controls (OCXs) – expanding the market from Visual Basic to all of OLE. In a second step, OLE controls were reshaped into ActiveX controls, which also work with internet applications, expanding the market from the OLE-based desktop to the internet.

Economy of scale and distribution are important aspects in the creation of component markets. Profit margins on inexpensive products are easily eroded by fixed costs, such as production, marketing, and distribution. As manufacturers of components can concentrate on their core competency, production of components should be cheaper than the production of complete solutions. Regarding distribution costs, some components may not be able to command individually the prices that would make them viable. Bundling them with related components can help. Streamlining the distribution process can also help (it is not clear quite why software has to come in shrink-wrapped boxes. For example, there is an increasing number of "software kiosks" or "component warehouses" that sell components across the internet. Besides reducing the cost of distribution, the internet has also become an affordable marketing platform.

Proper business models for software component industries are still in their infancy. Further discussion follows in Part Five, Chapter 28.

2.2   Fundamental properties of component technology

Establishing component markets rests on technological feasibility. Although many of the required key technologies are finally available, a solid overall understanding of component software is still lacking. There are several deep technical issues that need to be addressed before mission-critical systems can responsibly be built on component technology.

There is a single key aspect of component technology that causes most technical problems. Components come from independent sources and are integrated by third parties. In the absence of countermeasures, a component system is only as strong as its weakest component. Fault isolation is thus an essential theme, as is safety of individual components.

In traditional software engineering processes, module development and testing is followed by systems integration and testing. This approach leaves room for errors that are merely a result of composition and which are not apparent at the level of individual components, but which should be detected during systems integration and testing. With third-party integration, the situation becomes more difficult, as integration testing of modules from different sources needs to be addressed.

Part of the potential of software components – and a reason for the failure of the IC analogy – is the possibility of late integration. Java applets are an example of the extreme kind, as, until a web page is requested by a browser, the applet code will not be integrated into the requesting browser. When late integration is used, integration testing is no longer feasible. For most integration tests, a negative result would come too late in the process as the components will have already been acquired and deployed. Version checks are among the few tests that are useful and essential at the stage of late integration. A load-time complaint about incompatible versions of locally available components is a reasonable diagnosis.

Even if late sanity checks are performed, they can at most come to the rescue of the user, but cannot directly help to improve the quality of the components involved. A component vendor faces a combinatorial explosion of possible system configurations against which to test a component. In an open market of independent component developers, the set of possible combinations is not even known to any one of the involved parties. Furthermore, the number of combinations continues to grow even after deployment of a system, as new components can be integrated as they become available.

Instead of full integration testing, testing against a few possible configurations is the best that can be done. More fundamentally, components need to be built in ways that allow for modular checking – that is, the analysis of component properties based only on the component and the interfaces it builds on. Therefore, component vendors need to strengthen the per component process. In many cases, this requires conservative engineering (defensive programming). The notion of component safety is important as, even if a component fails to function, it must not violate system-wide rules. Safety is the foremost reason to discriminate among otherwise equal methods of component construction. One of the critical decisions to be made is the proper choice of programming languages and tools. If a language and its implementation guarantee important safety properties, proof obligations can be taken off developers and costly safeguarding runtime measures can be eliminated (Chapter 6). Software development processes that do not depend on testing – such as Cleanroom (Dyer, 1992) – naturally gain importance, though they have yet to make significant inroads into the practice of software development.

Once safety properties are in place, functionality and performance have to follow. Broad classes of safety requirements can be covered by the choice of methodology and tools. There is no such magic bullet to achieve functionality, and the effects of independent composition on overall functionality are not fully understood. Conservatism again seems to be the only advisable strategy. For example, OMG recommends mixing and matching its various object services, claiming orthogonality and interoperability. Although these services were designed with this goal in mind, studies show that actual mixing is not easy and, in some situations, even impossible (Wallace and Wallnau, 1996).

Even where functionality and safety are firmly in place, performance remains a formidable problem. Performance of a component system is affected in non-trivial ways by the actual composition. Performance is primarily addressing the question "Is it fast enough?" However, problems of economical resource utilization are closely related, including demands for processing capacity, primary and secondary storage, or network bandwidth.

2.3 Market development

Market forecasts are about as reliable as weather forecasts – the reliability quickly decreases the longer the projected time period under discussion. The situation does not get better merely because the majority of forecasters agree. However, if what is predicted is possible and the right people agree, then the prophecy may well fulfill itself. The following are various excerpts from forecasts made by some of the leading augurs between 1994 and 2002, where the older forecasts are retained to trace the development of markets as seen by those aiming to look forward.

It turns out to be very difficult to classify early predictions as "right" or "wrong" because the predictors tend to rapidly evolve the basis for predictions – the way they categorize markets and products. For instance, the IDC data on middleware and components – itself a category newly introduced in 1999 – does not include many of Microsoft's offerings because Microsoft views many of these categories as mere parts of the operating system. As these parts are not separately available, IDC does not include them. However, it would probably be possible to determine market percentages nevertheless. Clearly, any analyst has to draw these lines somewhere and the point is not that doing so one way or another is, as such, an issue. Rather, it is the resulting difficulty of reintegrating the provided data into a single cohesive picture. Such comprehensive data integration would be a formidable undertaking on its own and is beyond the scope of this book. The reader should thus use the information in the following subsections as a mere starting point.

2.3.1 *Strategic Focus* (January 1995)

The January 1995 *Strategic Focus* report indicates that, as early as January 1995, already one fourth (23.9 percent) of developers were using component technology. This is not as surprising as it may sound – technologies such as Visual Basic opened up the component market quite early. The report predicted an almost linear increase in the percentage of developers using component technology, reaching coverage of 61.5 per cent by the end of 1996. While no follow-up study was available to verify the accuracy of this prediction, it meshes well with the Forrester finding (see below) that by the end of 1996 38 percent of major corporations had already decided on company-wide component technology strategies and a further 28 percent were close to doing so.

2.3.2 *Ovum* (1995)

The 1995 *Ovum* report on distributed objects (King and Carnelly, 1995) predicted a substantial growth in the component software market. It presented a breakdown of the growth sectors into object request brokers (ORBs), component assembly tools ("builders"), component-based business applications, and component frameworks. Figure 2.1 summarizes the *Ovum* predictions of the individual growth of these market segments. The market for ORBs is not expected to reach substantial volume, as ORBs will become part of every platform, such as operating systems or web browsers. Besides the expected success of business applications that use component technology, *Ovum* predicts substantial markets for component frameworks and component assembly tools.

2.3.3 IDC (May 1996)

The May 1996 IDC White Paper *Component Technology* (Steel, 1996) explains why software components are succeeding where objects so far have failed. It is that objects are too fine-grained and their deployment requires too much understanding of an object's working. The report observes that the main component thrust developed out of Visual Basic custom controls and later ActiveX controls. It states that, in early 1996, already three million programmers worldwide used Visual Basic.

The report describes why it became impossible to escape from component approaches once they took off. It is largely claimed that the cause of the rapid evolution of these technologies is what is called "mass market innovation" (MMI):

> "When simple technology is exposed to hundreds of thousands of technically aware users around the world, the level of innovation is bound to be several orders of magnitude greater than that created in a single company's development shop."

However, turning MMI into profit-bearing products is a different matter. The report states that the most successful component technology then was that around Microsoft's standards. The substantial component offerings

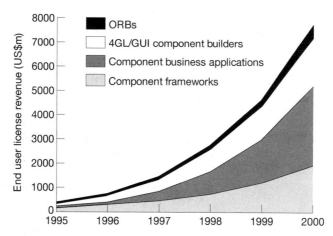

Figure 2.1 Annual global revenues based on end-user licenses in various component technology sectors.

from Microsoft itself combine forces with MMI-produced share or freeware and offerings from independent software vendors. A problem with MMI is quality control.

In the report, IDC distinguished five component types. First, "middleware components" – including ORBs, transaction-processing monitors, and database management systems – take care of the wiring. Second, "logic components," such as image-processing services, perform a specific non-visual service. Third, "vertical components," such as mini-applications, serve a specific domain. Fourth, "GUI components" enrich the toolset of user interface builders. Fifth, "container components" provide visual embeddings and environments for visual components (controls).

2.3.4 **Forrester Research (October 1996)**

In its software strategy report *Objects on the Net* (DePalma *et al.*, 1996), Forrester analyzes the current directions of object technology, based on interviews with 50 of the *Fortune* 1000 companies in the United States and with several of the leading manufacturers of operating and database systems. These companies want to use object technology, but see substantial problems, including the need to retrain their staff. Many of these companies view component technology as the opportunity when faced with this dilemma between old and new software technologies. Using the words of the report, there is a push from "elitist objects" to "populist components."

The report claims that, by the end of 1996, 24 percent of the companies decided to base their component solutions on Microsoft's COM/OLE,

14 percent wanted to use OMG's CORBA, 28 percent were about to make a decision, and 36 percent were in the middle of the decision process.

Furthermore, the report predicted that, by 1998, the various component models would stabilize and components would then find their way from the desktop to the back-end, where component-based solutions would replace older architectures. Also, it predicted that, by 1999, the current gaps between competing component worlds would have closed. In hindsight, we notice that the first prediction – the capturing of the server space – was accurate: Microsoft's COM+ and Sun's Enterprise JavaBeans successfully took components to the server. The second prediction is partially accurate, although the timeframe seems off by a few years. Consolidation did happen and, by 2001, the CORBA and Java spaces have largely joined forces, while Microsoft's COM+ and now .NET continue their own way. Interoperation between these worlds is now well supported by a number of products.

2.3.5 IDC (April 1999)

In the report *Components, Objects, and Development Environments* (Garone and Cusack, 1999), IDC reports on markets in 1998 and predicts development until 2003. The total market volume for software components worldwide was $440 million in 1998 and was predicted to reach $2.4 billion by 2003 – a compound annual growth rate of 40 percent. Windows-based components were expected to grow from 50 percent market share in 1998 to 60 percent by 2003. Unix-based components – the number two in 1998 at 29 percent – were predicted to fall to 10 percent in 2003 (still a growth in revenue from $128 to $240 million). The market for platform-independent components, today almost entirely in the Java space, held 10 percent in 1998 and was predicted to grow to 22 percent by 2003.

In 1998, the worldwide market for software components was fairly fragmented, with ILOG at $45.8 million revenue and 10.4 percent market share holding place one, followed by Rogue Wave Software at $41.2 million and 9.4 percent. No other company went beyond 3.5 percent market share. In the space of supporting middleware, the markets were more clearly divided. BEA Systems held 45.3 percent ($221.8 million in revenue) of the transactional middleware category, followed by IBM with 9.4 percent ($60 million) in second place. IONA held 34.5 percent ($57.5 million) of the CORBA ORB market, just beating Inprise at 30 percent ($50 million), with no other company holding more than 4 percent. Obviously, these figures would require much more careful analysis to understand what exactly was attributed to which category. However, the trend in 1998 was clear – components and supporting middleware had achieved market sizes that allowed them to be analytically tracked in their own categories.

2.3.6 **ComponentSource (2001)**

ComponentSource is the largest marketplace for software components and development tools. The site (www.componentsource.com) provides running bestseller statistics. In early 2002, the component market (as seen from statistics compiled by the author from online data at ComponentSource) is still largely ActiveX-oriented. Practically all of the top 50 and all of the top 5 products listed in March 2002 were COM (ActiveX) components or related. Table 2.1 shows the distribution of components and tools listed on ComponentSource in December of 2001. Figure 2.2 illustrates the distribution. VCL is Borland's Visual Component Library – visual components for Delphi and C++ Builder.

Table 2.1 – Products offered at ComponentSource.

ComponentSource (December 30 2001)			
	categories		
		authors	
			products
platform			
COM	95	376	934	75.5%
VCL	47	46	119	9.6%
.NET	42	37	85	6.9%
JavaBeans	40	52	70	5.7%
EJB	12	18	27	2.2%
CORBA	2	2	2	0.2%
total:			**1237**	

As the ComponentSource figures emphasize, the market for client-side components is by far the most mature. Server-side components are not yet regularly acquired and, instead, more typically made in-house.

2.3.7 **Flashline (2001)**

Flashline is another large online component marketplace. Compared to ComponentSource, Flashline has a stronger focus on server-side development and a preference for Java-based technologies. On its site (www.flashline.com), it maintains a running comparison chart of J2EE application server products. In December 2001, Flashline listed a total of 38 vendors, offering 78 different J2EE application server products that range in price from free to $75,000 per CPU. At the time, 22 of the 78 server products carried a J2EE license, certifying that they had passed the J2EE test suite.

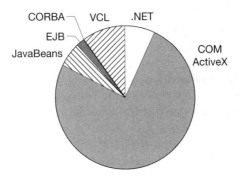

Figure 2.2 Market share at ComponentSource.

Flashline goes beyond a component marketplace and also offers market functionality for services. For instance, Components-by-Design is an auction-based
service that allows organizations in need of components to outsource development efforts. Flashline also offers a certification service for JavaBeans and EJB
components.

CHAPTER THREE

Standards

For component markets to develop, component standards must be in place. Standards are useful for establishing agreement on common models, enabling interoperation in principle. Standards can also be used for creating agreement on concrete interface specifications, enabling effective composition. Finally, standards can be used for ensuring agreement on overall architectures to assign components their place in a larger picture of composition and interoperation.

The following sections present a more detailed discussion of the need for standards, on the possible coexistence of multiple standards, and the danger of overemphasizing universal "wiring" or "plumbing" standards. The chapter then concludes with a brief overview of current technical approaches to software components and some of the more general open problems.

3.1 The utmost importance of (quasi) standards

For a component to find any reasonable number of clients, it needs to have requirements that can be expected to be widely supported. It also needs to provide services that can be expected to be widely needed. How wide? The answer depends on the domain addressed by a component. A component needs to hold a significant portion of a market specific to its domain. If that market is truly large, a small portion of it may be enough for economic viability. If the market is only small, then even a total monopoly may not be enough to justify the investment. The size of a market depends on both the number of potential clients and the price that a client is willing to pay.

If a component viably addresses a market segment covering a small number of clients, the component vendor may exactly understand the individual client's needs and deployment environments. The vendor then makes sure that the component will function as required in these environments. Obviously, the extreme case is the development of components for just one purpose and just one client. This extreme is normally called not component construction, but modular construction of fully client-specific solutions.

As the number of potential uses and potential clients grows, the chances that any component could possibly address all needs while being deployable in all environments decrease rapidly. The unavoidable middle ground that both clients and vendors need to seek is based on environment standards. It is totally irrelevant whether a regular standardization body has approved such a standard. The most successful standards have all been created where and when needed by those parties needing them. Such so-called industry standards are not second-class. On the contrary, it is a strange and ill-advised idea that standards are created by a committee, only to find out later if they address the right problem.

Often the "standard" is just the approach taken by the "innovator," the first successful vendor in a new market segment. With any workable standard in place, the growing number of clients is usually quickly paralleled by a growing number of vendors. The initially proprietary approach turns into an industry standard. Increasing pressure from customer groups further reduces the proprietary nature of the new standard by pushing for release of control to a neutral standards organization. The resulting competition raises the quality of the components, lowers prices, and attracts further clients. Until superseded by far superior approaches – that is, new standards – the created market will continue to thrive.

A standard should specify just as much about the "interfacing" of certain components as is needed to allow sufficiently many clients and vendors to work together. To draw from an analogy, the standards for parts such as screws specify not only a raster of diameters, lengths, and so on, but also acceptable deviations, so-called tolerances. The cost of making a part increases dramatically with decreasing tolerances. The equivalent in the software world would be a standard specifying levels of detail that lead to "friction" when combining different software parts.

For software components, the need for standards was recognized a long time ago. One approach is to build working markets first, followed by the formulation and publication of standards. In the software component world, Microsoft (OLE, ActiveX, COM+, .NET) is the most prominent player following this approach. Another player is Sun Microsystems (Java, JavaBeans, EJB, J2EE). A different approach is to build standards first and then build the markets. The prime player in this arena is a huge industry consortium – the Object Management Group (OMG). The various OMG standards are organized in the object management architecture (OMA). The most prominent part is the common object request broker architecture (CORBA). Other parts are the various standards for object services and facilities.

Where markets are created first, working products need to come before established standards. The result can be a technological suboptimality. Products using ad hoc solutions may be sold before a full understanding of all ramifications is reached. To upgrade to better solutions without losing the established base of customers, products need to be evolved carefully. Almost all successful standards, independent of the discipline area, emerged this way.

Where standards are created first, technologically optimal solutions can be prescribed if such optimality can be reached with the current level of understanding. Whether or not such standards have possible and, most importantly, viable implementations is open until demonstrated by a conforming realization.

3.2   Wiring standards are not enough

The problems to be addressed by standards are enormous. In particular, the vast number of domain- and application-specific aspects threatens to interfere with the standard and standardization process. It is tempting to concentrate on levels that are free from the semantic problems of such higher-level areas. Good candidates are standards at the "plumbing" or "wiring" level. It is obvious that components need to be connected with each other to be useful. It is also obvious that such connections need to follow standards to make it at all likely that any two components have compatible connection points (sometimes called "ports").

Connection standards solve an important problem. At first, it would seem that it is necessary to agree on a single connection standard. At second glance, however, a look at the world as it is reveals that this may not be the case. Almost all countries in the world have their own standard for power outlets, voltage levels, frequencies, and so on. Clearly, a common standard is desirable, but it does not seem essential as long as the remaining market per standard is large enough and bridging technology is available when needed.

On the drawing board, it would be trivial to design such common connection standards. What is more, it would be trivial to design compatible connection points to join totally incompatible services. Consider a system that used the same outlets and plugs for water and gas, or for power and telephone lines. For a dramatic example, consider the oxygen and nitrogen pipes in hospitals – one uses clockwise the other counter-clockwise threads.

Clearly, wiring compatibility is an important area. Getting it right can have enormous economic benefits. However, if everything works except for the actual wiring, then people usually find a way around this problem – and call it an adapter.

Where an approach that starts with standards and proceeds on to products is adopted, it is natural that the first standards to arrive deal with the "wiring" level. If nothing real exists that could be built on, it is difficult to engage in domain- or application-specific standardization efforts. Thus, OMG released CORBA first (the common object request broker architecture). CORBA is a wiring standard that enables communication among objects that are programmed in different languages and supported by different operating systems. Initially, CORBA solved the connection problem only per CORBA implementation, which is quite similar to the above example of country-specific power outlets. This defect was fixed with CORBA 2.0.

In contrast, Microsoft first had OLE (then OLE 1) and Visual Basic – two directly marketable and successful high-level technologies. Only later did Microsoft introduce COM, generic OLE (initially OLE 2), ActiveX, Visual Basic for Applications, and other technologies to broaden and generalize its options. Only then did they start to release some of these as "standards" to encourage other vendors to follow suit. These standards are now maintained by the Microsoft-initiated non-profit organization Active Group, a part of the Open Group. With the Common Language Infrastructure (CLI), Microsoft is now following a more aggressive path towards standardization. The CLI specification was adopted by ECMA in the fall of 2001, several months before the release of the first CLI-based Microsoft product – .NET Common Language Runtime (CLR), part of the .NET Framework.

Current component standards have now reached two main areas of application. The older one around compound-document applications – at the level of spreadsheets, word processors, graphing and presentation packages, and various interactive controls – is largely following the COM/OLE/ActiveX technologies. The newer area is server-side components, often offering transactional behavior. Here, the two competing technologies today are Enterprise JavaBeans and COM+. CLR holds promises in both areas (and potentially other, yet untapped, areas for component technology), but the impact needs to be seen.

The standardization of compound document applications and builders extends above simple "wiring," but is still not domain-specific. Domain-specific elements are added by "scripting" components, which is really programming rather than mere "plug-and-play" composition (see Chapter 10). However, all current software component camps need to strengthen their domain-specific standards. Some of the most capital-intensive markets are of the kind in which a smaller number of clients operate in a field of high specialization. Banking, medical services, factory automation, corporate management and entertainment industries are some examples.

3.3   Too many competing standards are not useful

Who will win the standardization race in component technology? Interestingly, there is no need for a single winner. As long as market shares remain large enough, multiple standards can coexist and compete. Even in highly mature engineering disciplines, it is more the rule than the exception that there are several alternative standards for a given situation.

Thus, well-meaning attempts to get it right the first time by standardizing an area that has yet to be populated by products, may be less than ideal. Nevertheless, it can be successful and lead to superior products that then gain large market shares. However, there are only a few actual examples of this. Whether in the area of programming languages (for example Algol, Ada), operating systems (for example OSF/1), communication protocols (for example

ISO OSI), or elsewhere, constructed, rather than derived, standards rarely took off.

An interesting exception to this rule is the IEEE floating point standard. This standard was forged out of thin air to overcome the useless variety and incompatibility across vendors found at the time. Several other contenders for standardization existed, all of which were backed by strong commercial players. However, that was exactly the problem. None of the vendors was willing to buy into a standard that had been defined (and already implemented!) by the competition.

All this would have led to a persisting number of incompatible standards. After all, we still live with ASCII and EBCDIC encodings of character sets. We still live with big and little endian encodings of integers. In all these cases, the conversion between the different representations is a nuisance and a technical inefficiency, but it is possible. In the case of floating point representations, the situation is different. In many cases, it is actually impossible to convert values from one floating-point format to another without loss of precision. Thus, the pressure for uniform international standardization had reached critical limits.

Today, all but a few supercomputers follow the IEEE floating point standard. For the purposes of data exchange, the level of agreement satisfies most demands. Apple Computer was probably the first company to take this standard very seriously. The Standard Apple Numerical Environment (SANE) implements the standard to painstaking detail – and has been available since the times of the Apple II machine!

3.4   Where is software component technology today?

Most standardization efforts in the component arena are either at the "wiring" or intra-component levels. Examples of wiring standards have been mentioned above. Intra-component standards aim at the innards of a component, rather than the aspects of component interoperation. Intra-component standards are the focus of traditional software engineering efforts. This is because traditional software engineering fully concentrates on the production of monolithic systems, with few provisions for interoperability.

Examples of intra-component standards are those concerned with programming languages or class and template libraries. Other examples are processes aimed at the production of monolithic software, such as the waterfall lifecycle model, the concept of integration testing, and the idea of complete requirements. The obvious question has to be, if all these established and proven things do not help with component-oriented programming – that is, programming beyond monoliths – what else would? The answer is less obvious and, in many cases, still subject to ongoing research. For some answers – and more problems – see Part Four.

It seems clear that domain-specific components will become the most profitable of all and that substantial markets will be created. However, domain-specific standards today raise the most questions. Should the standards come before the products and markets, or vice versa? There are already a few products in the direction of business objects (Sims, 1994). Also, there are standards-first attempts by the OMG's special interest groups. Neither the products nor the sketches of standards have reached a level of maturity or impact that would allow any predictions today. Some more detail can be found in Chapter 18, including an attempt to explain why these efforts have had limited success so far. However, the biggest promise is perhaps the emerging domain standards around XML.

3.5 What's next?

With a slowly developing maturity of software components comes a slow liberation from overly traditional objects. Nevertheless, much can be learned from object technology, and some of it can be generalized or transformed to serve components.

Particularly urgent matters revolve around architectural concepts in a component world. It is far too simplistic to assume that components are simply selected from catalogs, thrown together, and magic happens. In reality, the disciplined interplay of components is one of the hardest problems of software engineering today. Questions arise such as "How can the abstract interaction of components be described?", "How can variety and flexibility be covered?", "How can critical system-wide properties be guaranteed in the presence of arbitrary third-party components?", or "How can performance be guaranteed?"

A particularly powerful approach is beginning to take shape – that of component frameworks. A related approach is part of the object technology repertoire, namely class or application frameworks (Deutsch, 1989; Lewis, 1995). Beyond the similar names, almost identical visions, and superficially similar construction principles, component frameworks are very different from class frameworks. Essentially, a component framework is a set of interfaces and rules of interaction that govern how components "plugged into" the framework may interact. Typical component frameworks also provide an implementation that partially enforces these rules of interaction. The implementation of the component framework and those of the participating components remain separate.

Approaches to important component engineering problems are covered in Part Two. Component frameworks are briefly covered in Chapter 8, and discussed in detail in section 9.1.6. Part Four covers new approaches and case studies of first "componentware," including component architecture, programming, and assembly. Case studies of some component frameworks are presented in Chapter 21.

Foundation

The first part opened the scene and provided a broad initial perspective. It is now time to consider sharper technical detail and concepts. This part may prove to be difficult reading. As outlined in the Preface, some readers may wish to read only some chapters of this part.

Chapter 4 picks up the vague definition of components from Chapter 1 and refines it to a more solid definition. Chapter 5 introduces the particular semantics problems that occur in interacting state-based systems. This is important, as all mainstream component software approaches introduce state. Together with Chapter 6, on polymorphism, the presented material helps to understand the role of object technology in the context of component software. Chapter 7 contrasts object and class composition – a distinction essential to the understanding of many of the current approaches to component software. Much space is granted to the discussion of various approaches of "disciplined inheritance," an issue of utmost relevance when using orthodox object technology to construct component software. Chapter 8 presents a list of criteria that can be used to partition a system design into components. Chapter 9 briefly explains the important concepts of reuse in software, including object-oriented patterns and frameworks, but also system architecture. Some understanding of these concepts helps to relate claims about component software to understood and established techniques. Chapter 10 explores the wide spectrum of programming tasks in component systems, ranging from simple scripting to distributed computing. Finally, Chapter 11 draws together a number of other definitions or remarks on component software as found in the literature.

CHAPTER FOUR

What a component is and is not

The terms "component" and "object" are often used interchangeably. In addition, constructions such as "component object" are used. Objects are said to be instances of classes or clones of prototype objects. Objects and components are both making their services available via interfaces, and interfaces are of certain types or categories. As if that was not enough, object and component interactions are described using object and component patterns and prescribed using object and component frameworks. Both components and frameworks are said to be whitebox or blackbox, and some have even identified shades of gray and glassboxes. Language designers add further irritation by also talking about namespaces, modules, packages, and so on.

This plethora of terms and concepts needs to be reduced by eliminating redundancies or it needs to be unfolded, explained, and justified. The next section considers this universe of terms and concepts and provides brief explanations, relating the concepts to each other. The goal is to establish some degree of order and intuition as a basis for further discussions. Then, a refined definition of the term "component" is presented and discussed. Finally, the linkages to standards for horizontal and vertical markets are summarized.

4.1 Terms and concepts

Some degree of familiarity with most of the terms covered in this section is assumed – and so is some degree of confusion about where one term ends and another starts. One way to capture the intuitive meaning of a term is to enumerate characteristic properties. The idea is as follows: something is an A if it has properties a1, a2, and a3. For example, according to Wegner's (1987) famous definition, a language is called object-oriented if it supports objects, classes, and inheritance.

Unfortunately, the concepts relevant to component technology encompass many aspects. The massive overloading of the term object is the best example. Over time, the notions of module, class, and component have all become embraced by the term "object." (More recently, the same is done to the term "software component" – even to a point where plain old objects are now called components!) Combining several terms into one can simplify things superficially, but not to good advantage beyond the simplest thoughts. As precision and richness of the vocabulary decrease, so does the richness of expressible and distinguishable, yet concise, thoughts. It is essential to strive for a balance, preserving conciseness and intuition. The following subsections thus present definitions of some key terms and relate them to each other.

4.1.1 Components

The characteristic properties of a component are that it:

- is a unit of independent deployment;
- is a unit of third-party composition;
- has no (externally) observable state.

These properties have several implications. For a component to be independently deployable, it needs to be well separated from its environment and other components. A component, therefore, encapsulates its constituent features. Also, as it is a unit of deployment, a component will never be deployed partially. In this context, a third party is one that cannot be expected to have access to the construction details of all the components involved.

For a component to be composable with other components by such a third party, it needs to be sufficiently self-contained. Also, it needs to come with clear specifications of what it requires and provides. In other words, a component needs to encapsulate its implementation and interact with its environment by means of well-defined interfaces.

Finally, a component should not have any (externally) observable state – it is required that the component cannot be distinguished from copies of its own. Possible exceptions to this rule are attributes not contributing to the component's functionality, such as serial numbers used for accounting. The specific exclusion of observable state allows for permissible technical uses of state that can be crucial for performance without affecting the observable behavior of a component. In particular, a component can use state for caching purposes (a cache is a store that can be eliminated without any consequence, except possibly reduced performance).

A component can be loaded into and activated in a particular system. However, due to the stateless nature of components, it makes little sense to have multiple copies in the same operating system process as these would be mutually indistinguishable anyway. In other words, in any given process (or other loading context), there will be at most one copy of a particular component. Hence, it is not meaningful to talk about the number of available copies of a component.

In many current approaches, components are heavyweight units with exactly one instance in a system. For example, a database server could be a compo-

nent. If there is only one database maintained by this class of server, then it is easy to confuse the instance with the concept. An example would be the payroll server of a company. For example, the database server, together with the database, might be seen as a module with an observable state. According to the above definition, this "instance" of the database concept is not a component. Instead, the static database server program is, and it supports a single instance – the database "object." In the example, the payroll database server program may be a component, while the payroll data is an instance (an object). This separation of the immutable "plan" from the mutable "instances" is essential to avoid massive maintenance problems. If components were allowed to have observable state, then no two installations of the "same" component would have the same properties.

It is important to avoid a common confusion at this point. The component concept argued for here does not in any way promote or demote the use of state, observable or not, at the level of objects. Also, it is unrelated to the lifetime of such object state (per call, per session, or persistent). These are all object-level concerns that are not tied to the component concept, although components can be used to provide objects of any of these natures.

4.1.2 Objects

The notions of instantiation, identity, and encapsulation lead to the notion of objects. In contrast to the properties characterizing components, the characteristic properties of an object are that it:

- is a unit of instantiation, it has a unique identity;
- may have state and this can be externally observable;
- encapsulates its state and behavior.

Again, a number of object properties directly follow. Because an object is a unit of instantiation, it cannot be partially instantiated. Since an object has individual state, it also has a unique identity that suffices to identify the object despite state changes for its entire lifetime. Consider the apocryphal story about George Washington's axe. It had five new handles and four new axe heads, but was still George Washington's axe. This is a good example of a real-life object of which nothing but its abstract identity remained stable over time.

As objects are instantiated, there needs to be a construction plan that describes the state space, initial state, and behavior of a new object. Also, that plan needs to exist before the object can come into existence. Such a plan may be explicitly available and is then called a class. Alternatively, it may be implicitly available in the form of an object that already exists – that is, sufficiently close to the object to be created, and can be cloned. Such a pre-existing object is called a prototype object (Lieberman, 1986; Ungar and Smith, 1987; Blaschek, 1994).

Whether using classes or prototype objects, the newly instantiated object needs to be set to an initial state. The initial state needs to be a valid state of the constructed object, but it may also depend on parameters specified by the client asking for the new object. The code required to control object creation and initialization can be a static procedure – usually called a constructor if it is part of the object's class. Alternatively, it can be an object of its own – usually called a factory object, or factory for short if it is dedicated to this purpose. Methods on objects that return freshly created other objects are another variation – usually called factory methods.

4.1.3 Components and objects

Obviously, a component is likely to act through objects and therefore would normally consist of one or more classes or immutable prototype objects. In addition, it might contain a set of immutable objects that capture default initial state and other component resources.

However, there is no need for a component to contain classes only, or even to contain classes at all. Instead, a component could contain traditional procedures and even have global (static) variables (as long as the resulting state remains unobservable), or it may be realized in its entirety using a functional programming approach, or using assembly language, or any other approach. Objects created in a component – more precisely, references to such objects – can leave the component and become visible to the component's clients, usually other components. If only objects become visible to clients, there is no way to tell whether or not a component is "all object-oriented" inside.

What, then, is the difference between state maintained by objects created by a component and state maintained by a component? This is a subtle but critically important point. State maintained by an object is abstracted by that object's reference. A component that does not maintain observable state cannot (observably) maintain references even to the objects it created. A reference to the component itself (the component's fully qualified name) cannot be used to retrieve any objects. Interestingly, this property can be achieved in a non-object-oriented setting. A functional component can create closures and a procedural component can maintain tables of stateful records that are only manipulated in table indices, which themselves are not kept by the component. Whether or not any such state (in objects, closures, or tables) is persistent across component activations is a separate question, the correct answer to which depends on the intended use of a particular component.

A component may contain multiple classes, but a class is necessarily confined to being part of a single component. Partial deployment of a class would not normally make sense. Of course, just as classes can depend on other classes using inheritance, components can depend on other components – this is an import relation.

The superclasses of a class do not necessarily need to reside in the same component as the class itself. Where a class has a superclass in another component, the inheritance relation between these two classes crosses component

boundaries, forcing a corresponding import relationship between the two underlying components. Inheritance of specifications is an essential technique for establishing correctness, as, by referring to the same specification, two components establish a common basis. Whether or not inheritance of implementations across components is a good thing is the focus of a heated debate between different schools of thought. The deeper theoretical reasoning behind this clash is interesting and close to the essence of component orientation. Further detail and arguments follow in Chapter 7.

4.1.4 Modules

From the discussions so far, it should be clear that components are rather close to modules, as introduced by modular languages in the late 1970s (Wirth, 1977; Mitchell *et al.*, 1979). The most popular modular languages are Modula-2 (Wirth, 1982) and Ada. In Ada, modules are called packages, but the concepts are almost identical. An important hallmark of truly modular approaches is the support of separate compilation, including the ability to type-check across module boundaries properly.

With the introduction of the language Eiffel, it was claimed that a class is a better module (Meyer, 1988). This seemed to be justified, based on the early ideas that modules would each implement one abstract data type (ADT). After all, a class can be seen as implementing an ADT, with the additional properties of inheritance and polymorphism. However, modules can be used, and always have been used, to package multiple entities, such as ADTs or, indeed, classes, into one unit. Also, modules do not have a concept of instantiation, whereas classes do. (In module-less languages, this frequently leads to the introduction of "static" classes that essentially serve as simple modules.)

In more recent language designs – such as Oberon, Modula-3, Component Pascal, and $C^{\#}$ – the notions of modules (or assemblies in $C^{\#}$) and classes are kept separate. In all cases, a module can contain multiple classes. (In languages such as Java that do not have a separate module concept, modules can be emulated to a degree by using nested classes.) Where classes inherit from each other, they can do so across module boundaries. As an aside, it should be mentioned that in Smalltalk systems, it was traditionally acceptable to modify existing classes to build an application. Attempts have been made to define "module" systems for Smalltalk capturing components that cut through classes – for example Fresco (Wills, 1991). Composition of such modules from independent sources is not normally possible, though, and this approach is therefore not further followed in this book.

Unlike classes, modules can indeed be used to form minimal components. Even modules that do not contain any classes can function as components. A good example is traditional math libraries that can be packaged into modules and are of a functional rather than object-oriented nature. Nevertheless, one aspect of fully fledged components is not normally supported by module concepts.

There are no persistent immutable resources that come with a module, beyond what has been hardwired as constants in the code. Resources parameterize a component. Replacing these resources allows the component to be configured without the need to rebuild its code. For example, resource configuration can be used for localization. The configuration of resources seems to assign mutable state to a component. However, as components are not supposed to modify their own resources, resources fall into the same category as the compiled code that also forms part of a component. Indeed, it is useful to regard a localized version of a component as a different (but related) component. Tracking the relationship between a component and its derived localized versions is similar to tracking the relationship between different release versions of a component.

It is instructive to explore cases where modules do not qualify as components. Under the definition used here, components do not permit observable state, while modules can clearly be built to use global (static) variables to expose observable state. Furthermore, modules tend to depend statically on implementations in other modules by importing direct interfaces from other modules. For components, such static dependencies on component-external implementations are allowed but not recommended. Static dependencies should be limited to contractual elements, including types and constants. Dependencies on implementations should be relegated to the object level by preferring indirect over direct interfaces in module dependencies to enable flexible compositions using multiple implementations of the same interface.

To summarize, modularity is a prerequisite for component technology, but rules beyond the traditional modularity criteria are needed to form components rather than just modules. Many modularity criteria go back to Parnas (1972) and include the principle of maximizing cohesion of modules while minimizing dependencies between modules. Modularity is thus certainly not a new concept. Unfortunately, the vast majority of software solutions today are not even modular. For example, it is common practice for huge enterprise solutions to operate on a single database, allowing any part of the system to depend on any part of the data model. Adopting component technology requires adoption of principles of independence and controlled explicit dependencies. Component technology unavoidably leads to modular solutions. The software engineering benefits can be sufficient to justify initial investment into component technology, even when component markets are not foreseen in the mid-term.

4.1.5   Whitebox versus blackbox abstractions and reuse

Blackbox and whitebox abstraction refer to the visibility of an implementation "behind" its interface. In an ideal blackbox abstraction, clients know no details beyond the interface and its specification. In a whitebox abstraction, the interface may still enforce encapsulation and limit what clients can do, although implementation inheritance allows for substantial interference. However, the implementation of a whitebox is fully available and can thus be studied to enhance the understanding of what the abstraction does. (Some authors further distinguish between whiteboxes and glassboxes, with a whitebox allowing for manipulation of the implementation and a glassbox merely allowing study of the implementation.)

Grayboxes are those that reveal a controlled part of their implementation. This is a dubious notion, as a partially revealed implementation could be seen as part of the specification. A complete implementation would merely have to ensure that, as far as was observable by clients, the complete implementation performs as the abstract partial one. This is the standard notion of refinement of a specification into an implementation. Indeed, specification statements can be seen as graybox specifications (Büchi and Weck, 1997).

Blackbox reuse refers to the concept of reusing implementations without relying on anything but their interfaces and specifications. For example, in most systems, application programming interfaces (APIs) reveal nothing about the underlying implementation. Building on such an API is equivalent to blackbox reuse of the implementation of that API.

In contrast, whitebox reuse refers to using a software fragment, through its interfaces, while relying on the understanding gained from studying the actual implementation. Most class libraries and frameworks are delivered in source form, and application developers study the classes' implementation to understand what a subclass can or has to do.

The serious problems of whitebox reuse are analyzed in detail in Chapter 7. For now it suffices to say that whitebox reuse renders it unlikely that the reused software can be replaced by a new release. Such a replacement will probably break some of the reusing clients, as these depend on implementation details that may have changed in the new release.

A definition: software component

From the above characterization, the following definition can be formed:

> "A software component is a unit of composition with contractually specified interfaces and explicit context dependencies only. A software component can be deployed independently and is subject to composition by third parties."

This definition was first formulated at the 1996 European Conference on Object-Oriented Programming (ECOOP) as one outcome of the Workshop on Component-Oriented Programming (Szyperski and Pfister, 1997). The definition covers the characteristic properties of components discussed before. It has a technical part, with aspects such as independence, contractual interfaces, and composition. It also has a market-related part, with aspects such as third parties and deployment. It is a property unique to components, not only in the software world, to combine technical and market aspects. (An interpretation of this definition from a purely technical point of view is presented in Chapter 20.)

From a more modern point of view, this definition requires some clarification. The contract of a deployable component specifies more than dependencies and interfaces, it specifies how the component can be deployed, how, once deployed (and installed), it can be instantiated, and how the instances behave through the advertised interfaces. This latter aspect goes beyond a mere sum of per-interface specifications – an instance maintains an invariant that couples the per-interface specifications. In fact, the per-interface specifications need to be seen in isolation from any particular component that provides or requires an implementation of such an interface.

For example, consider a queuing component that requires stable storage via one interface and provides enqueue and dequeue operations via two further interfaces. The component contract states that what is enqueued via one interface can be dequeued via the other – a correlation that the individual interface's specifications cannot provide. The component contract also states that the component, once instantiated, can only be used by connecting it to a provider implementing the stable storage interface. This latter notion of connecting components that have matching provided and required interfaces needs to be effected by the composition rules of a supporting component model. The details of deployment and installation need to be supported by a specific component platform.

Interfaces are discussed in more detail in the following subsection. A discussion of context dependencies follows in the subsequent subsection.

4.1.6 Interfaces

Part One has already introduced the basic market aspects of component technology. Chapters 5–7 cover the aspects of interfaces, contracts, semantics, and composition in detail. For the following, more market-oriented, discussion, it suffices to consider the interface of a component to define the component's access points. These points allow clients of a component, usually components themselves, to access the services provided by the component. Normally, a component will have multiple interfaces corresponding to different access points. Each access point may provide a different service, catering for different client needs. Emphasizing the contractual nature of the interface specifications is important because the component and its clients are developed in mutual ignorance, so it is the contract that forms a common middle ground for successful interaction.

What are the non-technical aspects that contractual interfaces have to obey to be successful?

First, as mentioned in Part One, the economy of scale has to be kept in mind. A component can have multiple interfaces, each representing a service that the component offers. Some of the offered services may be less popular than others, but if none is popular and the particular combination of offered services is not popular either, the component has no market. In such a case, the overheads involved in casting the particular solutions into a component form may not be justified.

Notice, however, that individual adaptations of component systems may well lead to the development of components that themselves have no market. In this situation, extensions to the component system should build on what the system provides, and the easiest way of achieving this may well be the development of the extension in component form. In this case, the economic argument applies indirectly in that the extending component itself is not viable, but the resulting combination with the extended component system is.

Second, undue fragmentation of the market has to be avoided as it threatens the viability of components. Redundant introductions of similar interfaces have thus to be minimized. In a market economy, such a minimization is usually the result of either early standardization efforts among the main players in a market segment or fierce eliminating competition. In the former case, the danger is suboptimality due to "committee design" and, in the latter case, it is suboptimality due to the non-technical nature of market forces.

Third, to maximize the reach of an interface specification and components implementing this interface, there need to be common media to publicize and advertise interfaces and components. If nothing else, this requires a small number of widely accepted unique naming schemes. Just as ISBN (International Standard Book Number) is a worldwide and unique naming scheme to identify any published book, a similar scheme is needed to refer abstractly to interfaces "by name." Just as with an ISBN, an interface identifier is not required to carry any meaning. An ISBN consists of a country code, a publisher code, a publisher-assigned serial number, and a checking digit. Although it reveals the book's publisher, it does not code the book's contents. Meaning may be hinted at by the book's title, but titles are not guaranteed to be unique.

An interesting variation on the theme of interface standardization is the standardization of message formats, schemas and protocols. Instead of formalizing interfaces as collections of parametric operations, the focus is on what is passed back and forth. This viewpoint is sometimes described as the "viewpoint of the wire" or as "wire formats," alluding to the importance of standardizing message schemas, formats, and protocols when interconnecting machines in a network. Standardization of message formats, schemas and protocols is indeed the main approach of internet (IP, UDP, TCP, SNMP, and so on) and web (HTTP, HTML, and so on) standards. To achieve broader semantic coverage, it is useful to standardize message schemas in the context of a single generic message format. This is the rationale behind XML, a single generic format, the large number of related standards (including SOAP and several XML web services standards), and the growing number of XML schema standardization efforts (see Chapter 18).

4.1.7　Explicit context dependencies

Besides the specification of provides interfaces (more commonly called required interfaces), the above definition of components also requires components to specify their needs. In other words, the definition requires specification of what the deployment environment will need to provide so that the components can function. These needs are called context dependencies, referring to the context of composition and deployment. They include the component model that defines the rules of composition and the component platform that defines the rules of deployment, installation, and activation of components. If there were only one software component world, it would suffice to enumerate requires interfaces (more commonly called required interfaces) of other components to specify all context dependencies (Magee *et al.*, 1995; Olafsson and Bryan, 1997). For example, a mail merge component would specify that it needs a file system interface. Note that, with today's components, even this list of required interfaces is not normally available. The emphasis is usually just on provides interfaces. (Note that the more common terms of provided and required interface aren't quite accurate. Interfaces sit between components and are, as such, neither required nor provided.)

In reality, there are several component worlds that partially coexist, partially compete, and partially conflict with each other. For example, today there are three or four major component worlds, based on OMG's CORBA, Sun's Java, and Microsoft's COM and CLR. In addition, component worlds are themselves fragmented by the various computing and networking platforms that they support. This is not likely to change soon. However, from another perspective, these worlds collapsed to only two – the CORBA+Java world and the Microsoft world (including COM+ and .NET/CLR). Yet, despite this apparent culmination in just two poles, there is a surprising diversity at the level of actual offerings, even including an open source effort to independently implement the CLI specification underlying CLR (www.ximian.com).

Just as the markets have so far tolerated a surprising multitude of operating systems, there will be room for multiple component worlds. In a situation in which multiple component worlds share markets, a component's specification of context dependencies must include its required interfaces as well as the component world (or worlds) that it has been prepared for. There will, of course, also be secondary markets for cross-component world integration. By analogy, consider the thriving market for power plug adapters for portable electrical devices. Thus, chasms are mitigated by efforts to provide bridging solutions. Examples are OMG's Interworking standard (part of CORBA since version 2.0, July 1996 revision), which forms a bridge between Microsoft's COM and CORBA, and OMG's EJB interoperation specification that has formed part of the CORBA Component Model since CORBA version 3.0. Nevertheless, such bridging will always compromise where the bridged worlds are too different for the gap to be closed fully. To a degree, it is even demonstrably impossible to bridge separate component worlds completely (Smith *et*

al., 1998). When having a single universal standard offers overwhelming benefits, a "shake-out" effect is likely to eliminate most competing standards, as
happened with VCR standards (for a detailed discussion see Messerschmitt and
Szyperski, 2002). Following the same example, the ongoing emergence of new
media for video storage and recording, along with new standards (CD, CD-R,
CD-RW, DVD, DVD-RAM, memory stick, compact flash, and so on), also
suggests that such convergence is not necessarily durable in the presence of
technological evolution.

4.1.8 Component "weight"

Obviously, a component is most useful if it offers the "right" set of interfaces
and has no restricting context dependencies at all – in other words, if it can
perform in all component worlds and requires no interface beyond those the
availability of which is guaranteed by the different component worlds.
However, only very few components, if any, would be able to perform under
such weak environmental guarantees. Technically, a component could come
with all required software bundled in, but that would clearly defeat the purpose of using components in the first place. Note that part of the
environmental requirements lie with the machine that the component can execute on. In the case of a virtual machine, such as the Java VM, this is a
straightforward part of the component world specification. On native code
platforms, a mechanism such as Apple's "Fat Binaries," which packs multiple
binaries into one file, would still allow a component to run "everywhere."

Instead of constructing a self-sufficient component with everything built in,
a component designer may have opted for "maximum reuse." To avoid redundant implementations of secondary services within the component, the
designer decided to "outsource" everything but the prime functionality that
the component offers itself. Object-oriented design has a tendency toward this
end of the spectrum, and many object-oriented methodists advocate this maximization of reuse.

Although maximizing reuse has many oft-cited advantages, it has one substantial disadvantage – the explosion of context dependencies. If designs of
components were, after release, frozen for all time, and if all deployment environments were the same, then this would not pose a problem. However, as
components evolve, and different environments provide different configurations and version mixes, it becomes a showstopper to have a large number of
context dependencies. With each added context dependency, it becomes less
likely that a component will find clients that can satisfy the environmental
requirements. To summarize:

> **Maximizing reuse minimizes use.**

In practice, component designers have to strive for a balance. When faced with
requirements that specify the interfaces that a component should at least provide,

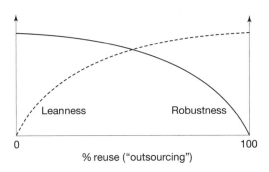

Figure 4.1 Opposing forcefields of robustness (limited context dependence) and leanness (limited "fat"), as controlled by the degree of reuse within a component.

a component designer has a choice. Increasing the context dependencies usually leads to leaner components by means of reuse, but also to smaller markets. Additionally, higher vulnerability in the case of environmental evolution must be expected, such as changes introduced by new versions. Increasing the degree of self-containedness reduces context dependencies, increases the market, and makes the component more robust over time, but also leads to "fatter" components. Figure 4.1 illustrates the optimization problem resulting from trading leanness against robustness.

The effective costs of making a component leaner, compared with making it more robust, need to be estimated to turn the qualitative diagram of Figure 4.1 into a quantitative optimization problem. There is no universal rule here. The actual costs depend on factors of the component-producing organization and of the target markets for the component. The markets determine the typical deployment environment and client expectations, including component "weight" and expected lifetime.

Note that it is not just coincidence that Figure 4.1 and Figure 1.1 (p. 6) are so similar. The discussion in this section focused on the "outsourcing" of parts of a component. In contrast, the discussion in Chapter 1 concentrated on the outsourcing of parts of a system – that is, the outsourcing of components. The former is about reuse across components, whereas the latter is about reuse of components.

4.2   Standardization and normalization

The "sweet spot" of the optimization problem introduced above can be shifted toward leaner components by improving the degree of normalization and standardization of interface and component worlds. The more stable and widely supported a particular aspect is, the less risky it becomes to make it a specified requirement for a component. Context dependencies are harmless where their support is ubiquitous. For example, only 50 years ago it would have been a bad idea in many cases to form a business that depends on its customers having access to a telephone. Nowadays, in many areas of the world, this is clearly safe. (In some areas and cases it is now even safe to assume that customers have internet and web access. Assuming broadband connectivity will be next.)

4.2.1   Horizontal versus vertical markets

When aiming for the formation of standards that cover all areas representing sufficiently large markets, it is useful to distinguish standards for horizontal and vertical markets. A horizontal market sector cuts through all or many different market domains; it affects all or most clients and providers. A vertical market sector is specific to a particular domain and thus addresses a much smaller number of clients and providers. For example, the internet and the world wide web standards are both addressing horizontal market sectors. In contrast, standards for the medical radiology sector address a narrow vertical market sector, which, as in this case, can have a substantial market volume all the same.

Standardization is hard in horizontal market sectors. If a service is relevant to almost everyone, the length of the wish list tends to be excessive. Consider, as an example, the situation that standards committees for general-purpose programming languages have to face. At the same time, it is the horizontal market sectors in which a successful standard has the highest impact. The web is one of the best examples of this.

Surprisingly, standardization in vertical sectors is just as difficult as it is in horizontal ones, but for different reasons. The number of players is smaller, so the likelihood of finding a compromise should be higher. However, the vertical sector considered for a standard has to be wide enough for a viable market. Also, with a smaller number of players, the mechanisms of market economies work less well and it is less likely that good, cost-effective solutions are found within a short time.

4.2.2   Standard component worlds and normalization

Component approaches are most successful where the basic component world and the most important interface contracts are standardized and these standards are sufficiently supported by the relevant industry. However, for standardization to help, it is important to keep the number of competing standards low. With a single strong international standardization body, a single strong company, a strong coalition of companies, or other organization behind a standard, this can work. However, more likely than not, standards will compete. A particularly dramatic explosion of "mutually unaware" competitors can arise if vertical fragmentation leads to the reinvention of standards in allegedly different sectors when the same standard would suit multiple sectors. For example, it is conceivable that several image-processing standards in, say, medical radiology and radio astronomy could be shared.

The risk of having large numbers of competing standards – and thus small markets for many of them – can be reduced by means of normalization. By publishing and cataloging "patterns" of common design, it is likely that otherwise mutually unaware standardization bodies will discover mutual similarities in their target domains. It is, of course, a matter of scale whether discovery and exploitation of such similarities are worthwhile – that is, cost-effective – or not.

CHAPTER FIVE

Components, interfaces, and re-entrance

Semantics is defined as the actual meaning of things beyond their outer form or appearance. As component technologies are all about interoperation of mutually alien components, the meaning of the whole becomes a difficult issue. This chapter presents the subtleties and problems of software component semantics. Some current approaches are discussed, not ignoring that this area is still a focus of ongoing research.

This chapter and the next two are likely to be quite tough reading for many. It is safe to only skim over them at a first reading. However, the material presented is essential to an understanding of the rationale behind many contemporary approaches and technologies. Both chapters contain several hints for readers who wish to skip some of the material.

This chapter has two parts. The first introduces the important concept of contractual specifications of interfaces. The second part, starting with section 5.4, focuses on the specific problems of contractual specifications of interfaces in a component setting. In essence, it will become obvious that recursive and re-entrant calls across component boundaries introduce many of the complexities of concurrent programming. This second part is technical and subtle. It is safe to "fast forward" to section 5.8. Many of the arguments in later sections and chapters build on the following discussions. It may thus be preferable to quickly read the following sections, concentrating on the examples, to improve understanding.

The material in this chapter is supported by examples developed in two programming languages – Java and Component Pascal. Appendix A presents a brief comparison of these two languages. Both languages have a familiar appearance, even for readers not versed in them. A precise understanding of these languages is not required to follow the examples. More subtle details are explained as they occur.

5.1 **Components and interfaces**

Interfaces are the means by which components connect. Technically, an interface is a set of named operations that can be invoked by clients. Each operation's semantics is specified, and this specification plays a dual role as it serves both providers implementing the interface and clients using the interface. As, in a component setting, providers and clients are ignorant of each other, the specification of the interface becomes the mediating middle that lets the two parties work together. It is therefore important to view interfaces and their specifications in isolation of any specific component that may implement or use such interfaces.

A component may either directly provide an interface or implement objects that, if made available to clients, provide interfaces. Interfaces directly provided by a component correspond to procedural interfaces of traditional libraries. There can be interfaces provided indirectly by objects that are made available by the component. Such indirectly implemented interfaces correspond to object interfaces. Components can be specified separate from interfaces and their specifications (for instance, D'Souza and Wills, 1999; Cheeseman and Daniels, 2000). A component specification names all interfaces that a component should adhere to and adds component-specific properties. For instance, two interfaces may be used for the input and output sides of a filter component. The filter specification would then say that the output is related to the input. Multiple component implementations can then conform to such a component specification.

It is also possible to focus on the interaction between components using certain interfaces. This is done by writing specifications that constrain data flows through a given set of interfaces. Hans Jonkers' interaction specifications (2001) follow this direction. The underlying realization here is that there is a dualism between specifying components and specifying the interactions between components – where interfaces serve as cut points in both cases. Interaction specifications "own" their interfaces such that they can assign constraints without risking a conflict with another interaction specification. That is, interfaces appear as the roles at the endpoints of an interaction specification and no interface can appear in more than one interaction specification. The traditional approach to specifying interactions is the world of protocols (see section 9.1.4 for more information). Traditional interface specifications can be seen as the degenerate case of interaction specifications (or protocols) focusing on the interactions between exactly two parties through exactly one interface.

5.1.1 **Direct and indirect interfaces**

Direct (procedural) and indirect (object) interfaces can be unified into a single concept. Essentially, the idea is to use static objects that can be part of a component. A procedural interface to a component is modeled as an object interface of a static object within the component. Most component implementations can be made to have their interfaces look like object interfaces. This is the traditional "workaround" of pure object-oriented languages, including Java.

Modeling all component interfaces as object interfaces, in which a single component may provide multiple object interfaces, helps simplify the grounds for discussion of semantics. However, it is important to remember the consequences of using a true object interface rather than a procedural interface. Since the early years of computing, procedural libraries have been used to provide a service through an interface to many clients. However, different library implementations were never competing with each other within any one given configuration. Library implementations would only vary across platforms or library versions. The situation is radically different with object interfaces.

An object interface introduces an indirection called method dispatch or, sometimes, dynamic method lookup. For a given object, its class determines the implementation of its interface. At runtime, a method invocation is resolved by retrieving the target object's class and directing the call to the method implementation in that class. Method dispatch can lead to the involvement of a third party. In particular, it can involve a third party of which both the calling client and the interface-introducing component are unaware. This is the case when the object implementing an interface belongs to a component different from the component with which the client seems to interact through the interface. Traditional procedural interfaces are always direct as the definition of the procedural interface and its implementation belong to the same component. Of course, explicit procedural indirection is possible by means of procedure variables (also called function pointers).

An example will make these things clearer. Consider a component TextServices that offers an interface ICheckGrammar. TextServices also offers a mediator that can be used to select a default grammar checker. A default grammar checker is selected by passing an object that implements the ICheckGrammar interface to the TextServices mediator. This installed third-party checker may then be used by other services implemented in TextServices, but also indirectly by clients of TextServices. Hence, a client that asks for a grammar checker might get one that is implemented outside TextServices. This is possible even though the client may only know about TextServices and TextServices itself may know nothing about the actual implementer of the grammar checker.

Figure 5.1 illustrates this scenario, the numbers indicating in which order objects are acquired. First, the grammar checker knows about the text service mediator. Second, the grammar checker registered itself as the default checker with the mediator – the mediator knows only about the abstract checker interface. Third, the word processor knows about the mediator. Fourth, the word processor acquires a reference to the current default checker from the mediator – just as the mediator, the word processor, knows only the abstract checker interface.

The effective coupling of two dynamically selected parties via a well-defined interface is a powerful concept called late binding and is right at the heart of object-oriented programming. In a component system, the situation is the same but the proper working of the resulting dynamic configurations is harder to control. With components, not only are the two connected parties unaware of each other, but also it is likely that even the designers do not know each other. Thus, it is only the quality of the interface specification that holds things together.

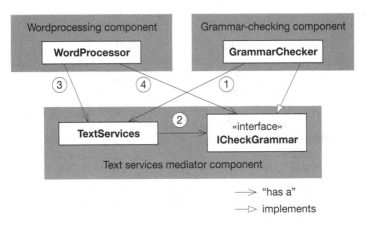

Figure 5.1 Example of direct and indirect interfaces.

5.1.2 **Versions**

In a component world, versions of components can be prolific. For example, many vendors may provide various "upwards-compatible," enhanced versions of a successful component. Traditional version management – often based on the assignment of major and minor version numbers – assumes that the versions of a component evolve at a single source. In a free market, the evolution of versions is more complex and management of version numbers can become a problem in its own right.

A subtle aspect of versioning arises when moving from direct to indirect interfaces – that is, to object interfaces. With direct interfaces it suffices to check versions at bind time, which is when a service is first requested. As discussed above, indirect interfaces couple arbitrary third parties. In a versioned system, care must be taken to avoid indirect coupling of parties that are of incompatible versions. For example, a client originally requesting a service may be capable of working with version 1 of that service. Once it holds an object reference, it may pass the reference on to another component. However, the latter component might require version 2 of the service. Unless versions are checked in every place where an object reference crosses component boundaries, version checking is not sound.

Few component infrastructures proposed so far address the component versioning problem properly. The goal is to ensure that older and newer components are either compatible or clearly detected as incompatible. The general strategy is to support a sliding window of supported versions. That is, ideally, once established compatibility is stable until an act of deprecation and finally removal ends compatibility cleanly for good.

One possible approach is to insist on immutable interface specifications. Instead of trying to maintain the complex compatibility relationship among various versions of interfaces, each interface, once published, is frozen and never changed again. Supporting multiple versions is then equivalent to supporting multiple interfaces. An outdated interface is simply no longer supported. Passing a reference of a particular interface version to other components is not a problem. The receiving component either accepts the reference because it can handle this particular interface or it expects a different version and thus a different interface and then it will not accept the reference. Using immutable interfaces is essentially the COM approach.

A more refined, but also more complex, approach is to allow mutation of definitions from one version to the next. Rules need to define precisely what changes are valid to retain backwards compatibility. Where such compatibility cannot be maintained, relevant parts of a definition should be deprecated. This way, outdated clients of such a definition can be isolated by analyzing their dependencies against what is provided. In general, interfaces and components can be used "side-by-side" – that is, multiple versions of a component can be loaded and instantiated in the same space. It is useful to distinguish components that should be used in the latest version from components that should always be used in the version that some client was built and tested against. This is essentially the CLR approach.

5.1.3 Interfaces as contracts

A useful way to view interface specifications is as contracts between a client of an interface and a provider of an implementation of the interface. The contract states what the client needs to do to use the interface. It also states what the provider has to implement to meet the services promised by the interface. (As pointed out by Wolfgang Weck, a contract binds two partners, who, in this case, are client and provider. Hence, the contractual specification of an interface really is just a contract template that is "instantiated" at composition time of client and provider. In theory, the contract could be refined or renegotiated at that time – an opportunity that is indeed commonly exploited in the form of dynamic type negotiations.)

On the level of an individual operation of an interface, there is a particularly popular contractual specification method. The two sides of the contract can be captured by specifying pre- and postconditions for the operation. The client has to establish the precondition before calling the operation, and the provider can rely on the precondition being met whenever the operation is called. The provider has to establish the postcondition before returning to the client and the client can rely on the postcondition being met whenever the call to the operation returns. Pre- and postconditions are not the only way to form contracts (add a specification to an interface). In addition, with pre- and postconditions alone not all aspects of an interface can be specified. Other forms of specifications are covered briefly further below.

Contracts are a simple idea but have subtle implications. Before delving into contracts for interacting objects, consider a simple procedural library. For example, a library that provides operations for text formatting. In addition, assume that the library's interface remains unchanged from one version to another, but that its implementation is revised. What effect do such implementation changes have on clients of the library?

This question can only be answered in the context of a precise specification stating what the library, in the abstract, is supposed to do. A contract is an appropriate approach, with pre- and postconditions attached to every operation in the library. If the revised implementation is not to break any old clients, it must respect the (unchanged) contract. This means that it can at most require less or provide more. (More technically, the implementation can weaken preconditions or strengthen postconditions. This will be explained in detail in Chapter 6.)

5.1.4   Contracts and extra-functional requirements

As long as an implementation respects its contracts, revisions pass unnoticed by clients. Contracts and procedural or functional libraries fit together very well. It is worth noting that typical contemporary contracts often exclude precise performance requirements. However, even for simple procedural libraries, a new release adhering to the original contract but changing performance can break clients. Consider a math library that is used by an animation package. Next, the math library is improved to deliver more accurate results, but at lower average speed. This "improvement" turns out to break the animation package, which now fails to deliver the required number of frames per second.

Take an example from the current practice that some Swiss banks put in place when subcontracting a component to a third party. The contractual specification consists of the functional aspects – interface syntax and semantics with invariants, and pre- and postconditions – but also a so-called service level. The service level covers guarantees regarding availability, mean time between failures, mean time to repair, throughput, latency, data safety for persistent state, capacity, and so on. Service levels are monitored and used to pay on the basis of component use. Failure to fulfill the service level is treated on the same grounds as a wrong result – the component (really the component vendor) broke its contract. It can be expected that this practice of including extra-functional specifications into a contract and monitoring them strictly will become more widely popular in the future.

5.1.5   Undocumented "features"

Note that it is always possible to "observe" behavior of an implementation beyond its specification. For example, the precise reaction to certain parameter values can be explored. Knowledge about an implementation derived through such exploration can be used to make clients dependent on a provider's implementation. It is not even necessary to have access to the implementation's source code to create such dependencies. A most insidious way of exploring an implementation's unspecified "features" is called debugging. While trying to fix problems, a debugger subtly reveals information that is not part of the contract. In practice, it is very difficult to avoid such non-contractual dependencies entirely. To minimize risks, a contract needs to maintain a balance between being precise and not being too restrictive.

5.2   What belongs to a contract?

The notion of contracts as interfaces – annotated with pre- and postconditions and, perhaps, invariants – is simple and practical. However, several important issues are not covered. For example, it is usually understood that an operation with a certain postcondition has to establish that postcondition before returning. However, it need not return at all! Simple pre- and postconditions on operations merely specify partial correctness and a partially correct operation either terminates correctly or does not terminate at all. The requirement that an operation should also eventually terminate leads to total correctness. This requirement can be added as a convention to all contracts. (The triple {precondition} operation {postcondition} is sometimes called a Hoare triple and is then indeed limited to partial correctness (Hoare, 1969). A popular notation for totally correct conditions is Dijkstra's weakest preconditions (1976) for an operation and a given postcondition, wp(S, Q). This is the weakest precondition for which execution of S is guaranteed to terminate eventually while meeting postcondition Q.

5.2.1 Safety and progress

The concept that something guaranteed by a precondition will lead to something guaranteed by a postcondition can be generalized. By separating pre- and postconditions from concrete operations, they can be made self-standing requirements of a contract. A common notation is the leads-to operator used to express progress conditions in a contract. For example, the clause "model update leads-to notifier calls" could be part of a contract between models and views. Progress conditions often rely on some form of temporal logic – providing logical operators such as leads-to (Chandy and Misra, 1988). They complement the safety conditions that can be expressed using invariants.

The notion of contracts can thus be formalized to capture safety and progress conditions, although still neglecting performance and resource consumption. Contracts of this style have been introduced by Helm *et al.* (1990) and taken further by Holland (1992). A different approach to expressing progress is specification statements, which use abstract non-deterministic statement sequences to specify safety and progress implicitly as abstract programs (Morgan, 1990). A brief discussion follows in section 5.10.

Object- and component-oriented practices still have to take advantage of such refined contract approaches on a regular basis. Pre- and postconditions, on the other hand, are widely accepted and usually combined with informal clauses to form complete contracts. The drawback of such semiformal approaches is the exclusion of formal verification.

5.2.2 Extra-functional requirements

The specification techniques looked at so far (conditions, contracts, histories, specification statements) are restricted to functional aspects. Contracts based on such techniques state what is done under which provisions. They do not state how long it would take or what other resources, besides time, would be consumed.

It is obvious that in most practical examples a violation of extra-functional requirements can break clients just as easily as a violation of functional requirements. If a provider is exceedingly slow in performing a function, the client itself will be slow in performing its duty. The effect can cause an avalanche, the result of which is that the entire system fails to perform satisfactorily. Unless performance is regulated by contracts, it can be difficult or impossible to pinpoint the underperforming components.

Besides time, a provider also has to respect other resource limitations. If a provider uses, say, excessive heap storage, then this can affect the entire system. Just as with underperformance, this can lead to aggregate effects causing the entire system to fail. Again, unless regulated by contracts, it is not easily possible to determine the components that misbehaved as there would not be any specified limits on resource usage.

5.2.3 Specifying time and space requirements

Ideally, a contract should cover all essential functional and extra-functional aspects. It is not yet clear how this can best be achieved, leaving room for ongoing and future research. However, first examples do exist. The C⁺⁺ Standard Template Library (Musser and Saini, 1996) bounds the execution time that legal implementations of a given abstract template function can take. Execution time is not specified in seconds, as that would be totally platform dependent. Instead, only the time complexity of legal implementations is bounded.

Specifying complexity bounds is an interesting compromise. For example, a contract might require a sort function to take no more than the order of $n \log n$ steps to sort n elements. This requirement rules out the use of most "bad" sorting algorithms, but it still does not refer to a particular platform's performance. Likewise, a contract could require the same sort function to take at most $\log n$ additional storage cells to perform the sort.

Assume that the complexity bounds of a provider are given by the contract. It is then often possible to determine absolute time and space bounds for a given provider on a given platform. To do so, usually a small number of measurements suffice. The reason is that, ideally, the various possible providers, constrained by the same bound, can at most differ by constant factors. If someone managed to implement a sort that takes just n steps, then the single measurement would not be enough. Fortunately, it is not possible to sort n arbitrary elements in less than $n \log n$ time using just $\log n$ space overhead.

For example, one sort function on a given platform might take 1 µs $n \log n$, whereas another on the same platform might require 2 µs $n \log n$. With a single measurement of a sufficiently large sorting task (large enough to avoid startup anomalies and so on), the constants (1 µs versus 2 µs) can be measured.

The gap between complexity bounds in a contract and absolute bounds (in seconds or bytes) on a specific platform needs to be bridged. An engineer performing component composition would need to know. Fortunately, at composition time, the selection of concrete providers would be known. Thus, if providing components came with the additional characteristics required, the composing engineer, or an automated composer, could compute absolute bounds for a given platform. For example, a sorting component could certify that it indeed sorts in $n \log n$ time. It might even list characteristic performance figures for various platforms or announce performance relative to a well-known component.

Note that the specification of worst-case bounds may not be the best choice. Instead, specification of average-case bounds may be preferable in many cases. For example, Quicksort (Hoare, 1961), the fastest known average-case sorting algorithm, has a worst-case time complexity of n^2 and can thus not be used with a contract requiring $n \log n$ time in the worst case. However, Quicksort has $n \log n$ time complexity in the average case and is more than twice as fast as the fastest-known sorting algorithm with worst-case $n \log n$ time bound (Heapsort – see Williams, 1964). Unfortunately, average case bounds have a drawback, which is that the constants of implementations cannot be simply measured and depend on platform and average input (for example, average distributions in the sorting case).

In summary, the specification of time and space complexity bounds in a contract, for both the average and the worst case, could significantly add to the practical value of that contract. By avoiding reference to platform-specific bounds (in seconds and bytes), the contract remains sufficiently universal. To fill the gap, components that provide a service under such a contract should come with the additional information required to determine absolute bounds. To become common practice, extra-functional specification techniques still have some way to go.

5.3 Dress code – formal or informal?

The above discussion suggests that interface contracts should be as formal as possible to derive all necessary information and to enable formal verification. Given the complexity of formal specifications, it is not surprising that they are rarely used in practice. Pre- and postconditions as shown before are used, but represent a semiformal style only. Just consider the numerous plain English "predicates" used where a formal predicate would first require the introduction of a much more precise formal model. However, it is worth noting that different parts of a system can be specified using different degrees of formality – the preciseness of the specification (and the cost incurred by it) have to be balanced against the criticality of the target part (and the risk incurred by using it).

The analogy that led to the name "contract" is, of course, a real-world contract. Such a contract, to be valid, has to stay within the rules prescribed by the relevant legislation. However, none of the real-world laws are formal. New "interpretations" are found every day and tested in court. This could well be the future for contracts between components or, rather, between providers of different components and their users.

It is clearly desirable to stay away from court resolution of cases wherever possible. Hence, formalizing contracts, where possible and agreeable, is a good idea. However, attempting to formalize everything can easily lead to totally unapproachable, and therefore unsalable, situations. It is important that a contract does not overspecify a situation. As in the real world, the enforcement of unnecessary requirements causes costs to increase dramatically and feasibility to diminish. The art of keeping contracts as simple as possible, but no simpler, has yet to develop in the young field of software components.

This concludes the first part of this chapter. The second part focuses on the specific problems of contractual specifications of interfaces in a component setting.

5.4   Callbacks and contracts

Contracts and procedural or functional libraries fit together very well. Unfortunately, the situation changes when introducing callback mechanisms to a library. A callback is a procedure that is passed to a library at one point, when the callback is said to be registered with the library. At some later point, the library then calls the callback. Figure 5.2 illustrates the call graph as it occurs in a system using callbacks. In a layered architecture, normal calls always originate in higher, more abstract, layers and then stay in their layer or move downwards. A callback usually reverses the direction of the flow of control, so

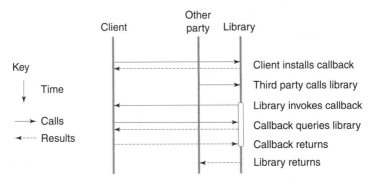

Figure 5.2 Call sequence between library and client in the presence of callbacks.

a lower layer calls a procedure in a higher layer. For this reason, callback invocations are sometimes called up-calls (Clark, 1985). The following detailed discussion of callbacks helps to build solid foundations for later ones concerning the more involved issues raised by objects.

Callbacks are a common feature in procedural libraries that have to handle asynchronous events. For example, some windowing libraries use a callback to notify a particular window's client code when the user resized the window. Alternatively, the client could poll the library for events continuously, a model that is also quite common.

What is so special about callback procedures? In a strict procedural library model, it is always the client calling the library. The library's operations always run to completion before returning control. Thus, the client never observes any intermediate states that the library might go through. The only relevant library states, as far as the client is concerned, are those just before and just after a call to the library. While the library procedure proceeds, the client's state does not change. As the client has full control over its own state when calling a library procedure, the library call can be understood simply from the client's state just before the call and the library procedure's pre- and postconditions.

In the presence of callbacks, the situation changes. The intermediate library state at the point of calling the callback may be revealed to clients. A library thus has to be careful to establish a "valid" state, as far as observable by the client, before invoking any callbacks. Furthermore, a callback may cause the library's state to change through direct or indirect calls to the library. Hence, the observable state of the library has to remain "valid" for as long as any callbacks are active. In Figure 5.2, this critical region in the library has been marked. Validity of the library state is again specified as part of a contract. The library defines the callback interface. Hence, the contract comes with the library and specifies what a callback can expect and, to a lesser extent, what it has to do.

Procedural code can generally observe state and state changes. A library can make part of its state observable by exporting variables or inspection functions. A library's client can thus observe the relative order in which callbacks are performed and in which the observable library state is changed. However, such ordering is not specified by normal pre- and postconditions, is not part of a normal procedural contract, and is therefore implementation dependent.

A simple way out would be to say that, as dependency on observable ordering is not part of the contract, a valid client must not depend on it. However, this is too rigid and would render callbacks quite useless. A callback procedure's role is all about state and state change. Most non-empty callbacks query the library and the client for further information – that is, observe more state, before taking appropriate action.

5.5 Examples of callbacks and contracts

Some examples will help to clarify these ideas. This section presents and discusses in much detail an example that relies on callbacks. The example is developed in several stages, simulating a natural progression in the development and evolution of actual software. The objective is to show that callbacks indeed introduce subtle dependencies that, even for simple examples, lead to unexpected complexities and error-prone situations. This section can be skipped or skimmed over on a first reading. The thorough reader is invited to work through the examples and predict the problems that are pointed out as the examples develop.

It is common practice to demonstrate pre- and postconditions by using examples that are effectively flat abstract data types (ADTs). Thus, stacks and queues are used instead of examples relying on callbacks or even webs of interacting objects. Although the raw concept of pre- and postconditions carries through, major points are missed when using trivial examples. The following examples thus start with a non-trivial scenario with callbacks. After examining these examples, the discussion continues with the closely related but more complex problems caused by cyclic object references.

5.5.1 A directory service

Consider a system that provides a basic directory service as part of a simple file system. The directory service supports callbacks to notify clients of changes in the managed directory. Such a notification service is useful, for instance, to keep a visual representation of the directory up to date.

Although this is only an example, it already represents an advance on the status quo of most current systems. The notification mechanism is exactly what would be needed to implement a file-and-folder metaphor on top of a file system in a reasonable way. Most current file systems do not support notification, and available "desktop" implementations are therefore forced to poll the file system to discover changes. Surprisingly, this is even the case with the Mac OS, although there never was any other user interface to the file system.

The example is sketched in Component Pascal notation, which should be readily accessible to most readers. Component Pascal would allow for an object-oriented formulation, but, again, this was intentionally not done for the example as the objective at this stage is to study direct rather than indirect interfaces.

```
DEFINITION Directory;
  IMPORT Files;  (* details of no importance for this example *)
  TYPE
    Name = ARRAY OF CHAR;
    Notifier = PROCEDURE (IN name: Name);  (* callback *)
  PROCEDURE ThisFile (n: Name): Files.File;
    (* pre  n ≠ "" *)
    (* post  result = file named n  or  (result = NIL and no such file) *)
  PROCEDURE AddEntry (n: Name; f: Files.File);
    (* pre  n ≠ "" and f ≠ NIL *)
    (* post  ThisFile(n) = f *)
  PROCEDURE RemoveEntry (n: Name);
    (* pre  n ≠ "" *)
    (* post  ThisFile(n) = NIL *)
  PROCEDURE RegisterNotifier (n: Notifier);
    (* pre  n ≠ NIL *)
```

(* **post** n *registered, will be called on* AddEntry *and* RemoveEntry *)
PROCEDURE **UnregisterNotifier** (n: Notifier);
    (* **pre** n ≠ NIL *)
    (* **post** n *unregistered, will no longer be called* *)
END Directory.

The simple directory service interface is grouped into two parts. The first part supports file lookup and addition or removal of named files, modeling a single flat directory for the sake of simplicity. The second part supports registration and unregistration of callbacks. Registered callbacks are invoked on addition or removal of a name. Each operation of the interface is specified using simple pre- and postconditions. State that is observable through a given interface but which is not mentioned in a postcondition is guaranteed to remain unchanged.

(To be useful in practice, this convention needs to be modified. It is often ambiguous as to which variables may change to establish a postcondition. Also, insisting that unmentioned variables remain unchanged can be too sharp. A common approach to resolving these issues is to introduce model variables – also called specification variables – that capture the abstract state relevant to a specification fragment. Then, pre- and postconditions on operations are augmented by modifies clauses. A modifies clause simply states which model variables may be changed by an implementation of the so-specified operation. This approach is not followed in this book for the sake of simplicity and approachability.)

5.5.2 A client of the directory service

Now consider a simple client that uses directory callbacks to maintain some visual display of the directory's contents.

```
MODULE DirectoryDisplay;   (* most details deleted *)
  IMPORT Directory;
  PROCEDURE Notifier (IN n: Directory.Name);
  BEGIN
    IF Directory.ThisFile(n) = NIL THEN
      (* entry under name n has been removed – delete n in display *)
    ELSE
      (* entry has been added under name n – include n in display *)
    END
  END Notifier;
BEGIN
  Directory.RegisterNotifier(Notifier)
END DirectoryDisplay.
```

The client's callback procedure involves first checking with the directory service to find out what change happened to the entry under the given name. Obviously, the notifier callback could get another parameter to pass this information directly. However, there is always a limit to what can be passed. It is thus highly realistic, as argued before, that a callback recursively invokes operations on the calling service.

There are several points left unclear in the directory contract. For example, on redefinition of an entry, is the notifier called at all, called once, or called twice? Not calling the notifier would be justified because the list of registered names did not change. One call would reflect the fact that the binding of the name has changed. Two calls would correspond to the implicit removal of the old entry, followed by the addition of the new entry. Such detail would need to be specified, but, although possible, this is difficult to achieve using only pre- and postconditions. Instead, a plain English by-clause is more likely to be used in practice – if such details are specified at all.

An even more difficult decision is whether to call the notifier before or after the directory itself has been updated. The design of the notifier with just the name as a parameter forces any useful callback to enquire for further information from the directory. Hence, the only sensible thing to do is call the notifier in implementations of AddEntry and RemoveEntry just before returning. Although in a sense obvious, this really ought to be added to the contract. Again, it is likely that such a clause would form part of the informal conditions in a contract.

5.5.3 Same client, next release

In a next stage, consider a variation of DirectoryDisplay that, on screen, uses a pseudo name "Untitled." This name is used for anonymous files that have not been registered with the directory, but have been announced to the display service. The assumption is that no registered file will ever be called "Untitled." Obviously, users would be confused if the directory ever contained an entry for a file named "Untitled." Assume that the implementer of DirectoryDisplay had a brilliant idea. Why not remove such an entry from the directory again as soon as the notification call arrives? Said and done:

```
MODULE DirectoryDisplay;   (* Version 1.0.1 *)
  IMPORT Directory;
  PROCEDURE Notifier (IN n: Directory.Name);
  BEGIN
    IF Directory.ThisFile(n) = NIL THEN
      (* entry under name n has been removed – delete n in display *)
    ELSE
      IF n = "Untitled" THEN
        (* oops – you shouldn't do that ...*)
        Directory.RemoveEntry(n)   (* ... gotcha! *)
      ELSE
        (* entry has been added under name n – include n in display *)
      END
    END
  END Notifier;
BEGIN
  Directory.Register(Notifier)
END DirectoryDisplay.
```

Is this not a clever hack? Of course, none of us would do such a thing. However, assume for a moment that someone did. Why would it be so bad? To make things clearer, consider the sketch given below of a possible implementation of Directory. The implementation is intentionally procedural and self-contained – that is, it does not rely on any collection library or similar.

```
MODULE Directory;
   IMPORT Files, Strings;
   TYPE
      Name* = ARRAY OF CHAR;   (* trailing * exports definition *)
      Notifier* = PROCEDURE (IN name: Name);
      EntryList = POINTER TO RECORD   (* linked list of entries *)
         next: EntryList;
         name: POINTER TO Name; file: Files.File
            (* an entry is a pair of a name and a file *)
      END;
      NotifierList = POINTER TO RECORD   (* linked list of notifiers *)
         next: NotifierList;
         notify: Notifier
      END;
   VAR
      entries: EntryList;   (* list of registered entries *)
      notifiers: NotifierList;   (* list of registered notifiers *)
   PROCEDURE AddEntry* (n: Name; f: Files.File);
      VAR e: EntryList; u: NotifierList;
      BEGIN
         ASSERT(n # ""); ASSERT(f # NIL);
         e := entries;   (* search for entry under name n *)
         WHILE (e # NIL) & (e.name # n) DO e := e.next END;
         IF e = NIL THEN   (* not found: prepend new entry *)
            NEW(e); e.name := Strings.NewFromString(n);   (* create new entry *)
            e.next := entries; entries := e   (* prepend new entry to list *)
         END;
         e.file := f;   (* fill in file – replaces old binding if entry already existed *)
         u := notifiers;   (* invoke all registered notifiers *)
         WHILE u # NIL DO u.notify(n); u := u.next END
      END AddEntry;
   (* other procedures not shown *)
END Directory.
```

Unlike a contract, an implementation answers all questions about the what, when, and where – obviously, this assumes sound and known semantics of the programming language used. The implementation details help to make the discussed problems concrete. Of course, this is only one of many possible implementations. It is therefore not appropriate to rely on implementation details when designing or implementing a new client.

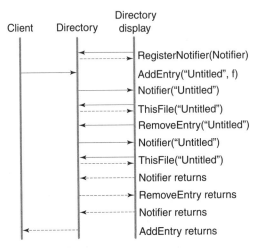

Figure 5.3 Call sequence between a client, the directory, and the directory display – version 1.0.1.

Figure 5.3 shows the flow of control in detail as it occurs when a client tries to insert a file named "Untitled" into a directory – an attempt undercut by the display notifier. The notifier is actually called recursively as a consequence of removing the entry from within the first notifier call. It is likely that this subtle interaction asked for some serious debugging. For example, a first attempt (version 1.0.1-alpha) might have been to catch and delete "Untitled" first thing in the notifier – that is, even before checking that the entry has actually been added rather than removed. Version 1.0.1-alpha terminated abnormally, reporting a stack overflow during a test insertion of an entry "Untitled."

5.5.4 A broken contract

Now recall the contract pertaining to AddEntry:

PROCEDURE **AddEntry** (IN n: Name; f: Files.File);
  (* **pre** n ≠ "" **and** f ≠ NIL *)
  (* **post** ThisFile(n) = f *)

The implementation of AddEntry in combination with the "hacked" Notifier procedure breaks this contract. When calling AddEntry("Untitled", someFile), the notifier immediately removes the newly added entry again. Thus, the post-condition ThisFile("Untitled") = someFile does not hold on return from AddEntry. A client relying on this postcondition would thus break. Unfortunately, the notifier is "out of the loop" then and the search for the culprit of the broken contract would naturally point to the directory implementation. Note that both the client and the directory implementation could have been deployed long before the component that installed the ill-behaved notifier was added.

5.5.5 **Prevention is better than cure**

How can a scenario of the kind analyzed above be regulated using contracts? What is missing is a contract between Directory and notifier implementations. Such a contract is difficult to capture, or at least the aspects that led to the above problems are difficult to capture. It is useful to think of callbacks as mechanisms that asynchronously observe and effect state changes. Asynchronously observable state, such as state observable by means of callbacks, allows contracts based on pre- and postconditions to fit less well. Asynchrony is more naturally dealt with by approaches developed to handle concurrency, such as process models. For example, histories of possible state changes could be used to specify the behavior of asynchronous systems (see section 5.9). Unfortunately, the resulting contracts are far less manageable than simple pre- and postconditions.

One aspect of the contract between Directory and notifier that can be captured is the requirement that a Directory instance has to notify all observers whenever the directory is changed. To specify this requirement, observers are abstractly modeled as holding an exact copy of their observed directory state and having the notifier as their only operation. A postcondition on all directory operations is then that these copies are again equivalent to the observable directory state. The only way the directory implementation can keep its part of the contract is to notify all observers after any change to the observable directory state. Another way to specify that directory operations call the notifiers is to incorporate abstract specification statements into postconditions. For example, Fusion uses the notation [[call1; call2]] to specify that call2 always occurs after call1 (Coleman *et al.*, 1993).

What is not captured by this contract is the condition that a notified observer must not change the notifying observed object. This is difficult to capture in a formal contract but could be specified in plain text. The problem is that such a restriction is of transitive nature. A notifier may invoke any other operation that internally, for whatever reason, uses the service that originally notified. The restriction imposed on the notifier needs to be applied also to such indirect invocations. It is difficult to capture such a global dynamic restriction using a strictly local and modular descriptive contract. For example, the simple rule that a notifier may not call any state-updating operations cannot be adopted as the very purpose of a notifier is to update the state of the notified entity.

An elegant middle ground is to equip a library using callbacks with state test functions. These tell whether or not a particular operation is currently available, without revealing too much of the library's internal state. Then, all library operations can include references to such test functions in their preconditions. Correct callback implementations may thus be dynamically restricted to the manipulation of only a part of the otherwise accessible state. If done carefully, this allows a callback to perform only its function without depending on particular library implementations.

5.5.6 **Proofing the directory service**

In the directory example, the addition of a test function InNotifier and its proper use in the preconditions of AddEntry and RemoveEntry would solve this particular problem. Version 1.0.1 of DirectoryDisplay would have to be rejected during conformance verification. The Directory interface refined below shows this use of test function InNotifier. Note that a missing postcondition, as in the case of Notifier, is equivalent to postcondition "true." An operation with such a trivial postcondition does not have any useful effect within the context of the contract.

```
DEFINITION Directory;   (* refined *)
   ...   (* unaffected parts omitted *)
   TYPE
      Notifier = PROCEDURE (IN name: Name);   (* callback *)
         (* pre  InNotifier() *)
   PROCEDURE InNotifier (): BOOLEAN;
      (* pre  true *)
      (* post  a notifier call is in progress *)
   PROCEDURE AddEntry (IN n: Name; f: Files.File);
      (* pre  (not InNotifier()) and n ≠ "" and f ≠ NIL *)
      (* post  ThisFile(n) = f *)
   PROCEDURE RemoveEntry (IN n: Name);
      (* pre  not InNotifier() *)
      (* post  ThisFile(n) = NIL *)
END Directory.
```

As stated, test functions are a mixed blessing. It would be preferable to resort to a more declarative form in the contract, rather than relying on an executable function that inspects state. However, test functions can be invoked by any client of a service and thus solve the problem of transitive restrictions. In the example, not InNotifier() is part of the precondition of AddEntry and RemoveEntry and thus binds any client of these procedures. As the precondition can be checked at runtime, clients can be implemented to behave correctly, even if dynamically, under a transitive restriction imposed by some other notified component.

5.5.7 **Test functions in action**

Test functions in interfaces are certainly not commonplace today – dynamic restrictions are often just stated informally. For example, operations such as AddEntry may have an informal clause stating that they are not to be called directly or indirectly from a notifier. Such a clause in a contract is "binding." However, it violates the principle that a client should be able to perform the same guarding tests that a provider would use to safeguard itself against ill-formed calls.

Test functions are nevertheless used sometimes, even if not made available to clients. A prominent example is the Java security manager, which is an object that protects critical services from being called by untrusted code. The situation is similar to that of the notifier example above. The security manager needs to prevent direct and indirect calls to critical code from within untrusted methods. To do so, the implementation inspects the runtime stack to determine whether or not there is an untrusted method's frame on the stack. The security manager may need to obtain further information, depending on the particular operation to be guarded. Thus, it may need to call some code outside the security manager's class. (In early versions of Java, to avoid problems resulting from recursive invocations to the security manager, the security manager itself had a test function (getInCheck) that returned true if the security manager was currently performing a security check. This has been fixed by allowing re-entrant calls into the security manager and deprecating the getInCheck call, which as of J2SE 1.4 is still available for compatibility reasons.)

This concludes the journey into the world of callbacks. The indirect recursion across abstractions caused by callbacks is a good basis from which to understand the similar difficulties introduced by webs of interacting objects.

5.6   From callbacks to objects

Object references seem to be simple and elegant. In reality, they are not simple, and some doubt their elegance. In any case, object references introduce linkage across arbitrary abstraction domains. Proper layering of system architectures thus lies somewhere between the challenging and the impossible – it is certainly not as natural as with procedural abstractions.

Understanding the implications of object references across a system is crucial. For example, the same object reference can be used at one time in a layer above that of the referenced object and at another time in a layer below that of the referenced object. A method invocation in the former case would correspond to a regular call, while one in the latter case would correspond to an up-call. With object reference there is thus no need for explicit callback constructs as every method invocation is potentially an up-call, every method potentially a callback.

This is again a good point at which to resort to an example. As with the example "session" on callbacks, it is safe to skip the rest of this section and the following section. A summary section after that will help to "resynchronize." However, again, studying the following examples carefully is recommended – the discussed problems do occur in practice and a good understanding is crucial to the full understanding of component technology.

Consider an interface for text processing. The interface is called TextModel because it supports only text manipulation, and not text display or a direct manipulation user interface. This time, for a change, the notation used is Java.

As with Component Pascal, most readers will find the Java notation intuitive enough, even if they are not Java programmers. (Where the syntax of Component Pascal resembles that of Pascal or Oberon, the syntax of Java resembles that of C or C++.)

```
interface TextModel {
  int max ();
    // pre  true
    // post  result = maximum length this text instance can have
  int length ();
    // pre  true
    // post  0 ≤ result ≤ this.max() and  result = length of text
  char read (int pos);
    // pre  0 ≤ pos < this.length()
    // post  result = character at position pos
  void write (int pos, char ch);
    // [ len: int; txt: array of char •
    //   pre  len := this.length(); (all i: 0 ≤ i < len: txt[i] := this.read(i)) :
    //        len < this.max() and  0 ≤ pos ≤ len
    //   post this.length() = len + 1
    //     and  (all i: 0 ≤ i < pos: this.read(i) = txt[i])
    //     and  this.read(pos) = ch
    //     and  (all i: pos < i < this.length(): this.read(i) = txt[i - 1])
    // ]
  void delete (int pos);
    // [ len: int; txt: array of char •
    //   pre  len := this.length(); (all i: 0 ≤ i < len: txt[i] := this.read(i)) :
    //        0 ≤ pos < len
    //   post this.length() = len - 1
    //     and  (all i: 0 ≤ i < pos: this.read(i) = txt[i])
    //     and  (all i: pos ≤ i < this.length(): this.read(i) = txt[i + 1])
    // ]
  void register (TextObserver x);
  void unregister (TextObserver x);
}
```

Note that, by convention, the notation x in an operation's postcondition refers to the value of variable x before entering the operation. For values returned by methods of objects, this notation becomes less sharp. To avoid this problem, the above preconditions of write and delete contain explicit assignments to capture state that the corresponding postcondition can then refer to. In particular, these preconditions capture the initial length and contents of the text.

The "local variables" used to capture the state form part of the specification, not an actual implementation.

A text model is a sequence of characters with random access to read, insert, or delete characters at arbitrary positions. At any one time, a text has a defined length, which can be zero. It also has an upper bound on its length. (The condition this.length() ≤ this.max() really is an invariant of the text model. Invariants are conditions that constantly hold with respect to a given program fragment. In the context of interfaces, invariants are conditions over state exposed by the interface. In cases where all state is only accessible by explicit operation invocations, such as with Java interfaces, invariants in interfaces can always be folded into pre- and postconditions. It may still be more readable to express invariants separately.)

A text model supports registration and unregistration of objects of type TextObserver. This is similar to the concept of registration and unregistration of notifiers, as explained in section 5.1. Whenever a text model is modified – that is, a character is inserted or deleted – the model notifies all registered observers. The observer interface is defined as:

```
interface TextObserver {
    void insertNotification (int pos);
        // pre character at position pos has just been inserted
    void deleteNotification (int pos);
        // pre character that was at position pos has been deleted
}
```

Any object implementing this interface can be registered. The implementations of insertNotification and deleteNotification can then take appropriate action to react to the models change.

The following interface, TextView, complements TextModel by facilitating the display and editing of text. The separation into model and view is a classic (p. 159). The traditional model view controller (MVC) separation has a third abstraction, controllers, to handle user interaction. For the sake of simplicity, some controller functionality is kept in the view and an explicit controller is left unspecified. Also, the detail of how a view acquires screen estate and how it draws to the screen has been left open.

```
interface TextView extends TextObserver {
    TextModel text ();
        // pre true
        // post result ≠ null
    int caretPos ();
        // pre true
        // post 0 ≤ result ≤ this.text().length()
```

```
    void setCaret (int pos);
      // pre  0 ≤ pos ≤ this.text().length()
      // post  this.caretPos() = pos
    int posToXCoord (int pos);
      // pre  0 ≤ pos ≤ this.text().length()
      // post  result = x-coordinate corresponding to text position pos
    int posToYCoord (int pos);
      // pre  0 ≤ pos ≤ this.text().length()
      // post  result = y-coordinate corresponding to text position pos
    int posFromCoord (int x, int y);
      // pre  (x, y) is valid screen coordinate
      // post  this.posToXCoord(result) = x and this.posToYCoord(result) = y
    void type (char ch);
      // [ caret: int •
      //   pre  caret := this.CaretPos() : this.text().length() < this.text().max()
      //   equiv  this.text().write(caret, ch)
      //   post  this.caretPos() = caret + 1
      // ]
    void rubout ();
      // [ caret: int •
      //   pre  caret := this.CaretPos() : caret > 0
      //   equiv  this.text().delete(caret - 1)
      //   post  this.caretPos() = caret - 1
      // ]
    void insertNotification (int pos);
      // inherited from TextObserver
      // repeated here for strengthened postcondition
      // pre  character at position pos has just been inserted
      // post  display updated and this.caretPos() = pos + 1
    void deleteNotification (int pos);
      // inherited from TextObserver
      // repeated here for strengthened postcondition
      // pre  character that was at position pos has been deleted
      // post  display updated and this.caretPos() = pos
}
```

Note that the notation **equiv** statement is used to indicate that the postcondition is the conjunction of the postcondition of the equivalent statement and the condition explicitly stated.

The view casts its text into lines and renders them on some unspecified display. The view also maintains a caret position (a marked position in the text, used for type and rubout commands from the user). The caret is also pictured on the display, say, as a vertical bar just before the character its position indicates. The mapping of character and caret positions to screen coordinates (and back) is also supported. Some user interface objects can use this mapping to interpret, for example, mouse positions.

Note that a text view interface is declared to extend the text observer interface introduced above. The concept of extending interfaces – also called subtyping – is explained in detail in Chapter 6. With its extended observer interface, a text view can thus be used to observe a text model. Many, possibly different, text observers can be connected to a single text model. For example, there could be a text view and a text statistics view, where the latter displays the number of words in the text.

Consider as a first scenario the interaction between a text model and a text view. Some program fragment gets hold of a reference to the text model and inserts a character at some position. The model then notifies its observers, including the text view. The text view removes the caret mark from the display, updates the text display, repositions the caret, and redisplays the caret in its new position. The view's notifier method then returns. Finally, the model returns control to the original client. This process is illustrated in Figure 5.4.

Everything seems to be straightforward. Note how simply ordering objects, as indicated by the vertical lines in the diagram, causes the illusion of some well-layered activity. The flow of control seems to be as simple as that known from procedural libraries layered on top of each other.

However, at a second glance, things are less simple. The transfer of control from the model to the view occurs through an installed notifier – although the notifier is a method of an object in this case. It is thus a strictly non-hierarchical transfer. Recall that a text view depends on a text model's state and not vice versa. Therefore, an ordering that better reflects dependencies is that shown in Figure 5.5.

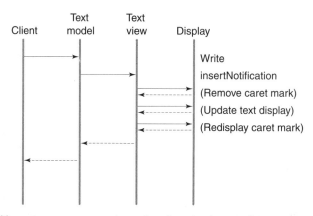

Figure 5.4 Message sequence occurring on insertion of a character into a text model that is displayed by a text view.

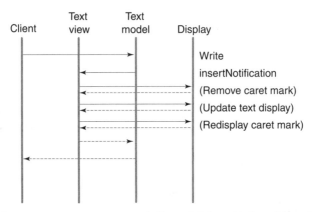

Figure 5.5 The same message sequence as in Figure 5.4, but with the ordering of objects.

Why does this rearrangement matter? It more faithfully reflects the actual hierarchy – and, when going into more detail – leads to fewer surprises. To see why, consider what a text view needs to do to perform its display updating functions. At the point where the old caret mark is removed, the display still shows the text as it was before the change. Hence, the caret needs to be removed using the old text position to screen coordinate mapping. This is important, because the mapping of text positions to screen coordinates depends on the actual text – for example, line-separating characters in the text force line breaks, characters may be of proportional width, the width of spaces varies in justified text, and so on.

Once the text display has been updated, it is time to redisplay the caret at its new position. This time the new (that is, updated) mapping of text positions to screen coordinates has to be used. If the text view, under certain circumstances, uses the wrong mapping, user irritation and display clutter are likely to result. As an aside, almost all commercial applications, including the most prominent ones, produce such screen rubble at times. This may serve as evidence that the series of examples presented here, and their problems, are far from being contrived.

To summarize, here are the steps a text view needs to take to react to a notifier call:

1 remove caret mark from outdated text display
  (a) map caret position to screen coordinates using mapping based on text before change
  (b) invert caret mark at computed display position;
2 re-cast text and update text display;
3 update caret position;
4 redisplay caret mark in updated text display
  (a) map caret position to screen coordinates usin g mapping based on text after change
  (b) invert caret mark at computed display position.

The text has already changed when the view is notified. Therefore, step 1a relies on a cached mapping. The text view has to keep the coordinates of the caret on the screen. For all other purposes, caching is not necessary – the coordinates can be recomputed whenever necessary, based on the text and the algorithm used to cast the text into display lines.

Whether indirectly, by means of a cache, or directly, by means of a computed mapping, steps 1a, 2, and 4a depend on the text model and, at least logically, access it in its present or previous state. Figure 5.6 presents a refined part of the message sequence chart, showing how these three steps interact with the model.

Yet, it would appear that the use of the correct mapping is simply a matter of using a correct text view implementation. However, remember that the text view makes its mappings between text positions and screen coordinates publicly available. The methods posToXCoord, posToYCoord, and posFromCoord use these mappings to perform their function. The text view cannot perform its display-updating duties without calling other objects. Hence, other objects take control while the view is still performing its update functions.

In any case, other objects may call one of the mapping methods before or during the view update. In this case, which mapping should the text view present to the outside – the one that reflects the status of the text or the one that reflects the status of the display? If the mapping that is made available is inconsistent with the display, then user interface events, such as mouse clicks, can be mismapped. If the mapping is inconsistent with the text, then positions in the text are calculated wrongly, potentially leading to wrong or even illegal modification attempts.

Perhaps the view should make two sets of mappings available? If the view can tell that the two are inconsistent, it could also refuse to perform the mapping – for example, by raising an exception. Whatever the choice, the flow of control against the layers of abstraction (up-call) clearly exposes inconsistencies

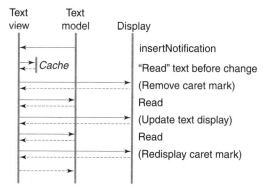

Figure 5.6 Message sequence in detail – interaction of text view and text model during update required by a change to the model.

to arbitrary other objects – a circumstance that should be reflected in the interfaces of text models and views but usually is not. For a discussion of how this could be done, see section 5.10.

5.7   From interobject consistency to object re-entrance

This section builds on the example developed in the previous section. Readers who skipped the previous section are thus advised to skip this section as well.

The model view scenario developed in the previous section shows how multiple objects can be subject to consistency constraints. Objects could be arranged in strict layers, with messages being sent only from objects located in higher layers to objects located in lower layers. Doing so would eliminate the problems of observable inconsistency as everything "below" is consistent and everything "above" is not observable. This is the main benefit of traditional layered architectures. For object systems, however, strict layering is rarely performed. Passing object references "down" and abstractly dealing with upper objects in lower layers is one of the most powerful aspects of object orientation. Harnessing this potential, however, is a major challenge.

Recall the text model and view example? One of the problems with view consistency affecting display and model was that other objects might call one of the view's mapping methods before or during the view update. On closer inspection, things are even worse – multiple observers could be registered with the text model. If another observer was notified before the text view, other objects could gain control before the text view became aware that the underlying text had changed. This might even lead to another text model change before the text view learned of the first change. This issue of ordering in event-based systems is discussed in detail in section 10.6.

The real problem is observation of an object undergoing a state transition with inconsistent intermediate states becoming visible. As objects encapsulate state, such observation is limited to what the object reveals. In other words, inconsistencies can only be observed by entering an object's method. (In some languages, objects can directly make some of their attributes accessible. Obviously, this can always be replaced by accessor methods in which observable inconsistencies become an issue.)

The situation is most intricate when considering object re-entrance – that is, the situation in which an object's method is invoked while another method is still executing. It is, if anything, the right of an object's own method to cause a state transition for that object. If, while in progress and before reaching consistency again, the intermediate state is observed by means of re-entrance, maintaining correctness becomes difficult.

As an example, consider the method type of a text view, as introduced above (interface on p. 69). This method is called by some user interface component when receiving, say, a key-press event. The text view reacts by inserting the character at the current caret position into the view's text model. From there on, the activities unfold as described before. Figure 5.7 shows the message sequence.

The view is now re-entered by the model notification while it is still processing the type message. Recall the specification of method type (from interface TextView):

```
void type (char ch);
   // [ caret: int •
   //   pre   caret := this.caretPos() : this.text().length() < this.text().max()
   //   equiv  this.text().write(caret, ch)
   //   post  this.caretPos() = caret + 1
   // ]
```

Therefore, in addition to inserting the typed character into the text, the method is also supposed to update the caret position. Luckily, the notifier already does the desired update. Recall its specification as well:

```
void insertNotification (int pos);
   // pre  character has been inserted at position pos
   // post display updated and this.caretPos() = pos + 1
```

The type method therefore performs all of its duties simply by calling the write method of its text model, which calls the insertion notifier. This is a rather subtle consequence of the specifications and the actual interplay of the text view methods involved.

Now consider the case where the notifier's specification is relaxed to maintain the caret position wherever possible. In particular, the caret should not

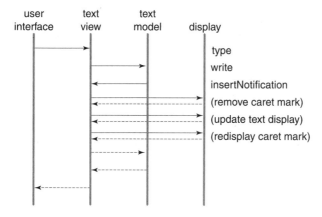

Figure 5.7 Message sequence caused by a request to insert a typed character.

move if it is located before the position of insertion. Also, it should be adjusted (by adding 1 to its current position) if it is located at or behind the position of insertion. The aim is that programmed text changes should not interfere with the caret – a user interface element.

Here is the changed insertion notifier specification:

```
void insertNotification (int pos);
    // [ caret: int •
    //   pre  caret := this.caretPos() :
    //          character has been inserted at position pos
    //   post  display updated
    //      and  caret < pos ⇒ this.caretPos() = caret
    //      and  caret ≥ pos ⇒ this.caretPos() = caret + 1
    // ]
```

Now a programmed text change no longer interferes with the caret position. Of course, a program could still call the view's setCaret method. However, the type method also needs a modification. As type is supposed to reflect a user event, it should still update the caret position. As the notifier no longer does this, the type method has to change the caret itself. A first difficulty at this point is that the type method needs to be changed at all, but things get worse.

By now, the example has developed into a fully fledged re-entrance scenario. Consider the following implementation of the type method:

```
void type (char ch) {
    int pos = caretPos();
    setCaret(pos + 1);
    text().write(pos, ch);
}
```

Innocent as it seems, this implementation breaks its contract. It is wrong. The reason is that, in an attempt to keep the caret at a consistent position, the notifier called indirectly by text().write may still change the caret. However, it assumes that the caret is still positioned where it was before the insertion took place. Assume that the caret sits at position 3 when a character is typed in. The type method sets the caret to position 4 and then inserts the character at position 3. If the notifier left the caret alone, everything would be fine. However, the notifier detects that the caret is at or behind the position of insertion (it is actually behind that position). Therefore, the notifier does its duty and increments the caret position, leaving it at position 5.

For a programmer seeing all detail, the solution is obvious. The order of actions in the type method needs to be reversed:

```
void type (char ch) {
    int pos = caretPos();
    text().write(pos, ch);
    setCaret(pos + 1);
}
```

Deriving this necessity from an inspection of all presented specifications would be possible, but is quite involved. The type method could be further simplified by deleting the call to setCaret entirely, provided the postcondition of insertNotification remains as it is. As the position of insertion is invariably that of the caret, this postcondition guarantees advancement of the caret position by 1. Some might still prefer the redundant call to setCaret, as it makes the type method more robust under evolution of the other method specifications. Obviously, a tradeoff between robustness and performance would be required if setCaret was an expensive operation. As can be seen, object re-entrance poses difficult problems even in this relatively simple example.

5.8 Self-interference and object re-entrance: a summary

Re-entrance of methods can pose problems, as objects normally have state and thus are not automatically re-entrant. A simple solution would be to require all invariants of an object to be established before calling any method. In other words, all state needs to be made consistent before calling a method. However, this is not possible where a state transformation requires a sequence of method calls. Unfortunately, this is commonly the case. At least self-recursive method calls (those to the current object) should thus be possible, even if not all invariants hold.

In addition, there are examples where objects are in a cyclical dependency. Desired invariants covering multiple objects in such a cycle cannot always be maintained. Such conditions can only be invariants for clients that cannot observe the transitory inconsistencies. Unfortunately, the observation of intermediate state can be difficult to prevent, as became apparent in the previous examples.

One way to address re-entrance problems caused by self-recursion or cyclical dependencies is to weaken invariants conditionally and make the conditions available to clients by means of test functions. Such conditions then allow for transitory violations of the original "invariant," leaving room for its re-establishment in cases in which multiple objects are involved. Note how such conditions are equivalent to the construction of test functions introduced for callback patterns (p. 65).

For example, in the model view or the observer design pattern that was used in the examples above, there is an "invariant" stating that the view presents part of what is represented by the model. However, when the model is modified, it first has to notify its views of the change. On receipt of the notification, a view updates itself accordingly.

Clearly, the simple invariant "a view presents the contents of its model" cannot be upheld and needs to be refined. A possible solution is to add a time stamp to the model, recording the most recent change to it. The view also gets a time stamp, recording the version of the model that it currently reflects. The invariant then becomes "a view that has the same time stamp as its model presents the contents of its model."

Now consider a refinement of the view. In addition to the representation of part of its model's contents, the view also displays some sort of marks. A caret mark was used above; selection marks would be another example. The precise position on the display depends on the marked model's contents. If the model changed, the marks may have to be moved or removed. On receipt of a notification that the model has changed, a view cannot rely on the model to compute the location of the old marks. Thus, it either has to cache all required information or the marks have to be removed before a model can be changed. The former way was taken in the above examples. Both approaches can be found in contemporary frameworks.

Such a subtle aspect is easily missed in the design of a complex object system unless all contracts are refined to ensure that they properly cover re-entrance conditions. A significant number of design and implementation errors – often hard to find and correct – go back to unexpected recursive re-entrance of objects. The recursion leading to such re-entrances is obscured either by subtle interactions of classes in an inheritance hierarchy or subtle interactions of objects.

Contracts based on pre- and postconditions can capture the conditions to allow for safe interactions, even in the presence of recursive re-entrance. The above time stamping used to weaken an invariant can also be applied to pre- and postconditions. However, such conditions are missing in almost all published interface specifications, pointing at a severe problem yet to be addressed in practice.

By now it should be clear that dealing with recursion and re-entrance is difficult enough in situations where the recursion is explicit and part of the design. However, self-recursion within a single object can be almost arbitrarily affected by class inheritance and thus leads to recursive re-entrance patterns that are neither explicitly specified nor necessarily expected. This thread is picked up again in Chapter 7.

Recursion and re-entrance become an even more pressing problem when crossing the boundaries of components. You will recall that the problem in the type method (p. 75) was solved after stepping back and inspecting the overall situation. With components, this can be impossible to do as a component system, by definition, does not have a final form. The specification problems encountered in recursive re-entrant systems need to be solved in a modular way to cater for components. In other words, each component must be independently verifiable based on the contractual specifications of the interfaces it requires and those it provides.

5.9   Processes and multithreading

The problems of recursive re-entrance of objects and concurrent interaction of processes are similar – even identical in the case of objects interacting across process boundaries. The idea can be taken to the extreme, by assigning full process semantics to every object. "Actors," as proposed by Hewitt and refined by Agha (Agha and Hewitt, 1987), go even further and turn every object invocation into a separate process! However, the current consensus is that doing so is not efficient. Instead, objects and processes are kept separate and processes are quite often populated by multiple threads.

It would seem that making an object system thread-safe – that is, protecting it against unwanted interferences from concurrent activities – would also solve the re-entrance problems. This turns out not to be the case. It must be possible for a thread to re-enter areas that it itself has locked. Otherwise, self-recursion and re-entrance patterns would simply lead to deadlocks – sometimes called self-inflicted deadlocks (Cardelli, 1994).

Assume that a thread had locked an object and, under self-recursion or indirect recursion, tries to re-enter that object. There are really only two possibilities. First, the thread can be treated as any other thread and has to wait for the locked object to be released. Of course, the locked object will never be released as the lock is held by the thread that now waits. Therefore, the thread deadlocks and all objects that it locked remain locked indefinitely. This is not acceptable, as re-entrance in the presence of abstraction cannot be prevented.

Alternatively, a thread may be granted access to locked objects if the lock is held by just that thread. This rule avoids deadlocks and, indeed, is found in many concurrent object-oriented languages, including Java. Unfortunately, relaxing the locking rules to allow re-entrance by the same thread also reintroduces all the problems of re-entrance. Understanding and properly addressing the issues of re-entrance in object systems does not become any simpler by introducing processes or threads.

5.10   Histories

Another approach to capturing the legal interactions among objects is the specification of permissible histories. This approach has its origin in algebraic specifications of abstract data types (ADTs). Histories, in the technical sense, are traces of states of a variable or a set of variables. Valid state transitions can then be specified by restricting the set of permissible traces. In other words, the specification is a formally captured set of permissible traces. For example, to specify that a variable's value can only stay the same or be increased, the specification could state that, in any permissible history of that variable, the recorded values are non-decreasing. By recording pairs of values in a trace, a history constraint can specify invariant relationships between two variables, and so on.

In most history-based specification techniques, permissible traces or histories are specified indirectly. In addition to a specification of valid initial states, a set of transformations is given. Each transformation takes any permissible trace, transforms it, and yields another, usually longer, permissible trace. This transformational approach led to the name algebraic specification.

For example, suppose it is intended that it is always permissible to increment a certain variable by 1. In this case, a transformation would take any non-empty trace of that variable. This transformation would return a trace that is identical to the one taken, with the most recent value incremented by 1 and appended to the end of the trace.

When considering substitutability (Chapter 6), some further complications arise. In terms of traces, an object is substitutable for another if all traces of the new object, projected to the states and operations of the old object, are explicable in terms of the old object. This is similar to the notion of behavioral subtyping (America, 1991; Liskov and Wing, 1994) and ensures that a client expecting the old object cannot observe that the new object is used. More generally, if traces were used to specify an interface, then any class implementing this interface would have to satisfy the substitutability criterion. For example, if an interface specification states that some event A will always be followed by an event B, then all implementations of that interface have to ensure that this is observed.

The idea of trace-based specifications can be incorporated into type systems such that substitutability can be verified automatically. Obviously, where such types would require equivalence of computed results, the type system would no longer be decidable. Unfortunately, even when concentrating only on permissible sequences of operations, the resulting system is undecidable as the number of legal states is, in general, unbounded (Hüttel, 1991). By introducing type systems that merely specify approximate bounds on traces, decidable type systems that help to check substitutability conservatively can indeed be found (for example, Nierstrasz, 1993). As with all practical type systems, these systems rule out some correct substitutions, but never permit incorrect ones. Specifications and type systems for objects are still an area of much ongoing work.

Combining the notions of history-based specification with that of stream-processing components leads to interesting specification and composition approaches. Probably the oldest example in this area is flow-based programming (FBP; Morrison, 1994). FBP has its roots on IBM mainframes in the 1970s, primarily driven by J. Paul Morrison and his group at IBM Canada. The idea is to focus on asynchronous processes that communicate by producing and consuming streams of data items. FBP introduced the concept of a coordination language to describe the composition of such processes, yielding composite components. Coordination languages describe connections between processes external to these processes. This is similar to connection-oriented programming (section 10.3) and architecture description languages (section 21.1.2).

FOCUS (Broy and Stølen, 2001) is a more recent example of a method in this direction. FOCUS establishes a mathematically rigorous foundation and a specification framework to specify components in a modular way. Like FBP, FOCUS uses data streams to establish communication links between component instances. FOCUS offers an interesting selection of modes of abstraction, such as glassbox versus blackbox composites. A glassbox reveals its internal composition structure and thus prevents refinements from changing this structure, while a blackbox does not reveal such structure and therefore allows for a wider choice of refinements. FOCUS adds a unique concept of global discrete time, modeled by inserting "clock tick" symbols into streams that can be used to specify and verify certain time-related properties. As a particularly strong point, FOCUS supports a spectrum of pragmatically useful modeling and specification tools, all of which are grounded in the same single underlying semantic model.

5.11   Specification statements

In the example of TextModels above (section 5.6), it suffices to specify when notifiers will be called and what a notifier is allowed to do. In particular, all notifiers are called after completion of a text-modifying operation and notifiers are not themselves allowed to modify their notifying text. These conditions can be captured neatly by using a specification that takes an imperative but high-level and non-deterministic form. Such specifications are sometimes called specification statements, as their form is somewhat similar to that of statement-oriented imperative languages. It is possible to insert specification statements into a sequence of normal statements. Unlike normal statements, specification statements state as much about an implementation as needs to be stated to capture the specification, while normal statements have to remove nondeterminism and accommodate many technical implementation decisions. Specification statements can then be refined into correct implementations ("refinement calculus"; Morgan, 1990).

A specification of TextModels (attributable to Emil Sekerinski and Wolfgang Weck; see also Büchi and Weck, 1997) is given below. Readers who are not interested in formal specifications may safely skip the remainder of this chapter.

The specification largely follows Morgan's notation (Morgan, 1990), with the addition of a few intuitive constructs – namely, class, keep, invariant over several classes, for ... do ... od. The class construct is similar to Morgan's module construct.

```
class TextModel;
  var text: seq char; observers: set Observer; max: N •
  procedure Max (result m: N) =
    m: [true, m ≥ max]; max := m;
  procedure Length (result l: N) =
```

```
    l := #text;
  procedure Read (pos: N; result ch: char) =
    ch := text[pos];
  procedure Write (pos: N; ch: char) =
    {max > #text} ;
    text := text[0 ... pos - 1] + <ch> + text[pos ... #text - 1];
    for o ∈ observers do o.InsertNotification(pos) od;
  procedure Delete (pos: N) =
    text := text[0...pos - 1] + text[pos + 1...#text - 1];
    for o ∈ observers do o.DeleteNotification(pos) od;
  procedure Register (obs: Observer) =
    observers := observers + {obs} ;
  procedure Unregister (obs: Observer) =
    observers := observers - {obs} ;
    initially text = <>; observers = { } ; max = 0
  end
class Observer;
  var text: TextModel •
  procedure InsertNotification (pos: N) =
    keep text^ ;
  procedure DeleteNotification (pos: N) =
    keep text^
end
invariant
    o: Observer; t: TextModel • o ∈ t.observers ⟺ o.text = t
```

Here are a few notes on the notation used.

- The selector operations on sequences s[i] and s[i...j] imply the precondition $0 \leq i \leq j < \#s$.
- The condition keep text^ means that none of the observable state according to the specification of text must be changed during this operation.

The specification of Max indicating the specific TextModels capacity is completely non-deterministic but points out that the values returned by Max are non-decreasing. Variable max is used for the sole reason of enforcing this constraint. This is important for max to be used in the precondition of Write at all, but has been left unspecified in the more informal specifications presented earlier in this chapter.

The specification of notifiers exhibits the problem mentioned earlier. It prohibits the notifier from modifying its notifying text. However, this precludes invocation of operations for which confined analysis – that is, analysis over a confined context – cannot establish that the notifier does not indirectly modify this text. Global analysis solves this but is in conflict with components and independent extensibility.

CHAPTER SIX

Polymorphism

Polymorphism is the ability of something to appear in multiple forms, depending on context, and the ability of different things to appear the same in a certain context. These are the two flip sides of the polymorphic coin. A refinement occurs once it is accepted that something does not have to be only what it appears to be. Then, dynamic exploration of what is behind the static appearance becomes possible.

This chapter sheds some light on the consequences of the above, somewhat philosophical, statements. In particular, the notion of substitutability is explained and related to the concepts of types and subtypes. Types lead to the notion of interfaces and their important role for components. As components are independently deployed, it is of utmost importance that the deployment environment accepts components that independently extend this environment. The important paradigm of independent extensibility is introduced to capture this requirement. The discussion of independent extensibility naturally leads to questions of security, safety, and trust. The chapter concludes with a discussion of different dimensions of independent extensibility, aspects of software evolution, and a short summary of some other forms of polymorphism not previously discussed in this chapter.

1.6 Substitutability – using one for another

Self-standing contractually specified interfaces decouple clients and providers. The same interface may be used by large numbers of different clients but also be supported by a large number of different providers. To avoid reducing the spectrum of possible clients and providers unnecessarily, an interface must be specified carefully. It should not require too much from either its clients or its providers. However, if it requires too little from them, the interface is just as useless.

If an interface requires too little from clients – for example, no non-trivial preconditions – it can overburden providers. In particular, such an interface can be hard or even impossible to implement. Also, it can be impossible to implement it

efficiently. On the flip side, if an interface requires too little from providers –
for example, no non-trivial postconditions – it is of no use to clients.

A carefully crafted interface requires no more than is essential for the service
to be provided. Such interfaces usually leave significant headroom for clients
and providers. In particular, clients and providers are always free to overfulfill
their contract. A client may establish more than is required by the precondition or expect less than is guaranteed by the postcondition. Likewise, a
provider may require less than is guaranteed by the precondition or establish
more than is required by the postcondition.

Pre- and postconditions are usually specified using predicates. The notion of
expecting less than is guaranteed takes the form of a logical implication – guarantees imply expectations. Likewise, an implication can be used to express that more
might be provided than is required – the provided implies the required. Using
the common symbol for implication ($\Rightarrow$), the above can be summarized as:

> established by certain client
> $\Rightarrow$ demanded by interface (precondition)
> $\Rightarrow$ required by certain provider

> established by certain provider
> $\Rightarrow$ guaranteed by interface (postcondition)
> $\Rightarrow$ expected by certain client

Here is an example. Consider the interface TextModel as introduced in Chapter
5 (p. 67). The relevant section of the interface is repeated below.

```
interface TextModel {
    int max ();   // maximum length this text can have
    int length ();   // current length
    char read (int pos);   // character at position pos
    void write (int pos, char ch);   // insert character ch at position pos
        // [ len: int; txt: array of char •
        //  pre    len := this.length(); (all i: 0 ≤ i < len: txt[i] := this.read(i)) :
        //         len < this.max() and 0 ≤ pos ≤ len
        //  post this.length() = len + 1
        //      and (all i: 0 ≤ i < pos: this.read(i) = txt[i])
        //      and this.read(pos) = ch
        //      and (all i: pos < i < this.length(): this.read(i) = txt[i - 1])
        // ]
    ...
}
```

Notice how the interface requires callers of operation write to make sure that the
character to be written is inserted within the current range of the text. An implementation GreatTextModel may relax this by allowing insertions to happen past

the end of the current text, by padding with blanks where necessary. Thus, a provider's implementation of write may have the following weakened precondition and strengthened postcondition (the changes are emphasized).

```
class GreatTextModel implements TextModel {
    ...
    void write (int pos, char ch) {
        // [ len: int; txt: array of char •
        //   pre    len := this.length(); (all i: 0 ≤ i < len: txt[i] := this.read(i));
        //          len < this.max() and  0 ≤ pos < this.max()
        //   post this.length() = max(len, pos) + 1
        //      and  (all i: 0 ≤ i < min(pos, len): this.read(i) = txt[i])
        //      and  this.read(pos) = ch
        //      and  (all i: pos < i ≤ len: this.read(i) = txt[i - 1])
        //      and  (all i: len < i < pos: this.read(i) = " ")
        // ]
        ...
    }
    ...
}
```

The precondition of the interface TextModel.write does indeed imply that of the implementation GreatTextModel.write:

    this.length() < this.max() **and** 0 ≤ pos ≤ this.length()
⇒
    this.length() < this.max() **and** 0 ≤ pos < this.max()

The postcondition of the implementation GreatTextModel.write does indeed imply that of the interface TextModel.write, provided the stronger precondition of the interface held. If it did not, the interface makes no statement at all about possible postconditions:

    (*from precondition:*
      len := this.length(); max := this.max();
      (**all** i: 0 ≤ i < len: char[i] := this.read(i))
)
    len < max **and** 0 ≤ pos ≤ max
and
    this.length() = max(len, pos) + 1
    and (**all** i: 0 ≤ i < min(pos, len): this.read(i) = char[i])
    and this.read(pos) = ch
    and (**all** i: pos < i ≤ len: this.read(i) = char[i - 1])
    and (**all** i: len < i < pos: this.read(i) = " ")
⇒

```
this.length() = len + 1
and  (all i: 0 ≤ i < pos: this.read(i) = char[i])
and  this.read(pos) = ch
and  (all i: pos < i < this.length(): this.read(i) = char[i - 1])
```

In both cases, the verification of these implications is straightforward and left as an exercise to the reader so inclined. Readers preferring not to go into this level of detail may safely skip this exercise.

There are, surprisingly, many further possible ways in which providers can interpret the interface contract. For example, a provider may accept arbitrary positions, including negative ones, in all operations, simply by first clipping the specified position to the currently valid range. Alternatively, a provider may decide to grow a text dynamically, making max return a non-constant value. Equally, a provider may decide to create the illusion of an infinitely long text, preinitialized with all blanks.

Obviously, clients based on the interface contract will not be able to benefit from any of the above implementation refinements. However, the same implementations could also support another interface contract that reveals more general capabilities.

On the client's end of an interface, the same sort of relaxation is possible. A client may guarantee more than is required and expect less than is provided. For example, a client of TextModel.write may use the operation only to append to a text:

```
{ TextModel text; int pos; char ch;
  ...
  if text.length() < text.max() {
    text.write(text.length(), ch);
    // expect  text.read(text.length() - 1) = ch
  }
  ...
}
```

Notice how pre- and postconditions make it fairly difficult to express conditions such as: "if text.length() < text.max() at one time, then this will continue to hold for as long as text.length() does not change." Such a condition is vitally important to avoid a "race condition" with precondition checks – the example above, for instance, depends on it. Owing to its notions of abstract time and sequencing, a history or statement-based specification technique as introduced in Chapter 5 can naturally cover such detail.

As is again easily verified, the client-established condition, together with the TextModel.length postcondition, implies the TextModel.write precondition. Also, the TextModel.write postcondition, together with the client's guarantees, implies the client's expectation:

text.length() $\geq$ 0
and
text.length() < text.max() **and** pos = text.length()
$\Rightarrow$
text.length() < text.max() **and** 0 $\leq$ pos $\leq$ text.length()
(*from precondition:*
   len := this.length(); max := this.max();
   (**all** i: 0 $\leq$ i < len: char[i] := this.read(i))
)
pos = len
and
text.length() = len + 1
and (**all** i: 0 $\leq$ i < pos: text.read(i) = char[i])
and text.read(pos) = ch
and (**all** i: pos < i < text.length(): text.read(i) = char[i - 1])
$\Rightarrow$
text.read(text.length() -1) = ch

Understanding the flexibility introduced by requiring only implications, instead of equivalences, becomes very important when considering interactions of multiple providers and clients. Figure 6.1 illustrates the pivotal role of the interface contract when considering multiple clients and multiple providers of the services advertised by an interface.

Libraries always supported the concept of a service provider catering for many clients. However, in any one given configuration, there is only one implementation of a library interface and the only concern on the provider's side is versioning. As explained above, the situation has changed dramatically with the introduction of self-standing interfaces and dynamic dispatch (late binding).

When is it legal to substitute one service provider for another? An unknown number of clients may rely on the service simply by relying on what is contractually promised by the service interface. Therefore, another service provider can come in if it satisfies the same contract. If a provider satisfies the same contract as another, the former is said to be substitutable for the latter.

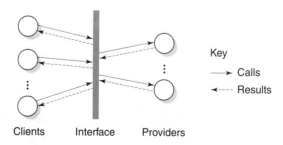

Figure 6.1 Pivotal role of interface contracts, coupling many clients with many providers.

6.2   Types, subtypes, and type checking

Ideally, all conditions of a contract would be stated explicitly and formally as part of an interface specification. In addition, it would be highly desirable to have a compiler or other automatic tool check clients and providers against the contract and reject incorrect ones. In practice, this ideal is quite far from attainable. Fully formalizing the interface contracts is a first major obstacle. Doing so is difficult and often considered too expensive.

However, even where a formal contract is available, automatic checking remains a major challenge of ongoing research. It is known that an efficient general-purpose verifier is not feasible. Therefore, research concentrates on tools that use heuristics to automate most of the manual proof process. Such tools are called theorem provers. Theorem proving will be too expensive to be done in a production compiler for years to come, and it requires manual assistance by an expert.

Today's compilers cannot check most conditions in a contract. Some cannot even be checked efficiently at runtime. However, it is worthwhile aiming for the earliest possible error checking to rule out potentially catastrophic faults. Hence, compiler-time checking is better than load-time checking, load-time checking is better than runtime checking, and runtime checking is better than no checking. However, sometimes later checking is the only possibility. For example, version conflicts among independently provided components can only be checked at configuration or load time. Likewise, index range errors can, generally, only be detected at runtime.

A class of errors that can lead to particularly disastrous results is memory errors. A memory error occurs when a program reads a memory cell based on a wrong assumption of what the cell contains. The program may expect, say, an object reference, whereas the cell really contains either something different – for example, a floating-point number – or has not been initialized at all. Memory errors are among the worst because they can affect entirely unrelated parts of a program, are notoriously hard to track down, and can be arbitrarily destructive.

Fortunately, there is a way to deal automatically with those conditions that need to be verified to eliminate memory errors. The idea is to group all values of related semantics, such as all integers, into sets. Such sets are called types. A type system ensures that all memory accesses are type compatible. By combining a type system with automatic memory management and certain runtime checks, a language implementation can fully eliminate memory errors – and some other error classes as well. Many modern languages, including Smalltalk, Java, C#, Oberon, and Component Pascal, fall into this category. However, many others, including Object Pascal, Modula-2, C, and C++, do not.

Basic types, such as INTEGER or REAL, can be understood as sets of values. In the context of objects and interfaces, a type is best understood as a set of objects implementing a certain interface.

A type names all operations of an interface and the number and type of parameters and the type of returned values of each of the operations. The types of input and in–out parameters form a part of an operation's preconditions. The types of output and in–out parameters plus the type of returned values form a part of an operation's postconditions. However, other pre- and postconditions that are likely to be part of the underlying contract are not part of a type. Thus, a type is an interface with a simplified contract.

As a type is a simplified contract, it is possible that a program that passes type checking still violates some contracts. This is an important point and is discussed below in section 6.5.

An object may implement more than the interface required in a certain context. It may implement additional interfaces or a version of the required interface extended with additional operations or both. For instance, the interfaces View, TextView, and GraphicsView below are in such an extension relation. TextView and GraphicsView are both interfaces that implement all operations in View, but also add operations specific to text and graphics viewing respectively. A more complete set of TextView operations has already been presented in Chapter 5 (p. 69).

```
interface View {
  void close ();
  void restore (int left, int top, int right, int bottom);
}
interface TextView extends View {
  int caretPos ();
  void setCaretPos (int pos);
}
interface GraphicsView extends View {
  int cursorX ();
  int cursorY ();
  void setCursorXY (int x, int y);
}
```

Under what circumstances can an object implementing one type be used in a context expecting another type? The answer follows directly from the above discussion of contracts. A client expecting a certain type really expects an object fulfilling a contract. Thus, all objects fulfilling the contract could be used. On the level of types, this includes all extended types as long as the understanding is that objects of an extended type respect the base contract.

Obviously, a TextView object or a GraphicsView object can be used wherever a View object is expected. As the set of text views is a proper subset of the set of views, TextView is called a subtype of View. Likewise, GraphicsView is a subtype of View.

The view examples show the formation of a subtype by defining a new interface and naming a base interface that is to be extended by the new interface.

This is called interface inheritance and is the most common way to form subtypes. Another way is structural subtyping, in which no base interface is named. Instead, operations are repeated and a subtype is said to be formed if a subset of the operations coincides with operations defined for another type.

A variable of type View can refer to objects of type View, TextView, GraphicsView, or other subtypes. This is called polymorphism, and the variable is said to be of a polymorphic type. As there are several different forms of polymorphism, this particular one is also called subtype or inclusion polymorphism. The latter name refers to the inclusion of subsets in their base set.

As far as the type system is concerned, objects of a subtype are substitutable for objects of a base type. However, again a warning: just as types simplify contracts, so does subtype polymorphism simplify substitutability. The fact that an object is in a proper subtype relationship does not guarantee that the object's implementation respects the base contract, or, for that matter, any contract. On the other hand, it is fair to say that types and subtyping rules can statically prevent many of the outright "dangerous" violations of contracts.

6.3 More on subtypes

The types of the parameters and the return value of an interface's operations form part of the pre- and postconditions of that operation. Discussion on "overfulfilling a contract" by a service provider helps to understand what legal modifications to the types of an operation a subtype interface may apply. (It would be logical to talk about subcontracts when referring to the contracts associated with subtypes. Unfortunately, subcontract has an entirely different and well-established meaning.)

Note that this section mostly presents straightforward consequences of what has been discussed above, but is quite technical in nature. It can be safely skipped, especially on a first read.

Types of output parameters and return values form part of an operation's postconditions. A provider may establish more than is required by a contract. Hence, a subtype interface can replace the types of output parameters and return values by something more specific – that is, by subtypes. In other words, the types of output parameters and return values may be varied from types to subtypes when moving from an interface of a certain type to an interface of a subtype of that type. As the types of output parameters and return values can thus be varied in the same direction as the types of the containing interfaces, this is called covariance.

Types of input parameters form part of an operation's preconditions. A provider may expect less than is guaranteed by a contract. Hence, a subtype interface could replace the types of input parameters by something more general – supertypes. In other words, the types of input parameters may be varied from types to supertypes when going from an interface of a certain type to an interface of a subtype of that type. As the types of input parameters can thus be varied in the opposite direction of the types of the containing interfaces, this is called contravariance.

The requirements of co- and contravariance can be illustrated graphically by showing how a function could be substituted for another if it covers the same or a larger domain and if it has the same or a smaller range. Figure 6.2 illustrates this. In terms of domain and range, function g in the figure could be used in places where function f was expected.

Finally, types of in–out parameters simultaneously form part of an operation's pre- and postcondition. From a combination of the arguments for types in pre- and postconditions developed above, it follows that types of in–out parameters cannot be varied at all in a subtype interface. This phenomenon is sometimes called invariance of in–out parameter types. If, in addition to operations, an interface is also allowed to contain modifiable attributes, these also have invariant types.

Here is an example. Consider adding an operation getModel to interface View. In the case of a text view the model is of type TextModel, and this could be reflected by covariantly redefining getModel in TextView. The same can be done for getModel in GraphicsView.

```
interface View {
    ... // as above
    Model getModel ();
}
interface TextView extends View {
    ... // as above
    TextModel getModel ();
}
interface GraphicsView extends View {
    ... // as above
    GraphicsModel getModel ();
}
```

This is obviously useful. Clients that care only about View will get a generic Model when they ask for the views model. However, clients that know they are dealing with a TextView object will get a TextModel.

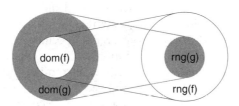

Figure 6.2 Contravariance of the domain and covariance of the range of a function g that could, in terms of domain and range, be substituted for a function f.

Next, consider an operation setModel used to connect a view to a certain model. If part of View, setModel would have to take an object of type Model.

```
interface View {
  ... // as above
  void setModel (Model m);  // is this a good idea?
}
```

However, a TextView object needs a TextModel object as its model and a GraphicsView needs a GraphicsModel. If covariant change of input parameters was safe, setModel could be changed in TextView to accept a TextModel and in GraphicsView to accept a GraphicsModel.

Using a subtype interface allows substitution of a subtype object for a base type object. Thus, a text view would have to expect to be used in a context that knows only about interface View. Within that context, the precondition of setModel simply requires, as far as types are concerned, a Model object. Thus, even if TextView were allowed (incorrectly) to modify covariantly the type of setModels input parameter, it would not help. The best that could happen is a dynamically caught type violation error.

Some type systems allow the introduction of typings that are coupled to the interface inheritance hierarchy. In other words, part of the precondition of the base operation is that subtype operations may covariantly modify certain parts that normally would fall under the contravariance restriction. Such type systems have to introduce other restrictions to remain sound, that is, to continue to allow claims about absence of certain errors in well-typed programs.

For example, for static checking, the original Eiffel type system (Meyer, 1990) required a conservative global analysis of entire programs including all libraries used. Such a global analysis was called system-level type checking, and it clearly defeats the ideas of modular checking (p. 77). A library may type check on its own and thus be delivered to clients. Then, the combination of client and library code may lead to type errors in the library. Such type errors are indirectly caused by the addition of the client code, but are hard to explain. Modular checking requires monotonicity, which means that if one module is determined to be internally type correct, then the addition of other modules cannot affect this result.

Type matching (Bruce *et al.*, 1997) and the revised Eiffel type system (Meyer, 1996) both allow for modular type checking of individual operations but require a more specific typing of variables. In particular, type matching requires that covariant changes in contravariant positions can occur only where the typed variable is declared to be monomorphic – that is, cannot refer to an object of a subtype. Similarly, revised Eiffel requires that such covariant changes can only occur where the typed variable can be conservatively determined to be monomorphic. Sather is another object-oriented language that requires variables to be declared as either monomorphic or polymorphic (Szyperski *et al.*, 1994; Omohundro and Stoutamire, 1996).

6.4 Object languages and types

Some languages, such as Smalltalk, do not have an explicit type system. In some of these cases, a compiler can still derive types by inspection of strictly local program fragments, such as in the Smalltalk dialect StrongTalk (Bracha and Griswold, 1993). In such languages, avoidance of explicit typing is a matter of convenience – there is less to write. The compiler can still check a program's typing and static type safety is preserved. Adding explicit typing is still useful, as it makes important architectural and design decisions explicit.

In other cases, including original Smalltalk, type inference is not possible without relying on global analysis of the entire code body (Palsberg and Schwartzbach, 1991). Type checking in Smalltalk and similar languages is thus deferred to runtime. For example, a Smalltalk expression x insert: 4 at: 3 requires that variable x refers at runtime to an object that understands the message insert:at:. However, in the general case, this cannot be verified statically. As a result, x may refer at runtime to an object that does not understand the message insert:at:. At least, this is checked dynamically and a "message not understood" exception is raised at runtime in such a case.

More modern languages, such as Java and Component Pascal, use an explicit type system and statically check programs at compile time. In addition, they check narrowing type casts at runtime. (A narrowing cast is a cast in which the programmer asserts that a variable of a certain type really refers to an object of a subtype of that type. The cast narrows a set to a subset.)

For readers who followed the co-/contravariance story above, it is interesting that few of the mainstream languages support any changes in types of operations when forming subtypes. In C^{++}, covariant return types were introduced only in early 1994 (Ellis and Stroustrup, 1994, p. 421). Java and C$^{\#}$ still do not support any type changes. (The Java 1.0 beta specification allowed for covariant return values, while neither the alpha specification nor the final 1.0 or 1.1 specification does.) Like C^{++}, Component Pascal supports covariant change of return values, but no other co- or contravariant changes.

6.5 Types, interfaces, and components

Some programming languages do not require the programmer to specify types and, instead, infer the most general types that still allow a program fragment to be type correct. Of course, this approach is impossible where interfaces are self-standing. At the time of creation of such an interface, there may be no implementations available. Indeed, clients may be programmed before the first provider implementing the interface becomes available. To keep clients and providers independent, a self-standing interface has to be fully and explicitly typed to benefit from type checking.

Other programming languages establish subtype compatibility between two types structurally. Assume that an interface of one type happens to contain all operations contained by another type – and the operations in the two interfaces themselves are appropriately typed. In this case, the former type is inferred to be a subtype of the latter. As, in this case, subtyping is based on type structures, this is sometimes called structural subtyping in contrast to declared subtyping. Obviously, in situations in which all types are inferred, types do not have names and subtyping has to be based on structural compatibility.

When viewing types as simplified contracts, it becomes clear that structural subtyping is dangerous. The structure of a type covers only part of a contract – the part that can be expressed in the used type system. A named type refers to the full contract. If another type is then considered to be a subtype of this type, it has to respect the contract of its base type, in addition to its own contract. As the full contracts are only referred to, proper subtype relations cannot be inferred automatically. Thus, a programmer should explicitly declare whether or not a type should be considered a legal subtype of another type. If so declared, the programmer accepts the obligation to verify that the subtype relation is indeed justified.

Many articles (for example, Magnusson, 1991) describe the apocryphal tale of a graphics editor that accepted all objects that happened to have a method draw. Unfortunately, the user program failed horribly after accidentally inserting a cowboy object into the graphics editor, which then caused the editor to redraw all objects.

It is sometimes argued that accidental structural subtyping is not likely in practice. The argument is that, for this to happen, all operations of the base type, including all of their parameter numbers and types and their return types, accidentally need to agree. For substantial interfaces this is indeed unlikely. Indeed, even for the draw example above, it is not likely that a graphics objects draw method would do without any parameters – as is likely to be the case for a cowboy object's draw method.

For small interfaces, and these are typical at the roots of subtype hierarchies, the situation is different. Quite often, root types have no or only a few very basic operations. Additionally, root types tend to be designed by following common design patterns. Thus, it is indeed possible and likely that accidentally derived subtypes lead to objects in positions where they, unknowingly, break their contracts.

For example, base types for interfaces such as Event and Property are likely to be empty. Alternatively, they may contain an operation to get some "owner" object – the event source or the object having the property. Thus, the structure of base types, say, Event and Property may coincide. Deriving a subtype relationship from that is unacceptable, of course, as an event is not a property and vice versa.

Another aspect of components is their potential support of multiple interfaces. It is sometimes necessary to specify a required set of interfaces and then accept any component that provides at least these required interfaces. Such interface sets are sometimes called categories. For example, Microsoft's COM

IDL has been extended to support such categories. This can be used to support one-stop tests, such as checking that a component implements all interfaces required to make it an ActiveX control.

In Java and C# (and most other CLR-targeting languages), even objects can implement multiple interfaces and interfaces can extend multiple interfaces. An example would be the merger of the two TextView examples presented above (pp. 69 and 89) – a TextView interface would have to extend both the TextObserver and the View interface. In Java, this is possible. However, Java has no concept of categories and an object's implementation of a set of interfaces must therefore be tested one by one. However, since category-like sets of interfaces are known ahead of time, they can be expressed as empty interfaces that derive from the set of interfaces in question. Testing whether or not an object implements a particular category then amounts to checking if it implements the category's interface. This approach works only if the object in question has been equipped to actually implement the category's interface rather than just implementing all the individual interfaces required by the category. Using a notion of structural interface sets and checking for the matching of such sets solves this problem. An example is Büchi and Weck's compound types (1998).

6.6 The paradigm of independent extensibility

The principal function of component orientations is to support independent extensibility.

A system is independently extensible if it is extensible and if independently developed extensions can be combined (Szyperski, 1996). For example, all operating systems are one-level independently extensible by loading applications. However, many applications themselves turned into independently extensible systems. Extensions to applications are sometimes called plugins. Applications, such as Netscape's Navigator or Internet Explorer, slowly turn into platforms by supporting an increasing number of increasingly complex plugins. The first examples of plugins supporting "sub-plugins" have already arrived. One such example is Gazelle, a browser plugin that supports downloading of Component Pascal "applets" that execute in a local blackbox component framework (Paznesh, 1997). Java is by now part of many browsers, but where that is not the case, Sun's Java Activator plugin is another example.

As applications are fragmented and turned into extensible architectures, operating systems do not stand still either. A radical design reduces the operating system itself to a minimal kernel, called a micro-kernel, and farms out almost all OS functionality to application-level servers. Micro-kernels were originally driven by research operating systems such as Mach (Accetta *et al.*, 1986) that by themselves never really made it on to the more general markets. However, the micro-kernel design also influenced industrial-strength operating system designs, including Microsoft's Windows NT (Cutler, 1993), which led to Windows 2000 and Windows XP, and recently Apple's Mac OS X (www.apple.com/macosx/), which is directly based on Mach.

Combining the "dekernelization" efforts of operating system architects and the modularization efforts of application architects leads to a new vision for overall system architectures – components everywhere! However, it is not only about being able to construct the equivalent of the traditional operating system combined with a handful of applications. It is all about forming a system architecture that is independently extensible on all levels. It is about independent extensibility as a recursive construction principle applied uniformly. Such systems have been explored in research projects (for example, the Ethos system; Szyperski, 1992a) and also in industrial projects. One of the most ambitious approaches, Taligent, failed. To understand why, it is helpful to return first to the early attempts to develop micro-kernel designs for operating systems.

Partitioning of systems into smallest components (to maximize reuse) conflicts with efficiency, but also with robustness when facing evolution and configurational variety. This was discussed in detail in Chapter 4. An argument similar to that for robustness can be made for performance. Micro-kernel architecture enforces total isolation of application-level processes to establish system safety and support security mechanisms. However, isolation comes at a price, and frequent crossing of protection domain boundaries can severely affect performance. (There are memory management units that separate address space management from protection domains, for example the ARM MMU (Furber, 1996). However, hardware support for many lightweight protection domains has yet to make it into the mainstream. Software alternatives exist (Wahbe *et al.*, 1993), but have yet to gain the degree of trust that a hardware protection mechanism commands.) In the end, for an operating system to be viable, its architects have to strive for a balance between flexibility on the one hand and performance and robustness on the other.

After initial waves of euphoria, many operating system experts now agree that extreme "micro-kernelism" is not the optimal design for an operating system. After all, flexibility and configurability are only one side of an operating system's characteristics. The other side, and at least as important, is delivery of overall system performance. It is the latter requirement that directly conflicts with extreme micro-kernel designs. For example, starting with version 4.0, Microsoft moved significant parts of the display driver code into the NT kernel to improve substantially the performance of graphics-intense applications. This move, unfortunately, also introduced a major threat to the robustness of NT – faulty display drivers would literally render polygons across kernel memory. Starting with Windows 2000, Microsoft is now publishing driver test suites and encourages driver manufacturers to get their drivers certified by independent third-party services. The certification authority cryptographically signs certified drivers – unsigned drivers of unknown quality status are, by default, rejected by Windows (as of Windows XP).

How can component technology and independent extensibility as a recursive system design concept ever be viable if performance is so severely affected? The answer to this question would seem extremely important for the future of component technology. In reality, however, it turns out to be the wrong question.

The true question to be answered is "Why is performance so severely affected?" The obvious answer is "because it is expensive to perform cross-context calls." Whenever an invocation crosses contexts (processes and so on), the operating system has to ensure several things. It has to make sure that security policies are respected – that is, check whether or not the call happens under proper authorization. Further, it has to adjust the hardware protection mechanisms by switching from caller to callee context. Finally, it has to make sure that the call parameters are transferred from the caller to the callee context. Once the called function returns, the process has to be reverted. In addition to the unavoidable basic costs, the switch also affects the processor caches. On some machines, the caches even have to be flushed for security reasons.

All this is expensive – a cross-context call on well-tuned operating systems is still easily a hundred times more expensive than a local in-process call. This is not the operating system's fault. Most architectures rely on hardware-supported process isolation to guarantee safety. An example of this is protecting a process in the presence of another out-of-control process that is trying to write to arbitrary memory addresses. Given a properly "sealed" operating system and proper set-up of authorizations, even a maliciously ill-formed program written directly in the machine's assembly language cannot harm other programs executing on the same machine.

The cost of hardware protection is high but can be tolerated if the switching can be limited to, for example, a few hundred switches per second. This is the case under normal time-sharing operations of traditional operating systems. In this case, inter-process communication (IPC) is usually based on pipelining data streams that decouple source and destination and reduce the frequency of context switching. Clearly, for tightly interacting components, "intercomponent communication" happens at much higher frequencies and is much more synchronous – the source component often has to wait for the result before it can continue.

On machines built for interactive use and made from cheap commodity items, called personal computers, this has long led to the utilization of rather different operating systems. Neither the Mac OS nor MS-DOS had a true process model. Hardware protection was mostly ignored. A malicious program could easily "crash" the entire system. This was, and occasionally still is, considered acceptable as these machines typically serve a single user who is in charge and who can avoid the crash simply by avoiding the use of unreliable applications.

At the same time, these machines and operating systems perform very well when it comes to typical interactive use. System extensions or plugins are called directly, with no context switches involved. Component architectures in specialized areas have been in mainstream use for some time. For example, Apple's QuickTime included plugin modules from the start, even though QuickTime's multimedia services are among the most performance-critical a system can offer.

Is it possible to have your cake and eat it too? Could there be a third way, with efficient component composition that also offers the sort of safety already demanded in section 2.2? One way is to choose carefully the granularity of components. If most interactions stay within a component's boundaries, the cost incurred when crossing component boundaries may be tolerable. Chapter 8 continues a discussion of various aspects governing component granularity. Another way is to guarantee statically that a component will be safe. This is discussed further in the next section.

6.7   Safety by construction – viability of components

The discussion on type safety points in the right direction. After all, hardware protection "just" eliminates memory errors – it prevents one part of a system from accessing (reading, writing, or executing) any other part of the system for which it has no authorization. In a totally type-safe system, the equivalent reading is that no part can access any other part to which it has not been given a reference or that is not in its static scope of visibility.

Here is an example. The Java class files (Java's portable compiled format) and the Java virtual machine have been crafted to interact in a way that prevents type-unsafe applets from being executed in a non-local environment. Java is a type-safe language. It provides automatic memory management using garbage collection. Finally, it performs runtime checks on all operations that are "dangerous," but cannot be statically checked, such as array bounds checks. Together, these techniques guarantee that memory errors cannot occur. As class files, produced by the Java compiler, could be tampered with, the virtual machine rechecks them when loading one coming from a non-local site, such as across the internet.

Component Pascal is another example. The language offers similarly strong guarantees. Here the execution environment receives an intermediate portable form produced by the compiler that is based on an entirely different approach. This form is also rechecked, but then compiled into a local cache of binaries and future references to the same component directly use the cached binary. Like Java, Component Pascal is also fully garbage collected. Unlike Java, Component Pascal neither has nor needs an interpreter or a virtual machine.

A third example is the Microsoft .NET Common Language Runtime (CLR). CLR also uses late compilation and avoids interpretation, eliminating the notion of a virtual machine. It defines an intermediate language that has been designed to support a wide variety of programming languages and still map efficiently to a wide variety of processors. Some 15 to 20 languages have been investigated and many of them implemented (in a large international collaborative effort called "Project 7") in order to validate the claim of support for many languages.

All three examples share one feature, which is that strong safety properties can be established at compile-time, checked at install, load, or JIT compile-time, and then be relied on without further checking while executing the resulting efficient code.

6.7.1 Module safety

However, type safety and elimination of memory errors are not enough, although it is assumed that the language respects object encapsulation. Without any additional measures, it would still be possible for a program to call arbitrary services present in or loadable into the system. This would be all that is required to acquire references to arbitrary objects in the system and thus "legally" (as far as the type system is concerned) to perform arbitrary manipulations. For example, there are ActiveX controls that shut down Windows.

The one additional requirement, also met by Java, Component Pascal, and CLR is module safety (Szyperski and Gough, 1995). A component has to specify explicitly which services – from the system or other components – it needs to access. This is done in the form of module (or package) import lists. The language and system do not allow access to any non-imported module. Hence, if that list contains only permissible modules, then it is safe to load and execute the new component. This is like access control in file systems, but on a per module (or per class) basis, rather than a per object basis. Objects are too dynamic to be identified explicitly for purposes of static access control.

With module safety in place, abstractions of entire multiobject services can be formed. Unlike classes, modules can enforce invariants across tightly interacting objects (Szyperski, 1992a). In a language not supporting any higher granularity of packaging than classes, access protection would have to be per class, offering class safety instead of module safety.

Module safety is not quite as simple as it sounds. In component systems it is important that other components (and services) can be retrieved by name. The name itself may be made available to a component after that component has been compiled, checked, and loaded – that is, at runtime. A clean and popular way to support component retrieval by name is a reflection service. Java, Component Pascal, and .NET CLR all offer such services. Where access to components is to be restricted, reflection services require special attention so as not to create a security loophole.

6.7.2 Module safety and metaprogramming

It should be impossible for a component to retrieve references to other components to which it has not been granted access. For example, in Java, a special security manager object is used to inspect whether or not the caller of a critical function has proper authorization. To do so, the call stack is traversed and checked for any untrusted activation record. If there is none, the call can proceed as it cannot serve any untrusted component. The call to the security manager is performed by the critical operation itself to protect itself against unwanted calls. The security manager throws a security exception if it does not authorize access for the direct or one of the indirect callers.

As admitted in the JavaBeans standard document (Sun, 1996), this approach can be undermined by a carelessly programmed but trusted service that performs asynchronous requests on behalf of clients (a so-called event adapter). In such a case, the true client will not be active at the time of the safety-critical call, only the trusted service will be. Another loophole would be if a critical object were registered in an unprotected registry. In this case, anyone guessing the access key or name or, if it were supported, anyone enumerating all registered objects, could retrieve the critical object under a generic supertype, such as Object. It would then be simply a matter of type test and cast to regain access to the critical object.

Even if a component legally accesses some module, it must not gain any access to the private (non-exported) parts of that module. For direct access, this is guaranteed by the language semantics. However, where meta-programming interfaces exist, these need to be explicitly restricted such that these services do not break encapsulation. This is contrary to some of the typical usages of meta-programming, such as debugging or data structure serialization services. Indeed, a system may offer two metaprogramming interfaces – one that is module safe and open for general use and another that is module unsafe and restricted to trusted components.

The BlackBox Component Framework (used with Component Pascal) is currently a unique example of a system offering a dual metaprogramming service. The type- and module-safe service is open for general use, whereas the module-unsafe service is used by trusted components, such as the BlackBox portable debugger. The Java JDK includes metaprogramming facilities that are normally module safe (package safe). Some limited module-unsafe operations are available to trusted callers, subject to security manager validation.

An interesting twist is added by the .NET CLR. This is the possibility of adding custom meta-attributes to methods that restrict the set of callers based on scope (calling code from a specific manufacturer or from a specific other component only) or security demands (calling code has to provide acceptable credentials). Several of these demands are checked at load-time, some can only be checked at runtime. The load-time checks are particularly interesting and unique.

6.7.3 Safety in a multilanguage environment

Component technology allows the selection of different programming languages for the implementation of different components. Mutual protection of components in the same hardware protection domain thus requires type and module safety properties that are common to all languages used in such a configuration. Sufficiently strong interface definition languages (IDLs) can solve this problem. It is therefore unnecessary to restrict a system to a single programming language approach simply to benefit from language-level type and module safety. However, the strength of the overall approach will depend on the strength of its weakest part – that is, the weakest of the languages used, including the IDL. The CLR provisions for establishing type safety, module safety, and security integrity across all supported languages show that the choice of language is second to the establishment of underlying firm principles compatible with many languages. Note, however, that requiring strong CLR safety properties limits the used languages to their safe subsets. For instance, $C^{\#}$ supports unsafe methods, which are those that cannot be automatically checked for their safety. A component written using $C^{\#}$'s unsafe methods (or similar facilities in other CLR-supporting languages) will be rejected by the automatic safety checks unless that component is equipped with the credentials that declare it as trustworthy. Unlike the ActiveX Authenticode approach, where components are either fully trusted or not executed at all, and like Java components, CLR components are preferably usable without requiring such levels of trust.

6.8   Safety, security, trust

Type safety, module safety, and absence of memory errors – what makes this language–semantics-based approach trustworthy? The answer depends on the circumstances. If the target is a set of components, installed locally, interacting on a personal computer, then this approach may already be close to satisfactory. If the target was the highest security level, then this approach would be totally unacceptable. If the target is a low- to medium-security system that moves components across the internet, this approach is probably at its limits.

What is wrong? First, and above all, this approach fully relies on the tight semantics of the programming language used. To be fully trustworthy, a formal semantics of the language together with formal proofs of the claimed safety properties would be required. Also, of course, the formal method itself needs to be trusted, including the tools that may be used to construct lengthy proofs semiautomatically. Very few programming languages satisfy this requirement and there is no mainstream object-oriented language.

Even if a language fully satisfies this criterion, its implementation could still break any proved property. Hence, to go all the way, the language processors and the language runtime systems again need to be formally specified and verified. This is quite a feat to achieve. Consider that language processing includes tools such as a compiler, an interpreter, or a byte code verifier. The language runtime includes mechanisms such as a virtual machine, a garbage collector, or a security manager. Obviously, this may lead to a bootstrap problem where the tools used to build the used tools again need to be formally verified, and so on. None of the widely available language implementations satisfies these criteria, not even in cases where the implemented language itself satisfies its safety criterion.

In the end, trust is a matter of reducing the unknown to the known and trusted, and doing so in a trusted way. This is obviously primarily a sociological process. For example, the way the Unix security mechanism was introduced played a major role in it being trusted. The designers of the mechanism published its details in full and encouraged everyone to try to break it. After years, the mechanism gained (or, better, earned) the trust it currently receives. This trust can be justified probabilistically. It is highly unlikely that a loophole remains undiscovered under the uncoordinated (stochastic) evaluation by many over an extended period of time.

The Java designers also publicized their security strategies early on and encouraged serious research groups (McGraw and Felten, 1997) to challenge the approach. In this way, known loopholes are published and fixed (see "Frequently asked questions – Java security," www.java.sun.com/sfaq). After years of steadily decreasing reports of found problems, people will increasingly trust the approach. Today, limitation of trust is appropriate, whatever the proponents claim, and even if they are right.

6.9   Dimensions of independent extensibility

In traditional class frameworks, extension happens by virtue of specialization: classes of the framework are subclassed to add the required behavior. If the framework does not offer the right abstractions, such a specialization may not be possible. However, the notion of implementation inheritance, as interpreted in most object-oriented languages, allows for quite radical changes to the classes introduced by the framework. Quite often, the required functionality can be forced on the framework.

Traditional class frameworks are specialized at application construction time and thereafter disappear as no longer separable parts of the generated application. The only conflict resulting from "forced" specialization is that migration of the application to the next release of the independently evolved framework may be difficult or impossible.

The situation is very different for independently extensible systems. Using a single component framework, extensions from independent sources can be combined. Forcing specialization would endanger the interoperability of independent extensions. Thus, even more so than for class frameworks, independently extensible systems require a clear statement of what can be extended. Each particular feature of an independently extensible system that is open for separate extension is called a dimension of (independent) extensibility (for example, Weck, 1997).

Note that dimensions of extensibility are not necessarily orthogonal – the same effect may be achieved by extending along one of several possible dimensions. This is not normally desirable, as it offers designers of extensions an unwanted choice. Perfect orthogonality of dimensions is difficult to achieve and a total exclusion of possible overlaps may excessively restrict individual dimensions. The result would be a system that is orthogonal but not complete. As a result, important extensions become impossible. The theoretical ideal would be to form orthogonal dimensions of independent extensibility that together form an extension space that is complete with respect to extensibility requirements.

In practice, extensible systems rarely have orthogonal dimensions of extensibility. For example, the same system may support extensible abstractions for object serialization and object persistence. Although not identical, these two services certainly overlap. Multiple dimensions of extensibility form a product space (the set of all combinations of extensions along the individual dimensions). Where the dimensions are orthogonal, the resulting space is a Cartesian product. (A Cartesian product, also called cross-product, of n sets is the set of n-tuples containing all possible permutations of the elements of the n sets. The number of effectively different permutations is reduced if the original sets overlap and then the corresponding dimensions are non-orthogonal.)

6.9.1 Bottleneck interfaces

If a system was independently extensible "from scratch" – that is, no fixed infrastructure would exist, then independent extensions could not interoperate at all. There would not be any common ground for them to interact. A common ground after the fact could not generally be provided as the extensions come from independent and mutually unaware sources. Component frameworks provide the required shared understanding that couples extensions. A component framework opens a number of dimensions for extending components. Also, a component framework may enforce some of the rules of interactions between extensions.

Interfaces introduced to allow the interoperation between independently extended abstractions are sometimes called bottleneck interfaces (for example, Szyperski, 1992b). A bottleneck interface is a self-standing contract. As a bottleneck interface couples independent extension families, it cannot itself be extended. This is one of the arguments behind the claim that such an interface, once published, can only be withdrawn or replaced but not extended. Bottleneck interfaces, once published, are immutable (see also the next section). Obviously, components may be mutually aware of their extensions and engage in special interaction. In poorly designed component frameworks, such mutual awareness is sometimes required for two components to interact properly. In other words, such component frameworks require seemingly independent components to enter into a "conspiracy."

6.9.2 **Singleton configurations**

A component framework may open dimensions of extensibility but require a singleton configuration for some of the dimensions. A configuration is a singleton configuration, regarding a specific compulsory dimension, if it provides exactly one component that extends that dimension. For optional dimensions, a singleton configuration provides at most one component. For example, a system may allow for the installation of a security manager, but may insist on having at most one such manager in a configuration at any one time.

6.9.3 **Parallel, orthogonal, and recursive extensions**

Normally, for most or even all of its dimensions, a component framework would not require singleton configuration. Thus, a configuration can contain many components that all extend along the same dimension. This is called parallel extension (Weck, 1997). The main problem of systems allowing for parallel extension is peaceful coexistence. Two components extending along the same dimension are in danger of asking for the same resources. A component framework allowing for parallel extension has to define rules and provide means for arbitration. An example is a set of multiple controls embedded into the same container of a compound document system. Necessarily unique resources, such as the current focus for keyboard input, need to be arbitrated when requests from multiple controls collide.

Separate extending components may also address orthogonal dimensions of a component framework. This is called orthogonal extension (Weck, 1997). The main problem with orthogonal extension is the provision of proper bottleneck interfaces to allow interaction between the orthogonal extensions. Again, using the example of controls and containers in a compound document, controls and containers are addressing orthogonal dimensions. A single component may address both dimensions simultaneously, so, for example, it could be control and container at the same time. A component framework for compound documents has to define and support the bottleneck interfaces that allow arbitrary controls to talk to arbitrary containers and vice versa. A typical interface of this kind is used by controls and containers to negotiate for screen space.

Both parallel and orthogonal extensions are flat – that is, extending components are mutually independent. Recursive extensions are also possible. A component can itself introduce a component framework. Components extending this new framework obviously depend on the framework-introducing component or at least the abstractions introduced by this component. Note that recursive extensions do not necessarily create a well-layered architecture. It is possible that a component simultaneously extends dimensions introduced by recursive extensions at different levels. For example, a system might have a component framework for distributed resource management. One of the components extending this framework may itself be a framework for compound documents. It is possible that, say, a container component extends dimensions of both the resource management and the compound document framework.

6.10 Evolution versus immutability of interfaces and contracts

A contract – an interface together with its specification – mediates between independently evolving clients and providers of the services the interface makes accessible. As soon as a contract has been published to the world, it (the interface and its specification) can no longer be changed. This holds for clients and providers bound by a specific contract.

A provider can always stop providing a particular interface. It will then potentially lose part of its client base – the part that has not yet been migrated to some newer interface. However, a provider can never change the specification of an existing contract as that would break clients without any obvious indication. Also, a client cannot change its understanding of the contract without risking breaking with some existing providers.

The cornerstone of even arguing about contracts and changing contracts is a way to name uniquely the contracts that clients and providers refer to. As a contract, with all its informal bylaws, is itself quite difficult to capture, the name of the associated interface is commonly used.

6.10.1 Syntactic versus semantic contract changes

Changes to a contract can take two forms. Either the interface or the specification is changed. If the interface is changed, this is referred to as a syntactic change. If the specification is changed, this is called a semantic change. As providers are often "in charge" of a contract, and typical providers in object-oriented settings are classes, the problem caused by contract change is sometimes referred to as the fragile base class problem. The syntactic and semantic variations of the fragile base class problem are discussed in detail in section 7.4.

A simple way to avoid these problems is to refrain from changing contracts once they have been published. Of course, there is no problem with changing contracts (syntactically or semantically), as long as all bound providers and clients are under control. Thus, evolution of contracts within a tight organization is usually not an issue. However, by releasing clients or providers to the open market, the contracts involved become uncontrollable. Then, change has to stop and the contracts have to be frozen, made immutable.

It is again helpful to consider the analogy of traditional contracts. No clause in a contract, once signed, can be changed without the agreement of all involved parties. Of course, once there is an uncontrollable number of parties, gaining agreement can become difficult or impossible. Examples are contracts between all employers and employees covered by some tariff union. However, such contracts do have mechanisms that allow for change. The two fundamental mechanisms are: acknowledging existence of overriding law and instances and statement of a termination time. (Thanks to Wolfgang Weck for pointing out this analogy.)

It is noteworthy that, today, only Microsoft's COM declares all published interfaces to be immutable. Even Microsoft itself adheres to the principle and introduces new interfaces instead of modifying existing ones that almost fit. Support for the older interfaces is upheld for a while to maintain backwards compatibility, but eventually such older interfaces can and should go. IBM's SOM did something different. By explicitly supporting a release order, clients of different releases (versions) of an interface can coexist. Essentially, the explicit release order guarantees for every method a fixed index into a lookup table. For this to work, a new release can only add to an interface, it cannot take functionality away. A more detailed discussion of the two approaches can be found in Chapter 13 (SOM) and Chapter 15 (COM). SOM has since been deprecated. Ironically, many newer approaches discussed in this book, including J2EE's EJB and CORBA 3's CCM, follow the SOM approach of supporting release-to-release binary compatibility models. The .NET CLR supports both – the COM approach of side-by-side existence of interface (and class), versions that therefore can be kept immutable, as well as the SOM approach of release-to-release compatibility.

6.10.2 Contract expiry

Some of the current component infrastructures offer licensing services and it is a natural property of licenses that they expire after a preset date. Hence, it would seem straightforward to couple service provision under certain contracts with license agreements and their expiry date. The result would allow for a controlled evolution in which clients and providers can blindly trust the validity and existence of a service under a certain contract until the expiration date is reached. Thereafter, manufacturers of clients and providers would have to renegotiate: a contract's lifetime could be extended or the contract could be replaced or refined.

Using contracts with "use-by dates" has effects on users. Software systems can no longer be used indefinitely – or at least for as long as that outdated PC can be kept alive. However, there is also an advantage. Instead of supporting legacy contracts forever, adding more and more baggage to providers and clients, there is a clean way to cut off the past. As noted above, it is always possible to stop support for an aged contract. However, without mutually agreed expiry dates, this will always come as a surprise to some users.

6.10.3 Overriding law

What about the other mechanisms in traditional contracts, overriding law? Overriding law in this sense can mean the depreciation of clients or providers conforming to the old interpretation of a contract. In acts of self-justice, strong companies or organizations often apply this principle. A more moral way to achieve the same is interception by an accepted independent organization. Typical examples are the International Standards Organization (ISO), the American National Standards Institute (ANSI), the European Computer Manufacturers Association (ECMA), the British Standards Institution (BSI), the German institute for industrial standards (DIN), and so on.

6.11 Other forms of polymorphism

There are other forms of polymorphism besides the subtype (or inclusion) polymorphism introduced above (section 6.2). These other forms are discussed briefly below. For thorough coverage, see Abadi and Cardelli (1996).

Although subtype polymorphism is a dynamic scheme, the other forms are static and resolvable by a compiler. There are higher-order type systems, where some of these other forms may also require dynamic resolution. Such type systems have not yet reached mainstream languages. Overloading, as supported by languages such as C^{++}, Java, and $C^{\#}$, is a form of polymorphism that groups otherwise unrelated operations under the same name. Overloading is sometimes called ad hoc polymorphism because it establishes only a superficial similarity that is based on neither typing nor shared implementation.

The third form of polymorphism focuses on using the same implementation to serve a variety of types. For example, a list implementation can be parametrized with the type of the list elements. Any one instance of the list will serve one specific type, but the list implementation itself is generic and provided only once. This is called parametric polymorphism and is similar to generics in Ada. Properly implemented, parametric polymorphism does not lead to an explosion of generated code. A particularly lightweight variant that always produces exactly one copy of code has been proposed for Oberon (Roe and Szyperski, 1997) and may in the future be supported by Component Pascal. Note that parametric polymorphism is also similar to C^{++} templates. However, C^{++} templates lead to code explosion as a template is necessarily compiled to different code for each instantiation. Also, templates cannot be statically type checked as type checking cannot occur before parameters are supplied.

It is sometimes useful to specify constraints on type parameters. Parametric polymorphism does not allow this – any type can be used to parameterize a parametric abstraction. For example, a parametric list can be used to form lists over arbitrary types. For lists, that is fine. Consider a parametric container component. It accepts controls of a certain type, determined by the type parameter. However, whatever the type parameter will be, it has to be a subtype of Control, that is, only control types are acceptable.

A stronger polymorphic form that accepts bounds in the form of minimal supertypes is called bounded polymorphism. Bounded polymorphism combines subtype and parametric polymorphism. For example, using subtype polymorphism, a list of control objects can be constructed, but the same list implementation cannot be further constrained to contain only text controls. Using parametric polymorphism, the latter can be achieved, but the list could also be parametrized to contain only models (or any other type of objects) – the subtyping property that each element is at least a control is lost.

In the control container example, control-specific operations need to be applied to all list elements. For such operations to be statically safe, a combination of subtype and parametric polymorphism would be required and bounded polymorphism could be used. The list would be parametrized with a type that has to be a subtype of the control type. The control type places a bound on acceptable parameter types. An interesting challenge for the late integration into existing languages is the necessity to coexist with existing code that does not know about bounded polymorphism. A further challenge is the desire to fully support runtime reflection of type information even via variables of bounded polymorphic type. Proposals to integrate bounded polymorphism into Java (Myers *et al.*, 1997; Odersky and Wadler, 1997; Bracha *et al.*, 1998; Cartwright and Steele Jr, 1998; JCP, 2001) and into CLR and C$^{\#}$ (Sime and Kennedy, 2001) exist and most of the challenges are now addressed in practical ways, indicating that these concepts will make it into mainstream languages soon. A fascinating opportunity for JIT-compiled languages like Java and C$^{\#}$ is the possibility of selective code expansion at specific types. Instead of bloating parametric code by template-expanding it at compile-time, the same code can be selectively expanded at JIT compile-time, possibly taking into account runtime profile information to fine-tune performance.

CHAPTER SEVEN

Object versus class composition or how to avoid inheritance

Before entering any discussion of inheritance, some definitions are necessary. Inheritance would seem – from the literature for and against it – to be one of the most sacrosanct terms in object-oriented vocabulary. Several different mechanisms are embraced within the term inheritance, so any discussion that does not begin by clarifying precisely which mechanisms are referred to is guaranteed to be misleading.

This chapter begins by discussing the various aspects of inheritance and their manifestation in different object models and object-oriented languages. A detailed discussion of the problems introduced by some of these aspects follows. In particular, the facets of the fragile base class problem are covered in detail. Some of the problems can be avoided by adopting a highly disciplined approach to inheritance – and a number of such "disciplines" are introduced in this chapter. A more radical way to solve these problems is to avoid (implementation) inheritance altogether and use object instead of class composition. This possibility and its ramifications are discussed in detail. The chapter concludes with a brief review.

7.1 Inheritance – the soup of the day?

If Simula 67 (Dahl and Nygaard, 1970) is taken as the origin of the concept, then inheritance combines three aspects: inheritance of implementation, inheritance of interfaces, and establishment of substitutability. However, if Smalltalk 80 (Goldberg and Robson, 1983) is considered the origin, then inheritance only combines inheritance of implementation and inheritance of interfaces, while substitutability is not required (although recommended). This may come as a surprise, but even the original Smalltalk 80 class library contains several well-known examples in which a class defines objects that are not substitutable for those of its superclass.

It is important to distinguish the Simula and Smalltalk interpretations of subclassing (inheritance). As explained before (p. 94), neither a language nor a compiler can enforce substitutability. However, a mechanism such as inheritance may be intended to be used to imply substitutability, or not. In Simula – and also in C^{++}, Java, and Component Pascal – a subclass is supposed to guarantee substitutability and, in theory, a proof liability for the programmer follows.

The story becomes even more complex when considering further interpretations of inheritance. For example, in Eiffel it was originally possible to undefine inherited interface features. A class may thus not even be interface-compatible with its superclass, ruling out substitutability completely. (In current Eiffel, undefining a feature simply makes that feature abstract.) Furthermore, in languages such as Emerald (Hutchinson *et al.*, 1987), Sather, Java, or C$^{\#}$, interface inheritance and implementation inheritance have been separated. In this case, it is possible to inherit a pure interface with no implementation (coded behavior) at all. And, finally, COM and OMG IDL are pure interface definition languages outside the realm of any implementation. Thus, they support only interface inheritance (subtyping).

To summarize, there are three cardinal facets of inheritance:

1 subclassing – that is, inheritance of implementation fragments/code, usually called implementation inheritance;
2 subtyping – that is, inheritance of contract fragments/interfaces, usually called interface inheritance; and
3 promise of substitutability.

It is surprising that the three facets are usually omitted, or at least not clearly distinguished, when starting heated discussions on the pros and cons. Part of an explanation might be the irrational discussion between "objectionists" and "hybridists." Alternatively, is it fundamentalists/purists against technocrats/pragmatists? The former usually refer to the prime directive that object models shall support inheritance (although which of the inheritance facets they insist on is often left open). The latter argue that nothing is impossible and everything may have its place.

Subtyping, contracts, and substitutability have been covered in Chapters 5 and 6. Some of this material will be considered in more depth in this chapter. The "how to avoid inheritance" promise refers solely to implementation inheritance, sometimes also referred to as code inheritance or subclassing. Also, despite the provocative chapter title, there is no intention of banning implementation inheritance outright. Rather, it seems appropriate to analyze carefully what implementation inheritance gives, what it costs, and where the tradeoffs are. The deeper implications of implementation inheritance on components rather than objects need to be worked out clearly.

7.2 | **More flavors to the soup**

As if the above splitting into often-unmentioned facets were not enough, even implementation inheritance comes in many flavors. For the following discussion it is not necessary to explore fully the endless list of variations. However, a few essential notions need to be covered to create a common basis for later comparisons.

7.2.1 Multiple inheritance

In principle, there is no reason for a class to have only one superclass. Why not mix and match by inheriting from a number of classes? The idea seems promising. There are two principal reasons for supporting multiple inheritance. The first is to allow interfaces from different sources to be merged, aiming for simultaneous substitutability with objects defined in mutually unaware contexts. (Multiple interface inheritance is sometimes called multiple subtyping.) The second is to merge implementations from different sources.

Establishing compatibility with multiple independent contexts is important. Multiple interface inheritance is one way to achieve this, although it is not the only one. OMG IDL, Java, and C$^{\#}$ are examples of approaches that explicitly support multiple interface inheritance. In C^{++}, multiple inheritance of abstract classes can be used. Microsoft COM does not support multiple interface inheritance, but allows a component to support multiple interfaces simultaneously, to much the same effect. A detailed discussion of these approaches follows in Part Three. For now, it suffices to state that multiple interface inheritance does not introduce any major technical problems beyond those already introduced by single interface inheritance (which is covered in detail further below).

Mixing implementation fragments by means of multiple implementation inheritance is a different story entirely. If the superclasses all come from totally disjoint inheritance graphs (that is, graphs that do not share any classes), and name clashes are properly resolved, the new class merely concatenates the inherited implementations. However, the superclasses are usually not guaranteed to be disjoint, with tricky semantic problems as a result. As illustrated in Figure 7.1, two superclasses may inherit code from a shared superclass. In general, superclasses may directly or indirectly share any number of classes further up the inheritance graph.

Figure 7.1 uses UML notation to depict inheritance relations among classes. In the figure, class C inherits from classes B1 and B2, both of which inherit from class A. The diamond shape of the inheritance graph in Figure 7.1 gives rise to the name the "diamond inheritance problem." This problem has long been documented in the object-oriented literature, and numerous "solutions" have been proposed. The problem is really twofold, centered on both state and behavior.

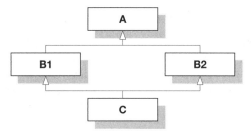

Figure 7.1 Superclasses may inherit code from a shared superclass further up the inheritance graph.

For state, the basic question is "Do both superclasses B1 and B2 get their own copy of the state defined by the shared superclass A?" The two superclasses may operate independently on this state. If the state is shared, the two classes are coupled, one observing state changes caused by the other. Obviously, this breaks encapsulation. If the state is not shared – that is, if each inheriting class gets its own copy – then consistency of a joined subclass C is in danger: which copy does it see? Would it need both superclasses to share some of the inherited state but not all? Generally, the client class C cannot fix the problem without fully understanding the implementation of the two superclasses.

Some approaches grant a class designer limited control over the sharing of inherited state. For example, in C^{++} a superclass can be made "virtual." This indicates that the superclass state should be shared with other subclasses that inherit from the same superclass and declare it "virtual." However, it is very difficult to decide whether or not a superclass should be made "virtual" without fully understanding its implementation. (Also, at least in C^{++}, there is a price to be paid – a method of a virtual superclass cannot recover the original object identity, that is, has its own "this.")

The behavior of the shared class A – that is, its method implementations – adds another dimension to the problem. If B1 or B2 or both override some of A's methods, what behavior should then make it to C? Assume that B1 overrides a method that B2 left unchanged. Should a call to that method, in the implementation inherited from B2 into C, call the overriding code in B1? As for inherited state, the correct answer might even be different from method to method.

In some approaches, following the early example of Common Lisp Object System (CLOS) (DeMichiel and Gabriel, 1987), the multiple implementation inheritance is disciplined by prescribing a linear order of inheritance. The order artificially arranges classes such as B1 and B2 in a way that one takes precedence over the other. Such an ordering scheme allows programmers to predict precisely what the effects of multiple implementation inheritance will be, provided the inherited code is known and understood. Abstraction and encapsulation suffer.

Approaches to the semantics of multiple inheritance usually stay close to the implementation strategy chosen. For example, the scheme used for C^{++}

(Stroustrup, 1987; Ellis and Stroustrup, 1994) is based on an earlier proposal for Simula (Krogdahl, 1984). This proposal aims at maintaining the integrity of subobjects, which are the pieces of the state space inherited from the various superclasses. Rossi and Friedman formalized this concept (1995) to remove direct implementation dependency, but it still remains mostly at the level of explaining effects of "feature interactions" rather than forming abstractions.

The designers of Java came up with an interesting solution: Java supports multiple interface inheritance but is limited to single implementation inheritance. The diamond inheritance problem is thus elegantly solved by avoidance without giving up on the possibility of inheriting multiple interfaces. CLR follows a similar approach and also supports multiple interface, but only single implementation inheritance. The OMG IDL and COM do not support implementation inheritance at all. IBM's system object model (SOM) was the only mainstream object model to support multiple implementation inheritance (and thus to address the diamond implementation inheritance problem).

7.2.2 Mixins

Multiple inheritance can be used in a particular style called mixin inheritance (Bracha and Cook, 1990). The idea is that a class inherits interfaces from one superclass and implementations from several superclasses, each focusing on distinct parts of the inherited interface. The latter classes are called mixins, as they are used to mix implementation fragments into a class. The following example shows how an interface Window introduces three separate "protocols" (sets of methods). The first protocol is used to handle a window as a whole, the second to handle its borders (title bar, scroll bars, and so on), and the third to handle its contents.

```
interface Window {
    // whole window:
    void drawWindow ();
    // window borders:
    void drawBorders ();
    void handleMouse (Event ev);
    // window contents:
    void drawContents ();
    Rect getVisibleSection ();
    Rect getContentsBox ();
    void scrollTo (Rect newVisible);
}
```

Each of the three protocols is now separately implemented by a mixin class:

```
abstract class StdWindowShell implements Window {
    void drawWindow () {
        drawBorders; drawContents;
```

```
      }
   }
   abstract class MotifWindowBorders implements Window {
      void drawBorders () {
         ...  // draw title bar
         Rect visible = getVisibleSection();
         Rect total = getContentsBox();
         ...  // draw scroll bars (compute thumbs using visible and total boxes)
      }
      void handleMouse (Event ev) {
         ...
         if (scroll bar thumb moved) {
            ...  // compute new visible region
            scrollTo(newVisible);
         }
         ...
      }
   }
   abstract class TextWindowContents implements Window {
      void drawContents () { ... }
      Rect getVisibleSection () { ... }
      Rect getContentsBox () { ... }
      void scrollTo (Rect newVisible) { ... }
   }
```

Each of the three mixin classes implements one of the protocols in one partic-
ular way. Alternative mixins would implement the same protocols differently.
For example, a mixin WindowsWindowBorders would implement those for
Windows instead of Motif.

The mixin classes are all abstract – they implement only one of the protocols, but use any of the other protocols as well. To form a concrete class, a
mixin is selected for each protocol and a new class is written that inherits from
each of the selected mixins. The following class MotifTextWindow combines the
three mixins sketched above. Note that this is pseudo-Java, as Java does not
support multiple implementation inheritance:

```
   class MotifTextWindow   // pseudo Java
      extends StdWindowShell, MotifWindowBorders, TextWindowContents {
   }
```

In this example, there is nothing left to do as the composition of the complete
set of three mixins fully implements a window that displays text and has the
look and feel of a Motif window.

As mixins address independent implementation aspects, their combination
by means of multiple inheritance is supposed to be straightforward. However,
unless programming languages and object models start enforcing the inde-

pendence of mixins, this is left as a convention for programmers to follow. Also, it is not clear whether or not insisting on total independence of mixins is acceptable as this would rule out a mixin that itself inherits from some standard library's class. (Other mixins might inherit from the same library class.)

7.3 Back to basic ingredients

The above exploration of some of the ramifications of multiple implementation inheritance should suffice to understand that an apparently simple and useful generalization could have subtle and possibly unexpected consequences. For the purposes of describing the further problems with inheritance of interfaces and code, the single inheritance case suffices. The underlying structure is thus simplified from an abstract inheritance graph – a directed acyclic graph or heterarchy – to a much simpler inheritance or class hierarchy.

To go further, two additional aspects need to be considered – how to get classes right and how to make them robust. Getting a class right is a static issue – how can a class be implemented to ensure its correctness? Getting it robust is a dynamic issue – how can a class be implemented to tolerate evolution and versioning of its superclasses and subclasses? The discussion of both of these issues led to the formulation of the so-called fragile base class problem.

7.4 The fragile base class problem

Fundamentally, the question is whether or not a base class can evolve – that is, appear in new releases without breaking independently developed subclasses. Considering the scenario in which the base class forms part of an operating system's interface, the importance of this question becomes clear. In the example, if independent release changes are not possible, a separation of operating system and applications fails. This potentially tight dependency of independently developed subclasses on their base class is called the fragile base class problem.

To confuse things, different positions have been taken based on two different interpretations of the problem – syntactic and semantic. Consider the following two quotations:

> "The problem is that the 'contract' between components in an implementation hierarchy is not clearly defined. When the parent or child component changes its behavior unexpectedly, the behavior of related components may become undefined."
>
> Sara Williams *et al.*, Microsoft (1995)

> "By completely encapsulating the implementation of an object, SOM overcomes what Microsoft refers to as the 'fragile base class problem', i.e., the inability to modify a class without recompiling clients and derived classes dependent upon that class."
>
> Frank Campagnoni, IBM (1995)

The first quotation refers to a problem of semantics of inheritance under release changes of the involved classes. The second quotation refers to a problem of binary interface compatibility or syntactic stability across release changes. It should be obvious that merely requiring or not requiring recompilation cannot solve a semantic problem. In the following, the two interpretations of the fragile base class problem are looked at and their relationship to inheritance is established.

7.4.1 The syntactic fragile base class problem

The syntactic fragile base class problem (syntactic FBC) is about binary compatibility of compiled classes with new binary releases of superclasses. This is sometimes referred to as release-to-release binary compatibility. It has nothing to do with the semantics of inherited code.

The idea is that a class should not need recompilation just because purely "syntactic" changes to its superclasses' interfaces have occurred or because new releases of superclasses have been installed. For example, methods may move up in the class hierarchy. However, as long as they remain on the inheritance path and retain a compatible list of parameters and return types, a subclass should not care and thus should not require recompilation. Likewise, new intermediate classes may be inserted or new methods added.

By initializing method dispatch tables at loading time, the syntactic FBC can be solved. IBM's SOM is doing just that and offers release-to-release binary compatibility of classes even under quite radical restructuring or extension of their superclasses.

It is interesting to see that a 1994 SOM White Paper (IBM, 1994) thereby declared the FBC problem solved, whereas SOM really only addressed the syntactic FBC problem. Binary compatibility is an important problem, and addressing it in full generality is certainly a major achievement for SOM's designers (Forman *et al.*, 1995). However, the semantic FBC problem goes much deeper and, ironically, seems to be best addressed by avoiding some of the mechanisms that initially led to the syntactic FBC problem.

7.4.2 The semantic fragile base class problem

The essence of the semantic FBC problem is how can a subclass remain valid in the presence of different versions and evolution of the implementation of its superclasses? (If the interface also changes, then the syntactic and semantic FBC problems occur in combination.) To answer this question, the very nature of implementation inheritance needs to be understood first.

The remainder of this and the following sections take a long detour to explain the semantics of implementation inheritance. For many, this is probably difficult reading, and skipping this material is safe. However, the material is required for a serious discussion of some of the deepest differences that occur between currently proposed object and component models.

The FBC problem is that a compiled class should remain stable in the presence of certain transformations of the inherited interfaces and implementations. Separating the syntactic from the semantic FBC problem allows elegant technical solutions (to the syntactic FBC problem) but is nevertheless questionable. The separate treatment and the infrastructural complexity required to solve the syntactic facet alone is costly and must be fully justified. The cost is only justified if, in practice, it is found to be common to rearrange interfaces or replace superclass releases without observably changing superclass behavior. If a superclass changed semantics from one release to the next, this would probably break subclasses. On the other hand, there remain many possible changes of a "syntactic" nature that cannot be addressed by a SOM-like scheme. Examples are splitting a method into two, joining two methods into one, or changing the parameter list of a method.

For immature class libraries, the point can probably be made that solving the syntactic FBC problem by itself eases library evolution. However, it is less likely that longer-term evolution of more mature libraries follows the same pattern. Minor syntactic changes, by themselves, such as refactoring of superclass chains, are less of an issue for more mature libraries – that is what maturity is all about. Further evolution, once required, can be expected to require changes to the syntax as well as the semantics of the library. This is where the semantic FBC problem comes into play.

Before analyzing the additional intricacies contributed by implementation inheritance, recall the situation with traditional libraries, callbacks, and object webs discussed in Chapter 5. As argued there, things become tricky as soon as the transition from simple "down-call only" libraries to libraries with callbacks or up-calls is made. In conjunction with observable state, this leads to re-entrance semantics close to that of concurrent systems. Arbitrary call graphs formed by interacting webs of objects abolish the classical layering and make re-entrance the norm. As discussed in Chapter 5, this leads to quite complex semantics and substantial subtleties in contracts.

7.5 Inheritance – more knots than meet the eye

Implementation inheritance is usually combined with selective overriding of inherited methods – some of the inherited methods being replaced by new implementations. The new implementations themselves may or may not call the overridden code. A special case is the overriding of abstract methods as there is no overridden code that could be called. Another example is methods that are, by interface declaration, empty.

The separation of models and views, as used in the previous examples, can be overkill in cases where complexity is low enough and where exactly one

view per model is required anyway. Simple controls fall into this category.
Consider a class Text that combines the roles of text models and text views as
described in Chapter 5. Text is an abstract class, while the actual text rendering
and display of the caret mark are left to subclasses. Here is a partial sketch of
the implementation of class Text. (The notation used is again Java and should
be readily accessible to the reader.)

```java
abstract class Text {
    private char[] text = new char[1000];
    private int used = 0;
    private int caret = 0;
    int max () {   // maximum length of text
        return text.length;
    }
    int length () {   // current length of text
        return used;
    }
    char read (int pos) {   // read character at position pos
        return text[pos];
    }
    void write (int pos, char ch) {   // insert or append ch at position pos
        // shift trailing characters right:
        for (int i = used; i > pos; i − −) {  text[i] = text[i - 1]; }
        used++;
        if (caretPos() >= pos) setCaret(caret + 1);
        text[pos] = ch;
    }
    void delete (int pos) {   // delete character at position pos
        used--;
        // shift trailing characters left:
        for (int i = pos; i < used; i++) {  text[i] = text[i + 1]; }
        if (caretPos() >= pos) setCaret(caret - 1);
    }
    int caretPos () {   // current caret position
        return caret;
    }
    void setCaret (int pos) {   // set caret position
        caret = pos;
    }
    abstract int posToXCoord (int pos);   // map position to x coordinate
    abstract int posToYCoord (int pos);   // map position to y coordinate
    abstract int posFromCoord (int x, int y);   // map coordinates to position
    void type (char ch) {   // insert character ch at current caret position
        int pos = caretPos();
        write(pos, ch); setCaret(pos + 1);
```

```
    }
    void rubout () {   // rubout character before current caret position
        int pos = caretPos();
        delete(pos - 1); setCaret(pos - 1);
    }
}
```

Class Text is a merger of the relevant methods from the TextModel and TextView interfaces (pp. 67 and 69), enriched by partial implementations. Methods marked abstract have no implementation. A non-abstract method may call an abstract method of the same class; the abstract method is then called a hook method. For brevity, the pre- and postconditions have been left out; they are similar to the ones attached to the TextModel and TextView interfaces. (Proper Java programming style would be to throw exceptions on violation of most of the preconditions. Again for brevity, such precondition checking is not included in this example.)

Obviously, class Text has most of the subtle interactions discussed earlier for separate text models and views. In particular, the setting of the caret in the methods write and type interacts in exactly the same way. However, as all inter-actions are now kept within one class, one could argue that the situation is less severe. This is indeed the case as long as no subclasses are formed, that is, no other class inherits parts of Text's implementation.

Next, consider a subclass SimpleText that inherits from Text, implements all abstract methods, and refines some of the concrete methods. The following section of code fully glosses over details such as partial visibility or scrolling, but it does show how the concrete method setCaret is refined to adjust the visual caret mark. (Note how a guard in method setCaret shortcuts this operation in the case where the caret is set to the position it already is at. This is done mainly to show how screen flicker and overheads can be controlled without demanding avoidance of redundant calls to methods despite their idempotency.)

```
class SimpleText extends Text {
    // cached coordinate of caret mark:
    private int cacheX = 0; private int cacheY = 0;
    void setCaret (int pos) {
        int old = caretPos();
        if (old != pos) {   // if caret position does indeed change
            hideCaret();   // remove caret mark at old caret position
            super.setCaret(pos);   // update caret position
            showCaret();   // redisplay caret mark at new caret position
        }
    }
    int posToXCoord (int pos) {
        ...   // compute x coordinate of anchor point of rendered
              // character stored at position pos
    }
```

```
int posToYCoord (int pos) {
    ...  // compute y coordinate of anchor point of rendered
         // character stored at position pos
}
int posFromCoord (int x, int y) {
    ...  // compute text position of the character whose bounding
         // box contains point (x, y)
}
void hideCaret () {
    // remove caret mark – asumes caret is visible
    int x = cacheX; int y = cacheY;
    ... // draw caret mark in invert mode at point (x, y)
}
void showCaret () {
    // displays caret mark – assumes caret is invisible
    int pos = caretPos();
    cacheX = posToXCoord(pos);
    cacheY = posToYCoord(pos);
    int x = cacheX; int y = cacheY;
    ... // draw caret mark in invert mode at point (x, y)
}
}
```

Figure 7.2 shows the complex message sequence occurring between Text and SimpleText as a result of a call to method type. For the sake of clarity, the message sequence caused by a showCaret call has been factored into a separate diagram (Figure 7.3). A hideCaret call relies on the cached coordinates of the preceding showCaret call and is thus simpler (and not shown).

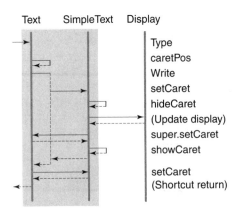

Figure 7.2 Callback-like message sequence between class and subclass in the presence of overridden inherited methods.

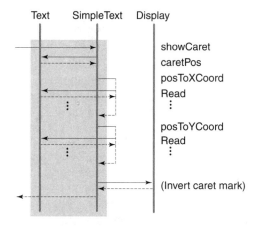

Figure 7.3 Message sequence subchart of *showCaret* in Figure 7.2.

When comparing with Figure 5.7 (p. 75), it should become obvious that invocation of an overridden method from within a class is very similar to invoking a callback from within a library. Call recursion freely spans class and subclass in both directions. The reader will no doubt be able to detect many critical subtleties, based on the discussions of callbacks. One recurring example is the need to cache display coordinates in the presence of model changes.

Where does the class scenario differ from the one using callbacks? In a class, every method can potentially call any other method. In combination with subclasses and overriding, literally any method can become a callback operation for any other method. Obviously, there is no problem if the superclass of a class is fully abstract, that is, it has abstract methods only. The method interaction is then fully and solely defined by the subclass. For example, Java interfaces are restricted to the introduction of constants and fully abstract methods. Thus, a Java interface is a fully abstract class. (Java also has abstract classes, but these need not be fully abstract. For a discussion of the Java language, see Chapter 14.)

With the examples developed above, it is possible to see consequences of the semantic fragile base class problem (section 7.4.2). Class SimpleText overrides method setCaret to update also the display of the caret. This relies on class Text never manipulating the caret position directly – that is, without calling setCaret. For example, assume a new version of Text with improved performance of method write:

```
void write (int pos, char ch) {    // insert or append ch at position pos
    for (int i = used; i > pos; i--) { text[i] = text[i - 1]; }
    used++;
    if (caret >= pos) caret++;
    text[pos] = ch;
}
```

Of course, this is a programming error breaking subclasses. In the example, this error is obvious enough as directly incrementing the caret variable leaves the visual caret mark in an incorrect state. In more involved interactions between classes and subclasses, such errors are much harder to spot and avoid. The real question is "Why is the above improvement of write illegal? The requirement that write ought to call setCaret is not easily expressed using post-conditions. What is needed is a specification for the specialization interface – that is, the interface of a class to its subclasses.

The following section looks at the slow but steady research progress made in this direction. While reading on, it should be remembered that there is always more than one object – even in systems using implementation inheritance. Hence, the two facets of the re-entrance problem, through inter-object and through intra-object recursion, really appear in combination. All approaches looked at in the following section address only the specialization interface of a single class and thus the (simpler) case of intra-object recursion. There is a significant opportunity for research targeting the more general problems of inter-object recursion.

7.6   Approaches to disciplined inheritance

The problems of implementation inheritance illustrated in the previous section have been known for quite a while. As early as 1986, Alan Snyder noted that inheritance breaks encapsulation (Snyder, 1986). The problems spotted at the time mostly pointed at weaknesses of programming languages, all of which have been addressed in the meantime. However, the general claim still holds – a subclass can interfere with the implementation of its superclasses in a way that breaks the superclasses. Likewise, an evolutionary change of a superclass can break some of its existing subclasses.

This section covers a number of attempts to discipline the implementation inheritance mechanisms. Obviously, many think that this powerful mechanism should not be given up on, but should instead be augmented by rules or conventions that help to reduce the risk of using this mechanism. This section is lengthy and it is safe to skip or just skim over it. However, it is strongly recommended that the reader continue with the next section – on object versus class composition – rather than the next chapter.

7.6.1 The specialization interface

In 1992, Gregor Kiczales and John Lamping described the problem in more detail and pointed out its importance in the context of extensible software systems (Kiczales and Lamping, 1992). They named the special interface between a class and its subclasses the specialization interface of that class. Distinguishing between the client and the specialization interface is important for approaches supporting implementation inheritance.

C^{++}, Java and C$^{\#}$, for example, support the notion of protected features of a class (Ellis and Stroustrup, 1994; Gosling *et al.*, 1996; ECMA, 2001a). A protected feature is accessible only to subclasses, not to regular clients of the class that only see the public features. The specialization interface of a C^{++} or Java class is the combination of the public and the protected interface. The client interface consists of only the public (non-protected) interface. In addition, the class can keep parts of its interface private. Private features can be used to solve the problems pointed out by Snyder.

In C^{++}, Java and C$^{\#}$, a private feature is private to a class, not an object. Therefore, these languages maintain classes as the unit of encapsulation, not objects. Smalltalk is different in that it encapsulates at the object level – access to fields of another object, even of the same class, has to occur through method calls. Java, C$^{\#}$ and Component Pascal also support the important notion of package-private (or internal or module-private) interfaces. These allow encapsulation of certain aspects on the level of packages (assemblies, modules), allowing direct access between multiple classes located in the same package (assembly, module). The same can be achieved in C^{++} in a less structured way using friend declarations.

7.6.2 Typing the specialization interface

Given the specialization interface of a class, what are the legal modifications a subclass can apply? As described at some length in the sections above, overriding methods needs to be done carefully to ensure correct interactions between a class and its subclasses. However, the introduction of protected interfaces merely excludes non-subclass code from using such interfaces. It does nothing to control the usage by subclasses.

In 1993, John Lamping proposed a type system approach to improve the control over specialization interfaces (Lamping, 1993). The idea is to declare statically which other methods of the same class a given method might depend on. Where dependencies form acyclic graphs, methods can be arranged in layers. Where dependencies form cycles, all the methods in a cycle together form a group.

If a method needs to call another method, it either has to be a member of the called method's group or of a higher layer's group. In such an approach, a subclass has to override methods group by group. Either all methods of a group are overridden or none. A subclass can redefine dependencies for overridden or new methods as it offers a fresh specialization interface to its subclasses. However, a subclass has to propagate unmodified parts of the specialization interface where inherited methods are used.

Grouping and layering of methods, as captured by Lamping's dependency declarations, is seen as a design activity. The designer of a class specifies the permissible call dependencies between the methods of a class. Below is an example of a specialization interface, based on the class Text (p. 118). For clarity, the return types and signatures (parameter lists and types) have been left out. For each method that depends on other methods, the set of those methods is written immediately after the dependent method. In addition, two "state abstractions" (caretRep and textRep) are used to refer abstractly to the state of class Text.

```
specialization interface Text {
    state caretRep
    state textRep
    abstract posToXCoord
    abstract posToYCoord
    abstract posFromCoord
    concrete caretPos   { caretRep }
    concrete setCaret   { caretRep }
    concrete max   { textRep }
    concrete length   { textRep }
    concrete read   { textRep }
    concrete write   { textRep, caretPos, setCaret }
    concrete delete   { textRep, caretPos, setCaret }
    concrete type   { write, caretPos, setCaret }
    concrete rubout   { delete, caretPos, setCaret }
}
```

In this example, the entire dependency graph is acyclic and therefore every method forms its own group. Several methods are affected only where representations are changed (textRep or caretRep). The dependencies specify the relative layering of the methods. The above interface is topologically sorted, which means that a dependent method always follows the methods it depends on. Note how the abstract caret mapping methods have no declared dependencies. A subclass might decide to add dependencies when implementing an abstract method. For example, the caret mapping methods might then depend on method read. As no method in Text depends on these mapping methods, such a change would be legal in a subclass implementing the caret mapping.

Obviously, Lamping's simple system can be based on static declarations and conformance can be statically checked. (A set of methods is the structure of a simple interface type.) That is why Lamping calls it a typing of the specialization interface. Despite its simplicity, today no language directly supports Lamping's specialization interface typing. However, corresponding conventions have been proposed as a recommendation for C++ programmers (Taligent, 1994).

Franz Hauck (1993) proposed an approach quite similar to Lamping's, at the same conference. Like Lamping, Hauck concentrates on typing self – that is, the type of the self-recursive structure of a class.

7.6.3 **Behavioral specification of the specialization interface**

Although Lamping's proposal improves the information available to subclass designers, it does not address semantic issues of implementation inheritance. After all, the approach aims at type system support, and type systems rarely address semantic issues. As described earlier, most semantic problems specific to implementation inheritance are related to problems of re-entrance caused by self-recursion. Recall that the problems of re-entrance do not occur in simple layered procedure libraries. The reason is that, in such a layered system, calls can only be made within (a part of) a layer or to a lower layer, but not upwards to a higher layer. In other words, a layered system performs no up-calls.

In 1995, Raymie Stata and John Guttag presented an approach to the behavioral (semantic) aspects of implementation inheritance (Stata and Guttag, 1995). They observed that the key requirement to be satisfied by any disciplined use of implementation inheritance would be the preservation of modular reasoning. It should be possible to establish properties of a class formally without a need to inspect any of the subclasses. Modular reasoning is of paramount importance for extensible systems, in which the set of subclasses of a given class is open. Any reasoning based on global inter-class analysis necessarily fails in extensible systems. It is interesting that layered systems are particularly well suited to modular reasoning.

Stata and Guttag propose to view a class as a combined definition of interacting part objects. In their paper, they name such part objects divisions of labor or method groups. Essentially, each such division owns part of the variables and methods of a class. No division can directly access the variables of another division. Subclasses have either to inherit or replace a method group as a whole. In addition, Stata and Guttag use algebraic specification techniques and the notion of behavioral subtyping (America, 1991; Liskov and Wing, 1994) to specify precisely what a subclass is allowed to do when overriding an inherited method group.

It is worthwhile looking closely at Stata and Guttag's approach. They split state and behavior defined by a class into groups, requiring strict abstractional barriers between these groups. Note that this is different from Lamping's approach. Stata–Guttag method groups encapsulate part of the state, whereas Lamping allows any dependency of methods on state. Effectively, Stata–Guttag groups can be viewed as separate classes, with the exception of one detail: all part classes together introduce a single "self." (This strict compartmentalization, leading to the almost total separation of the groups within a class, had previously been rejected by Lamping in his proposal. Lamping, 1993, pp. 207–208.)

It is interesting to compare the Stata–Guttag approach with a hypothetical one that introduces just one group per class and uses object composition instead of class composition. (Object composition is covered in detail in section 7.7.) If all classes consist of just one Stata–Guttag group, then subclasses either can change nothing or have to replace everything. Obviously, this makes implementation inheritance a useless mechanism in the hypothetical approach. Instead of forming a subclass that replaces everything, one could create a new class that is merely a subtype of the same type as the old class. Figure 7.4 illustrates this, the diagram on the left showing class B inheriting from class A (and replacing everything). The diagram on the right shows independent classes A and B that simply implement the same type, that is, the same interface. In other words, instead of introducing a class and opening it for implementation inheritance, a fully abstract class, that is a pure interface or type, is introduced. In this case, multiple classes can implement this interface. The result fully decouples implementation decisions but maintains polymorphism by means of the shared supertype.

To close the circle, consider what needs to be done to transform a Stata–Guttag class (one that contains multiple groups) into a set of classes that each contains a single group. Essentially, the lost "self" needs to be compensated for. The common "self" in a Stata–Guttag class allows methods in each of the groups of the class to invoke methods in each of the other groups of the class. The binding by a common "self" allows such calls to refer to the most specific overriding version of a group, just as is true for any self-recursive invocation of methods of an object.

Conceptually, to transform a Stata–Guttag class into a set of single-group classes, each of the group classes receives an instance variable referring to instances of each of the other group classes. Figure 7.5 illustrates this transformation for a Stata–Guttag class with three groups.

Obviously, all essential properties of the transformed class have been preserved. "Subclasses" can still be formed by replacing some of the single-group classes. Inter-group recursion within the original class is replaced by inter-object recursion. Clients now refer to instances of several classes, so the concept of object identity needs to be treated with care. By making any one of the part classes the main part, this problem can be overcome. The identity of the whole is then just the identity of the main part (part A in Figure 7.5).

As can be seen from the above transformation, classes in the Stata–Guttag approach are essentially reduced to providers of "self." Dropping classes (and therefore implementation inheritance) leads in the Stata–Guttag setting to

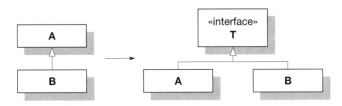

Figure 7.4 The Stata–Guttag approach to inheritance (left) and independent classes (right) decoupling implementation decisions but maintaining polymorphism.

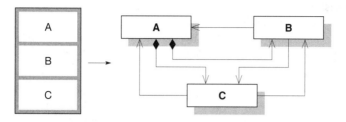

Figure 7.5 Transforming a Stata–Guttag class with three groups into a set of single-group classes.

compositions that are object-based (instead of class-based). There is no loss of functionality, although the increase in perceived complexity can be notable. The resulting object composition approach is more dynamic, as the part objects can be chosen at instantiation time rather than at class compilation time. Where meaningful, the object composition could even be changed during the composite's lifetime.

The enclosing Stata–Guttag class has cost advantages. All part objects of such a class are instantiated simultaneously and can therefore be allocated contiguously. With all offsets between part objects statically known, there is no need to maintain references between part objects. Object composition is more dynamic and makes such optimizations far more difficult to implement.

Another disadvantage of object composition seems to be the quadratic number of references required between part objects. However, this is easily solved. Without significant loss in performance, it suffices to have all part objects refer to an arbitrarily chosen main part (as above for identification purposes). The main part maintains references to all other part objects. The resulting number of inter-part references is linear, and inter-part access cost merely increases from a single to a double indirection.

To summarize the above, closer analysis of the Stata–Guttag proposal leads to a surprising insight. Attempts at tight semantic control over classes and implementation inheritance naturally lead to a model that is much closer to object composition than to traditional class composition, that is, implementation inheritance. This first glimpse at object composition should suffice at this point. A detailed coverage of object composition techniques follows below in section 7.7.

7.6.4 **Reuse and cooperation contracts**

Stata and Guttag's work advocates a fairly restrictive use of implementation inheritance, much along the lines of object composition. However, there is room for less restrictive forms of implementation inheritance. For this to be manageable, a much better understanding of the coupling between classes and subclasses is required. In particular, a better understanding of base class evolution and its consequences for subclasses is required.

In 1996, Patrick Steyaert, Carine Lucas, Kim Mens, and Theo D'Hondt returned to the idea of statically verifiable annotations of the specialization interface (Steyaert *et al.*, 1996). They named the annotated interface a reuse contract with the intention that classes are reusable assets. Reuse contracts then determine how reuse happens. As with all contracts, reuse contracts bind at least two parties – classes and their subclasses. They coarsely specify structural aspects of a base class, so that subclasses can build on this specification. The aim is to gain a better understanding of the effects of what Steyaert *et al.* called parent class exchange – another name for the fragile base class problem.

Although following in the tradition of Lamping's (and Hauck's) work, reuse contracts are quite different. A reuse contract specifies only the transitive hull of the part of a call structure in a class that subclasses may rely on. In other words, self-recursive calls, used in an implementation of a class, do not necessarily form part of the contract between that class and its subclasses. A reuse contract also mentions only those methods that should be relied on by subclasses. In contrast, Lamping (and Hauck) specified the total call structure observable by clients, regardless of whether or not clients are allowed to rely on that call structure. Below is the reuse contract of class Text.

```
reuse contract Text {
  abstract
    posToXCoord
    posToYCoord
    posFromCoord
  concrete
    caretPos
    setCaret
    max
    length
    read
    write   { caretPos, setCaret }
    delete  { caretPos, setCaret }
    type    { write, caretPos, setCaret }
    rubout  { delete, caretPos, setCaret }
}
```

Class Text does not define any methods that should be hidden from subclasses. Thus, none of Text's methods have been omitted. The listed dependencies are only among methods – Lamping's or Stata and Guttag's state representations or state partitions are not mentioned at all. Except for the concept of dropping information that ought to be irrelevant to subclass implementers, a reuse contract is just a specialization interface specification with less information.

The real innovation of the reuse contract approach is a set of modification operators. Using a sequence of applications of these operators, a contract can be modified to take a different shape. Changes described by such operator applications can explain the differences between base classes (base class evolution) as well as the differences between a subclass and its base class. The six operators introduced by Steyaert *et al.* are:

- concretization (its inverse is abstraction) – replace abstract methods by concrete methods (replace concrete methods by abstract methods);
- extension (its inverse is cancellation) – add new methods that depend on new or existing methods (remove methods without leaving methods that would depend on the removed methods);
- refinement (its inverse is coarsening) – override methods, introducing new dependencies to possibly new methods (removing dependencies from methods, possibly removing methods that now are no longer being depended on).

Steyaert *et al.* then argue that, by recording the sequence of operations applied when constructing a subclass and when constructing a new base class, the compatibility of an existing subclass with the new base class can be checked. As reuse contracts and associated operators say nothing about semantics (and do not even refer to actual typing of methods), this check can only be conservative. However, they claim that it does eliminate a large number of errors that typically occur in practice.

Figure 7.6, which is adapted from Steyaert *et al.* (1996), shows how both an abstract class and its concrete subclass implement a reuse contract, and how these two reuse contracts are themselves related. In the figure, the sequence "Op1; Op2; ..." refers to the sequence of operations applied to the base class's reuse contract to construct the subclass' reuse contract.

Figure 7.7, again based on Steyaert *et al.* (1996), shows how contract operators couple the reuse contracts of a class, its replacement, and one of its subclasses – before and after the replacement. In the figure, the labels Ops(derive) and Ops(exchange) refer to the sequences of operator applications that derive the subclass and the exchange base class respectively.

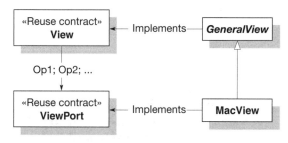

Figure 7.6 A class and its subclass implementing a reuse contract and how contracts are related. (Adapted from Steyaert, P., Lucas, C., Mens, K., and D'Hondt, T. (1996) Reuse contracts: managing the evolution of reusable assets. *Proceedings, OOPSLA '96*, ACM SIGPLAN Notices 31(10) 268–285.)

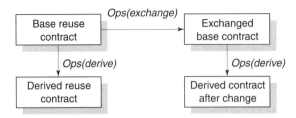

Figure 7.7 Exchange of a base contract. (Adapted from Steyaert, P., Lucas, C., Mens, K., and D'Hondt, T. (1996) Reuse contracts: managing the evolution of reusable assets. *Proceedings, OOPSLA '96,* ACM SIGPLAN Notices 31(10) 268–285.)

Steyaert *et al.* explain in detail what changes to a base contract would interfere with what derivations of subclasses. They claim that, where such interferences do not occur, a subclass will remain operational after the analyzed base class exchange. As the entire reuse contract approach is based merely on the transitive closure of relevant self-recursion, such a claim is not perfect. For example, a subclass may depend on the ordering of calls – as demonstrated in the SimpleText class (p. 119). Such a dependency can be broken by a base class exchange without being noticed by reuse contracts.

Reuse contracts represent an interesting tradeoff. On the one hand are the conditions that can be formally expressed and statically checked (for example, by a compiler). On the other are the conditions sufficient to capture formally the behavior of a class. However, in the general case, a compiler cannot statically verify these.

A later proposal by Mira Mezini (1997) calls for cooperation contracts that build on the ideas of reuse contracts and also those of specialization interfaces and Stata–Guttag groups. Like reuse contracts, cooperation contracts are not a fully formal approach. Unlike reuse contracts, cooperation contracts are closed at the metalevel through a metaobject protocol (Kiczales *et al.*, 1991) of the implementation environment.

7.6.5 Representation invariants and method refinements

In a generalization of the Stata–Guttag approach, Stephen Edwards (1996) demonstrated that the overriding of individual methods in a method group is permissible if the subclass maintains the representation invariant of the group's variables. The idea is to explicitly associate invariants with a class specification that refers to protected variables, which are variables that are only accessible by class and subclass code (but not external client code).

By separating the notions of subtyping and subclassing, Raymie Stata (1999) also allows the partial overriding of methods inside Stata–Guttag groups. Unlike his earlier work (Stata and Guttag, 1995) and Edwards (1996), he allows supercalls if each overriding method is a proper refinement of its corresponding base class method. This condition ensures that the specification of a base class method is met by the calling subclass method.

Stata's approach does not handle problems caused by mutually recursive methods or side-effects that are not captured by the base class' method specification (Ruby and Leavens, 2000).

7.6.6 Disciplined inheritance to avoid fragile base class problems

Leonid Mikhajlov and Emil Sekerinski (1998) defined a set of rules for disciplined inheritance that, if followed, avoid the semantic fragile base class problem. That is, their rules allow for the construction of subclasses based on a superclass specification such that the subclasses remain valid if the superclass implementation is changed (while still meeting its specification). Essentially, Mikhajlov and Sekerinski focus on eliminating the introduction of new cyclic method dependencies between the superclass and its subclasses when moving from the original to a new version of the superclass implementation. To achieve this, their rules require that superclass instance variables be private and that subclasses do not introduce new instance variables. While their restrictions are rather draconian, they enabled a rigorous formalization and formal proof that is in itself an interesting contribution.

7.6.7 Creating correct subclasses without seeing superclass code

Blending many of the ideas summarized in the previous sections, Gary Leavens *et al.* (1999; 2000) define their Java Modeling Language (JML) to enable the specification of class-based interfaces in a way suitable for class implementation, subclass implementation, and class use.

Building on the JML approach, Clyde Ruby and Gary Leavens (2000) focus on what seems to be the inverse problem of the semantic fragile base class (FBC) problem. They assume a given blackbox base class and ask what rules a programmer needs to follow to create a correct subclass, as far as the base class goes. This is an inverse of the FBC problem in the sense that the FBC problem assumes existing but unavailable subclasses that need to be preserved in the face of requested base class changes. Their problem formulation is thus close to that of behavioral subtyping (America, 1991; Liskov and Wing, 1994), which focuses on valid subtypes for a given type (rather than valid modifications of a type that preserve the validity of existing but unknown subtypes). Ruby and Leavens also call the problem they address the "fragile subclass problem", but that seems only partially appropriate.

Ruby and Leavens provide three parts to a class specification, all expressed using their JML, that together ensure that a subclass can be safely created without requiring access to the source code of the base class. These first two parts split the class specification into a public and a protected part. The protected part reveals information such as invariants over protected variables and conditions on protected methods. The third part is unusual in that it is based on an automatic analysis of the initial source code of the base class. The result of the analysis provides information on which variables are accessed and which methods are called by any given method and this information is incorporated into the JML specification of the class. This information is thus almost exactly the same as that provided by specialization interfaces (section 7.6.2), but split into public and protected and conservatively differentiating five different kinds of method calls and two different kinds of variable accesses.

Before looking at an example, reflect on this third part of their class specifications, which they call the subclassing contract. It might seem that this third part could be combined with the protected specification (their second part, which is similar to a specialization interface specification). However, Ruby and Leavens argue that exactly those call dependencies actually present in the base class implementation need to be known to enable safe implementation of subclasses. Therefore, this information cannot be changed once the base class has been released. It is this third part of the Ruby–Leavens specification that exposes the deep implementation dependency of code inheritance. The downside of exposing what would normally be seen as implementation detail of the base class is unavoidable. This is also the link between subclassing contracts and the FBC problem. Obviously, if the correctness of subclasses can be established based on just the public and protected class specification combined with the subclassing contract, then a change to a base class that continues to meet all three specifications cannot break existing subclasses. However, Ruby and Leavens do not explore this further.

Ruby and Leavens derive two sets of rules – one for library implementers and one for subclass implementers – that, if followed, allow for the safe implementation of subclasses. These rules are interesting and listed in the following. For a detailed discussion and a definition of all terms, see Ruby and Leavens (2000).

A class library implementer should ensure that for each class in the library:

- methods should not directly access any instance variables from unrelated classes;
- methods should not call the public methods of an object while temporary side-effects have not been restored in that object; and
- overriding methods should refine the method being overridden.

In addition, a class library implementer should ensure that, for each class that can be subclassed (is not final in Java, is not sealed in $C^{\#}$, is extensible in Component Pascal):

- there should be no mutually recursive methods;
- methods should not pass a self-reference as an argument when calling a method of a related class;
- methods should not self-call or super-call non-pure public methods;
- non-public methods should not call the public methods of a related class; and
- if a protected concrete instance variable of type T cannot hold all values of type T, then its domain should be described in a protected invariant.

Among other consequences, the rules for library implementers assign all methods to one of three layers – public non-pure, public pure, and non-public. Calls are only permitted within a layer and into a lower layer, where public non-pure is the highest and non-public the lowest layer.

A subclass implementer should ensure that, for each subclass:

■ additional side-effects are avoided when overriding non-public methods that modify superclass instance variables;
■ no group of mutually recursive methods is created that involves a method of a superclass;
■ overriding methods refine the overridden methods; and
■ the protected invariant of the subclass implies the protected invariant of the superclass if superclass instance variables have been exposed to the subclass or other classes.

An interesting result of Ruby and Leaven's work is that they can determine cases where it is not possible to write verifiably correct subclasses just based on their three-part specification, although a correct subclass could be written if the base class implementation was fully inspected. Concretely, they observe that such cases can only be avoided by disallowing the use of non-overridable methods (final in Java, sealed in $C^{\#}$) and by also disallowing the use of private instance variables. In other words, they find a clash between the otherwise good practice of designing classes that minimize exposure of implementation detail (by preventing overrides and hiding fields) and the necessity to expose skeletal implementation detail (their subclassing contract) to ensure safe subclassing.

7.7 From class to object composition

A prime motivation for implementation inheritance is the potential for flexible code reuse. In particular, it is usually emphasized that, in an inheritance-based scheme, evolutionary improvement of parent classes automatically improves subclasses. It is definitely true that the modification of parent classes leads to an automatic modification of subclasses. It is a different matter whether this leads to an improvement of the subclasses or not. The implicit web of self-recursive re-entrant invocations is difficult to control and could well stand in the way of evolution.

Object composition is a much simpler form of composition than implementation inheritance. However, object composition shares several of the often quoted advantages of implementation inheritance. What exactly is object composition? The idea is very simple and very much in the style of objects. Whenever an object does not have the means to perform some task locally, it can send messages to other objects, asking for support. If the helping object is considered a part of the helped object, this is called object composition. An object is a part of another one if references to it do not leave that other object. The part object is usually called an inner object because it can be seen as residing inside its owning object, the outer object.

Sending a message on from one object to another object is called forwarding. Note that, in the literature, the term delegation is also used in this context. However, technically, delegation has a different meaning, as will be explained further below. The combination of object composition and forwarding comes fairly close to what is achieved by implementation inheritance. However, it does not get so close that it also has the disadvantages of implementation inheritance.

An outer object does not reimplement the functionality of the inner object when it forwards messages. Hence, it reuses the implementation of the inner object. If the implementation of the inner object is changed, then this change will "spread" to the outer object. The difference between object composition with forwarding and implementation inheritance is subtle. This difference is called "implicit self-recursion" or "possession of a common self." If an object is an instance of a class, then it has exactly one identity – its "self," even if its class inherits from many other classes. However, if an outer object uses composition and forwarding, it does not share identity with its inner objects. There is no common "self" to a composition of objects.

The difference does not show until a self-recursive invocation is studied. In the case of implementation inheritance, control in a self-recursive invocation always returns to the last overriding version of any method. That is, control can return from any of the involved superclasses back to any of the involved subclasses. Method invocation can cause up-calls in the subclass hierarchy. (In most diagrams, subclasses are drawn below their superclasses – up-calls in such a diagram point downwards. This convention unfortunately clashes with that of drawing layered architectures, where base layers are drawn below "higher" layers. The latter convention led to the name "up-call" – see p. 58.) This is different in the case of forwarding. Once control has been passed from an outer to an inner object, self-invocations stay with the inner object. The outer object cannot possibly interfere with the flow of control inside the inner object.

To see why the lack of a common "self" is a severe if subtle difference, consider the previous example of classes Text and SimpleText (p. 118). A naive attempt to implement the functionality of SimpleText by composing a Text object with a simpleText object using forwarding would fail. The implicit self-recursive return of control from Text to SimpleText that is possible with inheritance does not occur under a forwarding regime. Hence, the subtle coupling between classes Text and SimpleText, as illustrated in Figures 7.2 and 7.3, cannot be reproduced using object composition and message forwarding alone. Figure 7.8 repeats a simplified version of the inheritance message chart of Figure 7.2 on its left. On its right, Figure 7.8 shows the forwarding message chart that would result from a SimpleText object forwarding to an unmodified Text object. (Note that class Text has abstract methods; assume that the text object is an instance of a subclass of Text that provides an arbitrary implementation for these methods.) Note that the chart on the right represents a malfunctioning simpleText object – its hideCaret and showCaret

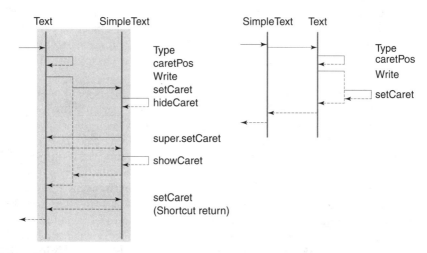

Figure 7.8 Comparing the control flow under inheritance (left) and forwarding (right) regimes.

methods are not invoked. A working version based on object composition is introduced further below.

Obviously, the inner object (text) can be designed with interference of an outer object (simpleText) in mind. For example, the outer object's reference can be added to some of the operations as an additional parameter. For Figure 7.8, such a parameter on method write would solve the problem. Alternatively, the outer object could be registered with the inner object. Regardless of how it is achieved, the point is that recursion across multiple objects needs to be designed in, whereas in the case of implementation inheritance it can be patched in. This is sometimes called planned versus unplanned reuse. One could also say that it is about expected versus forced use. A more constructive view follows in the next section.

As a strong advantage, object composition is also naturally dynamic. An inner object can be picked at the time of creation of an outer object. In some cases, the inner object can even be replaced while the outer object continues to function. This sort of dynamics can be added to inheritance models as well, although this is not normally done. For example, Objective-C (Pinson and Wiener, 1991; Apple Computer, 2000) allows specification of the superclass "object" at object creation-time.

7.8   Forwarding versus delegation (or making object composition as problematical as implementation inheritance)

Objects composed using object references and forwarding of messages lack the notion of an implicit common "self." As explained in the previous section, if such a common identity is required, it has to be designed in. This has far-reaching consequences. If an object was not designed for composition under a common identity, it cannot be used in such a context. An object may not have the mechanisms built in that are required to resend messages to an outer object. If so, it cannot be used as an inner or part object without affecting the common "self."

As argued above, the lack of an implicit common "self" is a major strength of object composition based on forwarding. In contexts in which all part objects are under the control of a single organization or team, the requirement to make a common "self" explicit everywhere may be considered overkill. After all, implementation inheritance works well for moderate numbers of classes, all of which are under local control and thus are whiteboxes. However, object composition has a second advantage over inheritance – it supports dynamic and late composition. Implementation inheritance can be augmented to approach the same degree of flexibility. Some examples of dynamic inheritance were briefly covered in the previous section. Making the "inheritance link" dynamic blurs the distinction between class and object composition and eliminates the implementation advantages of (static) class composition. Languages that take this path include Objective-C (Pinson and Wiener, 1991) with its dynamic superclasses and Modula-3 (Nelson, 1991) with an option to bind methods at object creation-time.

There is another way to close the gap between forwarding-based object composition and implementation inheritance-based class composition. Instead of making inheritance more dynamic, forwarding could be strengthened. The resulting approach to message passing is called delegation. To repeat, in much of the popular literature, the line between forwarding and delegation is not clearly drawn. The difference is of such a fundamental nature that the price for this imprecision is a resulting lack of understanding.

The concept of message passing by delegation is relatively simple. Each message-send is classified either as a regular send (forwarding) or a self-recursive one (delegation). Whenever a message is delegated (instead of forwarded), the identity of the first delegator in the current message sequence is remembered. Any subsequently delegated message is dispatched back to the original delegator. Figures 7.9 and 7.10 illustrate the difference between forwarding and delegation. The two objects involved, niceText and text, are expected to

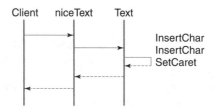

Figure 7.9 Forwarding.

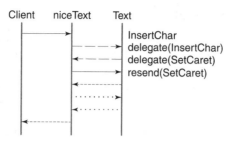

Figure 7.10 Delegation of messages InsertChar and SetCaret.

share a common part of their interface. In terms of object composition, niceText is the outer object and text is the inner object. The idea is that niceText has a "nicer" way to display marks, such as the caret. Messages from text to this shared interface are, under the delegation regime, rerouted to niceText. In the case of forwarding, this does not happen. For delegation to work, the delegator must share the delegate's delegation interface, much as a subclass shares the specialization interface of its superclass.

Delegation requires one further concept. Besides being able to send to the current "self," a method implementation should be able to call the base method in the object down the delegation chain. This is much like a "super call" in class-based schemes. For example, niceText gets control when text delegates SetCaret. However, niceText does not fully implement the caret state and wants to invoke also the SetCaret code of text. This is not a normal forwarding send, as the current "self" needs to be retained. It is also not a delegating send, as that would lead to an infinite regress (niceText is the current "self;" under delegation it would just reinvoke its own SetCaret).

The mechanism that performs the equivalent of a "super call" for objects is called message resending. As can be seen in Figure 7.10, niceText uses a resend to invoke text's SetCaret from within its own SetCaret. It is immediately obvious from the figures that the complexity of message sequences explodes when moving from forwarding to delegation. The interaction diagram looks similar to that in an implementation inheritance relation. As far as recursion structures are concerned, implementation inheritance and delegation are indeed equivalent (Stein, 1987).

Obviously, in the example shown in Figure 7.9, niceText will not function properly when using forwarding. By forwarding the InsertChar message to text, niceText loses control until this call returns. However, text reacts to InsertChar by calling SetCaret to update the caret position – something that niceText really needs to know to update its caret display. If forwarding is the only option and text had not been designed with recursion through outer objects in mind, the programmer of niceText would have to resort to workarounds. For example, niceText could check on returning calls to text whether or not the state that it depends on has changed.

7.9 A brief review of delegation and inheritance

Delegation is a powerful programming tool. The point made so far has been that delegation introduces the same "evils" as implementation inheritance. However, just as implementation inheritance is certainly an established and useful tool within components, so delegation could be put to use within similarly controlled units of encapsulation. The dynamics of a system based on object composition and delegation so gained is often cited as a prime advantage. It allows for direct manipulation systems that aim to make construction of software artifacts "tangible" (for example Smith and Ungar, 1995). In such systems, objects are directly combined to form larger solutions, instead of separating compile-time and runtime (classes and objects).

Languages that are based purely on objects, object composition, and delegation are usually called prototype-based languages as objects that are cloned and then modified take the role of classes. The original proposal to investigate such languages goes back to an article by Henry Liebermann (Liebermann, 1986). The first concrete language proposal soon followed, leading to the introduction of the language Self (Ungar and Smith, 1987). Since then, interest in delegation-based languages has increased, but none of these approaches has yet made it into mainstream commercially supported languages. This could change if the two approaches of inheritance and delegation are no longer seen as mutually exclusive philosophies. Dutoit *et al.* focused on smoother transitions from delegation-based prototyping to inheritance-based production code (1996). In addition, it has been noted that the design spectrum between delegation and inheritance is more diverse than was previously thought (Malenfant, 1995).

To quote Gamma *et al.* (1995, p. 21):

> "Delegation has a disadvantage that it shares with other techniques that make software more flexible through object composition: dynamic, highly parametrized software is harder to understand than more static software. [...] Delegation is a good design choice only when it simplifies more than it complicates. [...] Delegation works best when it is used in highly stylized ways – that is, in standard patterns."

Günter Kniesel showed how delegation can be incorporated into statically typed object-oriented languages (1999). Another focus of research has been the disciplined use of delegation (for example, Bardou and Dony, 1996). As delegation can be used to form a common "self" across webs of objects, one could term such webs themselves as objects of a higher order. Such "objects" are often called split or fragmented objects. In other words, instead of weaving arbitrary and overlapping domains of "self" across webs of objects, a disciplined approach aims at structure and hierarchy. In a sense, delegation-based technology is lagging behind inheritance-based technology when it comes to aspects of discipline and modularity (for example Ungar, 1995). Inheritance-based approaches lag behind in the area of system dynamics and late composition. (This is considered further in Chapter 25.)

CHAPTER EIGHT

Aspects of scale and granularity

Partitioning a design into components is a subtle process that has a large impact on the success of the resulting components. Obviously, it is the exception that all components in the partitioning are designed from scratch. Fresh construction is usually acceptable only in the absence of usable components. Construction of a generalized component is only reasonable if it is expected that the component will find further applications. In the case of a mature component market, most necessary components can be acquired rather than constructed. The process of partitioning is then driven by two considerations – the requirements and the catalog of available components.

Nevertheless, as pointed out several times before, there are substantial benefits to introducing a component approach even in cases where component markets or in-house component reuse is not yet foreseeable. Component-based architectures are inherently modular and, as such, have significant software engineering advantages. In particular, good modular architectures make dependencies explicit and help to reduce and control these dependencies. Also, good modular architectures are naturally layered, leading to a natural distribution of responsibilities. Once modularity has been established, it is easier to migrate part of a system to components by adopting relevant component interface standards. It is also possible that an outcome of the modularization effort is proposals for new component interface standards.

Where component frameworks or even entire component system designs can be adopted, the granularity of components in a system is predetermined. Today, this is the exception rather than the rule, and modularization is often the first step that needs to be taken. The important question of proper granularity then needs to be addressed.

The best size of a component depends on many different aspects. A system can readily be partitioned into units of varying size and coherence. Traditional units are procedural libraries, classes, and modules. The rules governing the partitioning vary from case to case. In particular, it is important to understand the implications of the granularity of a particular partitioning. This chapter covers a number of aspects of granularity and discusses the principal related concerns for an architect of a component-based system. It is argued that almost all relevant aspects governing granularity demand fairly coarse-grained partitioning. Individual procedures or classes are thus frequently ruled out as components.

8.1   Units of abstraction

Abstraction is perhaps the most powerful tool available to a software engineer. Abstraction aims at reducing detail, making the thing that has been subjected to abstraction simpler to handle.

- With abstraction, less becomes possible in theory, but more becomes possible in practice.

The main benefit of an abstraction is the design expertise embodied in it, ready for reuse. Traditional abstraction aims at capturing functionality, resources, or state spaces. Objects are examples of abstractions that combine functionality and state. Abstractions usually build on lower-level abstractions, leading to a layered hierarchical design.

However, from a software architect's point of view, the hardest design problem is how abstractions such as objects should interact. To keep complexity under control, it is desirable to isolate objects as much as possible. However, if a library can handle complex interactions, the complexity for the library's clients may be reduced considerably. Thus, a focus of more recent efforts is to study object interactions in their own right.

Indeed, interaction patterns themselves can become the focus of abstraction. Examples in this category are interaction specifications (Jonkers, 2001) at a specification level and "active" libraries (those using callbacks) or frameworks (Chapter 9) at an architecture and implementation level. Frameworks are libraries that define part of the interaction between certain objects. There is a deep conflict between the tight coupling required for effective interaction and the weak coupling required for strong and independent object abstractions. Frameworks address this conflict as objects within a framework are coupled much more tightly than are objects across different frameworks.

A framework may completely hide its implementation, and only provide an abstract interface. Such a so-called blackbox framework (Johnson, 1994) acts as a unit of abstraction. Its classes are rarely meaningful if considered individually. Thus, the entire blackbox framework may form a component, where the classes that constitute it cannot. Of course, for a framework to serve as a useful component, it needs to be a possible unit of deployment. Such a framework component thus needs to come with useful defaults. As such, a framework component can be specialized by plugging in components; it is also a component framework. Most conventional frameworks are not separately deployable and require specialization using class inheritance. Then, instead of being components, they simply serve as prefactored implementation fragments to be completed by a programmer before deployment.

Nested frameworks constitute another challenge to component formation. Can an inner framework be a component in its own right? Obviously, the answer depends on the abstraction of the outer framework. If the outer framework can do without the inner, then there is no cyclic dependency. Without a cyclic dependency, both the inner and the outer frameworks can be components themselves, with the inner component listing the outer one as a prerequisite for it to function.

8.2 Units of accounting

In large systems, as are typical for enterprise solutions, the actual cost incurred by individual parts of a system and their use may need to be monitored. It thus becomes important to partition a system into units of accounting. If the chosen granularity is too fine, the accounting overhead becomes significant. If the granularity is too coarse, accounting is not precise enough to trace costs back to their exact causes.

As components are the units of deployment, it makes sense also to make them the units of accounting. In this way it becomes possible to link costs and benefits to acquired components and their vendors.

8.3 Units of analysis

Any system of at least medium size needs to be hierarchically partitioned into smaller units, and the coupling between those units should be as weak as possible. Only a good partitioning allows us reliably to construct (synthesize) or to understand (analyze) a complex system. Examples where analysis of system parts is required are for verification according to a specification, testing, type checking, version control, re-engineering, and so on. Analysis is really the converse of synthesis. In fact, all phases of a software lifecycle ask for one sort of analysis or the other.

The coupling between units determines the extent to which any form of analysis of one unit needs to take properties of other units into account. In an unstructured system in which all units are tightly entangled with all other units, separate analysis of units is hopeless and a global analysis must be undertaken.

Partitioning a system into bounded units of analysis is necessary in practice when a system becomes too large for a global analysis to be feasible. Even more important, partitioning into bounded units of analysis is necessary in principle, when a system is meant to be independently extensible. As the client adds components on demand in such systems, there is no meaningful systems integration phase that the software engineer can rely on. Global analysis therefore cannot take place before it is too late (see Chapter 6).

Some forms of global analysis are unavoidable. A typical example is the final version check when integrating a component on demand. However, those "last-minute" checks should only flag problems that are meaningful to the user, such as the correctable problem of a version mismatch.

It is advisable to aim for the smallest units of analysis possible. In some cases, such as local type checking, individual classes or even individual methods can form the units of analysis. Quite often, the units need to be larger and encompass interacting groups of objects bound by a certain contract. It can be useful to form strong static hierarchical boundaries, such as erected by modules or whole subsystems. However, the unit of analysis can never be bigger than the unit of deployment; thus a component is the largest possible unit of (complete) analysis.

8.4 Units of compilation

Compilation is a quite fundamental aspect, and many gradual variations between full interpretation, mixed compilation and interpretation (Gough *et al.*, 1992), just-in-time compilation, and fully static compilation are possible. As compilation involves checking and can thus be used to establish safety properties and the like, it is worthwhile considering the possible choices of units of compilation.

Incremental compilation can speed up the edit–compile–link–run cycle considerably. Increments can be applications, modules, classes, or statements. In a component software world, complete applications no longer exist, and thus the application as a unit of compilation is not relevant to this discussion.

Units of compilation relate to the units of analysis discussed above. The extent of the compiler's involvement is limited to confrontation of a tradeoff when dealing with compilation units of finer granularity, such as classes. In particular, tight interaction with auxiliary constructs that are located outside the class but within a "natural" module enclosing the class may require combined analysis. This can be simplified when compiling at the level of modules. For even larger units, compilation speed becomes an issue. Given a fast compiler (for example, Wirth and Gutknecht, 1992), both modules and classes appear as reasonable units of compilation. Translating individual statements is only practical in interpreted languages.

To enable more global optimizations, compilation units should be as large as practically feasible. Components are the upper limit; modules may be a better compromise than classes. However, this performance argument becomes weaker when it is considered that just-in-time compilation or compilation on the fly (Franz, 1994) allows for cross-component optimization even after deployment.

8.5 Units of delivery

This section refers to units of delivery when it comes to the distribution of goods in a marketing sense. Today, applications, and sometimes components, are the typical units of delivery. Individual objects (or, better, classes) are rarely worth the administrative effort and cost of delivery. Surprisingly, the need to have clear and established interface contracts in place, to provide catalog entries, to market, and to maintain components adds significant cost to something inherently as cheap to replicate as a software component. At the other extreme, it also costs to bundle just "everything." Such "fatware" leads at least to tremendous training costs.

Individual classes are also rarely sufficiently self-contained to allow for separate deployment. In a system in which classes are the only structuring facility, it becomes very difficult to extract and package a suitable subset of classes, to ship them as a component. In practice, it becomes almost impossible to extract meaningful collections of classes from an unstructured collection that consists of thousands of classes. What is needed is a static higher-order structuring facility, such as a module construct (Wirth, 1982; Szyperski, 1992a; Cardelli, 1997). Even modules may prove insufficient, and constructs such as systems (Cardelli, 1989), libraries (Apple, 1992), or subsystems may have to be introduced for more complex components.

8.6 Units of deployment

Deployment is the process of readying a unit for operation in a particular environment. In simple cases, deployment is a trivial step and thus often confused or identified with installation (section 8.12). Deployment as a separate step became prominent with the introduction of context/container-based component platforms. For instance, in Enterprise JavaBeans a bean is not ready for installation as such. Instead, it carries a deployment descriptor that describes what requirements the bean has. A deployer takes a bean with its deployment descriptor and deploys it for a particular EJB container/server using tools provided with that container/server. These tools are free to generate additional code required to operate the deployed bean within the given container or to even rewrite the compiled bean. The actual installation of deployed beans is a separate step that makes the deployed bean available on a particular hardware configuration.

Units of deployment can be individual classes with their deployment descriptor, but usually are larger collections of classes, resources, and descriptors.

8.7 Units of dispute

If a system composed of several components fails, component vendors tend to blame each other for the problem. To minimize this undesirable effect, it is vital that errors remain contained in individual components. This means that they should be clearly attributable to their particular component, and they should not endanger the system as a whole ("bug containment"). The most severe non-local errors are violations of memory integrity – that is, dangling pointers and memory leaks.

In technical terms, safety means that invariants can be guaranteed. For a detailed discussion, see section 6.8. Information hiding on the level of objects (classes) allows invariants to be guaranteed over the hidden instance variables. For example, whenever the width of a rectangle is changed, the method that changes the width can also update an instance variable that contains the rectangle's area. In this way, the invariant "area equals width times height" can be maintained. Safety can be increased if more global invariants (Holland, 1992) can be specified and enforced by a closed unit – that is, if static information-hiding barriers can be erected. This is possible if information hiding is done at the level of modules or entire components, rather than at the level of individual objects or classes.

Languages either prevent errors or allow the component that caused the error that occurred to be pinpointed exactly. In a system composed of independently developed components, this helps clients to find out which vendor's software has failed. Pinpointing erroneous components at compile-time can be subtle, even at the level of type checking (Findler and Felleisen, 2001), but it is that much harder at runtime. If a component's identity (boundary) could not be clearly determined, it would become very difficult or even impossible to determine which vendor was the culprit. An interesting problem is the propagation of exceptions across component boundaries. Normally, components should handle exceptions themselves, as no other component can be expected to have the inside knowledge to do so. However, some exceptions cannot be handled locally and need to be propagated. If the propagated exception had been declared as part of the contract, then calling components are expected to handle such exceptions in an orderly manner (or propagate them properly). Otherwise, the calling component failed. Exceptions that are propagated across components but not stated in the contract represent a failure of the propagating component.

It is the latter case that is really exceptional – the called component's abstraction is unable to express what went wrong. (Java-style checked exceptions are really syntactic sugar for special return values – useful sugar, though, as the calling code can be checked for not ignoring these special return values.) The proper handling of "unchecked exceptions" – that is, real failures of a called component – requires architectural attention. In the general case, the caller will be unable to resolve such a situation. Instead, an encapsulating scope must be used to contain the consequences of the failure. A typical example is the use of a transaction monitor (or transactional container) that, upon detection of such a failure, aborts the current transaction, thus containing the impact that the failure may have. Error-handling policies, such as retry or fail and report to user, can be used to act properly on the occurrence of a failure-containment event.

8.8 Units of extension

A component may not provide completely new functionality, but, instead, extend existing functionality or implement existing interfaces. Typically, several objects must be extended simultaneously. The coupling between the objects forming an extension is tighter than between extending and extended components. After all, under the paradigm of independent extensibility (Chapter 6), it is desirable to allow for the coexistence of several extensions of the same base.

For example, the file abstraction of an object-oriented operating system may define separate abstractions for files and for file access paths. A concrete implementation of the file abstraction would contain hidden information about the disk sectors occupied by the file. An implementation of the access path abstraction would contain the current position and hidden information, such as the disk sector of the current position. To implement these objects in an efficient and safe manner, it is necessary that the implementation of the access path object has direct access to the implementation of the file object. However, access to either implementation from outside the component must be prevented.

The lack of an access control scope that can enclose several objects is a fundamental weakness of most object-oriented programming languages. Notable exceptions are modular languages such as Modula-3 (Nelson, 1991), Oberon, Java, and Component Pascal. The designers of C^{++} acknowledge the problem by allowing private parts of a class to be selectively exposed to certain explicitly named "friends" (Ellis and Stroustrup, 1994). Although perfectly general, this approach is entirely unstructured. The namespace construct that has been added to C^{++} merely provides units of name space management – it does not provide any access control. Java's packages are also interesting in that they are open. Thus, merely by declaring package membership of a new compilation unit, that unit gains full access to all package private and protected features of classes in that package. Java does not support closed packages – that is, modules.

A unit of analysis must not be broken up into several units of extension. Otherwise, an extension could be integrated into a target system with incomplete context – in other words, with a different context from that at the time of analysis. For example, a particular object may be less general than its interface seems to indicate because its implementation "conspires" with another object's implementation that was part of the same unit of analysis. Analysis showed that these two objects, if used together, would have the required properties. However, if the object was deployed individually and some entirely different implementation would serve for the second object, then the former object is likely to fail. Hence, it would not be wise to sell this object as an individual product.

8.9 Units of fault containment

Distributed systems must take into account classes of faults that are not under the control of any particular software component. For example, machines can fail and networks can have temporary or permanent communication failures. In such a situation, it is not a matter of isolating the "guilty" component – such as discussed in section 8.7.

Instead, the question is how system architecture can provide for subsystems that can contain certain classes of faults and thus shield the rest of the system. A fault-containing subsystem must itself be fault tolerant – that is, it must tolerate and effectively mask the faults that it is meant to contain. The two ways to mask faults are physical or temporal redundancy. With physical redundancy, the critical parts of a fault-containing subsystem are replicated and the subsystem uses a highly reliable voting mechanism to present majority results to clients of the subsystem – the rest of the system. The use of redundant network resources allows recovery from faults using forward error correction techniques. With temporal redundancy, the subsystem has sufficient time to roll back to a checkpoint and restart. Transaction monitors are a good example in this category.

Units of fault containment are very important on the level of overall system architecture. As indicated above, such units are usually of coarse granularity as they require explicit resourcing decisions and policies.

Related to fault containment is the inverse – fault exposure. If a component fails to meet its contract, then that fact cannot be reported within the frame of the contract. A way to deal with such a situation is to throw an exception or contact an out-of-band error-handling mechanism. Either way, the important observation is that regular callers of such a component cannot be expected to deal with such an error. After all, the situation escapes the abstraction and contract that bind the caller and the component. Therefore, such exceptions cannot be declared (made "checked exceptions" in Java lingo).

8.10 Units of instantiation

The standard unit of instantiation is an object. Larger or smaller units of instantiation would be conceivable with some object definitions. However, the one presented in this book leaves no choice – being a unit of instantiation is one of the defining characteristics of objects.

A component may package multiple classes (and required resources). It is not a useful unit of instantiation as the contained classes need to be instantiated individually and independently. Forcing a component to contain exactly one class is not useful.

8.11 Units of installation

Installation is a platform-specific activity that makes an installed unit available for use on a particular hardware configuration supported by that platform. The typical unit of installation is a tree of files, possibly gathered and compressed into an archive or cabinet file. In the simplest case, installation requires no more than copying such a tree of files into a file system (sometimes referred to as "xcopy install" following the xcopy file-copying utility on Windows systems). Installation is different from deployment (see section 8.6) as deployment involves actions required to ready a unit for a particular platform, while installation takes such a readied (deployed) unit and makes it available on a particular hardware configuration.

Install-time is a unique opportunity for a platform to perform critical checks that otherwise would need to be performed at a later time. For instance, the Windows device driver installation mechanism (starting with Windows XP) performs install-time checks of signatures to verify that a driver has not been tampered with and, if so signed, has passed driver certification criteria. A generalization of this idea is found in the .NET global assembly cache (part of the .NET Frameworks installation and part of Windows starting with Windows.NET).

Installation may be deferred by merely "installing" a remote location reference (the extreme case is installation on demand). For some platforms, such as JVMs with a special class loader, the installation step can be empty. Then, given some Java class available from a remote location, a class loader may immediately load such a class, skipping any installation steps.

8.12 Units of loading

Once a component has been installed (see section 8.6), it may be loaded on demand. In a networked environment, the component might not even be locally installed. Instead, the component is fetched from a remote site when needed (Arnold and Gosling, 1996). However it is done, a dynamic linking facility (DLLs) must be available. As classes in a component typically interact closely, loading one class would immediately cause the loading of the other classes. It is usually more efficient to load the whole component as a unit.

When loading a new component into an already running system, the version of the new component must be checked first. Loading must be prevented if the new component uses other components that are not available in this environment or which are of an incompatible version. Incompatibility due to version mismatches is the syntactic fragile base class problem. In essence, the problem is to "avoid breaking clients that do not depend on details that have changed in a service's release or its interface" (see section 7.4.1). For maximum compatibility, version checking should occur per class or interface or even per method, rather than per component (Crelier, 1994).

Delaying version checking from load-time to runtime, as is done in Java, is problematic. Incompatibilities will then be detected only at unexpected moments midway through execution. This is too late to provide generic handling, as the executing code may have already committed changes. Hence, Java programmers would have to catch the version mismatch exception wherever a method invocation crosses load units. In Java, that would be on every call to a method of a public class, except for the one public class that can be local to a load unit.

When objects of different origins are loaded, name collisions may occur. There must be a mechanism to prevent such collisions. The safest way is to define a hierarchical naming scheme, where the top-level names are registered with a global naming authority. This is the case with Java or the BlackBox Component Framework (Oberon microsystems, 1997b) and its predecessor Oberon/F (Oberon microsystems, 1994). See Jordan and Van de Vanter (1997) for an account of the Java-related issues.

Microsoft's COM uses 128-bit numbers – so-called globally unique identifiers (GUIDs) – to prevent name collisions. The scheme is part of the Open Software Foundation's distributed computing environment (OSF DCE), where such numbers are called universally unique (UUIDs). GUIDs are constructed out of the creating machine's network ID, the time of creation, and some other almost random sources. The algorithm makes it extremely unlikely that two GUIDs that have been generated independently will ever be the same. (In the latest revision, the generated GUIDs are postprocessed using an SHA-1 hashing algorithm, yielding another 128-bit number that is also highly likely to be unique, but that doesn't allow extraction of network IDs or creation time – information in older GUIDs that has been used to perform correlations that raise privacy concerns.)

The CLR solution to the problem blends the best properties of the hierarchical namespace approach and GUIDs. All CLR names are defined in a namespace hierarchy. For any given definition of a name and the definition's version (!) the definition is located in an assembly (a .NET component) that is tagged itself with a unique root name, which is the public key of a public/private key pair. The assembly is also signed using that same key pair. Key generators make it extremely unlikely that the same key is generated twice and signing eliminates the possibility of tampering with the root name of an assembly (or any other aspect of the assembly's contents).

The loading of new objects must not invalidate other already loaded objects merely by the fact of loading. This rules out the use of languages the type systems of which require global analysis for type checking, such as in original Eiffel (Meyer, 1990; Szyperski, 1996). Newer versions of Eiffel correct this problem (Meyer, 1996). Languages that explicitly expect dynamic loading are sometimes called dynamic languages (Apple, 1992).

Like COM (by convention), but unlike most other systems, CLR supports full side-by-side installation and loading of multiple versions of a component.

Side-by-side loading of multiple versions of a component requires that the component does not manage an external resource and that it does not maintain observable state (in global/static variables). Such side-by-side coexistence is essentially unavoidable if component dependencies lead to the transitive dependence of multiple versions (Meijer and Szyperski, 2002). For example, a component B may depend on version 1 of component A while another component C might depend on version 2 of component A. If B and C expose definitions from A in their signature (by, for example, using a type from A in exposed methods), then a component D that needs to use B and C will force the side-by-side coexistence of versions 1 and 2 of component A.

8.13 Units of locality

This section covers aspects of distributed computing. To avoid confusion with units of delivery, the term unit of distribution has been avoided. Microsoft coined the term remoting for distribution in this sense.

Component integration standards such as CORBA, DCOM, Java RMI, or CLR provide facilities to access objects on a remote machine. In the resulting systems, locality to minimize communication cost is traded against distribution to maximize resource utilization. Modern distributed systems are arranged in a hierarchy of networks: from system-area networks connecting processors within cabinets, local-area networks (LANs), and various possible intermediate networks (wide-area networks – WANs), right to the internet.

The communication cost increases with the network level used. Cross-process method invocations are significantly slower than in-process calls. Cross-machine calls across a LAN are even slower, and so on. Improving technology can be expected to deliver sustained bandwidth even over long distances. However, the high communication latency and therefore long observed round-trip delays over long distances will not change significantly. In other words, respecting locality preferences becomes increasingly important when moving up the network hierarchy.

Respecting locality essentially means keeping tightly coupled objects close together. Objects supported by the same component are likely to be coupled more strongly than objects in different components. It is therefore normally a useful strategy not to split up components across processes or machines.

A related aspect is the dynamic granularity of requests to a service. If a typical client needs to invoke many operations of a service to complete a single logical operation as seen by the client, then it is expensive to split client and service across machine boundaries. Hence, it is useful to design interfaces of units of locality – that is, interfaces meant to serve cross-machine requests, in a way that minimizes the number of individual requests. For distributed computing, this is an important design rule. For example, attributes of objects can be grouped to be retrieved together rather than by calling a sequence of accessor methods, and operations can be offered in "vector form" to perform the same operation on an array of arguments (Eichner *et al.*, 1997).

8.14   Units of maintenance

Software products are rarely perfect on release. Usually it is necessary to distribute updates that correct errors, which are more efficient, or add new features. If an update changes the inner workings of the component, depending client components may break because they relied on a particular behavior of the classes from which they inherited. This is the semantic fragile base class problem: "changing the inner workings of a provider, without violating the explicit contract, may still break clients" (section 7.4.2).

8.15   Units of system management

Certain parts of a system may require explicit management that goes beyond maintenance, as discussed above. To manage a system, it is useful to partition it into units of management, each of which can be individually monitored for availability, load, and so on.

Units of management can be individual components, but this solution may turn out to be too fine-grained to allow for efficient management of a large system. More likely, units of management will be subsystems located on server machines.

8.6   Summary

The many aspects discussed in this chapter lead to different natural unit granularities. In the majority of cases, fairly coarse-grained units are the best match. It is difficult to reduce these observations to a rule of thumb as to what granularity is right. Instead, it is probably best to use the discussed aspects to perform a detailed analysis for specific cases. For example, when aiming to develop component software targeting small mobile devices, the criteria are likely to be very different from those found when aiming for clusters of enterprise servers.

CHAPTER NINE

Patterns, frameworks, architectures

The discussions in the previous chapters should have helped to make one point clear: programming with objects and components is complex. Also, some of the ramifications in the case of large and complex systems are not yet fully mastered or even understood. A common reply to this generic concern is, "So what? It works!" – but does it? The surprising answer is "yes," object-oriented programming does get you quite far. In view of the major problems covered in the previous chapters, how can this be explained?

The simple answer is that software engineers follow guidelines and good examples of working designs and architectures that help to make successful decisions. Instead of being based on a sufficiently strong theory and "calculating" software designs, software engineers combine a little theory with a lot of experience. Reuse of architectural and design experience is probably the single most valuable strategy in the basket of reuse ideas. Also, it is not necessarily the hallmark of an immature engineering discipline to build firmly on examples and experience. All engineering disciplines are the same there – the creation of products that need to satisfy technical and non-technical criteria, including in-time production and marketing, cannot be based solely on theoretical "calculation." An educated mix is essential. Reuse of proven designs is the way in which *society* learns.

For a discipline to form a solid foundation grounded in experience, effective mechanisms need to be in place to communicate working examples. Software engineering spans a wide spectrum, from the extremely small – one bit is about as small as anything can get – to the very large. Design reuse addresses an equally wide spectrum.

The architecture of component-based systems is significantly more demanding than that of traditional monolithic integrated solutions. In the context of component software, full comprehension of established design reuse techniques is most important.

This chapter briefly reviews the established approaches that help to reuse design on those levels that are relevant to component software. In particular, traditional design "in-the-small" addressing individual algorithms or data structures is not covered. Full utilization of all presented design reuse methods assumes an established component-based culture. Initially, this is not the case, and the chapter therefore concludes by reviewing the issues of interoperability, legacy integration, and systems re-engineering.

9.1   Forms of design-level reuse

Reusing proven designs is essential, but there is no single reuse approach that covers all levels of granularity that software engineers have to face. Experience of how best to program "in-the-small" needs to be conveyed very differently from that on how to best program "in-the-large." There is a huge difference between the problem of sorting a list of values and that of building complex interacting systems.

Design reuse can be understood as the attempt to share certain aspects of an approach across various projects. The following list names some of the established reuse techniques and for which sharing level they are best suited.

- Sharing consistency: programming and scripting languages.
- Sharing concrete solution fragments: libraries.
- Sharing contracts: interfaces.
- Sharing individual interaction fragments: messages and protocols.
- Sharing interaction architectures: patterns.
- Sharing subsystem architectures: frameworks.
- Sharing overall structure: system architectures.

Each of these techniques will be covered briefly in the following sections.

9.1.1   Sharing consistency – programming languages

One of the oldest forms of reusing proven methods is their casting into programming or scripting languages. A programming language can make some things easy, others difficult, and yet others impossible. By doing so, the language encodes a dogma of how things should be done. Over time, the language dogma combines with a culture of proven ways of doing things using the language, it becomes the lingo of a field.

For example, if a language makes it difficult or cumbersome to implement dynamic hash tables or associative arrays, then the language designer is effectively saying that these should not be implemented anyway. Although this may sound a little harsh, this is the message that a programmer will get. Naturally, a language constructed in such a way that "everything goes" can largely eliminate such "language dictates." Most successful languages are somewhere in the middle, striving for a balance between enforcement of "good things" and flexibility to allow for the unforeseen. As projects grow in size and complexity, architecture gains importance. There is growing acceptance of the benefits of stringent languages, exemplified by the popular transition from C^{++} to Java.

A programming language cannot enforce good design, but it can exclude things that are likely to cause trouble. Thus, a programming language establishes consistency rails that protect programming efforts from certain classes of mistakes. It is known that a language – or, better, its implementation, the compiler – cannot statically verify a non-trivial program against its specification. Thus, enforcing correctness is out of the question. However, languages and their implementations can enforce static safety properties. The primary abstractional, structural, and compositional means of modern programming languages are:

■ static type systems, including higher-order mechanisms, such as parametric polymorphism or bounded polymorphism;
■ functions, higher-order functions, and functional composition;
■ closures or blocks;
■ lazy evaluation;
■ procedural abstractions;
■ exceptions and exception handling;
■ classes and implementation inheritance (subclassing);
■ dynamic type systems and inclusion polymorphism (subtyping);
■ support of an open object space (requires automatic memory management);
■ late binding and type-driven dispatch;
■ support for concurrency and synchronization;
■ metaprogramming and reflection;
■ module and package systems.

Hybrid object-oriented languages are the most successful in contemporary component-oriented programming. Therefore, the following sections will concentrate on the programming models of such languages. Nevertheless, it is worthwhile noting that other language models – in particular, the functional one – are promising. By the very nature of component-oriented programming, such alternative programming models could well start to blossom within components.

9.1.2 Sharing concrete solution fragments – libraries

Early programming languages attempted to provide all functions that should ever be used in multiple programs. An explosion of built-in functions was the result. For example, Pascal still had I/O concepts in the language (Wirth, 1971), while C no longer did (Kernighan and Ritchie, 1978). Since then, there has been a clear tendency to take specific functionality out of languages, in favor of abstractional and structural features. It was the birth of modular languages and their most prominent exemplar, Modula-2 (Wirth, 1982).

The central idea behind enhancing the sharing of proven solutions or, better, fragments thereof, is modular libraries or toolboxes. Such libraries can grow over time, without any need to change the language. For coverage of the essence of traditional libraries, see Chapter 5.

Libraries are naturally layered on top of each other. Some modular languages, such as Component Pascal, even enforce layering by excluding circular dependencies between modules. Layers are of foremost importance to system architectures and are covered in more detail in section 9.1.7.

9.1.3 Sharing individual contracts – interfaces

Once providers of a service and clients of that service come separately into existence and are combined freely, the binding contract between providers and clients gains self-standing importance (see Chapter 5). Attaching contracts, formal and informal ones, to a named interface leaves implementers of providers and clients with verification obligations. Where a contract has been carefully crafted, providers and clients from fully independent sources will be able to interact properly.

Interfaces with their associated contracts are logically the smallest contractual unit in a system. The individual operations of an interface do not have meaning of their own. (If they do, the interface is probably poorly designed.) The operations bundled into an interface together form a minimal basis for interaction between providers and clients. As such, an interface and its contracts say nothing about the larger organizational structures – the architecture – of a system.

Interfaces reside at the endpoints of interactions. An interface definition as such is neutral as to whether it refers to the provider or the client end. By differentiating requires from provides interfaces, the siding of such endpoint-assigned interfaces with endpoints is resolved. More precisely, while the same provides interface can be implemented by many providers, any particular instance of a provides interface is associated with one logical provider. Usually, this logical provider corresponds to one module for direct or one object for indirect interfaces (see section 5.1.1 for the distinction between direct and indirect interfaces). Symmetrically, a particular instance of a required interface is associated with one logical client, although multiple providers may be connected in a particular configuration.

Sets of interfaces can be bundled into composed contracts that are defined over sets of interfaces. An atomic interface bundles a set of operations that share the direction of invocation. Additionally, an atomic interface can be seen as a partial view on to one logical provider that, typically, can be used by multiple clients via that interface. A composed contract (Helm *et al.*, 1990) can combine interfaces of varied directionality and multiple logical providers. This notion of composed contracts covering multiple interfaces can be extended to the fairly recent notion of interface-based software architecture (Jonkers, 2001).

9.1.4 **Sharing individual interaction fragments – messages and protocols**

While interfaces reside at the endpoints of interactions, message schemas reside "on the wire" – that is, on the logical line between interacting parties. Messages are directional, traveling from a sender to a receiver. In the presence of gathering (collecting) or scattering (multicasting, broadcasting) interaction patterns, such logical lines can connect multiple senders and receivers.

While the communication line connecting senders and receivers is an abstraction that refers to endpoints, the communicated messages do not. A message schema describes a set of valid messages, usually with no constraints on particular senders or receivers. A particular message schema may require information in a message that identifies sender and/or receiver, but such identification is not a basic requirement for all messages. For example, a news message may be broadcast from an anonymous sender and received via subscription to the broadcast medium without any receiver identification in the message.

Message schemas can be described at the same two levels that characterize interfaces – a syntactic level that constrains the format of messages and a semantic level that captures the contractual nature of a message. Entirely analogous to interface definitions, message schemas use declarative notation to capture the syntactic level (including type-level constraints) and pre-agreed names to capture the semantic level.

A message can be made self-describing by tagging the message with the name of the message schema. Where such a schema is known at the point of inspection, its structural and typing details can be used to partially split the message into parts, while retaining meaning. This is equivalent to reflection systems that make objects self-describing by allowing the external extraction of an object's type name. Again, if that type name is known at the point of reflection, the syntactic part of the type definition (including types) can be used to explore that object further.

Interfaces and messages coexist in a subtle relationship. At one extreme, all interfaces could be reduced to holding a single "operation handle that" accepts a single self-describing message and returns another self-describing message. This is largely the style of web protocols that funnel all messages through a single hypertext transfer protocol (HTTP; IETF, 1999) port. At the other extreme, all interfaces have fully factored operations that only take and return non-self-describing arguments. This is largely the style of traditional application programming interfaces (APIs). There are many design points between these two extremes. For example, there are internet protocols such as telnet or ftp and their messages are meant for specific kinds of endpoints (often called ports) that offer specific interfaces.

Sets of interfaces correspond to protocols. Instead of focusing on the required and provided operations at endpoints, protocols focus on the valid sequences of messages exchanged between these endpoints. It is always possible to rewrite a protocol definition into a composed contract over sets of appropriately defined interfaces. The reverse is also true. When deciding which of these two dual approaches it is best to take, a number of factors need to be considered.

- ■ *Tradition* Many communications communities prefer messages and protocols while many computing communities prefer operations and interfaces. (This is changing as both communities grow together under the influence of the internet.)
- ■ *Emphasis* Protocols emphasize messages between endpoints, while interfaces emphasize operations on endpoints that accept and return messages.
- ■ *Synchronous v. asynchronous communication models* Messages and protocols more naturally describe asynchronous communication, while interfaces and operations more naturally describe synchronous communication. (Asynchronous operations on interfaces can be defined and synchronous constraints in protocols are also possible.)

9.1.5　Sharing individual interaction architecture – patterns

An attempt to collect and catalog systematically the smallest recurring architectures in object-oriented software systems led to the cataloging of design patterns (Gamma, 1992; Gamma *et al.*, 1995). Gamma *et al.* (1995) – also known as the "Gang of Four" or GOF – define patterns using the following four elements.

1 A pattern name.
2 The problem that the pattern solves.
　(a) Conditions that must be met for the pattern to be applicable.
3 The solution to the problem brought by the pattern.
　(a) Elements involved and their roles, responsibilities, relationships, and collaborations.
　(b) Not a particular concrete design or implementation.
4 The consequences (results and tradeoff) of applying the pattern.
　(a) Time and space tradeoff.
　(b) Language and implementation issues.
　(c) Effects on flexibility, extensibility, portability.

In their catalog, Gamma *et al.* identified 23 design patterns. Another interesting early collection of design patterns in the context of software architecture was published by Buschmann *et al.* (1996), followed by a second volume by Schmidt *et al.* (2000). Many more have since been identified and documented in an annual series of Pattern Languages of Programs (PLoP) conferences. The best are published in books (Coplien and Schmidt, 1995; Vlissides *et al.*, 1996; Martin *et al.*, 1997; Harrison *et al.*, 1999) and there is also the Patterns Series of books (Addison-Wesley). An example of a pattern already covered in the catalog by Gamma *et al.* that is particularly close to many examples in this book is the Observer pattern. It defines a one-to-many dependency between objects. This is that when the one object (the subject) changes, all its dependents (the observers) are notified to perform updates as required. Using the notation of Gamma *et al.*, Figure 9.1 shows the class diagram of the Observer pattern. The attached "notes" sketch implementations where this helps to understand the pattern. Otherwise, the notation is close to UML.

The idea is that, once the problem has been isolated, a proper pattern can be chosen. The pattern then needs to be adapted to the specific circumstances. For example, an observable subject may need to be observed by *n* observers which are themselves unknown to the subject. The Observer pattern is chosen, but the pattern's Update method may need an additional argument to inform observers of what it is that has changed. A pattern catalog should contain a discussion of the common variations on a patterns theme, as demonstrated by Gamma *et al.*

Design patterns are microarchitectures. They describe the abstract interaction between objects collaborating to solve a particular problem. They are quite different from frameworks (described in the next section). Gamma *et al.* list the following differences between patterns and frameworks (Gamma *et al.*, 1995, p. 28):

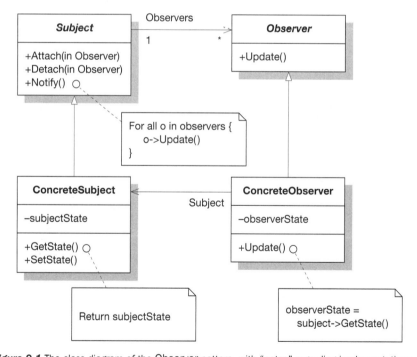

Figure 9.1 The class diagram of the Observer pattern, with "notes" regarding implementations.

■ "Design patterns are more abstract and less specialized than frameworks. Frameworks are partial implementations of subsystems, while patterns have no immediate implementation at all; only examples of patterns can be found in implementations."

■ "Design patterns are smaller architectural elements than frameworks. Indeed, some patterns live on the granularity of individual methods – examples are the Template Method and the Factory Method patterns; most frameworks utilize several patterns."

Design patterns and interfaces are orthogonal to each other. It is often useful for design patterns to only refer to parts of interfaces, while allowing any particular application of the pattern to exist in a larger context where the involved interfaces also cater to other purposes, possibly described by other patterns. The grouping of operations on interfaces should be driven by the contractual relationships among these operations, relative to one logical provider. The appearance of operations in patterns should be driven by their collaborative/interactive roles in the pattern.

Design patterns and message schemas are also orthogonal to each other. Design patterns can usefully refer to parts of exchanged messages, just as they can usefully refer to subsets of operations on interfaces.

To use design patterns, interfaces, and message schemas to their combined best effect, it is important to realize that these three abstractions all have a cross-cutting nature that describes slices of a system from a particular viewpoint. The nature of the crosscuts is different for each of the three.

■ Interfaces cut through and standardize partial views on to one logical provider, as seen by a typically open set of clients.

■ Message schemas cut through one logical line of communication between entities.

■ Design patterns cut through an architecture (a framework) separating out one concern for interaction.

It is possible, though difficult, to identify families of patterns that fit together in a harmonious way. If done properly, each pattern acts like a word in a well-chosen vocabulary. Adding the heuristics that guide the combination of patterns then forms a language – a pattern language. This idea originated in the realm of architecture – architecture in the classical sense (Alexander *et al.*, 1977). Many pattern languages for the realm of software architecture have been published – for example, pattern languages for relational databases and Smalltalk (Brown and Whitenack, 1995) or J2EE applications (Yang, 2001).

9.1.6 Sharing architecture – frameworks

Originally, frameworks were studied in the context of Smalltalk (Deutsch, 1989). Later, frameworks gained much attention as a general approach in object-oriented programming (Gamma *et al.*, 1995; Lewis, 1995). A framework is a set of cooperating classes, some of which may be abstract, that make up a reusable design for a specific class of software. Although frameworks are not necessarily domain specific, they are usually concept specific. For example, a framework for .NET Web Forms controls does not say much about the specific functions of parts, but embodies the concepts that make a piece of software a Web Forms control.

Frameworks keep a number of their classes open for implementation inheritance – that is, formation of subclasses. Some of these classes may be abstract, requiring implementation inheritance for the framework to work at all. Frameworks often provide default implementations to reduce the burden on lightweight usages of the framework. Instead of defining everything, a client merely needs to augment or replace those defaults that do not fit.

Traditional frameworks fully concentrate on classes and inheritance. However, there is no reason for a framework not to emphasize object composition instead. As implementation inheritance, even in the presence of reuse contracts (p. 127), tends to require knowledge of the superclass' implementations, it is often called whitebox reuse. Object composition, on the other hand, if based on forwarding rather than delegation, merely relies on the interfaces of the involved objects. It is therefore often called blackbox reuse. Frameworks are accordingly classified into whitebox and blackbox frameworks. Arbitrary "shades of gray" can be formed by partially opening a blackbox framework for whitebox reuse.

An important role of a framework is its regulation of the interactions that the parts of the framework can engage in. By freezing certain design decisions in the framework, critical interoperation aspects can be fixed. A framework can thus significantly speed the creation of specific solutions out of the semifinished design provided by the framework.

Most frameworks apply multiple patterns in their design. For example, the most famous framework of all, the Smalltalk model view controller (MVC) framework (Krasner and Pope, 1988), can be dissected into three principal pattern applications (Observer, Composite, and Strategy). In addition, there are also some others of lesser importance to the MVC framework (for example Factory Method and Decorator) (Gamma *et al.*, 1995).

The MVC framework is a classic because it defines a number of roles, each of which is immediately intuitive. Models represent information, views present information, and controllers interpret user manipulation. In most cases, the same information can be presented in many different ways. For example, a text model can be presented in outline form or in page preview form. Less obviously, it can also be presented as a statistical summary showing the word count, a Flesch Reading Ease score, and other measures. Similarly, a vector of numbers can be presented as a table, a bar or pie chart, or again as a statistical summary. Orthogonal to the presentation style, presentations can also be different in their aspect by using scrolling, panning, or zooming. These are just a few examples, of course. The point is that many views can be attached to a single model. Controllers mediate between a model–view pair and manipulative actions taken by a user. Controllers are usually attached one-to-one to views. Figure 9.2 shows the resulting class diagram.

The small number of classes (Model, View, Controller) in Figure 9.2 may suggest that MVC could be seen as a pattern rather than as a framework. However, the figure is intentionally simplified. The apparently simple relationship between model and view alone is covered by a pattern of its own – the Observer pattern (p. 157). The relationship between view and controller is also non-trivial. A controller has to interact tightly with the way in which the view presents data. Thus, a controller directly depends on a specific view. The controller augments the functionality of the view by adding a strategy of how to interpret user events and map them to view operations. Gamma *et al.* (1995) call the corresponding pattern Strategy. Note that the controller and view pairwise refer to the same model – this is not easily shown in a class diagram. (This redundancy could be avoided by requiring the controller to acquire the model indirectly from the view.)

Figure 9.2 displays further relationships. First, it shows how user-triggered events reach a controller and how view presentations reach the display. What is more important, it also shows that arbitrary, other "client" classes can directly operate on model, view, and controller. Remembering these "other" players is important in the context of a framework, whereas it is of less importance in the context of patterns.

A framework integrates and concretizes a number of patterns to the degree required to ensure proper interleaving and interaction of the various patterns' participants. Indeed, a framework can be explained in terms of the patterns it uses (Johnson, 1992). Thus a framework not only adds a higher level of architecture, but also the infrastructure that integrates the lower-level abstractions, often usefully described as using patterns. The degree of enforcement of integration rules depends on the framework technology used. If the framework is a set of Smalltalk classes, there is no strict enforcement that a programmer could

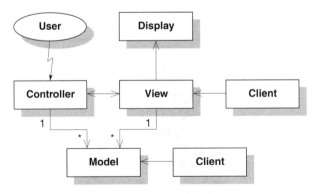

Figure 9.2 A controller has been added to the class diagram.

not breach. If the framework is encapsulated into "sealed" modules or packages the implementations of which are inaccessible, enforcement can be quite strict.

Framework design can be bottom up and pattern-driven (for example, Schmid, 1995), or it can be top down and target-driven. The bottom-up design works well where a framework domain is already well understood, such as after some initial evolutionary cycles. Starting from proven patterns and working one's way up has the advantage of avoiding idiosyncratic solutions in the small, problematic solutions that should be replaced by application of an established pattern. As with all bottom-up design work, there is a danger of constructing "shopping centers" of fragmentary solutions, without a sharp focus. (The term "shopping list" approach goes back to Meyer (1988), who advocated it as a good strategy for class design. This strategy does not work well in practice, though, as anything beyond trivial ADTs does not have a "complete" set of operations.)

Top-down design of a framework is preferable where a framework domain has not yet been sufficiently explored but where the target domain to be served by the framework is well understood. A framework domain is the set of rules and roles and their semantic models codified in a framework itself. A target domain is the set of interactions and entities found in a concrete outcome of a domain analysis effort. It is important to keep the two separated. Framework domains are technical, in a sense, "introverted," whereas target domains are application-oriented or "extroverted." A single framework is meant to address multiple concrete targets, otherwise the attempt to form a generalized architecture has failed.

An example will make this clearer. Assume that the ideas of the MVC separation were not yet known, but there was a firm understanding of what it means to edit some visualized data interactively in a window system. In this case, an entire family of target domains is understood, corresponding to the various kinds of documents to be edited. Also, the domains' entities are known – there are specific documents, windows, and users. Finding a family of closely related target domains is a good indication that a framework should be considered. Under the assumption that no such framework already exists, the question is "How can the target domain entities and their interactions be distilled to form the framework domain?" In the example, how can the abstractions and mutual interactions of models, views, and controllers (!) be found?

There is no simple answer. Concrete designs and implementations for specific targets can be found using one of the several object-oriented analysis and design techniques. However, substantial design and domain experience is required to determine what a good framework would be. Making the framework too rigid may unnecessarily rule out relevant targets. Making it too flexible will lead to inefficiency, undue complexity, and probably both. It is helpful for a first sketch to pick a small number of concrete targets and work on appropriate designs and implementations without aiming for a framework. Resting on this target domain expertise, a framework design can be attempted. Quite a number of iterations should be expected before a framework design settles and becomes stable.

9.1.7 Sharing overall structure – system architecture

A few basic principles can be learned from successful software architectures of the past:

- layering, strict and non-strict;
- hierarchies or heterarchies.

The idea of a strictly layered approach to software architecture is old. One of the first clear presentations of the idea, in the context of an operating system's architecture, was Dijkstra's article on the THE operating system (Dijkstra, 1968). ("THE" is the Dutch acronym of Technological University, Eindhoven – Dijkstra's affiliation at the time.) The benefits of layered architectures in terms of development effort and cost have been empirically verified (Zweben *et al.*, 1995). Software architecture as a discipline was first proposed by Perry and Wolf (1992). Shaw and Garlan (1996) published an introduction to some of the issues of software architecture (for a bibliography, see their architecture website: www.sei.cmu.edu/architecture/ and for more information on software architecture, see Chapters 21 and 24).

In a strictly layered system, the implementation of one layer can only be based on the operations made available by the layer immediately below. Figure 9.3 shows two popular ways to depict layered architectures.

The "onion model" emphasizes the encapsulating property of strict layers, but introduces a bias toward the expected relative size of the layers. There is no strict technical need for lower layers to be "smaller" than higher ones.

Strict layering introduces a very powerful property to a system's architecture. A layered system can be understood incrementally, layer by layer, whether bottom up or top down. This is possible because each layer can be fully understood by understanding its implementation, relative to the interfaces it uses from the layer immediately below, and the interfaces it offers to the layer immediately above.

Strict layering has several downsides however. It hinders extensibility and it can introduce unacceptable performance penalties. Extensibility is threatened because a new, higher-level component can only build on what is provided by

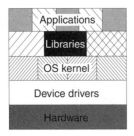 

Figure 9.3 Strictly layered architectures and the strict "onion model."

the next, lower layer. Although some layer further below – ultimately the hardware – may well support the new extension, the next lower layer may not. The percolation of requests through a deep hierarchy of layers can lead to performance problems. The extensibility issue can be addressed by allowing extensions on every level of the architecture. Where operations can be bundled and bulk requests can be issued, performance problems in a layered system can normally be resolved. If operations cannot be batched, and resulting latencies introduced by the layering cannot be tolerated, the number of layers has to be reduced.

Figure 9.4 shows typical depictions of extensible, layered architecture. In principle, the idea is that every extension should still reside on a single layer. Hence, if an extension on one layer needs to access services of a layer below the next lower layer, then intermediate extensions need to be devised. In practice, this principle is often breached. For example, instead of extending the clib (C library) layer, many UNIX applications directly access the kernel where required.

The practice of accessing not only the next lower layer but also any of the lower layers leads to non-strict layering. Figure 9.5 shows non-strict layering as it is often depicted. Non-strict layering can solve extensibility and performance problems by eliminating intermediate layers where useful. However, it destroys the main property of strict layering, which is that a layer creates an abstraction that is affected solely by the implementations forming that layer. In a non-strict layering, there is no obvious way to "slice" a component that extends down to lower layers to gather all implementations belonging to a given layer.

Obviously, a non-strict layering is harder to visualize – there can be conflicts that make a complete diagram of the shape used in Figure 9.5 impossible. Is this relevant? Architecture is very much about striving for balances between understandability, functionality, and economy, so it does matter if an architecture gets too complex to draw a simple overview diagram.

It has been advocated before that each level of a description should involve three to seven entities (the "seven plus or minus two" principle; Miller, 1956). The reasoning behind this range is sometimes based on the natural human ability to comprehend aggregates of up to around seven entities at once rather than sequentially and incrementally. An early proponent of this philosophy was

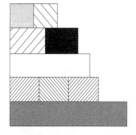

Figure 9.4 Extensible strict layering.

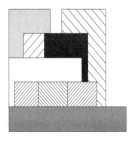

Figure 9.5 Non-strict layering.

Leo Brodie (1984). Many similar statements can be found in the literature on architecture or discussions about architecture. For example, Kent Beck wrote (Anderson *et al.*, 1993, p. 358):

> "The first test I apply [in my consulting practice] is whether staff can explain the system to me in 3–5 objects. If they can't, there is no explicit architecture. More often than not these projects are in trouble."

It may seem strange to base architectural decisions on such vague criteria of human perceptibility. All other aspects, such as functionality and cost-effectiveness, certainly ask for due attention as well. However, they all fade to gray when the perceived complexity of an architecture prevents understandability and thus prevents effective teaching, maintenance, and evolution. A first consequence is that it is much harder to establish architectural conformance of a given detailed design or implementation. In addition and often overlooked in a new project, complex architecture tends to deteriorate more rapidly over time as the architect has a much harder time to convey the guiding principles that would allow for proper evolution of the architecture.

9.1.8 Systems of subsystems – framework hierarchies

To what extent do patterns and frameworks address architectural concerns? Patterns are microarchitectures; frameworks are subsystem architectures. Most larger, fully functional systems will introduce multiple frameworks. However, interaction across frameworks is a difficult problem that needs to be addressed on a yet higher architectural level. If formation of good frameworks is difficult, then conception of good system architectures is truly hard.

There is a compelling reason not to stop at the architectural level of frameworks but to move on to entire systems. Independently designed frameworks are very difficult to combine as they each aim to take control (see next section). By the very nature of frameworks, they aim at the regulation and possibly enforcement of part interaction. Unless there is a clear higher-level view of where, when, and how parts of frameworks overlap or interact, there is no handle for the framework architect to ensure proper interframework cooperation.

Systems are usually modeled as a hierarchical composition of subsystems. It should thus be possible to lift the concept of frameworks to higher levels. Traditional class frameworks are partial combinations of classes – partial because they need to be completed when instantiating a framework. A logical extension of this approach leads to subsystem frameworks. Subsystem frameworks prestructure larger systems by partially combining the key subsystems. Just as class frameworks use abstract classes for combination of sets of concrete classes, subsystem frameworks could use abstract subsystems.

The above vision of hierarchies of frameworks sounds straightforward. Experience however teaches that moving from structures with a fixed number of abstractional levels on to general hierarchical structures can introduce substantial complication. For example, Chapter 21 contains an example of lifting the "flat" MVC framework to a hierarchical MVC framework. The result is not a framework hierarchy but a single framework covering a hierarchical structure. Nevertheless, the complexities introduced compared with plain MVC are truly substantial.

Another complexity of framework hierarchies needs to be faced. All previous attempts that aimed at merely replicating proven abstractional tools from a lower level to higher levels failed. For example, a class is not a procedural closure, a module or package is not a class, and a subsystem is not a module. In all these cases, the lower-level abstraction is not perfectly suited to capturing the higher-level needs. There are two reasons, and both can be understood as an "impedance mismatch." First, a lower-level abstraction is naturally closer to concrete detail, such as the execution order or the data representation. Retaining the lower level's degree of detail overburdens a higher-level abstraction. Second, a higher-level abstraction introduces new organizational roles, such as is required to increase the degrees of independence and autonomy of responsible producers. Ignoring the new organizational roles leads to a complete failure of the introduced abstraction. (Aiming to push such organizational roles down to lower-level abstractions will also fail, most likely by leading to bloated designs that cannot perform well. As an extreme example, consider equipping expression-level abstractions with module-quality explicit import/export declarations.)

The discipline area is still too young to venture a general attempt at framework hierarchies. The next step has to be a close study of what could be called second-order frameworks – frameworks of subsystems that each on its own can be structured and understood using traditional (first-order) frameworks. Attempts in this direction are component frameworks (see Chapter 21 for a detailed discussion).

To conclude, system architecture is a means to capture an overall generic approach that makes it more likely that concrete systems following the architecture will be understandable, maintainable, evolvable, and economic. It is this integrating principle – covering technology and market – that links software architecture to its great role model and justifies its name.

9.2   Interoperability, legacies and re-engineering

Existing solutions to problems are the cornerstone of working organizations. Such solutions naturally age and eventually become a "legacy" from earlier software engineering eras. Abrupt abandoning of legacy solutions and their instant replacement by something "new and better" is not normally an option. Instead, solutions must be sought that enable smooth transitions and gradual replacement (for example, Brodie and Stonebreaker, 1995).

A cardinal problem in many cases is the absence of a clear overall architecture of the legacy system, combined with refined architecture on lower levels of abstraction. Not surprisingly, some sort of architecture is usually present at the time a new system is first conceived. Naturally, this initial architecture proves inadequate as the system evolves, but, instead of carefully evolving the architecture as well, it is often left behind. As the system evolves independently of a maintained architecture, it "deteriorates" over time. Migration to new technologies then becomes a problem of re-engineering, and often even of reverse engineering in the absence of guiding high-level documents. Then, legacy becomes a major burden.

To prevent deterioration of architecture, systems need to be refactored periodically. A clear benefit of component-based architecture is the support of localized refactoring. Refactoring within a component is easiest, but a hierarchical overall architecture also enables selective refactoring of subsystems. Refactoring has increasingly widespread effects as it is taken further up the hierarchy of an overall architecture. It is thus useful to design a hierarchical architecture from the beginning with refactoring in mind. In particular, any form of coupling needs to decrease quickly when moving to higher levels of the hierarchy.

A separate but related aspect is interoperability across time and space. Interoperability across time is often called backward and forward compatibility. The issue is: how can two software systems, separated either by evolution over time or by independent development over space, cooperate? On a semantic level, this requires shared definitions. On an infrastructural level, it requires shared "wiring." It is the latter aspect that is often referred to as interoperability (Valdès, 1994).

Introduction of new technologies – without the simultaneous introduction of adequate architectural approaches addressing all relevant levels – can have disastrous effects. In the wake of early adoptions of object-oriented technology, architecture in-the-large has often been neglected. Objects were happily created and wired, all across a system. Layers were not introduced or not respected. Lines between a base and its extensions were not drawn or breached. The result is that object-oriented legacy is already a problem – sometimes after only a few years of adoption (for example Casais *et al.*, 1996). For example, the European Commission under the Esprit program funded a major project on evolution and re-engineering of "object-oriented legacy systems" (FAMOOS Consortium, 1996). The project ended in 1999 and delivered a number of techniques that help to recover from concrete framework implementations' lost architectural view information. Based on such information, framework refactoring is supported.

With the arguments presented in Chapter 7 in mind, it is not surprising that a lack of overall architecture in object-oriented systems is much worse than in traditional procedural systems. This is increasingly understood today and often leads to a shattering of initial "OO illusions." While it is a difficult task to move software to other procedural libraries, it is a truly formidable task to attempt migration to a different class framework. Very few traditional class frameworks have been designed to be compatible with other frameworks. Implementations that derive their classes from classes of a certain class framework are intimately coupled to their framework. Independent evolution of the framework is already a problem (see, for example, discussion of the fragile base class problem in Chapter 7). Exchange of the framework for another is almost impossible.

Interoperability on a global scale, as pushed by the internet and web, introduces a new dimension. Architecture on the top level now has to be global itself. It has to span borders, organizations, customers, and vendors alike. There is room for multiple architectures – not everything needs to integrate with everything else on the highest semantic level. For example, OMG's object management architecture (OMA) is one such ambitious attempt to standardize parts of a global architecture (Chapter 13).

CHAPTER TEN

Programming – shades of gray

It is sometimes thought that component software ends programming for most, leaving it to those specialists who create new components. The majority is expected merely to compose components – a task that is often called component assembly. If this were true, if programming were limited to the inside of a component, then this chapter and most of this book would be off-target.

What is programming? Programming a system is the activity of adding or changing functionality by combining or recombining existing or newly devised abstract entities according to a (programming) model. Programming can happen on all levels of a system. Programmable gate arrays lower the limits down to almost the gate level. Is there an upper limit? It is sometimes claimed that, from certain abstractional levels upwards, programming changes into scripting. Others claim that programming can be replaced by visual construction techniques. Such claims are not immediately helpful as their banishing of programming to the lower levels does no justice to this general concept.

In this chapter, the various forms of programming, as they are propagated today, are put into perspective and related to the theme of component software and software architecture.

10.1 Different programming methods for different programmers

It is helpful to differentiate between programming tasks of varying complexity and the audiences that are expected to perform these tasks. Here is a list of some exemplary activities that are not normally identified with programming, but which nevertheless are closely related:

- requirements engineering;
- work flow engineering and orchestration;
- visual application building and component assembly;
- scripting.

In all cases, the key is to consider the corresponding programming model. For requirements engineering, the programming model introduces entities of the application domain and ways to express relationships and transitions over time.

Executable requirement specifications are indeed preferable, especially in cases where ill-captured requirements can pose major safety threats (Leveson, 1995). The key difference to programming in the narrower sense is the total irrelevance of performance or resource consumption of the executable specification. Execution is merely used as a tool for validation.

Work flow engineering is the activity of capturing the flow of tasks and associated work items as defined by business processes and mapping such work flows into a descriptive form. In combination with an integration server, such work flow descriptions can then be executed to orchestrate business processes. This involves causing the automatic or semiautomatic sequencing of tasks along work stages, including the interaction with required computational services, the assignment of work items to people, and the gathering of results from peole. Overall, such orchestration leads to an integration of work done by people and information systems that is aligned with business processes. Despite the fairly high-level nature of this approach, it is nevertheless useful to view this activity as programming (of an entire enterprise, in the extreme). The latest development in this space aims to define standard work flow description languages for web services. IBM's WSFL and Microsoft's XLANG are two prominent examples (see section 12.4.5).

Visual application building rests on a programming model of plug-and-play of prefabricated components. The number of components that are combined is usually quite small and the mutual dependencies between these components take simple standard forms. Thus, visual builders are an option. Programming on this level concentrates mostly on functionality. It is expected that performance and resource consumption will be dominated by the components used, rather than by their particular "wiring."

Scripting is quite similar to application building. Approaches based on scripting admit that the actual "wiring" may need more than just "connections." Scripting allows programs to be attached to connections – either at the source end (events) or at the target end (hooks). Unlike mainstream component programming, scripts usually do not introduce new components but simply "wire" existing ones. Scripts can be seen as introducing behavioral coupling but no new state encapsulation (such as classes). Scripting is thus similar to traditional procedural or functional programming without global variables, and most scripting languages are indeed quite procedural in nature. Of course, there is nothing to stop a "scripting" language from introducing such state encapsulations – it then simply turns into a normal programming language. In fact, ECMAScript, Python/Jython, and Visual Basic have all gone this path. As for application building, it is expected that performance and resource consumption will be dominated by the components used rather than the scripts. The actual script execution engines therefore usually deliver mediocre to poor performance.

Scripts themselves are sometimes grouped into new abstract units – so-called script components (Nierstrasz et al., 1992). This terminology hints at the possibility of scripting scripts and ultimately at the fact that scripting is programming. In line with this observation, there is a strong trend for scripting languages to evolve into full programming languages. For example, the latest incarnation of Visual Basic, Visual Basic.NET, is fully equipped to define new classes and generate full .NET components (assemblies). However, a point could be made that it would be preferable to have separate scripting languages that are intentionally limited to not allow full programming. Such an approach leads to a cleaner separation of the composition and configuration nature of scripting versus the full manipulative power of programming (some approaches headed in this direction are discussed in section 24.1).

Following the above arguments, it is mainly the different programming models and the programming goals that make the difference. Scripting aims at late and high-level "gluing." Another dimension can be explored when considering graphical instead of textual programming, whether or not for scripting purposes. Graphical or visual programming is programming, and will remain programming, even if animation, virtual reality, and other media are used. This is so because the intellectual skills required are essentially the same. However, the audiences addressed by these different approaches to programming are likely to be quite different.

The proverb a picture says more than a thousand words comes to mind. Kristen Nygaard countered that the opposite is also true – a word says more than a thousand pictures (Nygaard's dinner speech "25 years Simula," ECOOP '92, Utrecht, The Netherlands). The point is that a true abstraction is necessarily represented symbolically, whereas a concrete real-world object may be represented (photo)graphically or by using its name. The photo may say much more than the name, but no picture can capture the full depth of the meaning of a symbol. (Nygaard challenged the audience by asking them to come up with a picture matching the word "vehicle.") Using icons instead of words merely adds new "words" to the language; icons and words are both symbols rather than direct presentations of the "real thing."

Symbols are not only appropriate but also inevitable when referring to abstraction as an abstraction is not a "real thing." The introduction of symbolic reference and abstraction is certainly among the foremost achievements of civilization. Without it, thinking remains at the level of the individual and concrete. Neither the future nor the past can be referred to and strategy, planning, generalization, and reflection remain out of reach. It would be a mistake to cripple general programming by insisting on total "concreteness" and "tangibility" of everything. In other words, graphical or visual programming cannot be about removing symbolism or eliminating metaphors used to visualize the abstract. Graphical notations, such as class diagrams, can indeed be entirely symbolic and unconcrete.

Graphical or visual programming can be the preferred method when the number of entities involved in any one "view" is relatively small. Such forms of programming can also be appropriate where the relations and interactions between these entities are mostly regular. Human perception can most efficiently spot minor irregularities in large and mostly regular structures. It can also evaluate "at once" all relations among a small number of entities. Another possibility is the visual presentation of a large number of attributes using carefully selected visual properties (dimensions), including color, texture, spatial distribution, and temporal patterns, such as flashing. Where such conditions are met, a graphical presentation can excel. In all other cases, more abstract methods, whether tabular, formula-based, or textual, are more appropriate. In particular, these methods are more economical in terms of space, easier to change, and tend to be more precise as to what is actually specified and what not. Finally, graphical notations do not lend themselves to formal reasoning. To tackle a common counterexample, in electrical engineering, graphical circuit schemata are used less and less frequently and usually only in high-level diagrams or individual patterns. The wiring of more complex circuitry is expressed and verified using special formal languages.

10.2   Programming to a system

The proper abstractions to support programming obviously depend on the programming model. Traditional programming models are primarily based on the composition of procedural abstractions provided by a library and a model of strict and immediate evaluation. In such a context, the programming style is caller-driven. Interfaces list call points, which are procedures, also called entry points. This does not change when moving from procedures to objects. As long as objects remain passive, computation remains caller-driven and interfaces list call points ("methods"). The model stays the same, even when considering higher-order programming, where procedure or object references are passed around, stored, and applied without static reference to the actual procedure or object.

The programming model changes when primarily looking at connections between objects rather than at callers. A connection is really just a binding between a caller and a callee. However, connections are symmetrical whereas traditional procedure invocation models are asymmetrically caller-controlled. Caller and callee are just the two ends of a connection. Neither of them is in charge of the actual binding. Interfaces in such a setting need to describe both call and calling points. A terminology introduced by Microsoft for its Connectable Objects approach is to speak of incoming and outgoing interfaces. Incoming interfaces are the traditional ones, listing call points. Outgoing interfaces declare what operations a component could invoke if it was properly connected. In other models, such outgoing interfaces are called raisable events or just events.

10.3   Connection-oriented programming

Components may need to call other components to perform. This corresponds to normal programming in which abstractions depend on other abstractions. It is also said that normal programmed calls correspond to a pull model of programming. The information is "pulled" in as needed. However, it may also be necessary for a component to be called by another component whenever that other component encounters a particular event. For example, in the observer pattern (Chapter 9) the observed object notifies its observers whenever its state has changed. However, it is not the observed object but the notified observers that depend on the notification. This is an important point. Notification or event propagation work in the reverse direction of traditional programming models – they implement a push model. Information is "pushed" out as it arises, rather than being pulled by a procedure call or method invocation.

In a traditional pull model, the caller knows what service to call. Increasing degrees of late binding or indirections can be used to generalize this model. With such indirections in place, it makes sense to say that caller and callee are "connected" by establishing the binding. In a push model, indirections are normally unavoidable as, in most cases, the pushing source cannot statically know the interested sinks. On an implementation level, indirections in push and pull models are handled in the same way. In procedural settings, procedure variables are used. In object-oriented settings, references to objects of base types can be used as a method invocation always introduces one level of indirection. Chains of call indirection can be formed using call forwarding, often implemented by proxy objects.

By replacing statically chained call dependencies by indirections that can be configured at runtime, connection-oriented programming is introduced. Increasingly, the connection mechanisms are factored out as separate services. Examples are event or message services. It is even possible, although restrictive, to build communication middleware entirely on the concept of messages and message distribution. This is called message-oriented middleware (MOM). However, in object-oriented middleware, such as Java 2, COM+, CORBA, or .NET, event and message services are of equal importance.

Connection-oriented programming is important when "wiring" prefabricated components or objects provided by such components. This is one occasion when an analogy with integrated circuits (ICs) helps. ICs have various pins, some of which carry input and others of which carry output signals. The technical documentation of an IC clearly and equally specifies the role of input and output signals. In traditional software systems there has been a bias toward "input signals." Connection-oriented programming requires symmetry of connection points (ports) for input and output. The corresponding interfaces are called incoming and outgoing interfaces – or, alternatively, provided and required interfaces. An incoming interface corresponds to traditional procedural or method interfaces. The analogy with IC signals is that calls come in on incoming interfaces, whereas calls go out on outgoing interfaces.

It is important to understand that the distinction between incoming and outgoing interfaces is about the direction of calls as seen by a component, not the flow of information. In particular, the parameters of a traditional incoming interface operation can, of course, be used to return values. It is thus easy to confuse return parameters with outgoing interfaces. The point is whether a call "through" that interface originates within or outside the component. Being incoming or outgoing is thus not a property of an interface in isolation. Every interface defines a clear call direction from interface client (caller) to interface provider (callee). Interfaces are incoming or outgoing with respect to a given component. Declaring outgoing interfaces of a component corresponds to declaring the events or messages that this component could emit.

The traditional model is asymmetrical. Although the callee does not know anything about the callers, a caller has to hold an explicit reference or static link to the callee. Interfaces on which a component depends are simply imported. Explicit parametrization using procedure references (callbacks) or object references are the only way to "connect" a caller dynamically to a callee. The idea of outgoing interfaces or event models is to normalize this approach and allow external tools – or third-party components at runtime – to connect objects with a given outgoing interface to objects supporting a matching incoming interface. In a type-safe setting, connections can only be made if the incoming interface is the same as or a subtype of the outgoing interface (see Chapter 6).

Figure 10.1 illustrates the connection of two objects by symbolically "wiring" outgoing to incoming interfaces using the COM notation (Chapter 15). Component object C1 has outgoing interfaces B and V and incoming interfaces A and U. Component object C2 has outgoing interfaces A and Y and incoming interfaces B and X. Connections have been established between the A and B interfaces of the two components.

Note that connections *per se* are independent of concepts of import, export, or layering. For example, a component framework may provide a common layer that defines various interfaces. A component for this framework imports the common layer and declares which of these interfaces it uses in incoming, outgoing, or both roles. It is then possible that several mutually independent components provide objects that, based on the common interface definitions, can be connected in a type-safe manner. These connections then exist horizontally within the layer of the components, or logically in a higher layer that establishes the connections. Such a separate connection layer (or the connected objects themselves) may need to provide persistence of connections. This is important when the connected objects themselves are persistent and the connections are supposed to persist as well. One approach is to group instance creation and connection descriptions into composites,

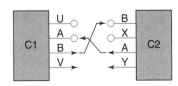

Figure 10.1 Connections, outgoing, and incoming interfaces.

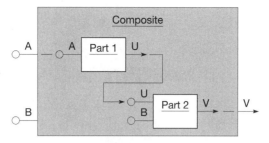

Figure 10.2 A composite over two subobjects.

which are objects that control the creation and connection of other objects. A composite instance does not contain the objects it creates and connects and neither does a composite component contain the components it instantiates. Figure 10.2 illustrates the nature of a composite. It shows a composite C that, when instantiated, creates two subobjects A and B, connects them to each other and to the composite's provided and required interfaces of the new composite instance.

Connection-oriented programming is a particular programming style that is especially useful when aiming for component-oriented programming. There are other styles that serve that same goal. Examples include attribute-based programming to drive automatic contextual composition (see section 21.1) and various forms of data-driven composition, where the arrival of a message of a certain type or with certain contents determines the next processing step. In the extreme case, data-driven programming leads to an actor model (Agha and Hewitt, 1987). Note also that connection-oriented programming as such does not imply component-oriented programming – the connected units may be of the wrong granularity or the established connections may not be backed by contractually specified interfaces.

10.4   Connection-oriented programming – advanced concepts

Once connections are emphasized as entities of their own, other connecting networks come to mind. For example, a single caller could be connected to a set of callees to create multicast connections. Intermediate abstractions, sometimes called channels or groups, can also be introduced, so that callers (sources) communicate through an additional indirection with a set of callees (sinks). Multiple callers can then use the same group. Callees can be added to or removed from such a group without contacting every caller currently using the group.

Figure 10.3 shows how C1's outgoing B interface can be connected to two incoming B interfaces. Technically, this requires a single call, here issued by C1, to be mapped to multiple calls, here to C2 and C3. Note that the connection of multiple outgoing interfaces to a single incoming interface is also possible and even quite common. This is nothing new – even the simplest procedural abstractions allow the same procedure to be called from many different call sites.

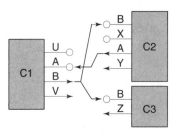

Figure 10.3 Multiple connections.

Figure 10.4 shows how an event channel or group can be used to decouple the connections callers-to-group and group-to-callees. Note that the group itself is represented by another component object, G. There is nothing special about groups or channels, except that they "promise," as part of their interface contracts, to relay incoming calls to outgoing interfaces. Obviously, this can be extended to provide other useful services. For example, a channel may filter, count, delay, log, or record calls for later replay. It is easy to see that such abstract calling fabrics are very useful and their existence makes the connection model truly powerful.

Interesting questions arise when the issue is the construction of generic group or channel services. If a group supports a specific set of interfaces, such as interface B in Figure 10.4, then the group's implementation is straightforward. It simply passes on all incoming calls to the incoming interfaces of all callees registered with the group. It is not productive to construct simple multicasting services repeatedly for all sorts of interfaces. Even if a tool performs the construction automatically, it leads to a large number of logically identical objects to which callers and callees have to be connected.

To program generic group or channel services, calls of operations with arbitrary signatures need to be dealt with generically. A paradigm that fits well is that of typed message passing. If calls always go through the same procedures or methods when being relayed between components, but carry different messages, then the construction of generic group or channel services is easy. In the

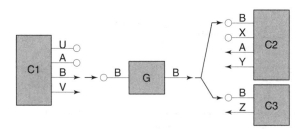

Figure 10.4 Separating the message target group from the message sources and sinks or, in message terms, separating the event chanel from the event sources and sinks.

presence of runtime type information, functionality such as message type-dependent filtering is also straightforward to realize. (Typed messages are often called event objects – see section 10.5.)

The following sample code illustrates this concept of message passing. The notation used is Component Pascal (Appendix A). Note that parametrization of types to express parametric polymorphism, as used in the following examples, is a proposed language extension (Roe and Szyperski, 1997) that has not yet been incorporated into Component Pascal. Similar proposals exist for Java and $C^{\#}$ and their future incorporation into the respective languages is likely. (Preview implementations of a generic Java version were made available by Sun in the second quarter of 2001.)

```
DEFINITION MessageGroups;
  TYPE
    Sink(A) = POINTER TO ABSTRACT RECORD
      (s: Sink(A)) Receive (VAR message: A), NEW, ABSTRACT
    END;
    Group(A) = POINTER TO ABSTRACT RECORD
      (g: Group(A)) Register (s: Sink(A)), NEW, ABSTRACT;
      (g: Group(A)) Unregister (s: Sink(A)), NEW, ABSTRACT;
      (g: Group(A)) Send (VAR message: A), NEW, ABSTRACT
    END;
END MessageGroups.
```

Component Pascal requires explicit naming and typing of the receiver object, called "this" or "self" in other languages. The receiver is specified in the form of an additional parameter list with exactly one parameter, placed before the operation's name. Methods have attributes. Attribute NEW marks a method as new – that is, as not overriding a base type method. (Note that a record declared with no base type has base type ANYREC.) Attribute ABSTRACT works as expected and marks the method as abstract.

In module Messages this is used to ensure that a group accepts only matching messages and sinks. Parametrization is achieved by naming any number of type parameters that can only be replaced by record types. In any specific context, all occurrences of a type parameter are guaranteed to refer to a type of identical bound. (The proposed parametric polymorphism is statically checked, does not conflict with separate compilation, has no runtime overhead, and does not lead to any object code duplication – see Roe and Szyperski, 1997.)

In this example, the types of groups and sinks are parametrized to show that these types could be used in conjunction with an arbitrary message base type. For example, a sink that only accepts messages of type MyMessage would be declared as:

```
TYPE
  MyMessage = RECORD ... END;
  MySink = RECORD (MessageGroups.Sink(MyMessage)) ... END;
```

With a slight modification, a similar declaration can be used to declare that sinks can accept messages of type MyMessage or any of its subtypes:

```
TYPE
  MyMessage = EXTENSIBLE RECORD ... END;
```

The attribute EXTENSIBLE indicates that, although MyMessage is a concrete record type, it is still open for extension – that is, not a final type. (Concrete types in Component Pascal are final by default.)

Below is the implementation of a module that offers a group implementation that broadcasts calls.

```
MODULE Broadcast;
  IMPORT Sets, MessageGroups;
  TYPE
    BCaster(A) = POINTER TO RECORD(MessageGroups.Group(A))
      sinks: Sets.Set(MessageGroups.Sink(A))
    END;
  PROCEDURE<A> SendOne (s: MessageGroups.Sink(A); VAR message: A);
  (* aux for Send *)
  BEGIN s.Send(message)
  END SendOne;
  PROCEDURE<A> (g: BCaster(A)) Register (s: MessageGroups.Sink(A));
  BEGIN g.sinks.Include(s)
  END Register;
  PROCEDURE<A> (g: BCaster(A)) Unregister (s: MessageGroups.Sink(A));
  BEGIN g.sinks.Exclude(s)
  END Unregister;
  PROCEDURE<A> (g: BCaster(A)) Send (VAR message: A);
  BEGIN Sets.Do(g.sinks, SendOne, m)
  END Send;
  PROCEDURE<A> New* (): MessageGroups.Group(A);  (* simple factory *)
    VAR bc: BCaster(A);
  BEGIN
    NEW(bc); bc.sinks := Sets.New();
    RETURN bc
  END New;
END Broadcast.
```

Note that in Component Pascal an identifier that is followed by an asterisk is exported from its defining module and thus visible in importing modules. In the example above, only procedure Broadcast.New is thus exported from module Broadcast. The group implementation in module Broadcast rests on a simple generic implementation of sets. The type parametrization of procedures (and methods) uses angular brackets rather than parentheses to indicate an important difference. Procedures are never explicitly parametrized. Instead, at every call site, the proper type arguments are inferred from the arguments passed to the procedure.

The definition of the Sets module, as used in this example, is shown below.

```
DEFINITION Sets;
  TYPE
    Set(A) = POINTER TO LIMITED RECORD
      (s: Set(A)) Include (elem: POINTER TO A);
      (s: Set(A)) Exclude (elem: POINTER TO A);
      (s: Set(A)) Contains (elem: POINTER TO A): BOOLEAN;
      (s: Set(A)) Size (): INTEGER
    END;
    Op(A,B) = PROCEDURE (elem: POINTER TO A; VAR arg: B);
    PROCEDURE<A> New (): Set(A);
    PROCEDURE<A,B> Do (s: Set(A); op: Op(A,B); VAR arg: B);
    (* other definitions deleted *)
END Sets.
```

In Component Pascal, the record attribute LIMITED prevents extension of the attributed record and restricts instantiation of such records to the defining module. In the example, only module Sets can allocate a new Set object. The broadcaster's method Send uses the procedure Sets.Do to call the auxiliary procedure SendOne once for each element of the set. Note that Group.Send, Sink.Receive, Broadcast.SendOne, and Sets.Do all take an arbitrary argument by reference (VAR mode in Component Pascal). Unlike Java, but like C#, Component Pascal can express "unboxed" constructed types and these can be passed by reference to generic procedures. The argument to such procedures can be allocated in the caller's stack frame, so heap allocation and subsequent garbage collection are thus optional.

Below is a simple test module that uses the above message group abstraction and broadcasting service.

```
MODULE TestClient;
  IMPORT Strings, Out, MessageGroups, Broadcast;
  TYPE
    Message = RECORD
      famousWords: Strings.String
    END;
    Sink = POINTER TO RECORD (MessageGroups.Sink(Message))
      name: Strings.String
    END;
  VAR
    sink1, sink2, sink3: Sink;
    group: MessageGroups.Group(Message);
    hello: Message;
  PROCEDURE (s: Sink) Receive (IN m: Message);
```

```
    BEGIN
      Out.String("sink " + s.name + " received message: " +
              m.famousWords); Out.Ln
    END Receive;
    PROCEDURE NewSink (IN name: ARRAY OF CHAR): Sink;
      VAR s: Sink;
    BEGIN
      NEW(s); s.name := Strings.NewFrom(name); RETURN s
    END NewSink;
  BEGIN
    Out.String("start of test"); Out.Ln;
    sink1 := NewSink("ONE");
    sink2 := NewSink("TWO");
    sink3 := NewSink("THREE");
    group := Broadcast.New();
    group.Register(sink1);  (* dynamic connect of sink1 to group *)
    group.Register(sink2);  (* dynamic connect of sink2 to group *)
    group.Register(sink3);  (* dynamic connect of sink3 to group *)
    hello.famousWords := Strings.NewFrom("Hello World!");
    group.Send(hello);   (* static connection here: source sends to group *)
    Out.String("end of test"); Out.Ln
  END TestClient.
```

The two remaining modules used by TestClient are Strings and Out. The relevant parts of their respective definitions are listed below.

```
DEFINITION Strings;
  TYPE String = POINTER TO ARRAY OF CHAR;
  PROCEDURE NewFrom (s: ARRAY OF CHAR): String;
  (* other definitions deleted *)
END Strings.
DEFINITION Out;
  PROCEDURE String (s: ARRAY OF CHAR);
  PROCEDURE Ln;
  (* other definitions deleted *)
END Out.
```

Executing TestClient will create three sample sinks, a broadcast group and a sample message. The three sinks are registered with the group. The message is then broadcast to all three sinks. Once TestClient terminates, the resulting output text will show the following five lines:

```
start of test
sink ONE received message: Hello World!
sink TWO received message: Hello World!
sink THREE received message: Hello World!
end of test
```

10.5 Events and messages

Events are occurrences that are localized in time and space. Messages are one way to communicate an event. Unfortunately, it has become common practice to call messages "events" if they communicate an event. This practice is somewhat acceptable, if at least the localization in time of the original event is retained by a timely message delivery mechanism. However, the fact that the arrival of a message is itself an event – occurring at the message-receiving endpoint – shows how unfortunate the blurring of the distinction between messages and events really is.

As can be seen from the example in the preceding section, all that is required to communicate events is to declare message objects and pass them around. With slight variations, this is the model of events in JavaBeans and of the Java Messaging Interface (Chapter 14), the CORBA Event and Notification services (Chapter 13), or of COM's connection points and the COM+ messaging service (Chapter 15). In the Component Pascal example above, a caller (a source) has to go through two steps:

1 create a message object and initialize its fields;
2 send the message object to the sinks.

With messaging services, accessed via the Java Messaging Interface, the CORBA Event or Notification service, or the COM+ messaging service, Step 2 is achieved via a channel abstraction. In JavaBeans or COM, such an indirection must be explicitly "wired" in. Otherwise, JavaBeans and COM events travel directly from source to sink, with no system-imposed indirection. COM uses separate sink objects per connection to the same receiving COM object, whereas JavaBeans uses a complex demultiplexing adapter approach to separate calls from different sources. In Java 2, COM+, CORBA 3, or .NET, both direct and indirect message distribution is supported.

The two-step approach of event signaling has three potential disadvantages:

1 making event objects first-class (heap allocated) can be expensive;
2 event objects of the wrong type could be passed;
3 event objects could be passed that have not been properly initialized.

All of these problems can be solved by proper programming language support. The first problem disappears where a language supports "unboxed" object types – and Java is among the few languages that do not. When using unboxed types (also known as value types), event objects can be allocated on the call stack, as with any other argument passed to a called procedure or method. (Note, however, that it is often required to treat messages polymorphically. Component Pascal is one of the few languages that support polymorphic passing by reference of unboxed types.)

In typed languages, for normal procedure or method invocations, the compiler statically checks the argument list. It is not possible to pass wrong numbers or ill-typed arguments. The second problem arises because of the desire to make event channels or groups generic. The JavaBeans specification, for example, recommends the use of specific event object types in event-handling methods. The same is possible with the CORBA Event Service. In C# or Java, it is not possible to construct generic channels or groups that are statically type safe. If the sources and sinks know the message's type, or at least a sufficiently narrow common base type, then parametric polymorphism solves the second problem. The above experimental version of Component Pascal supports parametric polymorphism; the MessageGroups and Broadcast examples above are parametrized with the message type and will handle only this message type or a subtype thereof.

It may be necessary to send a wide variety of messages through the same channel. The type parameter in such a case is necessarily imprecise – it could be as imprecise as the base type of all messages. If such an imprecise type bound is required, the second problem naturally remains, which is that a sink has to expect messages that it cannot handle and therefore should ignore. If such a message is sent erroneously instead of one that the sink would understand, then hard-to-track errors occur. Unfortunately, a sink cannot simply raise an exception when it receives a message that it does not understand. Under the broadcasting discipline, some other sink addressed by the same message may well understand it.

The third problem – the use of only partially initialized event objects – is caused by code explicitly filling in fields of a new event object. Using message or event constructors can solve this problem. In Java or C#, this is achieved by making the fields of an event object non-public, providing accessor methods, and using a constructor to initialize the event object. This is workable, but expensive. The solution in Component Pascal would be to export message or event fields in a read-only mode. Initialization also happens in a constructor procedure, but access is as efficient as with public fields.

Unless raisable events or outgoing interfaces form part of the definition of a component, it is not clear what events a particular object may raise. The solution is to make such information part of a component's definition. JavaBeans achieves support for events without changing the language Java. Instead of introducing a notion of separate "outgoing interfaces," JavaBeans relies on the Java core reflection mechanism. Reflection is used to extract dynamically those methods from a Java interface that follow certain naming and signature conventions (Chapter 14).

For example, to allow the connection of callees (called listeners in JavaBeans), a bean's interface must contain a method for each event type that it is capable of "listening" to. These methods must not have a return value and take only one parameter of a type that is a subtype of java.util.EventObject. Event-handling methods that follow this "design pattern" can be singled out automatically by using the reflection facilities to traverse all methods of an interface and inspecting the methods' signatures and return types.

A similar "design pattern" is used to find methods that support addition and removal of listener registrations. Such methods must not return anything, have a method name that starts with "add" or "remove" followed by the name of the listener type, and take a single parameter of this listener type. JavaBeans also defines a mechanism for a bean to override the automatic inference of event sources and handlers (Chapter 14).

Comparable conventions to method naming are also used in CLR to enable the support of existing languages. C#, having been co-designed with CLR, provides explicit syntax and language support and doesn't expose the underlying CLR naming conventions. A C# event is a registration point on an interface or a class. Event handlers (called delegates in C#) can be added to or removed from such a registration point.

10.5.1 Message syntax and schema – XML

In the example above, messages have been interpreted as special objects and therefore a programming language's object definition tools have been used to define types of messages. However, it is useful to view messages as items of their own, independent of any programming language. In particular, it is useful to distill the difference between objects and messages:

- objects encapsulate a combination of state and behavior and may refer to any number of other objects;
- messages do not encapsulate but merely package the data they carry, they do not normally have any behavior attached, and they never refer to other message instances – object references embedded in a message need to be handled with special care.

Why make this distinction? Messages as self-standing items have the potential to serve a very wide spectrum of communication needs. By preferring open, structured types over closed, encapsulating types, messages can be interpreted by a wide variety of means, including semi-generic filters, transformers, routers, and so on. Avoiding attached behavior eliminates dependencies on an implicit execution environment. If a message needs to convey behavioral aspects, then it can always contain "code" as part of its contained data, requiring interpretation under rules defined externally to the message.

Finally, by paying special attention to embedded object references, messages can be made more robust against change in their environment. Object references tie a message back to the objects they refer to. However, these objects have their own lifetime, scoping, and ownership issues that affect the very meaning of a message carrying such references. Robustness is achieved where a resolving indirection is introduced. For example, instead of referring to a particular object, a message may contain a URL (universal resource locator) or a COM-style moniker.

Extensible markup language (XML; W3Cb, 2000) is the one approach to message syntax and schema definition that has rapidly gained almost universal acceptance. A detailed discussion of XML and description of the most important standards in the larger XML family of standards follows in section 12.4. At this point, a simple example suffices to show the flavor of XML messages and schemas.

Consider the following message (using actual XML syntax) used to communicate a customer record:

```
<?xml version="1.0" ?>
<n:customer xmlns:n="http://schemas.example.com/customer">
  <n:customerID id="123-321" />
  <n:name>
    <n:familyName s="Duck" />
    <n:givenName s="Donald" />
    <n:title s="Mr." />
  </n:name>
  <n:remarks>
    Mr. Duck is an exceptionally friendly customer.
  </n:remarks>
</n:customer>
```

Perhaps most striking, the message is in clear text. There are efforts to standardize binary compressed versions, but basically XML is a text-based approach. Nothing in the above message's syntactic form even reveals that this is a message. Indeed, XML is a generic approach to describing data, not just data used to form messages, and XML calls all such data capture documents.

The example also uses the XML Namespaces standard to refer to tag names (such as "n:name") in an unambiguous fashion. Details can again be found in section 12.4.

The example shows how XML is used to capture the structure of data. A schema definition can be used to describe the required and optional elements and attributes of an XML document. Here is a possible schema underlying the above example, using XML Schema (W3C, 2001b/c):

```
<?xml  version="1.0" ?>
<xsd:schema   xmlns:xsd="http://www.w3.org/2001/XMLSchema">

<xmlns:n="http://schemas.example.com/customer">

<xsd:annotation>
    <xsd:documentation  xml:lang="en">
      Customer schema for VapourWare.com.
      Copyright 2002 VapourWare.com.
    </xsd:documentation>
  </xsd:annotation>
  <xsd:element  name="n:customer"  type="n:customerType"/>
  <xsd:complexType  name="n:customerType">
```

```
<xsd:sequence>
  <xsd:element  name="n:customerID"  type="n:customerIDType"/>
  <xsd:element  name="name"  type="n:nameType"/>
  <xsd:element  name="remarks"  minOccurs="0"/>
</xsd:sequence>
</xsd:complexType>
<xsd:complexType  name="n:customerIDType">
  <xsd:attribute  name="n:id" type="xsd:decimal"/>
</xsd:complexType>
<xsd:complexType  name="n:nameType">
  <xsd:sequence>
    <xsd:element  name="n:familyName"  type="xsd:string"/>
    <xsd:element  name="n:givenName"  type="xsd:string"/>
    <xsd:element  name="n:title"  type="xsd:string"  minOccurs="0"/>
  </xsd:sequence>
</xsd:complexType>
</xsd:schema>
```

10.5.2 Events versus calls

Firing an event is similar to calling a procedure or method. However, the target of the event is totally unknown to the source of the event and there can be multiple targets for a single event fired. Event firing is not normally expected to return any results. Firing events is done as a service to other objects, not to fulfill local needs. Event models can be seen as a generalization of notification mechanisms, such as the one introduced in the Observer design pattern (p. 157).

At times, however, it is useful for an event mechanism to be able to return a result. For example, an event can be fired to check whether or not any of the unknown listeners satisfies a certain criterion. Pure event services, such as the CORBA Event Service or JavaBeans, do not allow for the return of values. The motivation is simple – as events may be sent to multiple listeners, it is not clear what to do if multiple listeners want to return a result. There is an obvious solution, however. An event object can carry a reference to a collector object, which is often identical with the object that fired the event. Event sinks can then send results back to the collector object.

Other mechanisms, such as COM's Connectable Objects, directly support the returning of results in the event object. With interposed channels or other intermediate objects, special care is required. A typical approach is to set a flag in the event object, indicating that a result is returned. If the flag was set on arrival of an event, an event handler can no longer return a result. In this way, the first event handler with a result can report it. Other strategies that resolve conflicts among multiple replies are also possible, such as returning the largest or smallest value, or simply allowing the last handler to win.

10.5.3 Call syntax and protocol – SOAP

The simple object access protocol (SOAP) – submitted for standardization to
W3C (W3C, 2000a) – supports the invocation of services by using two other
standards: XML to describe the invocation and its arguments and HTTP
(hypertext transfer protocol; IETF, 1999) to issue invocations and pass the
describing XML.

A SOAP invocation corresponds to the passing of a message. The message is
an XML document made up of the following three XML elements:

- a mandatory SOAP envelope defining the message – it contains some
  information, such as the encoding used, and may contain a SOAP
  header and must contain a SOAP body;
- a SOAP header – it may contain extra definitions to be used to process
  the body and can also contain mandatory requirements and processing
  instructions for intermediaries;
- a mandatory SOAP body with call or response information – it either
  contains the information needed by the recipient to process the request,
  or – on the way back – the generated reply or an error indication (a
  SOAP fault).

For example, the following SOAP request (embedded in an HTTP "Request")
queries the name of a customer by ID:

```
<SOAP-ENV:Envelope>
  <SOAP-ENV:Body>
    <xmlns:n="http://schemas.example.com/customer" />
    <n:getName>
      <n:customerID id="123-321" />
    </n:getName>
  </SOAP-ENV:Body>
</SOAP-ENV:Envelope>
```

A corresponding SOAP response (embedded in an HTTP "Response") would
take the following form:

```
<SOAP-ENV:Envelope>
  <SOAP-ENV:Body>
    <xmlns:m="http://schemas.example.com/customer" />
    <n:getNameResponse>
      <n:familyName s="Duck" />
      <n:givenName s="Donald" />
      <n:title s="Mr" />
    </n:getNameResponse>
  </SOAP-ENV:Body>
</SOAP-ENV:Envelope>
```

In line with the observations about robust messages in section 10.5.1, SOAP does not even have a notion of object references. Multiple objects can be sent by value in a single SOAP message, including references between objects in the same message. For any form of external reference encodings such as URLs must be used. See section 12.4.4 for further details on SOAP.

10.6   Ordering of events – causality, races, and glitches

Event-based communication is asynchronous. The relative order in which events arrive at their sinks is not well defined in most cases. Consider the scenario in Figure 10.5. Source A fires event e1 while sinks B and C are listening. Sink B receives event e1 and immediately fires event e2, for which C and D are listening.

The ordering of events, as observed by C, is not defined. For example, in a single-threaded system it is likely that e2 arrives at C before e1. The event passing is handled by an invocation on B that, before it returns, causes an invocation on C to deliver e2. It is common that an event service specifies the relative event ordering only weakly. It is usually guaranteed that a sink receives events from the same source in the order in which they were sent. Figure 10.6 illustrates two possible arrival orders – of the events e1 and e2 – at sink C.

The top ordering in Figure 10.6 is the natural order (breadth first), that is, the order that is closest to the intuition behind event distribution. The bottom ordering is the recursive call order (depth first) – that is, the natural ordering in systems that do not use intermediate buffers and separate threads to distribute events.

There is one substantial difference between these two orderings. The natural order preserves causality, whereas the recursive call order does not. The firing of event e2 by B is caused by C's receipt of e1. In a causality-based logic, the receipt of e1 happened before the sending of e2. C should therefore first receive e1 and then e2. Preserving causality in group-communication mechanisms has been studied thoroughly in the context of distributed systems (for example Birman, 1985), and yet it is not normally considered a feature in event services. Unfortunately, the natural emergence of the recursive call order makes it much cheaper to implement than any other ordering.

Consider the following example. A model notifies its two views. As a result of the notification, the first view fires an event that, among other targets,

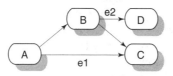

Figure 10.5 Event propagation.

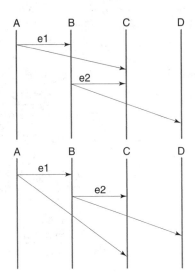

Figure 10.6 Event ordering – natural order (top) versus recursive call order (bottom).

reaches the second view. If the second view receives this event before it received the original model notification, it may not be in a consistent state and ready to handle the event. The situation becomes very severe in systems that support recursive embedding of document parts. For a particular solution provided by the BlackBox component framework see Chapter 21.

The asynchronous nature of event models can be compared with the asynchronous propagation of signals in electronic circuits. It can happen that an event reaches its target "just before" the target moves to a consistent state. After receiving the event, the target may make this inconsistency observable to other objects for a short time, before reaching a consistent state again. In an electronic system, this transitory condition is referred to as a glitch and resulting errors can be difficult to track down. As with electronic systems, introduction of a delay mechanism can solve the problem. In a software system, such a delay is introduced by buffering the event and propagating it only after doing whatever is required to bring the event target up to date.

Another effect with an analogy in electronic systems is a race condition. If the relative ordering of event arrivals depends on dynamic conditions, then the events may arrive in the right order in some cases and in a wrong order in others. In a sense, the events compete in a "race" to reach their targets first. In electronic systems, race conditions are affected by the inherent non-determinism of the exact timing of signals. This is not an issue in software systems. The analogy holds nevertheless as the very large number of possible state sequences in a complex component software system replaces non-determinism in time.

Preserving sufficiently strong order – such as causal order – and avoiding glitches and races is a tricky but important aspect of a component system's architecture. In some cases, component frameworks can be used to enforce well-formed interactions that avoid these problems (Chapter 21). In other cases, special programming methodologies can be used to avoid such problems from the outset (Chapter 22).

10.7 Very late binding – dispatch interfaces and metaprogramming

Connection orientation, notifications, and events are all cases of late binding. The binding between caller and callee is not established before runtime, although the type of interface is known at compile-time. Occasionally, it may even be necessary to find out at runtime the types of interfaces that a connected object supports. It may therefore even be necessary to delay type checking until runtime.

A typical example is a system in which a top-level interpreter can dynamically invoke precompiled operations. If these precompiled components are acquired dynamically, then runtime exploration of their interfaces may be necessary. A good example is a web browser that supports scripting of documents that contain arbitrary controls or applets. The script author and the control "know" what is involved, but the intermediate web browser, serving as a container for the embedded controls, does not.

Provided that a component comes with enough information to be self-describing, the interfaces supported by the component can be dynamically explored. The means to do so differ from approach to approach, but the fundamental problem is always the same – preserve information available at compile-time for inspection at runtime. Making such information about a system available within that system is called reification. A system that uses this information about itself in its normal course of execution is said to be reflective. Programming a system to not only use reified information but also to manipulate this information is called metaprogramming. (For a good treatment of the issues involved, see the literature on metaprogramming. For example, Kiczales *et al.*, 1991.)

Few mainstream services support full metaprogramming. One of the early examples was IBM's late system object model (SOM), which fully supported metaprogramming. For example, a program based on SOM can define new interfaces, synthesize matching new classes at runtime, and then create instances of the new classes. SOM goes as far as allowing for the interception of the actual execution model. This was used by distributed SOM (DSOM), which was really just a library sitting on top of SOM and using SOM's metaservices to intercept operations and transparently support distribution.

Flavors of metaprogramming are, to a lesser degree, supported by all approaches. Since version 1.1, Java provides the Java Core Reflection Service. The name has been well chosen as the service does not allow interception or manipulation at the metalevel (although the newer Proxy class permits interception in certain ways). However, it extends the rudimentary runtime type information available in the Java language (instanceof operator, p. 277). The Java language facilities merely allow an object to be probed for implementation of statically known interfaces. The reflection services allow enumeration and inspection of all facets of an object, a class, or an interface. For example, it is possible to write code that, for a particular method, inspects the signature, assembles the required parameters, and invokes the method. Obviously, this takes the compiler's type checking out of the loop and the reflection service has to perform checks at runtime.

The approach taken for COM is quite similar. A COM component can be equipped with a type library. Although the COM standard does not support full metaprogramming, the COM library does support dynamic inspection of all interfaces revealed in type libraries. Interfaces of a certain canonical form, called dispatch interfaces, can be invoked dynamically. This is more restrictive than the Java, CLR, or CORBA approaches, which all allow for dynamic invocation of any method in any interface or class. A dispatch interface essentially has just one interesting operation – Invoke. Operation Invoke takes an operation selector, called "dispatch ID," and a generic variant structure with the selected operation's arguments. However, this variant restricts the types of possible arguments to dispatch operations.

Using dispatch interfaces is substantially more expensive than calling operations directly. Component providers are thus encouraged to make dispatch interface operations also available in standard method form. An interface that offers both forms is called a dual interface (p. 347). Dual interfaces can be synthesized automatically, given a normal interface that respects the restrictions on signatures imposed by dispatching. This takes a substantial burden and source of error off the programmer. Microsoft's J++ compiler synthesized dispatch interfaces and so does CLR's COM-interoperation layer.

Dispatch interfaces make it easy to construct generic relay or adapter services, as discussed in the section on message groups above, without the need to synthesize special proxies or other non-generic code. All dispatch interfaces use the same single binary calling convention. Invocations can therefore be stored, forwarded, logged, filtered, or duplicated at will and generically for all possible dispatch interfaces. Similar generic implementations based on reflection services are possible but far less efficient. A dispatch interface thus sits in the middle between regular interfaces and fully dynamic reflection-based operation.

Some vendors of high-level components have taken the strategic decision to support only dispatch interfaces. Considering automatic generation of dispatch interfaces from given regular interfaces, this decision does not seem wise. It amounts to always using reflection services in Java, even when the interface is statically known. For operations that individually are quite expensive, this can be justified and is the justification for inefficient scripting engines. Otherwise, it simply cripples efficient direct programmability of components and should be avoided. Dual interfaces, where possible, are the best compromise – and are often recommended for COM.

In CORBA, interface repositories serve the purpose of reflection. The interface repository reifies all OMG IDL information. This information can be used to check whether or not a certain object implements a specific interface. Dynamic invocation interfaces and dynamic stub interfaces allow calls to be dynamically dispatched either at the client's or at the object server's end. With the introduction of meta-object facility (MOF, version 1.3; OMG, 2000), the CORBA standard supports the systematic storage and manipulation of metamodels.

Finally, the CLR frameworks include full support for reflection, some support for interception, and also quite extensive support for dynamic code synthesis – classes can be synthesized on demand and compiled down either into the running system or into loadable units (assemblies). In combination with dynamic loading, unloading, and call interception infrastructure, these facilities can be used to implement most techniques usually associated with full metaprogramming, but not quite all. In particular, the behavior of an already loaded and instantiated class cannot be changed to affect all existing instances.

Beyond the sometimes vexing details of the various approaches, and beyond being less efficient, reflection-based approaches and dispatch interfaces share another disadvantage over regular interfaces. They are also statically less type safe than regular interfaces. Runtime type safety can be and still is enforced, but at the cost of additional runtime overhead and the possibility of exceptions. To put it differently, the nature of fully dynamic resolution of method calls is largely that of Smalltalk message sends. Nothing is known before runtime, errors are detected late, and a noticeable cost is incurred. This cost is unavoidable for truly dynamic situations requiring very late binding. However, reflection and dispatch interfaces should be avoided where regular interfaces would do.

It is useful to view the different calling and binding styles as a spectrum. The calls on one end of the spectrum are bound and checked statically at compile-time – procedure calls and static method calls. The calls at the other end of the spectrum are bound and checked dynamically at runtime – these are reflective calls. In between these two extremes lies the important case where checking is done statically but binding is dynamic – procedure variables and method dispatch. The spectrum is illustrated in Figure 10.7.

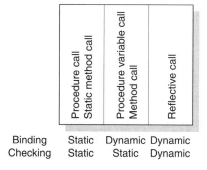

	Procedure call / Static method call	Procedure variable call / Method call	Reflective call
Binding	Static	Dynamic	Dynamic
Checking	Static	Static	Dynamic

Figure 10.7 Spectrum of checking and binding times.

10.8 Degrees of freedom – sandboxing versus static safety

The importance of safety in a software component world has been stated repeatedly already. The issue is of such vital importance that the selection of programming languages that guarantee safety does play a key role in component-oriented programming. Safety guaranteed by a language does not necessarily interfere with efficiency. Effects on efficiency are negligible or even positive when a combination of compile-time and load-time checks is used to establish safety in a largely static way. This is the strategy taken by Java, Component Pascal, and all CLR-targeting languages that have an explicit safe subset, such as C# or Visual Basic.NET. Provided that the language implementation can be trusted, the final component can execute efficient compiled native in-process code.

If the implementation language does not provide strong guarantees or its implementation cannot be trusted, lower-level runtime protection is required. Traditionally, operating systems achieved this objective by means of process isolation. By using hardware protection facilities to separate processes fully, mutual interference, even in the case of erroneous or malicious processes, can be controlled. For component software, such strict isolation is often too expensive. Components need to interact frequently and efficiently.

An approach pioneered by Wahbe *et al.* (1993) is called software-based fault isolation or sandboxing. The idea is to augment component code at load-time to prevent it from accessing addresses for which it has no authorization. Somewhat surprisingly, it turns out that the overhead incurred is lower than for hardware protection schemes, while at the same time supporting protection at a much finer level of granularity.

The ideas of load- or install-time checking can be generalized beyond the verification abilities of current JVM or CLR implementations. To enable verification, components contain information besides the loadable code, typically in the form of metadata such as types. Verification is essentially a redundancy check – that is, under some conservative check, is the provided code guaranteed to be consistent with the provided additional information. Hence, verification can be viewed as proof checking in that the additional information is proof of properties of the provided code. This is the idea of proof-carrying code (PCC; Necula and Lee, 1996; Necula, 1997). A proof checker is fundamentally much simpler than a theorem prover that has to come up with a new proof. Checking merely entails establishing that the proof is step-by-step within a given framework of proof rules. It is therefore possible to run such a checker at load- or install-time of an untrusted component.

10.9 Recording versus scripting

Event models and dispatch interfaces support the logging of activities. Replay while all involved objects are still "alive" is also straightforward, although the replayed sequence may not make sense, depending on the state of the objects involved. A useful application of operation recording and replay is user-controlled multilevel undo and redo of commands. Other examples are systems that use checkpointing and replay to provide fault tolerance. Yet another is the automatic support of queued asynchronous communication, such as provided by Microsoft's COM+ Queued Components and Sun's Enterprise JavaBeans 2.0, where calls and returns are automatically converted to and from messages queued in a messaging system.

Unfortunately, recording of events is not enough in the case of automatic creation of scripts. Many scriptable systems provide utilities that record user activities and turn them into scripts for later replay. The key requirement over the low-level recording discussed so far is that a recorded script should be applicable in similar rather than identical situations. It is thus too precise to record the object identities of objects involved in the recorded command. Instead, it is essential to use a symbolic object reference that is understood in the object's context. On replay, a script is then interpreted within the current context and symbolic references are resolved within this context.

One of the few, fully generic scripting architectures that supports this level of genericity is the open scripting architecture (OSA), derived from the older AppleScript. To a lesser degree of generality, COM also supports a scripting service, ActiveX Scripting, that solely relies on COM dispatch interfaces and uses COM monikers to record logical object references. (See Part Three for more information on these approaches.)

CHAPTER ELEVEN

What others say

The literature offers a number of definitions of what software components are or should be. Definitions range from the term component to the semantics of components and component systems. Most of these definitions are close to the ones used in this book, but not all are, and the various differences are certainly worth a closer look. For comparison, the definition from Chapter 4 is repeated here:

> "A software component is a unit of composition with contractually specified interfaces and explicit context dependencies only. A software component can be deployed independently and is subject to composition by third parties."

Note that a corollary of this definition, as explained in Chapter 4, is that software components are executable units of deployment that are composed without modification. (Compatible definitions at a more technical level are explored in section 20.3.)

This chapter displays various authors' views on the (software) component term in a chronological order. On this timeline, the first edition of this book appeared between sections 11.9 and 11.10.

11.1 Grady Booch (1987)

In his book *Software Components with Ada: Structures, Tools, and Subsystems*, Booch (1987) states:

> "A reusable software component is a logically cohesive, loosely coupled module that denotes a single abstraction."

This definition fully ignores environmental dependencies, except for stating that there should be few ("loosely coupled"). Independent deployability is not required. Also, Booch concentrates on source-level components (although that isn't apparent from the brief quote above).

11.2 Oscar Nierstrasz and Dennis Tsichritzis (1992 and 1995)

In their 1992 *Communications of the ACM* article, Nierstrasz *et al.* discussed component software in a form already quite close to the viewpoint taken in this book. They discussed the issues of component composition and scripting. They introduced the notion of script components that allows scripts to be encapsulated.

The book *Object-Oriented Software Composition* (Nierstrasz and Tsichritzis, 1995) contains an article by Nierstrasz and Dami with the following compact definition:

> "A software component is a static abstraction with plugs."

"Plugs" refers to the in and outgoing interfaces. The static aspect is according to the definition in this book; it allows components to be stored in repositories. Independent deployability is not covered. However, as composition and composability are central to their discussion, third-party composition is among the requirements.

The emphasis is on composition at system build-time. This leaves aside issues of late composition at runtime. Market issues are not touched on.

11..3 Gio Wiederhold, Peter Wegner, and Stefano Ceri (1992)

In their seminal 1992 article "Megaprogramming," Wiederhold *et al.* state:

> "Megaprogramming is a technology for programming with large modules called megamodules that capture the functionality of services provided by large organizations like banks, airline reservation systems, and city transportation systems."

Megamodules correspond to subsystems – that is, "large" components. They further state:

> "Megamodules are internally homogeneous, independently maintained software systems [...]. Each megamodule describes its externally accessible data structures and operations and has an internally consistent behavior."

They indirectly capture the contractual nature of such "megamodule" interfaces by emphasizing:

> "Megamodules are [...] managed by a community with its own terminology, goals, knowledge, and programming traditions. [...] The concepts, terminology, and interpretation paradigm of a megamodule is called its ontology."

They then discuss aspects of megamodule composition, megaprogramming system architecture, and even megaprogramming languages and compilation. Despite their unusual terminology, at least in the context of this book, they described a large number of important issues of component software and component-oriented programming. Given the underdeveloped state of middleware in 1992, this article showed quite some foresight.

11.4   Ivar Jacobson (1993)

In his book *Object-Oriented Software Engineering*, Jacobson (1993) states:

> "By components we mean already implemented units that we use to enhance the programming language constructs. These are used during programming and correspond to the components in the building industry."

Jacobson's definition deviates from the one in this book. His component concept is wider and includes "components" such as macros or templates. This makes sense if components are seen as only appearing during "programming," whereas the software components as understood in this book retain their isolatable character at product deployment time.

11.5   Meta Group (1994)

In a 1994 white paper, the Meta Group states (in the context of OpenDoc):

> "Software components are defined as prefabricated, pretested, self-contained, reusable software modules – bundles of data and procedures – that perform specific functions."

The basic notion is in line with this book, but the refinement "bundles of data and procedures" is not. Simple procedural modules are possible components, but a component can encompass more powerful abstractions than just "data and procedures." In particular, a component can provide object-oriented abstractions and can be backed by its own set of resources. Also, the inclusion of data suggests statefulness at the component level – a possibility that is excluded in the component definition in this book. Finally, the Meta definition does not mention required services and other dependencies. A set of procedures, for instance, forms only a component if it does not call any other procedures outside the set unless these dependencies are fully documented. (Traditional procedures tend to treat dependencies on other procedures as "implementation details.")

11.6   Jed Harris (1995)

In their book on distributed objects, Orfali *et al.* cite Jed Harris (then the president of the former Component Integration Labs, which looked after OpenDoc and maintained registries for extensions). Jed Harris is quoted as defining a component as follows:

"A component is a piece of software small enough to create and maintain, big enough to deploy and support, and with standard interfaces for interoperability."

Once again, there is no mentioning of required services and other dependencies.

11.7 Ovum Report on Distributed Objects (1995)

In its 1995 report, Ovum defines "componentware" as:

"Software designed to enable application elements to work together that were constructed independently by different developers using different languages, tools and computing environments."

Individual components are viewed as:

"Small blocks of code that can collaborate at runtime."

Furthermore, it emphasizes the importance of object-oriented middleware, such as CORBA ORBs or Microsoft's DCOM:

"It is only with the availability of ORBs that componentware becomes technically feasible. This is because ORBs provide a way of bridging some of the differences inherent in assembling applications from components written in different languages on and for different operating systems."

11.8 Robert Orfali, Dan Harkey, and Jeri Edwards (1995, 1996)

In a February 1995 *Datamation* article, Orfali and Harkey state:

"A component is a factory-debugged software subsystem."

In their book *The Essential Distributed Objects Survival Guide*, Orfali *et al.* (1996) broaden the definition of components by listing a number of minimal requirements (pp. 34–35). They also present a number of desirable requirements (pp. 36–37). The following is a brief summary of their minimal and desirable requirements. Note the lack of separation between objects and classes and thus the positioning of components as "better" objects.

"A 'minimalist component:'

- is a marketable entity: self-contained, shrink-wrapped, binary;
- is not a complete application;
- is usable in unpredicted combinations: 'plug-and-play' within 'suites of components;'
- has a well-specified interface: can be implemented using objects, procedural code, or by encapsulating existing code;

- is an interoperable object: can be invoked across processes, machines, networks, languages, operating systems, and tools;
- is an extended object: supports encapsulation, inheritance, and polymorphism."

They move on to define:

"A 'supercomponent' adds support for: security, licensing, versioning, lifecycle management, support for visual assembly, event notification, configuration and property management, scripting, metadata and introspection, transaction control and locking, persistence, relationships, ease of use, self-testing, semantic messaging, and self-installation."

11.9 Johannes Sametinger (1997)

In his book *Software Engineering with Reusable Components*, Sametinger (1997) has a surprising definition of component, and one that is somewhat at odds with this book:

"Reusable software components are self-contained, clearly identifiable pieces that describe and/or perform specific functions, have clear interfaces, appropriate documentation, and a defined reuse status."

This is followed by a statement:

"We clearly take the (conservative) approach of defining existing abstractions as components."

Code fragments, such as individual functions or macros, are explicitly included as candidates for components. Also included are pieces that merely "describe" rather than "perform" (implement) functionality. Sametinger explains:

"We use the term piece in our definition to indicate that components can have a variety of different forms, for example source code, documentation, executable code."

His notion of software components is thus a vast superset of the one considered in this book. He claims that his superset conforms to the definitions given in the NATO standard for the development of reusable software components (Brown, 1994).

The essential aspect of independent deployability is indirectly covered by the requirement for self-containedness and identifiability. Clear provided interfaces are mentioned. Required interfaces are handled implicitly as a part of self-containedness. In particular, Sametinger distinguishes between execution and composition platforms. An execution platform is the environment required for a component to execute – obviously not an issue for documentation components. A composition platform is the environment within which a component can interoperate with other components. For example, the Java VM is an execution platform, whereas a specific framework is a composition platform.

11.10   UML 1.3 Standard (1999)

The UML 1.3 specification (OMG 1999) defines components as follows:

> "Component: A physical, replaceable part of a system that packages implementation and provides the realization of a set of interfaces. A component represents a physical piece of implementation of a system, including software code (source, binary or executable) or equivalents such as scripts or command files."

This definition is close to the spirit of the one in this book by emphasizing the "physical" nature of software components. However, discrepancies are the inclusion of non-executable code (by listing "executable" as an alternative to "source" and "binary"), the non-mentioning of resources, and the emphasis on realized interfaces (but skipping dependencies and requires interfaces).

11.11   Desmond D'Souza and Alan Wills (1999)

Desmond D'Souza and Alan Wills define in their book *Objects, Components, and Frameworks with UML: The Catalysis Approach* (1999):

> "Component (general) – A coherent package of software artifacts that can be independently developed and delivered as a unit and that can be composed, unchanged, with other components to build something larger.
>
> Component (in code) – A coherent package of software implementation that (a) can be independently developed and delivered, (b) has explicit and well-specified interfaces for the services it provides, (c) has explicit and well-specified interfaces for the services it requires from others, and (d) can be composed with other components, perhaps customizing some of their properties, without modifying the components themselves."

The former notion is far more general than the one of software components in this book. The latter notion, however, is quite close. It would seem fair to therefore equate their "component (in code)" with software component as defined here. (More information on and around Catalysis can be found at www.catalysis.org.)

11.12   Krzysztof Czarnecki and Ulrich Eisenecker (2000)

In their book *Generative Programming*, Krzysztof Czarnecki and Ulrich Eisenecker (2000) state:

> "We define software components simply as building blocks from which different software systems can be composed. [...] We want them to be plug-compatible by design and to be combinable in as many ways as possible. We want to minimize code duplication and maximize reuse."

This definition is wider than the one in this book in that it does not emphasize the potential for independent production of components. It is also narrower in that emphasizing code minimization and reuse maximization ignores the larger tradeoffs discussed in this book.

From this initial definition they continue:

> "These and other properties determine the quality of components, but, in general, are not necessary or sufficient for a component to be a component. A component is always a part of a well-defined production process. For example, a brick is a component in the process of building houses, not cars. The often-cited criteria, such as binary format, interoperability, language independence, and so on are always relative to the production process. For example, if you need containers in C^{++}, STL components, which are source level, are just fine to use."

Including source-level components is in direct contrast to this book. While a component concept can be defined anywhere where a composition operator can be found, the notion of "software component" (rather than source component, specification component, and so on) is more specific. From their broader, inclusive perspective they continue:

> "Trying to come up with a general classical definition for software components is not only futile, but harmful. We have a classical definition for objects. A classical definition means that we can provide a single set of necessary and sufficient properties to define an object: An object has an identity, state, and behavior.
>
> The concept of a 'component' has a completely different quality. It is an example of a natural concept, rather than an artificial, constructed concept. [...] Most natural concepts do not have a classical definition. As an example, try to define the concept of a 'table.'"

Their argument is grounded in the theory of formal concept analysis (Ganter and Wille, 1999) and the observation that it is impossible to enumerate a fixed agreeable set of features that is necessary and sufficient for a natural concept such as "component" or, their example, "table." This is correct – and feature-enumerating definitions such as those in Chapter 20 are unavoidably narrower than necessary (as is explained there).

Nevertheless, natural concepts can be defined – not by means of feature enumeration, but by means of stating the intention for their introduction and then exploring the technically inevitable consequences, much in the way Czarnecki and Eisenecker do in the first quote above. Listing aspects of intent needs to be done carefully – simply claiming "maximized reuse" as an intention can have undesirable consequences. Broad definitions, such as the one given in Chapter 4, are based on captured intentions.

So, what about "table?" Simple, a table is a device that is used to place things on in a non-permanent way, such that they are in easy reach for someone requiring access to these things. While such a statement clarifies the intention, it cannot yield a complete list of defining features. Technical consequences are relative to the concrete use scenarios. (For instance, Scott Crawford, when reviewing this definition of "table" suggested that the intention should be augmented with the criteria that a table, first, is in reach for someone who is seated – or else "counter" fits just as well, and, second, that access is shared by multiple people – or else "desk" would qualify.) However, they will generally include limits on the design, height, strength, and size of a table. These are technical constraints, not features – and so are the characteristic properties postulated for components in Chapter 4.

11.13   Peter Herzum and Oliver Sims (2000)

In their book *Business Component Factory*, Herzum and Sims (2000) claim:

> "In summary, we can state four essential characteristics of a
> component model: the component, the component socket, the
> ability of components to cooperate with other components, and the
> user of the component."

They explain:

> "1 A component is a self-contained software construct that has a defined use, has a runtime interface, can be autonomously deployed, and is built with foreknowledge of a specific component socket.
>
> 2 A component socket is software that provides a well-defined and well-known runtime interface to a supporting infrastructure into which the component will fit. A design-time interface alone is necessary but not sufficient because it does not exist in the runtime unless it's implemented by some piece of software, that is, by the infrastructure.
>
> 3 A component is built for composition and collaboration with other components.
>
> 4 A component socket and the corresponding components are designed for use by a person with a defined set of skills and tools."

If "socket" is read as component framework (combined with component platform), then their first three characteristics are largely in line with this book. The fourth emphasizes that, in a world of component software, people play different roles that require different skill sets (see Chapter 27 for a discussion along these lines).

They then move on to identify a subset of components that they call business components (or enterprise components, earlier in their book) and characterize these as follows:

> Business components "address the enterprise challenge. [...] They have what we call network-addressable interfaces [...] They are medium to very large granularity. [...] They isomorphically represent a business concept."

Then they define:

> "A business component is the software implementation of an autonomous business concept or business process. It consists of all the software artifacts necessary to represent, implement, and deploy a given business concept as an autonomous, reusable element of a larger distributed information system."

Business components are not identified as a specific category in this book. However, component frameworks or component-based architecture may well map concepts of a particular domain (in this case entities and relations of an enterprise model) in a one-to-one manner. If that is the case, it is plausible and useful to directly identify the involved components with the model entities they represent. Unlike Herzum and Sims, there is no claim made in this book that such isomorphic mapping of high-level modeling domains to components is the preferred approach in all cases.

11.14　CBSE Handbook (2001)

The best-practice handbook *Component-Based Software Engineering: Putting the Pieces Together* (Council and Heinemann, 2001) uses the following definitions:

> "A software component is a software element that conforms to a component model and can be independently deployed and composed without modification according to a composition standard.
>
>　A component model defines specific interaction and composition standards. A component model implementation is the dedicated set of executable software elements required to support the execution of components that conform to the model.

> A software component infrastructure is a set of interacting
> software components designed to ensure that a software system or
> subsystem constructed using those components and interfaces will
> satisfy clearly defined performance specifications."

To capture (machine) executability, the following clarification is provided:

> "A software element contains sequences of abstract program
> statements that describe computations to be performed by a
> machine. A software element is machine-executable if: (1) the
> machine directly executes the program statements or (2) a machine-
> executable interpreter directly understands the program statements
> and the machine directly executes the interpreter."

Note that the inclusion of interpreters in the definition effectively introduces a virtual machine concept. By merely dropping the last constraint ("and the machine directly executes the interpreter"), the definition would be more general and allow for hierarchies of interpreters. Leaving such details aside, the overall tenor of these definitions is in line with this book. Indeed, the definitions from this book's first edition were one of the inputs provided when the above definitions were formed. In this book, the notion of component platforms allows explicitly for infrastructure that is itself not necessarily made up of software components.

The handbook provides some discussion of the concepts of interaction standards, composition standards, component models, and component model implementations. In particular, an interaction standard specifies the type of explicit context dependencies a component may have. A composition standard specifies how a set of components can be composed. A component model defines how a component is constructed and can globally constrain how components can communicate and interact with each other. A component model implementation is the dedicated set of executable software necessary to support the execution of components within a component model. Unfortunately, the handbook does not provide as sharp a distinction of these underlying concepts as the definition above might suggest.

PART THREE

Component models and platforms

This part presents a survey and analysis of the current best practice of component technology. Three main approaches (CORBA, Java, COM+/CLR) are looked at in some detail and set into technical and strategic perspective. A common theme – XML and web services – is first covered separately and then woven into the three main technologies. As CORBA and Java have co-evolved to draw heavily on each other, these two chapters are best read in combination. To a lesser degree, some co-evolutionary coupling can also be identified between CORBA/Java on the one hand and COM+/CLR on the other, as supported by many cross-references. The technically detailed presentations help to form a solid understanding of each of the approaches – as is required for any useful comparison and evaluation.

CHAPTER TWELVE

Object and component "wiring" standards

Wiring is the fabric that connects electrical components. Plumbing is essentially the same whether it is for gas, water, or sewage systems. Standards on this level are important for components to be connectable at all. However, care must be taken not to overestimate the value of wiring standards. It would, for example, be easy to have identical plumbing standards for oxygen and flammable gases. There is a very good reason for making these two standards totally incompatible. Sometimes, compatibility would obviously be useful, but has never been achieved: the enormous worldwide spectrum of phone jacks is an example. Another example of even greater annoyance to the traveler is overly diverse cellular technology – even the once-praised unifying GSM standard has now split into three frequency bands (900/1800 and 1900MHz).

This chapter reviews the features of software component wiring and the emerging world of XML-based standards that promise to develop into a universal adapter. The following chapters then go into the details of the more prominent wiring standardization attempts.

12.1 Where it all came from

For a long time, interoperability of software was limited to binary calling conventions at the procedural level. Every operating system defines calling conventions, and all language implementations respect the calling conventions of their platforms. Surprisingly, however, none of the traditional operating systems supported procedural calls across process boundaries. Even system calls to an operating system's inner services frequently follow non-standard calling conventions. To grant regular language implementations access to such services, OS vendors usually provide standard libraries that shield system calls.

As procedural interactions were confined to process boundaries, operating systems support a wide variety of mechanisms for interprocess communication (IPC). Typical examples are files, pipes, sockets, and shared memory. Apart from BSD-Unix sockets, by now a quasi-standard supported on most platforms, none of these mechanisms is portable across platforms.

An advantage of all IPC mechanisms – with the exception of shared memory, which has scaling problems – is that they can easily be extended to work across networks right up to the internet. This is a direct consequence of the traditional process model, in which each process creates the illusion of a separate virtual machine on a shared physical host.

All these IPC mechanisms operate on the level of bits and bytes – quite far from the well-ordered world of procedures with typed parameters. Implementing complex interactions on top of such mechanisms is painful and error-prone. This was soon recognized and remote procedure calls were proposed as early as 1984 (Birrel and Nelson, 1984).

The idea is to use stubs at the ends of the local callee and the remote caller. The caller uses strictly local calling conventions and seems to call a local callee. In reality, it calls a local stub that marshals (serializes) the parameters and sends them to the remote end. At that end, another stub receives the parameters, unmarshals (deserializes) them, and calls the true callee. The callee procedure itself, just as the caller, follows local calling conventions and is unaware of being called remotely. The marshaling and unmarshaling are responsible for converting data values from their local representation to a network format and on to the remote representation. In this way, format differences, such as byte ordering of number representations, are bridged.

The distributed computing environment (DCE), a standard of the Open Software Foundation (part of the Open Group), is the most prominent service implementing remote procedure calls (RPCs) across heterogeneous platforms. At the other extreme, lightweight RPC variations can be used for interprocess communication on a single machine. Windows (since NT), for example, supports lightweight RPCs across processes and, with DCOM, full RPCs between machines. DCE also supports version control by attaching major version numbers to every service. Clients can specify what version of a service they expect.

A simultaneous advantage and burden of RPCs is the potential for transparency. Where the RPC "glue" is automatically generated, neither clients nor providers need to be aware of non-local calling. This is an advantage as it simplifies the programming model by mapping all levels of communication (in-process, interprocess, and intermachine) on to a single abstraction – that of a procedure call. It is also a burden, as it hides the significant cost difference between a local, an interprocess, and an intermachine call. On most current architectures, interprocess calls are ten to a thousand times slower than local calls. Intermachine calls are, again, ten to ten thousand times slower than interprocess calls (the latter factor being closer to most mainstream implementations).

To automate the creation of stubs, DCE introduced an interface definition language (IDL). For each remotely callable procedure, IDL specifies the number, passing modes, and types of parameters, as well as the types of possible return values. To ensure that communication across machine boundaries works, any IDL has to fix the ranges of basic types, such as specify that integers are 32-bit 2's complement values (a 2's complement is a mathematical scheme to represent negative numbers in binary form). DCE also introduced the concept of universally unique identifiers (UUIDs) – names synthesized using an algorithm that, for all practical purposes, guarantees uniqueness (until year 3500; Rogerson, 1997). UUIDs are unreadable and meaningless to people. They are much like social security or license plate numbers.

Procedure calls, with their binary calling conventions, provide a well-proven "wiring" standard. However, they do not directly support remote method invocations as required by objects. If combined with dynamic link libraries (DLLs), remote procedure calls get close to forming a useful basis for component wiring. Services can be located by name (the name of the DLL), are bound dynamically rather than at compile time, and can be remote. Why did procedural libraries not take off as major software component forms? In fact, they did. Procedural libraries are still one of the most successful forms of software components. Such libraries can be and are sold in executable form. So, instead of asking why RPC and procedural libraries didn't take off, it is more appropriate to explore the limitations of this approach.

12.2 From procedures to objects

Object invocations differ from procedural invocations primarily in their very late, data-driven selection of code to call. A method call, unless optimized, inspects the class of the receiving object and picks the method implementation provided by that class. Also, a method always provides, as another parameter, a reference to the object to which the message was sent. Most advantages of object-oriented programming result from these two properties of method calls. (Many remote procedure call models share these two properties, though. In a sense, a remote machine is an object and its RPC entry points are its methods. To put it differently, every object can be seen as a possibly tiny virtual machine.)

It is interesting to see that current object invocations do not follow standard platform calling conventions. The reason is simple. It is that, as contemporary operating systems and their libraries have procedural interfaces, there never was a need for OS vendors to define method-calling conventions. As a result, code compiled using different compilers does not interoperate, even if implemented in the same language. To be generally useful, an object-oriented library must thus be distributed in source form. This is a simple reason for executable (rather than source) class libraries being far less popular in such instances than in the procedural case.

It is possible to implement method calls on top of the machinery that implements procedure calls. For example, IBM's System Object Model did just that (section 13.1.3). In SOM, all language bindings simply called SOM library procedures and the SOM runtime then dynamically selected the methods to be called. CORBA ORBs (Chapter 13) are another example – the last versions of SOM were actually CORBA compliant. Microsoft's COM (Chapter 15) is also quite close to just using procedural calling conventions, although it does rely on tables of procedure variables, also called dispatch tables, containing function pointers. This is not a problem as procedure variables have been part of calling conventions for a long time. For example, some DLL loaders rely on procedure variables to perform dynamic linking.

Another possibility is to define a new virtual machine level with built-in support for method calls. This is the approach followed by the Java virtual machine (JVM, Chapter 14) and the .NET common language runtime (CLR, Chapter 15). However, unlike library support and system-wide calling conventions, a virtual machine can prevent or hinder interoperation beyond its own boundaries. Thus, both JVM and CLR provide special support for interoperation across VM boundaries.

12.3 The fine print

If, at the executable level, procedural calling conventions almost suffice, why have so many different and competing proposals? There are other important aspects that need to be considered and standardized to achieve interoperability. Questions to be answered include "How are interfaces specified? How are object references handled as they leave their local process? How are services located and provided? How is component evolution handled?"

12.3.1 Specification of interfaces and object references

What exactly is an interface? All current approaches uniformly define an interface as a collection of named operations, each with a defined signature and possibly a return type. The signature of an operation defines the number, types, and passing modes of parameters.

What does an interface connect to? Here, the approaches differ. Those based on traditional object models define a one-to-one relation between interfaces and objects (CORBA 2, SOM). An object provides the state and implementation behind one interface. Other approaches associate many interfaces with a single object (Java, CLR) or many interfaces with many part objects in a component object (COM, CCM in CORBA 3). Obviously, as soon as there can be multiple objects behind an interface, the question of identity arises and needs to be addressed (COM and CCM provide a special interface for this purpose).

How are interfaces specified? Traditionally, all approaches followed the DCE lead and used an IDL. Unfortunately not *the* IDL, as there are several competing proposals. In particular, OMG IDL and COM IDL are the two strongest competitors. There is no IDL for Java or CLR – the corresponding information is kept as metadata and can be projected to any of the supported languages. Instead of learning an IDL besides their preferred language, programmers can view interface and other type definitions using the means of their language. The so-called Java IDL is actually a CORBA ORB callable from Java combined with an IDL-to-Java compiler. Java is supported by a mapping from Java types to the OMG IDL (and back). A similar bidirectional mapping has been defined between OMG IDL and COM IDL. Presently, there is no similar mapping between OMG IDL and CLR types – or the more specific types of $C^{\#}$.

What are object references? How are they handled when passed as an argument in a remote method invocation? Again, the approaches differ, but all have mechanisms to map locally meaningful references to references that retain meaning across process, machine and network boundaries.

12.3.2 Interface relationships and polymorphism

All approaches provide for polymorphism. In all cases, an entity with a known interface can be one of many different possible implementations. Also, in all cases an implementation can provide more than is specified by the interface.

When it comes to details, the approaches all differ. CORBA 2 follows a traditional object model. An object has a single interface, although this interface may be composed of other interfaces using multiple interface inheritance. The actual interface provided may be a subtype of the interface expected. The additional capabilities can be explored dynamically. CCM in CORBA 3 supports multiple interfaces and dynamic navigation among them. CCM also explicitly supports required interfaces besides the commonly supported provided interfaces. COM has immutable interfaces that, once published, cannot be extended or modified. Single interface inheritance is supported to introduce new interfaces derived from previously published ones. However, a COM object can have multiple interfaces. For a particular object, the set of provided interfaces can vary over time and can be explored dynamically. COM supports required interfaces through conventions. A Java object can also implement multiple interfaces, although this is closer to multiple interface inheritance than to COM's totally separate interfaces; the set of interfaces implemented by an object is statically determined by the object's class. The same is true for CLR objects. The multiple inheritance heritage of Java interfaces leads to a problem when attempting to support interfaces with clashing method names – a Java object cannot support more than one of such interfaces. Both COM and CLR keep methods on different interfaces separate at the implementation level, regardless of method names. The CLR model goes beyond COM in also supporting multiple interface inheritance, like Java or CORBA. Like COM, Java and CLR resort to supporting required interfaces by means of conventions only.

12.3.3 Naming and locating services

How are interfaces named? How are they related to each other? No two approaches agree. COM draws on DCE's UUIDs, called globally unique identifiers (GUIDs) in COM. GUIDs are used to name a variety of entities uniquely, including interfaces (IIDs), groups of interfaces called categories (CATIDs), and classes (CLSIDs). OMG CORBA originally left unique naming to individual implementations, relying on language bindings to maintain program portability. In CORBA 2.0, globally unique Repository IDs have been introduced. These can either be DCE UUIDs or strings similar to the familiar universal resource locators (URLs) used on the worldwide web. Java fully relies on unique name paths established by nested named packages. CLR provides similar qualified names to establish a readable naming scheme, but ultimately grounds all names in so-called strong names of assemblies – in essence, the public half of a private/public key pair that is, with very high probability, unique. That is, whereas repository IDs back individual names with unique IDs, CLR backs entire families of names with a single unique ID, as long as such a name family is co-published in a single assembly (a CLR software component).

Given a name, all services provide some sort of registry or repository to help locate the corresponding service. On top of this directory-like function, all approaches offer some degree of meta-information on the available services. The minimum that is supported by all is the runtime test of the types of the offered interfaces, the runtime reflection of interfaces, and the dynamic creation of new instances.

12.3.4 Compound documents

Among the first practical approaches to software components were compound document models. Compound documents are a model in which components and composition are intuitively meaningful to those composing, namely the users. The Xerox Star system was first, based on research results of the Xerox Palo Alto Research Center (PARC), but failed to capture significant market and mind share. A first breakthrough was Apple's Hypercard, with its simple and intuitive composition and usage model, but creating new components was a pain. Microsoft's Visual Basic followed, with a reasonable programming model for Visual Basic controls (VBXs). General documents followed, with Microsoft's OLE and Apple's OpenDoc. Later, web pages with embedded objects, such as Java applets and ActiveX controls, added a new dimension. Apple's CyberDog integrated the web and documents and so did Microsoft's Internet Explorer.

The concept is simple. Instead of confronting users with many different applications, each with their own "self-centered" idea of what a document is, users deal only with documents. If parts of a document need the support of different "applications," then it is the system's problem to find and start these where needed. For this document-centric paradigm to be intuitive, it is necessary that embedded document parts can be manipulated in-place, even if they are supported each by a different "application." Figure 12.1 shows a compound document – in this case, a form embedded in text. In the form, there is

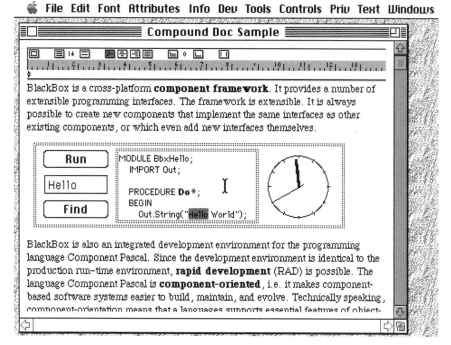

Figure 12.1 Compound document (this example was created using the OpenDoc-like look-and-feel of BlackBox for Mac OS).

other text, some controls, and a clock. The inner text has focus and is ready for in-place editing.

In Visual Basic, all documents are forms. However, a form can contain controls and the list of possible controls is open. Users become component assemblers simply by placing controls in forms and adding some Basic scripts to connect controls. The resulting flexibility and productivity created one of the first software component markets. What was called "control," with simple things such as selection boxes and entry fields in mind, turned out to be a powerful concept. The market quickly offered entire spreadsheets and process automation tools as Visual Basic "controls."

In OLE, the concept was taken a step further. First, arbitrary containers were allowed. Besides the Visual Basic forms, Word texts, Excel spreadsheets, PowerPoint slides, and so on, all became OLE containers. Also, the concept of "control" was generalized to arbitrary document servers. However, the biggest change was that components could be document containers and servers at the same time. As a result, a Word text can be used to annotate a PowerPoint slide, which again might be embedded in another Word text. (Embedding miniaturized PowerPoint slides in PowerPoint slides is actually a common and useful practise to summarize points made on previous graphical slides.)

The ultimate example of a compound document is the web with objects embedded in HTML pages. Browsers present a uniform document model for all web pages. The embedded objects, such as Java applets, can then add specifics as needed. Although a more recent development, web pages can be seen as a step back from OLE to Visual Basic. Web containers are as static as Visual Basic forms. Worse, the embedded objects cannot themselves be containers and therefore are rather like original Visual Basic controls. (The later versions of Visual Basic fully support ActiveX objects, which can be containers.) However, there are powerful server-side web programming models such as Sun's Java server pages (JSP) or Microsoft's active server pages (ASP) and now ASP.NET. It is this server-side model where modern web pages go well beyond OLE when it comes to synthesizing a compound document based on a combination of backend data and user input.

12.4 On the wire – the rise of XML

Only introduced in 1998, XML (extensible markup language; W3C, 2000b) has succeeded where numerous previous attempts have failed. Partially, that is because of some interesting properties of XML; partially it is because of proper timing. The arrival of XML coincided with a growing number of areas that genuinely needed standardization at that level, most of which can be summarized as e-business.

XML is useful for representing any structured or semistructured data. Any such data structured and formatted following XML rules is called an XML document. Unlike the schemas known from relational databases that prefer tabular data, XML prefers tree-shaped data, but accommodates all other sorts of data shapes as well. Like relational schemas, XML is not ideal to contain unstructured bulk data. It is possible to embed unstructured data, even binary data using a standard encoding, but for anything but small blocks of such data it is preferable to keep bulk data out-of-line and refer to it from within the XML-framed structured data.

Since XML is useful for representing any (semi-)structured data, new applications of XML arise by the day. Besides messages, web pages, and traditional documents, XML is now commonly used for configuration data. Even if such data is never produced or read by any other application than the one the schema was defined for, using XML can still be useful. Browsers such as Internet Explorer directly support displaying and exploring XML documents. There is also a wide range of tools that offer other forms of generic support for XML-based data, including editors, schema checkers, and schema-driven translators. ("Generic support" is just saying that the data will still be consumed by other applications.) Without exception, the greatest benefits arise when XML is used as a syntactic lingua franca (common language) among applications of independent origin and operation. In a sense, XML takes the notion of wiring standards from the level of protocols and wire formats to the level of durable data representation.

12.4.1 **XML, XML Namespaces, XML Schema**

XML is a relatively simple set of textual syntactic conventions that can be used to create structured documents. The important qualifier extensible – lending the leading "X" to all the acronyms in the XML family – states that the notation itself is formed to allow for independent extensions that do not interfere with documents created before such extensions were introduced. While rooted in the much older SGML (standard generic markup language; ISO, 1986), it is the full support for extensibility that makes XML stand out. Extensibility at the level of a notation such as XML is not entirely novel, though. The venerable S-expressions (symbolic expressions) of Lisp (formed 1956–1962; McCarthy, 1979) had most of XML's potential already – a uniform simple syntax for everything (for a modern rendition, see the language Scheme; Abelson *et al.*, 1998). Beyond details and the key provisions for extensibility, it is mostly a matter of the unprecedented, almost universal, adoption of XML that makes XML so special. Obviously, the world was ready for a single, uniform, and extensible notation to capture semistructured information.

Structure of XML

There are three important categories: XML elements, XML attributes, and unstructured text. Elements and attributes are similar to those in HTML, but are strictly nesting and regular. It is fairly straightforward to insist on regularity in HTML as well. The HTML standard that does just this is called XHTML (W3C, 2001d). Like HTML, XML requires that unstructured text is properly quoted – that is, encoded to avoid accidental inclusion of XML metacharacters. There are really only two critical metacharacters, which are the opening angle bracket "<", quoted as "<", and the ampersand "&", quoted as "&". The ampersand is only reserved because it is used to introduce a quoting sequence. The standard also requires quoting of the closing angle bracket ">" (>) in certain cases – CDATA sections – and provides quoted forms for apostrophes (') and quotes (").

An XML document has a single unique root element, which typically contains a hierarchy of nested elements. An element is introduced by the form <tag ...> and either includes a slash just before the closing angular bracket (as in <tag ... />) or it opens a scope that must end with </tag>. Two special kinds of elements are formed using the patterns <? ... ?> and <!— ... —>. The former are called processing instructions and indicate meta-information about the XML document (such as the XML version used or instructions to a particular processor) and the latter are comments.

Within an element's scope, nested elements or unstructured text can be placed. Multiple nested elements can have the same tag. XML is ordering sensitive, so the ordering of nested elements matters. Attributes are the "parameters" of elements and an element can carry any number of attributes following its opening tag: <tag attr1="val1" attr2="val2">. The attributes of an element form a set – that is, for a particular element, no two attributes can have the same name and the relative attribute ordering is irrelevant. Attribute values are always plain strings as they are themselves not structured at the level of XML, although there is a convention to interpret white-space separated substrings as a list of simple values.

XML documents – with their elements that can have nested subelements and so on – thus form trees. The nodes of such a tree are attributed. A common question is whether some information should be cast into attributes of an element or into subelements of that element. A first criterion is whether the particular information could occur more than once or not. If so, elements are the only option. A second criterion is if, at the level of XML, the information needs to be substructured. If so, elements are again the only option. A third criterion is whether or not default values should be provided in the case of optional information items. If so, attributes are the only option. A fourth criterion is the size of the information item. Even if it isn't structured, it is usually considered "bad style" to use a very long string value as an attribute value. Unstructured text within elements is the preferred option. If, however, the information item at hand occurs at most once per element, is itself unstructured, reasonably small, and likely to play the role of a key (in the database sense), then attributes are usually preferred for their more compact representation in XML and their support in navigation standards such as XPath (see section 12.4.2). Within these bounds, it is a matter of style and consistency is the most important guiding rule.

Obviously, there is a need to describe the rules that lead to well-formed XML documents for a particular purpose. The following kinds of rules need to be expressible to constrain XML documents:

- the set of elements that can appear at the top level – if there is only one element valid at the top level, the resulting documents are called rooted as they form trees with an explicit root node;
- for each element, the set of valid attributes and nested elements;
- for each optional attribute of an element, the default value if the attribute is omitted;
- the allowed ordering of peer elements, both at the top and at any nesting level;
- the required and allowed number of appearances of an element, both at the top and at any nesting level;
- for each element, whether or not it can contain unstructured text (called "CDATA").

XML document types

Following the SGML roots of XML, DTDs (document type descriptors) were originally used to capture these rules. An XML document that carries or references a DTD is valid if the document obeys the constraints expressed in the

DTD. DTDs are syntactically somewhat cryptic and fairly limited in their expressiveness, but fairly compact. Here is a simple DTD example:

```
<?xml  version="1.0" ?>

<xmlns:n="urn:schemas-sample-org:Customer">

<!ELEMENT n:Customer (n:CustomerID, n:Name, n:Remarks )>
<!ATTLIST n:CustomerID n:ID CDATA #REQUIRED >
<!ELEMENT n:Name (n:FamilyName, n:GivenName, n:Title ) #REQUIRED >
<!ELEMENT n:Remarks (#PCDATA )>
<!ELEMENT n:FamilyName (#PCDATA ) #REQUIRED >
<!ELEMENT n:GivenName (#PCDATA ) #REQUIRED >
<!ELEMENT n:Title (#PCDATA )>
```

The xmlns:n notation introduces prefix n: to be used in element and attribute tags that draw their names from the namespace indicated by the URI http://schemas.example.com/customer. When used without a suffix, xmlns defines the default namespace to draw from if a name without prefix is found.

XML Schema

The main disadvantage is that the DTD form itself is not extensible. As extensibility is the hallmark of XML itself, new approaches based on XML itself have been under development for several years. An early approach by Microsoft – called XML Data Reduced (XDR) – is used in some Microsoft products (most notably in BizTalk Server 2000). A new approach under the name XML Schema – a logical superset of XDR – reached the status of a W3C Recommendation in May 2001 and is likely to become the universally accepted standard in this space. XML Schema can replace DTD for most practical purposes (exceptions include DTD "entities"), improving on DTD in many important ways:

- XML Schema itself is extensible and schemas expressed using XML Schema are also extensible;
- XML Schema is much richer and more expressive than DTD;
- part of XML Schema is a flexible and expressive data type description system;
- XML Schema supports instance-level annotations and, in particular, the explicit attribution of elements with types;
- as a schema document is an XML document, it can be subject to a metaschema, and the XML Schema standard defines the metaschema for all schema documents (using XML Schema itself);
- XML Schema interacts well with other important XML-related standards and standard proposals, such as XML Namespaces and XPath (there are hickups, though – several of these standards were established before XML Schema was finished, leading to some discrepancies that the W3C will likely sort out eventually).

Here is the above DTD example expressed in XML Schema form:

```
<?xml  version="1.0" ?>
<xsd:schema  xmlns:xsd="http://www.w3.org/2001/XMLSchema">

  <xmlns:n="urn:schemas-sample-org:Customer">

  <xsd:element  name="n:Customer"  type="n:CustomerType"/>

  <xsd:complexType  name="n:CustomerType">
    <xsd:sequence>
      <xsd:element  name="n:CustomerID"  type="n:CustomerIDType"/>
      <xsd:element  name="Name"  type="n:NameType"/>
      <xsd:element  name="Remarks"  minOccurs="0"/>
    </xsd:sequence>
  </xsd:complexType>

  <xsd:complexType  name="n:CustomerIDType">
    <xsd:attribute  name="n:ID" type="xsd:decimal"/>
  </xsd:complexType>

  <xsd:complexType  name="n:NameType">
    <xsd:sequence>
      <xsd:element  name="n:FamilyName"  type="xsd:string"/>
      <xsd:element  name="n:GivenName"  type="xsd:string"/>
      <xsd:element  name="n:Title"  type="xsd:string"  minOccurs="0"/>
    </xsd:sequence>
  </xsd:complexType>

</xsd:schema>
```

XML Schema defines two namespaces. One is for schema-level names and the other for names to be used at the instance level – that is, at the level of XML documents that describe particular instances of a schema. By convention, the aliases xsd and xsi (XML Schema definition and XML Schema instance) are used for these two namespaces. The schema-level definitions are organized into two parts – structural schemas (W3C, 2001b) and data types (W3C, 2001c). The structural part is concerned with the constraints discussed so far – that is, which elements and attributes can or must occur and, in the case of elements, how often and in what order. Such structural constraints largely take the shape of regular expressions augmented with simple counting (minimal and maximal required occurrences). In particular, complex types can be formed using three compositors (all, choice, and sequence) to capture the nesting constraints of valid element trees. Complex types are, by default, available for derivation of restricted or extended types, but they can be marked final to prevent restriction, extension, or both. Factoring of common subdefinitions is supported by attribute groups (sets of attribute definitions) and model groups (sets of constraints over trees formed using the complex type compositors).

The data-type part of XML Schema covers simple types and is itself extensible in several ways. Simple data types include integer, decimal, date, and string, but also lists and unions of such types (but not lists of lists). Simple types are always representable as XML-level unstructured text and can thus describe attribute values as well. All simple data types are derived from their parent type (with anySimpleType as their root) by means of restriction. A restriction subsets the set of values or value representations allowed by the parent type. For example, negativeInteger derives from nonPositiveInteger by excluding the value zero. Data types, at a detail level, are characterized by sets of facets (such as the length of a string) and restrictions are applied to these facets in order to derive a new data type. In addition to atomic values, simple data types can be defined to cover white-space-separated lists of values and unions of values.

XML extensibility and namespaces

The overall extensibility of XML rests on three pillars. First, a restriction to uniform and simple syntax only, which eliminates syntactic collisions among extensions; second, a rigorous approach to naming and name resolution, which eliminates name collisions among extensions; and, third, a generic rule that states that if an element is encountered that, under the prevailing schema, isn't understood, it can be safely ignored. (A schema can demand that only defined attributes or subelements may occur to close a particular element, ruling out any extensions.) The last pillar is obviously creating the foundation for extensibility, but it is also subtle. In particular, authors of extending elements need to understand that ignoring their elements is a valid option. The combination of the second and third pillars allows multiple, independently created extensions to coexist. Central to the second pillar – the XML naming approach – is XML Namespaces (W3C, 1999a), a flexible yet fundamentally simple approach to unambiguously organizing and referencing names.

In XML, names appear in two positions, as element and attribute names. An XML namespace groups a set of names. XML documents refer to XML namespaces by "pointing" to the namespace (more below) and optionally assigning a local alias. XML documents can use names in two variations. These are names qualified with a namespace alias explicitly bound to the specified namespace, unqualified names either bound to a document-wide default namespace, or those that remain unbound if no such default has been declared. (Unbound names can be bound later when textual inclusion establishes a default namespace frame. While powerful at first sight, this technique is actually dangerous as it leads to degenerated XML fragments that are semantically meaningless macros.)

The above XML Schema example already included examples of using namespaces. Attributes and elements of the form xmlns:alias="<urn>" introduce a new local alias name for the namespace logically named by the given URN (universal resource name). A URN refers to the subset of URI required to remain globally unique and persistent even when the resource ceases to exist or becomes unavailable (IETF, 1998). GUIDs are an example and carefully formed URIs patterned after URLs (universal resource locators) are another. It is increasingly becoming common practice to use URNs that are also URLs formed around domains of special organizations (such as w3.org), as these can also point to an actual web location hosting the documents supporting a particular namespace. A convention adopted by the W3C is to incorporate time information to indicate the version of a namespace. Consider the following line from the above example:

<xsd:schema xmlns:xsd = "http://www.w3.org/2001/XMLSchema">

The xmlns (XML Namespaces) attribute binds the alias xsd to the namespace named "http://www.w3.org/2001/XMLSchema." Inclusion of /2001 indicates that this is the first version of the XML Schema specification made available in the year 2001. (Month and day information is included only where required to distinguish a version from an older one in the same year or month. For example, the previous XML Schema specification was labeled /2000/10 for October 2000.)

The scope of a namespace definition is the entire scope of the element that has the namespace attribute. Note how in the example the bound alias is used to qualify the element name itself, xsd:schema. This qualification indicates that schema is a name defined in the namespace bound to the alias xsd. If xmlns is used directly, instead of as a qualifier, it introduces a default namespace for its scope.

12.4.2 XML support standards

The XML family of standards and proposed standards is quite well developed. This section briefly introduces some of the more important standards.

Symbolic navigation through XML documents is supported by XPath (W3C, 1999d). XPath is designed to be used by both XSLT and XPointer and is also used by many newer XML standards, such as XML Schema and XQuery. XPath paths can be formed using a fairly rich set of syntactic forms. Elementary paths look like the paths known from file systems, with tags separated by slashes ("/"). As XML elements can have any number of child elements, some or all of which may share the same tag, XPath allows for contents-based selection and the formation of result sets. For example, a path step can be augmented with qualifiers to select based on attribute values. XPath even includes a small expression language with Boolean, integer, and string types, a set of operators over these, and a mechanism to define and use simple functions, complemented by a library of predefined functions. The predefined functions enable the operation on sets of nodes, the processing of strings, and the manipulation of names and namespace names. XPointer (W3C, 2001f), a proposed extension of XPath, extends the sets of identifiable locations in XML documents. XLink (W3C, 2001e), another related proposal, focuses on links among XML documents, subsuming HTML-style unidirectional hyperlinks and adding more sophisticated links.

The XML stylesheet language (XSL) augments XML documents with presentation information. The XSL transform (XSLT) standard enables the definition of declarative transformation rules that, when applied, transform an XML document into another form. Originally intended to guide the transformation of XML documents into presentation forms, such as XHTML, XSLT is actually quite general and can be used for many other transformation purposes. For example, integration servers can use XSLT to transform SOAP (simple object access protocol) requests and replies to mediate between systems conforming to different XML schemas. In variations and not necessarily using XSLT as the transformation description language, this approach is used by integration servers from many vendors.

12.4.3 XML document object and streaming models

XML documents can be seen as the external representation of a data structure. For programs to access and manipulate XML documents it is useful to define a standard way of presenting XML documents as abstract data structures or objects. This is what the XML document object model (DOM) standard does (W3C, 2000c). DOM essentially maps every element of an XML document to an object. Such an object has methods to access the element's attributes and navigate the document – that is, methods to locate the parent element and enumerate the child elements.

For smaller XML documents, it suffices to load the entire document and eagerly convert it into a tree of objects. However, this approach does not scale well. For large documents, it is useful to follow an approach of lazy evaluation – parts of the XML document that haven't been requested aren't fully processed or mapped to objects. The standard XML document format with its textual nature makes such optimizations only partially possible as elements simply cannot be located without parsing most of their context. This can be different in the case of binary encoded XML, which could provide indexing information to enable rapid navigation. However, the WAP binary XML content format (W3C, 1999c) merely aims for compactness and does not support random access. Dodds (2001) provides a good discussion of the many issues surrounding binary XML encodings.

A general assumption when using DOM is that random access is a requirement. In reality, many applications require a single linear scan of an XML document to extract required information. Likewise, some applications can generate XML documents in a single linear pass. For such applications, using DOM is not optimal. The entire web of objects representing the XML document is effectively produced in vain. The alternative in such cases is to use an XML streaming model such as SAX (simple API for XML, see www.saxproject.org). In a streaming model, sequential reading and writing of XML documents is supported; the effective traversal order is depth-first. SAX in particular works by first registering various event handlers with a SAX parser and then invoking the parser, which will call these handlers as it parses the XML document. It is always possible to build a DOM-style tree of objects as a side-effect of the execution of SAX-style handlers. It is thus appropriate to view a SAX-style interface as being at a lower level than a DOM-style one.

DOM- and SAX-style services are available for Java, COM+, and CLR. The DOM interfaces in their standardized form are defined using OMG IDL. Language mappings for Java and ECMAScript are also provided. The actual value of establishing DOM-level standards in isolation is not clear – the W3C describes its DOM standard as a "platform- and language-neutral interface." As part of the OMA, such standards would make sense, as similar standards for other platforms would. However, it is unclear what benefits could be derived from having an implementation that claims "DOM compliance" on a platform that doesn't support OMG IDL, a matching ORB, or call semantics. In fact, it is not even clear that fine-grained DOM-style interfaces are at all appropriate in the CORBA space, raising the question of whether OMG IDL is the appropriate notation to use or not. Issues include the lifetime management of DOM-generated node objects and the performance implications of finest-grain operations through an ORB.

SAX follows a different path by initially focusing on Java and later adding further languages/environments, each with their own peculiarities. SAX can therefore benefit from Java's support for garbage collection and efficient local invocations.

12.4.4 SOAP

XML documents can be used as self-describing messages. An interesting application of such individual messages is remote object invocation. A restrictive basic encoding for RPC-style requests and replies is XML-RPC (www.xmlrpc.com). Its successor SOAP (simple object access protocol) is a proposal for an XML-based standard (W3C, 2000a) that enables invocations on remote objects, typically using HTTP (hypertext transfer protocol; IETF, 1999). The SOAP standard provides standard ways to:

■ describe the addressee of an invocation;
■ encode a wide range of typical programming data types into invocation messages;
■ define what parts of a message must be understood or can be ignored.

An example of a request/response sequence using SOAP messages can be found in section 10.5.3. The SOAP standard defines namespaces for SOAP envelopes (schemas.xmlsoap.org/soap/envelope/) and for SOAP encoding and data types is (schemas.xmlsoap.org/soap/encoding/). SOAP messages must use these envelope and encoding namespaces. The SOAP body contains encoded typed values. Types can be simple, such as integers, strings, enumerations or complex, including compound types such as structs (type contructors for record-shaped instances; called records in Pascal) or arrays. References between values that form part of a single SOAP message can be encoded. The simple types are the ones described in XML Schema (Part 2: Datatypes; W3C, 2001c). SOAP itself is independent of HTTP, but standard bindings for the use of SOAP within HTTP are defined with two variants – one with and one without HTTP extensions (IETF, 2000).

SOAP contains one interesting twist. Although objects and references between objects are supported, this only extends to objects that are marshaled (communicated) "by value" in an open way (only public fields) and is restricted to object references closed under the objects sent with one SOAP message. In other words, a SOAP message can contain a graph-shaped data structure, but no references to message-external objects. If a sender wishes to pass a logical object reference to some receiver, then SOAP requires the use of an XLink-compliant naming scheme (W3C, 2001e) as an indirection. Typically, the names used are URLs (universal resource locators) that can be used by the receiver to locate some suitable "object" at the sender's end.

However, there is no built-in guarantee that the URL will indeed refer back to an object actually live at the sending process, the sending machine, or even the sending site. There is also no guarantee that two successive resolution requests for the same URL will yield the same object. In fact, most likely they will not. URLs thus do not represent object identity. This is a feature. Communicating "naked" object references (absolute object identities), as is commonly done in traditional remote method call protocols, such as Java RMI, DCOM, or IIOP, creates a fragile dependency of the communicated message on the sending party's computational state (section 10.5.1). Such a dependency can be appropriate and even preferable for synchronous communication within tightly coupled computer clusters. It is practically never useful for communications in web-like, loosely coupled, cross-organizational, asynchronous, load-balanced, multifailure-mode systems. Hence, instead of saying "uses this specific object," SOAP messages say "here is where an appropriate object can be found."

As of late 2001, SOAP-based invocations incur around ten times the latency of traditional RPC technologies. They also require higher communication bandwidth to not incur communication latencies due to the less compact XML encoding. On wide-area or internet connections, these differences tend to be masked by the substantial latency introduced by such networks.

12.4.5 XML web services: WSDL, UDDI, WSFL, XLANG

With SOAP in place, web services can be established, which are services offered by web servers. (Strictly speaking, such services are XML web services as there could be non-XML web services, but, for the purposes of this book, "web service" shall mean "XML web service.") Unlike traditional web servers that serve web pages for consumption by people, web services offer computational services to other systems. For example, an online bookstore could offer its database as a web service in such a way that other services (or websites targeting people) can build on it. Services can be seen as a pair of deployed components and a service provider (with its infrastructure). A service provider makes services available based on service-level agreements that offer guarantees at the provider's end for a price paid at the client's end. Services enable very flexible pricing models from pay per use, to flat subscription, to pay once (for details, see section 28.2).

Web services are similar to deployed components from a client point of view as they offer features via standard interfaces. However, services do not reveal their implementation's platform and infrastructure requirements. They also, today, do not reveal explicit dependencies on other services. In other words, web services are far more self-contained than typical components or even applications and thus reside at the very heavy end of Figure 4.1 (the left side in this figure). By being almost completely self-contained, services cannot be reused in different contexts, but are merely good to be used as is. To enable reuse, services would have to have explicit context dependencies and offer reconfiguration by binding their required interfaces against selected provided interfaces of other services. This step goes beyond current thinking about web services and requires care. Much of the flexibility of component models cannot be transferred easily to a loosely coupled world such as the web.

Web services are open for business on the web, but what is the business model of web services? While a very important question, and well within the scope of this book, the answer is not to be found at the level of standards such as SOAP. SOAP assumes that the validity of a particular exchange has been established beforehand or that it is checked as a part of the exchange. In other words, authentication of communicating parties, encryption of exchanged information, and compensation agreements, such as subscription or billing, are not addressed at the level of SOAP. Instead, these issues are left to be addressed by other standards, existing or to be created.

Web services description

Web services need to be described, much like interfaces required description using an IDL or suitable metadata. A proposed standard for this purpose, WSDL (web services description language; W3C, 2001a), builds on XML and defines an extensible framework to describe web services. Here is an example of a simple WSDL document (taken from the proposed WDSL standard document) that describes a service that accepts HTTP requests for stock quotes and uses HTTP responses to return the requested quotes:

```
<?xml version="1.0"?>
<definitions name="StockQuote"
     targetNamespace="http://example.com/stockquote.wsdl"
     xmlns:tns="http://example.com/stockquote.wsdl"
```

```
    xmlns:xsd1="http://example.com/stockquote.xsd"
    xmlns:soap="http://schemas.xmlsoap.org/wsdl/soap/"
    xmlns="http://schemas.xmlsoap.org/wsdl/"
>

  <types>
    <schema
        targetNamespace="http://example.com/stockquote.xsd"
        xmlns="http://www.w3.org/2001/XMLSchema"
    >

      <element name="TradePriceRequest">
        <complexType>
          <all> <element name="tickerSymbol" type="string"/> </all>
        </complexType>
      </element>

      <element name="TradePrice">
        <complexType>
          <all> <element name="price" type="float"/> </all>
        </complexType>
      </element>

    </schema>
  </types>

  <message name="GetLastTradePriceInput">
    <part name="body" element="xsd1:TradePriceRequest"/>
  </message>

  <message name="GetLastTradePriceOutput">
    <part name="body" element="xsd1:TradePrice"/>
  </message>

  <portType name="StockQuotePortType">
    <operation name="GetLastTradePrice">
      <input message="tns:GetLastTradePriceInput"/>
      <output message="tns:GetLastTradePriceOutput"/>
    </operation>
  </portType>

  <binding name="StockQuoteSoapBinding"
      type="tns:StockQuotePortType"
  >
    <soap:binding style="document"
      transport="http://schemas.xmlsoap.org/soap/http"
    />
```

```
        <operation name="GetLastTradePrice">
          <soap:operation
            soapAction="http://example.com/GetLastTradePrice"
          />
          <input> <soap:body use="literal"/> </input>
          <output> <soap:body use="literal"/> </output>
        </operation>
      </binding>

      <service name="StockQuoteService">
        <documentation>My first service</documentation>
        <port name="StockQuotePort" binding="tns:StockQuoteBinding">
          <soap:address location="http://example.com/stockquote"/>
        </port>
      </service>

    </definitions>
```

Web service discovery

How can a web service be discovered in the first place? A website that implements a web service need not support discovery. Any other site could be
describing the service, such as a web services directory. Alternatively, there may
not be a public means of finding the service at all.

UDDI (universal description, discovery, and integration) details one possible
directory service to discover web services in the first place. UDDI was originally
proposed by Ariba, IBM, and Microsoft, but had found over 200 supporting
companies and organizations by mid 2001 (see www.uddi.org). UDDI defines
four types of data entries. A business entity represents information about a business. Each business entity contains a set of business service entries, which
describe the services offered by the business. Each business service entry contains
a set of binding template entries, which provide pointers to the service access
points. A binding template also refers to a type model ("tModel"), which represents the technical specification of the service type. UDDI maintains a global
registry of well-known tModels, identified by UUIDs.

A UDDI service is itself a regular web service as every UDDI enquiry is an
XML message wrapped in a SOAP envelope. For instance, to find all businesses registered under a certain name, the following simple message can be
used (shown inside a SOAP envelope):

```
    <?xml version="1.0" encoding="UTF-8"?>
    <Envelope xmlns="http://schemas.xmlsoap.org/soap/envelope/">
      <Body>
        <find_business generic="1.0" xmlns="urn:uddi-org:api">
          <name>Example</name>
```

```
  </find_business>
 </Body>
</Envelope>
```

The result returned is an XML document similar to the following example (from here on, SOAP envelopes are no longer shown):

```
<businessList generic="1.0" operator="Your Friendly UDDI Shoppe"
    truncated="false" xmlns="urn:uddi-org:api">
 <businessInfos>
  <businessInfo businessKey="8FA16E6B-419F-4BC8-9958-
                            7CA17D2D3F90">
   <name>Electronic Coffee</name>
   <description xml:lang="en">
    Zero caffeine and pure bits for everyone.
   </description>
   <serviceInfos>
    <serviceInfo businessKey="8FA16E6B-419F-4BC8-9958-
                             7CA17D2D3F90"
     serviceKey="6C914879-0C2F-4CDC-AB92-6F03A961654A">
     <name>Supersized fat-free bits</name>
    </serviceInfo>
   </serviceInfos>
  </businessInfo>
 </businessInfos>
</businessList>
```

Using the following enquiry, the binding templates for a specific service can be requested:

```
<get_serviceDetail generic="1.0" xmlns="urn:uddi-org:api">
 <serviceKey>6C914879-0C2F-4CDC-AB92-6F03A961654A </serviceKey>
</get_serviceDetail>
```

As a result, the following binding templates are returned:

```
<serviceDetail generic="1.0" operator="Your Friendly UDDI Shoppe"
    truncated="false" xmlns="urn:uddi-org:api">
 <businessService businessKey="8FA16E6B-419F-4BC8-9958-
                              7CA17D2D3F90"
 serviceKey="6C914879-0C2F-4CDC-AB92-6F03A961654A ">
  <name> Supersized fat-free bits </name>
  <description xml:lang="en">Any number of 100% recycled
                    bits</description>
  <bindingTemplates>
   <bindingTemplate bindingKey="313C2BF0-021D-405C-8149-
                               25FD959F6F0B"
```

```
        serviceKey="6C914879-0C2F-4CDC-AB92-6F03A961654A">
        <description xml:lang="en">Publish wisdom</description>
        <accessPoint URLType=
                "https">https://uddi.example.com/publish</accessPoint>
        <tModelInstanceDetails>
          <tModelInstanceInfo
            tModelKey="uuid:64C756D1-3374-4E00-AE83-
                    EE12E38FAE63">
            <description xml:lang="en">Wisdom Publication
                            Interface</description>
          </tModelInstanceInfo>
        </tModelInstanceDetails>
      </bindingTemplate>
      <bindingTemplate bindingKey="A9CAFBE4-11C6-4BFE-90F5-
                            595970D2DE34"
        serviceKey="D2BC296A-723B-4C45-9ED4-494F9E53F1D1">
        <description xml:lang="en">Find wisdom</description>
        <accessPoint URLType=
                    "http">http://uddi.example.com/find</accessPoint>
        <tModelInstanceDetails>
          <tModelInstanceInfo
            tModelKey="uuid:4CD7E4BC-648B-426D-9936-
                    443EAAC8AE23">
            <description xml:lang="en">Wisdom Retrieval
                            Interface</description>
          </tModelInstanceInfo>
        </tModelInstanceDetails>
      </bindingTemplate>
    </bindingTemplates>
    <categoryBag>
      <keyedReference keyName="KEYWORD" keyValue="API"
        tModelKey="uuid:A035A07C-F362-44DD-8F95-E2B134BF43B4" />
      <keyedReference keyName="KEYWORD" keyValue="SOAP"
        tModelKey="uuid:A035A07C-F362-44DD-8F95-E2B134BF43B4" />
      <keyedReference keyName="KEYWORD" keyValue="XML"
        tModelKey="uuid:A035A07C-F362-44DD-8F95-E2B134BF43B4" />
    </categoryBag>
  </businessService>
</serviceDetail>
```

Table 12.1 illustrates how the three protocol layers of SOAP, WSDL, and UDDI stack up to support web services and how they build on established transfer and transport protocols underneath.

Table 12.1 The core web services protocol stack

Discovery	UDDI	Itself a web service, UDDI serves as a directory for web services.
Description	WSDL, WSFL/XLANG, others to come	Given one or more web services, describe properties at a metalevel.
Access	SOAP, SOAP with attachments	Given a web service instance, access it via messages.
Transfer	HTTP, SMTP, others	Transfer SOAP messages, incl. Attachments.
Transport	TCP/IP, UDP, others	Transport data.

To further enhance coordination among web services involved in some common task, ideas from work flow engines can be used. Such languages allow for the behavioral specification of web services and protocols used to combine web services. Two attempts in this direction are IBM's WSFL (web service flow language; Leymann, 2001) and Microsofts XLANG (pronounced "slang"; Thatte, 2001).

12.4.6 Web services and programming models

WSDL ports describe input and output messages. Ports are grouped into WSDL services. Ports on services are similar to methods on interfaces. It is thus tempting to model web service invocations as synchronous remote method calls. Likewise, it is tempting to think of web service implementations as classes that implement the ports of a service as methods.

To see if such approaches are appropriate, it is important to recall the special nature of web-distributed services. Latencies can be significant and unpredictable, actual host selection must be flexible to enable load balancing, and failures can occur at any time. For instance, as web services above the HTTP layer never refer to particular hosts, there is no guarantee that the result will be processed on the same host that sent the request – such a redirection would be under the control of the logical client and not the called web service, of course.

Implementing a web service port as a method on a class can be appropriate, depending on the server-side programming model. In particular, if a web service doesn't draw on other web services or otherwise slow resources, then a web service implemented using synchronous classes would perform well.

Calling a web service is a different matter, though. Assuming substantial round-trip latencies and possible message queuing on the way, a caller would run into severe performance issues when using blocking synchronous calls on web services. A client programmed this way would have to draw on a large number of concurrent threads to deal with large numbers of outstanding call results or else would simply not do anything useful while a call was pending. A better model uses asynchronous call models against web services, similar to those found in message queuing systems.

Many other issues need to be addressed in the world of web services that have previously been addressed in remote procedure, distributed object, and messaging approaches. Microsoft's proposal for a global XML web services architecture (GXA) is one attempt to consolidate this space. GXA, as defined in early 2002, comprises WS-Inspection, WS-License, WS-Referral, WS-Routing, and WS-Security specifications. These support service reflection (inspection), rights certification (licenses), message self-routing, multi-hop message forwarding, and security, respectively. Freshly inaugurated in early 2002, the W3C working group on web services architecture can be expected to develop standards in a direction similar to GXA.

Also founded in 2002, the new WS-I (web service interoperability; www.ws-i.org) standardization body aims to define profiles of sets of web-service standards. A first proposed profile consists of XML Schema 1.0, SOAP 1.1, WSDL 1.1, and UDDI 1.0. Given such a profile, WS-I plans to provide test suites, sample implementations, and self-certification guidelines that should help ensure interoperability across implementations.

12.5   Which way?

Based on the above developments and ideas, a number of approaches and technologies are trying to capture their share of the emerging component markets. The next three chapters (Chapters 13 to 15) present a detailed technical account of the three major approaches followed today. These are the CORBA-centered standards, which emerged mainly from the world of enterprise computing and legacy application integration; Sun's Java-centered standards, with origins stemming from the internet and the web in particular, and which are now especially strong in the application and web server space; and, finally, the COM+ and now .NET-centered standards, which evolved out of Microsoft's strong position in the desktop area. Chapter 16 briefly covers a few further approaches and Chapter 17 presents a strategic comparison of the main approaches. Chapters 18 and 19 conclude with hints at ongoing efforts on domain-specific standards and at a number of open problems.

Overarching all developments and permeating many aspects of technology is the growing connectivity and interoperation on a global, cross-organizational scale brought by the web. Web standards, such as XML and web service models, are forming a new layer of unprecedented integration potential that relativizes all individual technology families, including the component software technologies discussed in the following chapters.

CHAPTER THIRTEEN

The OMG way: CORBA, CCM, OMA, and MDA

The Object Management Group (OMG), founded in 1989, is by far the largest consortium in the computing industry. OMG operates as a non-profit organization aiming at the standardization of "whatever it takes" to achieve interoperability on all levels of an open market for "objects." Early 2002, around 800 member companies had joined OMG.

13.1 At the heart – the object request broker

Originally, OMG's efforts concentrated on solving one fundamental problem – how can distributed object-oriented systems implemented in different languages and running on different platforms interact? Far from the problems of distributed computing, such simple phenomena as total incommunicado between codes generated by two C++ compilers on the same platform stopped integration efforts right at the start. Differing object models from language to language made this worse. Differences between platforms coupled by low-level socket communication or – in better cases – by remote procedure call (RPC) packages completed the picture of deep gaps everywhere. The first years of OMG went into tackling these basic "wiring" problems. The outcome was the Common Object Request Broker Architecture (CORBA) in its initial version, 1.1, released in 1991, followed by minor improvements in version 1.2. Today's highly successful standard is CORBA 2, version 2.0, released in July 1995 and updated in July 1996 (OMG, 1997a). The current version is 2.6, released in December 2001. The CORBA 3 specification is, as of early 2002, largely finalized but still pending. While numerous contributions originally scoped in CORBA 3 have been released in successive CORBA 2 increments, the biggest contribution, the CORBA component model (CCM), remains CORBA 3 proper and pending.

From the beginning, the goal behind CORBA was to enable open interconnection of a wide variety of languages, implementations, and platforms. Thus,

OMG never settled on "binary" standards (standards at the level of deployable executables) – everything is carefully standardized to allow for many different implementations and for individual vendors of CORBA-compliant products to add value. The downside of this very open approach is that individual CORBA-compliant products cannot interoperate on an efficient binary level, but must engage instead in costly high-level protocols. The most prominent, although only moderately efficient, interoperability protocol is OMG's inter-net inter-ORB protocol (IIOP), standardized with CORBA 2.0 in July 1995. Any ORB claiming interoperability compliance has to support IIOP. In the July 1996 update of the CORBA 2.0 standard, an interworking standard was added, which specifies the interworking of CORBA-based systems with systems based on Microsoft's COM (see Chapter 15).

CORBA essentially has three parts: a set of invocation interfaces, the object request broker (ORB), and a set of object adapters. Invocations of object-oriented operations – also called method invocations – require late binding of the implementation. The method implementing the invoked operation is selected based on the object implementation to which the receiving object's reference refers. Invocation interfaces enable various degrees of late binding. They also marshal an invocation's arguments such that the ORB core can locate the receiver object and the invoked method and transport the arguments. At the receiving end, an object adapter unmarshals the arguments and invokes the requested method on the receiver object. Figure 13.1 illustrates the basic CORBA structure in simplified form.

For invocation interfaces and object adapters to work, two essential requirements need to be met. First, all object interfaces need to be described in a common language. Second, all languages used must have bindings to the common language. The first condition enables construction of generic marshaling and unmarshaling mechanisms. The second allows calls from or to a particular language to be related to the common language. This common language formed an essential part of CORBA from the beginning and is called OMG interface definition language (OMG IDL). Here is an example of an OMG IDL specification:

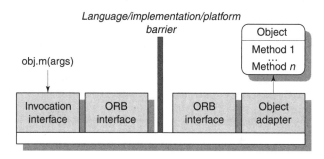

Figure 13.1 Simplified structure of an ORB-based system.

```
module Example {
  struct Date {
    unsigned short Day;
    unsigned short Month;
    unsigned short Year;
  }
  interface Ufo {
    readonly attribute unsigned long ID;
    readonly attribute string Name;
    readonly attribute Date FirstContact;
    unsigned long Contacts ();
    void RegisterContact (Date dateOfContact);
  }
}
```

Bindings to OMG IDL are available for several languages, including C, C++, Smalltalk, PL/1, COBOL, and Java. Once interfaces are expressed in OMG IDL, they can be compiled using an OMG IDL compiler and deposited in an interface repository, which every ORB must have. By means of the ORB interface, compiled interfaces can be retrieved from the interface repository. Also, when compiling program fragments that can provide implementations of such interfaces, these program fragments, called object servants, can be registered with the ORB's implementation repository. An ORB is capable of loading and starting an object servant when receiving invocation requests for an object of that servant. An object adapter is responsible for telling an ORB which new object is served by which servant. Multiple servants can execute in a shared server environment, typically a process.

To enable efficient marshaling and unmarshaling of arguments, an ORB-specific OMG IDL compiler must be used to generate stubs and skeletons. A stub can be instantiated and then looks like a local object, but forwards all invocations through the ORB to the real target object. In other approaches, stubs are called (client-side) proxy objects. A skeleton receives invocations, unmarshals arguments, and directly invokes the target method. Although not mentioned so far, a skeleton also accepts return values, marshals these, and sends them back to the stub for unmarshaling and final returning. In other approaches, skeletons are called (server-side) stubs.

Stubs and skeletons are good solutions when dealing with regular method invocations. However, sometimes this binding is too static and the operation to be invoked needs to be selected at runtime. CORBA provides a dynamic invocation interface (DII) for this purpose, while CORBA 2.0 added a dynamic skeleton interface (DSI). These interfaces allow for the dynamic selection of methods either at the client's end (DII) or at the server's end (DSI). Both interfaces use a universal data structure for arguments to cater for methods of arbitrary signature. Older versions of IONA's Orbix, for example, generated stubs that translate static invocations to non-local objects into sequences of DII calls. These Orbix ORBs then handled only the universal dynamic invocation structures. Significant performance improvements can be gained by ORBs that implement SII/SSI directly and, since the introduction of IIOP, this is now commonly done. Figure 13.2 gives a more detailed view of CORBA and its interaction with the OMG IDL.

It is important to understand that the separation into calling client and called object does not impose an asymmetric architecture, such as client–server computing. The same process can be both issuing and receiving calls. Distribution of functionality to machines is left to the system's architect using CORBA. The object adapter introduces the only asymmetry. Programs that need to function as object servants need to register with the ORB via the object adapter. In theory, there can be different object adapters for the same ORB and these could even be used concurrently to serve different kinds of objects. Originally, OMG standardized the basic object adapter (BOA). In 1998, the BOA specification was deprecated and replaced by the specification of the portable object adapter (POA). The main problem with BOA was its underspecification that forced vendors to provide proprietary extensions, eliminating any hope for porting CORBA object implementations from one ORB to another.

Once an object servant is registered with an ORB, the ORB "knows" how to activate that servant when needed. (To be precise, the ORB draws on the services of object adapters to activate servants.) To determine on which machine to activate the servant, each registered object has a home machine that is used to start the servant on. Pure application programs that only call objects (but do not export any of their own), do not register with an ORB and therefore cannot be started by an ORB.

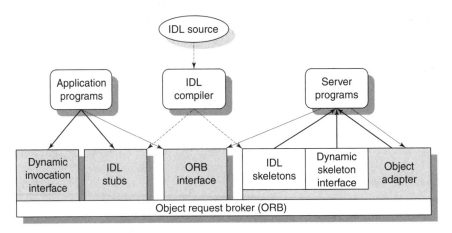

Figure 13.2 CORBA and OMG IDL.

The OMG IDL distinguishes between basic and constructed data types and CORBA object references. Data types include integers, floats, characters, strings, structures, sequences, and multidimensional fixed-size arrays. All data types are passed by value. Before CORBA 2.3, CORBA objects themselves could not be passed, only references to CORBA objects could. Starting with CORBA 2.3, objects can also be passed by value and a standard mapping of such values to XML is defined. CORBA object references are opaque types and different from the references used within a bound language; they are much larger and cost more than the native references. Again starting with CORBA 2.3, there is a standard way to form an object reference as a URL (as in corbaloc::www.example.org/CoolService).

The ORB interface provides operations to turn a native reference into a CORBA reference and back. It also provides operations to turn a CORBA reference into a unique but proprietary ORB-specific string and back. Such strings can be used to store CORBA references – and are typically used within IIOP exchanges. A CORBA reference is defined to have an indefinite lifetime – that is it will never be reused. The attempt to retrieve the associated object may of course fail if that object has been deleted in the meantime.

Almost all CORBA standards are, in the end, specified over interfaces defined using OMG IDL. With CORBA 3.0, OMG is moving beyond IDL by introducing two new languages that focus on class rather than interface properties. The first is the persistent state definition language (PSDL) that primarily captures storage types (records with typed fields) and storage homes (factories) – for more information see the discussion of the persistent state service in section 13.2.2. The second new language is the component implementation definition language (CIDL), itself an extension of PSDL, adding components, component homes, composition entities, composition processes, and executors (for details see section 13.3).

13.1.1 From CORBA to OMA

CORBA 2-compliant ORB implementations are available from several vendors on many platforms, but CORBA 3-compliant implementations were slow to materialize (as of early 2002). The above discussion should have made clear that an ORB is essentially a remote method invocation service. As such, ORBs promise a much cleaner model to program distributed systems than services based on remote procedure calls or even lower-level abstractions. Indeed, the most common use of ORBs in industry is to replace sockets and remote procedure calls in applications spanning several server machines. The pure "wiring" standard established with CORBA is thus successful. However, above this basic "wiring," programmers were still left alone before CORBA 3. Although the communicating ends may be on different machines and implemented in different languages, they need to share many conventions to interoperate. As a result, the ends are still most likely to be developed by the same team.

Being aware of this shortcoming, OMG started to broaden its focus long ago. Since CORBA 2, the OMG's overall effort is called the object management architecture (OMA) (OMG, 1997b). Today, it revolves around the CORBA 3 specification, including OMG IDL, language bindings, invocation interfaces, object adapters, interface and implementation repositories, object servants, and component infrastructure. The OMA adds three new areas of standardization, which are a set of common object service specifications (CORBAservices), a set of common facility specifications (CORBAfacilities), a set of application object specifications, and, since CORBA 3, the CORBA Component Model (CCM), also called CORBA components. Figure 13.3 presents an overview of OMA.

Object services support all CORBA-based programs in a way that is independent of specific domains or application models. Object services concentrate on the fundamental building blocks of any distributed solution, such as event propagation, transactions, or naming. Common facilities are either horizontal or domain-specific. Horizontal facilities are domain-independent, but focus on specific application models – these are increasingly de-emphasized and play almost no role in CORBA 3. For example, the once prominent (and most complex) standardized horizontal facility – OpenDoc, supporting compound documents – is now effectively defunct. Vertical facilities with their focus on specific domains, on the other hand, had a slow start but are now growing strongly.

Finally, application objects add domain-specific entities that could be plugged into component frameworks. The most prominent class of application objects is business objects. These are objects that directly represent abstractions used in specific businesses. Today, this category is essentially void. No specifications of application objects are presently part of OMA.

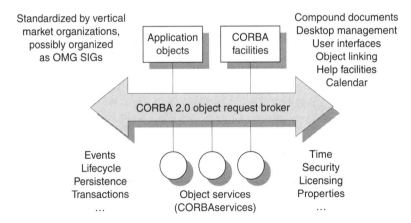

Figure 13.3 The OMG's object management architecture (OMA).

13.1.2 **CORBA timeline**

The following list places the CORBA versions on a timeline (unexpanded acronyms are explained elsewhere in this book – see glossary and index):

CORBA 1.0 – October 1991
IDL, DII, Interface Repository, C mapping
CORBA 1.1 – February 1992
BOA and memory management; clarified Interface Repository as well as object model.
CORBA 1.2 – December 1993
Several clarifications, especially in memory management and object reference comparison.
CORBA 2.0 – February 1997
DSI, initial reference resolver for client portability, extensions to Interface Repository, interoperability architecture (GIOP, IIOP, DCE CIOP), layered security and transaction services, data type extensions for COBOL, scientific processing, wide characters, COM and OLE Automation interworking, language mappings for C++ and Smalltalk.
CORBA 2.1 – September 1997
Secure IIOP, IIOP over SSL, language mappings for COBOL and Ada, interoperability revisions and IDL type extensions.
CORBA 2.2 – July 1998
Server portability enhancements (POA), DCOM interworking, language mapping for Java, reverse mapping Java to IDL.
CORBA 2.3 – December 1998
Revisions of: language mappings for C/C++/Java, ORB portability, COM and automation interworking, CORBA Core, ORB interoperability, and security.
CORBA 2.3.1 – October 1999
CORBA 2.4 – October 2000
Several quality of service (QoS) specifications. Contains asynchronous messaging, Minimum CORBA, and real-time CORBA specifications.
CORBA 2.4.1 – November 2000
CORBA 2.4.2 – February 2001
CORBA 2.5 – September 2001
Fault-tolerant CORBA, portable interceptors.
CORBA 2.6 – December 2001
New secure interoperation specification and general interoperability improvements.
CORBA 3.0 – pending
Java and internet integration (objects passable by value and XML mappings, allow Java RMI objects to interoperate over the network as CORBA objects, standard URL protocol corbaloc for non-binary object references, firewall specification); quality of service control, real-time and fault-tolerant CORBA; and the CORBAcomponents architecture (CORBAcomponents and CORBAscripting, mappings for scripting languages).

CORBA 1 was all about object request brokers and IDL is its hallmark contribution. CORBA 2 focuses on interoperation (and interworking) and IIOP is its hallmark. CORBA 3 aims to focus on component and system integration and CCM is its hallmark. This timeline exposes a fairly steady process, even if often much slower than initially hoped. For instance, CORBA 3 was originally scheduled to be finalized by late 1998.

In early 2002, the CORBA 3.0 specification was still not formally released. However, as they have been formalized one by one, several of the items targeted for CORBA 3.0 have been incorporated into CORBA 2.3 to 2.6 releases. In particular, objects passable by value, XML mappings (see section 13.7), and Java RMI interoperation were incorporated in CORBA 2.3, which marked the beginning of the mutual Java-CORBA co-evolution. Object reference URLs, asynchronous messaging, minimum, and real-time CORBA are part of CORBA 2.4. CORBA 2.5 added fault tolerance and portable interceptors; CORBA 2.6 secure interoperation. A Python mapping has been formalized (Python is a popular scripting language); IDLscript is pending. The main contribution of CORBA 3.0, the component model, was essentially complete by the end of 2001.

13.1.3   A bit of history – system object model (SOM)

IBM's System Object Model was deprecated in 1998 (the SOM 3.0 distributions for AIX, OS/2, and Windows NT are available as freeware from www.ibm.com/software/ad/som). The following brief discussion is kept as there are several historic references to SOM throughout this book.

SOM was originally developed independently from CORBA as part of the OS/2 workplace shell. Later, it was made first CORBA 1.2- and then CORBA 2-compliant. In fact, distributed computing is supported by the distributed SOM (DSOM) libraries, which build on SOM. In this section, DSOM is considered to be an integral part of SOM. SOM implemented a superset of the CORBA 2 standard and supported metaservices that are still not on the CORBA map. In addition, SOM defined a binary standard.

Two features of SOM stand out – its support for metaprogramming and support or binary compatibility across binary releases. The SOM metaprogramming model largely follows the Smalltalk example (Goldberg and Robson, 1983), so every class is itself an object and as such an instance of a metaclass. All metaclasses are instances of a single class, Metaclass, which is its own metaclass. SOM goes beyond the reflective capabilities of CORBA as SOM allows classes to be constructed or modified dynamically. For example, it is possible to add a new method to an existing class without disturbing any of the existing instances of that class – these existing instances will immediately support the new method. There is at present no other mainstream component platform that supports a similar level of metaprogramming. Runtime code synthesis is supported elsewhere (CLR, Java), but these do not support modifications that affect already existing instances.

Versioning and binary compatibility are supported by the notion of a release order (Forman *et al.*, 1995). For example, adding new methods to a later release does not alter the dispatch indices used by code compiled against an older release. SOM comes with precise rules as to which changes in a release maintain, and which other changes break, binary compatibility with previous releases. Binary compatibility is a very important issue in a component world. It is unthinkable to ask all vendors of dependent components – and the vendors of components dependent on these components, and so on – to recompile and redistribute within any reasonable time. This is the syntactic fragile base class (FBC) problem (section 7.4.1). JVM and CLR incorporate similar notions of release-to-release binary compatibility.

SOM guarantees binary compatibility across a large number of base class changes, including refactoring of class hierarchies, as long as the required methods remain available and of compatible signature. As a special case, SOM guarantees that, if no interface changes took place, then building the next release of a component is guaranteed to preserve binary compatibility with clients compiled against the previous release. This effectively solves the syntactic FBC problem, but obviously cannot address the semantic FBC problem. (Tackling the semantic FBC problem requires full support for side-by-side existence of multiple versions of interfaces and implementations, as originally established by COM and fully supported by CLR. See Chapter 15.)

13.2 Common object service specifications (CORBAservices)

CORBAservices currently specifies 16 object services, one of which (the notification service) is formally part of the telecommunications domain facility. The following sections present brief summaries of these services, in two categories. Per category, the order follows the much more detailed discussion by Siegel (2000). The first category covers the services relevant for today's enterprise computing applications using CORBA. These applications typically use CORBA objects as modules and CORBA as a convenient communications middleware. The relevant services are those that support large-scale operations. The second category covers the services aiming at finer-grained use of objects. These are today seen as being of lesser practical importance. One potential exception with a particularly turbulent history could be the persistent state service (PSS) of CORBA 3 that replaced the CORBA 2 persistent object service (POS). While yet to be adopted by products, PSS is one of the three pillar services underlying the CORBA Component Model (described in section 13.3); the other two are the object transaction and the notification service (described in the next section). It is noteworthy that large CORBA-based systems frequently use only a few CORBA services, with the exception of naming and some sort of security and, to a lesser degree, transactions and trading. This reality is reflected in available ORB products, which tend to not support the full spectrum of CORBA services.

13.2.1 Services supporting enterprise distributed computing

Many large enterprise systems use CORBA essentially as an object bus, relying on ORBs to attach a wide variety of systems. Naming is the one key service that all such systems build on.

Naming service, trader service

Objects always have a unique ID used internally. The naming service also allows arbitrary names to be associated with an object. Names are unique within a naming context and naming contexts form a hierarchy. The resulting naming tree is quite similar to directory structures in file systems.

The trader service allows providers to announce their services by registering offers. Clients can use a trader to locate services by description. A trader organizes services into trading contexts. Clients can search for services, based on parts of descriptions and keywords, within selected contexts. The trader returns a list of offers that match the query. The OMG trader service specification was simultaneously adopted by the ISO (ISO/IEC 13235-1) and the ITU (ITU-T recommendation X.950).

The naming service can be compared to White Pages and the trader service to Yellow Pages.

Event service, notification service

The event service allows event objects that can be sent from event suppliers to event consumers to be defined. Event objects are immutable in that information flows strictly in one direction, from supplier to consumer. Events travel through event channels that decouple supplier from consumer. Events can be typed (described using OMG IDL) and channels can be used to filter events according to their type.

The event channel supports both the "push" and the "pull" model of event notification. In the "push" model, the event supplier calls a push method on the event channel, which reacts by calling the push method of all registered consumers. In the "pull" model, the consumer calls the pull method of the event channel, effectively polling the channel for events. The channel then calls a pull method on the registered suppliers and returns an event object if it found a supplier that returned an event object.

In 1998, the specification of the notification service added several critical features to the event service (Siegel, 2000) – quality of service (QoS) specification and administration; standards for typed and structured events; dynamic event filtering based on type and QoS; filtering at source, channel, consumer group, and individual consumer level; and event discovery among source, channel, and client. Note that, technically, the notification service is not a CORBA service but a CORBA facility introduced as part of the efforts of the telecommunications domain taskforce (TelDTF).

Object transaction service

The object transaction service (OTS) is one of the most important services to build distributed applications. OTS was standardized by OMG in December 1994, and now forms part of most ORBs and several J2EE servers. An OTS implementation must support flat, and optionally can support nested, transactions. It is possible to integrate non-CORBA transactions that comply with the X/Open distributed transaction- processing standard. Integration with transactions spanning multiple and heterogeneous ORBs is also possible.

In the context of component-based systems, nested transactions seem unavoidable. It should be possible for a component implementation to create a transactional closure for a sequence of operations without having to declare this in the component interfaces. The principle of independent extensibility then requires support of nested transactions. Flat transactions, the only ones guaranteed to be supported in a compliant OTS implementation, are of limited value in a component system. However, this is a common shortcoming as practically no mainstream transactional systems today support nested transactions.

The OTS automatically maintains a current transaction context that is propagated along with all ORB-mediated requests and passed on to non-ORB transactional activities. For CORBA objects, the context is passed to any object that implements interface TransactionalObject. The current context can be requested from the ORB and thus is always available. The transaction operations begin, commit, and rollback are defined on the current context.

All objects that are modified under a transaction and require transactional control register with the OTS coordinator object. The relevant coordinator can be retrieved from the current context. A resource can indicate that it understands nested transactions. Resources have to implement the interface Resource, which is used by the coordinator to run a two-phase commit protocol. (It is known that two-phase commit may deadlock in a fully distributed implementation unless it can be built on a specific kind of broadcast protocol; three-phase commit protocols are known to avoid this problem, but at a higher cost per transaction (Mullender, 1993). The OTS approach requires the coordinator to be logically centralized.)

Instead of providing transaction control as a separate service, as promoted by the OTS design, it is now most popular to integrate transaction and other services into a context or container abstraction provided by an application server. (The CORBA model to do so is the new component model (CCM) described in section 13.3.)

Security service

A robust security service is clearly of paramount importance for distributed systems spanning more than a single trusted organizational domain. The security service needs to be pervasive. All interoperating ORBs, and other interworking systems, need to collaborate, and a security policy needs to be established for all involved organizational units.

The CORBAsecurity specification defines a number of services for tasks such as authentication, secure communication, delegation of credentials (also known as impersonation), and non-repudiation. Very few products actually support the full spectrum of security services in this specification. A few, such as BEA's WebLogic Enterprise and IBM's WebSphere go quite far. Many other products simply rely on Netscape's secure sockets layer (SSL) – especially in the case of standalone ORBs as compared to fully integrated application servers. Using SSL is fine to establish simple authentication and secure communication properties. However, it does not support more advanced concepts such as delegation or non-repudiation.

13.2.2 Services supporting architecture using fine-grained objects

Out of the following list of services, several have not made it into products, including the collection, externalization, and query services. The reasons range from loose specification, as in the case of the query service, to impractical assumptions, as in the case of the collection service (Siegel, 2000). The following is, nevertheless, a complete list and brief description of all object services presently covered by the OMA.

Concurrency control service

This service supports acquisition and release of locks on resources. Locks can be acquired either within a transactional context (see object transaction service below) or within a non-transactional context. Locks acquired on behalf of a transaction will be released as part of a transaction's rollback. Locks can be acquired in one of several lock modes, such as read, write, and upgrade. A read lock allows for multiple readers whereas a write lock ensures single writers. An upgrade lock is a read lock that can be upgraded to a write lock because it guarantees mutually exclusive read access.

Locks are acquired out of locksets. Each protected resource holds a lockset that determines what kind of locks and how many of them are available. A lockset factory interface supports creation of new locksets. Locksets are either transactional or non-transactional and can be related to other locksets. A lock coordinator object can be used to release all locks held in related locksets.

Licensing service

As soon as components are used to assemble solutions, there needs to be a way to obtain licenses for all but freeware components. The licensing service supports a variety of different licensing models. The service defines just two interfaces (abstractions) – license service manager and producer-specific license service. If an object is bound by a license agreement it can itself use the license service manager to find out whether or not its use is legitimate.

A licensed object contacts the license service manager and obtains a reference to a producer-specific license service object. All further activities are with this specific object. The licensed object informs the specific service object that its use has started and passes information such as the component name and version, the object reference, and a user context. The specific service object checks whether or not a valid license exists for this user context and advises the licensed object about actions to be taken. For example, the licensed object may switch to demo mode or offer a grace period if no valid license exists or if the license has expired. The actual licensing policy is thus fully encapsulated by the licensed object and the producer-specific license service object.

Once operating, the producer-specific license service object periodically sends event notifications to the licensed object, which replies by reporting usage statistics. Alternatively, the licensed object could actively report at regular intervals. The reports can be used to maintain a usage profile or implement license expiration policies. Finally, if the user stops using the licensed object, it informs the specific service object, which then stops sending events.

Lifecycle service

This service supports creation, copying, moving, and deletion of objects and related groups of objects. Containment and reference relations used to handle groups of objects are described using the relationships service outlined below. Where containment relations are used, copies are deep – all contained objects are also copied. To support object creation, the lifecycle service supports registry and retrieval of factory objects. Once the needed factory object has been retrieved, it can be used to create new objects.

Surprisingly, the lifecycle service offers a destroy operation to get rid of objects or groups of objects but does not help to determine when to destroy objects. This is a significant shortcoming of CORBA as subtle distributed memory management issues are simply left for higher levels to solve. By comparison, DCOM supports distributed reference counting and Java and CLR even support a form of distributed garbage collection based on remote reference leases that expire unless used or renewed.

In current enterprise applications built using CORBA, this is not normally an issue for several reasons. For one, certain "objects" are of unbounded lifetime and simply represent a traditional server program. In such a setting, CORBA is used as a communication middleware for modules distributed across a networked environment. Also, to be fair, distributed reference counting or garbage collection works well as long as there are no network or machine failures. To solve the distributed memory management problem in the presence of such failures requires embedding in a transaction context. Long-lived transactions are necessary to manage the lifetime of longer-lived objects in a proper fashion and long-lived transactions do not form part of mainstream offerings. Therefore, a different approach is commonly used. This involves building on short-lived transactions and keeping all relevant state in transacted stable stores (databases). The lifetime of objects is then either delineated by the lifetime of transactions or by that of database entries. In the latter case, the object itself is merely a reconstructable cache of the database state.

Relationship service

The relationship service was meant to allow general relationships between objects to be specified and maintained. Rather than resorting to language-level pointers or references, this service introduces an associative model that allows relationships over objects to be created without changing the involved objects at all. However, the relationship service is rarely used or even implemented and is likely to be replaced by support for relationships among business objects based on CCM (Siegel, 2000).

Persistent state service

Object persistence is the property of an object to survive the termination of the program that created it. Starting with CORBA 2, the persistent object service (POS) was meant to support persistence of CORBA objects. Despite being a key service standardized by OMG in early 1994, it took implementations until mid 1996 to appear in the first beta releases. Some reports on implementation attempts even pointed out severe technical problems with the specification and its expected interoperation with other object services, such as that with the object relationships service (Kleindienst et al., 1996). In addition, it emerged that the POS did not solve the "right" problems. In particular, it was still left to application code to request object storage. The POS specification was finally deprecated and replaced in CORBA 3 by the new persistent state service (PSS).

The fundamental idea behind any persistence service is to provide an abstraction layer that shields persistent objects from the persistence mechanism. For example, objects can be stored in files, in relational or object databases, or in structured storage as used by compound document architectures. There are only two basic operations, which are storing an object and retrieving an object. However, three properties of objects make these operations a non-trivial undertaking.

First, objects have an observable identity – that is, they are not referentially transparent. A persistence service must thus ensure that object integrity is preserved. If an object that has been stored before is stored, then the original copy is updated and a reference to that is stored. Likewise, if an object that has been retrieved before is retrieved, and is still reachable, then a reference to the previously retrieved object is returned.

Second, objects refer to each other and thus form an object web. These references need to be maintained across persistent storage of objects in a web. It must be possible to distinguish between essential and transitory object references; otherwise a large number of temporary objects would be dragged into the persistent store. Also, if multiple persistent stores are used, relationships must be kept across such stores. In addition to programming language-level references, a POS must also support relationships introduced using the object relationships service.

Third, objects are units of encapsulation. Despite their storage in persistent stores, an object's contents should be protected against direct manipulation, bypassing the object's encapsulation barrier. Of course, this level of protection is only feasible with certain persistent stores.

The original POS aimed to resolve these issues by means of protocols between persistent objects and persistent data services. As these protocols require the cooperation of the involved objects with the persistence service, they were sometimes called conspiracies (Orfali *et al.*, 1996). The resulting design would have led to an entangling of objects to be persisted and the various stores – probably one reason for the failure of the POS attempt.

With the new PSS, the approach to determining what to store for a given object type has been made explicit and declarative. Either a programming language, such as Java, is used that has built-in support for persistency declarations on fields of objects, or a separate persistence declaration is written using the OMG persistent state definition language (PSDL). Essentially, declarations in either form establish a schema for the storage representation, split into abstract storage types and concrete storage types that implement one or more abstract storage types. This model is quite close to the distinction between abstract and concrete classes, or interfaces and classes. Instead of focusing on the abstraction of operations, PSDL focuses on the abstraction of persistable state. In addition, PSDL supports abstract and concrete factories (called storage homes) for instances of given storage types.

Externalization service

This service supports mapping of an object web to a stream and back. The process of first externalizing the objects and then internalizing them again creates a copy of the corresponding object web. The externalization service does not maintain referential integrity. It merely preserves the references between objects externalized together. Externalization can thus be used to copy object webs by value. References to other objects can be maintained explicitly by using ORB provided string identifiers for these references.

To become externalizable, an object needs to implement the Streamable interface. Externalization of an object is requested by invoking an externalize method on an object implementing the Stream interface. This stream object invokes the externalize_to_stream method of the streamable object and passes an object implementing the StreamIO interface. The streamable object can then use this streamIO object to write any of the OMG IDL-defined data types or to write embedded objects. The streamable object can also externalize an entire graph of objects defined using the relationship service.

Properties service

This service allows arbitrary properties to be associated with objects that implement at least interface PropertySet. Properties can be added, retrieved, and deleted individually or in groups. If an object also implements interface PropertySetDef, properties can be further controlled to be of one of four property modes. Properties can thus be normal (can be modified or deleted), read-only (can be deleted but not modified), fixed-normal (can be modified but not deleted), or fixed-read-only.

The property service does not interpret any of the properties associated with an object. Properties are useful for programs that, generically, need to attach information to arbitrary objects. An important example is system administration tools that attach "stickers" in order to track objects efficiently.

Object query service

This service helps to locate objects by attributes. It is similar to the object trader service, but instead of locating servers it locates object instances. Queries are based on the attributes that objects make public or accessible via operations. Two query languages are supported, namely the Object Database Management Group's ODMG-93 object query language (OQL) and SQL with object extensions. A single common query language is under development.

The query service defines its own simple collection service – a subset of the general collection service. Collections are used while processing queries to form result sets and are then returned to the querying client. These simple collections provide ordered set semantics, including operations to add and remove elements or sets of elements. The service also provides an Iterator interface to support enumeration of the elements of a collection.

The query service defines four entities – query objects, query evaluators, query managers, and queryable collections. A query object encapsulates the query itself and operates in two stages. First, the query is prepared and then the query is executed. A query evaluator can take a query and operate over a queryable collection to process the query and return a result, which, again, is a collection. A query manager creates query objects and delegates queries to the relevant query evaluators. The querying client finally uses an iterator to work through the collection of returned results.

Object collections service

The collection service supports collections of various abstract topologies, such as bags, sets, queues, lists, or trees. The role model is the Smalltalk collection-classes library (Goldberg and Robson, 1983, 1989). It is debatable whether or not the CORBA collection service – based on the relatively heavyweight model of CORBA objects – can ever be competitive with native object collection libraries. At the same time, object databases may be better suited to transfer "collections" of various shapes and with various properties across ORBs.

Time service

This service deals with the inaccuracies inherent in a distributed system with multiple asynchronous clocks. In many applications, realtime information is used to correlate internal events, such as creation of files, with universal time. A time service has to ensure that such correlation is possible within reasonable error margins and that non-causal correlation is avoided. As an example, consider the creation of a new object as a reaction to another object firing an event. Non-causal time-based information would result when assigning a "date of birth" time stamp to the new object that predates the first object – a typical result of a non-causal time service.

13.3 CORBA Component Model

CORBA 3 is the latest incarnation of the suite of CORBA standards (Siegel, 2000). Although, as of mid 2002, the final set of specifications is still forthcoming, substantial strides have already been made to improve on almost all aspects of CORBA 2. Besides an overhaul of many object services, the single biggest contribution is probably the new CORBA Component Model (CCM) – although the release of the final CCM specification is itself still pending. (Occasionally, CCM is also referred to as CORBAcomponents.)

CCM is an ambitious logical extension of Enterprise JavaBeans (see section 14.5.2). CCM introduces several novel features, promises a fully compatible embedding of existing EJB solutions and aims to maintain the original CORBA tenet of being both language and platform independent.

It remains to be seen if CCM can break free from being a mere paper extension of EJB   that is, whether or not viable CCM-compliant products will emerge. Such products would go beyond the current tendency of J2EE application servers that largely use CORBA only as an interoperable connectivity standard via IIOP. Although the CCM specification was close to being finalized in mid 2001, only a few commercial implementations had been announced by then. Most notably, IONA committed to delivering a CORBA 3-compliant implementation almost in synchrony with the finalization of the specification.

The following subsections cover the most important CCM features, including the portable object adapter (POA) that is essential for several CCM features.

13.3.1 Portable object adapter

The main function of a CORBA object adapter is to mediate between an ORB and the actual implementation of an object receiving incoming calls and returning results. Replacing the now outdated basic object adapter, the current object adapter specification is that for portable object adapters. Presently, there is no other object adapter specification. An instance of the portable object adapter accepts requests on behalf of a group of objects. In any server process supported by an ORB there will be at least one POA instance; but there may be as many as one per serviced object in that process.

Clients direct calls to object references. Object references are created by POAs at the server side and then passed to clients. To enable clients to talk to any objects, a set of well-known objects is made available by ORBs on the client side, typically including an object providing the naming service. The object reference contains the information needed for a client ORB to locate the server ORB, which then receives the client's call. Furthermore, the object reference contains the name of the POA that created the object reference and an object ID that is valid only relative to that POA. A POA's name is assigned on initial creation in a server, while ORBs maintain a registry of such named POAs and can reactivate POAs if necessary.

A POA instance handles an incoming request by handing it off to a servant. Servants are the implementations of CORBA objects. Figure 13.4 shows a typical tooling scenario, where, starting from an IDL definition, a client-side stub, a server-side POA skeleton and a server-side servant template is generated. A developer can then fill in the implementation details by completing the generated template. A CORBA object is not necessarily implemented using object-oriented languages and servants are therefore not necessarily classes. If object-oriented languages are used, servants are instances of classes.

POAs create servants following a number of different possible policies. Objects, and with them their servants, can be activated explicitly by, for example, a server startup program. Explicit object activation yields the fastest response times but also has the highest impact on resources. In addition, it precludes load balancing, which requires an inactive object. Alternatively, a single servant can be used for all objects of a kind with either one servant per type or one servant for multiple types. In this case, the servant can implement resource management mechanisms to keep only active objects in memory. A servant itself can also be activated on demand by an ORB for either the duration of a single method call or for the lifetime of the hosting server process.

13.3.2 CCM components

A CCM application is an assembly of CCM components, each of which may be custom-built or off-the-shelf, in-house or acquired. Enterprise JavaBeans (EJB; see section 14.5.2) components and CCM components can be combined in a single application. (For readers unfamiliar with EJB, it may be

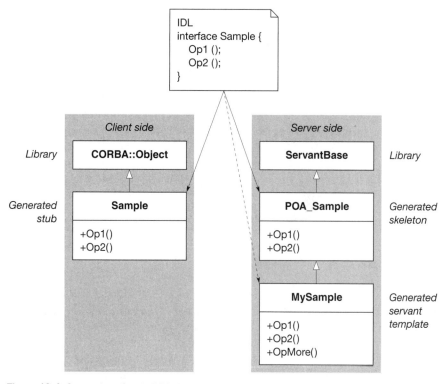

Figure 13.4 Generation of stub, POA skeleton, and servant template from given IDL specification*.

preferable to read relevant parts of Chapter 14 before proceeding.) Individual components are shipped in component packages that contain an XML document detailing their contents, which can include binaries for multiple platforms. CCM assemblies contain an XML document describing the set of component packages they refer to and the deployment configuration of these.

A CCM component itself can consist of multiple segments. CCM runtimes load applications at the granularity of segments (see Figure 13.5). As CCM requires special server-side support, CCM applications can only be executed on CORBA 3-compliant ORBs. Perhaps surprisingly, a CORBA 3 ORB is also required at the client end to achieve full CCM fidelity. CCM does support so-called component-unaware clients on pre-CORBA 3 ORBs, but such clients will not have access to several CCM features, such as navigation operations.

A CCM component is classified into one of the four categories of service, session, entity, and process components. (The session and entity categories correspond to stateful session and entity beans in EJB, respectively.) A CCM application provides declarative information on component categories and component factories. A POA uses this information to create and assign servants to component instances. Service components are instantiated per

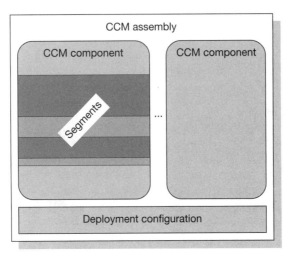

Figure 13.5 Assemblies, components, and segments in CCM.

incoming call and thus cannot maintain state across calls (they correspond to EJB stateless session beans). Instances of session components maintain state for the duration of a transactional session and allow for multiple calls within such a session. Across session boundaries, instances of session components lose their state. Instances of process components have persistent state – their lifetime corresponds to the lifetime of some process they are servicing and is as such arbitrary. Entity components finally have persistent instances that correspond to entities in some database – they can be accessed by presenting the database entity's primary key.

A CCM component is programmatically characterized by a number of features (Figure 13.6).

- Ports that are classified into facets, receptacles, event sources, and event sinks. A facet is a provided interface and a receptacle is a required interface. A component instance's receptacles are connected to other instances' facets. Event sources and sinks are similar, but instead of being connected to each other, they are both connected to event channels.
- Primary keys, which are values that instances of entity components provide to allow client identification of the instances.
- Attributes and configuration, which are named values exposed via accessors and mutators.
- Home interfaces, which provide factory functionality to create new instances.

A special facet (interface) of a CCM component is the equivalent interface, which enables navigation between the different facets of a CCM component. Each facet interface can be provided by a part object with its own reference

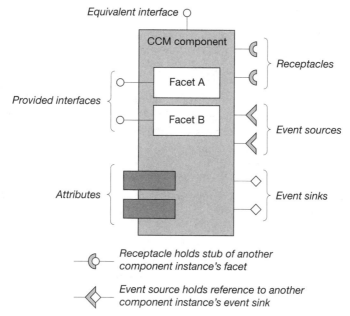

Equivalent interface

CCM component

Receptacles

Facet A

Provided interfaces

Facet B

Event sources

Attributes

Event sinks

Receptacle holds stub of another
component instance's facet

Event source holds reference to another
component instance's event sink

Figure 13.6 CCM components with their many features and two styles of explicit connections*.

that is encapsulated by the CCM component's outer instance. The support of multiple facets and navigation via a joint equivalence interface is very similar to the COM design (Chapter 15) of aggregation and navigation based on the IUnknown interface. Clients require special ORB support to be able to navigate the facets of a CCM component instance. Such component-aware clients need to run on a CORBA 3 ORB.

Receptacles provide connect and disconnect operations and internally correspond to object references to other objects of appropriate type. Connections can be made declaratively in CCM deployment configurations or made or broken dynamically at runtime.

Configuration interfaces support initial configuration of new component instances. They are described as IDL attributes with set and get operations. (CORBA 3 extends IDL to allow for exceptions being thrown by attribute setters and getters.) A special call signals completion of configuration as, before that, calls on operational interfaces are disallowed and, after that, calls on configuration interfaces are disallowed.

The home interface is provided by a component, not its instances, and supports the creation of new instances. Home interfaces also have other lifecycle-related operations for the objects they manage, such as lookup operations based on primary keys or destructor operations. A component provides at least one, but can provide multiple home interfaces.

13.3.3 CCM containers

CORBA 3 defines a component implementation framework (CIF), which includes generators that accept CIDL (component implementation description language) input and generate implementation code that completes explicitly provided component code.

In addition, every component instance is placed inside a CCM container (Figure 13.7). Components interact with POA as well as transactions, security, persistence, and notification services via interfaces on their container. A container also has receptacles that accept callbacks into the component instance.

A number of options are available for each of the four services that CCM packages. Transaction control can be container-managed or self-managed. In the container-managed case, a component configuration states if transactions are supported, required, required new, or not supported. The container will begin and end transactions to meet these requests. Similarly, persistence can be declared as container-managed or self-managed. In the container-managed case, PSDL is used to declare what needs to be persisted. For security, required access permissions can be declared on operations in CIDL and will be checked by the container.

13.4   CORBA-compliant implementations

By early 2002, several CORBAservices had not been adopted widely nor had they even been implemented seriously. Such service specifications may be retired in the near future. Also, most service implementations are bundled with ORBs and not sold as separate products, but there are exceptions. Moreover, most ORBs aren't sold as individual products either, but bundled in larger application server products, such as IBM's WebSphere, BEA's WebLogic Enterprise, IONA's Orbix E2A Application Server Platform, or Borland's Enterprise Server, all of which combine a J2EE application server with

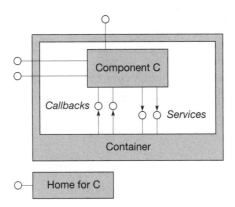

Figure 13.7 CCM containers*.

CORBA ORB and service functionality. It is noteworthy that IBM's WebSphere and BEA's WebLogic are also the premier implementations of J2EE in the market (in early 2002). IONA continues to provide several stand-alone CORBA ORB products and specializes on reaching a broad spectrum of platforms, including mainframes.

On the CORBA 3 front, activities looked slow in early 2002. However, in May 2002, the Internet Component Management Group (iCMG) announced the availability of its K2 Component Server 1.2, a server-side infrastructure based on CCM (www.icmgworld.com/corp/k2/k2.overview.asp). Inter-working with EJB was still at the level of EJB 1.1 – as was then still mandated by the CCM specification.

The following brief descriptions of some available CORBA-compliant products may help to gauge the reach of CORBA (at the time of writing). Beyond that, the descriptions are neither comprehensive nor is the list of products in any way complete.

13.4.1 BEA's WebLogic

The BEA WebLogic Platform is a family of products including a J2EE application server (WebLogic Server), an integration server (WebLogic Integration), and a web server (WebLogic Portal). A dedicated integrated development environment (WebLogic Workshop) enables creation, testing and deployment of applications and web services built using the WebLogic products. Under the umbrella WebLogic Enterprise Platform, BEA subsumes WebLogic products as well as its Tuxedo product. (Starting with version 8.0, Tuxedo includes the former WebLogic Enterprise 5.1 "T-Engine," while all Java and EJB-related technology is exclusively located in WebLogic products.)

The WebLogic Server integrates with BEA's Tuxedo transaction processing monitor via the WebLogic Tuxedo Connector at the levels of IIOP connection pooling, transactions, and security. As today's IIOP doesn't cover all requirements (especially in the area of security), WebLogic also supports BEA's proprietary T3S protocol. Tuxedo includes a CORBA 2-compliant ORB for C++ and Java, including implementations of object lifecycle, naming, notification, security, and transaction services. An interface repository is supported. Tuxedo supports C/C++ and Cobol applications based on procedural, CORBA and ATMI (application to transaction manager interface) programming models. Tuxedo also supports the CORBA specification for distributed application development. Finally, ActiveX clients can access the Tuxedo ORB via COM automation interfaces.

Tuxedo supports load balancing of objects and requests across replicated server processes and server groups. Routing of requests can be data-driven (ATMI only) or factory-based (CORBA). Multiple incoming client connections can be multiplexed. Multithreaded servers can be constructed. Tuxedo has a pluggable security framework that can be customized to integrate with external security systems. As of WebLogic Server 7.0 and Tuxedo 8.0, both products use the same pluggable security framework, easing their integration.

13.4.2 IBM's WebSphere

The WebSphere Applications Server family of products includes standard, advanced, and enterprise editions. (A number of other IBM products are also branded WebSphere, but these are less relevant here.) The standard edition is essentially a web server supporting Java servlets, Java server pages, and XML. The advanced edition adds J2EE application server capabilities by supporting EJB. The enterprise edition, finally, incorporates a CORBA 2-compliant ORB.

The WebSphere advanced edition's J2EE implementation stood out in early 2002 for its support for EJB 2.0 container-managed persistence and relationships in a way that integrates tightly with the DB2 caching system. This is important as container-managed persistence and relationships reduce an application programmer's control over performance characteristics by either manifesting too many entity instances (eager) or too few (lazy). Integrating with the database cache reduces the impact on performance.

WebSphere enterprise edition builds on IBM's ComponentBroker, an approach to packaging existing software into components and supporting simple set-up of connections between such components. In original ComponentBroker announcements, IBM stated that an "estimated 70 percent of all code written today consists of interfaces, protocols and other procedures to establish linkage among various systems." ComponentBroker supports CORBA and Java to enable connectivity. In addition, ComponentBroker provides a system-wide management facility to control aspects such as security, adequate resourcing to satisfy demands, and proximity of location to improve performance.

ComponentBroker consists of CBToolkit and CBConnector. The toolkit facilitates development of components whereas the connector enables connection and management of components. The ComponentBroker programming model is to separate business objects from client views. Business objects encapsulate functionality according to business functions. Client views are visual objects. Each business object can be presented by one or more client views to users.

The Object Builder, part of CBToolkit, generates source code skeletons for business "objects" based on OMG IDL and further specifications, targeting Java or C++. Client views can also be generated to use ActiveX interfaces and live within ActiveX containers. The CBConnector-managed object framework is provided so that new classes can inherit all standard management interfaces and functionality. Services covered by this framework are lifecycle, externalization, naming, security, event, persistence, concurrency, and transaction services. A CB-specific service, the identity service, allows objects to be uniquely identified based on references relative to managed CBConnector domains.

The CBConnector application adapter framework can be used to create components that wrap existing applications and make them available to ComponentBroker-based solutions. An integrated transaction monitor concentrates and dispatches high volumes of requests. Clients are dynamically associated with their applications, supporting distribution across resources, scalability, and high availability. The main downside of ComponentBroker is that it is difficult to use in combination with other CORBA-compliant products because of the special role played by the adapter framework.

13.4.3 IONA's Orbix E2A Application Server Platform

IONA's Orbix (in its current version, Orbix 2000) is an ORB that is available for a particularly large number of platforms. It supports C++, Smalltalk, Java, and Object COBOL bindings. Orbix is implemented as a pair of dynamic link libraries – one for the client and one for the server interface. In addition, a daemon process is used to handle activation on demand for incoming requests.

IONA's Orbix E2A application server is the result of integrating Orbix 2000 with IONA's iPortal application server supporting J2EE and development of web services. The Orbix E2A ORB is CORBA 2.4-compliant and supports C++ and Java. The application server is available in Standard, Enterprise, Mainframe, and J2EE Technology editions. Included in Orbix E2A is COMet, an Orbix implementation that runs under Windows and implements CORBA/COM interworking via local COM interfaces, including support for COM dual interfaces (Chapter 13).

ORBacus 4.1 is a CORBA 2.4-compliant ORB distributed as source code that is available in C++ and Java. ORBacus also supports some of the CORBA 2.5 features, including portable interceptors. ORBacus supports several CORBAservices, which are Names (interoperable naming service), Events, Properties, Times (time service), Trader (trading service), and Notify (OMG Telecom Domain Task Force's notification service).

Orbix/E 2.1 (previously ORBacus/E) is a lightweight ORB for embedded applications in C/C++ or Java that complies with a CORBA 2.3 subset to minimize memory needs. (Orbix/E requires 100Kb 100Kb for clients and 150Kb for servers and significantly outperforms fully compliant ORBs.) Like ORBacus, Orbix/E is distributed in source code. The C/C++ version supports the plain C language mapping. The Java version adds support for Sun's J2ME with the connected device configuration (CDC) and foundation profile classes. Orbix/E 2.1 implements a basic POA and includes embedded Naming and Event services. Fault tolerance can be achieved via multiple profiles, each object reference consisting of one or more profiles, each of which designates a different protocol and/or a different server. If a request fails, Orbix/E switches to the next profile.

13.4.4 Borland's Enterprise Server

Visibroker is Borland's ORB implementation. Visibroker was originally developed by Visigenic, which was later acquired by Borland. (Note that Borland was renamed Inprise at one stage, but later reacquired its original name.)

Visibroker initially attracted some attention when Netscape announced that it would use Visibroker for Java as the in-built ORB in its Communicator product. While this happened, the impact of supporting CORBA on web clients remains minimal.

Like Orbix/E for Java, Visibroker for Java is a CORBA 2-compliant ORB implementation written entirely in Java. Visibroker for C++ is an equally native ORB for C++ programmers. Visibroker uses IIOP for all requests – in other words, also for those between two Visibroker ORBs. An interesting feature of Visibroker is its support for multiple object replicas. Client requests are forwarded to one of the replicas to balance load and survive server crashes. CORBA for Fault Tolerance standardized a similar feature in CORBA version 2.5.

Visibroker provides an integrated transaction service (ITS) that is compliant with the CORBA transaction service, implements logging and recovery, connectivity with database and legacy systems, and administrative facilities. Furthermore, the following services are supported, not all of which are CORBAservices – security, firewall, naming, and event.

Borland offers its Enterprise Server in three tiered variants – Web Edition, VisiBroker Edition and AppServer Edition. The Web Edition does not include Visibroker and focuses on delivering web pages. The VisiBroker Edition adds automatic fail-over, the Visibroker ORB, visual administration tools, and a naming service. The AppServer edition is J2EE 1.3 certified, including full support of EJB 2.0, and adds integration with Borland's JBuilder development environment, SonicMQ (Borland's Java message service [JMS] implementation), and application partitioning.

13.4.5 Non-for-profit implementations

A number of popular CORBA implementations are free. Two are certified CORBA-compliant by the OpenGroup (MICO and OmniORB). OmniORB is a CORBA 2.3-compliant implementation provided by the former AT&T Lab in Cambridge, UK (www.uk.research.att.com/omniORB/). The open source implementation MICO (www.mico.org) is CORBA 2.2-compliant. Another open source project, ORBit (orbit-resource.sourceforge.net) is also a CORBA 2.2-compliant ORB with C and Perl bindings. Early versions of bindings are also available for C++, Lisp, Pascal, Python, Ruby, and TCL. ORBit supports POA, DII, DSI, TypeCode, Any, IR and IIOP. The core ORB is written in C. The TAO ORB (www.theaceorb.com/product/index.html) is sold in its version 1.2, but version 1.1 is available as open source.

13.5   CORBAfacilities

CORBAfacilities can be split into facilities for horizontal (general) and vertical (domain-specific) support. In both cases, a facility defines a specific component framework that can be used to integrate components. Initially, OMG attempted to standardize horizontal facilities in four areas – user interfaces, information management, system management, and task management. These efforts all folded and today the OMA category of horizontal facilities is only weakly populated. It is retained, however, as the vertical facility work is likely to yield facilities that are not really domain-specific and should thus be factored. Examples for horizontal facilities that are either standardized or under consideration include the internationalization service, mobile agents, time, and printing facilities.

Domain taskforces define vertical facilities. In early 2002, there were ten such taskforces active – business enterprise integration; command, control, computers, communications, and intelligence; finance; healthcare; life science research; manufacturing; space; telecommunications; transportation; and utilities. For more on these taskforces, see section 18.1.

13.6 Application objects

This is the top category in the OMA. Application objects serve a specific application domain. The standardization process is handled by the OMG Domain Technology Committee. For an overview of the DTC taskforces, see section 18.1.

Business objects are application objects that directly make sense to people in a specific business domain. Common examples are customer or stock objects. More interesting examples are truly domain-specific. For example, an object might represent a chemical reactor, a portfolio, or a car in a company's fleet. Although this has been an area of great interest for years, the standardization process in this space has been very slow.

Application and business objects are obviously the most long-term aspect of the OMA. They cannot be fully specified before the underlying infrastructure, with all necessary services and facilities, is in place. Several evolutionary cycles for each application object standard are realistically required to get it roughly "right." Evolution needs to be based on use experience. Evolution cannot take place before robust and practical implementations of services and facilities are available and deployed. With such conditions being met in many cases, the work of the DTC taskforces has led to a quickly growing number of standard proposals and standards since around 1999. Actual adoption varies widely (for details see section 18.1).

A radically different example is the component-oriented realtime operating system Portos and its development environment, developed by Oberon microsystems (1997) and furthered and marketed as JBed by esmertec, now as an embedded Java solution. Although rewritten to target Java, JBed still follows the overall architecture and contributions of Portos. Portos supports application objects for industrial control systems. It uses an unconventional programming model that makes the individual components and the interaction of their instances natural and intuitive for process engineers (often trained electrical or mechanical engineers rather than software engineers). See Chapter 21 for more information on Portos.

To summarize, despite several successful examples of application object models, the time is probably not yet right for general standards. For example, GTE's Michael Brodie, a long-time advocate of object technology, conceded that "distributed object computing" in general still requires highly trained staff to deliver it at all, and costs are currently likely to exceed benefits (Brodie, 1996). In more confined areas, this is changing, though. The advent of application servers that present a component model within a well-defined context (or container) model finally made object-oriented components in the enterprise arena both viable and popular. Interestingly enough, these systems do not promote a model of uniform distributed objects, but rather refined multi-tier architecture with different kinds of components and objects in different places and tiers. Such distinctions are manifest in the top-level architecture of J2EE and .NET. While the CORBA component model follows this direction, there is no comparable standard or standardization effort within the OMG for overall multitier architecture.

13.7   CORBA, UML, XML, and MDA

The unified modeling language (UML) has been adopted as an OMG standard. Firmly based in the tradition of object-oriented analysis and design, UML inherits many aspects of older modeling languages and approaches – OMT in particular. The support for component software in UML 1.1 is weak though possible by means of the careful use of conventions (Cheeseman and Daniels, 2000). Started in mid 2001, work on UML 2.0 is progressing and better support for components is among the expected improvements.

The W3C document object model (DOM) standard for accessing XML via interfaces uses OMG IDL to define those interfaces, yet it took a while for XML to play any significant role in the CORBA space itself. A first stride was made with the adoption of the XML/Value Type specification in April 2001. This specification details how CORBA value types, including objects passed by value, are mapped into XML documents.

The second area of XML influence is the component model. In CCM, XML documents are used uniformly to encode component configurations and deployment descriptors of component assemblies.

The third area is the adoption of the XML metadata interchange (XMI) standard included in CORBA 2.3. XMI defines how meta-information as captured by the metaobject facility (MOF) is mapped to XML documents. The present XMI standard has a few shortcomings that hint at its early adoption (relative to the evolving XML world), such as the fact that XMI uses DTD instead of XML Schema and does not use XML Namespaces to actually enable safe extensibility (the X in all XML-related standards). These issues could be addressed in a revision of the XMI specification, but at the cost of incompatibility with existing XMI-based solutions.

A fourth area is the common warehouse metamodel (CWM) – a specification that describes metadata interchange among systems for data warehousing, business intelligence, knowledge management and portal applications. Based on the meta-object facility (MOF, described below), CWM establishes a common basis for metamodels, enabling them to coexist in joint repositories and facilitating the integration of applications across differing models.

13.7.1 Meta-object facility

The meta-object facility organizes descriptive information in four layers, called M0 to M3. M0 is the instance layer containing regular runtime instances; M1 is the model layer that contains the model types, the instances of which can be found at M0. M2 is the metamodel layer that contains the entities of the modeling language used at M1 – the most prominent modeling language is UML, another OMG standard. Finally, M3 is the metametamodel layer that contains the MOF modeling entities used to describe the model of the modeling language at M2.

At M3, the MOF is fixed and fairly frugal. This model, called the MOF Core, is a subset of the UML core (dropping AssociationClasses, Qualifiers, and N-ary associations). Reduced to its essence, the MOF Core contains MOF::Class and MOF::Association. The few M3 entities are instantiated to create the diverse set of modeling entities found in typical modeling languages such as UML. For example, UML::Class, UML::Component, and UML::Operation all derive from MOF::Class.

The XMI specification in its present form prescribes some warped mappings as it relies on XML DTDs that cannot express subtype relations. A future version of XMI could be updated to use XML Schema (see section 12.4.1).

CCM introduces two new MOF M2 metamodels – one for OMG IDL and one for CIDL.

13.7.2 Model-driven architecture (MDA)

In an attempt to build on several OMG specifications – including UML, XMI, and CORBA – the OMG architecture board introduced a new approach called model-driven architecture (MDA) in July 2001. In September 2001, OMG members voted to make MDA the base architecture for all forthcoming OMG specifications. Essentially, this requires specifications to be written at two levels, namely platform-independent models (PIMs) and corresponding platform-specific models (PSMs) with the corresponding PIM-to-PSM mappings. The hope is that business processes and entities can be modeled at the PIM level to a degree of precision that then enables the automatic generation of large parts of implementations for a variety of platforms, driven by PIM-level models and PIM-to-PSM mappings for the target platform.

It is a declared MDA goal to "embrace CORBA, J2EE, XML, .NET and other technologies" (OMG, 2001). The extent to which such a wide-ranging promise can be met remains to be seen. It is plausible that generative approaches can span implementation-level detail differences in technologies (platforms) that otherwise adhere to mostly identical architectural principles. For instance, bridging CCM and J2EE would appear easier than bridging J2EE and .NET. While a concrete CCM implementation will likely have its peculiarities, it is the intention of the CCM specification to be a J2EE superset that gives rise to hope here. Effective bridging of divergent technologies and platforms at the level of MDA remains a largely untackled challenge. A further cautionary remark: the MDA approach requires PIM-level models to be precise, leading to a need to use a fully formalized modeling language. The UML as it stands is semiformal and efforts to underpin it with sufficiently strong formal semantics have been ongoing for years. One of the difficult tradeoffs in this space is to retain the flexibility that enables the use of UML for a wide spectrum of modeling activities while allowing precision where it is needed.

CHAPTER FOURTEEN

The Sun way – Java, JavaBeans, EJB, and Java 2 editions

Java is a true phenomenon in the industry. It is one of the very few success stories of the 1990s – a new programming language, which, together with its own view of the world, really made an impact. Sun released Java in alpha form in early 1995 and, although it was hardly known and very little used before early 1996, it is now one of the most commonly used buzzwords. It seems that the time was ripe for the message that there is more to come in the way of programming languages than was at first commonly believed. However, it was not the language that attracted attention originally. Other, and perhaps better, languages had failed before. The real attractor was the concept of applets, mini applications that function within a web page.

This chapter presents a detailed account of the Java language, the Java component models that have been formed so far (JavaBeans, Servlets, Enterprise JavaBeans in four flavors, and J2EE Application Components), and a selection of the large number of relevant Java services. In line with the arguments of component safety by construction, the safety features of Java and their interaction with the Java security mechanisms are explored in detail. The introduction to the Java language is important because much of each Java component model directly builds on the properties of the language.

14.1 Overview and history of Java component technologies

As observed above, the applet was the initial factor of attraction and breakthrough for Java. Indeed, much of early Java was designed specifically to allow an untrusted downloaded applet to execute in the same process as a client's web browser without posing an unacceptable security threat. For this purpose, language Java was designed to allow a compiler to check an applet's code for safety. The idea is that an applet that passes the compiler's checks cannot be a security threat. As the compiled code can still be tampered with, it is again checked ("verified") at load-time. The verified applet is then known to be safe and can thus be subjected to strong security policies. None of this would be possible with most of the established programming languages, including C⁺⁺ and Object Pascal. Security policies can, of course, be enforced for languages that are usually interpreted, such as Smalltalk or Visual Basic. Java, however, was designed to allow for the compilation to efficient executables at the target site. This is done by so-called just-in-time (JIT) compilers.

As an aside, it is possible to base security policies on trust in applet vendors. Authentication techniques can be used to make sure that a received applet has not been tampered with and, indeed, comes from the announced vendor. If that vendor is trusted, the applet can be loaded, even if it has come in binary form. This is largely the approach taken by Microsoft's ActiveX ("Authenticode"). An obvious disadvantage is that no one will ever trust the large number of small developers providing the web community with applets. A combination of the two approaches is best and is now also supported by Java, known as "signed applets." If a downloaded applet is signed and authenticated as coming from a trusted source, it can be given more privileges than an applet that does not pass this test. The set of trusted sources is under the user's control.

The second winning aspect of Java is the Java virtual machine (JVM). Java compilers normally compile Java into Java byte code, a format that is understood by the JVM. By implementing the JVM on all relevant platforms, Java packages compiled to byte code are platform independent. This is a major advantage when downloading applets from the internet. The true advantage is not so much the JVM but the Java class-file and JAR archive formats (see section 17.3).

None of the advantages of Java are technically new. Safe languages existed before, including efficiently compilable ones (Reiser and Wirth, 1992). Virtual machines with byte code instruction sets go back to the early times of the Pascal p-machine (Nori *et al.*, 1981) and the Smalltalk 80 virtual machine (Krasner, 1983). Even the concept of object integration into the web had been demonstrated before. The principal achievement with Java was to pull it all together and release it in a very timely fashion.

14.1.1 Java versus Java 2

While the initial Java specification suite was much under the influence of the early applet idea, the Java 2 platform (introduced in late 1998) breaks free and relegates applets to a marginal side role. Java 2 introduced the notion of platform editions, which are selections of Java specifications that together address the concern of a particular class of Java users. Figure 14.1 shows the organization of the Java 2 space; more information on the Java 2 editions can be found in the following sections.

The flagship platform edition – J2EE (Java 2 platform, enterprise edition), first released end 1999 – is the most successful. With the specification of Enterprise JavaBeans (EJBs) at its heart, J2EE is the suite of specifications underlying a large

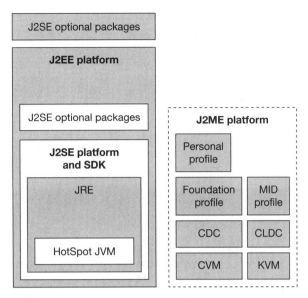

Figure 14.1 Organization of the Java 2 space.

number of application servers from a large number of different vendors. (The two largest such vendors are IBM, with its WebSphere products, and BEA, with its WebLogic products, but, by the end of 2001, there were almost 40 vendors listed on the Flashline.com comparative matrix, with prices running anywhere from free/open source to $75,000 per CPU.) The micro edition is also fairly successful, especially in the mobile phone sector. However, it is the enterprise edition that establishes a rich environment for component software, making it the most relevant with regard to the scope of this book.

Besides editions, Java 2 also formalized the notions of runtime environment (RE), software development kit (SDK), and reference implementation. Runtime environments are implementations of the JVM and the mandatory J2SE API specifications. An RE is typically paired with an SDK of a matching version that contributes development tools, including compiler and debugger. Confusingly, the 1.x numbering of the older "Java 1" specifications is continued for runtime environments and SDKs in Java 2. So, for example, a particular RE might be referred to as "Java 2 Runtime Environment, Standard Edition, v1.4."

14.1.2 Runtime environments and reference implementations

The Java runtime environment (JRE) is included in the J2SE platform, which itself is a subset of the J2EE platform. The JRE includes the runtime, core libraries, and browser plugin. Sun's reference implementation of the JRE 1.4 builds on its HotSpot runtime and HotSpot JIT compilers, which perform online re-optimization of JIT-compiled binary code. Separate HotSpot compilers are available for client and server environments, respectively. They differ in their optimization target function with differing tradeoffs for memory footprint, startup-time, throughput, and latency. The Java SDK 1.4 includes JRE 1.4, as well as the Java compiler, debugger, platform debugger architecture APIs (JPDA), and a tool to generate documentation (javadoc). Figure 14.2 outlines the structure of the J2SE platform as of v1.4.

There is no standard RE or SDK for J2EE (beyond the included J2SE and J2SE options) as J2EE is meant to be a specification to be implemented by many vendors. Instead, Sun provides a reference implementation as a proof of concept and to clarify specifications. They are available in source code at a danger of making the reference implementation's exact semantics be the standard. Sun refers to this as the reference implementation serving as an

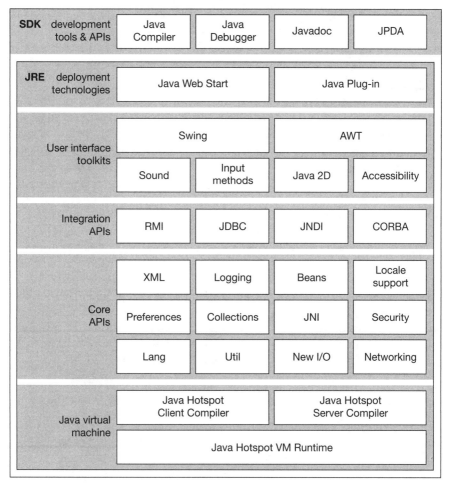

Figure 14.2 Organization of the Java 2 platform, Standard Edition v1.4. (From **java.sun.com**)

"operational specification." Reference implementations are not meant to be used as such – for example, tradeoffs are made in favor of clarity instead of performance. Instead, reference implementations ought to be used to verify that a proposed new implementation is indeed compliant.

The reference implementations are also useful to provide a complete environment for a new implementation of some Java standard. Compatibility test suites are provided to help validate implementations and these test suites themselves have been validated against the corresponding reference implementations. Java BluePrints is a collection of design guidelines and patterns that can be used to map certain classes of enterprise applications to the space of J2EE technologies.

14.1.3 Spectrum of editions – Micro, Standard, and Enterprise

Originally, Sun announced special packagings of Java to address the demands of various markets, such as Personal Java, Enterprise Java, Embedded Java, or Smartcard Java. With the arrival of the Java 2 restructuring of the overall organization of the Java specifications, this space has also been tidied up, so, as of mid 1999, Java 2 defines three packagings – the micro, standard, and enterprise editions. (The Java Smartcard space remained, catering for the particularly resource-constraint nature of these devices.) The micro edition is a family of specifications that aim at a spectrum of small and embedded devices (see Figure 14.1). At the foundation are a lightweight implementation of the full JVM (called CVM) and a trimmed-down JVM (called KVM – "K" stands for kilobyte, an indication of aiming for severely constrained devices). APIs on top of these two VMs are organized into configurations and profiles – cut-down sets of classes and interfaces appropriate for different device configurations. At the core is either the connected devices configuration (CDC) or the configuration for limited devices (CLDC). Device-specific profiles, such as the mobile information device profile (MIDP) augment the core configurations.

The standard and enterprise editions target the client-only and the multitier solution space, respectively. The standard edition is a proper subset of the enterprise edition. The micro edition does not establish any such upwards compatibility to other editions, acknowledging that most components will not usefully scale from such special small devices to more generic computing platforms. (JavaCard is addressing even smaller devices – smartcards – but it does not form a formal tier in the Java 2 classification.)

Java 2 Standard Edition

The size of J2SE has grown substantially over the first five years since its introduction in 1997. From 212 classes and interfaces in v1.0 (1997) on to 504, 1781, 2130, and now 3395 (in over 130 packages) in v1.4, released early in 2002. Included in v1.4 are 578 classes and interfaces defined by the Apache group, W3C (DOM interfaces), and by the SAX project. J2SE 1.4 comprises 2606 classes and 789 interfaces, clustered into the following packages, grouped by functional areas.

- java.lang, java.lang.ref, java.lang.reflect Basic types of Java language, foundation classes for class loading and runtime reflection, support for various special references to partially control garbage collection, and extended reflection support.
- java.applet Applet base class and support types.
- java.awt, java.awt.color, java.awt.datatransfer, java.awt.dnd, java.awt.event, java.awt.font, java.awt.geom, java.awt.im, java.awt.im.spi, java.awt.image, java.awt.image.renderable, java.awt.print AWT (Abstract Windowing Toolkit); the original Java user interface construction framework; augmented and partially superseded by Swing for user interfaces and specialized printing packages.
- java.beans, java.beans.beancontext JavaBeans base classes and support types.
- java.io, java.nio, java.nio.channels, java.nio.channels.spi, java.nio.charset, java.nio.charset.spi Character and bytestream readers and writers, files and channels. Service provider interfaces (SPIs) for channels and character sets.
- java.math Augments the basic library of math functions in class java.util.Math with implementations of big integers and decimals.
- java.net, javax.net, javax.net.ssl Networking support – sockets, HTTP, SSL.
- java.rmi, java.rmi.activation, java.rmi.dgc, java.rmi.registry, java.rmi.server, javax.rmi, javax.rmi.CORBA Remote method invocation (RMI), late-bound construction (activation), distributed garbage collection, distributed service registry, server support, and RMI over CORBA IIOP.
- java.security, java.security.acl, java.security.cert, java.security.interfaces, java.security.spec, javax.security.auth, javax.security.auth.callback, javax.security.auth.kerberos, javax.security.auth.login, javax.security.auth.spi, javax.security.auth.x500, javax.security.cert, org.ietf.jgss Security manager, access control lists (ACLs), certificates, authentication, Kerberos, login, and X500 directory.
- java.sql, javax.sql Support for SQL-based access to relational databases.
- java.text Text manipulation.
- java.util, java.util.jar, java.util.logging, java.util.prefs, java.util.regex, java.util.zip Various utilities, Java archive (JAR) file access, logging, preferences, regular expressions, and ZIP file access.
- javax.accessibility Accessibility.
- javax.crypto, javax.crypto.interfaces, javax.crypto.spec Cryptography – MD5, SHA-1, DES.
- javax.imageio, javax.imageio.event, javax.imageio.metadata, javax.imageio.plugins.jpeg, javax.imageio.spi, javax.imageio.stream Image I/O support.

- javax.naming, javax.naming.directory, javax.naming.event, javax.naming.ldap, javax.naming.spi Naming and directory access; LDAP.

- javax.print, javax.print.attribute, javax.print.attribute.standard, javax.print.event Printing support.

- javax.sound.midi, javax.sound.midi.spi, javax.sound.sampled, javax.sound.sampled.spi Sound support; MIDI, sampled sound.

- javax.swing, javax.swing.border, javax.swing.colorchooser, javax.swing.event, javax.swing.filechooser, javax.swing.plaf, javax.swing.plaf.basic, javax.swing.plaf.metal, javax.swing.plaf.multi, javax.swing.table, javax.swing.text, javax.swing.text.html, javax.swing.text.html.parser, javax.swing.text.rtf, javax.swing.tree, javax.swing.undo Swing user interface construction framework, including platform-specifc and Java-generic look-and-feel, undo/redo, HTML and RTF support.

- javax.transaction, javax.transaction.xa Transaction support; XA.

- javax.xml.parsers, javax.xml.transform, javax.xml.transform.dom, javax.xml.transform.sax, javax.xml.transform.stream, org.w3c.dom, org.xml.sax, org.xml.sax.ext, org.xml.sax.helpers XML parsing, XSLT, DOM 2, SAX.

- org.omg.CORBA, org.omg.CORBA_2_3, org.omg.CORBA_2_3.portable, org.omg.CORBA.DynAnyPackage, org.omg.CORBA.ORBPackage, org.omg.CORBA.portable, org.omg.CORBA.TypeCodePackage, org.omg.CosNaming, org.omg.CosNaming.NamingContextExtPackage, org.omg.CosNaming.NamingContextPackage, org.omg.Dynamic, org.omg.DynamicAny, org.omg.DynamicAny.DynAnyFactoryPackage, org.omg.DynamicAny.DynAnyPackage, org.omg.IOP, org.omg.IOP.CodecFactoryPackage, org.omg.IOP.CodecPackage, org.omg.Messaging, org.omg.PortableInterceptor, org.omg.PortableInterceptor.ORBInitInfoPackage, org.omg.PortableServer, org.omg.PortableServer.CurrentPackage, org.omg.PortableServer.POAManagerPackage, org.omg.PortableServer.POAPackage, org.omg.PortableServer.portable, org.omg.PortableServer.ServantLocatorPackage, org.omg.SendingContext, org.omg.stub.java.rmi Standard CORBA interfaces and ORB binding.

An interesting category of packages are so-called service provider interfaces (SPIs). These are of interest to implementers of a particular service, rather than to clients. The idea is that a Java standard framework sits between such service providers and clients and mediates. Examples are the SPIs for I/O channels, character sets, authentication, and naming.

Java 2 Enterprise Edition (J2EE)

J2EE includes all of J2SE, including optional packages. Since, in early 2002, J2EE 1.4 had not yet been released, the following numbers cover J2EE 1.3 and, thus, J2SE 1.3. In version 1.3, J2SE comprises 2606 classes and 789 interfaces. To that J2EE 1.3 adds 243 classes and 198 interfaces. J2EE also includes 279 classes and 182 interfaces based on CORBA specifications as well as 673 classes and 92 interfaces contributed by a number of Apache projects. All this adds up to a total of 3801 classes and 1261 interfaces, or a grand total of 5062 types.

Table 14.1 shows the required support of various Java standards in the J2EE versions 1.2.1 and 1.3 (Sun, 2001). Most notably, EJB 2.0 (with its substantial improvements over 1.1) is required and Connector, JAAS, and JAXP have been added to the list of requirements. JNDI and RMI-IIOP are no longer specific to J2EE as they have been reclassified as J2SE optional packages, although they are required in J2EE. As of 1.3, J2SE also includes Java IDL and JDBC Core. The JDBC 2.0 Extensions are optional in J2SE, but required in J2EE. As can be seen in the table, there is a separate evolution of individual Java specifications and the umbrella platform specifications. As long as each individual specification maintains perfect backwards compatibility that is not a major issue.

At the heart of the J2EE architecture is a family of component models. To be precise, there are three groups of component models with a total of nine variations on the component theme, which are, on the client side, application components, JavaBeans, and applets; on the web server tier, servlets and JSPs;

Table 14.1 Matrix of specification versions under two consecutive J2EE platform versions.

J2EE	1.2.1	1.3.1	Interfaces	Classes
J2SE	1.2	1.3	789	2606
EJB	1.1	**2.0**	17	11
JAF	1.0	1.0	4	13
JavaMail	1.1	1.2	12	85
JDBC	2.0 Ext.	2.0 Ext.	12	2
JMS	1.0	1.0	43	15
JNDI	1.2	(1.2)		
JSP	1.1	1.2	6	19
JTA	1.0	1.0	7	10
RMI-IIOP	1.0	(1.0)		
Servlets	2.2	2.3	20	16
Connector	–	1.0	24	13
JAAS	–	1.0	5	23
JAXP	–	1.1	39	36
			189	**243**

on the application server tier, EJB in four variations (stateless session, stateful session, entity, and message-driven beans). Using different kinds of components (rather than just different components) is a mixed blessing. On the one hand, it helps to have component models that fit well with a particular architectural area. On the other hand, it makes it harder to refactor an overall system as boundaries of component models may need to be crossed. It is also somewhat unclear how such a fine and diverse factoring of component models caters to the evolution of overall systems architecture. Will the number of J2EE component models continue to grow?

The J2EE architectural overview in Figure 14.3 separates the areas that J2EE supports using specialized component models. Figure 14.3 does not mention JavaBeans. The reason is that JavaBeans components, although pre-equipped with options to perform in the user interface space, aren't really confined to any particular tier. Instead, JavaBeans and its core technologies could be used in almost any of the spaces shown in the figure. Furthermore, note that the arrows in the figure represent characteristic cases of control flow. They are not meant to be complete. Data flow typically follows the same lines, but in both directions. A binding substrate underpinning all parts of a J2EE system is the naming and directory infrastructure accessible via JNDI (Java naming and directory interface). A second integration plane is the messaging infrastructure accessible via JMS (Java message service). Both JNDI and JMS

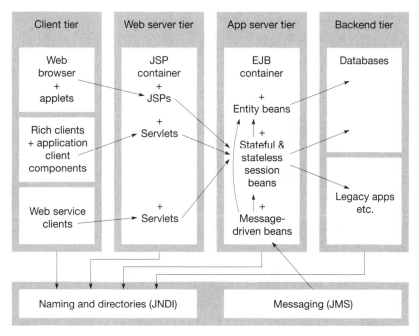

Figure 14.3 Architectural overview of J2EE.

are discussed in section 14.6.3. With the help of message-driven beans in an EJB container, messages can trigger processing on arrival. Messaging and naming/directories are two important integration layer services, but there are also others, such as transactional coordination and security services, that are not covered in Figure 14.3 for the sake of clarity. They are, however, discussed under the heading of enterprise services later.

A detailed discussion of JavaBeans follows in section 14.3. Basic services and advanced services for JavaBeans are discussed in section 14.4. Switching to the enterprise scale, section 14.5 comprises a discussion of the EJB component models. Some details of the most important enterprise services follow in section 14.6.

14.2   Java, the language

Java is an almost pure object-oriented language. It makes some admissions – not everything is an object, for example. All Java code resides in methods of classes. All state resides in attributes of classes. All classes except Object inherit interface and implementation from exactly one other class. Non-object types are the primitive types (boolean, byte, char, short, int, long, float, double) and interface types. Objects are either instances of classes or arrays. Objects can be created but not explicitly deallocated (Java uses an automatic garbage collector for safety). A class can implement any number of interfaces and interfaces can be in a multiple interface inheritance relationship.

All Java classes and interfaces belong to packages. (As of Java 1.1, a class can also be nested inside another class or even inside a method.) Packages introduce a level of encapsulation on top of that introduced by classes. The default mode for access protection allows arbitrary access across classes in the same package. Packages form a hierarchy, but only the package immediately enclosing a class or an interface affects encapsulation and protection. Outer packages merely serve to manage namespaces. All naming in Java is relative to the package name paths formed by appending the names of inner packages to those of outer packages. It is recommended that a globally unique name be used for a top-level package, a typical candidate being a registered company name.

A fully qualified name of a feature of a class takes the form package. Type.feature. Here, package is the path name of the package, Type is the name of the class or interface, and feature is the name of the method or attribute referred to. If internet domain names are used, a package name can take a form such as org.omg.CORBA. Although originally recommended, it is now commonplace to use company-name.productname prefixes for packages, relying on the stability and uniqueness of company instead of domain names. To use another package, the using package can always use fully qualified names to refer to the other package. However, such names can become quite lengthy. By explicitly importing some or all the types of the other package, these type names become directly available in the importing package – Type.feature then

suffices. The unfortunate use of the period to separate all package name parti-
cles, top-level type names, nested type names, and features makes the Java
notation a.b.c subtle to parse and possibly difficult to understand to the
human reader. (C# shares this unfortunate design.)

Figure 14.4 shows the graphical notation used here for Java packages, interfaces, classes, attributes, and methods. The notation follows UML static
structure diagrams with a non-standard extension for final classes, which are
those that cannot be further extended – that is, they cannot be inherited from.
In addition, and not shown in the notational overview, Java methods can be
final (not overridable) or static (class instead of instance methods). Attributes
can also be final (immutable after initialization) or static (class instead of
instance attributes). Interfaces extend any number of other interfaces. Classes
extend exactly one other class, except for class java.lang.Object, which has no
base class. Classes can also implement any number of interfaces.

Figure 14.5 uses the concrete example of (part of) the java.awt.image package
and its relation to the java.lang package. Note that java.awt.image is a subpackage
of java.awt. As stated before, there is no special relationship between a package
and a subpackage that goes beyond the structure added to the namespace. In particular, both java.awt and java.awt.image contain interfaces and classes.

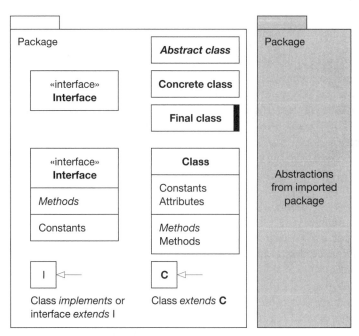

Figure 14.4 Java structuring constructs – names of abstract classes and abstract methods are
set in italics.

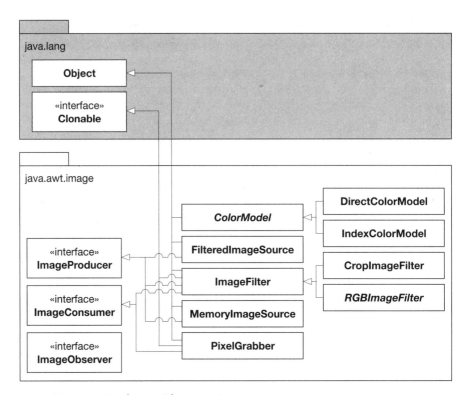

Figure 14.5 Part of the java.awt.image package.

The line between the Java language and some of the fundamental class libraries is not easy to draw. In particular, there are three packages required by the Java language specification (Gosling *et al.*, 1996) – java.lang, java.util, and java.io. The package java.lang is even deeply intertwined with the language specification itself. Many classes and interfaces in this package receive special treatment by the language rules. It would be fair to say that the otherwise modestly sized language Java really includes the definition of java.lang. Unfortunately, in JDK 1.4, java.lang alone defines 82 classes and interfaces, all of which are available in any Java package automatically.

The interweaving of language and standard package constructs is worse than it seems. Not only are all interfaces and classes of package java.lang automatically injected into any other package, but also the language itself builds on some java.lang classes. In particular, these are the classes Object, String, and Throwable, which are entangled with the null reference, the array type constructors, the string literals, and the throw statement respectively. Under the transitive closure over the types used in the signatures of Object, String, and Throwable, the list expands to include classes Class, ClassLoader, and several subclasses of Throwable.

Because Java supports arbitrary and possibly circular dependencies across packages, java.lang can and does have dependencies on other packages. This has been the case since the first release and has worsened in all following releases. The class Throwable relies on types java.io.PrintStream and java.io. PrintWriter, in a debugging method called printStackTrace. This method indirectly causes the classes PrintStream, PrintWriter, FilteredOutputStream, Writer, OutputStream, and IOException from package java.io to be pulled into the language itself. More such dependencies were woven into later versions. So, for example, in J2SE 1.4, java.lang.ClassLoader depends on java.security. ProtectionDomain, java.lang.Process depends on java.io.InputStream, and java.lang.SecurityManager depends on java.net.InetAddress, java.io.FileDescriptor. These pull in many other definitions. In JDK 1.4, the transitive closure of all classes and types directly reachable from the Java language specification contains 146 classes and interfaces!

Java defines two access levels for top-level interfaces and classes – default (package-wide) and public. In the former case, the interface or class is accessible only within its defining package, not even within sub- or superpackages, but in the latter case it is accessible everywhere. The default limitation to intra-package accessibility is not enforceable by the language implementation – anyone can drop a new definition into an existing package. The definition and enforcement of access rights for entire packages is left to the environment. Access rights can be further controlled on the level of class features – that is, nested types, methods and fields. Java defines four levels of static access protection for features of a class, which are private, default (package-wide), protected, and public. Private features are accessible only within their defining class. Default accessibility includes all classes within the same package. Protected features can, in addition, be accessed within all subclasses of the defining class. Finally, public features are globally accessible, provided the defining class is. (Environment-enforced access constraints may exclude access even if the respective definition is declared public.)

Fields can be final, effectively making them constants once initialized. Final methods cannot be overridden. Static features belong to the class rather than to instances of the class. Interface fields are implicitly public, static, and final, making them global constants. Interface methods are implicitly public and abstract. With these restrictions enforced, Java interfaces introduce neither state nor behavior – they are pure types.

14.2.1 Interfaces versus classes

Probably the most innovative aspect of Java is its separation of interfaces and classes in a way that permits single implementation inheritance combined with multiple interface inheritance. This separation eliminates the diamond inheritance problem (p. 111) while preserving the important possibility of a class being compatible with multiple independent interfaces. The diamond inheritance problem is eliminated because interfaces introduce neither state nor behavior. Thus, there can be no conflicts beyond name clashes in a class that implements multiple interfaces.

Java offers no complete solution to the name conflict problem. If two interfaces introduce methods of the same name and signature but of different return type, then no class can simultaneously implement both interfaces. Clashes of method names among independently defined interfaces are difficult to avoid entirely, but don't seem to pose a significant problem in practice. One reason is that many method names contain the interface name – generally an unfortunate choice. A different scenario, however, literally forces such name clashes. If an interface is versioned, it is likely that the old and new version will share some method names. As pointed out in section 5.1.2, it is essential that components support sliding windows of versions – that is, that they support the interfaces of multiple version generations. In Java, doing so requires us to change the name of an interface for a new version *and* change the name of all methods logically retained in the new version. This requirement is cumbersome enough that it is not part of best practice. Java classes are thus not normally able to simultaneously support multiple versions of their contracts.

Leaving this quite fundamental problem of Java aside, there are other potential pitfalls for designers using a mix of single class and multiple interface inheritance. These are not limited to Java and equally apply to other languages following a similar design paradigm, such as C#. Consider the following example involving both classes and interfaces. The standard package java.util defines the class Observable and the interface Observer, as shown below.

```
package java.util;
public class Observable extends Object {
    public void addObserver (Observer o);
    public void deleteObserver (Observer o);
    public void deleteObservers;
    public int countObservers ();
    public void notifyObservers ();
    public void notifyObservers (Object arg);
    protected void setChanged ();
    protected void clearChanged ();
    public boolean hasChanged ();
}

public interface Observer {
    void update (Observable o, Object arg);
}
```

The idea is that observable objects are instances of classes that extend (inherit from) Observable. Class Observable maintains a list of observers and a flag indicating whether or not the observable object has changed. Observers have to implement interface Observer. All registered observers will be called when the observable object calls notifyObservers. Figure 14.6 shows a simple class diagram using Observable and Observer to implement a straightforward model view scheme. (The asterisk at the end of the line, from Observable to Observer, is the UML notation showing that one Observable instance can be associated with many observers.)

Observable and Observer aim to support the observer design pattern (Gamma *et al.*, 1995). This pattern is most prominently used in conjunction with model view separations in user interfaces (see Chapter 9). The Observer interface certainly demonstrates a good use of interfaces in Java. However, the Observable class has a design flaw. (Observer and Observable are not used in any of the standard Java packages, although the definitions have never been deprecated. They were superseded by the event and event-listener concepts introduced with the JavaBeans specification described in section 14.3; Sun, 1996.)

The problem is that Observable is a class and not an interface. This forces restructuring of a class hierarchy in cases where a class already depends on a superclass that is different from Object and where instances of this class now should become observable. Why was this done? Observable as it stands does too much. It contains a concrete implementation of the list of observers and the notification broadcast. It also implements an "object has changed" flag. (This flag itself has a few design problems. For instance, at least up to v1.4, the specification states that it is cleared after notifying observers, so re-entrant changes are not notified and no exception is thrown either. In reality, since v1.2, the implementation clears this flag before notifying observers. Another problem is that Observable isn't synchronizing. Concurrent threads may enter race conditions that can lead to inconsistent handling of notifications.)

A simple solution is not to use the Observer/Observable approach. However, to study some further aspects of Java, assume that the interface Observable should be used, but that the observable object already extends some other class. Class Observable cannot therefore be used directly. The astute reader will notice that, again, using object composition can save the situation. To do so, a trivial subclass of Observable needs to be implemented:

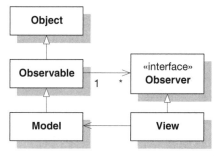

Figure 14.6 Model view construction using Observable and Observer.

```
package fix.it;
public class ObserverRegistry extends java.util.Observable {
  public readonly Object observable;   // reference to actual observable object
  public ObserverRegistry (Object observable) {   // constructor
    this.observable = observable;
  }
  public void setChanged() {
    super.setChanged()
  }
  public void clearChanged() {
    super.clearChanged()
  }
}
```

This trivial subclass removes the protected access mode from methods setChanged and clearChanged. Instances of ObserverRegistry can now be used as part objects of observable objects. Because observers get a reference to an Observable, ObserverRegistry's read-only field observable provides a reference to the object that has actually changed. The registry's constructor sets this reference. For example:

```
package fixed.it;
import fix.it.*;
public class StringBufferModel extends StringBuffer {
  private ObserverRegistry obReg = new ObserverRegistry(this);
  public ObserverRegistry getObserverRegistry () {
    return obReg;
  }
  public void setLength (int newLength)
      throws IndexOutOfBoundsException
  {
    super.setLength(newLength);
    obReg.setChanged();
    obReg.notifyObservers();   // could tell them what has changed ...
  }
  // other StringBuffer methods
}
```

Class StringBufferModel extends the standard class java.lang.StringBuffer, a helper class to support composition of strings. As a string buffer is a mutable object, it is a good candidate for a model-view scenario. For example, a text entry field could be implemented as a view on a string buffer. Unfortunately, StringBufferModel cannot extend Observable directly, as it already extends StringBuffer. StringBuffer was not designed to serve as the superclass of something observable and so extends Object instead of Observable. StringBufferModel solves this by using an ObserverRegistry object instead. Below is the sketch of an observer object displaying a StringBufferModel object's contents.

```
package fixed.it;
import java.util.*;
public class StringBufferView implements Observer {
  private StringBufferModel buf;
  public StringBufferView (StringBufferModel b) {
    buf = b;
    b.getObserverRegistry().addObserver(this);
  }
  public void update (Observable o, Object arg) {
    ObserverRegistry reg = (ObserverRegistry)o;   // checked cast
    Object observable = reg.getTrueObservable();
    if (observable != buf) throw new IllegalArgumentException();
      ... // get changes from buf and update display
  }
}
```

This concludes the example on how to use interfaces and object composition in Java. The example showed only classes implementing a single interface, but the extension to multiple interfaces is straightforward. Where unresolvable naming conflicts occur, a Java compiler rejects a class trying to implement conflicting interfaces. In all other cases there is no interference whatsoever between multiple implemented interfaces. One question remains to be answered, though. How can a client having a reference of a certain interface or class type find out what other interfaces or classes the referenced object supports? The answer is two-fold. Java provides a type-test operator – instanceof – that can be used to query at runtime. Java also has checked type casts that can be used to cast the reference to another class or interface. Here is an example:

```
interface Blue { ... }
interface Green { ... }
class FunThing implements Blue, Green { ... }
```

A client holding a Blue reference can test whether or not the object also supports a Green interface, although Blue and Green themselves are totally independent types:

```
Blue thing = new FunThing ();
Green part = null;
if (thing instanceof Green)   // type test
  part = (Green) thing;   // checked type cast, from Blue to Green
```

It is not possible to statically state that a variable refers to an object implementing both Blue and Green without introducing a common subtype of these two interfaces. The late introduction of such a common subtype for this purpose (say, Cyan extends Blue, Green) does not solve the problem. For instance, class FunThing above should qualify (it implements both Blue and Green), but doesn't as it does not implement the artificially introduced common subtype

Cyan. What is needed is a notion of requiring structural compatibility with a set of interfaces. Büchi and Weck (1998) call such interface sets compound types and identify non-support of compound types as a common problem in all contemporary mainstream languages.

14.2.2 Exceptions and exception handling

The Observer/Observable example above introduced another feature of Java – exception handling. Exceptions and runtime errors are reflected in Java as exception or error objects. These are either explicitly thrown, such as the throw statement in StringBufferView, or thrown by the runtime system, such as on out-of-bounds indexing into an array. All exception and error objects are instances of classes that are derived from class Throwable. A catch branch of a try statement can catch such throwable objects. For example, the notifyObservers method in class Observable could be protected against exceptions raised by notified observers:

```
public void notifyObservers () {
   for (Observer ob = first(), ob != null, ob = next()) {
      try {
         ob.update(this, null);   // observer may throw an exception
      }
      catch (Exception ex) {
         // ignore exception and continue with next observer
      }
   }
}
```

In the example, it is not apparent just by looking at the declaration of method update that it might throw an exception. Exception types for which this is legal are called unchecked exceptions. Java also has exception types that can only be thrown by a method's implementation, if the method declaration announced this possibility. Such declared exceptions are called checked exceptions. For example:

```
class AttemptFailed extends Exception { }
class Probe {
   public void goForIt (int x) throws AttemptFailed {
      if (x != 42) throw new AttemptFailed();
   }
}
class Agent {
   public void trustMe (Probe p) {
      p.goForIt(6 * 7);   // compile-time error!
   }
}
```

Class Agent cannot be compiled. Method trustMe neither declares that it may throw the user-defined exception AttemptFailed nor catches this exception should it be thrown. Note that this check based on static annotations adds a degree of robustness to software. In the example, Agent happens to "know" what Probe needs to avoid failure. Hence, Probe will actually never throw an exception when called from within trustMe. However, a future version of Probe may do so. After all, this possibility has even been declared and is thus part of the contract between Probe and Agent.

14.2.3 Threads and synchronization

Java defines a model of concurrency and synchronization and is thus a concurrent object-oriented language. The unit of concurrency is a thread. Threads are orthogonal to objects, which are therefore passive. Threads can only communicate through side-effects or synchronization. A thread executes statements and moves from object to object as it executes method invocations. Threads can be dynamically created, pre-empted, suspended, resumed, and terminated. Each thread belongs to a thread group specified at thread creation time. Threads belonging to separate thread groups can be mutually protected against thread state modifications. Threads can be assigned one of ten priority levels and can be in either user or demon mode. A thread group may impose limits on the maximum priority of its threads. However, priorities are hints only – some virtual machines ignore them while others differ in their interpretation. Thread termination is not automatically propagated to child threads. A Java application terminates when the last user thread has terminated, irrespective of the state of demon threads. Figure 14.7 shows the states in which a thread can exist and the possible state transitions. The states and transitions are explained below.

Java's threads are lightweight as, on any given virtual machine, they all execute in the same address space. A JVM is free to schedule processing resources by pre-empting executing threads at any time, but JVMs don't have to implement time-slicing. (If progress depends on scheduling, a thread should call Thread.yield – see below.) As threads may be pre-empted, this raises the question of how concurrent access is regulated. The language specification requires atomic ordering of access operations on values of primitive types and reference types. (As a concession to efficient implementation on contemporary 32-bit architectures, there are no such requirements for Java's 64-bit types long and double. However, long and double variables can be declared volatile to prevent interleaved access.) For consistent access to larger units, such as multiple fields of an object or multiple objects, explicit synchronization is required.

Java supports thread synchronization either on entrance to a synchronized method or at a synchronized statement. Synchronization forces a thread to acquire a lock on an object before proceeding. There is exactly one lock associated with each object. If the thread in question already holds a lock on that object, it can continue. (This is an important rule avoiding deadlocks in a

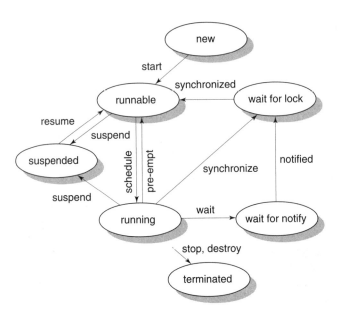

Figure 14.7 States and state transitions of Java threads.

common situation – a thread re-entering an object. Cardelli introduced this approach to avoid what he called self-inflicted deadlocks, 1994.) Synchronized methods use the lock of the object to which they belong. Below is an example of a wrapper for the unsynchronized stacks provided by the standard library class java.util.Stack:

```
class SynchStack {
    private java.util.Stack stack = new java.util.Stack();
    public synchronized void push (Object item) {
        stack.push(item);
    }
    public synchronized Object pop () {
        return(stack.pop());
    }
    public synchronized boolean empty () {
        return(stack.empty());
    }
}
```

The synchronized statement takes the object to be locked as an argument:

```
...  // thread may or may not already hold a lock on obj
synchronized (obj) {
    ...  // thread now holds lock on obj
}    // lock released, unless it was already held by current thread
```

Without any further measures, a thread waiting for an event would have to poll variables. To avoid inefficiencies, Java allows threads to wait on any object, either indefinitely or up to some specified timeout. For this reason, class Object defines methods wait, notify, and notifyAll. These methods can only be called by a thread that holds a lock on that object. While waiting, the lock is released. On notification, a thread first reacquires the lock before proceeding – by doing so it has to compete with all other threads trying to acquire the lock. Normally, the lock is still held by the notifying thread. Once the lock becomes available, any one of the threads trying to acquire the lock will be chosen. If multiple threads have been notified (or even all that have been waiting by using notifyAll) or if other threads attempt to acquire the same lock, then they will compete for the lock and acquire it, in any order, as soon as the previous owner of the lock releases it.

There is, however, a significant and dangerous subtlety attached to the use of objects as synchronization signals. If an object used for synchronization is accessible to threads from multiple subsystems, then it is unlikely that these threads agree on the semantics of wait/notify on that object. As a result, the same object may end up being used accidentally as a synchronization object by two subsystems. This is especially likely when using a global object. For instance, a widespread pattern uses the meta-object attached to some type for purposes of locking and synchronization. Another danger is that an object is used for conflicting locking and synchronization purposes at base class and derived class levels. To avoid these problems, it is recommended to predominantly use objects that aren't widely accessible for synchronization.

A thread is associated with an owning object at thread creation time. It is through this object that a thread can be suspended, resumed, or terminated. The owning object can also be used to move a thread between user and demon status before the thread is first started. Objects that own a thread are instances (of a subclass) of class java.lang.Thread. Below is an excerpt:

```java
public class Thread implements Runnable {
    public static Thread currentThread ();
    public static void yield ();
    public static void sleep(long millis) throws InterruptedException;
    public Thread ();                          // default constructor; use method run
    public Thread (Runnable runObject);        // use method run of runObject
    public void run ();
    public void start ();
    public void stop ();                       // deprecated
    public void suspend ();                    // deprecated
    public void resume ();                     // deprecated
    public void interrupt ();
    public static boolean interrupted ();
```

```
public boolean isInterrupted ();
public void setPriority (int newPriority);
public void setDaemon (boolean on);
public final boolean isDaemon ();
public void destroy ();              // unsafe, not implemented
public final void checkAccess ();    // check caller permissions
// other methods deleted ...
}
```

A thread object can itself define the outermost method to be executed by the new thread – method run in class Thread. Alternatively, the thread object is constructed with a reference to an object that implements interface Runnable. In the latter case, thread execution starts by calling the run method of that other object. Either way, the thread terminates if the outermost method returns. A thread also terminates when its outermost method throws an exception.

The definition of class Thread also contains means to control a thread. Static methods are provided for a thread to affect itself by yielding the processor or by sleeping for some set time. Threads that are waiting for a lock or sleeping can be interrupted by another thread, which causes an InterruptedException to be thrown. If a thread is interrupted while not waiting or sleeping, its interrupted flag is set, which can be polled by calling isInterrupted or polled-and-cleared by calling interrupted.

A thread can be terminated by calling its owning object's stop or destroy methods. (Method stop sends a ThreadDeath exception to the thread, whereas destroy terminates the thread immediately and with no clean-up. Objects locked by a destroyed thread remain locked. This is the last resort in case a thread catches ThreadDeath and thereby refuses to terminate.) However, all these methods have been deprecated with v1.2, and one of them has actually never been implemented (destroy). The reason for this deprecation is that these methods are unsafe. Suspending a thread can lead to unavoidable deadlocks if the suspended thread holds a lock that the suspending thread needs to acquire. Stopping a thread causes that thread to release all its locks, potentially leaving the previously locked objects in an inconsistent state. Destroying a thread would leave arbitrary locked objects locked for good.

As of 1.2, the recommendation is to use polling of variables to signal suspension or termination requests. Long-running threads should poll such a variable periodically and, if set, gracefully return to a consistent state and release locks. This is a form of cooperative multitasking that requires the programmer to have substantial insight at a global level.

14.2.4 Garbage collection

Java provides a number of mechanisms to allow programs to interact with the JVM's garbage collector. The first such mechanism is object finalization. It is used by overriding protected method Object.finalize. This method is called by the collector at some time after an object has been found to be unreachable, but before its memory is actually reclaimed. Unless it is known with certainty that the superclass doesn't have a non-empty finalizer (versioning fragility!), a finalize method should always call the super-finalize method. Unlike object constructors, this chaining is not enforced by the Java language.

The implementation of a finalize method can reach objects that are otherwise unreachable (including its own object!), but it may also reach objects that are still reachable. By assigning a reference from one of the previously unreachable objects to a field of one of the still reachable objects, a previously unreachable object can be "resurrected." That is, after the call to the finalize method, some previously unreachable objects may again be reachable. To prevent endless finalization efforts, the Java garbage collector will call the finalize method of an object exactly once before reclaiming its storage. (The "exactly once" semantics is only guaranteed if an object does become unreachable and if the JVM doesn't fail catastrophically.)

The best finalization strategy is thus to avoid resurrection and to only use finalizers to release external resources. For instance, if an object holds some platform handle to, say, an open database connection, then a finalizer can be used to ensure that the connection is closed eventually. However, note that this guarantee is still fairly weak as there is no guarantee how long it will take before the JVM detects unreachability and before it calls a finalizer. A garbage-collection pass can be "encouraged" by calling System.gc. A best-effort finalization pass can be requested by calling System.runFinalization(). If used with care at strategic points, this can help ensure swift release of critical resources. However, forcing finalization effectively forces partial garbage collection (to detect unreachability) and can thus be expensive. The negative impact on overall performance can be dramatic.

The finalize methods are called on an unspecified thread that is merely guaranteed to not hold any client-visible locks. The specification even allows for multiple concurrent threads to cause concurrent finalization. (In early JVM implementations this led to a subtle security hole, which was that if the thread used was a system thread with high privileges, then the finalize method ran with these privileges and could thus undermine security policies.)

For objects holding internal resources – that is, resources modeled using Java objects – there is no need to implement a finalizer as such internal resources are themselves subject to garbage collection, and finalization if required. The vast majority of Java classes do not require a finalizer.

A second mechanism that helps to steer the garbage collector are special references introduced in SDK 1.2. There are three kinds – soft, weak, and phantom references. Note that standard Java language-level references are now also called strong references. An object is strongly reachable if a sequence of strong references from a root variable leads to that object. It is softly reachable if a sequence of strong and soft references leads to that object. A need to go through at least one weak reference to reach an object makes it weakly reachable.

Finally, if at least one phantom reference is on every path to an object, then that object is phantom reachable.

A soft reference is an instance of class java.lang.ref.SoftReference or its subclasses. A soft reference holds an encapsulated reference to some other object, its referent. If the JVM is under memory pressure, it is free to clear soft references, provided their referents are no longer strongly reachable (reachable via normal Java references only). Although not required, the specification encourages JVM implementations to choose least recently used soft references first. The specification requires a JVM to clear all soft references before throwing an out-of-memory exception. Once cleared, a soft reference will return null when asked for its referent. It is also possible to register reference objects with reference queues. The garbage collector enqueues registered reference objects when clearing their referent. It is usually more efficient to poll or block on a reference queue than to periodically poll all soft references to determine which ones have been cleared. Soft references are useful to implement object caches.

If an object is only reachable via soft or weak references and its soft references have been cleared, then it can be finalized. A weak reference does not ask for holding a referent unless there is a memory shortage – if a weakly referenced object can be collected, then its weak references are cleared and it is readied for finalization. Reference queues work for weak references as well. As a last straw, phantom references can be used to keep the last trace of a finalized but not yet reclaimed object. Phantom references never return their referent (to prevent resurrection), but can be used as unique "names" of their referents in canonicalization algorithms. Reference queues are the only means to extract useful information from phantom references. They are primarily useful to perform a post-finalization cleanup of name tables used for canonicalization. For instance, if a particular object should only be created if no other object has already been created in a certain place, then a phantom reference is a cheap way to account for this condition without keeping any objects unnecessarily alive. However, a memory leak can occur if phantom references, once enqueued, aren't cleared.

It should be clear by now that the garbage-collection steering mechanisms discussed in this section are highly problematical. Slight misuse can lead to significant performance degradation or program misbehavior, although memory safety is always preserved. Luckily, the majority of classes can be written without ever touching on any of these mechanisms.

14.3 JavaBeans

Initially, Java targeted two kinds of products – applets and applications. The composition models are rudimentary, however. Applets can be composed by placing them on the same web page and then, within one applet instance, using class AppletContext to find another applet instance by name. While different applets can be used to fill such named positions, there is no way to determine statically what type such applets must have. There is also no standardized way to "rewire" applets on a page. In the case of plain Java applications, Java provided even less: Composition there depended entirely on facilities of the operating system. Beyond simplistic cases, applets are not suitable as separately sold components.

JavaBeans fills some of this gap and makes a new kind of product possible – Java components, called "beans" (Sun, 1996). It is unfortunate that the clear distinction between class and object in Java is not carried through in JavaBeans. Although a bean really is a component (a set of classes and resources), its customized and connected instances are also called beans. This is confusing. Thus, in the following, bean refers to the component and bean instance to the component object. "Bean object" would be too confusing, because a bean usually consists of many Java objects.

A bean can be used to implement controls, similar to OLE or ActiveX controls. JavaBeans provides a protocol to handle containment (see section 14.4.5). In addition, JavaBeans has been designed to also enable the integration of a bean into container environments defined outside Java. For example, there is an ActiveX bridge available from Sun that allows a bean instance to function as a control in an ActiveX container.

Beans have been designed with a dual usage model in mind. Bean instances are first assembled by an assembly tool, such as an application builder, at "design-time," and are then used at "runtime." A bean instance can customize appearance and functionality dynamically by checking whether or not it is design-time or runtime. One of the ideas is that it should be possible to strip the design-time code from a bean when shipping an assembled application. A bean instance can also enquire, at "runtime," whether or not it is used interactively, that is, whether or not a graphical user interface is available. Thus, a bean instance can behave differently when being run on a server or as part of a batch job, rather than interactively.

The main aspects of the bean model are the following.

- *Events* Beans can announce that their instances are potential sources or listeners of specific types of events. An assembly tool can then connect listeners to sources.
- *Properties* Beans expose a set of instance properties by means of pairs of getter and setter methods. Properties can be used for customization or programmatically. Property changes can trigger events and properties can be constrained. A constrained property can only be changed if the change is not vetoed.
- *Introspection* An assembly tool can inspect a bean to find out about the properties, events, and methods that a particular bean supports.
- *Customization* Using the assembly tool, a bean instance can be customized by setting its properties.
- *Persistence* Customized and connected bean instances need to be saved for reloading at the time of application use.

14.3.1 Events and connections

Events in the JDK 1.1 terminology – and as used in JavaBeans – are objects created by an event source and propagated to all currently registered event listeners. Thus, event-based communication generally has multicast semantics. However, it is possible to flag an event source as requiring unicast semantics – such a source accepts at most one listener at any one time. Event-based communication is similar to the COM Connectable Objects approach and also can be seen as a generalization of the Observer pattern (Chapter 9).

An event object should not have public fields and should usually be considered immutable. Mutation of event objects in the presence of multicast semantics is subtle. However, where mutation of an event object during propagation is required, these changes should be encapsulated by methods of the event object. The JavaBeans specification gives coordinate transformations as an example, so a mouse-click event may need to be transformed into local coordinates to make sense to a listener.

Listeners need to implement an interface that extends the empty "marker" interface java.beans.EventListener and that has a receiving method for each event the listener listens to. (Marker interfaces are also known as tagging interfaces. They are themselves empty and serve as a mark [or tag] on the type that extends or implements them. This is a form of simple binary meta-attribution. In the case of event listeners, the marker is used to find listeners via introspection.) For example:

```
interface UserSleepsListener extends java.util.EventListener {
    void userSleeps (UserSleepsEvent e);
}
```

A listener can implement a given event listener interface only once. If it is registered with multiple event sources that can all fire the same event, the listener has to determine where an event came from before handling it. This can be simplified by interposing an event adapter. An event adapter implements a listener interface and holds references to listeners. Thus, an event adapter is both an event listener and an event source. A separate adapter can be registered with each of the event sources. Each adapter then calls a different method of the listener. Thus, event adapters can be used to demultiplex events. In principle, event adapters can perform arbitrary event-filtering functions. Note that, in the absence of method types and method variables, event adapters lead either to an explosion of classes or to slow and unnatural generic solutions based on the reflection service. Such generic demultiplexing adapters were indeed proposed in the JavaBeans specification (Sun, 1996, pp. 35–37). Since Java 1.1, this problem has been reduced by supporting in-line construction of lightweight adapter classes – so-called anonymous inner classes, somewhat similar to Smalltalk blocks. A more modern approach uses nested classes to implement the required functionality directly rather than forwarding calls, which minimizes code redundancy.

An event source needs to provide pairs of listener register and unregister methods:

```
public void addUserSleepsListener (UserSleepsListener l);
public void removeUserSleepsListener (UserSleepsListener l);
```

If a source requires unicast semantics, it can throw a TooManyListenersException:

```
public void addUserSleepsListener (UserSleepsListener l)
    throws java.util.TooManyListenersException;
```

Event propagation in a multicast environment introduces a number of subtle problems (see the discussion of callbacks and re-entrance in Chapter 5). The set of listeners can change while an event is propagated. JavaBeans does not specify how this is addressed, but a typical way is to copy the collection of registered listeners before starting a multicast. Also, exceptions may occur while the multicast is in progress. Again, JavaBeans does not specify whether or not the multicast should still continue to address the remaining listeners. Finally, a listener may itself issue an event broadcast on reception of an event. This raises the difficult problem of relative event ordering; JavaBeans does not specify any constraints on the ordering of event delivery (see section 10.6 for a detailed discussion of the ordering issues of event-based programming).

Event ordering issues are aggravated in multithreaded environments such as Java. For example, an event source may hold locks that are required by event listeners to process events. The result would be a deadlock if the event listener uses a separate thread to acquire such locks. Indeed, the authors of the JavaBeans specification (Sun, 1996, p. 31):

> "strongly recommend that event sources should avoid holding their own internal locks when they call event listener methods."

This is clearly subtle. For one, problems only arise if the event listener uses additional threads besides the one carrying the event notification, because the notifying thread continues to hold all the locks held by the event source, which would prevent deadlocks. Also, it is not even clear if this recipe can be followed generally without breaking encapsulation. It may not be at all easy to determine whether and which locks the event source already holds. More precise advice continues:

> "Specifically, [...] they should avoid using a synchronized method to fire an event and should instead merely use a synchronized block to locate the target listeners and then call the event listeners from unsynchronized code."

As indicated above, "to locate the target listeners" is best interpreted as performing a synchronized copy of the collection holding references to the target listeners. Otherwise, if listeners were added or removed during an ongoing notification, then standard Java collections would throw a ConcurrentModificationException, following the "fail fast" pattern. Although this specific advice clearly needs to be followed, it is not sufficient to avoid subtle deadlocks that result from a combination of multithreading and event-based communication. More effective advice is to not use event-based models in combination with multiple threads. (For a discussion of Java threading in general, see section 14.2.3.)

14.3.2 Properties

A bean can define a number of properties of arbitrary types. A property is a discrete named attribute that can affect a bean instance's appearance or behavior. Properties may be used by scripting environments, can be accessed programmatically by calling getter and setter methods, or can be accessed using property sheets at assembly time or runtime. Typical properties are persistent attributes of a bean instance. Property changes at assembly time are used to customize a bean instance. A property change at runtime may be part of the interaction with the user, another bean instance, or the environment.

Access to properties is via a pair of methods. For example, the setter and getter methods for a property "background color" might take the following form:

```
public java.awt.Color getBackground ();
public void setBackground (java.awt.Color color);
```

To optimize the common case where an array of property values needs to be maintained, indexed properties are also supported. The corresponding setter and getter methods simply take an index or an entire array of values:

```
public java.awt.Color getSpectrum (int index);
public java.awt.Color[] getSpectrum ();
public void setSpectrum (int index, java.awt.Color color);
public void setSpectrum (java.awt.Color[] colors);
```

A property can be bound. Changes to a bound property trigger the firing of a property change event. Registered listeners will receive an event object of type java.beans.PropertyChangeEvent that encapsulates the locale-independent name of the property and its old and new value:

```
public class PropertyChangeEvent extends java.util.EventObject {
    public Object getNewValue ();
    public Object getOldValue ();
    public String getPropertyName ();
}
```

The methods required to register and unregister property change listeners are:

```
public void addPropertyChangeListener (PropertyChangeListener x);
public void removePropertyChangeListener (PropertyChangeListener x);
```

The interface java.beans.PropertyChangeListener introduces the method to be called on property changes:

> void **propertyChange** (PropertyChangeEvent evt);

A property can also be constrained. For a constrained property, the property setter method is declared to throw PropertyVetoExceptions. Whenever a change of a constrained property is attempted, a VetoableChangeEvent is passed to all registered vetoable-change listeners. Each of these listeners may throw a java.beans.PropertyVetoException. If at least one does, the property change is vetoed and will not take place. If no veto exception is thrown, the property is changed in the usual way and a PropertyChangeEvent is passed to all change listeners.

The methods required to register and unregister vetoable property change listeners are:

> public void **addVetoableChangeListener** (VetoableChangeListener x);
> public void **removeVetoableChangeListener** (VetoableChangeListener x);

The interface java.beans.VetoableChangeListener introduces the method to be called on property changes:

> public void **vetoableChange** (VetoableChangeEvent evt)
>   throws PropertyVetoException;

Normally, properties are edited by property editors as determined by a java.beans.PropertyEditorManager object. This object maintains a registry to map between Java types and appropriate property editor classes. However, a bean can override this selection by specifying a property editor class to be used when editing a particular property of that bean. Furthermore, where customization of a bean is complex or involves many properties, a bean can also nominate a customizer class that implements a specific customization interface. A customizer will normally take a separate dialog window, whereas typical property editors are controls. Thus, property editors can be used in the dialog implemented by a customizer.

14.3.3 Introspection

Events and properties are supported by a combination of new standard interfaces and classes. Examples are EventListener, EventObject, EventSetDescriptor, and PropertyDescriptor (for more information on the property and event models, see the following sections). The use of interfaces such as EventListener allows an assembly tool using the reflection services (see below) to discover support of certain features by a given bean. In addition, JavaBeans introduces the new notion of method patterns. (In the JavaBeans specification, these are called "design patterns"; Sun, 1996. This is confusing. The term "method pattern" used here is much closer to what is meant.) A method pattern is a combination of rules for the formation of a method's signature, its return type, and even its name. Method patterns allow for the lightweight classification of individual methods of an interface or class. For example, here is the method pattern used to indicate a pair of getter and setter methods for a specific property:

```
public <PropertyType> get<PropertyName> ();
public void set<PropertyName> (<PropertyType> a);
```

For a property "background" of type java.awt.Color, this pattern yields the following two methods:

```
public java.awt.Color getBackground ();
public void setBackground (java.awt.Color color);
```

The use of conventional names in method patterns can be avoided – a bean can implement interface java.beans.BeanInfo. If this interface is implemented, an assembly tool will use it to query a bean instance explicitly for the names of property getters, property setters, and event source registration methods. The signatures prescribed by the patterns still need to be followed, of course, as otherwise the assembly could not take place. The following excerpts from class BeanInfo and related classes (JavaBeans as in JDK 1.4) hint at how BeanInfo information can be used to find out about the supported events, properties, and exposed methods:

```
package java.beans;
public interface BeanInfo {
    // some constants elided

    public BeanInfo[] getAdditionalBeanInfo ();
        // current info takes precedence over additional bean info
    public BeanDescriptor getBeanDescriptor ();
    public int getDefaultEventIndex ();
    public int getDefaultPropertyIndex ();
    public EventSetDescriptor[] getEventSetDescriptors ();
    public Image getIcon (int iconKind);
    public MethodDescriptor[] getMethodDescriptors ();
    public PropertyDescriptor[] getPropertyDescriptors ();
}

public class FeatureDescriptor {
    public Enumeration attributeNames ();
    public String getDisplayName ();
    public String getName ();
    public String getShortDescription ();
    public boolean isExpert ();    // feature for expert users only
    public boolean isHidden ();    // feature for tool-use only
    public boolean isPreferred ();    // important for human inspection
```

```
    public Object getValue (String attributeName);
    public void setValue (String attributeName, Object value);
        // setValue and getValue allow to associate arbitrary named attributes
        // with a feature
    // other set-methods elided
}

public class BeanDescriptor extends FeatureDescriptor {
    // constructors elided
    public Class getBeanClass ();   // the class representing the entire bean
    public Class getCustomizerClass ();   // null, if the bean has no customizer
}

public class EventSetDescriptor extends FeatureDescriptor {
    // constructors elided
    public java.lang.reflect.Method getAddListenerMethod ();
    public java.lang.reflect.Method getRemoveListenerMethod ();
    public java.lang.reflect.Method getGetListenerMethod ();
    public java.lang.reflect.MethodDescriptor[] getListenerMethodDescriptors ();
    public java.lang.reflect.Method[] getListenerMethods ();
    public Class getListenerType();
    public boolean isInDefaultEventSet ();
    public void setInDefaultEventSet (boolean inDefaultEventSet);
    public boolean isUnicast ();
        // this is a unicast event source: at most one listener
    public void setUnicast (boolean unicast);
}

public class MethodDescriptor extends FeatureDescriptor {
    // constructors elided
    public java.lang.reflect.Method getMethod ();
    ParameterDescriptor[] getParameterDescriptors ();
}

public class ParameterDescriptor extends FeatureDescriptor {}

public class PropertyDescriptor extends FeatureDescriptor {
    // constructors elided
    public Class getPropertyEditorClass ();
    public Class getPropertyType ();
    public java.lang.reflect.Method getReadMethod ();
    public java.lang.reflect.Method getWriteMethod ();
    public boolean isBound ();
        // change of bound property fires PropertyChange event
    public boolean isConstrained ();   // attempted change may be vetoed
    // set-methods elided
}
```

Method patterns are an interesting deviation from the established Java design principles. Normally, a Java class that has a certain property, or implements certain functionality, signals this by implementing a corresponding interface. Consider the following hypothetical substitution of the method pattern for property getters and setters. A standard empty interface Property is provided. For each property, a subinterface is defined. A bean class that has some of these properties then has to implement the corresponding property interfaces:

```
interface BackgroundProp extends Property {    // hypothetical!
    public Color getBackground ();
    public void setBackground (Color color);
}
```

The names of the set and get method should still contain the property name to avoid conflicts with set and get methods from other property interfaces. Java reflection could now be used directly to look for property interfaces in a class. The triggering key would be extension of interface Property rather than detection of methods of a certain pattern. It is not clear why this straightforward use of interfaces and reflection, instead of method patterns, was not used for the specification of JavaBeans. This is particularly surprising as a similar approach is used for event listener interfaces.

The feature introspection mechanism of JavaBeans allows attachment of arbitrary named custom attributes (name-value pairs) to features of a bean. As of SDK 1.4, this mechanism became fragile – class Introspector now uses soft references to hold on to BeanInfo instances. As a result, any bean-info object can be garbage collected as soon as the last client reference is gone. Sun recommends checking attribute attachments every time a bean-info object is acquired – and re-attaching attributes in case they aren't there any more (because the previous info object has been collected). Doing so can become quite tedious and requires keeping all attachment code central. The option to use attached attributes to communicate between separate parts of a system is essentially gone.

14.3.4 JAR files – packaging of Java components

Java class files were the only pre-beans means of packaging Java components in pre-1.1 JDKs. All that a Java class file can contain is a single compiled class or interface. A class file also contains all meta-information about the compiled context. Resources cannot be included in a class file. To ship a component, many separate files would need to be distributed.

The problem is solved by using Java Archive (JAR) files to package a JavaBean. JAR files were originally introduced to support JavaBeans, but have since been used to package all other Java components as well. Technically, a JAR file is a ZIP-format archive file that includes a manifest file. Manifest files

are used to provide information on the contents of an archive file (see below). The archive may include:

- a set of class files;
- a set of serialized objects that is often used for bean prototype instances;
- optional help files in HTML;
- optional localization information used by the bean to localize itself;
- optional icons held in .icon files in GIF format;
- other resource files needed by the bean.

The serialized prototype contained in the JAR file allows a bean to be shipped in an initialized default form. Serialization is performed using the object serialization service (see section 14.4.2). New instances of such a bean are created by deserializing the prototype, effectively producing a copy.

There can be multiple beans in a single JAR file – potentially, each of the contained classes can be a bean and each of the serialized objects can be a bean instance. The manifest file in the JAR file can be used to name the beans in the JAR file.

14.4 Basic Java services

Over the years, there have been many additions to the services standardized for Java. This section covers reflection, object serialization, and the Java native interface (JNI).

14.4.1 Reflection

The Java core reflection service is a combination of original Java language features, a set of support classes (introduced with JDK 1.1), and a language feature to support class literals (expressions of type Class, such as MyFoo.class, introduced with JDK 1.2). The reflection service, curbed by the active security policy, allows:

- inspection of classes and interfaces for their fields and methods;
- construction of new class instances and new arrays;
- access to and modification of fields of objects and classes;
- access to and modification of elements of arrays;
- invocation of methods on objects and classes.

The reflection service thus now covers all the Java language's features. The Java language-level access control mechanisms, such as privacy of a field, are enforced. (Unrestricted access can be useful to implement trusted low-level services, such as portable debuggers. A special interface for such unrestricted access is part of the Java platform debugger architecture – JPDA.) To enable reflective operations, the reflection service introduces a package java.lang.reflect. (The default import of java.lang into all packages makes java.lang itself effectively inextensible as otherwise there would be a risk of name clashes with existing packages imported using the package.* syntax. The introduction of java.lang.reflect, instead of introducing the new classes into java.lang itself, avoids the conflict. This is somewhat unfortunate as the original JDK 1.0 reflection classes, such as Class, are in java.lang. Also, once compartmentalized, further additions that aren't about reflection didn't logically fit into java.lang.reflect – as of J2SE 1.4 there's also java.lang.ref to support special references; see section 14.2.4.)

Classes Field, Method, and Constructor provide reflective information about the field, method, or constructor that they describe and allow for type-safe use of this field, method, or constructor. All three are final and without public constructors. All three implement interface Member, which makes it possible to find out how the member is called and determine the member's modifiers and to which class or interface it belongs. Below are excerpts of some of these interfaces and classes:

```
package java.lang.reflect;
public interface Member {
   public abstract Class getDeclaringClass ();
   public abstract String getName ();
   public abstract int getModifiers ();
      // decodable using class java.lang.reflect.Modifier
}

public final class Field implements Member {
   public Class getType ();
   public Object get (Object obj)   // if static field, obj is ignored
         throws NullPointerException, IllegalArgumentException,
         IllegalAccessException;
   public boolean getBoolean (Object obj)
         throws NullPointerException, IllegalArgumentException,
         IllegalAccessException;
   // similar for all other primitive types; avoids wrapping in get
   public void set (Object obj, Object value)
         throws NullPointerException, IllegalArgumentException,
         IllegalAccessException;
   public void setBoolean (Object obj, Boolean z)
         throws NullPointerException, IllegalArgumentException,
         IllegalAccessException;
   // similar for all other primitive types; avoids wrapping in set
}

public final class Method implements Member {
   public Class getReturnType ();
   public Class[] getParameterTypes ();
   public Class[] getExceptionTypes ();
   public Object invoke (Object obj, Object[] args)
```

```
      // returns null if return type is void
      throws NullPointerException, IllegalArgumentException,
        IllegalAccessException,
        InvocationTargetException;      // wrapper for exception thrown
            // by invoked method
}
```

Class Class (still in java.lang, not java.lang.reflect) has methods to return instances of these classes when querying for the features of a particular class. The important methods of class Class are:

```
public final class Class {
    public static Class forName (String className)
        throws ClassNotFoundException;
    public Object newInstance ()
        throws InstantiationException, IllegalAccessException;
    public boolean isInstance (Object obj);
    public boolean isInterface ();
    public boolean isArray ();
    public boolean isPrimitive ();
    public String getName ();
    public int getModifiers ();   // decodable using java.lang.reflect.Modifier
    public ClassLoader getClassLoader ();
    public Class getSuperclass ();
        // null if primitive, interface, or class Object
    public Class[] getInterfaces ();
    public Class getComponentType ();
        // type of array components; null if not array
    public Class getDeclaringClass ();
        // next outer class, if this is an inner class or interface
    public Class[] getClasses ();
        // public inner classes or interfaces, incl. inherited ones
    public Field[] getFields () throws SecurityException;
        // public accessible fields, incl. inherited ones
    public Method[] getMethods () throws SecurityException;
        //public methods, incl. inherited ones
    public Constructor[] getConstructors () throws SecurityException;
        // public constructors
    public Class[] getDeclaredClasses () throws SecurityException;
        // all inner classes or interfaces, excl. inherited ones
    public Field[] getDeclaredFields () throws SecurityException;
        // all fields, excl. inherited ones
    public Method[] getDeclaredMethods () throws SecurityException;
        // all methods, excl. inherited ones
```

```
  public Constructor[] getDeclaredConstructors () throws
SecurityException;
      // all constructors
    // further methods to get resources and
    // (declared) field, method, constructor, or class by name
  }
```

There are several constant objects (public static final) for the languages primitive types. For example, there is an object java.lang.Boolean.TYPE that is the Class object for primitive type boolean. While still supported, the preferred and universal way to get to a Class object since JDK 1.2 is the form boolean.class. Class Array supports dynamic construction and use of arrays. Class Modifier simplifies the inspection of modifier information on classes, fields, and methods.

```
  package java.lang.reflect;
  public final class Modifier {
    public static boolean isPublic (int modifiers);
      // true if modifiers incl. public
    // similar for private, protected, static, final, synchronized, volatile,
    // transient, strictfp, native, interface, abstract
    // note that "interface" is viewed as a class modifier!
  }
```

14.4.2 Object serialization

Up to JDK 1.0.2, Java did not support serialization of objects into bytestreams – only primitive types were supported. If an application wanted to write an entire web of objects to an output stream, it needed to traverse and serialize the objects itself, using some ad hoc encoding scheme. The Java object serialization service overcomes this by defining a standard serial encoding scheme and by providing the mechanisms to code and decode ("serialize" and "deserialize") webs of objects.

To be serializable, an object has to implement interface java.io.Serializable. In addition, all fields that should not be serialized need to be marked with the modifier transient. This is important, because fields may refer to huge computed structures, such as caches, or values that are inherently bound to the current JVM incarnation, such as descriptors of open files. For objects implementing Serializable, sufficient information is written to a stream such that deserialization continues to work, even if different (but compatible) versions of classes are used. Methods readObject and writeObject can be implemented to control further what information is written or to append further information to the stream. If these methods are not implemented, all non-transient fields referring to serializable objects are automatically serialized. Shared references to objects are preserved.

To make serialization safe and configurable, methods readObject and writeObject are private! Therefore, there can be one such method per subclass level. Reflection is used to find these methods for each extension level. If these methods exist, they should call a method defaultReadObject (or defaultWriteObject) before handling additional private data. The reason is that readObject and writeObject on a given class extension level handle only the fields introduced in this level, not those in subclasses or superclasses.

As an alternative to implementing interface java.io.Serializable, a class can implement interface Externalizable. Then none of the object's fields is automatically handled and it is up to the object to save and store its contents. Externalizable has methods writeExternal and readExternal for this purpose. These methods are public, and objects implementing Externalizable open themselves for access to their state that bypasses their regular public interface. This requires some care to avoid safety problems.

A simple versioning scheme is supported – a serializable class can claim to be a different version of a certain class by declaring a unique serial version unique ID (SUID). A SUID is a 64-bit hash code ("fingerprint") computed over the name of a class and all implemented interfaces' features of that class, including the features' types or signatures. It does not cover superclasses, because each extension level has its own serial version ID and is responsible for its own evolution. The serial version ID is computed automatically when an instance of a class is serialized and that class does not declare a serial version ID. However, if it does, then the class declares itself to be compatible with the class that originally had this ID. The readObject method can be used to read serialized state from other versions and thus preserve compatibility with serialized versions.

Object serialization must be used with care to avoid security holes. For example, if a serialized stream can be tampered with, then it can be arranged to deserialize a critical object in a way that its internal subobjects are shared by some rogue object. These alias references can then be used to bypass security checks of the critical object. Before J2SE 1.4, it was recommended to eagerly copy such private subobjects after deserialization in order to break unwanted aliases. Such a deep copy is expensive and non-trivial to implement. In version 1.4, new methods readUnshared and writeUnshared are provided to solve this problem.

Object serialization creates a stream of bytes in a single-pass process – that is, with no back-patching. Hence, while still serializing a web of objects, the part of the stream that has been produced already can be forwarded to filters or the destination. The stream is fully self-describing down to the level of Java primitive types – a tag that describes the type of the following item precedes every value in the stream. Compared with compact native formats, this can be quite costly. However, the added robustness of the serial format probably outweighs the higher cost.

A major drawback of the current serialization service is the missing support for graceful degradation in the case of missing or incompatible classes at the receiving end. For example, if the serialized object is a document, then it should be possible to deserialize and use that document even if some of its embedded objects cannot (currently) be supported on the receiving platform. The current service simply throws a ClassNotFound exception and does not offer means to resynchronize and continue deserialization. In the document example, it would also be desirable if an unsupported object could be kept in serialized form to include it when serializing the document again. This is also not supported by the current serialization service.

14.4.3 Java native interface

The Java native interface (JNI) specifies, for each platform, the native calling conventions when interfacing to native code outside the Java virtual machine. JNI also specifies how such external code can access Java objects for which references were passed. This includes the possibility of invoking Java methods. JNI does not specify a binary object model for Java – that is, it does not specify how fields are accessed or methods are invoked within a particular Java virtual machine. Interoperation between Java virtual machines on the same platform remains an unresolved issue, as does interfacing with services such as just-in-time compilers. JNI allows native methods to:

- create, inspect, and update Java objects;
- call Java methods;
- catch and throw exceptions;
- load classes and obtain class information;
- perform runtime type checking.

The actual layout of objects is not exposed to native code. Instead, all access is through so-called JNI interface pointers (Figure 14.8) that use a runtime structure identical to that of COM (p. 331).

Despite the superficial closeness to COM, JNI is different and not automatically compatible with COM. A JNI interface pointer is used only to refer to a thread-specific context and does not correspond to an individual Java object. The JNI interface does not include standard COM functions QueryInterface, AddRef, or Release. If these are added, the entire JVM could function as one

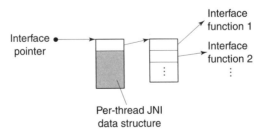

Figure 14.8 JNI interface pointer.

COM component object. A native method is called with a JNI interface pointer as its first argument. Other arguments, including Java object references, are passed directly, but all access to Java objects is via functions provided by the JNI interface pointer.

For the Java garbage collector to work, the JVM keeps track of all references handed out to native methods. References are handed out as local references, and these are released by the JVM on return of the native method. Native code can turn a local into a global reference. It is the responsibility of the native code to inform the JVM when a global reference is no longer needed.

All access to fields or invocation of methods of Java objects from native methods is performed using one of several accessor functions available via the JNI interface pointer. Below are two sample JNI functions that show how to invoke a Java object's method, using C++ notation:

```
JNIEnv *env;  // the JNI interface pointer
jmethodID mid = env->GetMethodID (classPtr, methodName,
                 methodSignature);
  // methodSignature is a string representing the mangled signature
jdouble result = env->CallDoubleMethod(obj, mid, args);
  // factoring of GetMethodID useful to avoid repeated method lookup
```

JNI specifies how to "mangle" signatures of methods. In the above example, this is used to resolve overloaded methods when performing a method lookup. As JNI does not reveal how a JVM implements objects or dispatches methods, access is relatively expensive.

14.4.4 Java AWT and JFC/Swing

The Java abstract windowing toolkit (AWT) and Java foundation classes (JFC) are central to any Java development providing a graphical user interface. Here is a brief summary.

- *Delegation-based event model* Perhaps the most dramatic change in JDK 1.1. The previous event model was based on inheriting from component classes and overriding event handler methods. The subtle interaction of super-calls, open lists of possible events, and local handling decision procedures was found to be too complex and error-prone. (The 1.1 model has been described in section 14.3.1.) "Delegation-based" is a misnomer, following the unfortunate example of the use of the term delegation in COM. The 1.1 JDK really provides a forwarding-based event model. Object connection and composition are used in favor of implementation inheritance.
- *Data transfer and clipboard support* Like the COM universal data transfer service, AWT defines the notions of transferable data items.

Internet MIME (multipurpose internet mail extensions) types are used to interact with non-Java applications. Data transfer between Java applications can also directly use Java classes.

- *Drag and drop* Support for drag and drop among Java and non-Java applications (by hooking into the underlying system's drag and drop protocols, such as the OLE one on Windows).

- *Java 2D* Classes for advanced 2D graphics and imaging. Java 2D covers line art, text, and images. Supported features include image compositing, alpha blending (transparency), accurate color space definition and conversion, and display-oriented imaging operators.

- *Printing* The printing model is straightforward. Graphical components that do not explicitly handle printing will be printed using their screen-rendering methods. Thus, for simple components, printing is free. However, the printing model does not address the subtleties resulting from printing embedded contents that need to spread over multiple pages. (This is addressed, for example, by the ActiveX printing model, which allows embedded controls to print across several pages in cooperation with their container. This is a complex model, though, and few if any ActiveX containers actually implement this advanced printing protocol.)

- *Accessibility* Interface that allows so-called assistive technologies to interact with JFC and AWT components. Assistive technologies include screen readers, screen magnifiers, and speech recognition.

- *Internationalization* Based on the Unicode 2.1 character encoding, support is provided to adapt text, numbers, dates, currency, and user-defined objects to the conventions of a locale, as identified by a pair of language and region identifiers.

- *Swing components and pluggable look and feel* In JDK 1.0, most user interface components (buttons, list boxes, and so on) relied on native implementation in so-called "peer classes." This has the advantage that a Java application truly looks and feels like a native one. Introduced later, so-called Swing components (which are JavaBeans) are independent of native peers and support pluggable look-and-feel. Whatever look-and-feel is selected, it will be consistent across all platforms. Swing components are written entirely in Java, without relying on native window-system-specific code.

14.4.5 Advanced JavaBeans specifications

The following four specifications generalize the JavaBeans model – the containment and services protocol, the Java activation framework (JAF), the long-term persistence model, and the InfoBus specification. Each is described briefly below.

Containment and services protocol

The containment and services protocol supports the concept of logically nesting JavaBeans bean instances. All beans can assume the services of the JVM and core Java APIs. With the containment and services protocol, a nested bean can acquire additional services at runtime from its container and a container can extend services to its nested beans.

Java activation framework (JAF)

JAF is used to determine the type of arbitrary data (by following the MIME standard), the operations ("commands") available over that type of data, and to locate, load, and activate components that provide a particular operation over a particular type of data. The central piece of a JAF implementation is a command map – a registry for components that is indexed by pairs of MIME types and command names.

Long-term persistence for JavaBeans

Long-term persistence – also called archiving – is an alternative to object serialization (see section 14.4.2). The file format created by this archival process is XML with a DTD or one of two proprietary Java file formats. While object serialization aims to fully persist the entire state held in a graph of objects, archiving only captures the part of the state that can be set through public properties. As such public interfaces are far more stable over time than the object's implementations, it is much less likely that a future version of a component can no longer read the state written by an older version (or, indeed, the other way around.)

The process of creating and consuming such archived state is interesting. It uses the same basic infrastructure as object serialization, but limits itself to publicly settable properties. To prevent the writing of default values, the proposed persisting form is immediately read again to create a copy of the original object graph. Any attempt to set a property to a value that it already has (because of defaults) is detected and such values are eliminated from the persisted form. This approach compresses persisted forms nicely, but it also introduces a new form of implementation dependency. If a particular default value wasn't picked according to a bean's specification, but merely for implementation convenience, then it may be different in a future bean implementation. Error handling is also done in an original way – exceptions during reconstruction from persisted form are effectively ignored – in a hope that a partially reconstituted object graph is better than none. This is problematical and a protocol should be provided to allow the detection and handling of inappropriate reconstruction failures.

InfoBus

The InfoBus specification creates a generic framework for a particular style of composition. The idea is to design beans to be InfoBus-aware and categorize beans into data producers, data consumers, and data controllers, all of which can be coupled by an information bus determining data flow.

The InfoBus protocol distinguishes six steps. First, any Java component can connect by implementing InfoBusMember, obtaining an InfoBus instance, and having the member join it. Second, members receive notifications by implementing an interface and registering it with the InfoBus. Two event listener interfaces are defined to support data consumers receiving announcements about data availability and data producers receiving requests for data. Third, based on the name of some data item, data producers and data consumers rendezvous to exchange data. Fourth, to allow producers and consumers to operate in terms of their internal data representations, the InfoBus provides a set of interfaces for various standard protocols, which are used to create data items with common access. Fifth, data values are typically of primitive type or collections to minimize dependencies between consumers and producers. Sixth, a consumer can attempt to change data items, but the producer can enforce policies as to what changes are acceptable.

Data controllers implement the InfoBusDataController interface and participate in the distribution of InfoBusEvents to consumers and producers on an InfoBus. Multiple controllers can be added to the bus in order to optimize communication, not interfere with actual data item exchange between producers and consumers. A data controller can intercept requests and, for instance, implement a cache for data items from an expensive producer. Requests from consumers and producers are offered to controllers in sequential order – the first controller to declare the request handled stopping further propagation. A default controller at the end of this chain handles all remaining requests.

14.5 Component variety – applets, servlets, beans, and Enterprise beans

The Java universe defines five different component models, and more may arrive in the future. Besides the applet and JavaBeans models (both part of J2SE), there are Enterprise JavaBeans, servlets, and application client components (all part of J2EE). This section presents a brief overview of these different component models.

The two critical contributions to the J2EE server-side models are servlets/JSPs and EJBs. These are covered in more detail in following subsections. All components in the J2EE space are packaged into JAR files, which can be included in a J2EE application. An important aspect of all J2EE components is the support of deployment descriptors. These are XML files co-packaged with a component that describe how a particular component should be deployed. Deployment is the act of readying a component for an actual deployment context – a step that can be, and often is, separate from the notion of installation. (It is possible to deploy a component once and then install it many times. See sections 8.6 and 8.11.) The detailed nature of deployment descriptors depends on the particular component model. For instance, the descriptor of an EJB entity bean (see section 14.5.2) may request container-managed persistence and detail how properties of the entity bean should be mapped to tables in a database.

Applets were the first Java component model, aiming at downloadable light-weight components that would augment websites displayed in a browser. The initial applet security model was so tight that applets could not really deliver much more than "eye candy" – an area that was rapidly captured by other technologies, such as GIF89a animated images, Macromedia's Shockwave and Flash technology, JScript, and refinements to the HTML world itself, including the introduction of DHTML (dynamic HTML). Taking advantage of such browser-level technologies, most J2EE-based applications use servlets and JSPs to generate scripted HTML pages instead of sending applets.

The second Java component model, JavaBeans, focuses on supporting con-nection-oriented programming and is, as such, useful on both clients and servers. Historically, JavaBeans are more popular in the scope of client-side rich applications and sometimes perceived as being replaced by EJB on the server. This view is, technically, wrong. EJB, beyond its name, shares little with JavaBeans. JavaBeans remain useful when building client-side applications as they explicitly support a visual application design mode. (As of J2SE 1.3, a bean can also be an applet. However, so far the support is limited – bean applets will always receive an empty applet context and stub.)

EJB, Java's third component model, focuses on container-integrated serv-ices supporting EJB beans (components) that request services using declarative attributes and deployment descriptors. In a later revision, a container model was added to JavaBeans as well, but JavaBeans containers are very different from EJB containers. The former are a mere mechanism for containment, while the latter are partially driven by declarative constructs. As JavaBeans does not require the presence of an interactive user outside of design-time, it is con-ceivable to use JavaBeans to construct more complex EJBs. (JavaBeans and EJBs correspond roughly to component classes and serviced component classes in the .NET Framework.)

The fourth Java component model is servlets. These pick up the spirit of applets, but live on a server and are (usually) lightweight components instanti-ated by a web server processing, typically, web pages. A matching technology, Java ServerPages (JSP), can be used to declaratively define web pages to be generated. JSPs are then compiled to servlets. (Servlets and JSP correspond roughly to page classes and pages in ASP.NET; see section 15.13.3.)

J2EE introduces a fifth Java component model – application client compo-nents. These are essentially unconstrained Java applications that reside on clients. A client component uses the JNDI enterprise naming context (see section 14.6.3) to access environment properties, EJBs, and resources on J2EE servers. Such resources can include access to e-mail (via JavaMail) or databases (via JDBC).

At a distribution and deployment format level, J2EE enterprise applications are packaged in .ear (enterprise archive) files that contain .war and .jar files. Servlets and JSPs are packaged in .war (web archive) files; applets, JavaBeans, and EJBs are packaged in .jar files. All these files follow the ZIP archive file format (www.pkware.com).

J2EE deployment descriptors serve two purposes. First, they enable the component developer to communicate requirements on the side of the component. Requesting container-managed persistence is an example. Second, they enable the component deployer to fill in the blanks. For example, for a component that requests container-managed persistence, a deployer would specify exactly how the state of that component's instances should be mapped to particular relational tables. The role of the deployer is distinct and often served by a person different than the component developer, potentially in a separate organization. (For comparison, in COM+ and CLR, the equivalent of deployment descriptors shows in two different places, aligned with these two different roles. Deployment information provided by the developer is capture in attributes that are closely aligned with the code. In the CLR case, these are conveniently attached using language-supported custom attributes. Deployment information that is modified or provided by the deployer is kept in separate XML-based configuration files.)

The variety of supported Java component models is a reflection of different needs. However, to actually establish component markets in these various areas, deeper standardization of domain-specific concepts has to happen. Today, only a few EJB components, to name just one case, are used beyond even the one enterprise application for which they were developed.

14.5.1 Java server pages (JSP) and servlets

Serving web pages and other formatted contents can be viewed as a combination of three core functions. First, incoming requests for such contents need to be accepted, checked for proper authorization, and routed to the appropriate components ready to handle a particular request. Second, such components need to draw on information sources and processes to retrieve or synthesize the requested contents. Third, the retrieved or generated contents need to be sent to the requesting party.

The prototypical model handling these three steps is that of a web server. Incoming HTTP requests are received by a web server that interprets the request and the target URL, including possible parameters. A simple web server will either find a static HTML page, typically in the local file system, or use the URL to activate a component via a simple interface called CGI (common gateway interface). The component receives the URL (and, in particular, the parameters that it may include) and generates an HTML page. In both cases, the server will then send the HTML page back to the client, typically a web browser.

The same model can also be used to serve up content that is not in HTML format. For instance, a web server can be used to provide XML web services. In that case, incoming SOAP requests are routed to the right component, processed, and SOAP replies are sent back.

A common property of the above scenarios is that the web server infrastructure is common up to the point where specific components need to take over to process requests and retrieve or synthesize replies in a customizable way. For instance, the Windows internet information service (IIS) handles incoming HTTP requests, determines whether or not to send back information found in a file directly, or activate an appropriate component and send back the results produced by that component.

Writing the customizing components requires not much more than a simple interface to the server infrastructure – at least when aiming for simple cases only. An example of such an interface in the context of IIS is ISAPI (internet server API), an efficient low-level interface that enables high performance, but that is quite demanding on the developer of a customizing component. To simplify this situation for the bulk of website requirements, Microsoft introduced ASP (active server pages), a model that allows raw web pages to include server-side script code. The ASP server executes such scripts, which will typically synthesize HTML fragments as their result. ASP then places computed HTML fragments where the script used to be and returns the resulting HTML page to the client.

Java server pages (JSP) improved on the ASP model by compiling JSP pages (pages containing HTML with inserted Java fragments) into servlets. A JSP server activates servlets as needed to handle requests. In addition, servlets are also supported by explicit API definitions. It is possible and common to implement servlets instead of writing JSP pages. The result is an inversion of the page programming model. At the level of ASP and JSP pages, code fragments reside in line in HTML (or other markup, such as XML). At the level of servlets, HTML (or other markup) resides in line in Java source code. (This is a simplified description as, in both cases, the in line fragments can be included by reference to separate files.) The following simple example shows how a doGet method on a servlet produces a simple HTML result:

```
import javax.servlet.*;
import javax.servlet.http.*;
public class HelloWorld extends HttpServlet {
    protected void doGet (HttpServletRequest request,
                          HttpServletResponse response)
        throws ServletException, java.io.IOException
```

```
    {
        java.util.Calendar calendar = new java.util.GregorianCalendar();
        int hour = calendar.get(currTime.HOUR);
        int minute = calendar.get(currTime.MINUTE);
        ServletOutputStream out = response.getWriter();
        out.print("<HTML><BODY>\r\n");
        out.print("The time is: " + hour + ":" + minute +
                " – or it was when I looked.\r\n");
        out.print("</BODY></HTML>\r\n");
    }
}
```

As can be seen, the servlet programming model is quite natural if relatively small static HTML (or other markup) fragments need to be combined with computed results. The servlet container supports servlets by providing simple access to HTTP Request parameters and by managing sessions. However, if large amounts of static markup contents need to be produced with print calls, readability quickly suffers. In addition, if the markup fragments need to be open for localization (such as translation into another language), then embedding these fragments as string literals into source code is a bad choice. The fragments can be factored into separate files to enable reasonable localization, but that leads to further reduction of code readability.

The dual model to embedding markup in source code is to embed source code in markup. This is exactly what a JSP page does, where the content of <% ... %> tags is interpreted as Java source code. The following example shows a JSP page that leads to the same result as the servlet above. Note the use of tag <%= ... %> to request evaluation of a Java expression and output of the result by printing to the page stream.

```
<HTML> <BODY>
<%
    java.util.Calendar calendar = new java.util.GregorianCalendar();
    int hour = calendar.get(currTime.HOUR);
    int minute = calendar.get(currTime.MINUTE);
%>
The time is: <%= hour %>:<%= minute %> – or it was when I looked.
</BODY></HTML>
```

When processed, this JSP page causes the generation of, essentially, the servlet above. It is thus appropriate to always think of web page and other contents handling as being performed by servlets, even if the source is kept in the form of JSP pages. To keep JSP pages largely contents-oriented and maintain both readability and localizability, it is useful to minimize code in JSP pages. Unlike contents, Java code is supported by natural abstraction mechanisms – packages, classes and methods. Thus, instead of embedding large pieces of Java code in JSP pages, it is preferable to keep most code in separate Java packages and reduce code in JSP pages to the necessary glue – invocation of methods on appropriately created objects and insertion of results into page streams. This helps avoid another source of possible confusion – server-side Java and client-side JavaScript may coexist in the same JSP page, which clearly does not help readability.

By means of special and custom tags, JSP can go further towards eliminating server-side code in JSP pages. For instance, there is a set of tags to create JavaBeans instances and access their properties from JSP pages. Custom tag extensions can be added easily, for instance by implementing just two methods (doStartTag and doEndTag) on a class derived from class javax.servlet.jsp.tagext.TagSupport. In the following example, two custom tags are used to retrieve the current hour and minute, respectively, and insert the value into the page output stream.

```
<% taglib uri="/hour" prefix="calendar" %>
<% taglib uri="/minute" prefix="calendar" %>
<HTML><BODY>
The time is: <calendar:hour>:<calendar:minute> – or it was when I looked.
</BODY></HTML>
```

The JSP standard tag library (JSTL) includes control flow tags such as iteration and conditionals, tags for manipulating XML documents, internationalization tags, and SQL tags. JSTL also introduces an expression language to simplify page development and a framework for integrating existing custom tags with JSTL tags.

When combining the servlet concepts with libraries that support the processing of XML, JSP servlets can be used to implement simple web services. To do so, the JSP server itself needs to be augmented with support for the underlying web service protocols (essentially SOAP and possibly web service standards for security and other aspects). This is essentially the path that ASP.NET follows to support web services (see section 15.13.3).

Servlets do not have to directly produce the contents stream eventually output by the server to the client. Instead, a request can be handled by one servlet that contains relevant business logic. Once such logic has been processed, that servlet can hand off output generation to another servlet class. In other words, it is possible to factor servlets, yielding more specialized and easier to maintain components.

If web requests are only one point of entry into larger enterprise applications or if complex integration across applications is required, it becomes useful to further factor the approach. To do so, servlets can build on the services of EJBs (see the next subsection). Where such a separation is performed, it is important to recognize the overheads naturally introduced by building on two separate component models and their (partially) separate infrastructure. It is possible to colocate a JSP server and an EJB container on the same machine and even in the same process, sharing the same JVM instance. However, it is equally possible to distribute JSP and EJB processing across separate machines, potentially enabling better scalability – but at an increased base overhead.

14.5.2   Contextual composition – Enterprise JavaBeans (EJB)

The naming of Enterprise JavaBeans suggests a close relationship to JavaBeans (see section 14.3). This is, in fact, not the case. The JavaBeans approach to composition is connection-oriented programming or, as it is sometimes called, wiring. Beans can define both event sources and event listeners. By connecting one bean instance's listener to another bean instance's event source, events flow. Later improvements of the JavaBeans model introduce support for hierarchical container structures (see section 14.4.5), so, instead of placing all bean instances in a flat space and relying on peer-to-peer connections only, containers allow the hierarchical creation of subsystems. Another addition to JavaBeans, the InfoBus, allows for a flexible decoupling of event sources and event listeners by routing some or all communication through a bus structure that allows for the interception of messages and application of policies without requiring cooperation from the event source or listener and without a need to re-wire. With JavaBeans containment and services infrastructure in place and the availability of the InfoBus, JavaBeans could move beyond connection-oriented composition to forms of contextual composition and data-driven composition. In practice, this potential is rarely exploited as, while the infrastructural design is in place, the critical mass of contextual services or messaging infrastructure is not.

EJB follows an entirely different path. There are no provisions for connection-oriented programming at all. (Adding these is one of the main improvements of CCM over EJB; see section 13.3.) Instead, EJB components (e-beans) follow a relatively conventional model of object-oriented composition. For example, if an e-bean instance needs a fresh instance of another e-bean, it simply creates one. If it needs to communicate with another e-bean instance, it simply calls methods. That is, EJB is not about systematically improving compositionality of e-beans via wiring of connections. E-beans are just as composable as their specific design made them and the generic EJB architecture does little to improve or hinder. For the remainder of this subsection, e-beans will be called just beans for brevity and to align with the common EJB lingo. It is important, however, to remember that EJB beans and JavaBeans beans are entirely different.

If EJB is weak at the connection-oriented composition level, it is strong at the level of contextual composition. (Since EJB 2.0, data-driven composition is also well covered; see the following subsection.) Contextual composition is about the automatic composition of component instances with appropriate services and resources (see section 21.2 for a theoretical discussion). Two important examples of services in the EJB space are the handling of transactions and security policies. An EJB container configures services to match the needs of contained beans. These needs are expressed declaratively in a bean's deployment descriptor (see section 14.5). The skeleton of an EJB deployment descriptor has the following form:

```
<!DOCTYPE ejb-jar PUBLIC
    "-//Sun Microsystems, Inc.//DTD Enterprise JavaBeans 2.0//EN"
    "http://java.sun.com/dtd/ejb-jar_2_0.dtd">
<ejb-jar>
  <enterprise-beans>
    <session> ... </session>
    <entity> ... </entity>
    <message-driven> ... </message-driven>
  </enterprise-beans>
  <relationships>
    <ejb-relation> ... </ejb-relation>
  </relationships>
  <assembly-descriptor>
    <security-role>
      <description> ... </description>
      <role-name> ... </role-name>
    </security-role>
    <method-permission>
      <role-name> ...as defined in a security role entry... </role-name>
      <method>
        <ejb-name> ...bean name... </ejb-name>
        <method-name> ...method name or * for all methods...
                                        </method-name>
      </method>
    </method-permission>
    <container-transaction>
      <method> ...as above... </method>
      <trans-attribute> ... </trans-attribute>
    </container-transaction>
  </assembly-descriptor>
</ejb-jar>
```

In this example skeleton, three different beans (a session, entity, and message-driven bean) are described (with all details elided). The following relationships map declares relationships among entity beans, which are used by the container to manage relationships and persistence of entity beans. For example, the container can use declared relationships to automatically find the entity bean instance at the other end of a relationship of an entity bean instance. The application descriptor section covers security and transaction requirements. For instance, it might grant the right to call a particular set of methods to anyone acting in a particular named role. (Mappings from role names to specific roles in the deployment environment are declared separately using a deployment tool.) Likewise, the transaction attribute might be set to Required, which instructs the container to create a new transaction if the bean's caller isn't already enlisted in one. As deployment descriptors can get long and detailed, good tool support at development and deployment-time is essential. (One issue here is that a lot of information appears redundantly in multiple places. For example, the name of a method on an EJB object interface appears in the deployment descriptor, on the object interface – twice if local and remote are supported – and on the bean class. All four occurrences cannot be checked by the compiler for mutual consistency.)

Deployed beans are contextually composed with services and resources by an EJB container. Contextual composition works by placing a hull around instances and intercepting communication from and to that instance. The hull itself can be thought of as a wall of proxies placed on all references to and from the instance inside the hull. To enable interaction between services and an instance, contextual access to services is provided to the instance – thus contextual composition. That is, the instance receives some form of reference to its context. The combination of the service implementations, intercepting hull, and context is referred to as a container in EJB. EJB containers are provided by servers. In the case of J2EE, the standard architectural enclosure for EJB, this server is a J2EE application server that will also provide containers for servlets (see previous subsection).

EJB realizes the hull around beans by not allowing any direct access to a bean's fields, methods, or constructors from any other bean, including beans colocated on the same server in the same container. Instead, all access to beans is required to go through one of two interfaces – the EJB home interface for lifecycle operations and the equivalent of static methods and the EJB object interface for all methods on the bean instance. Non-local clients will see these interfaces implemented on stub objects that use RMI or RMI-over-IIOP to communicate with the corresponding EJB container, which then relays calls to bean instances it contains. As of EJB 2.0, local clients can request local versions of both home and object interfaces. Local clients are still not allowed to access other beans directly and, as home and object interfaces never return anything but home and object interfaces of other beans, there is actually no way to do so. (Technically, a local bean could use reflection to subvert containment. However, a server implementation could use deployment-time code inspection and run-time checking techniques to discover and prevent such attempts.) Figure 14.9 shows how client, server, container, bean, home, and object relate in EJB.

The EJB specification does not detail how a particular container wraps bean instances. As part of the deployment process, tools provided with a container implementation take a bean in a JAR file, including the compiled interfaces and classes defining the bean and its deployment descriptor. These tools generate the bean's EJB object and EJB home. They are free to either generate classes implementing the local and remote EJB object and home interfaces

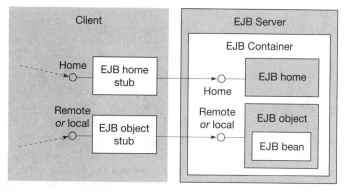

Figure 14.9 Isolation of EJB beans in containers via EJB home and EJB object interfaces. After Fig. 2-2 in Monson-Haefel, R. (2001) *Enterprise JavaBeans, 3rd Edition*, reprinted by permission of O'Reilly and Associates, Inc.

that wrap the bean's class, to synthesize subclasses that combine container-supplied object and home code with the code found in the bean's class, or even to synthesize classes that directly combine the implementation of the bean's class and the container-specific code. (In the latter cases, reflection would reveal additional members on the bean's class and, again, the EJB server could take deployment and runtime measures to prevent that.)

Beans of many flavors

There are four kinds of EJB beans – stateless session, stateful session, entity, and message-driven beans. Message-driven beans are new in EJB 2.0 and somewhat different from session and entity beans (they are described in the following subsection). The three flavors of session and entity beans are covered in more detail further below. They are all united by a common top-level contract between beans and containers and their use of deployment descriptors. Session and entity beans in addition share the design of EJB object and EJB home interfaces. (These are not standardized Java interfaces but are synthesized according to a standard pattern for any given bean.)

Every EJB home interface has a standard method create to instantiate a bean. In the case of entity beans it also has a standard method findByPrimaryKey to locate an existing instance by its primary key. A home interface can have additional, bean-specific methods as specified in the deployment descriptor. As such methods are not associated with any specific bean instance, they roughly correspond to static methods on a Java class. The methods on an EJB object interface are all bean-specific as specified in the deployment descriptor.

The EJB container cycles beans through defined lifetime stages. Immediately after creation, setEntityContext or setSessionContext is called to establish a backlink to the container's context for the new bean. Then ejbCreate is called, which is matched by a call to ejbRemove just before a bean instance is finally released. For entity beans, removal also implies deletion from the database as, unlike session beans, entity beans are thus only removed when their deletion is explicityly requested (via their home interface). As a container may need to keep many bean instances logically around, but parked at some low-cost level, it can call ejbPassivate to request release of any non-essential resource held by a bean instance. Then the container serializes a stateful session bean to some exterhal store or writes an entity bean back to the database, respectively. The container calls ejbActivate to return a bean to a ready state, after deserializing it from external store or loading it from a database.

Although the container context is attached to a bean in such a special way, it hasn't been designed in a particularly durable way. Of its ten methods, three have been deprecated. The remaining seven allow a bean some control over the current transaction, limited access to the security context, and access to the bean's own local and remote home. However, the "mother of all contexts" is not available – the initial context of JNDI (section 14.6.3). Instead, every bean has to find this initial context in a way that, up to EJB 2.0, is not portable.

An EJB container serializes all invocations of beans, so there is no need to synchronize within beans and the use of the synchronized keyword on bean methods and the creation of new threads is even illegal. The container also protects beans from re-entrant calls (with the exception of entity beans that explicitly declare that they can tolerate re-entrancy; see below), throwing an exception whenever a re-entrant call is attempted. Finally, the container isolates faults, so if a bean throws an exception, its EJB object is immediately invalidated and the offending bean instance destroyed, the remove method having not been called.

Session beans

A session bean is created by a client as a session-specific contact point. For instance, a servlet may create a session bean to process web requests that the servlet received. A stateless session bean does not maintain state across multiple invocations – a container can therefore decide to keep instances in a pool instead of creating new ones for every invocation in every session. A stateful session bean, on the other hand, remains associated with the one session for its lifetime and thus can retain state across method invocations.

The deployment descriptor of a session bean, in skeleton form, has the following form:

```
<session>
    <ejb-name> ...name of the session bean... </ejb-name>
    <home> ...name of EJB home interface... </home>
    <remote> ...name of EJB object interface... </remote>
    <local-home> ...name of local EJB home interface... </local-home>
    <local> ...name of local EJB object interface... </local>
    <ejb-class> ...name of class implementing this EJB... </ejb-class>
    <session-type> ...Stateless or Stateful... </session-type>
    <transaction-type> ...Container or Bean... </transaction-type>
```

<ejb-ref> ...*import of other beans referenced by this bean...* </ejb-ref>
<security-identity> ...*run-as role-name or use-caller-identity...*
</security-identity>
</session>

Besides assigning a name to the session bean itself, the descriptor assigns names to the EJB home and object interfaces and, if supported, their local counterparts. (A bean that does not declare local interfaces will not receive any when deployed.) The EJB class is the main class implementing the bean. The session type determines whether or not the container will associate the bean with a particular session and, therefore, whether the container will create a new instance per call or not. Session (and message-driven) beans have an option to explicitly control transactions – so-called bean-managed transactions – or follow the default of container-managed transactions. Explicitly control-ling transactions is subtle and error-prone, but it allows for covering scenarios where the container-managed approach does not work. This is usually the case only when interfacing with external systems that are not coordinated with the container. The list of EJB references is like an import clause in that it lists the names of other beans and their local and remote EJB home and object inter-faces. During deployment, this list is used to make sure that a deployed bean refers to the right synthesized interfaces and classes. Finally, the security iden-tity field (new in EJB 2.0) allows a bean to either run under the caller's identity or under some specified role.

Entity beans

The idea behind entity beans is to use objects corresponding to database enti-ties and encapsulate access to actual database records. An entity bean can correspond to a single row in a relational table, but more likely it corresponds to a row in the result of a join operation. The mapping of entity beans to and from database rows is called persistence. Entity beans can manage their own persistence by directly using JDBC to operate over databases. Alternatively, they can use container-managed persistence driven by object-to-table map-pings defined during the deployment process.

Entities in a database schema are related to each other. Thus, there is a need to find entity bean instances by navigating entity relationships. The correspon-ding mechanisms can again be either bean or container-managed relationships, as selected by the deployment descriptor. It is interesting to note that con-tainer-managed relationships map entity relationship (ER) models straight into object models. The database model is no longer relational, but instead of net-work-style. Network databases were introduced well before relational ones and they can have performance advantages. However, as they do not support con-cepts of normalization, network databases are known to be fragile. If the schema changes, client code needs to change as well. By keeping the data in normalized form (in a relational database), ER model changes will only affect the code inside entity beans.

An entity bean is either newly created or located by its primary key. In the former case, a new entity bean is created and associated with a new primary key. In the latter case, the container checks whether or not the corresponding bean instance is already available. If so, it is returned. If not, the container creates a new instance and associates it with the primary key. Then either the container or, in the bean-managed case, the bean class locate the underlying data in a database in order to initialize the new instance.

The deployment descriptor for an entity bean takes the following skeleton form:

```
<entity>
    <ejb-name> ...name of the entity bean... </ejb-name>
    <home> ...name of EJB home interface... </home>
    <remote> ...name of EJB object interface... </remote>
    <local-home> ...name of local EJB home interface... </local-home>
    <local> ...name of EJB object interface... </local>
    <ejb-class> ...name of class implementing this EJB... </ejb-class>
    <persistence-type> ...Container or Bean... </persistence-type>
    <prim-key-class> ... </prim-key-class>
    <reentrant> ...True or False... </reentrant>
    <abstract-schema-name> ... </abstract-schema-name>
    <prim-key-field> ...field name... </prim-key-field>
    <cmp-field> <field-name> ...field name... </field-name> </cmp-field>
    <security-identity> ...run-as role-name or use-caller-identity...
                        </security-identity>
</entity>
```

The initial fields match those of session bean descriptors. The persistence type can be container- or bean-managed, as discussed above. The primary key class defines which Java class to use to hold primary key values. This can range from java.lang.Integer to complex compound key types. The re-entrance field can be used to enable re-entrant calls as, by default, re-entrance of EJB beans is prohibited and causes the container to throw an exception. This cannot be overridden for session beans, but entity bean designers can decide to support re-entrancy as it can be difficult to prevent cases of re-entrance when navigating from entity to entity along the relationship graph. The abstract schema name is one that is unique to the particular bean that is used in EJB's query language (EJB QL; see below). Each field descriptor for container-managed persistence is interpreted as the name of a property (as of EJB 2.0) that has a setter and a getter method to be called by the container.

Entity relationships and database mapping

As mentioned above, combining the descriptors for relationship among entity beans and those for container-managed persistent fields yields an abstraction for a flexible object-to-relational mapping. This approach is at the heart of the improved portability of entity beans in EJB 2.0 from one J2EE server product to another. (EJB 1.1 introduced a container-managed persistence model that was severely limited and essentially made portable entity beans non-existent. While not described in this book, EJB 1.1 persistence lives on, but to enable backwards compatibility, an EJB 2.0 container has to also implement EJB 1.1 persistence.)

EJB 2.0 supports one-to-one, one-to-many, and many-to-many relationships – all in both unidirectional and bidirectional versions. In addition, EJB 2.0 introduced a query language similar to SQL called EJB QL. This language is used in deployment descriptors to declaratively specify additional find methods for the home interfaces of entity beans. For example, to define a find method that locates an entity by name (rather than by primary key), the following fragment could be added to a deployment descriptor:

```
<entity>
  ...
  <query>
    <query-method>
      <method-name>findByName</method-name>
      <method-params>
        <method-param>java.lang.String</method-param>
      </method-params>
      <ejb-ql>
        SELECT OBJECT(x) FROM Employee e WHERE e.name = ?1
      </ejb-ql>
    </query-method>
  </query>
</entity>
```

This descriptor fragment causes the implementation of a findByName method that takes a single string-typed argument. The SELECT statement is similar to SQL; ?1 refers to the first (and, in this case, only) method argument. In EJB 2.0, the specification of EJB QL still has a number of shortcomings (Monson-Haefel, 2001). For example, it is not possible to select rows in sorted order and it is not possible to properly handle dates. The lack of support for sorted order, especially, is a significant drawback for high-performance applications.

Container-managed persistence and relationships, as defined in EJB 2.0, are a powerful abstraction of the data-mapping machinery. However, there is a danger that developers lose touch with actual performance. At the time of writing, IBM's WebSphere implementation of J2EE 1.3.1 was one of the few that integrated the EJB 2.0 container mechanisms with the caching system of the database server. Without such a deep integration, container-managed persistence and relationships can lead to surprising performance problems because entities are brought in either in small increments or at once – both of which can seriously degrade performance.

14.5.3 Data-driven composition – message-driven beans in EJB 2.0

With the introduction of EJB 2.0, support for data-driven composition was added to the EJB model. In essence, this is done by adding an entirely new e-bean type – message-driven beans (md-beans). Like session and entity beans, md-beans reside inside an EJB container. Like session bean instances, they have no container-managed peristent state. Unlike session and entity beans, they also don't have a remote or local interface or home interface. The only way to instantiate and use an md-bean is to register it for a particular message queue or topic as defined by the Java message service (JMS, see section 14.6.3). An md-bean can be registered with exactly one such queue or topic only, requiring external collection of messages meant to be handled by an md-bean into a single queue or topic.

When the container schedules a message in a queue or topic for processing, it creates a new instance of any bound md-bean (or recycles an existing instance) and then calls its ejbCreate method. The container calls setMessageDrivenContext to associate the new md-bean with its context. Then the actual message handling is requested by calling the one central method of any md-bean – onMessage. An md-bean handling a message behaves a bit like a stateless session bean handling an incoming method call – it does not maintain specific state when returning from onMessage. The container is free to recycle an md-bean instance to handle multiple messages. Eventually, the container cleans up by calling the ejbRemove method, allowing the md-bean to release any resources it might have acquired. Unlike any other bean, an md-bean cannot return invocation results. To have any permanent effect whatsoever, an md-bean draws on other beans including entity beans. It can also draw on any resource accessible via its context, which, in EJB 2.0, has to include a JMS provider via which the md-bean can send messages. There are many more options, such as accessing databases or other external resources via JDBC or JCA resource connectors, respectively (see section 14.6.3).

It is possible to write all application logic using md-beans. The resulting message-queue-oriented design is fully asynchronous and thus not suitable for serving interactive sessions. However, the gained flexibility at the message queuing and scheduling level leads to a composition model that is well suited to workflow-oriented automatic distribution of work items.

14.6   Advanced Java services

This section covers Java support for distributed computing at an enterprise scale. There are actually four different models supporting distributed computing in Java – RMI, RMI over IIOP, CORBA, and EJB containers (that themselves build on RMI or RMI over IIOP). EJB was covered in the previous section; this section covers the remaining approaches, followed by the most important services supporting distributed applications.

14.6.1 **Distributed object model and RMI**

Distributed computing is mainly supported by the object serialization service (as described above) and the remote method invocation (RMI) service, both introduced with JDK 1.1. This subsection describes RMI and RMI over IIOP, which are subtly different.

A distributed object is handled via references of interface type – it is not possible to refer to a remote object's class or any of its superclasses. Interfaces that can be accessed remotely have to be derived from java.rmi.Remote. A remote operation can always fail as a result of network or remote hardware problems. All methods of a remote interface are therefore required to declare the checked exception java.rmi.RemoteException. Parameter passing to remote operations is interesting. If an argument is of a remote interface type, then the reference will be passed. In all other cases, passing is by value – that is, the argument is serialized at the call site and deserialized before invoking the remote interface. Java objects are not necessarily serializable. An attempt to pass a non-serializable object by value raises a runtime exception. If Java RMI conventions were made parts of the language, then the compiler could statically enforce that only serializable objects are passed by value and that all methods declare RemoteException.

The Java distribution model extends garbage collection as well. Fully distributed garbage collection is supported, based on a careful bookkeeping of which objects may have remote references to them. The collector is based on the work for Network Objects (Birrel, 1993). Distributed garbage collection is the most outstanding feature of Java RMI compared with almost all other mainstream approaches today. The only other approach that also builds on Network Objects and the idea of leased references is CLI remoting (see section 15.13.1), which was introduced about four years after the debut of Java RMI.

The Java distributed object model has a number of quirks, however. First, Java RMI interferes with the notion of object identity in Java. Second, Java RMI interferes with the Java locking system's semantics, which normally prevents self-inflicted deadlocks. These two problems are explained below. (Both of these problems are solved by the CLI approach.)

Java RMI affects object identity as a result of its model of implementing remote references. If a remote interface reference is passed around, proxy objects are created on remote sites. A reference to a remote interface, once passed in a remote method invocation, is thus not a reference to the remote object but to the local proxy of that object. Even if such a remote reference is sent back to the object's home server, it will still point to a proxy – one that is in the same server that the object itself is residing in. It is thus not possible to send out a reference, get it back, and compare it against a local object to see whether or not the returned reference matches that of the local object. (In contrast, DCOM and CLR maintain object identity on proxies. That is, they do not create multiple proxies for the same remote object in the same client context.)

Self-inflicted deadlocks are caused by locking systems that do not allow a thread to re-enter an area locked by that same thread. In regular Java, threads can acquire locks any number of times without causing a deadlock. In Java RMI, the situation is different. The notion of a thread identity does not span multiple machines. If a remote invocation performs a nested remote invocation back to the original requester, then a distributed deadlock can occur. Such a deadlock is caused by the original requester holding locks that are also needed by the recursive callback. (Compare this to logical threads, supported by DCOM and CLR, that can span process and machine boundaries.)

The special handling of identities by Java RMI has further effects. Several methods defined in java.lang.Object had been introduced with the Java object identity model in mind. Under Java RMI, the Object method's equivalents, hashCode and toString, need to be implemented differently. Proper handling can be achieved by extending class java.rmi.RemoteObject when creating a class that implements remote interfaces. Obviously, this precludes extending some other class and it may therefore be necessary to override these three methods "manually."

The situation is somewhat worse for the Object methods getClass, notify, notifyAll, and wait. These are declared final in java.lang.Object and cannot be adjusted by RemoteObject or another class. Although none of these methods malfunctions in the context of Java RMI, they all have potentially unexpected semantics. When operating on remote references, all these methods operate on the proxy object. For getClass, this makes the synthesized proxy class visible, instead of returning the real class of the remote object. For the wait and notify operations, there is no synchronization between the local proxy and the remote object. (The latter is usually desirable, as remote locking would be a fairly inefficient operation.)

14.6.2 Java and CORBA

An OMG IDL to Java binding and, an OMG first, a Java to OMG IDL reverse binding were defined in 1998 as part of CORBA 2.2 (see section 13.1.2). An important reason to incorporate CORBA into Java projects is to enable the use of IIOP for communication with non-Java subsystems. For access to CORBAservices it is usually more convenient to go through Java-specific access interfaces that can map to CORBA-compliant and other service implementations. Several of these Java service interface standards are discussed in the following subsections.

CORBA and Java usually coexist in almost all application server products today. It is therefore often reasonable to assume the presence of CORBA mechanisms (for interoperation) when implementing for the application server tier.

RMI is normally implemented using a proprietary protocol (Java Remote Method Protocol – JRMP), which limits the use of RMI to Java-to-Java com-

munication. The RMI-over-IIOP specification was introduced in 1999 and is part of the JDK since J2SE 1.3. It supports a restricted RMI variant to be used over the CORBA IIOP protocol, reaching any CORBA 2.4-compliant ORB. This specification requires a recent addition to CORBA that enables the sending of objects by value – that is, the sending of a copy of the object rather than the sending of a reference to the object staying behind.

RMI-over-IIOP does not support the RMI distributed garbage collection model and thus falls back on CORBA's lifecycle management approach to deal with the lifetime of remote objects explicitly. In addition, RMI-over-IIOP creates proxies that do not allow normal Java instanceof/cast mechanisms to be used to discover interfaces or subclasses. Instead, a service method must be called to determine whether or not some type is supported – and, if so, that method returns a new proxy. The fact that a new proxy instance may be returned does, as such, not add new complications as RMI is already removing the object identity property and several proxy instances may refer to the same remote object.

With J2SE 1.4, introduced in 2002, support was added for POA (portable object adapter), portable interceptors, INS (interoperable naming nervice), GIOP 1.2 (general interoperability protocol), and dynamic any's. J2SE 1.4 also includes a tool to remotely manage a persistent server and an ORB daemon (ORBD) that enables clients to transparently locate and invoke persistent objects on CORBA-supporting servers.

14.6.3 Enterprise service interfaces

Important parts of the J2EE architecture are several suites of interfaces that address enterprise-level services. Such service interfaces could also be established via CORBA (see section 14.6.2). However, Java-CORBA integration necessarily introduces some friction. In contrast, the Java-centric interfaces discussed in this section are designed to minimize any such friction, both from a client's and an implementer's point of view.

Java naming and directory interface (JNDI)

A universal problem in computing systems is the location of services by exact name or attributes. Naming services address the former and directory services the latter problem. Examples of naming services include the internet domain name service (DNS), the RMI registry, and the CORBA naming service. Examples of directory services include LDAP-compliant directories such as Novell's eDirectory, Microsoft's Active Directory, or the open source OpenLDAP (www.openldap.org).

JNDI provides uniform APIs for naming (javax.naming) and directory (javax.naming.directory) services. The most commonly used interface – Context – makes a particular naming context available on which method lookup can be used to locate objects by name. A naming context can also be used to list all bindings in the context, remove a binding, or create and destroy subcontexts. An important naming context for EJB beans is the environment naming context (ENC) provided by the EJB container. It enables access to environment properties, other beans, and resources.

Interface DirContext extends Context to provide directory functionality of examining and updating attributes associated with an object listed in the directory and searching a directory context by value. As DirContext extends Context, a directory context is also a naming context. Most contexts are themselves found by recursive lookup on another context. The starting point is the initial context that is always accessible by instantiating class InitialContext.

JNDI also defines an event API (javax.naming.event), an LDAP API (javax.naming.ldap) that supports the LDAP v3 features that go beyond the DirContext features, and a service provider interface (javax.naming.spi) that enables providers of naming and directory services to hook into JNDI. The event mechanism is used to register for change notifications. J2SE 1.4 comes with four built-in service providers – CORBA naming, DNS, LDAP, and RMI.

Java message service (JMS)

Asynchronous messaging enables composition models that decouple and overlap operations of the instances communicating by messages. Transacted message queues establish the level of reliabilty that normally requires synchronous call-based models. Flexible message routing, multicasting, and filtering further improve flexibility. JMS is a Java access mechanism to messaging systems – it doesn't implement messaging itself. JMS support message queues for point-to-point delivery of messages. It also supports message topics that allow for multiple targets to subscribe. Messages published to a topic are delivered to all subscribers of that topic.

JMS supports a variety of message types (bytes, streams, name-value maps, serialized objects, and text). Using declarations that are close to the SQL WHERE clause, message filters can be set up.

Java database connectivity (JDBC)

JDBC followed the popular Microsoft ODBC (open database connectivity) standard in establishing a common way of interacting with a database. The JDBC API is split into the core API (found in package java.sql and part of J2SE) and the JDBC optional package (found in javax.sql and optional in J2SE, but mandatory in J2EE). Like ODBC, JDBC depends on drivers to map the JDBC API to the native interfaces of a particular database.

There are four types of JDBC drivers. Type 1 and Type 2 drivers use native (non-Java) code accessed via JNI. Type 1 drivers use native code with a common interface, while Type 2 allows for database-specific interfaces. The most common Type 1 driver is the JDBC-ODBC bridge included in the JDK – it maps JDBC calls to ODBC calls. This is relatively slow as ODBC uses its own driver model to access specific databases. Type 3 and Type 4 drivers are pure Java. Type 3 accesses a database indirectly via a network protocol and a database gateway, while Type 4 accesses a database directly. Drivers can be selected without affecting client code as the JDBC API itself is unaffected by the choice of driver. In terms of typical performance, Type 4 is usually the best, followed by Type 2, then Type 1, and finally Type 3.

Available JDBC drivers are tracked by the driver manager. Typically, a driver registers with the driver manager using a static initializer. That is, merely loading a driver suffices to cause registration. The following statement is commonly used to load a driver – the JDBC-ODBC bridge driver in this example.

```
Class.forName("sun.jdbc.odbc.JdbcOdbcDriver");
```

Once a driver has been located, the Driver interface can be used to create a database connection, which is reflected by a returned object that implements interface Connection. The Connection interface is the main JDBC hub – it can be used to retrieve meta-information about the database itself, create database statements (SQL statements), and manage database transactions. Statements come in three variants – plain, prepared, and callable statements. Prepared statements are effectively SQL templates, which are SQL commands with variables. Before executing a prepared statement, these variables are filled in by calling methods that associate a variable with a value. Callable statements invoke SQL stored procedures. Some statements perform a database command that has no results (such as deleting a row of data), but most yield a result. Results are objects that implements interface ResultSet. Unless a result is read-only, it can be updated and pushed back to the database.

Database connections (and open statements per connection) are a relatively expensive resource and most systems impose tight limits. This is an area where reliance on the JVM's garbage collector is not acceptable practice. Instead, developers must take care to explicitly call the corresponding close methods to ensure release of such resources as soon as they are no longer needed. There are further complications in this space. For instance, while prepared statements are good candidates for shared use – they can be created once and then used repeatedly with variable bindings – they are always associated with a single specific connection. However, connection pooling is a common technique to enhance performance, forcing the creation of a new statement every time as the connection instance will vary.

Java transaction API and service (JTA, JTS)

While transaction management is almost always delegated to an EJB's container, there are cases where explicit transaction management is required. The CORBA object transaction service (OTS) or its Java implementation (JTS) can be used for this purpose. However, a much simpler interface was introduced with EJB, namely the Java transaction API. It comprises a low-level XA interface

(the X/Open transaction API standard) used by server/container implementations and a high-level client interface accessible to EJB beans implementations.
The most common high-level interface is javax.transaction.UserTransaction
with six simple methods (with exception lists elided for brevity):

```
package javax.transaction;
public interface UserTransaction {
    void begin () throws ...;
    void commit () throws ...;
    int getStatus () throws ...;
    void rollback () throws ...;
    void setRollbackOnly () throws ...;
    void setTransactionTimeout (int seconds) throws ...;
}
```

The use of JTS (or OTS) requires explicit and careful enlistment of resources
in transactions and, thus, the explicit demarcation of transaction boundaries.
With the high-level JTA interfaces, this error-prone function is performed by
the EJB container. However, explicit transaction management is still error-
prone and can lead to inconsistencies or inefficiencies due to resources held by
long-running transactions.

J2EE connector architecture (JCA)

Introduced with J2EE 1.3, JCA standardizes connectors between a J2EE
application server and enterprise information systems (EIS) such as database
management, enterprise resource planning (ERP), enterprise asset management (EAM), and customer relationship management (CRM) systems.
Enterprise applications not written in Java or within the J2EE framework are
also candidates for JCA connection. The JCA is defined in package
javax.resource and its subpackages (cci, spi, and spi.security). (JCA is a case of
frontal acronym collision as the same acronym is also used for the Java cryptography API.)

JCA defines resource adapters that plug into a J2EE application server –
one such adapter per EIS type. Resource adapters interact with an application
server to support connection pooling, security, and transactions. This collaboration is formalized by three corresponding JCA system contracts that specify
how application servers and application components establish connections as
well as security and transaction contexts. In addition, the JCA common client
interface (CCI) defines a client API for application components that need to
access an EIS. The CCI is preferably used by enterprise application integration
(EAI) frameworks and by tools.

In early 2002, nine J2EE application servers supported JCA, including
BEA's WebLogic, IBM's WebSphere, Borland's Enterprise Server and Oracle's

9iAS application server (java.sun.com/j2ee/connector/products.html). At the same time, 16 EIS and EAI products supported JCA, with an additional 16 announced or in beta. Connectable EIS include BEA's Tuxedo, SAP's R/3, IBM's CICS, IMS, and MQ/Series, JD Edward's, Oracle's, Peoplesoft's and SAP's ERP systems, and Siebel's CRM system.

14.6.4 Java and XML

Sun has been one of the early promoters of XML. Yet, initially, XML support for Java was limited to interfaces supporting the processing of XML documents, presenting the XML document (DOM) and XML streaming (SAX) models. More complete support for XML, including XML Schema, and support for web services standards has been added as a pre-release ("early adoption") in early 2002.

The Java Architecture for XML Binding (JAXB) provides an API and tools that automate the mapping between XML documents and Java objects, although the early access version released in early 2002 only supports DTDs, not XML Schema.

Java API for XML messaging (JAXM) is a J2SE optional package that implements the simple object access protocol (SOAP), v1.1 with attachments. Messaging profiles are included to enable pluggability of higher-level protocols.

The Java API for XML-based RPC (JAX-RPC) supports the construction of web services and clients that interact using SOAP and that are described using WSDL.

Java API for XML processing (JAXP) is a collection of DOM, SAX, and XSLT implementations.

Java API for XML registries (JAXR) provides uniform and standard access to different kinds of XML registries, including the ebXML registry and repository standard and the UDDI specification.

14.7 Interfaces versus classes in Java, revisited

Java separates and supports classes and interfaces, where an interface is essentially a fully abstract class. As Java classes can be fully abstract, Java programmers have to choose whether to use an interface or an abstract class. It is interesting to observe the current trend away from the use of classes and toward the increasing use of interfaces. As interfaces rule out implementation inheritance, this trend also favors object composition and message-forwarding techniques. A few examples of this ongoing trend are described below.

JavaBeans still allows classes to surface on bean boundaries. Even implementation inheritance across bean boundaries is commonly used, although usually to inherit from base libraries, not from other beans. However, the JavaBeans specification (as of v1.00-A) recommends not using the Java type test and

guard operators (instanceof and checked narrowing cast). Instead, programmers should use the methods isInstanceOf and getInstanceOf in class
java.beans.Beans. The intention probably was to provide a hook for post-1.00
beans that can be represented to the outside by more than one object, similar
to the QueryInterface mechanism in COM, although this has yet to happen.

The Java AWT event model has been changed from an inheritance-based
solution in JDK 1.0 to a "delegation-based" (really a forwarding-based) solution in JDK 1.1. In addition to the resulting advantages and increased
flexibility, it was admitted that the 1.0 approach led to undue complexity and
was a source of subtle errors.

Whereas the non-distributed Java object model supports classes and interfaces, the distributed Java object model (based on RMI; see section 14.6.1)
restricts remote access to interfaces. In other words, where distribution is
used or planned for, direct use of classes is not advisable and all access should
be via interfaces.

Enterprise JavaBeans also restricts bean access to interfaces, but it goes even
further than RMI as there can be only one remote interface on an EJB bean. If
an EJB bean would need to implement multiple interfaces, it suffices to define
a single interface extending these interfaces.

It is interesting to see how the tension between interfaces and classes shaped
up as the Java specifications evolved. For instance, the ratio of classes to interfaces has markedly shifted from almost exclusive use of classes in the early Java
packages to much heavier use of interfaces in later Java specifications. A Sun
initiative, code-named "Glasgow," aimed to generalize JavaBeans. Besides
other enhancements (see sections 14.4.4 and 14.4.5), this specification was
supposed to support object composition based on containment and aggregation. While Glasgow did add many new features to JavaBeans and the larger
user interface toolkit, including an interesting container design, it did not
deliver aggregation support.

14.8   JXTA and Jini

JXTA and Jini address a similar problem – the federation of systems over
loosely coupled distributed systems. Jini focuses on Java everywhere, with a
preference for (although not a strong restriction to) Java-specific networking
protocols such as RMI (www.sun.com/software/jini/; www.jini.org; Arnold *et al.*,
1999). Jini also moves Java components to where they are needed. Thus, Jini
requires the Java runtime environment on at least some of the involved computers and devices. The surrogate project (www.jini.org) created the Jini
surrogate architecture, a design that enables non-Java endpoints to be hooked
into a Jini federation by having a Jini surrogate act on their behalf. (In standard networking terminology, a surrogate is a protocol bridge.) For instance, a
surrogate could be used to bridge between a Jini federation and a Universal
Plug-and-Play federation.

JXTA (pronounced "juxta", short for juxtaposition; Gong, 2001) is a Sun initiative that aims at open peer-to-peer computing, preferring XML-based conventions and protocols on the network (wwws.sun.com/software/jxta/; www.jxta.org; Brookshier, 2002). There is no requirement that JXTA participants run Java, although JXTA naturally defines how Java-based endpoints can be formed. The Jini surrogate architecture can be used to bridge between JXTA and Jini.

Jiro is another Java-based approach that aims to use federation to specifically aid systems management. As it stands in early 2002, Jiro focuses even more specifically on the domain of managing storage systems. See section 18.5 for a brief discussion of Jiro.

All three initiatives (Jini, JXTA and Jiro) have some overlap with the space of web services. Jini's and Jiro's reliance on sending Java components across the network limits it to non-XML web services. JXTA builds on XML conventions and protocols, but, as it stands, does not use the standard protocols of XML web services, such as SOAP, WSDL, and UDDI (see section 12.4.5).

14.8.1 Jini – federations of Java services and clients

Jini is a specification that describes how federations of Java services and clients of such services can be formed over loosely coupled systems. Three problems need to be addressed – how clients locate services, how services make themselves available, and how the overall system copes with partial failure and reconfiguration. Jini addresses the problems of locating and publishing services and partially addresses the problems of robustness under various failure modes.

Jini defines special services called lookup services that serve two purposes. First, clients query the lookup services in order to find specific services and, second, services publish themselves by registering with lookup services. This introduces a bootstrap problem – how do clients and services locate lookup services? Jini defines both a broadcast protocol for lookup service location within smaller networks that support such broadcasts and a unicast protocol to hierarchically locate lookup services in larger networks that don't support full broadcasts.

When a Jini service registers with a lookup service, it specifies a desired lease period. This is similar to the RMI distributed garbage collection scheme (see section 14.6.1) as, once the lease expires, the lookup service removes the registration entry of that service. A lookup service is free to constrain the lease period and grant a lease only to an upper bound it can accommodate. In particular, Jini lookup services will never grant an infinite lease period.

A Jini service can register with more than one lookup service and multiple Jini services can register under the same service type. A Jini client can consult multiple lookup services. Hence, it is possible – and in a larger federation even likely – that a client locates multiple services that could be used. It then picks one of them and establishes contact. Once a client has located a service, Jini is out of the loop. If a service fails while a client is connected, then it is that client's responsibility to either take appropriate measures or else simply fail as well. As Jini services can be – and often are – clients of other Jini services, such failure propagation can cause a ripple effect.

The dynamic proxy mechanism introduced in J2SE 1.3 can be used to isolate clients from certain service failures (Ledru, 2002). The idea is to automatically fail over from a failed service to an equivalent one and do so inside a proxy, such that a client doesn't observe such a change. Clearly, there is a strong assumption to be made – that the failed session didn't build up any session-specific or even longer-term state in the service. If such state existed, it would be lost on fail over. In other words, even with such smart proxies in place, it is still the responsibility of the developer of Jini services and clients to deal with partial failure modes at a state level properly.

14.8.2 JXTA – peer-to-peer computing

JXTA is supposed to span programming languages, platforms (such as Unix versus Windows), and networking infrastructure (such as TCP/IP versus Bluetooth). The JXTA protocols establish a virtual network on top of existing networks, hiding their underlying physical topology. Peer discovery and organization into peer groups is performed over this virtual network. The JXTA protocols also address the advertising and discovery of resources and communication among and monitoring of peers. The following five abstractions form the JXTA virtual network – uniform peer ID addressing, peer groups, advertisements, resolvers, and pipes. JXTA defines a search approach that helps to locate peers and resources efficiently in large networks.

Figure 14.10 shows the main layering of the JXTA architecture (Gong, 2001). JXTA comprises the following core protocols – peer discovery, peer resolver, peer information, peer membership, pipe binding, and endpoint routing. Peers and resources are identified uniformly by UUIDs (128-bit "flat" unique IDs). XML documents are used to advertise services and resources. Peers are required to support a set of peer-level protocols. In addition, groups of peers can form a virtual entity that supports additional group-level protocols. Communication is by means of messages sent via pipes. Pipes are directed, unreliable, unicast or multicast constructs that deliver messages between peer endpoints. Thus, a pipe can be seen as a named unreliable message queue. Higher-level communication semantics, such as reliable delivery, can be built on top of basic pipes. The motivation is to get as close as possible to the physical networks (say, UDP instead of TCP/IP), which usually do not provide reliable communication.

The peer discovery protocol serves a peer to discover its peers, peer groups and advertised resources (by discovering the describing advertisement, an XML document). If no ID is specified, this protocol will return all advertisements of a particular peer or peer group. By starting with a unique world peer

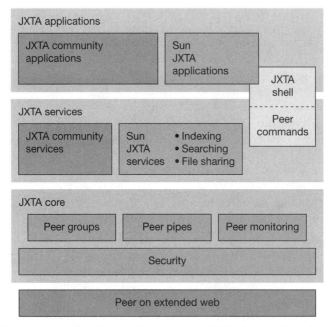

Figure 14.10 JXTA architectural layering. (From Gong, L. (2001) Project JXTA: A Technology Overview. Sun Microsystems, Palo Alto, CA. (**www.jxta.org/project/www/docs/TechOverview.pdf**).)

group, a system can be bootstrapped. Notice that this is conceptually very similar to the internet's domain name service (DNS) supported by a hierarchy of DNS servers, where nodes are identified by their IP address, which as of IPv6 is also a flat 128-bit value.

The peer resolver protocol is used to implement advanced search functionality. It is typically implemented by peers that maintain repositories. The peer information protocol can be used to retrieve status (liveness) and capability information on other peers. The peer membership protocol allows peers to discover credentials required to join a particular group, apply for membership, update membership and credential information, and cancel membership. Protection is provided in the form of authentication and security credentials.

The pipe-binding protocol allows peers to bind a pipe to one of their endpoints. Pipes can be created, opened, closed, or deleted. An open pipe can be used to send and receive messages. Opening a pipe binds it to an endpoint; closing it causes unbinding. Endpoints specify the actual sources and sinks of messages within a peer implementation. The peer endpoint protocol enables peers to become routers. Thus, if a peer needs to determine how to reach another peer, it uses this protocol to discover possible routes. Any peer that implements the protocol indicates that it can route messages over certain networks to certain other peers.

On reflection, JXTA is a bit like a virtual internet over the internet. While creating a clear opportunity for redesign of this space, it is not yet clear whether or not the benefits of a hopefully cleaner design can outweigh the disadvantages of separation from the internet via this abstraction layer. The internet was designed to scale to enormous size and has certainly successfully done so. Its protocols may show signs of their age, but they don't seem to show fundamental flaws that would indicate an approaching end of scalability. In particular, the large computers from the early days of the internet are now matched by the capabilities of even the smallest devices. Useful implementations of SNMP, HTTP, and TCP/IP can now be squeezed into tiny devices (www-ccs.cs.umass.edu/~shri/iPic.html; www.ipsil.com). It might well be that JXTA would be more effective by complementing the existing internet protocol family, including the emerging web services protocols.

14.9 Java and web services – SunONE

SunONE (Sun open network environment) is an extension of J2EE that relies on specialized servlets to handle web service protocols. SunONE also incorporates the J2EE server products formerly marketed by iPlanet (note that the alliance between Netscape and Sun that was called iPlanet expired in early 2002, leaving the iPlanet products with Sun. In early 2002, iPlanet accounted for around 7 percent market share in the J2EE space, following IBM's WebSphere and BEA's WebLogic at 34 percent each and closely followed by Oracle at 6 percent.)

With the release of early adopter versions of the Java web services developer pack (Java WSDP) in early 2002, Sun provides support for SOAP, WSDL, and UDDI. Java WDSP includes the Java APIs for XML messaging (JAXM), XML processing (JAXP), XML registries (JAXR), and XML-based RPC (JAX-RPC). It also includes the JSP standard tag library (JSTL), the Ant build tool, the Java WSDP registry server, the web application deployment tool, and the Apache Tomcat web server container.

CHAPTER FIFTEEN

The Microsoft way:
COM, OLE/ActiveX, COM+, and .NET CLR

In a sense, Microsoft is taking the easiest route. Instead of proposing a global standard and hoping to port its own systems to it, it continually re-engineers its existing application and platform base. Component technology is introduced gradually, gaining leverage from previous successes, such as the original Visual Basic controls (VBX – non-object-oriented components!), object linking and embedding (OLE), OLE database connectivity (ODBC), ActiveX, Microsoft Transaction Server (MTS), or active server pages (ASP).

In the standards arena, Microsoft focuses mostly on internet (IETF) and web (W3C) standards. More recently, some of its .NET specifications (CLI and $C^{\#}$) where adopted by ECMA – a European standards body with a fast track to ISO (ECMA, 2001a, 2001b). Microsoft is not trying to align its approaches with OMG or Java standards. While Java figured prominently in Microsoft's strategy for a while, it has been relegated to a mere continuation of support of its older Visual J^{++} product – in part as a result of a settlement between Sun and Microsoft. In addition, under the name Visual $J^{\#}$ .NET, Microsoft offers a migration tool to .NET, primarily targeting users of Visual J^{++} 6.0.

As part of the .NET initiative, Microsoft is promoting language neutrality as a major tenet of CLR and aims to establish a new language, $C^{\#}$. $C^{\#}$ adopts many of the successful traits of Java, while adding several distinctive features of its own (such as value types) and not supporting key Java features (such as inner classes). $C^{\#}$ is positioned as a CLR model language, but as an equal alongside with several other languages, including an overhauled Visual Basic .NET, Managed C^{++} (an ANSI-compliant extension of C^{++}), and many languages supported by other vendors and organizations.

In the space of contextual composition (see section 21.2), the spiral between Microsoft, OMG, and Sun technologies is fascinating. Contextual composition was first sketched in COM's apartment model, ripened in the Microsoft Transaction Server (MTS), then adopted and improved in Enterprise JavaBeans, independently matured in COM+, next adopted and refined in the CORBA Component Model (CCM), and finally taken to an extensible and open mechanism in CLR, while – again in parallel – EJB 2.0 overtakes the meant-to-be superset CCM, indicating a required "maintenance step" of the CCM specification.

As COM is likely to be of continuing importance for years to come and CLR interoperability with COM is particularly strong, the following discussion of the Microsoft approach begins with an introduction to COM. COM+ added services to COM, many of which are still not redundant as the first CLR release uses COM interoperation to provide the COM+ services.

15.1   The first fundamental wiring model – COM

COM is Microsoft's foundation on which all component software on its platforms is based. In addition, COM is made available on the Macintosh by Microsoft and on many other platforms by third parties, such as Software AG, and Hewlett-Packard. However, it would be fair to state that COM has never gained much support beyond the Microsoft Windows platforms. The basic ideas behind COM had, at the same time, quite some influence. For example, the Mozilla project's XPCOM is very similar to a simplified core of COM (Scullin, 1998) and Groove's Transceiver is built using COM, but not using the full COM infrastructure (www.groove.net). Even the design of the recent CORBA component model (CCM, see section 13.3) shows some influence (the CCM equivalence interface and the supported interface facets are very similar to COM's QueryInterface and aggregation, respectively – more on both further below).

This section provides a detailed and technical account of the inner workings of COM. Although, at the heart, COM is simple, it is also different from standard object models, and a detailed understanding helps to compare COM with other approaches.

COM is a binary standard – it specifies nothing about how a particular programming language may be bound to it. COM does not even specify what a component or an object is. It neither requires nor prevents the use of objects to implement components. The one fundamental entity that COM does define is an interface. On the binary level, an interface is represented as a pointer to an interface node. The only specified part of an interface node is another pointer held in the first field of the interface node. This second pointer is defined to point to a table of procedure variables (function pointers). As these tables are derived from the tables used to implement virtual functions (methods) in languages such as C^{++}, they are also called vtables. Figure 15.1 shows a COM interface on the "binary" level.

The double indirection – clients see a pointer to a pointer to the vtable – seems odd. Indeed, very few descriptions of COM in the literature that are not of the most technical nature explain what this extra indirection is for. To understand this point, it is necessary to elaborate on another detail of COM –

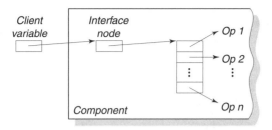

Figure 15.1 Binary representation of a COM interface.

the calling convention, which is the specification of what exactly is passed when calling an operation from an interface.

Methods of an object have one additional parameter – the object they belong to. This parameter is sometimes called self or this. Its declaration is hidden in most object-oriented languages, but a few, including Component Pascal, make it explicit. The point is that the interface pointer is passed as a self-parameter to any of the interface's operations. This allows operations in a COM interface to exhibit true object characteristics. In particular, the interface node can be used to refer internally to instance variables. It is even possible to attach instance variables directly to the interface node, but this is not normally done. It is, however, quite common to store pointers that simplify the lookup of instance variables and the location of other interfaces.

A COM component is free to contain implementations for any number of interfaces. The entire implementation can be a single class, but it does not have to be. A component can just as well contain many classes that are used to instantiate objects of just as many different kinds. These objects then collectively provide the implementation of the interfaces provided by the component. Figure 15.2 shows a component that provides three different interfaces and uses two different objects to implement these.

In Figure 15.2, object 1 implements interfaces A and B, whereas object 2 implements interface C. The dashed pointers between the interface nodes are used internally as it must be possible to get from each node to every other node. The unusual layout of objects and vtables is just what COM prescribes if such an n-to-m relationship between objects and interfaces is desired. However, without proper language support, it is not likely that many components will take such a complex shape. What is important, though, is that there is no single object part that ever leaves the component and represents the entire COM object. A COM component is not necessarily a traditional class and a COM object is not necessarily a traditional single-bodied object. However, a COM object can be such a traditional object and all of its interfaces can be implemented in a single class by using multiple inheritance (Rogerson, 1997).

There are two important questions to be answered at this point. How does a client learn about other interfaces and how does a client compare the identity

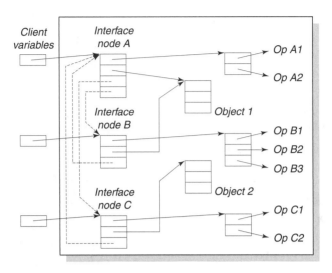

Figure 15.2 A COM object with multiple interfaces.

of COM objects? Surprisingly, these two questions are closely related. Every COM interface has a common first method named QueryInterface. Thus, the first slot of the function table of any COM interface points to a QueryInterface operation. There are two further methods shared by all interfaces. These are explained below.

QueryInterface takes the name of an interface, checks if the current COM object supports it, and, if so, returns the corresponding interface reference. An error indication is returned if the interface queried for is not supported. On the level of QueryInterface, interfaces are named using interface identifiers (IIDs). An IID is a GUID (Chapter 12), which is a 128-bit number guaranteed to be globally unique. COM uses GUIDs for other purposes also.

As every interface has a QueryInterface operation, a client can get from any provided interface to any other. Once a client has a reference to at least one interface, it can obtain access to all others provided by the same COM object. Recall that interface nodes are separate and therefore cannot serve to identify a COM object uniquely. However, COM requires that a given COM object returns the same interface node pointer each time it is asked for the IUnknown interface. As all COM objects must have an IUnknown interface, the identity of the IUnknown interface node can serve to identify the entire COM object. To ensure that this identity is logically preserved by interface navigation, the QueryInterface contract requires that any successful query yields an interface that is on the same COM object – that is, establishes the same identify via queries for IUnknown. To enable sound reasoning, the set of interfaces explorable by queries must be an equivalence class. This means that the queries are reflexive in that if they ask for an interface by querying that same interface, they will succeed. They are also symmetrical in that if they ask for an interface, from where the current interface was retrieved, they will succeed. Further, queries are transitive in that if a third interface can be retrieved via a second that was retrieved from a first, then the third can be retrieved directly by querying the first. The final rule ensures stability. It is that if a query for an interface on a particular COM identity succeeded (failed) once, then it will succeed (fail) for the lifetime of that instance.

A common way to depict a COM object is to draw it as a box with plugs. As every COM object has an IUnknown interface (which also identifies the COM object), it is common to show the IUnknown interface on top of a COM object's diagram. Figure 15.3 shows an example of a COM object diagram – in this case, an ActiveX document object.

Back to the IUnknown interface. Of course, its "real" name is its IID "00000000-0000-0000-C000-000000000046," but for the sake of convenience all interfaces also have a readable name. By convention, such readable interface names start with I. Unlike IIDs, there is no guarantee that readable names are unique. Thus, all programmed references to interfaces use IIDs.

The primary use of IUnknown is to identify a COM object in the most abstract – that is, without requiring any specific functionality. A reference to an IUnknown interface can thus be compared to a reference of type ANY or Object in object-oriented languages. In a sense, IUnknown is a misnomer. It is not an unknown interface, but, rather, the only interface guaranteed always to be present. However, a reference to an IUnknown interface is a reference to a potentially otherwise totally unknown COM object, one with no known interfaces.

The IUnknown interface supports just the three mandatory methods of any COM interface. The first mandatory method is QueryInterface, as described above. The other two mandatory methods of any COM interface are called AddRef and Release. Together with some rules about when to call them, they serve to control an object's lifetime, as explained further below. Using a simplified COM IDL-like notation, IUnknown is defined as:

```
[ uuid(00000000-0000-0000-C000-000000000046) ]
interface IUnknown {
   HRESULT QueryInterface
      ([in] const IID iid, [out, iid_is(iid)] IUnknown iid);
   unsigned long AddRef ();
   unsigned long Release ();
}
```

The type HRESULT is used by most COM interface methods to indicate success or failure of a call. QueryInterface uses it to indicate whether or not the requested interface is supported. If an interface belongs to a remote object, then HRESULT may also indicate network failures.

Every COM object performs reference counting either for the object in its entirety or separately for each of its interface nodes. Where a COM object uses a single shared reference count, it cannot deallocate an interface node,

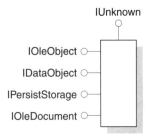

Figure 15.3 Depiction of a COM object.

although this particular node may have no remaining references. This is normally acceptable, and sharing of a single reference count is the usual approach. In some cases, interface nodes may be resource intensive, such as when they maintain a large cache structure. A separate reference count for such an interface node can then be used to release that node as early as possible. (This technique of creating and deleting interface nodes as required is sometimes referred to as "tear-off interfaces.")

On creation of an object or node, the reference count is initialized to 1 before handing out a first reference. Each time a copy of a reference is created, the count must be incremented (AddRef). Each time a reference is given up, the count must be decremented (Release). As soon as a reference count reaches zero, the COM object has become unreachable and should therefore self-destruct. As part of its destruction, it has to release all references to other objects that it might still hold, calling their Release methods. This leads to a recursive destruction of all objects exclusively held by the object under destruction. Finally, the destructed object returns the memory space it occupied.

Reference counting is a form of cooperative garbage collection. As long as all involved components play by the rules and cooperate, memory will be safely deallocated. At least, objects will never be deallocated while references still exist. Reference counting has the well-known problem that it cannot deal with cyclic references. Consider the two objects in Figure 15.4.

The two objects are, as a whole, unreachable as no other object still has a reference to any of the two. However, the mutual reference keeps both objects' reference counts above zero and thus prevents deallocation. Obviously, this is only a special case. The general case is a cycle of references

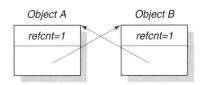

Figure 15.4 Cyclical references between objects.

via an arbitrary number of objects – all of which keep each other mutually "alive." As cyclical structures are very common, COM defines a set of rules that govern the use of AddRef and Release in the presence of cycles. These rules are complex and prone to error. In addition, they differ from situation to situation. The idea, however, is always the same – at least one of the objects in a cycle has another method that breaks the cycle, making the objects in the cycle collectible. The difficulty lies in specifying exactly when this extra method is to be called.

15.2 COM object reuse

COM does not support any form of implementation inheritance. As explained in Chapter 7, this can be seen as a feature rather than a weakness. (Note that COM does not define or "care about" how an individual component is internally realized. A component may well consist of classes that, within the component, use implementation inheritance.) In any case, lack of implementation inheritance does not mean lack of support for reuse. COM supports two forms of object composition to enable object reuse (Chapter 7). The two forms are called containment and aggregation.

Containment is just the simple object composition technique already explained in Chapter 7 – one object holds an exclusive reference to another. The former, also called the outer object, thus conceptually contains the latter, the inner object. If requests to the outer object need to be handled by the inner object, the outer object simply forwards the request to the inner object. Forwarding is nothing but calling a method of the inner object to implement a call to a method of the outer object.

For example, Figure 15.5 shows how an outer object's IStream interface is implemented by forwarding calls to methods Read and Write to an inner object. Figure 15.5a shows that containment is really no more than normal object use. Figure 15.5b uses a different depiction of the same situation, this time illustrating the containment relation.

Containment suffices to reuse implementations contained in other components. In particular, containment is completely transparent to clients of an outer object. A client calling an interface function cannot tell if the object providing the interface handles the call, or the call is forwarded and handled by another object.

If deep containment hierarchies occur, or if the forwarded methods themselves are relatively cheap operations, then containment can become a performance problem. For this reason, COM defines its second reuse form, which is aggregation. The basic idea of aggregation is simple. Instead of forwarding requests, an inner object's interface reference could be handed out directly to an outer object's client. Calls on this interface would then go directly to the inner object, saving the cost of forwarding. Of course, aggregation is only useful where the outer object does not wish to intercept calls to,

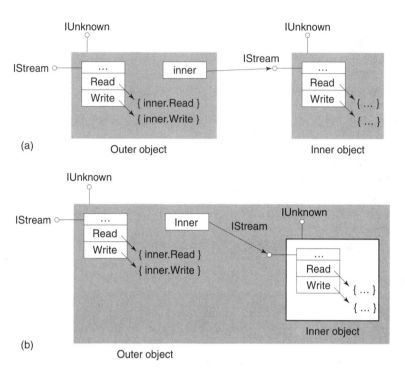

Figure 15.5 (a) Containment as seen on the level of objects. (b) Alternative depiction emphasizing the containment property.

for example, perform some filtering or additional processing. Also, it is important to retain transparency as a client of the outer object should have no way of telling that a particular interface has been aggregated from an inner object.

With containment, the inner object is unaware of being contained. This is different for aggregation, which needs the inner object to collaborate. A COM object has the choice of whether or not to support aggregation. If it does, it can become an aggregated inner object. Why is this collaborative effort required? Recall that all COM interfaces support QueryInterface. If an inner object's interface is exposed to clients of the outer object, then the QueryInterface of that inner object's interface must still cover the interfaces supported by the outer object. The solution is simple. The inner object learns about the outer object's IUnknown interface when it is aggregated. Calls to its QueryInterface are then forwarded to the outer object's QueryInterface.

Figure 15.6 shows how the scenario from above changes when using aggregation. Recall that the depiction of one object inside another, just as with containment, has merely illustrative purposes. The inner object is fully self-standing and most likely implemented by a different component than the outer object. The aggregation relation manifests itself in the mutual object references established between the inner and the outer object.

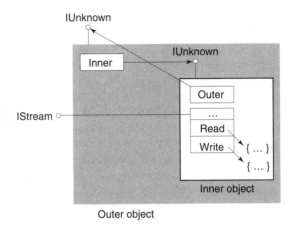

Figure 15.6 Aggregation.

Aggregation can go any number of levels deep. Inner objects, on whatever level, always refer to the IUnknown interface of the outermost object. For internal purposes, an outer object retains a direct reference to an inner object's original IUnknown. In this way, an outer object can still query for an inner object's interfaces without being referred to its own IUnknown. As is clearly visible in Figure 15.6, the inner and outer objects in an aggregation setting maintain mutual references. As explained above, such cycles would prevent deallocation of aggregates. Thus, COM has special, and again error-prone, rules about how to manipulate the reference counts involved in order for the scheme to work.

Aggregation, as a pure performance tool, if compared to containment, is probably meaningful only for deeply nested constructions. This is one of the reasons for aggregation in COM practice being less important than containment. Another reason is the increase in complexity. Nevertheless, aggregation can be put to work where efficient reuse of component functionality is needed. The resulting performance is as good as that of a directly implemented interface as aggregated interfaces short-circuit all aggregation levels.

Aggregation can be used to construct efficient generic wrappers ("blind delegation" of arbitrary interfaces). In particular, aggregation can be used to add support for new interfaces on otherwise unchanged objects. However, doing so requires great care as the new interfaces must not interfere with any of the (generally unknown!) interfaces on that object. This works if the potential use of aggregating wrappers and their added interfaces was already known when constructing the original objects (then interference is avoided by construction of these objects) or when the added interfaces are private to some infrastructure. For example, COM remoting builds up proxy objects that implement both the interfaces of some remote object and private interfaces of the COM remoting infrastructure. This technique makes aggregation a potentially powerful tool. However, the conditions for when this technique is safe are so subtle that it is better avoided where possible.

15.3 Interfaces and polymorphism

COM interfaces can be derived from other COM interfaces using (single) interface inheritance. In fact, all COM interfaces directly or indirectly inherit from IUnknown, the common base type of the interface hierarchy. Besides IUnknown, there are only two other important base interfaces that are commonly inherited from – IDispatch and IPersist. Otherwise, interface inheritance in COM is rarely used. Why is this?

Surprisingly, interface inheritance in COM has nothing to do with the polymorphism COM supports. For example, assume that a client holds a reference to an interface, say IDispatch. In reality, the interface the client is referring to can be of any subtype of IDispatch. In other words, the function table may contain additional methods over and above those required by IDispatch. However, and this point is important, there is no way for the client to find out! If the client wants a more specific interface, it has to use QueryInterface. It is of no relevance to the client whether or not the returned interface node is actually the one QueryInterface was issued on, but this time guaranteeing the extra methods.

The true nature of polymorphism in COM is the support of sets of interfaces by COM objects. The type of a COM object is the set of interface identifiers of the interfaces it supports. A subtype is a superset of interfaces. For example, assume that a client requires an object to support the following set of interfaces: {IOleDocumentView, IOleInPlaceActiveObject, IOleInPlaceObject}. An object that supports the set of interfaces {IOleDocumentView, IOleInPlaceActiveObject, IOleInPlaceObject, IOleCommandTarget, IPrint} obviously satisfies the client's requirements and could, thus, from a subtyping point of view, be used. Figure 15.7 illustrates this.

One way to test whether or not a COM object satisfies all requirements is to call QueryInterface once for each required interface. For example, an ActiveX document container may need to check that an object offered for insertion

Figure 15.7 COM types are sets of interface IDs, and subtypes are supersets.

into one of its documents satisfies the minimal requirements for an ActiveX container control.

15.3.1 Categories

Instantiating a COM object and issuing a large number of QueryInterface requests, just to verify that all the requested interfaces are indeed implemented, is too inefficient. To support efficient handling of sets of interfaces, COM defines categories. A category has its own identifier (CATID), which, again, is a globally unique identifier. Categories are roughly defined as sets of interface identifiers. A COM object can be a member of any number of categories, and categories among themselves are totally unrelated. Figure 15.8 illustrates the situation using set diagrams. The two categories A and B both require three interfaces. They overlap in that both require ITwo.

Categories have to serve a second purpose, one that is a little irritating. COM allows a component to return an E_NOTIMPL error code for any of the methods of an interface. This is quite catastrophic and subverts the idea of COM interfaces as contracts to some extent. A client still has to be prepared for a provider, despite its announced support of an interface, to choose not to implement one or the other method. The resulting coding style is ugly to say the least. Categories help to clean up this situation. A category specifies not only which interfaces must at least be supported, but also which methods in these interfaces must at least be implemented.

Finally, categories also have a contractual nature. For example, a category can specify not only that an object provides the universal data transfer interfaces, but also that it knows about specific data formats or media.

Categories also pose a problem – who maintains the list of categories? If categories are produced in large numbers, they become useless. Categories only make sense if a provider and a client agree in advance. Currently, the definition of categories is largely left to Microsoft. However, a strong vendor of, say, some innovative new container could cause a new category to become widely accepted. As CATIDs are GUIDs, no conflicts would arise.

Categories never achieved a major position in COM applications – one reason might be that objects don't normally answer a QueryInterface for a

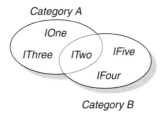

Category A

IOne

IThree   ITwo   IFive

IFour

Category B

Figure 15.8 COM categories.

CATID. It might sound surprising, but the QueryInterface specification actually allows for non-IID arguments and leaves open what would be returned in such cases. An object could, for example, answer a query for a CATID by returning IUnknown if it supports the category and the "E_NOTINTERFACE" error code otherwise. However, as no such protocol was ever included in the COM specifications, no generic client could ever rely on it.

15.3.2 Interfaces and versioning

Once published, a COM interface and its specification must not be changed in any way. This addresses both the syntactic and the semantic fragile base class problem (see Chapter 7) by avoidance. In other words, an IID in COM serves also to identify the version of an interface. As interfaces are always requested by IID, all participants in a system agree on the version of an interface. The problem of transitive version clashes mentioned in the CORBA discussion (Chapter 13) does not occur with COM.

A component may choose to implement several versions of an interface, but these are handled like any other set of different interfaces. Using this strategy, a COM-based system can concurrently support the old and the new while allowing for a gradual migration. A similar strategy would be hard or at least unnatural to implement in systems in which the multiple interfaces implemented by a single object are merged into the namespace of a single class. This is a problem with approaches to binary compatibility that are based on conventional object models, such as Java or CORBA. Despite its otherwise conventional object model, CLR avoids this issue by allowing the separate implementation of methods of the same name and signature on different interfaces implemented by the same class (see section 15.11.2).

15.4 COM object creation and the COM library

So far, the described COM mechanisms are self-sufficient. As long as COM components follow the rules, no further runtime support is needed. What is left unexplained, however, is how COM objects come to life. The question is "What information does some executing code have that could allow it to request a new COM object?

IIDs are obviously not enough. By the very definition of interfaces, there can be any number of different kinds of providers that support a specific interface. Asking for a service by asking for an interface is like asking for something with wheels without specifying whether this should be a bike, a car, a train, or something else. Instead of asking for a service by interface, the service should be retrieved by class.

To identify classes of COM objects, COM defines class identifiers (CLSIDs). A CLSID is also a globally unique identifier (GUID). COM defines a procedural library interface to request new object instances based on their

CLSID. As this interface is static and procedural, a bootstrapping problem is avoided. Programs can ask for objects without first having to know about an object that knows how to create objects.

The simplest way to create a new COM object is to call CoCreateInstance. (All COM library procedure names start with Co for COM.) This function takes a CLSID and an IID. It then creates a new instance of the specified class (CLSID) and returns an interface of the requested type (IID). An error indication is returned if COM failed to locate or start a server implementing the requested CLSID, or if the specified class does not support the requested interface.

When creating a COM object that is instantiating a COM class, COM needs to map the given CLSID to an actual component that contains the requested class. COM supports a system registry for this purpose, which is similar to the CORBA implementation repository. The registry specifies which servers are available and which classes they support. Servers can be of one of three different kinds. In-process servers support objects that live in the client's process. Local servers support objects on the same machine, but in a separate process. Remote servers support objects on a different machine. CoCreateInstance accepts an additional parameter that can be used to specify what kinds of servers would be acceptable.

CoCreateInstance consults the registry (via its local service control manager, SCM) to locate the server and, unless already active, loads and starts it. For an in-process server, this involves loading and linking a dynamic link library (DLL). For a local server, a separate executable (EXE) is loaded. Finally, for a remote machine, the service control manager on the remote machine is contacted to load and start the required server on that machine. (From a middleware point of view, the SCM performs a role similar to a CORBA ORB – see Chapter 13 and Pritchard, 1999.)

A COM server has a defined structure. It contains one or more classes that it implements. For each class, it also implements a factory object. (In COM, factory objects are called class factories. This name can be misleading, as a factory creates not classes but instances of classes.) A factory is an object that supports interface IClassFactory – or IClassFactory2, where licensing is required. COM needs to use factories because COM objects need not be of simple single-object nature and their creation therefore needs to be specified by their component rather than a system-provided service. Figure 15.9 shows a COM server that supports two COM classes (coclasses), each with its factory.

On startup, a self-registering server creates a factory object for each of its classes and registers it with COM. CoCreateInstance uses the factory objects to create instances. For improved performance, a client can also ask for direct access to the factory, using CoGetClassObject. This is useful in cases where many new objects are required.

Often, clients ask not for a specific class, but for something more generic. For example, instead of using the CLSID for "Microsoft Word," a client may

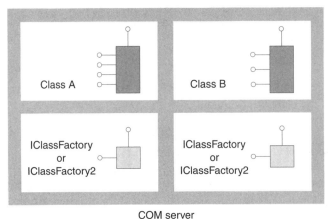

COM server

Figure 15.9 COM server with two coclasses, each with a factory.

use the CLSID for "rich text." To support such generic CLSIDs and enable configuration, COM allows one class to emulate another. Emulation configurations are kept in the system registry. For example, an emulation entry may specify that class "Microsoft Word" does the emulation for class "rich text."

15.5 Initializing objects, persistence, structured storage, monikers

COM uses a two-phase approach to object initialization. After creating a COM object using CoCreateInstance or a factory object, the object still needs to be initialized. This is like creating a new object in C++ or Java with a constructor that takes no arguments, the required storage being allocated, but no useful data loaded into the new object. Once created, an object must be initialized. There are many ways to do this and the client has control over which method to use. This two-phase approach is more flexible than the use of constructors.

The most direct way to initialize an object is to ask it to load its data from a file, a stream, or some other data store. For this purpose, COM defines a family of interfaces that are all derived from IPersist and named IPersistFile, IPersistStream, and so on. This direct approach is useful where a client wants to take control over the source of data to be used for initialization.

A standard place to store an object's data is in a COM structured storage. A structured storage is like a file system within a file. A structured storage simply is a tree structure. The root of the tree is called a root storage, the tree's other inner nodes are called storages, and the tree's leaf nodes are called streams. Streams are the "files" in a structured storage, while storage nodes are the "directories." From Windows 2000 on, COM's structured storages support simple transactions that allow an entire structured storage to be updated completely or not at all.

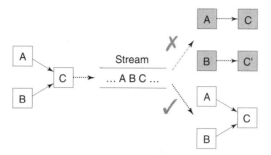

Figure 15.10 Preservation of sharing.

COM also defines a way to refer directly to a persistent object "by name." Such references can be used to ask the system to find and load the required server, create the referred object, and initialize the new object from its source. Such object names are called monikers (nicknames). Monikers are really objects in their own right. Rather than referring to an object using a unique ID, a moniker refers to an object by specifying a logical access path. For example, a moniker can refer to the spreadsheet object named "1997 Revenue," embedded in the document "The previous millennium," and stored at a certain place specified by a URL. Quite often, monikers refer to objects stored within a structured storage.

To summarize, COM does not directly support persistent objects. Instead, classes and data are kept separate and object identity is not preserved across externalization–internalization cycles. In other words, when attempting to load the "same" object twice, two objects with different identities may be created. Likewise, asking a moniker twice for an object may yield two different objects, although probably of identical class and with identical initial state. Therefore, where preservation of interobject relations is required, this needs to be handled explicitly. Consider the example illustrated in Figure 15.10, in which two objects (A and B) share a third (C). In this example, when loading the objects from a persistent store, C must be loaded only once and a reference to C must then be passed to A and B.

In the presence of shared references across component boundaries, the task of preserving sharing becomes involved. Without a general persistence service, COM offers just a building block – monikers.

15.6 From COM to distributed COM (DCOM)

Distributed COM transparently expands the concepts and services of COM. DCOM builds on the client-side proxy objects and the server-side stub objects already present in COM, where they are used only to support interprocess communication. DCOM services were already hinted at when mentioning remote servers above.

To support transparent communication across process boundaries or across machine boundaries, COM creates proxy objects on the client's end and stub objects on the server's end. For the communication between processes within a single machine, proxies and stubs merely need to map all simple data types to and from streams of bytes. As the sending and receiving processes execute on the same machine, there is no need to worry about how data types are represented. Things are slightly more complex when an interface reference is passed – still between processes on the same machine.

An interface reference sent across process boundaries needs to be mapped to an object reference that retains meaning across process boundaries. When receiving such an object reference, COM needs to make sure that a corresponding proxy object exists on the receiving end. COM then selects the corresponding interface of that proxy and passes this reference instead of the original one, which would refer to an interface in the "wrong" process. Figure 15.11 illustrates this approach.

Figure 15.11 shows a client issuing a call on object A. The called method takes a single parameter, referring to an interface of object B. As object A is in another process, a local proxy object mediates the call. The proxy determines an object identifier (OID) for object B and an interface pointer identifier (IPID) for the particular interface being passed. The OID and the IPID are sent together with the client process's ID to a stub in the server process. The stub uses the OID to locate the local proxy for object B and the IPID to locate the particular interface. The stub then issues the original call, on behalf of the client. It passes the interface reference of the local B proxy to object A, the receiver of the call.

The machinery used by DCOM is quite similar. There are two differences. These are that representations of data types can differ across machines and

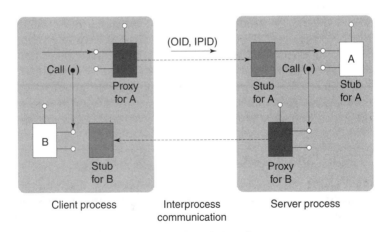

Figure 15.11 Marshaling and unmarshaling of interfacing references across processes on a single machine. (Simplified: in COM, proxies and stubs are per interface.)

object references need to contain more information than provided by just OIDs and IPIDs. To deal with differences in data representations, DCOM marshals data into a representation called network data representation (NDR), a platform-independent format. To form machine-independent object references, DCOM combines the OID and IPID with information that suffices to locate an object exporter. An object exporter is an object provided by DCOM that knows how to bind the objects exported by a server. Each object exporter has a unique ID (OXID), and this OXID is included in an object reference.

If the object exporter has been contacted recently, the OXID is known locally, together with contact information of the remote machine. This caching mechanism speeds up the resolution of object references, even in the presence of large numbers of objects. However, if the object exporter referred to in an object reference is seen the first time, a final field of the object reference is consulted. This field contains the symbolic information (a URL-like string binding) needed to contact the OXID resolver object on the remote machine. The remote OXID resolver is contacted and the contact information for the remote object exporter with the given OXID is retrieved.

In addition to this low-level machinery to connect COM objects across machine boundaries, DCOM also provides higher-level mechanisms to speed up remote operations, provide security, and detect remote machine failures (using "ping" messages). The security mechanism is quite involved and supports various levels of security at various levels of granularity. There can be default security settings for machines, individual COM servers on machines, and individual COM interfaces in servers. All accesses can be protected by access control lists (ACLs) and based on authenticated principles. Authentication can be done per connection, per message, or per packet. Exchanged data can be protected against unwanted access (encrypted) or just protected against tampering (fingerprinted).

15.7 Meta-information and automation

COM does not require the use of a specific interface definition language, as it really is a binary standard. However, to use the standard Microsoft IDL compiler (MIDL), it is necessary to use the COM IDL. Despite the similar name, COM IDL and OMG IDL are two different languages, related only by some common heritage from older IDLs (the IDL of DCE in particular). Once interfaces and classes have been described using COM IDL, the MIDL compiler is used to create stubs and proxies, but also to create type libraries. Other tools, such as Visual J++ and Visual C++, and also the CLR COM interoperability tools, generate stubs, proxies, and type libraries directly and thus completely bypass the need for a separate IDL.

COM uses type libraries to provide runtime type information for interfaces and classes. Each type library can describe multiple interfaces and classes. Using the CLSID of a class, clients can query the COM registry for type information on that class. If a corresponding type library exists, the registry returns an ITypeLib interface that can be used to browse the type library. For each interface or class, an ITypeInfo interface can be retrieved and used to obtain type information on that specific object. Available information includes the number and type of parameters of a method. Also available, from the registry, are the categories to which a class belongs. For each interface, attributes are available to indicate dispinterfaces (dispatch interfaces, see section 15.8.2), dual interfaces, outgoing interfaces, and more.

In the context of COM, "automation support" means programmability. Essentially, everything that provides COM interfaces, regular, dispatch, dual, or outgoing, is programmable in the sense of COM. Together with type libraries, services such as scripting systems can be built. COM automation fully relies on COM interfaces and type library information.

15.8 Other COM services

In addition to the aforementioned wiring and structured storage services, COM also provides several other general services. There is a trend for services originally introduced for OLE or some other higher-level technologies to move down into the COM domain to form a wide basis for other technologies. Important COM services include uniform data transfer, dispatch interfaces, and outgoing interfaces (connectable objects). These services are introduced briefly in the remainder of this section.

15.8.1 Uniform data transfer

Uniform data transfer allows for the unified implementation of all sorts of data transfer mechanisms. Examples are clipboards, drag and drop facilities, files, streams, and so on. All that is required of a COM object to participate in such a data transfer is to implement interface IDataObject. Objects doing so are called data objects and function as both universal data sources and targets.

Obviously, source and target need to agree on a number of things for such a transfer to work and make sense. This agreement is based on a mutually understood data format and a mutually agreed transfer medium. Both can be specified using parameters to the methods of IDataObject.

Some additional interfaces support drag and drop-like mechanisms and object linking, where a transfer target needs to be notified of future data source changes. As drag and drop has wider applicability than just compound documents, this machinery is now considered to be part of COM rather than OLE. Uniform data transfer also supports "lazy evaluation" of transferred data, meaning that large items can be kept at their source until they are truly needed. Finally, uniform data transfer defines a number of standard data formats.

15.8.2 Dispatch interfaces (dispinterfaces) and dual interfaces

Dispatch interfaces (dispinterfaces) have a fixed number of methods defined in the interface IDispatch. A dispinterface combines all methods of a regular interface into a single method: Invoke. Method Invoke uses a variant record type to combine all possible parameters into one. This record is self-describing to the extent that each field is a pair of type and value. The actual method to call is specified by a dispatch ID (DISPID), which is simply the number of the method. DISPIDs are unique only within one dispinterface. IDispatch adds only four methods to those defined in IUnknown. The arguments are stylized in the following summary and will vary depending on the language binding used.

```
interface IDispatch : IUnknown {
    HRESULT GetTypeInfoCount ([out] bool available);
    HRESULT GetTypeInfo (unsigned int itinfo, [out] ITypeInfo typeinfo);
    HRESULT GetIDsOfNames ([in] names[], [out] DISPID dispid[]);
    HRESULT Invoke ([in] DISPID dispID, [in] DISPPARAMS dispParams,
        [out] VARIANT result, [out] EXCEPINFO einfo, [out] int argErr);
}
```

Dispinterfaces have one principal advantage – they always look the same. It is therefore easy to implement services that generically forward or broadcast dispinterface calls. Very prominent examples of such generic forwarding mechanisms are found in interpreters such as Visual Basic. Using dispinterfaces, an interpreter can call arbitrary operations without requiring that the interpreter itself be compiled against all these interfaces. (However, all later versions of Visual Basic actually do support calling arbitrary operations on arbitrary COM interfaces. This is achieved by constructing and using required call frames directly.)

Dispinterfaces have several disadvantages. Obvious is the performance penalty. Furthermore, dispinterfaces restrict dispatch operations to parameters of a limited set of types (those covered by the VARIANT type), and to at most one return value (no support for multiple occurrences of out or inout). Finally, dispinterfaces introduce considerable complexity per interface implementation, instead of providing an adequate service that would factor this effort.

The performance disadvantage can be compensated for by so-called dual interfaces. A dual interface is both a dispinterface and a regular interface. It starts off with the IDispatch methods, including Invoke, and concludes by also providing all dispatched methods directly. With a dual interface, clients compiled against the interface can call methods directly, whereas other clients can use the more dynamic but less efficient dispatch mechanism.

Dispinterfaces could be avoided. Modern metaprogramming support would allow the same for arbitrary methods in arbitrary interfaces. By comparison, the CORBA dynamic invocation and dynamic stub interfaces support a much cleaner model for dynamic invocations at client or server end, without any of the dispinterface restrictions. Generic broadcasting and forwarding in CORBA can be achieved by using both the dynamic invocation and dynamic stub interface. As a result, the ORB transfers the abstract parameter list and other invocation information without performing a final dispatch to the target method. By using a static invocation via IDL-generated stubs and a dynamic skeleton interface at the server's end, the ORB can be used to translate a static invocation into a dynamic one that can then be used to forward or broadcast the request. The CLR remoting system is another example for smoothly supporting both static and dynamic binding, utilizing metadata in the latter case.

15.8.3 Outgoing interfaces and connectable objects

An outgoing interface is an interface that a COM object would use (rather than provide) if it were "connected" to an object that provides this interface. The intention is that, by specifying an outgoing interface, a COM object can announce that it could proactively provide useful information to any object that provided that interface. In essence, outgoing interfaces support the registration of other objects that wish to "listen" for notifications. Beyond this use, outgoing interfaces can also be used to realize configurable required interfaces as used in connection-oriented programming (section 10.3). Unlike notification listeners, such connections are mandatory for the object to function. Whether connection of an outgoing interface is mandatory or optional is part of that interface's contract.

To become a full connectable object, a COM object has to declare outgoing interfaces. It also has to implement interface IConnectionPointContainer. Finally, for each outgoing interface, it has to provide one connection point object that, in addition to calling the outgoing interface, also implements interface IConnectionPoint.

Using IConnectionPointContainer, the various connection point objects of a connectable object can be found and enumerated. For each connection point, IConnectionPoint can be used to establish, enumerate, and tear down connections. A connection is established by passing an interface reference of another object to the connection point. When it wants to call a method of an outgoing interface, a connectable object iterates over all presently registered connections. For each registered connection – that is, for each registered interface reference – the required method is invoked.

Connectable objects provide a uniform way to implement change propagation. As outgoing and incoming interfaces are matched, the propagation can take the form of regular method invocations instead of requiring the creation of event objects. Connections are thus efficient. Modeling individual connection points as objects managed via a container abstraction makes connectable objects somewhat heavyweight, though. More lightweight alternatives are the event source and listener approaches in JavaBeans (section 14.3) or the language-level support in $C^{\#}$ (section 15.11.4).

Compound documents and OLE

Object linking and embedding (OLE) is Microsoft's compound document standard. OLE was created to blend legacy applications, with their own application-centric view of the world, into a single document-centric paradigm. It is also possible to create objects that only exist within an OLE setting – ActiveX objects being the best example. However, OLE continues to also support standalone applications with varying degrees of OLE integration. This pragmatic aspect makes many OLE technologies rather complex. However, it also allows for a smooth transition path, protecting investments in developments and user training, and therefore preserving the client base.

As with every technology on top of COM, OLE can be summarized as a (large) collection of predefined COM interfaces. Several of the key technologies required by OLE are delivered by COM services. This includes structured storage, monikers, uniform data transfer, including drag and drop, connectable objects, and automation support (Chappel, 1996).

The OLE compound document's approach distinguishes between document containers and document servers. A document server provides some content model and the capabilities to display and manipulate that content. A document container has no native content, but can accept parts provided by arbitrary document servers. Many document containers are also document servers – that is, they support foreign parts but also have their native content. Most of the popular "heavyweights," such as Microsoft's Office applications, Word, Excel, PowerPoint, and so on, are combined servers and containers. For example, Excel has a native content model of spreadsheet-arranged cells of data and formulae. Excel is also a container. As such, it can accept, say, insertion of a Word text object.

Fundamental to the user's illusion of working with a single document is the ability to edit everything where it is displayed. This is called in-place editing. In the example, Excel would allow Word to take over when the user wants to edit the embedded text object. In fact, Word opens a window for this purpose; the window is opened just over the place where Excel was displaying the text object. It is not apparent to the user that Word opened a window. The user sees only the text being activated after double clicking on it, ready for editing using the familiar Word tools.

In-place activation is a tricky business. The container has to hand off part of the container's screen estate to the server of an embedded part. Also, and more difficult, the container and server have to agree on how to handle other parts of the user interface. For example, menus and toolbars need to be changed as well. The OLE approach to in-place activation is generally to change all menus, toolbars, and other window adornments to those required by the activated server. For menus and toolbars, container and server can agree on a merger. For example, the File menu stays with the (outermost) container, while filing operations normally operate on the entire document.

Besides embedding, OLE also supports linking of document parts. *Nomen est omen*. Linking rests on monikers, a container storing a moniker to the linked object. In addition, the linked object advises the container of changes. The technology to do so could be connectable objects, but, for historical reasons, a separate, less general, mechanism is used – sink advisory interfaces for data objects.

The OLE user interface guidelines do not allow in-place activation or editing of linked parts. Instead, a fully separate document window is opened to edit a linked part. This simplifies the user's view of things, as a linked part could be linked to multiple containers. Editing in a separate document window is also an option for embedded parts and is useful when embedded parts are too small for reasonable in-place editing.

15.9.1   OLE containers and servers

The interaction of containers and servers is complex by nature. A large number of details have to be addressed to enable the smooth cooperation required for a well-integrated document-centric "look and feel." In the case of OLE, things are further complicated by the support of standalone applications with OLE integration.

Recall that COM distinguishes between in-process, local, and remote servers. OLE has to provide ways to enable document integration for configurations of all three server types. As windows can only be written to by their owning processes, things are complicated for all but in-process servers.

For local (out-of-process) servers, the situation is quite different. There needs to exist a "representative" of the server object, executing in the container process. Such a representative is called an in-process handler. It implements functions that, among other things, draw to the container's window. A generic default in-process handler is part of the OLE infrastructure, but custom handlers can be used to fine-tune performance and functionality. Perhaps surprisingly, remote servers do not add a significant additional burden for the OLE programmer, as DCOM hides the details and the local server technology carries over. This transparency can be deceptive, however. Whereas a local server is unlikely to crash individually, a remote server may well become unreachable or fail. COM-based applications thus have to expect a potential error indication on each method invocation – to be prepared for interactions with a remote server.

The interaction between document containers and document servers is governed by two interfaces provided by a containers client site object and seven interfaces provided by a server's content object. That does not mean that servers are more difficult to implement than containers. In the end, containers have to call the operations of all the server interfaces. Indeed, it is generally more difficult to implement document containers. Figure 15.12 shows the split of interfaces across document container and server.

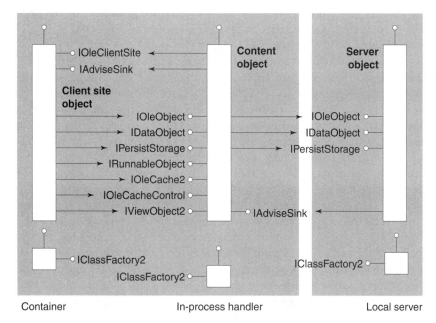

Figure 15.12 OLE document container and server interfaces.

Figure 15.12 also shows the interaction between the in-process handler, implementing the content object seen by the container, and the local server, implementing the actual server object. As can be seen, the in-process handler is really supporting a separate class with its own factory. The factories could also use the simpler IClassFactory interface. As IClassFactory2 supports licensing, and licensing is most useful for controls, this is the choice shown in the figure.

15.9.2 Controls – from Visual Basic via OLE to ActiveX

Visual Basic controls (VBXs) were the first successful component technology released by Microsoft – first after their operating systems, of course. Visual Basic uses a simple and fixed model in which controls are embedded into forms. A form binds the embedded controls together and allows the attachment of scripts that enable the controls to interact. Entire applications can be assembled rather than programmed, simply by composing controls into forms, although the final scripting, again, is a form of programming.

VBXs ranged from simple controls in the original sense of the word to "mini applications." For example, there are controls that implement entire spreadsheets, charting tools, word processors, or database connectivity tools. Despite this variety and the obvious potential, VBXs have some severe problems. The main disadvantages are the tight coupling of VBXs to Visual Basic, and Visual Basic's restrictive form model that a VBX cannot escape from. OLE controls (OCXs) were introduced to migrate the useful VBX concept to a more powerful platform – that of general OLE containers. OCXs are COM objects whereas VBXs are not.

To qualify as an OLE control, a COM object has to implement a large number of interfaces (Figure 15.13). Essentially, an OLE control implements all of an OLE document server's interfaces, plus a few more to emit events. The (good) idea was that a container could expect substantial functionality from a control. The unfortunate downside was that even the most minimal controls had to carry so much baggage that implementing OCXs was far less attractive than it was for VBXs. The extra baggage is particularly painful when considering competition with things as lightweight as Java applets. Downloading across the internet makes lean components mandatory.

When OLE controls were finally renamed ActiveX controls, the requirements were also revised. ActiveX control is therefore not just a new name for OLE control, but is also a new specification. An ActiveX control has to be implemented by a self-registering server. Self-registration allows a server, when started and asked to do so, to register its classes with the COM registry. This is useful where a server's code has just been downloaded, for example, from the internet. In addition, all that is required is the implementation of IUnknown.

ActiveX controls are really just COM objects supported by a special server. However, the ActiveX control specification is not empty. It does define a large number of features and interactions, but leaves all of them optional. A control supports only what is required for it to function. A full-blown control can even be a container itself, a so-called container control. Later extensions of the control specifications, dubbed "Controls 96," allow controls to take arbitrary,

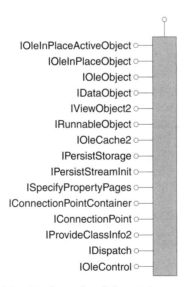

Figure 15.13 Mandatory interfaces of an OLE control.

non-rectangular shapes and to be "internet-aware" – that is, they are able to handle slow links.

ActiveX controls have regular COM interfaces, but they also have outgoing interfaces (p. 348). These are very important, as controls are sources of events that are used by the control to signal changes. Recall that an outgoing interface is essentially an announcement of the availability of a notification mechanism. All interested objects register matching incoming interfaces with the object implementing the outgoing interface. Unfortunately, there is a dilemma in this case.

Of course, ActiveX controls can announce any number and kinds of outgoing interfaces. These may very well make sense to other controls or to script programmers, but not to the container. The container cannot possibly provide all interfaces that some control might want to be connected to. The solution to this problem is the use of outgoing dispinterfaces, which, as with all dispinterfaces, have a fixed static form – the one defined in IDispatch (p. 347). A container can dynamically construct such dispinterfaces as needed by reading the control's type library. The dispinterfaces then allow for dynamic handling and forwarding by a container. This mechanism is the reason that an ActiveX control that wishes to signal events has to come with a type library.

Another important aspect of almost all ActiveX controls is that they have properties. Containers can also have properties. Properties are settings that a user or application assembler can use to fine-tune looks and behavior. ActiveX defines a number of interfaces that can be used to handle properties. These interfaces are used by controls to examine the properties of its container. They are also used by the container to examine and modify the properties of embedded controls.

An ActiveX container is an OLE container with a few additional properties. Such a container cannot rely on anything when interacting with an embedded control. Therefore, it has to inspect what interface a control supports and react accordingly. Testing for a large number of interfaces can be expensive, and the category identifiers (CATIDs, p. 339) come in handy. Although it is now trivial to implement a new ActiveX control, it is also much more difficult to implement a useful container. However, because the number of containers is much smaller than the number of controls, this is the right tradeoff. Unfortunately, many so-called ActiveX containers on the market today do not fully conform to the ActiveX specification and function only when embedded controls do implement the numerous OLE control interfaces.

15.10 Contextual composition and services

Like the various CORBAservices, Microsoft offers a number of key services that build on DCOM. A fundamental service in any distributed infrastructure is a directory service. The Windows Registry – a generalization of the system registry required by COM – serves this purpose. Security services are built into the DCOM extension of COM, as briefly outlined in section 15.6. A simple licensing service has been part of COM since the introduction of OCXs. Many of these older services have been replaced by new ones in CLR.

A class of services called "enterprise services" has been introduced originally in the form of Microsoft Transaction Server (MTS) and Microsoft Message Queuing (MSMQ) and later integrated with the overall COM infrastructure to form COM+. In its initial release, CLR uses the COM+ enterprise services via its COM interoperation layer instead of providing replacements native to CLR. The common property of these services is their contextual binding.

The support for contextual composition by various Microsoft technologies is elaborated further in the following. (For a discussion of the principle of contextual composition and its realization in multiple technologies, see sections 21.1 and 21.2.)

15.10.1 COM apartments – threading and synchronization

Apartments are, in many ways, the most surprising and most commonly misunderstood feature of COM. Often presented as a "hack" to make things work in a world that started out with single threading (the original Windows API), apartments really go much deeper. The idea is to not associate synchronization with individual objects, although this is commonly done and even part of the fundamental Java programming model ("synchronized" methods). Instead, synchronization is associated with synchronization domains, called apartments in COM. A process is partitioned by apartments and each apartment can have its own synchronization regime.

Originally, COM distinguished single threading and free threading apartments; rental threading was added later. A single-threaded apartment services all contained objects with a single thread. No further synchronization is required as using global variables and thread-local storage is safe. A rental-threaded apartment restricts execution to a single thread at a time, but as one thread leaves another can enter. Finally, a free-threaded apartment allows for any number of concurrent threads to coexist.

A programmer can declare constraints on classes to request that instances of that class be placed in certain apartments only. These class constraints are kept in the Windows registry. For example, a class can request single threading only, it can insist on free threading, or it can accept either.

Synchronization actions are inserted automatically by the COM infrastructure at apartment boundaries. In the case of free-threaded apartments, nothing needs to happen – threads can freely enter and leave. At the boundary of a rental-threaded apartment, a synchronization lock is acquired and released on return. However, at the boundary of a single-threaded apartment, the procedure is quire elaborate. Incoming calls are translated into messages and queued. The single thread inside the apartment is expected to periodically poll that queue for messages. If a message is in queue when polling, the poll call, as a side-effect, executes the method being called. To avoid deadlocks as a result of queue capacity limits, every outgoing message send also causes a poll. The cost of synchronization of single-threaded apartments is significantly higher than it is for the other apartment types. Rental threading is thus preferred for apartment-level synchronization.

When instantiating new objects, a program can either just rely on the constraints on the instantiated class or take some control of how objects are inserted into apartments. In the default case, objects are instantiated in the creating code's current apartment if that is acceptable, in a single free-threaded apartment per process if required, or in a new single-threaded apartment if single threading is required. It is possible to create multiple free-threaded apartments per process and direct creation of instances into some existing apartment. The latter requires that suitable handlers are already running in those apartments.

15.10.2 Microsoft transaction server – contexts and activation

The transaction server supports online transaction processing of COM-based applications. It maintains a pool of threads to control performance in the presence of large numbers of requests to large numbers of COM objects. Requests are queued until one of the pooled threads becomes available to handle it. The server also manages the mapping of components to server processes automatically. This can be used to group components according to security or fault isolation requirements. Like the thread pool, the server also maintains database connection pools, amortizing the cost of establishment and teardown of connections over large numbers of requests. Finally, the server supports multiple resource managers, such as multiple databases.

The transaction server currently does not address fault tolerance issues beyond the properties of transactions. Starting with COM+ and Windows 2000, load balancing across available machines is supported. The server supports Microsoft's SQL Server and databases with ODBC or OLEDB interfaces. Support for other protocols includes IBM's SNA LU6.2, transaction internet protocol (TIP), and XA.

An interesting feature of the transaction server is its transparent addition of transactional capabilities to existing COM components. By setting a property in the component catalog, a component can be marked transactional. At component object creation time, the transaction server then intercepts and adds transactional closures to the component's operations by creating a context object that wraps the object in a COM containment style. The server automatically detects references to other COM objects by a transactional component and extends transactional handling to these as well. Despite this automation, component developers need to be aware of transactions to keep exclusive locking of resources to a minimum. For components that need to be directly aware of transactions, a library call – GetObjectContext – is provided to retrieve the current transactional context. Also, an interface – IObjectContext – has been defined to access such a context.

15.10.3 COM+ – generalized contexts and data-driven composition

In October 1997, Microsoft had announced COM+, an extension of COM. COM+ was first released in mid 2000 (with Windows 2000 Server) and has since been a part of Windows Server releases. Causing some initial confusion at the time (and affecting the first edition of this book), COM+ 2.0 was also used as the target name for what is now the .NET Framework (see following section). What was called COM+ 1.0, in anticipation of this major next step, is now simply called COM+. Unlike COM+ 2.0 would have been, COM+ (1.0) is accurately named after COM as it is at the heart of COM+. COM+ integrates into COM previously separate and somewhat colliding support technology, such as transactional processing, asynchronous messaging, load balancing, and clustering. The most prominent predecessor products were the Microsoft Transaction Server (MTS) and the Microsoft Message Queue server (MSMQ).

The central idea, starting with MTS, is to separate declarative attributes about infrastructure requirements from the code of components and applications. Such infrastructure requirements can also be understood as aspects (in the sense of aspect-oriented software development) – concerns that cross-cut components and applications. Requirements such as synchronization and transactional closure require consistent implementation in all participating components. By merely declaring such requirements, the platform can intercept activities and inject appropriate calls to the infrastructure, such as acquiring a lock or committing a transaction. (For a general discussion of contextual composition see section 21.2.)

COM+ combines MTS and MSMQ declarative attributes with several new ones, leading to the following list of application-level attributes.

- Activation type: library (in process) or server (separate process).
- Authentication level: none, connect, call, packet, integrity, or privacy.
- Authorization checks: application-only or application-and-component.
- Debugger: command line to launch debugger.
- Enable compensating resource manager: on or off.
- Enable 3GB support: on or off.
- Impersonation level: identify, impersonate, or delegate.
- Process shutdown: never or n minutes after idle.
- Queueing: queued or queued with listener.
- Security identity: interactive user or hard-coded user/password.

At the component level, the following attributes are supported.

- Activation-time load balancing: on or off.
- Auto-deactivation: on or off.

■ Declarative authorization: zero or more role names.
■ Declarative construction: class-specific string.
■ Instrumentation events: on or off.
■ JIT activation: on or off.
■ Must activate in activator's context: on or off.
■ Object pooling: on (min. and max. instances, timeout) or off.
■ Synchronization: not supported, supported, required, requires new.
■ Transaction: not supported, supported, required, requires new.

The component-level attributes apply to classes, except for declarative authorization, which also applies to interfaces and methods, and auto-deactivation, which only applies to methods.

New with COM+, an attribution model is provided that allows for the automatic mapping between procedural invocations and message queuing. The idea is simple – a component can be marked as communicating via messages and the methods on all the component's interfaces can be restricted to one-way semantics (by not including return values, out or in-out parameters, and by not expecting error codes or exceptions relating to call completion). The COM+ context wraps such a component's instances with special proxies that accept incoming messages from MSMQ queues and send outgoing messages to MSMQ queues. In COM+, such components are called "queued components" – somewhat of a misnomer as neither the component nor its instances, but the messages to and from its instances, are queued. A similar concept was added in late 2001 to Enterprise JavaBeans 2.0, where the more appropriate name message-driven bean is used (see section 14.5.3).

15.11 Take two – the .NET Framework

The .NET Framework is part of the larger .NET space (see below). It comprises the common language runtime (CLR), a large number of partially interfaced, partially class-based frameworks, packaged into assemblies, and a number of tools. CLR is an implementation of the common language infrastructure (CLI) specification, adding COM+ interoperation and Windows platform access services. In particular, CLR offers dynamic loading and unloading, garbage collection, context interception, metadata reflection, remoting, persistence, and other runtime services that are fully language independent. Presently, Microsoft supports four languages on CLR: $C^\#$, JScript, Managed C^{++}, and Visual Basic.NET.

Assemblies are the units of deployment, versioning, and management in .NET – that is, they are the .NET software components. Side-by-side use of the same assembly in multiple versions is fully supported. Assemblies contain metadata, modules, and resources, all of which are expressed in a platform-independent way. Code in modules is expressed in CIL (common intermediate language) that roughly resembles Java or Smalltalk bytecode, or Pascal P code.

Unlike these earlier bytecode formats, the one used in assemblies deemphasizes interpretation. MSIL (Microsoft intermediate language) is a CIL-compliant superset, with instructions added to enable the CLR interoperation features that go beyond the CLI specification. CLR either compiles at install- or at load-time, always executing native code. CLR reflection and other type-based concepts cover a large type system space called CTS (common type system).

The following subsections cover details of these various .NET Framework-related technologies.

15.11.1 The .NET big picture

The Microsoft .NET initiative aims to align a wide spectrum of Microsoft products and services under a common vision of interconnected devices of many kinds, from servers to stationary and mobile PCs to specialized devices. At a technical level, .NET targets three levels:

- web services;
- deployment platforms (servers and clients);
- developer platform.

Web services aim for transitive programmability of the internet (that is, not just the traditional web, which targets human clients – the internet and web standards and proposed standards supporting the construction, location, and use of web services are discussed in section 12.4.) To bootstrap the space of web services, Microsoft plans to make available a number of foundational core services. A first such service has been available for a while – .NET Passport, a service to authenticate users. Another one, .NET Alerts, became active in early 2002. This is a generalized alert service that, at the time of introduction, delivers alerts via Windows Messenger. As part of the .NET My Services and other initiatives, Microsoft announced further services such as for storage.

The Microsoft platforms, beginning with the various server products and Windows.NET Server, are being transformed in a series of steps to natively and efficiently support and use web services and process XML.

Finally, and the focus of this chapter, there is a new developer platform comprising CLR, frameworks, and tools. CLR contributes a new component infrastructure that can (but doesn't have to) shield components from the details of the underlying hardware platform. Like JVM, CLR defines a virtual instruction set to isolate from particular processors. Unlike JVM, CLR also enables components that require tight integration with the specific underlying platform.

15.11.2 Common language infrastructure

The common language infrastructure (CLI) specification, jointly submitted to ECMA by Microsoft, Intel, and Hewlett-Packard, establishes a language-neutral platform, something like CORBA. Unlike CORBA, though, CLI also defines an intermediate language (IL) and deployment file format (assemblies), such as Java bytecode, class, and JAR files. Unlike CORBA and Java, CLI includes support for extensible metadata. The common language runtime (CLR), part of the Microsoft .NET Framework, is the Microsoft implementation of the CLI specification. CLR goes beyond CLI compliance and includes support for COM and platform interoperation (for details, see the following subsection.

CLI comprises the specification of execution engine services (such as loader, JIT compiler, and garbage-collecting memory manager), the common type system (CTS), and the common language specification (CLS).

CTS and CLS play two complementary roles. The CTS scope is the superset of many languages' core concepts in the type space. CLI-compliant code can operate over the entire CTS space. However, no two languages cover the exact same CTS subset. For code implemented in different languages to interoperate, the CLS space is useful. CLS is a strict CTS subset that is constructed in such a way that a wide variety of languages can cover it completely. In particular, if a definition is CLS-compliant, then any language classified as a CLS consumer will be able to make use of that definition. This is the simplest useful class of CLI-targeting languages. A language that can also introduce new definitions in the CLS space is called a CLS producer. Finally, a language that can extend existing definitions in the CLS space is called a CLS extender. CLS extenders are always also CLS producers and CLS producers are always also CLS consumers.

CTS defines a single root type – System.Object – for all types. Under Object, CTS distinguishes value types and reference types. All value types are monomorphic subtypes of type System.ValueType, itself a subtype of System.Object. Reference types are split into interfaces, classes, arrays, and delegates. (Technically, interfaces are modeled as special classes in CTS.) Classes are split into marshal-by-value and marshal-by-reference; marshal-by-reference is further split into context agile and context bound. See Figure 15.14 for an overview of the CTS type hierarchy.

There are no primitive types, so types such as integer or floating point ones are merely predefined value types. Multiple interface and single class inheritance relations are supported. Even value types can inherit (implement) multiple interfaces. Accessibility is controlled in two dimensions – that is, whether or not definition and use points are in the same location and whether or not definition and use points are related by class inheritance. For the former purpose, three location scopes are distinguished – class, assembly, and universe. The accessibility relation has thus six possible constraint combinations, although most languages support only a subset. For example, $C^{\#}$ does not support definition of protected access limited to less than universal scope. Some, like managed C^{++}, support all combinations.

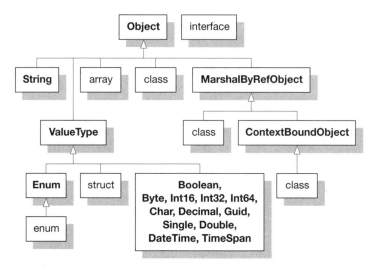

Figure 15.14 Top-level CTS type hierarchy.

Methods can be static, instance-bound, or virtual (which implies instance-bound). Overloading is supported on the basis of method names and signatures, but not return types. The overload resolution policies vary from language to language. (The CLI reflection mechanism thus introduces its own overload resolution policy.)

A class can implement multiple interfaces and can qualify method names with the name of the introducing interface. As a result, it is possible to implement two interfaces on the same class, even if a method name and signature appear identical on both interfaces, although they should be implemented differently. C#, for example, fully supports this notion of explicitly implementing an interface's method:

```
interface IShape {
  void Draw ();
}
interface ICowboy {
  void Draw ();
}
class CowboyShape : IShape, Icowboy {
  void IShape.Draw () { ... }
  void ICowboy.Draw () { ... }
}
```

While the above cowboy/shape example is widely used, it isn't actually covering an important case. Accidental name collisions happen and are a problem. However, much more significant is a different case, which is the release of new versions of an interface together with the desire to enable side-by-side support of

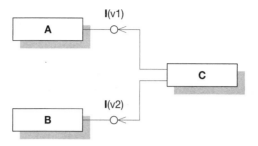

Figure 15.15 Side-by-side implementation of different versions of an interface.

components. Figure 15.15 shows how a class C needs to implement both interface I, version 1, and interface I, version 2, in order to properly interact with classes A and B that require interface I on objects, but differ in which version of that interface they need. CTS anchors all names of definitions in the names of their containing assemblies. Since an assembly's name includes version information (section 15.12), the two versions of interface I actually can be distinguished – the method names on them are likely conflicting, though. CTS enables the implementation of both versions of that interface on the same class – a significant step to supporting the side-by-side use of multiple versions of an assembly.

Various method naming conventions, such as property and indexer get–set methods (see C$^\#$ details in section 15.11.4), are part of CTS. The purpose of defining these conventions is to enable cross-language interoperation, regardless of explicit support for the conventionally named features in the various languages. For example, for a C$^\#$ property Foo the corresponding accessor methods are called get_Foo and set_Foo. C$^\#$ does not allow direct use of these method names, but other languages that do not support properties directly can simply call these methods to access properties.

Throwable exceptions are not part of CTS method signatures. Unlike Java or C^{++}, CTS has no provisions for static checking of throwable exceptions when calling a method. Languages are still free to perform such checks within their own realm. No two languages fully agree on the semantics of such declarations and checks, rendering cross-language checks useless even if the annotations were supported in CTS. (The issue to what degree such checking is actually useful is discussed in section 8.7.)

15.11.3 **COM and platform interoperation**

CLR includes substantial support for COM interoperation and direct access to the underlying platform, which is Win32 and other DLL-based APIs. By integrating support for both COM interoperation and platform invocation, the CLR execution engine can deliver almost optimal performance. For example, a platform invocation is JIT-compiled to a native code sequence that is practically identical to what one would find in traditional compiled code. COM interoperation is achieved by providing two kinds of automatically synthesized wrappers – COM-callable wrappers present CLR objects via COM interfaces and runtime-callable wrappers present COM objects via CLR interfaces.

To interoperate with COM, CLR tools can be used to create interop assemblies that define types matching those defined in a COM type library. The fact that CLR assemblies shared across .NET applications must have a unique strong name has a subtle consequence for COM interoperation. It is that it is possible for multiple parties to generate an interop assembly for the same COM interface (the same IID). However, the resulting interop assemblies then expose mutually incompatible types, although all these types correspond to the same COM interface with the same IID. To avoid this situation, primary interop assemblies (PIAs) are defined. A PIA should be produced by the publisher of the COM interface (the "owner" of the IID). An alternativee interop assembly can be generated if no PIA is available, but its types should only be used internally to an assembly. Exposing them in the signature of a new assembly would eventually lead to incompatibilities with other assemblies that rely either on the PIA or expose their reliance on another alternative interop assembly (see go.microsoft.com/fwlink/?LinkId=3355 for details).

COM interoperation is a subtle and complex problem, despite COM's surface-level simplicity. The reasons are the details of the COM calling conventions (including dispatch interfaces), its marshaling conventions (including rules as to who allocates and deallocates), and its support for low-level unsafe types (including pointers to arrays of unknown size). Remotable interfaces (those for which DCOM proxies can be generated automatically) are easier to handle, as proxies require roughly the same information as CLR wrappers do. Unfortunately, DCOM introduces its own puzzles – IDL annotations such as the [call_as(...)] attribute have procedural meaning only and cannot be automatically interpreted to generate appropriate CLR wrappers.

Amazingly, if interfaces are limited to "isomorphic types" (types that do not require transformations when crossing the CLR/COM boundary), then the overhead of a call to a COM method from managed code is in the order of only about 50 instruction cycles.

15.11.4 Exemplary .NET language – $C^{\#}$

$C^{\#}$ (pronounced "C sharp") is an object-oriented language that sits somewhere between Java (described in some detail in the next chapter) and C^{++}. (For readers unfamiliar with both Java and C^{++}, it may make sense to first read the sections on Java in section 14.2.) Designed to be an exemplary .NET language, $C^{\#}$ provides direct support for most – but not all – CLR features, some of which are unique to CLR. The $C^{\#}$ language specification is an ECMA standard, in parallel with the CLI specification (ECMA 2001a/b).

$C^{\#}$ distinguishes five kinds of top-level definitions – interfaces, classes (CTS reference classes), structs (CTS value classes), enums (CTS enumeration classes), and delegates (CTS reference classes). The corresponding CTS concepts are explained in the previous section. There are some built-in types that are distinguished by having corresponding constant literals in the language, such as integer or string literals. However, there are no real primitive types in the language; types such as int or decimal map to value classes such as System.Int32 and System.Decimal that are fundamentally no different from user-defined value classes. The appearance of special treatment is achieved by uniform support for value classes in combination with operator overloading. Hence, a+b could be an expression over the standard ints or an operation over some user-defined value class such as Example.Complex.

C# organizes names into namespaces. In line with the general CLI philosophy, namespaces are orthogonal to assemblies (the CLI software components), so a namespace can span multiple assemblies (and new assemblies can add new definitions to an existing namespace) and an assembly can add definitions to multiple namespaces. The mapping from names in namespaces to names in assemblies is established at compile-time. A C# compiler is presented with a list of assemblies to compile against. The names in the compiled source are then searched in these assemblies. The CLI definition allows the same readable name (including full namespace qualification) to appear in multiple assemblies that then can be loaded and used side-by-side. However, in its present version, C# (and most other CLI-compliant languages) have no means to refer to more than one of these identical names from within a given source text.

Unlike the Java reliance on naming patterns, C# includes syntax for properties. A property is an abstract field that has a get method, set method, or both. Properties can be defined on interfaces, classes, and structs.

```
interface IColored {
    System.Drawing.Color Color { get; set; }
}
class SampleGadget : IColored {
    System.Drawing.Color color;
    IColored.Color {
        get { return this.color; }
        set { this.color = value; }
    }
}
class UseGadget {
    SampleGadget gadget = new SampleGadget();
    gadget.Color = new System.Drawing.Color.RoyalBlue;
    ...
}
```

Note that, by not providing a getter or a setter, a property can be made write- or read-only. In either case, by abstracting a field as a property, proper action can be taken whenever the property value is accessed. In the example above, the second assignment invokes a getter on the right-hand side to get the value of the color from property RoyalBlue. Then, a setter is invoked on the left-hand side to set the gadget to this color value. When accessing a property, most field operations work as if a property were a field. However, properties do not have an address and thus cannot be passed by reference. (While the CLR would support the creation of delegates on property getters or setters, $C^{\#}$ does not.)

In addition to the abstraction of fields by properties, $C^{\#}$ also supports the abstraction of arrays by indexers. Indexers can be defined on interfaces, classes, and structs. In $C^{\#}$, an indexer has no name (the name this is uniformly used), so there can be at most one per interface, class, or struct. (As classes and structs can implement any number of interfaces without interference, classes and structs can implement multiple indexers if these are individually placed on different interfaces.) An indexer can have a getter, setter, or both. Unlike properties, an indexer takes any number of additional arguments that are meant to correspond to the indices of array access expressions. As these arguments can be of any type, indexers can be used to abstract semantic arrays. For example, an indexer can be a map from strings to strings:

```
interface IMapStrings {
    string this [string key] { get; set; }
}
using System;
class StringMapper : IMapStrings {
    Hashtable h = new Hashtable();
    string IMapStrings.this [string key] {
        get { return (string) h[key]; }
        set { h.Add(key, value); }
    }
}
```

$C^{\#}$ includes direct support for a simple form of connection-oriented programming – the "wiring" of method-level handlers for *events*. Classes and interfaces can declare event sources (example adapted from Gunnerson, 2000):

```
using System;
class TimerEventArgs : EventArgs {
    DateTime time;
    public TimerEventArgs (DateTime time) { this.time = time; }
    public DateTime Time {
        get { return this.time; }
    }
}
class TimerRelay {
    public delegate void TimerEventHandler (object sender, TimerEventArgs e);
    public event TimerEventHandler OnTickHandler;
    protected void OnTick (TimerEventArgs e) {
        if (OnTickHandler != null) OnTickHandler(e);
    }
```

```
public void Notify (DateTime time) {
  OnTick(new TimerEventArgs(time));
 }
}
```

Every such event source is multicast enabled and accepts the registration of any number of listeners. (This is different from the JavaBeans model, which distinguishes singlecast from multicast event sources.) A listener is a delegate on a method of matching signature. (As explained above, delegates are, in essence, function or method pointers.) C$^\#$ overloads the unary increment and decrement operators ($+=$, $-=$) to facilitate the registration and deregistration of listener delegates:

```
class TimerEventLogger {
  void LogEvent (object sender; TimerEventArgs e) {
    Console.WriteLine("Tick at {0}", e.Time);
  }
  public void Watch (TimerRelay timerRelay) {
    timerRelay.OnTickHandler +=
      new TimerRelay.TimerEventHandler(LogEvent);
  }
}
```

If more than one delegate is registered with an event source, events are multicast. The ordering of event delivery is not specified. If one of the delegates throws an exception, delivery to remaining delegates is not guaranteed.

Unlike delegates, which are special CTS types, events are mere syntactic sugar introduced by C$^\#$. The core ability to chain delegates to get multicast support is part of delegates themselves: any delegate can be chained to another delegate of the same type. The event keyword in C$^\#$ does not do more than introduce a protected delegate-typed field and overloaded $+=$ and $-=$ operators. Other CLI-compliant languages may provide different or more sophisticated support for connection-oriented programming.

C$^\#$ fully supports CLI custom attributes – user defined meta-attributes attached to interfaces, classes, structs, fields, methods, parameters, and so on. A good number of custom attributes are defined in various .NET frameworks. An example is the CLR COM interoperation support. In it, custom attributes are used to direct marshalling operations when calling between COM and CLR (section 15.11.3). However, custom attributes can be defined anytime; leaving open who or which tool will make use of them:

```
using System;
[AttributeUsage(AttributeTargets.Method, AllowMultiple = true)]
class SampleAttribute : System.Attribute {
  private string s;
  public string Meaning {
    set { meaning = value; }
```

```
    get { return meaning; }
  }
}
```

In this example, the new custom attribute SampleAttribute is defined by subclassing class Attribute, using the AttributeUsage attribute to allow the new attribute only on methods and the occurrence of more than one on the same method, and defining properties on the class that can be used to hold attribute arguments. The new attribute could then be used as follows (the conventional name suffix Attribute can be dropped when applying an attribute):

```
[Sample(Meaning = "life")]
[Sample(Meaning = "42")]
public void HitchHike (Galaxy g) { ... }
```

15.11.5 **Visual Studio .NET**

Visual Studio .NET (VS.NET) integrates most tools for the .NET Framework. By building on the CLR cross-language properties, VS.NET can support editing, building, and debugging of applications – all across multiple languages. It is possible to plug in specialized editors and debuggers. A wide variety of supportive tools, for tasks such as modeling, browsing or documentation, are also integrated. Remote and cross debugging are supported for development tasks that target distributed or embedded systems. There are several third-party profiling tools for the analysis of performance and resource consumption.

15.12 | **Assemblies – the .NET software components**

CLI deployment units are called assemblies. An assembly is a set of files in a directory hierarchy, roughly equivalent to the contents of a JAR file (see section 17.3). A mandatory part of an assembly is its manifest, which is a table of contents of the assembly. In the case of single-file assemblies, the manifest is included in that file; otherwise it may stand alone in a separate file. Files in an assembly can be split into module and resource files. Modules contain code and resources immutable data. Assemblies can be tagged with a culture label (in the sense of RFC3066 [IETF, 2001], so, for example, you would have "fr-CH" for Swiss French). To enable localization without duplication, assemblies can have satellite assemblies. A satellite assembly contains everything required for a specific culture and otherwise defaults to its main assembly. A satellite typically contains translated text material, but may also contain forms and other user-interface elements that require adjusting.)

An assembly is either private to a single application or shared among multiple applications. Shared assemblies are subject to a rigorous naming and name resolution scheme; private assemblies are not, assuming that an application is self-consistent with the parts that it contains but doesn't share.

A shared assembly is uniquely named by a strong name composed as follows:

Strong name = (publisher token, assembly name, version vector, culture)
Version vector = (major, minor, build, patch)

The publisher token is the SHA-1 hash of the public half of a public/private key pair. The assembly is signed by encrypting an MD-5 hash over the entire assembly using the private key. On download or install, the assembly hash is recomputed and the signature checked using the public key. Assemblies are thus protected from in-transit tampering. Furthermore, public keys are generated in a way that makes their uniqueness extremely likely. The SHA-1 hash preserves this uniqueness with very high probability. By including the publisher token in the strong name, name collisions at the level of the readable assembly name are immaterial. Inclusion of version and culture information disambiguates the assembly name fully. Unlike using a GUID to identify every defined item within an assembly, strong names are like assigning a GUID to the assembly and interpreting definition names relative to their assembly's strong name. (The downside is that packaging decisions have a lasting effect on naming.)

Assemblies list which other shared assemblies they statically require by listing their strong names. By making strong names structured rather than using a flat GUID, interesting configuration policies can be established. For example, by default, the CLR loader will load the assembly with exactly the same strong name, that is, the exact version requested. Publishers of assemblies, applications using assemblies, and system administrators at sites of deployments can tune this resolution policy. For example, if it is actually known that version 2 of some assembly can replace version 1 in the scope of a particular application, then the default policy can be spot-relaxed to allow loading of version 2 when running that application.

Shared assemblies are stored in the global assembly cache (GAC) – a facility provided by Windows, starting with XP. The GAC is effectively a database of assemblies, keyed by their strong names and equipped with policies. The three policy classes mentioned above are used to determine which shared assembly should be yielded by the GAC to service a request given a particular strong name. The first policy class is called publisher policy and is included in a shared assembly itself. With it, an assembly's publisher states, for instance, that this assembly is backwards compatible with some older version. Below is a simple example of a publisher policy that redirects dependents of myAssembly v1.0 to v2.0.

```
<configuration>
  <runtime>
    <assemblyBinding xmlns="urn:schemas-microsoft-com:asm.v1">
      <dependentAssembly>
        <assemblyIdentity name="myAssembly"
                 publicKeyToken="32ab4ba45e0a69a1"
                 culture="en-us" />
```

```
        <bindingRedirect oldVersion="1.0.0.0" newVersion="2.0.0.0"/>
      </dependentAssembly>
    </assemblyBinding>
  </runtime>
</configuration>
```

The second policy class is called application policy and is used by the provider of an application to express overriding requirements, such as the need to receive a particular version of an assembly, even if a newer version with its publisher policy claims compatibility. In the simplest case, an application policy will just state <publisherPolicy apply="no"> to disable publisher policies and get the exact version used at application build-time. The third policy class is called machine policy and is used by a machine's administrator to override both publisher and application policies where deemed necessary. Machine policies are a last resort to resolve integration or security problems that would result from applying publisher and application policy.

The Microsoft Windows Installer and the GAC cooperate to maintain a dependency graph among assemblies in the GAC and applications using these assemblies. This is used to collect and remove assemblies that are no longer used.

15.13   Common language frameworks

On top of CLR, the .NET Framework provides a large collection of frameworks. In the first .NET Framework release, the nature of these frameworks varies somewhat in style. Some frameworks emphasize customization by subclassing; others provide interfaces for that purpose. In both cases, the frameworks make use of sealed classes (classes that do not permit any subclassing and thus prevent overriding) to close the design in cases where the intricate nature of the implementation would make valid overriding very difficult. According to the asmstats tool by Mike Woodring (staff.develop.com/woodring/dotnet/), the first release comprises 69 assemblies with over 4000 public types (classes, interfaces, attributes, enums, delegates, and value types).

The following overview of the frameworks supported in the first release helps to get a sense of breadth of coverage. The detail ends at the level of almost 100 namespaces – though many of these namespaces contain tens and some even hundreds of class and interface definitions. A more thorough description is beyond the scope of this book. (For some frameworks, additional detail is covered in the following sections of this chapter.) The overview is organized by rough functional areas and further grouped by namespace families.

Framework foundation is as follows.

■ System Fundamental classes and base classes defining commonly used value and reference data types, events and event handlers, interfaces, attributes, and processing exceptions.

■ System.Collections, System.Collections.Specialized Various object collections: lists, queues, arrays, hash tables and dictionaries; in addition, specialized and strongly typed collections, such as a linked list dictionary, a bit vector and collections that contain only strings.

- System.Reflection, System.Reflection.Emit View of loaded types, methods, and fields, dynamically instantiate types and invoke methods. Emission of metadata and CIL into memory or into a newly generated portable executable (PE) file.
- System.Security, System.Security.Cryptography, System.Security.Cryptography.X509Certificates, System.Security.Cryptography.Xml, System.Security.Permissions, System.Security.Policy, System.Security.Principal Underlying structure of CLR security system, including permissions and policies; cryptographic services, including data encryption/decryption, secure hashing, random number generation, message authentication, and digital signing. Authenticode X.509 v3 certificates. XML model for CLR security system. Access control for access to operations and resources based on policy. Configurable sets of rules to determine which permissions to grant to code, based on the code's domain, user, and assembly. Principal object representing security context of executing code.
- System.Text, System.Text.RegularExpressions ASCII, Unicode, UTF-7, and UTF-8 character encodings; converting blocks of characters to and from blocks of bytes; manipulate/format strings without creating intermediate String instances. Regular expression engine.
- System.Threading, System.Timers Groups of threads, thread pools, timers, locks, thread scheduling, wait notification, and deadlock resolution.

Framework support for configuration, globalization, and management consists of the following.

- System.Configuration, System.Configuration.Assemblies, System.Configuration.Install Configuration in general, for an assembly, and for custom installers for components.
- System.Globalization Culture-related information, including language, country/region, calendars in use, format patterns for dates, currency and numbers, and sort order for strings.
- System.Resources Create/store/manage/use culture-specific resources of an assembly.
- System.Management, System.Management.Instrumentation Enable standard management of applications via CIM, WBEM, and WMI.

Framework support for platform access and COM interoperation is made up from the following.

- System.Drawing, System.Drawing.Design, System.Drawing.Drawing2D, System.Drawing.Imaging, System.Drawing.Printing, System.Drawing.Text GDI+ basic graphics functionality; design-time user interface (UI) logic and drawing; advanced two-dimensional and vector graphics; customize printing; advanced GDI+ typography, including creation and use of fonts.

- System.Runtime.InteropServices,
  System.Runtime.InteropServices.CustomMarshalers,
  System.Runtime.InteropServices.Expando Accessing COM objects and
  native APIs via attributes, exceptions, managed definitions of COM
  types, wrappers, type converters, and marshaling.
- System.ServiceProcess Install and run services: long-running
  executables without user interface; possibly to auto-start under a system
  account after computer reboot.

Framework support for I/O, messaging, remoting, and serialization includes
the following.

- System.Data, System.Data.Common, System.Data.OleDb,
  System.Data.SqlClient, System.Data.SqlTypes Constitutes ADO.NET,
  enables efficient management of data from multiple data sources.
  Common classes are shared by all .NET data providers (a collection of
  classes used to access a data source such as a database). Special support
  for OLE DB-compliant .NET and SQL Server data providers. Support
  for native SQL Server data types.
- System.DirectoryServices Directories – in particular, Active Directory.
- System.EnterpriseServices,
  System.EnterpriseServices.CompensatingResourceManager Integration
  of COM+ services, including access control, transactions and
  synchronization, messaging and queuing, load balancing, just-in-time
  activation and pooling. Support for creation of new compensating
  resource managers (managers of transactional resources).
- System.IO, System.IO.IsolatedStorage Synchronous and asynchronous
  reading/writing of datastreams and files. Creation and use of isolated
  stores supporting the reading/writing of data separated from the
  standard file system – data is stored in compartments isolated by current
  user and by assembly holding the saving code.
- System.Messaging Connect to message queues on the network and
  send/receive/peek messages.
- System.Runtime.Remoting, System.Runtime.Remoting.Activation,
  System.Runtime.Remoting.Channels,
  System.Runtime.Remoting.Channels.Http,
  System.Runtime.Remoting.Channels.Tcp,
  System.Runtime.Remoting.Contexts,
  System.Runtime.Remoting.Lifetime,
  System.Runtime.Remoting.Messaging,
  System.Runtime.Remoting.Metadata,
  System.Runtime.Remoting.MetadataServices,
  System.Runtime.Remoting.Proxies, System.Runtime.Remoting.Services
  For tightly or loosely coupled distributed applications – contexts, proxies,
  messages and channels (over HTTP or directly over TCP), supporting
  synchronous and various forms of asynchronous communication.

- System.Runtime.Serialization, System.Runtime.Serialization.Formatters, System.Runtime.Serialization.Formatters.Binary, System.Runtime.Serialization.Formatters.Soap Serializing/deserializing objects and graphs of objects for storage or transmission; binary and SOAP formats.

Framework support for debugging, compilation, and code generation consists of the following.

- System.Diagnostics, System.Diagnostics.SymbolStore Application debugging support, execution tracing, start system processes, read/write event logs, and monitor system performance using performance counters. Read/write debugging symbol information, such as sourceline to CIL maps.
- System.CodeDom, System.CodeDom.Compiler Object model to represent elements and structure of source code; generation and compilation based on the CodeDom for supported programming languages.
- System.Runtime.CompilerServices For compiler use only, involving attributes that affect the runtime behavior of the common language runtime.
- Microsoft.CSharp, Microsoft.JScript, Microsoft.VisualBasic Compilation and code generation for $C^{\#}$, JScript, and Visual Basic.
- Microsoft.Win32 Interoperation support for Win32 OS events and the Windows registry.

Framework support for internet and web protocols, web server access, and XML standards is made up from the following elements.

- System.Web, System.Web.Caching, System.Web.Configuration, System.Web.Security, System.Web.Services, System.Web.Services.Description, System.Web.Services.Discovery, System.Web.Services.Protocols Enable browser/server communication, including HTTP requests and responses; access to server-side utilities and processes; cookie manipulation, file transfer, exception information, and output cache control. Caching of server resources, including ASP.NET pages, web services, and user controls. Cache directory to store server application resources, such as hash tables and other data structures. ASP.NET configuration and security. Building and using web services. Description of web services using WSDL. Location and discovery of available web services on a web server. Protocols for data transmission to/from web services.
- System.Net, System.Net.Sockets Simple programming interface to many internet and web protocols; "pluggable protocols" to use internet resources parametrized over the protocol used. Sockets following the Winsock model.

- System.Xml, System.Xml.Schema, System.Xml.Serialization, System.Xml.XPath, System.Xml.Xsl XML processing, including DOM access, XML Schema, XPath, and XSL/XSLT. Serializing objects into XML documents or streams.

Framework support for component classes, web server support, and for client-side and web-based user interfaces, including the following.

- System.ComponentModel, System.ComponentModel.Design, System.ComponentModel.Design.Serialization Runtime and design-time behavior of component classes and controls; includes base classes and interfaces for attributes, type converters, binding to data sources, and component licensing. Design-time behavior and serialization at design time.
- System.Web.UI, System.Web.UI.Design, System.Web.UI.Design.WebControls, System.Web.UI.HtmlControls, System.Web.UI.WebControls Web forms space to create controls and pages as user interfaces. Standard controls, such as buttons and text boxes, and special purpose controls, such as a calendar; data-binding functionality for server controls; support to save view state of a control or page; parsing functionality for programmable and literal controls. Extensible design-time support for web forms and controls. HTML server controls that run on the server and map to HTML tags. Web controls that run on the server, including form controls, and that are more abstract than HTML controls: they do not necessarily reflect HTML syntax.
- System.Windows.Forms, System.Windows.Forms.Design – Rich Windows-style user interface features. Extensible design-time behavior for Windows Forms.

15.13.1 AppDomains, contexts, reflection, remoting

The CLR execution engine partitions a process into one or more AppDomains (application domains). An AppDomain isolates sets of objects from all objects in other AppDomains, but is more lightweight and thus cheaper than typical operating system processes. Communication across AppDomain boundaries requires marshalling (but can be optimized as all AppDomains within a process share the same address space). The CLR supports remoting across the boundaries of AppDomains, processes, and machines. The unit of execution is a logical thread that is mapped to a physical thread whenever entering an AppDomain. Logical threads retain identity, even when crossing machine boundaries.

AppDomains are also the scope of loading and unloading. In the first release, assemblies can be loaded into AppDomains at any time, but there is no support for individual unloading of assemblies. Instead, entire AppDomains can be deleted – unloading the corresponding AppDomains if they aren't still serving other appdomains in the same process. AppDomains are thus a convenient mechanism for sandboxing extensibility models, then a running application can, at any time, create a new AppDomain to host extension code. Although there is a price to pay (increased communication costs when crossing AppDomain boundaries), there is a significant advantage to this point – the use of resources (including the loading of further extending assemblies) can be controlled and all such resources can be collectively released by deleting the AppDomain.

Finer structuring of execution spaces beyond AppDomains is provided by contexts. A context is a partition of an AppDomain the member objects of which share the properties of their context. (For a more complete discussion, see section 21.2.) A CLI object is pre-classified as either context agile or context bound – this being determined by whether or not the object's class derives from the special class System.ContextBoundObject or not. Context-bound objects can make context demands by means of attribute-based programming (as introduced by MTS and now widely established in COM+ and EJB). The most direct way to make such demands is to use CLI's custom attributes on the class of a context-bound object. In the following example, a class requests placement in a synchronizing context:

```
using System;
public delegate void UpdateEventHandler(object sender);

[Synchronization(IsReEntrant=true)]
public class SynchSample : ContextBoundObject {
  private int sampleVar;
  public event ValueChange;
  public int SampleProperty {
    get { return sampleVar; }
    set {
      sampleVar = value;
      if (ValueChange != null) ValueChange(this);
    }
  }
}
```

The attribute used (System.SynchronizationAttribute) is parametrized to request that the context containing the SynchSample instance should synchronize (allow at most one thread to enter it) and be re-entrant (if the current thread calls out of the context, another thread can enter it). In the example, setting the property SampleProperty will cause a notification outcall, if any handlers are registered with the ValueChange event source. The thread setting the property will also service the event notification calls, causing it to possibly leave the current context. (Whether it actually leaves the context depends on whether the registered handler objects reside in a different context or not.)

It is instructive to compare this style of synchronization (which is only one of many uses of contexts) to the style of marking individual methods as "synchronized." The latter is the style built into Java, but also supported by CLI. In $C^\#$, a special custom-attribute on a method can be used to achieve the same, but synchronized methods do not attract special $C^\#$ syntax. Like Java's synchronized statement, $C^\#$ supports a lock statement to acquire a lock for the duration of a block. Synchronized blocks are a very fine-grained construct as their scope is fully under a programmer's control, but synchronized methods are somewhat in the middle in that they lock an entire object for the duration of a method call. Synchronizing contexts address a coarser level of granularity in that they lock all objects that share the same synchronizing context. The performance impact of using synchronizing wrongly can be substantial – and such an impact is likely to be greater when using synchronizing contexts that contain many shared objects. At the same time, it is exceedingly difficult (bordering on impossible) to design a system that is multithreaded and dynamically extensible if locking is limited to the scope of individual objects. In Java, EJB containers provide a comparable service of collectively locking all objects that share a container.

The interaction semantics of context-bound and context-agile objects forms a unique CLI property. Essentially, context-agile objects can be used by context-bound ones as if the agile objects resided in the same context. The same is possible in COM+ contexts. However, COM and COM+ contexts do not form strong isolation boundaries and programmers need to be careful not to "leak" references to agile objects to other contexts accidentally – a source of subtle errors. CLI improves on this situation by making the use of context-agile objects entirely safe. Whenever an agile object accesses a context-bound object, the CLI execution engine checks whether the call is on behalf of another context-bound object or not. If it is, then the engine checks if the calling context coincides with the called contexts. If so, the entire call-chain, through any number of agile objects in between, is considered a chain of calls within that context. Otherwise, the incoming call is considered to be crossing the context boundary of the called object and proper interception is performed.

The CLI reflection support grants full access to the type structure of loaded assemblies, including all attributes and custom attributes defined on these types. It also enables creation of instances of these types and invocation of methods on these types. The systematic support for custom attributes is a unique CLI feature. CLI reflection is moderated by permissions of the CLI security framework – if a reflection client has full reflection permissions, it can use reflection to access even private fields. If, at the other end of the spectrum, a reflection client has default permissions only, then reflection will only grant access to public features.

The CLI remoting support combines context and reflection infrastructure with flexible support for proxies, channels, and messages to provide building blocks for a wide variety of communication styles and patterns. At the synchronous end, a standard pattern is remote method calling using standard or custom marshalers over either binary or SOAP encodings. At the asynchronous end, method calls with polling and notifying completion information are supported, as well as various messaging semantics.

Synchronous remote method calls essentially share the semantics of DCOM. A logical thread is formed that links the physical calling and the physical called thread. This is in contrast to Java RMI, which does not have a logical thread concept. Logical threads are an important tool to handle self-inflicted re-entrancy (the remote method call leads to a nested remote method callback to the calling context; for more details, see section 14.6.1 on Java RMI). Unlike DCOM and like Java RMI, CLI remoting supports lease-based handling of remote references. That is, a reference to a remote object expires after a settable period of time, unless the lease is renewed in time. The owner of the object can rely on remote references either silently expiring or seeing explicit renewal requests before that happens. As a result, distributed garbage collection scales better – a result established by the seminal work on Network Objects (Birrel, 1993) that also inspired Java RMI. Unlike Java RMI, remote references are not scoped to an entire JVM activation, but to an AppDomain. Deleting an AppDomain thus systematically drops all remotely accessible objects and remote references held by the AppDomain, enabling controlled partial shutdown (as explained above for AppDomains).

15.13.2 Windows Forms, data, management

Windows Forms is the .NET Framework family that enables the construction of Windows applications using CLR-hosted managed code. The basic model of Windows Forms (and Web Forms discussed below) is component classes (classes that typically derive from System.ComponentModel.Component, but at least implement System.ComponentModel.IComponent). As a minimum, component classes support having a site, which is a helper object supplied by a container object. Sites are used to attach properties to component objects and enable a contained object to access its container. Beyond this basic hierarchical containment model, Windows Forms uses properties, events, and delegates to support connection-oriented programming.

At the level of component classes, Windows Forms covers dialogs, controls, collections, native windows, property types, cursors, data formats and data objects, clipboard, support for help and error handling, and support for the embedding of ActiveX controls in Windows Forms. (Only non-container ActiveX controls are supported in the first release, covering most ActiveX controls in use.) The palette of provided implementations is quite rich. Standard dialogs provided include those for color, file, font, page setup, print, and print preview. Standard controls and related widgets include button, checkbox, radio button, data grid, date time picker, group, label, list, combo, checked list, calendar, picture, print preview, progress bar, scrollable, form, property grid, up, down, panel, tab page, scroll bar, splitter, status bar, tab, text box, tool bar, track bar, tree view, image list, menu, context menu, icon, and tool tip.

Windows Forms components, such as JavaBeans, distinguish design time as a special stage of development, supported by the components themselves. Unlike JavaBeans, Windows Forms uses CLI custom attributes to attach design-time information and behavior to components. The following example shows how a custom editor is attached to a property:

```
class SuperTrackBar : ITrackBarProperties {
    [Editor(typeof(TrackBarDarkenByEditor), typeof(UITypeEditor))]
    int ITrackBarProperties.DarkenBy { get; set; }
    ...
}
```

In this example, an integer-typed property is attributed to request the selection of a special-purpose editor. Designer tools should instantiate and use this special editor, instead of their default editor for integer-typed properties. The requested editor is named using its class type, while the second attribute argument classifies the editor (usually an interface or base class of the editor's class; in the first release, only the base class System.Drawing.Design.UITypeEditor is defined).

15.13.3 Web Forms, Active Server Pages (ASP) .NET

Web Forms is a framework to build dialogs within ASP.NET. Web Forms works by "rendering" to DHTML (dynamic HTML) and relying on a remote browser to display forms and interact with users. This is in contrast to Windows Forms, which uses the Windows platform's functionality to render controls and interact with users. Web Forms aims to keep all application logic on the server and target any browser, but allows taking advantage automatically of browser-specific features for improved performance or user interface.

Web Forms uses the same connection-oriented programming model as Windows Forms (see previous section). The Web Forms framework fully abstracts the capture of an event on the client and its transmission to the server. Registered handlers are invoked as if the event was originated locally. Similar abstraction is provided when maintaining form state by sending updates to the client. The resulting programming model of Web Forms presents a form as a logical unit, despite the split into client versus server side. For most purposes, Web Forms and Windows Forms thus follow the same programming model and abstraction. The Web Forms framework leverages this level of abstraction to support scaling from single processor to web farm servers without changes to the application logic.

Technically, ASP.NET uses compilation of page descriptions to page classes that are then dynamically loaded and instantiated to achieve the combination of abstraction and performance. More detailed, ASP.NET parses the page description (an .aspx file) and its code, generates a new class (deriving from class System.Web.UI.Page) dynamically, and then compiles the new class. The dynamically generated class combines the page's code, bindings to required controls, and the page's static HTML text. This new class is inserted into a new assembly that is loaded by the server whenever the Web Forms page is requested. At runtime, an instance of the class processes incoming requests and responds by dynamically creating HTML and streaming it back to the browser. If the page contains web controls (as it typically would), the derived Page class acts as a container for the controls, and instances of the controls are created at runtime and, likewise, render HTML text to the stream.

The ASP.NET approach is a departure from the older ASP model. In ASP, the page consisted of static HTML interspersed with executable code. An ASP processor reads the page, extracts and runs (interprets) only the code, and then fits the results back into the static HTML before sending the results to the browser. ASP.NET is implemented as an ISAPI extension of IIS (the Internet Information Server that is part of Windows Server platforms). ISAPI (Information Server API) enables very high performance web servers, but it is based on native code that imperatively generates HTML and other contents requested by clients. The ASP.NET model yields a performance level closer to raw special-purpose ISAPI applications while providing a programming model that actually improves on that of ASP (which performs well below the levels of native ISAPI extensions or ASP.NET).

With ASP.NET page classes the entire page is turned into an object the output of which is HTML. The page object goes through a series of stages – initialize, process, and dispose. To cater for the unpredictable nature of web browsing (such as users navigating back and forth while having a half-completed form), page objects are initialized, processed, and disposed every time a round trip to the server occurs. (To improve performance, ASP.NET caches the information required to recreate the page.) As a final stage after regular processing and before disposal, a page object renders itself as an HTML stream. ASP.NET pages and page classes are similar to Java ServerPages (JSP) pages and Java servlets, respectively (see section 14.5.1).

Aside from the components supporting a page, ASP.NET provides a second kind of componentization at the page description level itself. So called pagelets allow modular use of reoccurring definitions and constructions in the contexts of multiple pages. Pagelets can hierarchically use other pagelets and are compiled into separate classes. ASP.NET supports the use of multiple languages on a page, but it is good practice to use a single language per pagelet.

15.13.4 **XML and data**

The world of data access and processing is now predominantly split into two halves – normalized, structured data in relational tables and semi-structured, self-describing data in XML trees. A second dimension is the distinction between online and off-line data access. The web data framework is designed around the four resulting quadrants, supporting online and off-line access and manipulation of relational and XML data. It also supports conversion of relational data into XML data and vice versa. The latter case is interesting as fairly effective heuristics are used to determine tabular shape in the absence of schema information. To support off-line data access and manipulation, the web data framework provides generic caching support.

Access to and manipulation of relational data is handled by a part of the framework called ADO.NET, which logically takes the place of the previous COM-based ADO (active data objects) technology. ADO.NET supports ODBC and OLEDB to access relational data sources.

Access to and manipulation of XML data is handled by another part of the framework. Beyond parsing and object model access, the framework supports validation against XML Schema, handling of XPath, XSL, and XSLT.

15.13.5 Enterprise services

In the initial release of the .NET Framework, so-called enterprise services continue to be handled by COM+ (section 15.10.3). However, it is actually easier to implement and use such services on the CLR than it used to be in COM. The following code fragment shows how custom attributes are used to request particular services:

```
using ES = System.EnterpriseServices;

[ ES.Transaction(ES.TransactionOption.Required) ]
[ ES.Synchronization(ES.SynchronizationOption.Required) ]
[ ES.JustInTimeActivation(true) ]
public class Account : ES.ServicedComponent { ... }
```

Simply placing the transaction-required attribute on a class and deriving from the ServicedComponent base class causes instances of Account to be placed in a COM+ transactional context – a new one if the caller didn't already have one. The example also requests all access to the Account instances to be synchronized and "just-in-time" (when actual calls arrived) activation of instances.

15.13.6 Web services with .NET

As outlined in section 12.4.6, web services with their WSDL-defined ports are similar to interfaces with methods. The .NET Framework takes direct advantage of this similarity and allows lightweight implementations of (simple) web services. Essentially, all that needs to be done is to define a method with appropriate parameter types and then place the WebMethod custom attribute on that method. The following example (taken from ASP.NET documentation) implements a simple web service that has a single port on which it receives two numbers and returns the sum of these.

```
<%@ WebService Language="C#" Class="SimpleMath" %>
using WS = System.Web.Services;
public class SimpleMath {
  [WS.WebMethod]
  public int Add(int a, int b) {
    return a+b;
  }
}
```

The special comment in the first line of the example addresses ASP.NET. By using ASP.NET, all additional steps are automated and the web service can go online with almost no further effort. The following SOAP message could be send to this simple service:

```
<?xml version="1.0" encoding="utf-8"?>
<soap:Envelope xmlns:soap="http://schemas.xmlsoap.org/soap/envelope/" >
  <soap:Body>
    <Add xmlns="http://tempuri.org/">
      <a>37</a>
      <b>5</b>
    </Add>
  </soap:Body>
</soap:Envelope>
```

The web service replies with the following SOAP message:

```
<?xml version="1.0" encoding="utf-8"?>
<soap:Envelope xmlns:soap="http://schemas.xmlsoap.org/soap/envelope/" >
  <soap:Body>
    <AddResponse xmlns="http://tempuri.org/">
      <AddResult>42</AddResult>
    </AddResponse>
  </soap:Body>
</soap:Envelope>
```

At this level of using ASP.NET, there is no need to understand XML, HTTP, SOAP or any of the other protocols used to build web services. However, for more advanced tasks, there are several tools available to build web services directly, without using ASP.NET. For instance, the disco.exe tool acquires WSDL contract documents from web services. The wsdl.exe tool generates code for web services and web service clients from WSDL documents, schemas, and discovery documents. The soapsuds.exe tool generates CLR classes from XML Schema types and vice versa (to simplify interoperation with schema-defined types within programs).

On the caller's side, the wsdl.exe tool generates proxy classes that internally call the SOAP infrastructure. For the above example, the proxy would have a method Add and, in addition, methods BeginAdd and EndAdd. Calling Add causes a synchronous blocking call to the web service (which is not generally a good idea). Calling BeginAdd initiates an asynchronous call and returns a handle (of type System.IAsynchResult). The caller can then use the handle to request updates on the status of the call. Finally, if the caller either determines that the result is available or that it has to block anyway, it calls EndAdd, passing in the handle. EndAdd returns with the result (and blocks until the result is available). It is also possible to pass a delegate to BeginAdd pointing at the method that should be called as soon as the asynchronous call completed. The asynchronous call mechanism is complete – it supports all parameter passing modes of the CLR (in, out, and in/out value, as well as by-reference). It is also type-safe as begin and end methods are generated by the compilers to ensure proper passing of arguments.

There is support for a service implementer to explicitly deal with asynchronous calls. This is only necessary if a service either issues asynchronous invocations itself or if it has to call on some other slow services. The support for asynchronous programming is quite systematic on the .NET platform. For instance, all of the following are supported asynchronously:

- File IO, Stream IO, Socket IO;
- networking – HTTP, TCP;
- remoting channels (HTTP, TCP) and proxies;
- XML web services created using ASP.NET;
- ASP.NET Web Forms;
- messaging message queues over MSMQ;
- asynchronous delegates (which can be requested on any delegate type – compilers and CLR cooperate to synthesize the asynchronous Begin... and End... methods with strongly typed signature.)

CHAPTER SIXTEEN

Some further technologies

Besides the main approaches covered in the previous four chapters (XML and web services, OMG standards, Java standards and technology, Microsoft standards and technology), there are many others. In this chapter, some of these approaches are described, briefly and non-exhaustively.

16.1 Computer Associates' Advantage Plex

Computer Associates' Advantage Plex is a model-driven environment that emphasizes integration with a wide variety of other technologies, including IBM's iSeries 400 and DB2, Java/EJB, and Microsoft server products (www.cai.com/products/). A COM "connector" bridges to Microsoft tools (such as Visual Basic) and server products. Java integration is supported by a built-in JRE (Java runtime environment). Advantage Plex creates native code for the platforms of Java servers with Win32 C++ or Java clients, JDBC Access; IBM iSeries 400 servers with Win32 C++ or Java clients, iSeries 5250 with SQL, JDBC, and DDS access to DB2/400; Windows NT/2000/XP with BackOffice-compliant Windows NT servers and Win32 C++ clients, Oracle8i and SQL Server.

Here's a bit of history. Texas Instruments Software developed the TI Composer, a widely used approach to the component-based construction of large enterprise applications. This division of TI was later acquired by Sterling Software, which itself was acquired by Computer Associates in 2000. Sterling developed component-based methods and tools under its COOL line of products and the composer under the name COOL:Plex. CA is now continuing this line under their Advantage Plex brand.

Starting from models that describe business processes and software architecture, details are refined until sufficient information is available to generate the actual deployable software. By providing collections of established patterns, software architects are guided toward designs that follow best practice. Without a need to undo the top-level models and designs, details can be changed to generate variants for different target platforms and technologies.

Models are defined by selecting, combining, and completing "patterns." Third-party patterns can be integrated. Model-level tools are provided that perform dependency analysis, change tracking and management, and impact analysis. Browser-style tools can be used to answer "What if?"-style questions and determine their likely impact on the system were the probed changes executed. Code generation can only go so far – it is not possible to generate the universe. Runtime integration server functionality – as provided by the CA Advantage Integration Server – is required to bridge gaps among existing deployed systems. Support is provided for extending applications to HTML and XML exchange as well as support for wireless operation (WAP and I-mode) and portal-style organization.

16.2   Hitachi Appgallery

Hitachi's Appgallery (www.hitachi.co.jp/Prod/comp/soft1/open-e/appgal/appgal.htm) is an environment supporting the visual assembly of user interfaces based on Microsoft's OLE, roughly in the tradition of Visual Basic. Applications are created by visually placing icons on a canvas. A "painted" canvas is translated into a module of program code, where an application may comprise multiple canvases.

All components are OLE objects, enabling integration with Microsoft Office and many other applications. Components are represented as icons on a component palette, sorted into sheets, where each sheet gathers components in a particular category. The palette organization is customizable – new categories can be defined and components can appear in multiple categories to ease their organization on the palette. Detailed information about selected components can be browsed. The creation of new components is supported by a component-builder tool that uses OLE automation interfaces.

While an Appgallery user can place and connect components manually, there is also support for automatic guidance by a mechanism called "wizard." For instance, if a user drags a component instance over another, the wizard asks a few questions and then establishes required connections automatically. The wizard is fully extensible to the extent that new components can be shipped with appropriate wizard routines to ease the proper use of the new components. In addition, the wizard monitors the Appgallery user's progress and offers advice and options on how to proceed or how to further connect component instances.

16.3   Groove Transceiver

With Groove Transceiver, Ray Ozzie, the designer of Lotus Notes, aims at a comprehensive and fully integrated group collaboration environment. The central idea is simple, which is that workspaces can be created that contain hierarchical structures of folders and tools. On a peer level, much as in the case of "buddy lists" formed by messenger services, collaborators can be invited to join a workspace. Groove uses presence protocols (again like messenger applications) to inform all connected collaborators of the status of the other members of a workspace. Work can continue off-line and Groove provides server capacity to synchronize changes in a loosely coupled way.

Groove Transceiver uses a cut-back version of COM as its component model, but standard and proprietary web-based protocols instead of DCOM for networking. New tools for Groove can be implemented using the cut-back version of COM and then downloaded and inserted into the transceiver. It is not yet clear how far such extensions can take the transceiver and, thus, the whole Groove approach. The somewhat proprietary component approach of the current transceiver may indicate a bootstrap problem where Groove has to develop almost all initial components to make the transceiver attractive enough for users and therefore for ISVs to create further components.

Strategic comparison

Given the abundance of technical detail that characterizes each of the approaches discussed so far, what are the significant differences and what are the essential shared attributes? What are the strategic consequences?

17.1 Shared attributes

Obviously, the shared attributes of the approaches discussed cannot help to make decisions as to which approach to follow. However, the rich sharing of attributes swings the decision in favor of using component software technology, whatever the concrete approach is. Understanding the shared attributes also helps to prevent fruitless arguments for minor points that are simply misunderstood as major differences.

All approaches rely on late binding mechanisms, encapsulation, and dynamic polymorphism (also called inclusion polymorphism or subtyping). All approaches support interface inheritance, although in the case of COM this is almost irrelevant. (COM's source of polymorphism is the interface class separation and the support of multiple interfaces for each class.) In other words, all approaches rely on some sort of object model.

In addition, there has been strong cross-fertilization over time. Most approaches now support:

- a component transfer format – Java JAR files, COM cab files, CCM: – ("– " means none), CLI assemblies;
- uniform data transfer;
- events and event connections or channels, single and multicasting;
- meta-information – introspection, reflection;
- some form of persistence, serialization or externalization;
- attribute-based programming or deployment descriptors;
- a specialized component model for application servers – EJB, COM+, CCM, CLR:COM+;
- a specialized component model for web servers (JSP/servlets, COM: –, CCM: –, ASP.NET).

An often overlooked development is that the non-COM approaches slowly converge to also support what COM always had, which was component objects that can present themselves to their clients via multiple distinct objects. Doing so opens up the possibilities of dynamic configuration. This has now been acknowledged. The CORBA component model's notion of equivalence interfaces is an almost literal adoption of the COM QueryInterface identity property. JavaBeans introduces a library indirection, java.beans.Beans, to replace the Java language's type tests (instanceof) and guards (checked casts). By doing so, future beans could present themselves to clients as a set of Java objects, rather than just a single object. Interestingly, CLI/CLR in their first version do not follow the COM lead and don't provide support or conventions to deal with multibodied instances, although a common design pattern uses $C^\#$ properties to get subobjects off of a main object.

17.2   Differences

Once the decision to utilize software components has been taken, the next step is to choose an approach. Alternatively, based on the wide spectrum of shared attributes of many approaches, it can be useful to follow a small number of different approaches simultaneously. Proponents and third parties are likely to provide bridging solutions between the major approaches in particular. There are several examples in this direction. IONA's Orbix 2000 COMet is a CORBA/COM integration tool. Sun's ActiveX bridge allows JavaBeans instances to be embedded into ActiveX containers. Says IONA's chief technology officer, Annrai O'Toole:

> "Our motto is incompatibility is business – it's a huge opportunity for us."

Here is a (non-exhaustive) list of significant differences between the approaches.

- *Binary interfacing standard per platform* A binary standard for component interaction is the heart of COM. (It should be noted that, although technically feasible and attempted at times, COM has never really left the realm of Windows – thus binary standard per platform.) Java avoids an actual binary standard by standardizing on bytecode instead. For binary interfacing, Java defines the Java native interface (JNI), the design of which is based on COM, but which is quite Java-specific. In particular, it is designed to create room for modern garbage collectors. CORBA still does not define binary standards. Binary standards are required by Direct-to-* compilers that map constructs of a specific language directly to binary interfaces. CLR (a CLI superset), like Java, stays one level removed from a binary standard and standardizes MSIL (a CIL superset) instead. Ahead-of-time compilation

CHAPTER SEVENTEEN

is supported, though, and efficient support for platform API invocation conventions and COM interoperation is provided.

■ *Source-level standards for compatibility and portability* CORBA is particularly strong in standardizing language bindings that ensure source code compatibility across ORB implementations. The large number of standardized service interfaces strengthens its position. The current practice of accessing ORB-specific functions on the object server side reduces the portability of CORBA-based servers. For Java, the agreement on the Java language specification solves the problem as long as no other languages are used to target the Java platform. Standardization of language bindings then becomes an issue as, otherwise, interoperation of bytecode generated from multiple source languages is jeopardized. The larger Java space covers a large set of (*de facto* Sun) standards. The J2EE suite of standards in particular has been targeted by dozens of companies providing implementations. COM does not have any concept of source-level standards or standard language bindings. The COM interface market is also not standardized beyond Microsoft's *de facto* standards. The .NET CLR provides the common language specification (CLS) to guide language bindings that yield a high degree of interoperability without actually prescribing the individual language bindings. The common language infrastructure (CLI) specification underlying the CLR, as well as a set of base class libraries and the $C^\#$ language, has been standardized by ECMA.

■ *Grown versus forged standards* COM, CORBA, Java, and the CLI standards (in that order) have had ever-shorter periods of evolution before forging "standards." Both COM (with OLE 1) and CORBA (1.2) have already gone through substantial revisions, with no true backwards compatibility. COM/OLE/ActiveX has many redundant mechanisms – for example, outgoing interfaces and connectable objects (but also change notification interfaces, also known as advice interfaces) and dispatch interfaces (but also verb interfaces and, since ActiveX, command target interfaces). A consequence of the varying lifetimes of the approaches is the difference in product variety on the markets today. There are several thousand ActiveX objects on the market, but there are only a few dozen beans. However, Enterprise JavaBeans components have found substantial support in the industry, though today they are mostly developed and used in-house. For CLI/CLR-compliant components, it is too early to report on market acceptance.

■ *Memory management, lifecycles, and garbage collection* CORBA today does not offer a general solution to the global memory management problem in a distributed object system. COM and DCOM rely on reference counting from the ground up – this works if every component plays by the rules, but does have scaling problems in large, open distributed systems. Java relies totally on garbage collection, and with the Java remote method invocation (RMI) service since JDK 1.1, Java also defines a distributed object model and supports distributed garbage collection, where the concept is based on "leases" – pre-assigned bounded lifetime of remote references. CLR also performs garbage collection combined with lease-based invalidation of remote references. In addition, CLR supports an open set of other communication and marshaling protocols, such as SOAP over HTTP.

■ *Container-managed persistence and relations* EJB innovated the space of container-managed persistence and, since EJB 2.0, also container-managed relations. CCM follows as far as it is a superset of EJB. Neither COM+ nor CLR provides such support so far. These mechanisms tend to still have rough edges, such as overly eager loading of all entities in a relation in J2EE servers, leading to poor performance for many applications. OLEDB (and thus COM+ and CLR) supports pluggable persistence mappings, allowing the persistence of data to many external stores, beyond pure databases. EJB, in version 2.0, does not yet include support for pluggable mappings, rendering the container-managed persistence and relationships mechanisms weak outside of pure database applications. Likewise, EJB 2.0 is limited when mappings require complex joins or stored procedures.

■ *Concepts of evolution and versioning* COM insists on freezing interfaces and their specifications once they have been published together with their interface ID. This solves both the version and the migration problem, but surfaces problems when attempting managed version compatibility policies at a particular site of deployment. CORBA does not directly address this issue, but supports the weak notion of major and minor version numbers. The CORBA solution has problems because it allows a reference to an object of some version to be passed on to another object that expects an object of a different version – version checking is performed only at initial object creation time. Java addresses versioning only on the level of binary compatibility, for which a painstaking list of rules is given. It would seem that some of these rules go too far. For example, changing a constant's value from one release to another has no effect on precompiled clients, which simply stick to the old value. Instead of declaring such a client as broken when interfacing to the new version, the old client remains usable, although it is likely to malfunction. Component Pascal implementations use a per-interface fingerprinting algorithm to maintain compatibility on a fine granularity (Crelier, 1994). The most complete approach to versioning can be found in CLI. CLI components, called assemblies, are each tagged with their own version information and also the set of versions of components they depend on. Policies can be used to establish tolerable ranges of matching versions. Side-by-side execution is supported to allow multiple versions of a component to coexist. This enables sliding windows of migration over time – not everything needs to move forward to a new version of a component at once. However, neither the initial .NET Framework nor the initial languages targeting the CLR take full advantage of the CLI versioning support.

■ *Concept of categories* Categories in COM are often overlooked as they are new and seem harmless, but, in fact, introduce the concept of contractual binding to specifications encompassing any number of interfaces. A component can belong to any number of categories and a framework or other component can use category membership as a high-level assertion. Neither Java nor CORBA has anything like it, although empty marker interfaces are used for a similar purpose in Java. CLI offers custom attributes to extend a component's metadata, so categorical and other meta-information can be captured using custom attributes.

■ *Availability of industrial-strength implementations and applications* Here, all approaches have their home fields. COM is strongest on the client/desktop side. J2EE and COM+ now dominate non-PC-based and PC-based server solutions. Web servers in particular heavily use JSP or ASP (and now ASP.NET). CORBA is strongest for traditional legacy integration at the level of enterprise computing. Both COM and CLR implementations are largely limited to those provided by Microsoft. CORBA and J2EE implementations are available from many vendors. While porting from one J2EE server to another is not trivial, it is certainly much easier than porting from J2EE to .NET or vice versa.

■ *Development environments* A wide range of strong development environments supports COM. Environments for Java are also mature. Environments for CORBA are still underdeveloped. CLR, the Microsoft CLI implementation, co-released with Visual Studio .NET, including support for Visual Basic, JScript, C#, and Managed C++.

■ *Services* CORBA now has a full set of standardized services, but most of these still lack commercial implementations. COM+ complemented COM with a rich set of key services, including transactions and messaging. A comparably wide set of services is part of Java 2 Enterprise Edition, which includes Enterprise JavaBeans. CLR offers deep interoperability support with COM+, including all COM+ services (now called Enterprise Services). However, these are not covered by the CLI specification. In the future, some COM+ services might migrate to become genuine CLR-hosted services. Support for distributed transaction coordination is available in CORBA and COM+ (and thus CLR), but not in the scope of the EJB 2.0 standard. Support in J2EE servers varies accordingly.

■ *Deployment* J2EE, COM+, CCM, and CLR all follow the MTS concept of attribute-based programming. EJB factored attributes out and placed them in separate XML-based deployment descriptors, enabling a clean object of manipulation for a specialized deployment step. J2EE broadens the deployment descriptor concept to several component models. CLR combines XML-based configuration with CLI-based custom attributes. Custom attributes simplify the alignment of code and metadata as the attribute is placed directly in the relevant source code. This factors the roles of developer (places custom attributes) and deployer (manipulates configuration files).

■ *Web service components* CORBA and COM don't have a specialized component model in this space. J2EE does – Java ServerPages (JSP) and its servlet components. The .NET Framework does – page component classes for ASP.NET. JSP followed some of the older ASP model, but innovated in the space of JSP pages versus servlets. ASP.NET followed some of the JSP model, but added target independence, so, instead of providing components that render HTML, ASP.NET encourages the use of provided controls that perform the rendering. Many ASP.NET components will, therefore, not emit a single line of HTML directly, making them independent of the requirements of particular target devices, such as rendering WML for mobile devices.

■ *On the wire* CORBA supports the IIOP as a standard "wire-level" protocol for inter-ORB interoperation. In addition, the OMG has adopted XML and its schema world for application-level wire format description. Java supports IIOP bindings, but natively supports its own RMI protocol. Java support for XML is improving. COM uses DCOM as its native wire protocol and COM+ adds support for multiple messaging formats. CLR continues support of all formats supported by COM and COM+ and adds support for XML schema definitions and SOAP invocation protocols.

17.3   Consequences for infrastructure vendors

One of the most fundamental differences among the four main approaches considered here (OMA, COM, Java, and CLI) is the degree of freedom they leave to implementers of the approach. To understand what is possible, it is useful to look at what exactly is fixed by an approach.

All four approaches define an object model and do so in different ways. OMG also defines language bindings, the OMG IDL, sets of standard interfaces in IDL, and interoperability protocols (IIOP in particular). COM defines binary calling conventions and binary interface definitions of a set of standard interfaces (the COM IDL is defined *de facto*, as explained below). Java defines standard interfaces, specified using the Java language. Additionally, Java defines the load file format, including all available meta-information, in class files and, since 1.1, Java archive (JAR) files. Finally, Java also defines the stream format of serialized objects – that is, objects externalized automatically using a standard strategy. CLI defines standard interfaces and class-based frameworks specified in a language-neutral way. Additionally and also in a language-neutral way, CLI defines a load file and extensible metadata format (assemblies), multiple serialization protocols (including XML), tooling, management, and development support interfaces.

What are the consequences of such subtle differences? They mainly govern the number of variants that need to be implemented to support the opened spectrum. The OMA does not define standards at the executable level. Hence, it is necessary for an ORB vendor to provide language-binding tools for each supported language. For COM, independent vendors can provide language implementations, including COM bindings, as COM defines a binary standard. COM still offers significant leeway for different COM implementations – COM library, type libraries, proxy and stub implementation and generation (including DCOM), and the implementation of standard services. However, no non-Microsoft implementations of COM have achieved relevance – although there are products such as EntireX from Software AG that supports DCOM on Linux (www.softwareag.com/entirex/download/). The Java standard merely requires one class file compiler per language targeting the Java class-file format, independent of platforms, but the standard is fine-tuned to support just one language (Java). Only very few other languages are in widespread use on JVMs. Of these, Jython, for scripting purposes, is probably the most important (Rappin and Pedroni, 2002). However, many other languages have been implemented to target the JVM, at varying levels of support (www.cs.tu-berlin.de/~tolk/vmlanguages.html). For further discussions, see Sessions (2001b) and Udell (2000). Finally, CLI follows a decoupling strategy similar to Java, but aims at a wide range of languages and, therefore, extensible metadata and cross-language interoperation. The potentially broad reach of the CLI will depend on its uptake by multiple vendors of languages and possibly platforms. By late 2001, there were two Open Source efforts ongoing to implement the CLI – the Mono project (www.go-mono.com) and the Open CLI Library project (sourceforge.net/projects/ocl). In addition, Corel and Microsoft announced that they were to provide a CLI implementation on FreeBSD UNIX.

A simple analysis shows that the above decisions work best for Java and CLI, second best for COM, and worst for OMA. Assume that there are L languages and P platforms to be supported. Ideally, for each language and each platform it should be possible to have multiple vendors.

With Java and CLI, each language vendor merely implements mappings to class files for Java and assemblies for CLI. With an average of VL vendors per language, L*VL language implementations are created. For each platform, the native Java or CLI services have to be provided, possibly including a just-in-time compiler. This leads to P*VP implementations, where VP is the average number of Java or CLI implementation vendors for each platform. With JDK 1.1, JNI has been standardized. It reduces the burden on platform-specific developments by defining a single standard binary interface for each platform. This interface allows a particular Java VM implementation to be connected with platform-specific "native" libraries that are themselves JVM-independent. In addition, J2EE leverages CORBA, avoiding reimplementation of those services provided by CORBA. Microsoft aims to support the CLI as a part of all its platforms, likely reducing VP to one on those platforms. Also, Microsoft does not leverage CORBA, which isn't very widespread on Windows platforms anyway. Otherwise the CLR and JVM calculations agree.

With COM, each language vendor implements native code generation. With VLP being the average number of language vendors for each language–platform combination, L*P*VLP language implementations are created. For each platform, a COM implementation needs to be devised. With VP average vendors per platform, this leads to P*VP implementations.

With CORBA, each language vendor implements native code generation. As with COM, this leads to L*P*VLP language implementations. For each platform an implementation of ORB and CORBAservices is required. However, CORBA vendors also need to provide language bindings, and these can differ between language vendors, even for the same language. This leads to L*P*VPL CORBA implementations that differ at least in their language bindings. Here, VPL is the average number of language binding plus ORB vendors per language–vendor–platform combination.

Note that language and CORBA vendors can be distinct and that language vendors are independent. However, CORBA vendors may need to provide different bindings for each language vendor, even for the same language, because there are no fixed calling conventions. In other words, if all CORBA vendors want to support all language vendors, L*P*VPL*VP implementations result.

Note that this is only part of the CORBA spectrum. Most ORB vendors deliver object adapters that go well beyond the common standard basic object adapter (BOA). Object servers therefore depend on the object adapter on which they were built. Switching from one ORB to another is thus an option only at the client end. (While this situation has improved at the level of the BOA, which has been replaced with the portable object adapter (POA), new fragmentation occurs at the level of component containers.)

What is wrong with potentially large numbers of offerings, as predicted for CORBA? In the absence of a single or very few lead vendors, this potential for variety is likely actually realized by numerous vendors. The market becomes fragmented and thus, astonishingly, the spectrum of options actually available is likely to be small. For example, picking a language that is not supported on all ORBs on all platforms restricts the options that a project would otherwise have. To support a language universally in the CORBA case, P*VP bindings are required. It is not likely that this investment will be made for a large number of languages. For example, there were several direct-to-SOM compilers on the market that bound directly to SOM, avoiding the indirection of the OMG IDL. The effort required for such a direct-to-ORB compiler is significant. As was to be expected, such support did not become available for most ORBs. At the other extreme, for the Java approach, the support of additional languages is cheap. Only one implementation per language is required to guarantee universal availability of that language, provided that there is at least one Java implementation for each platform. However, the Java platform is not well suited for languages other than Java – problems surface, for example, when using the reflection facility on non-Java code. This is where the CLI platform shows an advantage.

A possible argument against the above line of reasoning would be to claim that the mentioned VP will be small. Assume that there is only one service vendor per platform – VP=1. For COM, this is a likely scenario and leads to P service implementations. The number of language implementations is unaffected and remains L*P*VLP. For CORBA, even today, the number of competing ORB vendors is quite large on the more popular platforms. The assumption is therefore less realistic. Nevertheless, the assumption does not help. L*P*VPL service implementations are still required. However, VPL is now likely to become larger as the market share of the single CORBA vendor on a platform allows for the support of more languages and language vendors.

The above becomes more concrete by substituting realistic numbers. There are around 10 important platforms and around 10 important languages. In spite of the aim of Java to be a single-language approach, the Java platform today supports, besides Java, languages such as Ada 95 (Intermetrics, 1997) or REXX (IBM, 1997). However, the use of non-Java languages on the Java platform has never become really popular, perhaps with the exception of the scripting languages Jython/JPython. Java also already covers all major platforms. The COM model today supports all major languages, including Java, but also C++, Component Pascal, Object Pascal, Visual Basic, Object Cobol, ML, and so on. It also covers many major platforms (via DCOM ports), although it has never become popular beyond the Windows platforms. (The COM ideas have led to similar, but not compatible, approaches elsewhere, such as XPCOM as used in the Netscape Mozilla browser implementation.) The CLI supports about 20 languages, including Visual Basic, JScript, C#, C++, Component Pascal, Haskell, ML, Python, Perl, and many others. For the time being, a rich CLI implementation is only available for Windows platforms (Microsoft's .NET Framework), though a lighter version aimed at small devices is scheduled to follow (Microsoft's .NET Compact Framework). Microsoft have also released (2002) a shared source CLI implementation called Rotor that includes C# and JScript compilers. The Mono project (www.ximian.com) aims to develop an open source, Linux-based version of the CLI platform.

CORBA implementations are available for almost all platforms. Also, for many platforms, there is a choice between several ORB vendors. However, there is a tendency to support only a small number of languages. Often, C++ is the only language supported. Smalltalk used to be second choice but has rapidly lost support. Java has filled this gap. In fact, Java is the only language that enjoys both a traditional OMG IDL to Java mapping as well as a Java to OMG

IDL reverse mapping. (IONA's Orbix/Web is interesting in that it implements a minimal ORB in Java that travels with applets and uses IIOP to interact with other ORBs.) The number of languages available for a given ORB is usually small, despite the availability of OMG IDL mappings for several languages. Today there is only one language available on all ORBs across all platforms. It is C^{++}, although it is closely followed by Java. The above analysis makes this outcome plausible and, in hindsight, quite predictable.

In summary, if too many dimensions are coupled to support the widest variety of solutions, most solutions will be limited to a small niche market. This will result in pruning, and variety is first hurt where it is least welcome – in the spectrum of language–platform combinations supported uniformly. This can be summarized succinctly as:

■ maximizing the number of possible combinatorial variations minimizes the number of available variations.

In other words, where too much is possible, islands of mutual competition and partial incompatibility result and a component market becomes highly unlikely.

Thus, CORBA fails to deliver on one of its major promises, which is support of a wide variety of available (not just possible) solutions. CORBA was meant to be platform, ORB vendor, and language independent. Hence, it does not define sufficiently strong low-level integration standards that allow for efficient language-independent service and service-independent language implementations. Java seems to be the clear and obvious winner. However, there is one drawback. The Java class file format is tightly coupled to the language Java. Translation of other languages is suboptimal (Ada 95, Component Pascal) or impossible (C^{++}). (The Java position, although not that of the Java language, would improve further if Java class files and Java VM were carefully generalized – in ways that efficiently support concepts such as in-line allocated objects, reference parameters, and overflow checks, for example.) COM sits in the comfortable middle. It can support a very wide variety of languages at close to optimal efficiency. CLI widens the language-neutral support of COM, combines it with the strong decoupling established by an intermediate format, as with Java, and shares the strengths of CORBA when communicating via standard protocols.

A breakthrough for CORBA, beyond legacy integration, would require that a strong enough vendor fills the gap left by OMG and defines a *de facto* execution-level standard on all relevant platforms (or defines a virtual execution platform). However, supporting a variety of languages would still take time, especially as users of these languages have to retarget their applications first.

In the meantime, cross-language solutions can be built using the CORBA C binding and the fact that all reasonable language implementations today can call C functions. Using C as a lingua franca has substantial disadvantages, however. As C does not have a notion of objects, it offers a very low-level bridge between a safe object-oriented language and the safe and object-oriented

CORBA world. Note that C++ cannot be used as the lingua franca because platforms do not define C++ calling conventions and, thus, bindings to third languages rarely exist. Note also that the use of the CORBA C binding is hampered because some commercial ORBs such as Orbix (with the exception of Orbix/E) do not support the C binding.

The strongest point in favor for COM, besides the compromise described above, is its migration path for old application code. COM is simple enough to support effective wrapping of legacy code into COM components. For example, COM enabled the migration of the originally monolithic Microsoft Office applications to the still coarse-grained collection of components that they are in 2002. Wrappers for CORBA are possible, but are more involved and are ORB-specific in a subtle and complicated way (for example, Wallace and Wallnau, 1996). Wrappers for Java are possible, although the JNI can be in the way of efficient wrappers.

17.4 Consequences for component vendors

Another interesting difference is the degree of freedom left to an implementer of a component targeting one of the approaches. Designers have to face a very large number of decisions. Reducing the degrees of freedom of possible designs is a "good thing," as long as it does not affect feasibility. To cite Orfali *et al.* (1996, p. 522):

> "Only the consumer gets freedom of choice; designers need freedom from choice."

This citation is taken from an argument on why the more restrictive constraints of OpenDoc, as compared with OLE, speak in favor of CORBA and against COM. It is ironic that their argument does speak for particular aspects of OpenDoc, but also speaks against the generality of CORBA.

Most current approaches largely follow what could be called the "toolkit philosophy," as compared with one that defines frameworks or even system architectures. Despite their names, CORBA (common object request broker architecture) and OMA (object management architecture) are not architecture from the component vendor's point of view. CORBA is an architecture from the ORB implementer's point of view. The OMA does not go beyond the granularity of objects. It could be seen as a global architecture on the level of ants.

The new CORBA component model does go beyond individual objects and presents a component framework that integrates several previously separate object services. Once CCM-compliant products become available, it would seem possible that a market for CCM components forms. The main inspiration for CCM was the Enterprise JavaBeans (EJB) specification, which itself derived facets from the Microsoft Transaction Server (MTS) architecture (now part of COM+). Any market for CCM components would thus be likely patterned after those for EJB or COM+ components. However, by early 2002, both EJB and COM+ had failed largely to create a market for their respective components. One reason might be that the components used in EJB or COM+ (or CLR, or CCM) settings on the server side are predominantly encapsulating business logic – the application, domain, and enterprise-specific part of an enterprise application. Nevertheless, as business categories such as web order handling become more standard, supporting standard components seems more likely.

An early example from the area of compound documents and user interfaces is the BlackBox component framework. This was also, from the beginning, designed as a component framework and thus as an architecture for component vendors to target. Although BlackBox is still around, it failed to create a market. Most components that have been developed from BlackBox remain in-house or are informally exchanged among BlackBox users.

Some of the cornerstones of a component architecture include regulation of the interaction with other components, definition of the roles of components, and standardization of user interface aspects for assembly and use. Component frameworks are a partial answer – context frameworks (EJB, COM+, CCM, and CLR) and BlackBox are examples in this direction. Component frameworks are focused architectures whereas component system architectures consider interaction across frameworks. By analogy, consider the architecture of a single building compared with that of a master-planned city. Today, only few component system architectures in this sense exist. An older example is Windows DNA (Distributed Network Architecture). More recent ones are J2EE (Java 2 Enterprise Edition) and .NET. (For a detailed discussion of component architectures and frameworks, see Part Four.)

CHAPTER EIGHTEEN

Efforts on domain standards

The importance of domain-specific standards has been recognized and several efforts aim at such standards.

18.1 OMG Domain Technology Committee

This committee of the OMG organizes "domain taskforces" to oversee the standardization of domain-specific interfaces. The following domain taskforces (DTFs) were active in early 2002 – their adopted specifications are briefly listed after each DTF's name.

- *Business Enterprise Integration DTF* – negotiation facility, organizational structure (OSF), public key infrastructure (PKI), task and session, workflow management facility.
- *Command, Control, Computers, Communications and Intelligence (C4I) DTF* – none in early 2002.
- *Finance DTF* (includes banking and insurance) – currency, general ledger, party management.
- *Healthcare (CORBAmed) DTF* – Clinical image access service (CIAS), clinical observations access service (COAS), lexicon query service, person identification service (PIDS), resource access decision (RAD).
- *Life Science Research* – bibliographical query service, biomolecular sequence analysis (BSA), gene expression, genomic maps, laboratory equipment control interface specification (LECIS), macromolecular structure.
- *Manufacturing DTF* – computer-aided design (CAD) services, data acquisition from industrial systems (DAIS), distributed simulation systems, product data management (PDM) enablers.
- *Space DTF* – none in early 2002.
- *Telecommunications DTF* – audio/visual streams, telecoms log service, management of event domains, telecom service and access subscription (TSAS), CORBA-FTAM/FTP interworking.
- *Transportation DTF* – air traffic control, surveillance manager.
- *Utilities DTF* – utility management systems (UMS) data access facility.

18.1.1 OMG BODTF

Probably the oldest domain-specific OMG group is the Business Object Domain Task Force (BODTF), formerly called the Business Object Model Special Interest Group (BOMSIG). Business objects, as defined by BODTF, have the characteristic property of directly representing entities that, as such, make sense in a certain business process. Entities can be people, goods, concepts, places, organizations, and so on. A business object populates a conceptual level that directly matches that of people working in its target business domain. As units of manipulation, combination, and communication, they therefore individually make sense to involved staff. The first two such entity concepts that passed OMG standardization are task and session, both of which are already used in the negotiation facility of OMG's electronic commerce domain taskforce (ECDTF).

Business objects are still largely on the drawingboard. The few systems that truly aim at this level so far form relatively small islands. In all cases, the idea is that the object can be presented to the user directly. Presentation in the form of an icon is the minimum, custom user interaction the goal.

In all these examples, objects surface and become tangible for regular users. Allowing users to manipulate directly and compose such objects certainly has great potential. However, there is good reason to remain suspicious. Where are the domain-specific aspects? There is indeed fairly little there. In all cases all that is provided is an infrastructure that could be used to support domain-specific tasks.

The point, however, is missed. For business objects to collaborate in a way that truly solves domain-specific problems, these objects not only need to be domain-specific, but also need to follow domain-specific standards for interaction. Where these specifications are fully provided by an individual organization, the main gain is that of using a powerful infrastructure, rather than creating component markets.

Only where successful component-based solutions are opened, relevant specifications are published, and *de facto* standardization is aimed for, will specialized component vendors be able to benefit.

18.2   W3C

The world-wide web consortium (W3C) is the primary organization looking after web-related standards. Initially focusing on HTML, the W3C is now also the home for most XML standards, including the XML specification itself. Standards such as XML Schema or XQuery are evolved under W3C guidance.

At the level of domain-specific standards, the W3C largely plays the role of an enabler. In general, it does not look after individual domain-specific standards. There are exceptions, depending on how the term "domain" is understood. For instance, the W3C effort on MathML aims at a standard way to encode and present mathematical formulae. However, this could be seen as similar in spirit to – and thus as horizontal in nature as – other W3C efforts, such as SVG (structured vector graphics) or SMIL (synchronized multimedia integration language).

A new important activity at W3C, started early in 2002, is an effort to standardize web services beyond XML and SOAP.

To enable domain-specific standardization, the W3C has been working on several standards to enable the uniform capturing of metadata. The oldest effort is RDF (resource description framework; W3C, 1999b), a relatively simple and general framework to describe graphs of things – "resources" – and relationships between them. In early 2000, a new W3C effort called "the semantic web" was formed and incorporated the older RDF effort. The semantic web effort adds work on common web ontology, which is common words and ways to describe important concepts and their relationships.

18.3 | Business processes and documents

With the rise of XML as an almost universal data representation standard, several organizations arose that aim to use XML-based standardization to enable electronic commerce. Prominent examples are OASIS (www.oasis.org), RosettaNet (www.rosettanet.org), and the Microsoft BizTalk.org initiative (www.biztalk.org). While OASIS has its roots in SGML (standard general markup language), it is now focusing most of its efforts on XML. RosettaNet and BizTalk.org use XML exclusively.

18.3.1 OASIS and ebXML

In early 2002, OASIS – the Organization for the Advancement of Structured Information Standards – has around 190 organizational members (besides over 200 individual members). OASIS' efforts include ebXML (electronic business XML; www.ebxml.org). The ebXML suite of standards is developed jointly by OASIS and the United Nations Centre for Trade Facilitation and Electronic Business (UN/CEFACT; www.unece.org/cefact/). Technical committees for ebXML registry, messaging, collaborative partner, and implementation are hosted by OASIS, and business process and core component work continues at UN/CEFACT. In early 2002, OASIS joined four international standards organizations in a memorandum of understanding (MoU) on e-business. Founding members of the MoU include the International Electrotechnical Commission (IEC), the International Organization for Standardization (ISO), the International Telecommunication Union (ITU), and the United Nations Economic Commission for Europe (UN/ECE). This could be called the "Geneva Connection" as all these organizations have their headquaters in Geneva, Switzerland, which is thus placing itself on the global map of e-commerce facilitation.

The ebXML business process and information metamodel defines a set of design viewpoints. By drawing on several of the metamodel's viewpoints, the ebXML specification schema supports the specification of business transactions and their protocol arrangement into business collaborations. The specification schema draws on several of the metamodel viewpoints. The specification schema is available both as a UML profile and as a DTD. Each business transaction can be implemented using one of many available standard patterns. The specification schema comes with a set of standard patterns and a set of modeling elements common to those patterns. Combining a business process and information metamodel (specified against the specification schema) and an identification of the desired pattern(s) yields collaboration protocol profiles (CPPs) and agreements (CPAs).

The ebXML requirements specification (ebXML, 2001) aims for an architecture to establish a common ground for business processes, semantics (meaning) of business transactions, terminology (standard mapping from words to meaning), XML-level character encoding and structure, security implementations, data transfer protocols, and network layers. Several of these goals are achieved by agreeing on the use of some other established or emerging standard. For instance, while ebXML originally aimed to introduce its own message encodings, it later adopted SOAP as extended by SOAP messages with attachments (W3C, 2000d). At the level of registration mechanisms, a similar confluence with UDDI work is expected (www.uddi.org), where a UDDI service could be one possible implementation of an ebXML registry. Another possible point of convergence could be the use of the many business documents defined by the Open Applications Group (www.openapplications.org).

The core remaining ebXML contribution would seem to be twofold – to bring all these aspects together and to complete the picture at the level of standard terminology and process. As such, the ebXML effort is similar to the RosettaNet approach discussed next. Also related is the WS-I effort (www.ws-i.org), although WS-I stays at the level of horizontal infrastructure, without claims in particular domains, such as business processes. Finally, there is Microsoft's BizTalk initiative, discussed further below, that focuses on business processes captured via the exchange of XML business documents.

18.3.2 RosettaNet and PIPs

Founded in 1998 and 400 member-companies strong, RosettaNet is one of the oldest consortia in this space (www.rosettanet.org). Named after the famous Rosetta stone (found in 1799, it contained the same message in three languages, enabling the decyphering of Egyptian hyroglyphs), RosettaNet aims for standardization and homogenization of processes and terminology to enable electronic commerce. In early 2002, RosettaNet had more than 400 member organizations and four main domains – electronic components, information technology, semiconductor manufacturing, and solution providers.

RosettaNet defines partner interface processes (PIPs) that are based on the defined exchange of XML documents. Each PIP specifies terminology and business process in the form of a message exchange protocol. RosettaNet dictionaries provide a common set of properties for PIPs. The business dictionary designates the properties used in basic business activities and the technical dictionaries provide properties for defining products. Current PIPs cover the process areas of administration, partner, product and service review, product introduction, order management, inventory management, marketing information management, service and support, and manufacturing. At this level, RosettaNet competes with the ebXML approach discussed above. However, the emphasis of ebXML is to enable e-business for small and medium enterprises, while RosettaNet seems to focus on the interplay of large enterprises.

RosettaNet uses a formal validation process. Under that process, a group of RosettaNet partners commit to implementing a new standard on publication. The partners run the standard in production for a period of time, providing and reviewing feedback to enhance the standard, and ultimately attesting that the standard meets predefined requirements and has been successfully implemented in production. This process encourages rapid evolution of new standards to improve robustness and lower the frequency of change in the future.

RosettaNet also defines an implementation framework (RNIF) that provides exchange protocols for quick and efficient implementation of RosettaNet standards. RNIF was first released in mid 1999. A major 2.0 release followed in early 2001 and was validated in mid 2001. A minor release (2.0.1) followed in early 2002. RNIF specifies information exchange between trading-partner servers using XML, covering the transport, routing and packaging, security, signals, and trading partner agreement. At that level, RosettaNet competes with XML web services efforts based on SOAP, WSDL, UDDI, and the various protocols proposed as part of the global XML web service architecture (GXA). RNIF uses MIME and MIME/S standards to encode messages and then uses HTTP, HTTPS, SMTP, or other transfer protocols to exchange those messages. As of version 2.0.1, RDIF still fully relies on XML document type descriptors (DTDs), not XML Schema. To complement DTDs – in particular to provide constraints on number of occurrences – a proprietary informal "tree structure" notation is used. RNIF specifically addresses issues of authentication, authorization and non-repudiation, as these are of fundamental importance for electronic commerce. For instance, RNIF requires participants to store received business messages for an agreed period of time (typically three to seven years).

18.3.3 BizTalk.org

Established by Microsoft in 2000, BizTalk.org provides resources for using XML for enterprise application integration (EAI) and business-to-business (B2B) document exchange. Microsoft's BizTalk framework (2000) provides design guidelines for XML schemas and XML tags to be used in messages sent between applications.

The framework defines BizTalk documents as SOAP 1.1 messages in which the body of the message contains the business documents that themselves are not detailed by the framework but agreed on by business partners. The header contains BizTalk-specific entries to control message handling. In particular, documents are assigned an identity and definite lifetime (outside of which they must not be sent, accepted, processed, or acknowledged). The framework insists on the idempotence of business documents – that is, repeated reception of the same document (based on its identity) must not have any effect. It is therefore safe to repeat a transmission if there is any doubt as to whether the document arrived intact or not.

Reception is acknowledged by sending special receipts – themselves regular business documents, including idempotency. There are two kinds of receipts – acknowledgements of acceptance for delivery and acknowledgements of commitment. The former merely state that the document was, as such, properly addressed, while the latter indicates that all header fields marked "must understand" have been understood, that the correctness of their contents and the contents of the body has been verified, and that there is a commitment to process the document.

The most widely used BizTalk.org service is its library of schemas for many different business purposes in many different industries. As of early 2002, almost 500 such schemas had been registered in BizTalk.org's library. Out of these, only 8 use XML Schema while 471 use XDR (XML Data Reduced), an earlier schema design proposed by Microsoft that can be seen as a subset of XML Schema.

18.4 DMTF's CIM and WBEM

The Distributed Management Task Force (DMTF) is an industry consortium developing management standards for distributed desktop, network, enterprise and internet environments. In early 2002, DMTF had around 230 members, including almost 50 academic institutions.

DMTF has formalized a number of standards and initiatives. The common information model (CIM) is a standard implementation-neutral schema for describing overall management information in a network/enterprise environment. The desktop management interface (DMI) is a standard framework for managing and tracking components in a desktop PC, notebook, or server. Web-based enterprise management (WBEM) is a suite of standard technologies, including CIM, to unify the management of enterprise computing environments. The directory-enabled network (DEN) initiative aims to map concepts from CIM (such as systems, services and policies) to a directory and to integrate this information with other WBEM elements in the management infrastructure. The alert standard format (ASF) defines remote control and alerting interfaces that target lightweight clients. Finally, the system management BIOS (SMBIOS) specification defines how system vendors present management information about their products in a standard format by extending the BIOS interface on Intel architecture systems.

CIM follows an object-oriented modeling approach, with classes, subclassing, and attributes on classes. Relationships are expressed as pairs of attributes. The CIM core model defines managed entities (both logical and physical), their settings, configurations, and dependencies. Detailed models are defined for systems, devices, networks, and applications. All models have provisions for extensions.

Originally, the CIM definitions used the proprietary managed object format (MOF), which is an IDL derivative, but mappings of CIM to XML have since been standardized as the xmlCIM encoding specification. The mapping was defined before XML Schema was finalized and therefore rests on DTDs. Instead of attempting a direct mapping of CIM metadata to XML DTDs (or XML Schema), the CIM to XML mapping uses a metaschema mapping. There is one DTD that describes the CIM metaschema and both CIM instances and CIM classes are mapped to valid XML instance documents using that single DTD. That is, this single CIM DTD describes the notion of CIM classes and instances. CIM element names are mapped to XML attribute or element values rather than XML element names. This mapping choice is interesting as it allows a single mapping definition to cover the open-ended world of CIM. This is essential as CIM is extensible and many organizations have independently defined extension schemas.

WBEM builds on CIM and the xmlCIM encoding specification. In addition WBEM defines the concept of providers and the use of HTTP to run CIM operations on such providers. WBEM and CIM have received broad industry support. WBEM is part of the Solaris operating environment, starting with Solaris 8, and there is a Sun WBEM SDK for J2SE. WBEM has been implemented as part of the Windows management instrumentation (WMI), starting with Windows 2000. IBM's AIX includes WBEM infrastructure since its version 5.0. HP's HP-UX supports WBEM. The Open Group hosts the open source project Pegasus that aims to provide a WBEM implementation for multiple platforms (www.opengroup.org/pegasus/).

18.5 Java domain standard efforts

Two examples in the category of Java's domain-specific standardization efforts were briefly discussed in the first edition of this book – the Java electronic commerce framework (JEFC) (Sun, 1997) and the San Francisco project (www.ibm.com/Java/SanFrancisco). Both efforts have been discontinued since.

A newer, domain-specific, Java-based initiative is Sun's Jiro (www.sun.com/jiro/ and www.jiro.com). Jiro is a component framework aiming at federated resource management, with an initial emphasis on management of storage systems. Jiro defines a layer of components and services that connect managed resources with management applications. Such resources can be accessed using any standard management protocol, such as the WBEM (see section 18.4) or simple network management protocol (SNMP). Jiro builds on Java and Jini (see Chapter 14, particularly section 14.8) and adds a new component category called FederatedBeans, based on JavaBeans. Events in Jiro travel across networks. It is thus necessary to define event classes with awareness of RMI, the event service, and class loading on a remote device.

FederatedBeans enables management applications to distribute their services across a network of storage devices, provided these support Jini and the JRE. Jiro uses the federated management architecture (FMA) to supply basic management functions, such as fault notification, scheduling, distributed logging, and transaction rollback. In addition, Jiro uses Jini to provide enterprise-wide discovery and lookup to enable devices to announce their available resources to other devices and to management tools.

Two further domain-specific Java-based domain standardization efforts execute under Sun's Java community process (www.jcp.org) – JAIN (Java APIs for integrated networks) and OSS (operations support systems). Both suites of specifications support telecom products and services (java.sun.com/products/jain/, java.sun.com/products/oss/).

18.6   OLE for process control

An interesting example of domain-specific aspects that is completely off the track of desktop or typical enterprise solutions comes from industrial automation. An effort to create signaling standards for process control led to COM-based standards called OLE for process control (OPC; www.opcfoundation.org). In essence, OPC defines COM interfaces for classes of device drivers.

One of the oldest domain-specific component technology standardization efforts, OPC continues to be active, with over 300 member organizations in early 2002. According to the OPC foundation, at that same time there were over 250 manufacturers of OPC-compliant products.

18.7   Industry associations

According to an IDC white paper (Steel, 1996), two kinds of industry associations can be identified that aim to establish relevant component standards. The first are groupings of the information technology industry. The second are trade associations. A third, not mentioned in the white paper, could be general user associations.

18.7.1 Information technology industry groupings

Groupings of IT vendors have a simple interest in establishing interoperability standards. The members of the group can then believably position their products as pieces of a larger plan. As long as group members claim their own ground, they can join forces against their common competition. Some groupings are so large that they merely serve to push the envelope – examples are the OMG or the Open Group. The more relevant examples in the category of vendor groupings are much smaller in terms of their membership and, indeed, have the primary purpose of increased competitiveness.

An example in this latter category is the Open Applications Group, Inc. (OAGI). Founded in early 1995, by the end of 2001 it had nearly 60 members, including IBM Software, IONA, OMG, Oracle, PeopleSoft, Sun, and Vitria. The OAGI coordinates the standardization of interfaces for commercial domains and aims at the integration of business objects. To this end, the OAGI has created their business object document (BOD) architecture and their OAG Integration Specification (OAGIS). The aim is to enable the bridging of a very broad range of "wiring" standards, including CORBA and COM, but also older standards such as Edifact. Thus, the BOD defines requests and replies in terms of formatted documents, without insisting on any particular encoding standard, although XML is now the preferred encoding. In version 7.2.1, as of late 2001, OAGIS specifies 201 XML-based messages (business documents) in areas such as general ledger, accounts payable, accounts receivable, purchasing, sales order management, and plant data collection. The OAGI website covers all OAGI standards (www.openapplications.org).

Another example is OASIS, the Organization for the Advancement of Structured Information Standards (www.oasis-open.org), a non-profit consortium that creates interoperability specifications based on XML, SGML, and other standards related to structured information processing. Early in 2002, OASIS had around 90 sponsoring members, including Computer Associates, EDS, Microsoft, Oracle, SAP, Sun, Tibco, Vitria, and webMethods, and almost 100 contributing members. Jointly with the United Nations Centre for Trade Facilitation and Electronic Business (UN/CEFACT), OASIS has developed ebXML (e-business XML; www.ebxml.org) that comprises a technical architecture and specifications of business processes, collaboration protocol profiles (CPPs) and agreements (CPAs), a registry service (RS) and registry information model (RIM), and a messaging service (MS). For more details, see section 18.3.

Two recent examples in the space of web services are UDDI.Org (www.uddi.org) and WS-I (www.ws-i.org) focusing on the promotion and furthering of web services standards. In early 2002, UDDI.Org had over 220 members, including Ariba, BEA, Compaq, Dell, Documentum, EDS, Fujitsu, HP, Hitachi, IBM, Intel, IONA, Microsoft, Mitre, OAG, Oracle, Rational, SAP, Software AG, Sun, Tibco, Unisys, VeriSign, Vitria, and webMethods. Also in early 2002, WS-I had 55 members, including Akamai, BEA, Borland, Compaq, FileNET, Groove Networks, HP, IBM, Intel, IONA, Microsoft, Oracle, Rational, SAP, Sybase, VeriSign, and webMethods.

18.7.2 Trade associations

Users of information technology in a certain industry sector may form trade associations pushing for vertical standards that broaden the market for high-quality offerings that suit their needs. Again, the motive is obvious – the members of the association collectively gain strength against their competition.

Trade associations may control the quality of components and validate their standard compliance. Component vendors gain a competitive advantage where a trade association gave its approval.

An interesting example of a trade association moving into software is the Underwriters Laboratory (UL; www.ul.com) that establishes quality standards and certifies quality properties of products.

18.7.3 User associations

An association formed by component users can create a forum to exchange know-how and have a collective voice that will be heard by component vendors. In contrast to trade associations, user associations aim for very large memberships – mostly individuals or small organizations. It is conceivable that associations such as the ACM or the IEEE Computer Society could form branches that would represent the interests of component users in particular domains.

Strong user associations have already formed around several specific technologies, such as Linux, Python, Perl, and, in particular, Java, with Java User Groups (JUGs) having formed in many countries.

CHAPTER NINETEEN

Ongoing concerns

As has to be expected with a technology as young as that of component software, there are still various open problems. In this chapter, some of the more persistent problems are briefly reviewed.

19.1 Domain standards

The need to create working and accepted domain-specific standards was emphasized in the last chapter. Plumbing and wiring are not enough, but forging domain standards out of thin air is also not a good answer. The OMG "fast-track" mechanism to approve domain standards promises a normal turnaround of just six months. OMG insists that such proposals rest on proven technology. However, in a field in which even the wiring infrastructure moves rapidly (CORBA 3.0 has yet to be completed), how can anyone claim to have proven domain-specific technology? Proposals must necessarily be based on experience with other and older technology.

It is of vital importance not to rush into standards and risk credibility. There is a need for a time of fierce competition and evolution of approaches before any one of them can qualify for standardization. Processes that encourage independent exploration of markets and domains but also encourage submission of proposals for standardization later would be ideal. However, this is far from being realistic. Why would an organization that "got it right" and has established its market position want to release crucial information?

The idea is that pushing for domain standards based on established but proprietary technology promises to expand the target market. The reason is that more customers will be willing to build on standards than proprietary solutions. The proponent of a new standard is in a strong position based on products that already comply with the proposed standard. The relative market volume of the proponent is thus expected to grow, assuming that the proponent can defend its leading edge.

Unfortunately, things are not that easy. Initial competition for the best approach – and thus the absence of a single standard – benefits quick product evolution. Where incompatible standardization proposals emerge, the threat of "standards by compromise" follows. This entire phenomenon is only too well known in traditional industries that have lived with standards for a long time. Such traditional industries converge on standards slowly and often in painful shakeout processes. There is no fast track to working standards!

19.2 Rethinking the foundations of software engineering

From a software engineering point of view, component technology presents a number of novel challenges that question the applicability of many proven approaches. The key problem is the notion of independent extensibility that is so characteristic of any component-based system (Szyperski, 1996; see also Chapter 6). Late integration of components from independent sources eliminates the confidence usually drawn from integration testing in a traditional software engineering model. Also, extensibility needs to be "architected" and designed into a system and all its parts or else the resulting system will not be extensible – components will not be independently producible and deployable.

To summarize, all facets of software engineering and the entire underlying approach need to be rethought. It is not helpful to throw in large numbers of different technologies, each with even larger numbers of alternative ways of tackling a problem. There is an urgent need to unify methodologies, guiding architectures, and working examples. All this will take time to mature; investment in component technology at this time still needs to be seen as strategic rather than tactical.

19.3 But is it object-oriented?

Object orientation has been "evangelized" to such a degree over the past decade that, for some, it has become a synonym for quality rather than being a means to an end. Object-oriented usually means that everything is partitioned into objects, each of which encapsulates state and behavior. Objects are instances of classes, which themselves are related by (traditional) inheritance. Finally, objects can be used in polymorphic contexts (for example, Wegner, 1987). Wars of bitter arguments are fought over these requirements. It is interesting to subject the main approaches in the component field to these criteria.

Before looking at the various approaches, it is important to recall that Java adds a language model to its object one. In contrast, CORBA, COM, and CLR are all language neutral and, thus, simply cannot impose certain restrictions required to make something "object-oriented" in the genuine programming languages sense.

The Java approach is quite clearly object-oriented – with the defensible exception of some basic types, everything is done with objects. Objects are instances of classes. Classes can inherit implementation and interfaces. Polymorphism is introduced by subtype compatibility of both subclasses and "subinterfaces." Classes (not objects) are the units of encapsulation, although packages add a second level. The distribution technology (remote method invocation) makes object location transparent and allows for the free passing of Java's object references across process and processor boundaries. Object references in Java are not of a persistent nature, but persistence can be supported by a service.

COM bases everything on component objects that are accessible via sets of interface references; object references do not exist. COM objects are instances of classes, but classes are in no inheritance relationship. COM interfaces can be in a single interface inheritance relationship, but that is of little importance to COM. Polymorphism is introduced by allowing any number of classes to implement any set of interfaces. Encapsulation is addressed by limiting all interactions to object interfaces. Interface references can be transferred freely across process and processor boundaries. References are not of persistent nature and object identity across persistent forms is not a COM concept, but could be supported by a persistence service.

In CORBA, everything seems to be based on objects. Classes correspond to object implementations, but are not related by inheritance. Interfaces are related by multiple interface inheritance. This is also the basis for polymorphism in CORBA. Encapsulation is addressed by limiting all interactions to object interfaces.

Basic types are not CORBA objects, but neither are many complex data types, such as sequences and structures. All CORBA types, including object references, are collected into a generic type "any." Fully excluded are "small" objects – called serverless objects – for which the cost of the CORBA model could be prohibitive. CORBA does not make object location fully transparent as it distinguishes between local object references and CORBA object references. The latter are themselves not so small objects and can be converted into string form (and back). Object references and their "stringified" forms are guaranteed to be of indefinite validity. CORBA object references are too expensive to replace all component-internal references.

To make an object a CORBA object, its class needs to inherit from interface CORBA and the object needs to be registered with the ORB, which returns a fresh object reference. CORBA objects are too expensive to make all objects used within a component CORBA objects. A hidden mechanism to mediate automatically between internal and CORBA references, as available in Java RMI or DCOM, does not exist. OMG IDL does not allow the use of normal object references in operation definitions – only OMG IDL basic types, constructed types, and CORBA object references are allowed. A particular language binding could automatically call ORB services to map an internal reference to a CORBA reference (and back). This is possible as long as the referred object is a CORBA object – that is, registered with the ORB. For SOM, special direct-to-SOM compilers are available that make most ORB interactions transparent to the programmer.

In the CLR world, a unified type system rooted in root type Object covers value and reference types. Though basic types are not objects – just as in

CORBA – they can be manipulated like objects for most purposes. Objects are instances of classes that can singly inherit from another class and implement any number of interfaces. Object references are not persistent, but – as for Java – a service can provide persistence.

In summary, none of the discussed approaches is "object-oriented." Java and CLR come closest, but do not establish objects as the units of encapsulation. COM and CORBA units of encapsulation are, at best, individual object servers. Neither COM nor CORBA specifies at all how objects located in the same server can interact. CORBA separates internal references, such as those used by Java or C^{++}, from external references to from CORBA object references. For local invocations, some ORBs optimize the actual conversion to and from external references. However, the bipartite nature of the world of references and, thus, the world of objects cannot be hidden. All of Java, COM, and CLR exhibit local references and use external references only "under the hood" (in RMI, DCOM, and CLR Remoting) when marshaling references for remote calls.

It should be noted that it is not very relevant that none of the approaches is "object-oriented." The important question is "What can these approaches do and not do?" All four approaches seem to be able to carry the weight of coarse-grained partitioning, in which individual objects exposed by the approach are relatively large. COM, CLR and Java can also handle smaller objects efficiently, although it is most likely that only Java and CLR programmers will do so. COM naturally asks for clustering of multiple, and possibly many, non-exposed objects into one COM object. References to the non-exposed objects are of no meaning outside that COM object.

Having multiple non-COM objects within a single COM object is not an efficiency requirement. Clearly, COM is efficient enough to make all objects COM objects. (A COM method invocation on an interface in the same process is as cheap as or slightly cheaper than a C^{++} method invocation.) Microsoft's J++ took advantage of this and made any Java object a COM object. J++ mapped Java interfaces to COM interfaces and Java classes to COM classes. As COM does not directly expose classes, Java's implementation inheritance remains banned inside Java. J++ automatically implements QueryInterface and reference counting. Finally, J++ automatically synthesizes class factories and dispatch interfaces with all the argument checking required by COM.

The automation of QueryInterface and reference counting was pioneered by Oberon microsystems' Direct-to-COM compiler (DTC) and their Safer OLE technology, both extensions to the BlackBox component builder. DTC does not impose some of the restrictions of J++, such as ignoring the case of method names. DTC also faithfully models the COM notion of in, out, and in/out parameters that cannot be handled by Java.

Finally, CLR has been designed with fully integrated COM interoperation support built in. At a base cost of only a few machine instructions, a CLR method call can be mapped to a COM method call, and vice versa. The cost does not increase significantly as long as all arguments passed are of a primitive type. As soon as marshaling of arguments is required, CLR COM interop can become expensive. This is not surprising as the two object models are sufficiently different.

19.4 Object mobility and mobile agents

An issue not directly addressed by any of the mainstream approaches is object mobility. All assume that an object resides in some object server and that all that is passed around are references to that object. For objects providing services, this is a useful assumption. If required, the entire object server can be migrated to another machine, to rebalance load, for example.

However, there is another role that objects can play. An object can simply encapsulate data by means of a normalizing access interface. Where small amounts of data need to be communicated, it is often preferable to send the object itself rather than a reference. CORBA introduced a mode to send objects by value. Java RMI sends by value those argument objects that do not implement any remote interface. COM does not provide built-in support for by-value semantics, but has a fully customizable marshaling mechanism that can be used to custom marshal objects by value. The CLR explicitly distinguishes objects to be marshaled by value from those to be marshaled by reference.

A related issue is mobile "agents." In this case, the requirement is not the efficient and lightweight transfer of small objects but the transparent transfer of objects representing agents roaming across a network. Any fixed binding of objects to object servers needs to be avoided in this context unless, of course, the notion of object server is made so lightweight that an entire object server could become an "agent."

Java applets seem to be mobile objects. In reality, all that is mobile is the component implementing the applet. Java components are moved around in JAR files. As long as a component cannot modify the contents of the JAR file from which it was instantiated, the unit of mobility is still just a component, not an object. If a component could modify the JAR file from which it was instantiated, it would jeopardize other objects instantiated from the same file. To make an applet, a bean, or any other component instance a truly mobile object, new mechanisms are needed. Some research in this direction at IBM Japan went under the name of "aglets" (Lange and Chang, 1996).

Here, object serialization can offer an answer, if combined with proper infrastructure for orderly "beaming" of mobile objects. An object needs to be taken out of its current environment, not just serialized, and implanted into a new environment, probably after security checks. Then it needs to be revived. Parts of the answers have been pioneered at Digital's System Research Center with its work on network objects for Modula-3 (Birrel et al., 1994). At the same center, the approach has been taken further with the Obliq language and system. Obliq addresses safety-critical issues of mobile objects by imposing a static scoping rule across sites of activation (Cardelli, 1994).

19.5   Foundations – better contracts for better components

Component software and the widespread use of software components will dramatically increase the demands put on component developers. There are two reasons. First, the technology underlying component software is more complex than that underlying traditional software. Second, the use of third-party components encourages the "outsourcing" of risk in that customers will set much higher standards on bought components than on in-house developments.

As quality and, in particular, security are major concerns when using components on the internet, neither Java nor ActiveX objects has been doing particularly well in today's web. For example, a study in March 1997 showed that, out of 20 million web pages, only 30,000 used Java and fewer than 1000 used ActiveX objects (Leach and Moeller, 1997). This has likely shifted since, yet most web pages rely on embedded ECMAScript or use Macromedia's technologies for animation. Use of ActiveX to host controls that are already present on the client's system is quite popular, though. An example is the common embedding of the Windows Media Player control. (In early 2002, the .NET technologies including CLR hadn't been available for long enough.)

However, components can only be of high quality – and customers can only insist on such quality – if the requirements are clearly specified. The specifications of the contracts that bind components thus need to be improved much further. The current best practice of listing interfaces with informal descriptions is by no means enough for a stable component world. Where components already function, this is largely because of a strong vendor setting *de facto* benchmarks. For example, whatever the OLE specifications may say, an ActiveX component had better work with Word, Excel, PowerPoint, and Internet Explorer.

Compatibility and cross-implementation portability are ongoing issues for CORBA and Java specifications. The original basic object adapter in CORBA had to be replaced completely by the portable object adapter to gain any level of object implementation portability. The introduction of EJB 2.0 in J2EE 1.3 in mid 2001 was largely motivated by the improved portability of EJBs based on the new container-managed persistence scheme. Similar lessons can be expected once more than one implementation of the ECMA CLR specification exists. The summary conclusion here is that the underlying specifications of all these approaches are nowhere near precise enough to avoid compatibility and portability issues upfront. Instead, an implementation culture forms over time that helps separate implementers to converge on a common interpretation of the specifications.

Particular points that should be addressed in improved contract specifications are:

- specification of re-entrance conditions – sequential and concurrent cases need to be covered differently;
- specification of self-recursive patterns or, alternatively, abstaining from inheritance and implicit delegation across component boundaries, but, of course, explicit re-entrance patterns remain;

■ specification of bounds on execution time and resource needs – compositions break unexpectedly where parts have unspecified time or resource demands that can be satisfied for each part but not for the whole and the situation becomes very difficult where bounds of the whole are not additively related to bounds of parts;

■ specification of other extra-functional properties, as indicated in section 5.2.2.

Current IDLs describe contracts at the "plumbing" or "wiring" level. All that is firmly captured is what is required to marshal data properly when communicating across process, processor, or machine architecture boundaries. This is, of course, essential to enable "wiring" at all. Also, it should not be expected that significant parts of contracts will ever make it into the IDL parts processed by an IDL compiler. Contract specifications, formal or informal, will remain largely for the human programmer. Their precise specification, formal where reasonable, should nevertheless accompany the machine-level interfaces. An explicit and unambiguous link must exist between an interface and its contractual specification.

The COM requirement that a published interface has to remain immutable is grounded in the idea that an interface comes with a specification. Thus, the real requirement is that the specification must stay the same. A COM unique interface ID could thus be seen as linking a specification to an interface. The later introduction of categories into COM takes this one step further. A category identifier links a unique identifier to a specification spanning multiple interfaces of a component, conceptually promising its proper embedding into a larger pattern of interoperation, perhaps a component framework.

In a similar attempt, Java specifications rely more and more on the use of empty interfaces or classes, called marker or tagging interfaces. These are used to specify certain characteristics of a class derived from such a marker interface or class. For example, the interface java.lang.Clonable is empty. It should be "implemented" by a Java class that supports cloning – but cloning itself is based on the clone method in class java.lang.Object. Another example is java.util.EventListener to mark all classes that "listen" for events. Both COM's categories and Java's empty interfaces allow for runtime enquiries to check whether a certain component does or does not obey a certain contract.

CORBA finally defines repository IDs that associate a unique ID with an OMG IDL-specified type. The interoperation standard uses these IDs to match entries in interface repositories of independent ORBs. Although repository IDs are very similar to COM IIDs, they are not normally associated with interfaces at interface definition time. Although CORBA 2 introduced an IDL pragma (a special attribution syntax) to specify the repository ID of an interface, this is rarely used. Instead, repository IDs are usually automatically generated and assigned when registering an interface with an interface repository.

Obviously, this practice has to change for interoperation or interworking to work properly. A second transition is required in coding conventions – all code must refer to interfaces by repository IDs. Otherwise, version control is unsound (Chapter 12). Once these transitions are made, CORBA interfaces and COM interfaces will be much closer and the fundamental concept that meaning is attached to an interface by means of a unique identifier will have gained almost universal acceptance. Note that "IDL-free" approaches to CORBA programming, such as direct generation of IDL from Java source or direct-to-SOM compilation, will have to follow suit. Unique identifiers will have to be associated with the source code. In the COM world, this is already common practice, such as in Oberon microsystems' Direct-to-COM compiler or Microsoft's J^{++}.

In the CLR world, robust naming is achieved by associating unique identifiers with assemblies (as part of an assembly's strong name) that then serves as an anchor for all named definitions within these assemblies. CLR custom attributes can be used to attach arbitrary metadata to type definitions. The idea of Java-style marker interfaces is thus superseded by a more general meta-attribution mechanism. Custom attributes are themselves defined as classes (with certain constraints) and can be defined like any other type.

Moving from reliably named types and declarative meta-attribution to more explicitly formalized precise specifications has to be the next step. Tool and runtime environment support to leverage specification information for development, testing, certification, and runtime monitoring should follow. Some good progress has been made already in some of these directions. For instance, precise specifications with operational semantics can be grounded in abstract state machines (www.eecs.umich.edu/gasm/). The ASML project designs a specification language based on the ASM concept and explores tools for automated test oracles and generation of test cases (research.microsoft.com/foundations/#AsmL). Another example is the specialized Testing and Test Control Notation language (TTCN-3; www.etsi.org/ptcc/) standardized by ETSI, a standardization organization mostly focusing on the needs of the telecommunications industry based in France (www.etsi.org).

PART FOUR

Components meet architecture and process

This is the last technical part of the book. Combining the foundations laid in Part Two and the current approaches reviewed in Part Three, this part aims at opening perspectives for future technical development. The examples are naturally not taken from the future, but have been selected for their early adoption of one or another aspect expected to gain importance in the future. The chapters in this part are only weakly linked and can be read in any order. In particular, it is safe to skim over or skip any of the technical details.

Chapter 20 discusses the concept of component architectures and a set of technical definitions and a conceptual framework for component architecture are developed. Chapter 21 covers the important notion of component frameworks and presents three cases of such frameworks, namely contextual composition frameworks (as found in COM+, EJB, CLR, and CCM), an exemplary framework targeting visual objects, and one industrial automation. Chapter 22 covers a range of component development issues, including methodologies and aspects of programming languages. Chapter 23 briefly discusses the issues of component acquisition and distribution, the problem of finding components, and current attempts at solving this problem. Chapter 24 covers component assembly and Chapter 25 concludes with a discussion of some open problems.

CHAPTER TWENTY

Component architecture

As briefly outlined in Chapter 9, system architecture is the pivotal basis of any large-scale software technology and is of utmost importance for component-based systems. Only where an overall architecture is defined *and maintained* do evolution and maintenance of components and systems find the firm foundation they require. To name just a few of the cornerstones of a component architecture: interaction between components and their environment is regulated, the roles of components are defined, tool interfaces are standardized, and user interface aspects both for end users (where applicable) and for assemblers are regularized.

Where component vendors do not find a clearly established architecture, random architectures arise. For example, component vendors copy the sample implementations provided by infrastructure vendors or early adapters, without a precise understanding of what guided the various implementation decisions. The result is a quick blurring of even the crispest concepts; a component world emerges, full of redundancies, inconsistencies, and idiosyncrasies. Eventual collapse is preprogrammed.

It is not at all clear what a component architecture – better, a component system architecture – should look like. No current approach goes beyond individual component frameworks, as described in the next chapter. This chapter presents an attempt at conceptualizing the important area of component architecture. The driving point is to establish order within chaos. By carefully enabling independent extensibility in key areas of a system, degrees of freedom are introduced that remain for all time – that is, for the lifetime of the architecture. Such degrees of freedom limit overall understanding in principle.

20.1 The roles of an architecture

People claim to be key or principal architects of one or the other software architecture, but it is usually unclear what that means. While software architecture is still maturing, much can be learned from the role of architecture and architects in the "real world." In any system complex enough to ask for guiding rules for design and implementation, an architecture is needed. An architecture needs to create simultaneously the basis for independence and cooperation. Independence of system aspects is required to enable multiple sources of solution parts. Cooperation between these otherwise independent aspects is essential in any non-trivial architecture as the whole is more than the sum of its parts.

Architecture is about a holistic view of a system, often one that is yet to be developed. More technically, an architecture defines overall invariants – that is, properties that characterize any system built following this particular architecture. An architecture categorizes central resources to enable independence in the presence of competition for resources. Operating systems are a good example. An operating system partially defines the architecture for the overall system resting on it by defining how independent processes compete for resources.

An architecture prescribes proper frameworks for all involved mechanisms, limiting the degrees of freedom to curb variations and enable cooperation. An architecture includes all policy decisions required to enable interoperation across otherwise independent uses of the mechanisms. Policy decisions include the roles of components.

An architecture needs to be based on the principal considerations of overall functionality, performance, reliability, and security. Detailed decisions can be left open, but guidance regarding expected levels of functionality and performance is required. For example, an architecture may exactly prescribe some details to ensure performance, reliability, or security. All too commonly, aspects of performance, reliability, and security are ignored on architectural levels, emphasizing only functionality. The consequences can be fatal, literally, depending on the deployment context. Thus, emphasis of these so-called extra-functional aspects has a tradition in safety- or security-critical applications. To view all four aspects as prioritized facets of a whole in any software architecture remains an important goal.

20.2 | Conceptualization – beyond objects?

At a conceptual level, it is obviously useful to introduce layers, to single out components, and separate concerns. How much of this needs to "survive" in a concrete realization of an architecture? More controversially, are granularities beyond objects really needed? Interestingly, it is sometimes claimed that a prime strength of objects is the isomorphism of objects and object relations as they show up in requirements, analysis, design, and implementation (for example Goldberg and Rubin, 1995). This is true both if nothing but objects count in all these phases and if everything that is more than one object can be isolated. Doing so is largely the main thrust of "pure" object-oriented approaches.

It is obviously not true that everything is just an object. However, it is true that anything that requires a group of objects to interact can be abstracted by designating a representative object that stands for the interacting group. In this context, it becomes essential to distinguish between "has a" (or "contains a") relationships and "uses a" relationships. The representative object "has a" group of objects, whereas the objects in the group, possibly mediated by the representative, "use" each other. Relationships between objects can be modeled as graphs, whereas objects are nodes and a relationship introduces directed edges between such nodes. Distinguishing "has a" from "uses a" allows us to distinguish between intergraph and intragraph edges. Consider an externalization service that supports transfer of objects between contexts in time and space. Storing a compound document is an example. Intragraph edges need to be followed in typical externalization activities. Intergraph edges are not followed but abstractly maintained as "links," where links symbolically represent the target node of a directed edge. As a special case, links can also occur within a graph.

Unless particular care is taken, all objects are potentially in arbitrary "uses a" or "has a" relationships. (The "has a" relationship is also known as a "part of" relationship.) Arbitrary "uses a" relationships can introduce cyclical dependencies and threaten organizational structure. Arbitrary "has a" relationships can even be unsound as they must be acyclic. Hierarchical design is the key to mastering complexity. Unless objects are conceptually allowed to contain other objects in their entirety, there is little hope of mastering complexity in a pure object-oriented approach. As soon as hierarchical designs are introduced, the question arises "How could parts of such hierarchical designs be units of deployment?" It is therefore, and quite paradoxically, non-trivial to introduce the notion of components into object systems. The following section introduces definitions of structures at levels beyond objects (classes).

20.3 Definitions of key terms

The terms defined in this section help to construct an architectural terminology.

- A component system architecture consists of a set of platform decisions, a set of component frameworks, and an interoperation design for the component frameworks.

A platform is the substrate that allows for installation of components and component frameworks, such that these can be instantiated and activated. A platform can be concrete or virtual. Concrete platforms provide direct physical support – that is, implement their services in hardware. Virtual platforms – also called platform abstractions or platform shields – emulate a platform on top of another, introducing a cost–flexibility tradeoff. In practice, all platforms are virtual to some degree, and a sharp distinction is academic. The conceptual distance, or gap, between a virtual platform and its underlying platform generally has a tremendous impact on expected performance. Understanding this distance is thus very important.

- A component framework is a dedicated and focused architecture, usually around a few key mechanisms, and a fixed set of policies for mechanisms at the component level.

Component frameworks often implement protocols to connect participating components and enforce some of the policies set by the framework. The policies governing the use of the mechanisms that are used by the framework itself are not necessarily fixed. Instead, they can be left to higher-level architecture.

■ An interoperation design for component frameworks comprises the rules of interoperation among all the frameworks joined by the system architecture.

Such a design can be seen as a second-order component framework, with the (first-order) component frameworks as its plugin (second-order) components. It is quite clearly established by now that this second level is required – a single-component framework for everything is illusory. It is less clear if a third or even higher level will be needed, but the meta-architecture model hinted at here is scalable, allowing for growth. (For a more detailed discussion, see section 20.4.)

■ A component is a set of normally simultaneously deployed atomic components.

This distinction between components and atomic components caters for the fact that most atomic components will never be deployed individually, although they could. Instead, most atomic components belong to a family of components and a typical deployment will cover the entire family.

■ An atomic component is a module and a set of resources.

Atomic components are the elementary units of deployment, versioning and replacement. Although usually deployed in groups, individual deployment is possible. A module is thus an atomic component with no separate resources. (Java packages are not modules in this strict sense – the atomic units of deployment in Java are class files. A single package is compiled into many class files – one per public class.) The above technical definitions are in line with the broader definition of components in Chapter 4. In particular, there is room for other technical definitions that nevertheless respect the definition in Chapter 4.

■ A module is a set of classes and possibly non-object-oriented constructs, such as procedures or functions.

Obviously, a module may statically require the presence of other modules to function. Hence, a module can only be deployed if all modules that it depends on are also available. The dependency graph must be acyclical, or else a group of modules in a cyclical dependency relationship would always require simultaneous deployment, violating the defining property of modules. To enable external configuration and composition, modules used to construct components should limit static dependencies, preferably to pure types/interfaces only.

■ A resource is a "frozen" collection of typed items.

The resource concept could include code resources to subsume modules. The point is that there are resources besides those generated by a compiler compiling a module or package. In a "pure objects" approach, resources are externalized immutable objects – immutable because components have no persistent identity and duplicates cannot be distinguished (component instances have identity, of course).

20.4   A tiered component architecture

A fundamental notion of traditional software architectures is that of layers (Chapter 9). Layers and hierarchical decomposition remain very useful in component systems. Each part of a component system, including the components themselves, can be layered as components may be located within particular layers of a larger architecture. To master the complexity of larger component systems, the architecture itself needs to be layered. It is important to distinguish clearly between the layers formed by an architecture and those formed by a meta-architecture. The layers formed by a meta-architecture are thus called tiers. Multitier client–server applications are an example of tiered architecture. However, the tiers proposed in the following differ from the tiers found in client–server architecture.

A component system architecture, as introduced above, arranges an open set of component frameworks. This is a second-tier architecture, in which each of the component frameworks introduces a first-tier architecture. It is important to notice the radical difference between tiers and traditional layers. Traditional layers, as seen from the bottom up, are of an increasingly abstract and increasingly application-specific nature. In a well-balanced layered system, all layers have their performance and resource implications. In contrast, tiers are of decreasing performance and resource relevance but of increasing structural relevance. Different tiers focus on different degrees of integration, but all are of similar application relevance. Figure 20.1 illustrates the interplay of layers and tiers in a multilayer three-tier architecture. As depicted, higher tiers provide shared lower layers to accept lower tiers. Tiers are depicted beside each other, whereas layers sit on top of each other.

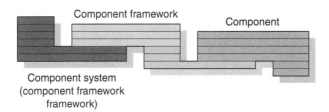

Component framework   Component

Component system
(component framework
framework)

Figure 20.1 A multilayer architecture with three tiers – components, component frameworks, and a component system.

Figure 20.2 shows how component instances communicate with each other either directly (for example, by using COM connectable objects, COM messaging service messages, CORBA events, or JavaBeans events) or indirectly via a component framework that mediates and regulates component interaction. The same choice recurs when component framework instances interact – the mediator in this case being a tier three instance. In Figure 20.2, CI stands for component instance, CFI for component framework instance, and CFFI for component system (or component framework framework) instance.

In a world still largely dominated by monolithic software, not even first-tier architecture is commonplace. Note that objects and class frameworks do not form the lowest tier. The tier structure starts with deployable entities – components! Traditional class frameworks merely structure individual components, independent of the placement in a tiered architecture. Objects and class frameworks can be found within components. There, depending on the components' complexity, they can readily form their own layering and hierarchies, such as MFC in OLE. However, all of a class framework's structure is flattened out when compiling a component. Unlike component frameworks, the line between a class framework and its instantiation is blurred as the framework is immaterial at runtime, whereas the instances do not exist at compile-time. This duality may explain the common confusion of the terms class and object.

As in the preceding section, it can be seen to be clearly established that a single first-tier architecture satisfying all demands of all components and all component applications will never emerge. Obviously, if it did, the tier model would be superfluous. What is more important, it is not even desirable to focus on a single unified first-tier architecture. Lightweight architecture that intentionally focuses on one problem rather than trying to be everything for all enables the construction of lightweight components. Such components can be constructed with restrictive assumptions in mind. Lightweight components are most economical if their guiding architecture opens an important degree of extensibility while fixing other decisions.

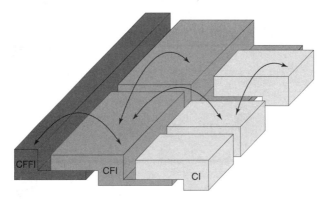

Figure 20.2 Free versus mediated interaction in a tiered architecture.

The ability to have lightweight components is important – it creates richness in a market in which heavier weights can also blossom. For example, the many ActiveX "heavyweights" become truly useful when combined with the many more lightweight objects, including controls in the original sense. Lightweight components can be made possible in two ways. First, by using multiple specialized component frameworks or, second, by allowing components to leave unimplemented those features that they do not require. In the first case, the question of interoperation among component frameworks arises and, thus, the concept of tiered architecture. In the second case, it becomes very difficult to compose components, as it is never clear which aspects are implemented. Indeed, most systems following the second approach simply do not even have a guiding first-tier architecture – there is no component framework at all.

20.5   Components and middleware

Middleware is a name for the set of software that sits between various operating systems and a higher, distributed programming platform. Middleware is sometimes categorized into message-oriented (MOM) versus object-oriented (OOM). However, most modern middleware blends both approaches. Also, there is a tendency for traditional operating systems to incorporate direct support. Operating systems have always included support for some communication protocols. The push for web services and its "inversion" of the programming world from a program- to a protocol-centric one makes much of the middleware value proposition split into two halves – support for suitable protocols and support structure that eases the local construction of services.

Isolated middleware products, such as message queuing systems, transaction processing monitors, or concentrators are slowly disappearing. Instead, specialized servers are emerging that combine middleware functions with specific component frameworks. Application servers combine application management, data transaction, load balancing, and other functions. Integration servers combine protocol conversion, data translation, routing, and other functions. Work flow and orchestration servers combine event routing, decision making, and other functions.

The application server market is served by almost 50 J2EE server implementations as well as by .NET/COM+ servers. The work flow and orchestration server market sees quite a variety of products, including IBM's MQ Series Workflow and Microsoft's BizTalk Server. The integration server market is perhaps the most fragmented, with products of many shapes and forms from many vendors, including CrossWorlds, IBM (WebSphere B2B Integrator), Microsoft (BizTalk Server), Oracle (XML Integration Server), SeeBeyond (eBusiness Integration Suite), Sun (SunONE Integration Server), Sybase (Integrator), Tibco (ActiveEnterprise), Vitria (BusinessWare), webMethods (Enterprise), and WRQ (Verastream). For some comparative information, see Sanchez *et al.* (2001).

All these server categories introduce their own component framework – usually built on top of one of the leading component platforms, which are J2EE or .NET (incl. COM+). In early 2002, the most successful example is EJB for J2EE application servers. This trend can be seen as a progressive replacement of middleware – which often took the form of traditional procedural or object-oriented libraries – by component frameworks.

20.6   Components versus generative programming

Generative programming aims at transformational approaches to the construction of software (Czarnecki and Eisenecker, 2000). Transformation as such is not new to software engineering. Compilers transform source code into target code; JIT compilers transform intermediate code into machine code. However, generative programming aims to go beyond such traditional transformation where the transformers are fixed. The idea is to allow programmers to define new transformers. One approach, explored by Czarnecki and Eisenecker (2000) in great detail, is to use C^{++} templates to define transformations. They also discuss many other approaches, including specialized generative techniques such as those in the GenVoca family (Batory and O'Malley, 1992). In a more general frame, Biggerstaff discusses the motives that support generative approaches (1998).

In a world of deployable components, generative approaches work best in two areas. They can be used to produce individual components and enhance composed systems. If used to produce individual components, generative approaches are "contained" by component boundaries. This approach is most useful when targeting the production of either fairly large components or the production of potentially large numbers of related components. It is important to carefully select techniques that can be parametrized with boundary conditions that are requirements for the generated component. In particular, it must be possible to precisely control the actual component boundary, including all provided and required interfaces. In addition, it must be possible to precisely control static dependencies on other components.

If generative approaches are used to enhance composed systems, they need to be positioned in such a way that they do not interfere with the unit of deployment characteristic of components. JIT techniques, as found in Java virtual machines or CLR execution engines, are a good example. Today's JIT technology is itself sealed by the manufacturer. However, it seems possible and useful to allow for extensions of this infrastructure itself. If done properly, new transformers could be introduced into the load-time or JIT stages. No systems provide such capabilities today.

CHAPTER TWENTY-ONE

Component frameworks

Component frameworks are the most important step for lifting component software off the ground. Most current emphasis has been on the construction of individual components and basic "wiring" support of components. It is thus highly unlikely that components developed independently under such conditions are able to cooperate usefully. The primary goal of component technology – independent deployment and assembly of components – is not achieved.

A component framework is a software entity that supports components conforming to certain standards and allows instances of these components to be "plugged" into the component framework. The component framework establishes environmental conditions for the component instances and regulates the interaction between component instances. Component frameworks can come alone and create an island for certain components, or they can themselves cooperate with other components or component frameworks. It is thus natural to model component frameworks themselves as components. It is also straightforward to postulate higher-order component frameworks that regulate the interaction between component frameworks. For a general discussion, see the preceding chapter on component architecture.

What precisely is it that a component framework contributes to a system architecture? If its purpose were to collect "useful" facilities, then it would be no more than a traditional "toolbox"-style library. As, by construction, a component framework accepts dynamic insertion of component instances at runtime, it also has little in common with class frameworks. In fact, implementation inheritance is not normally used between a component framework and the components it supports.

The key contribution is partial enforcement of architectural principles. By forcing component instances to perform certain tasks via mechanisms under control of a component framework, the component framework can enforce policies. To use a concrete example, a component framework might enforce some ordering on event multicasts and thus exclude entire classes of subtle errors caused by glitches or races that could otherwise occur.

Today, there are only few component frameworks on the market, but their number is growing. Since the appearance of this book's first edition, component frameworks have taken off in a particular area – contextual composition. Although higher-order component frameworks seem necessary and unavoidable in the longer run, only a few are on the market today (see section 21.2.4 below). This section therefore concentrates on first-order component frameworks, which is a two-tier component system architecture. Several component frameworks for contextual composition are discussed from a principled point of view. Then, a component framework for visual components is presented in some detail. Finally, a non-visual component framework for hard realtime control applications is presented briefly.

21.1   Contributions of contextual component frameworks

The concept of contextual composition is covered from various points of view in several sections of this book, including the state-of-the-art technology chapters in Part Three. This section revisits the theme of contextual composition from a more fundamental point of view and, in light of that, compares it with various other approaches.

21.1.1 Foundation and roots

From formal theories on compositional reasoning (with early roots in Gentzen's sequent calculus; Szabo, 1969), it is known that very little can be said about non-trivial composition unless the context of the composite can be constrained. In other words, the context of the elements being composed into some composite needs to be known at least partially to guarantee that the composite will have certain desirable properties or that it will not have certain undesirable properties. (The latter exclusion of undesirable properties is usually expressed in the positive by requiring properties that in their presence exclude the undesirable properties.) In compositional reasoning, this is achieved by defining well-formedness conditions over contexts and then introducing composition rules of the following form: if these given elements have these given properties, given a well-formed context, then the composite build using the following composition operator will have the following properties.

Note that compositional reasoning is the formal foundation of many widely used concepts, such as type systems. Let us take a concrete example. Given two values defined in a well-formed context (as defined for some language) that are both of type int, then the operator $==$ yields a new value of type bool. This sample rule in typical notation (where C is the context, $==$ the composition operator, x and y the elements and $(x == y)$ the composite):

$$\frac{C \vdash x{:}int \quad C \vdash y{:}int}{C \vdash (x == y){:}bool}$$

The power of contextual composition derives from three facts.

- Elements declare their constraints on acceptable contexts, but do not construct the context.
- Composition assumes well-formed contexts, minimizing the burden of describing and handling exceptional conditions. The application of composition operators successively builds contexts. (To be well-founded, there must be at least one composition operator that can start from an empty context, which therefore must be allowed under well-formedness.)
- Composites have certain properties by construction, as long as they have been formed using one of the valid composition rules.

These fundamental observations can be applied to composition at all levels of abstraction or granularity (for a warning see Lamport, 1997). For component software, the most interesting area of contextual composition is at the level of component frameworks. The elements of composition are instances created by components. The composition operators combine sets of such instances. Contexts collect sets of instances into domains of comparable properties.

Importantly, a mechanism that supports contextual composition of attributed components can be seen as a component framework. In particular, it forms a framework that composes instances not based on directly declared connections or derivations (such as inheritance of a framework class), but based on creation of contexts and placement of instances in appropriate contexts. For example, a component framework for transactional computation can be formed by supporting transactional attribution of components (such as "this component's instances need to be used inside a new transaction") and transaction enactment at the boundary of contexts. The same approach can be used to create frameworks for security, load balancing, management, and many other properties. These properties are sometimes called aspects as they tend to cross-cut a system, yielding system qualities that are not established by any single component in a system.

There are various academic roots to the approach of using contextual composition in software. Composition filters (Aksit *et al.*, 1994) are an early approach aiming at per-object wrapping, such that aspects are addressed separately from an object's functional implementation. Some extensions to this approach are explored in LayOM (Layered Object Model; Bosch, 1996).

The idea of co-containing several objects of different classes in a single container or context has also been explored in a number of approaches. In an early attempt, Hogg (1991) proposed to keep sets of objects in "islands" that are only accessible via special gateway objects. Schmidt and Chen's "kens" (1995), Almeida's "balloons" (1997), Bokowski and Vitek's confined types (1999), and other approaches are based on similar ideas. In all cases, special objects are designated as being visible from the outside of such sets, while all other objects in a set are not. This is different from contextual composition (in its general form), where any object can potentially be accessible from outside its context, but where the context boundary gets an opportunity to intercept all messages crossing the context boundary. The intercepting boundary objects themselves remain invisible to both external and normal internal objects.

The main problem with any factoring of aspect-specific code is one of orthogonality. No two aspects, as we know and understand them today, are truly orthogonal to each other. If they were, then any ordering of aspect-handling code would yield the same result. To see why this is a hard problem, consider the following example of two separate aspects. The first aspect is security and it is addressed by encryption at boundaries using session keys. The second aspect is tracability and it is addressed by call logging at boundaries. These two aspects seem about as independent as one can hope. However, they are not orthogonal at all. If programmed in isolation and then combined in any order, they will interfere such that the result is unacceptable. If, say, the encryption code runs first, followed by the logging code, then the logs will contain entries encrypted with long-lost session keys. Such logs are entirely unusable. If, in an attempt to fix this, the logging code runs first, followed by the encryption code, then it is quite likely that the log breaches the security barrier, unless the log files are themselves protected – an issue that the independent logging aspect code isn't supposed to worry about.

The solution to the composability problem when faced with non-orthogonal features is uniformly the same – a resolving third party needs to be placed in an architecture to allow for explicit resolution. In the case of the above logging and encryption aspects, such a third party might, first, order the two aspects in such a way that logging of outgoing calls runs first, followed by encryption, and, second, connect the logging component to a secure store, in line with the security policy that led to the selection of the encryption component. Such resolving parties can never be synthesized out of "thin air."

21.1.2 Contextual component frameworks versus connectors

Architecture Description Languages (ADLs) typically distinguish components and connectors. Components are meant to provide functionality while connectors focus on connectivity. As part of an architecture description, rules are formulated that state which connectors should support interaction between which components. Connectors can then perform actions of synchronization, encryption, authentication, and so on. The idea is to deal with aspects and system qualities in connectors, not in components. The roots of ADLs are Module Interconnection Languages (MILs), originally proposed to address the problems of programming-in-the-large (DeRemer and Kron, 1976). Also related are coordination languages that establish data flows in a composed system (Morrison, 1994). Probably the first ADL, and also the first to distinguish components and connectors, is Darwin (Magee *et al.*, 1995). Two more recent ones that support description of separate viewpoints are Rapide (pavg.stanford.edu/rapide; Luckham *et al.*, 1995) and ACME (www.cs.cmu. edu/~acme; Garlan *et al.*, 1997).

A connector, when zooming in, can easily have substantial complexity and really ask for partitioning into components itself. Also, functional behavior may well be required to implement the connectivity behavior of a connector. Therefore, it seems somewhat artificial to classify some components as connectors. The picture is a bit clearer when considering non-connector components as these aren't supposed to interact with other components directly. (Note that connectors aren't supposed to interact with other connectors directly either, creating an impression that the two concepts are actually dual.)

By introducing a pure connection-oriented approach (see section 10.3), all components are restricted to only interact with other components if connected appropriately. However, restricting all components leaves no room for special connector components. Instead, "connectors" turn into regular components and no special actions can be performed on the connections as such. Contextual component frameworks can then be used to reintroduce the intercepting behavior of connectors, but this time at the level of context boundaries. Contexts themselves are not instances of components, but all non-generic aspects of contexts are provided by parametrizing generic contexts with objects. These objects are created by regular components.

Early ADLs were restricted to static connectivity. Later ADLs added support for dynamic connectivity and dynamic reconfiguration. Occasionally, such architecture is called dynamic architecture, which is a bit of a misnomer as the architecture itself is static – it merely describes certain dynamic aspects of a system complying with the architecture.

A ground-breaking early approach to describing system configurations in the domain of realtime systems is ROOM (Realtime Object-Oriented Modeling; Selic *et al.*, 1994). ROOM uses the same model for all phases of the development process. In ROOM, component instances are called actors, which communicate by exchanging messages following protocols. Actors can nest and connections between actors can, but do not have to, respect nesting hierarchies. Actors can have behaviors described by ROOM charts, a variant of Harel's state charts (1987). Descriptions of actors, protocols, and behaviors can all be reused via inheritance. A ROOM derivative called UML-RT (Grosu *et al.*, 1999) has been proposed as a UML profile, where ROOM-style actors are now called capsules. Some groundwork has been laid with the standard UML profile for schedulability, performance and time (OMG, 2002). In the emerging UML 2.0, capsules may make it into the base UML specification (called UML 2.0 superstructure).

21.1.3   Contextual component frameworks versus metaprogramming

Metaprogramming has its roots in early Lisp systems. The idea is to allow a program (called a metaprogram) to inspect and manipulate another program and its execution. A systematic treatment of the capabilities of metaprogramming led to the notion of metaobject protocols (MOPs; Kiczales *et al.*, 1991).

The observation that metaprogramming can be applied hierarchically, modifying metaprograms with meta-metaprograms, led to metaprogramming hierarchies. Smalltalk is an early example of a system with a metaprogramming hierarchy, fixed to three levels. Perhaps the most dramatic project based on an open hierarchy of metalevels is Sony Research's experimental Apertos operating system (www.csl.sony.co.jp/project/Apertos). The OMG MOF (meta-object facility; OMG, 2000) is an approach to support modeling at four levels (called M0 to M3).

It has been proposed repeatedly (for example, De Volder, 1999) to use metaprogramming to separate aspect-oriented code from functional code. For example, method interception (sometimes called intercession) can be used to inject synchronization code into pre- and post-invocation handlers that wrap some method. Then, all calls to that method are synchronized without requiring any changes to either caller or callee code. The main problem with this approach is one of ordering and composability. If two aspects are independently realized using meta-interception, then it is very unlikely that the two will compose. (This problem is not unique to metaprogramming and is discussed in section 21.1.1 above.)

The idea of using systematic call interception to inject aspect-specific code into calls can be generalized to sets of objects. It should be clear that this is just another way of describing contextual composition. Today's context infrastructure does not, however, support the notion of hierarchical metaprogramming: the special objects assigned to a context boundary are themselves not supported by a higher-up context boundary. The problems of ordering and composability of a simple single-level context model are already quite overwhelming (section 21.2.4 below). Adding a hierarchical structure would complicate things further and seems, today, beyond practical reach.

21.1.4   Contextual component frameworks versus aspect-oriented programming

Aspect-oriented programming (AOP; Kiczales, 1994) is an attempt to factor aspect-specific code from functional code and "weave" the resulting code fragments into the actual code to be executed. As the weaving process is a pre-deployment processing stage, AOP can be viewed as static metaprogramming. The reflection and interception capabilities of a metaprogram are effectively available at weave-time, but not at runtime.

Predecessors of the AOP idea focused on specific aspects. For instance (and thanks to Christian Becker for providing this example), middleware layers such as DCOM or CORBA use an IDL to capture the remoting aspect separately. IDL compilers generate required proxies and are effectively the "weavers" for remoting aspects.

AOP can be viewed as belonging to the category of generative approaches (the weaver being the generator) and there are subtle interactions between component-oriented and generative approaches (see section 20.6). Fundamentally, AOP – like most generative approaches – works best if applied within a component. The handling of aspects in component-based systems is then left to component frameworks (including contextual ones) that bridge the "aspect gap" between components. In such a scenario, component frameworks (as pre-exiting artifacts) and aspect code interact. Reuse of aspect and functional code in various combinations yields a family of components, but only some of these target required existing other components and component frameworks. In detail, this interaction is not well understood yet.

The AOP team at Xerox PARC has cast AOP into a Java extension called AspectJ (aspectj.org). A more general approach followed at IBM Research led to the notion of hyperspaces and a Java-related realization called Hyper/J (www.research.ibm.com/hyperspace). A hyperspace aims to separate concerns in general – functionality, aspects, and packaging being examples of concerns. A hyperspace is structured into hypermodules, each of which introduces a set of hyperslices and corresponding composition rules. A hyperslice can, for instance, cover an aspect. It can also be seen as a generalization of the notion of subject in subject-oriented programming (Ossher *et al.*, 1995).

At first sight unrelated to AOP, but also in the category of static metaprogramming, are several proposals for flexible configuration, layering, and mixing of features at the level of languages. For example, Units support flexible modular composition and configuration in the space of hyper-order typed ("HOT") functional languages (Flatt and Felleisen, 1998). Knit supports flexible dependency configuration in C (Reid *et al.*, 2000). Jiazzi extends Java in a similar way but also adds flexible configuration of inheritance dependencies (McDirmid *et al.*, 2001). Mixin layers (Smaragdakis and Batory, 1998) are a similar approach that extends the concept of mixins (see section 7.2.2) to layers of mixins – special layer classes resolving mixin dependencies for an entire group of mixins. The claim is that this approach enables the construction of complex custom applications by selecting and configuring only a relatively small number of mixin layers (Smaragdakis, 1999).

21.2 Frameworks for contextual composition

This section explores current technology support for contextual composition. Probably the first commercially available support for contextual composition can be found in COM's apartment model. Indeed, the next iteration, MTS contexts, can be seen as the origin of all current contextual composition approaches – EJB containers, COM+ contexts, CCM containers, and CLR contexts.

As an aside, note that EJB and CCM containers closely correspond to MTS, COM+, and CLR contexts, but not to OLE or ActiveX containers. A container in the OLE or ActiveX sense does not intercept all incoming or outgoing calls to or from contained controls.

21.2.1   COM+ contexts

As discussed in section 15.10, COM+ contexts have their roots in COM apartments and MTS contexts. COM apartments are used to separate objects by threading model; MTS contexts are used to separate objects by transactional domain. COM+ unified these two notions and also added a large number of new context properties. In all cases, declarative attribution is used to drive the runtime construction of contexts and the placement of objects in appropriate contexts. In the case of COM apartments, the declaration takes the form of registry entries per COM class. The entry can request that instances of that class be placed in single-threaded apartments only, in multi-threaded apartments only, or in either of these. (COM+ adds the notion of rental-threaded apartments, which are also restricted to a single thread at a time, but different threads can enter a rental-threaded apartment in succession.)

Microsoft Transaction Server (MTS) introduced transactional contexts. COM classes configured for use with MTS carry declarative requests for their instances to execute only in non-transactional contexts, only in new transactional contexts, in new or existing transactional contexts, or in any transactional or non-transactional context. Given these declarations, MTS collaborates with the Distributed Transaction Coordinator (DTC) to create appropriate transactional domains. Objects within the same transactional domain share a single logical thread and a single shared set of transactional resources (such as database connections and locks). Once a thread returns from a transactional domain, the transaction either commits or aborts, the domain is destroyed, and the resources held by the domain are released.

To MTS transactional domains, COM+ adds the capability to return from a domain temporarily, retaining the status of the ongoing transaction, and continuing the transaction with the next incoming call. This model allows clients to enter into a dialog with a transactional service, using multiple call/return invocations. COM+ also dramatically widens the notion of context properties, domains, and declarative configuration. By incorporating the previously separate Microsoft Message Queue (MSMQ) service and adding several other new services, COM+ presents a large set of declarative properties (for more details, see section 15.10). COM+ introduced queued components, which are those that are instantiated on receipt of a message.

In COM+, two objects are in the same domain if they share a compatible set of context properties. For example, two objects are in the same transactional domain if they share the same transaction ID. Domains, as in MTS, can

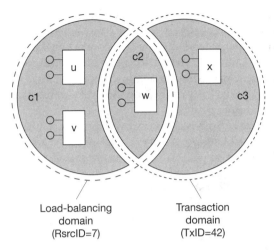

Figure 21.1 Domains and contexts.

span process and machine boundaries. Contexts themselves, also as in MTS, partition processes, they do not span process boundaries. Objects in the same contexts agree on all context properties. Domains are per-property groupings while contexts are based on property sets. Figure 21.1 shows three contexts, two of which belong to the same transaction domain (c2 and c3) and two others belonging to the same load-balancing domain (c1 and c2). The two domains overlap in the middle context c2. The figure shows four objects placed in these context. The objects u, v, and w share the same load-balanced resource (with resource ID 7), while objects w and x share the same transaction (with transaction ID 42).

Calls crossing context boundaries are intercepted and, depending on the context's properties, preprocessed, postprocessed, or rejected.

21.2.2 **EJB containers**

The Enterprise JavaBeans (EJB) model is introduced in the context of Java technologies in section 14.5. EJB provides containers for EJB instances. While these containers have been patterned after MTS contexts, they do add their own twist. An EJB container allows a class to be attributed to request explicit transaction control – that is, instances of such a class are expected to explicitly call on transaction APIs to begin, commit, or abort a transaction. Such explicit control makes these classes much harder to compose, but it enables an easier path when wrapping legacy transactional code that already contains such calls. Explicit control in COM+ is possible, but less straightforward. (Essentially, explicit control requires living outside COM+ transactional domains and direct interaction with the Microsoft distributed transaction controller – DTC.)

Furthermore, EJB containers support persistent objects by distinguishing session beans and entity beans. A session bean behaves much like a COM instance in an MTS context – its state is lost once its enclosing transaction terminates (abort or commit). An entity bean, however, is transferred to a transactional persistent store on transaction commit. That is, beans can be kept as persistent objects besides explicitly programmed database accesses – the only choice in MTS or COM+.

Since version 2.0, EJB provides improved container-managed persistence and relationships, improving portability of EJB entity beans from the container of one vendor's application server to that of another. EJB 2.0 also adds message-driven beans, a new category of EJB components that are entirely data-driven. Like stateless session beans, message-driven beans are instantiated on arrival of a message and destroyed immediately after message handling has been completed. This is similar to queued components in COM+. The concept of message-driven activation can be traced back to the transaction manager function of IBM's information management system (IMS) that activates and deactivates IMS programs to handle queued messages (IMS dates back to 1969; Blackman, 1998).

21.2.3 CCM containers

The CORBA Component Model (CCM) is introduced in the context of CORBA 3 specifications in section 13.3. Just as EJB builds on MTS concepts, CCM builds on EJB concepts. A CCM container is defined to be a full superset of an EJB container. (The fact that the EJB and the CCM specification evolve separately under different processes means that CCM will be chasing EJB unless EJB absorbs the CCM increment, fusing the two specifications into one.) It adds support for process components to the session and entity components introduced by EJB. More precisely, CCM session components correspond to stateful session beans in EJB, while stateless session beans are called service components in CCM. Instances of a service component do not retain state beyond a single method call. Instances of a process component have persistent state, but cannot be located by a primary key. Process components are thus useful to capture the state of an ongoing process rather than the state of an identifiable entity.

21.2.4 CLR contexts and channels

The CLR context infrastructure is probably the first mainstream attempt to provide a genuinely extensible infrastructure for contextual composition. Unlike MTS, COM+, EJB, and CCM containers, the list of so-called context properties is not closed. Third parties can contribute new properties that populate a context boundary if so requested by objects placed in that context. Context properties can intercept, act on, and manipulate any incoming and outgoing message as calls cross the context boundary.

When constructing a new context, CLR offers a one-time opportunity to populate the new context's boundary with properties. A particular context property can be added programmatically, for instance by some other property or by the object that requested creation of the new context. Alternatively, a new context property can be requested declaratively by an object being created and on whose behalf a new context is created. The declarative mechanism relies on CLR custom attributes – extensible metadata that can be placed directly on CLR classes. Similar to COM+ attributes or EJB deployment descriptors, such custom attributes make aspectual requirements explicit. For instance, a class may carry an attribute requesting synchronization. When instantiated, the system checks that the new object will reside in a context that has the synchronization property. The .NET Framework defines standard attributes for all COM+ enterprise services. This way, it is easy to create managed objects on the CLR side that, via the CLR-COM interop infrastructure, draw on COM+ services (see section 15.10.3 for a list.)

CLR objects come in four top-level flavors – value types, pass-by-value types, pass-by-reference types, and context-bound types. Value and pass-by-value types are marshaled by value when communicated across AppDomain boundaries. Pass-by-reference and context-bound types are marshaled by reference. For a discussion of AppDomains, see section 15.13.1, but the only aspect of them that is interesting here is that they create a flexible marshaling boundary. Marshaling is performed over channels and new channel types can be added. Standard types include marshaling over SOAP/HTTP and marshaling over DCOM. At the ends of channels, the system reconstitues pass-by-value objects while it places proxies for pass-by-reference objects. New proxy implementations can also be added.

Context-bound types always reside inside a context that is equipped with appropriate properties. All other objects reside outside of any context and so are context agile. COM has a similar notion of apartment-agile objects, but that notion is not safe. In the CLR, however, references to context-bound objects cannot "escape." Context boundaries intercept calls to or from a context-bound object exactly if the calls cross the boundary around that object. For example, when storing a context-bound object's reference in a field of an agile object, passing that into another context, and calling a method via that reference, the call will be intercepted. If the reference is then – by any means – passed back into the original context and another call is attempted, this second call will not be intercepted.

By default, a new object is placed in the same context as the object that requested creation. Alternatively, the creating object can select any other context (but requires "help" from another object inside that context) or create a new context. A new context is created automatically if the properties of the selected context don't match the object's declarative requirements.

As discussed in section 21.1.1, it is unlikely that context properties are perfectly orthogonal. As it stands, CLR offers no generic architecture to introduce resolving instances (see section 21.1.1). In other words, the context infrastructure can be used to create new closed worlds of properties and even to linearly extend an existing world. However, it cannot be used to combine independently created properties on a single context.

21.2.5 Tuple and object spaces

An approach to contextual composition that predates all of the above approaches is based on the concept of an omnipresent data space that can be used to communicate without explicit addressing. The seminal work by David Gelernter and his group at Yale University (www.cs.yale.edu/Linda/ linda.html) established this design space. In particular, the Linda coordination language by Nicholas Carriero and David Gelernter (1988) introduced the notion of tuple spaces. These are spaces that hold atoms of data called tupes. Linda defines only three fundamental operations over tuple spaces – adding a tuple to a space, matching and reading (polling) a tuple in a space, and matching and removing a tuple from a space. A current example following this idea is JavaSpaces (java.sun.com/products/javaspaces).

Coordination via data or object spaces has several appealing properties, including that there is no need to establish location awareness or dependencies among component instances and scheduling decisions are completely separate from the functional requirements on data flow. At the same time, these properties also pose some substantial challenges. For instance, to avoid a central bottleneck in a distributed implementation, the tuple space should not reside at a single physical location. However, to enable effective scheduling, information on available and requested data tuples or objects needs to be propagated to federated parts of the system. Requirements to keep tuple space operations atomic further complicate the demands on the infrastructure.

Tuple and object spaces have a potential to contribute to a refinement of contextual composition – data-driven composition. At the time of writing, such approaches have yet to leave research projects and impact mainstream technology. However, one could argue that the widespread use of directory infrastructure presents an interesting special case of tuple-space coordination. Examples in this space include the internet's domain name service (DNS), lightweight directory access protocol (LDAP) directories, Microsoft's Active Directory, or the web service universal description, discovery, and integration (UDDI) directory.

Directories assume a weak consistency model, that entries are replicated lazily, temporary update inconsistencies among replicas are tolerated, and the change frequency is much lower than the read frequency. These properties enable large-scale and even global scaling directory implementations. For example, DNS is implemented as a global hierarchy of DNS servers that federate to spread the workload of the constant and massive onslaught of hundreds of millions of machines requesting DNS-based name resolutions at a stunning rate.

Arguably, all major component approaches draw on the power of directories to enable certain forms of contextual composition. None of the mainstream approaches do so via a component framework, as the Linda coordination approach would suggest. Instead, directory services are made available via some API and coordination activities are left to the developer of client components.

More general data-driven component frameworks are also available. In the case of COM+ queued components or J2EE message-driven beans, data is distributed by message-oriented middleware (message queuing systems) and arriving messages cause the automatic activation of appropriate handler components that react by either causing some local effects or sending further messages.

21.3 BlackBox component framework

The BlackBox component framework (formerly Oberon/F; Oberon microsystems, 1994) is part of the BlackBox component builder, a component-oriented rapid development tool and component-oriented programming environment by Oberon microsystems (1997b). When first released in 1994, the BlackBox component framework (BlackBox for short) was one of the first component frameworks. Like many other early component approaches, BlackBox focuses on components for compound-document-based client applications with rich graphical user interfaces.

As the name suggests, BlackBox builds on the principles of blackboxes (abstraction) and reuse by means of object composition (a blackbox fully hides its concrete implementation behind its abstract interface). Figure 21.2 presents an overview of the BlackBox architecture. The framework consists of a core set of layered modules and an open set of subsystems. Each subsystem is itself a set of layered modules. The component builder is the component framework extended by a development subsystem (providing compilation, debugging, browsing facilities, repository services, as well as documentation and source wizards).

All parts of BlackBox, except for those shaded in Figure 21.2, are platform independent. The lightly shaded modules still have portable interfaces. Even the look and feel of the platform's native compound document architecture is abstracted from. Platform-specific features can be accessed, but components that refrain from doing so are themselves fully platform independent. The modules and subsystems on the left side of Figure 21.2 provide standard programming interfaces. Those on the right side are either optional (for example, SQL or a development subsystem), not normally imported by components (for example, module Windows), or platform-specific (for example, Host subsystem).

The BlackBox component framework focuses on visual components – a flexible concept, as proved by Visual Basic, OLE, ActiveX controls, and JavaBeans. The cornerstone of visual components is their visual appearance and interaction with their containing and contained components. The central abstraction in BlackBox is thus a view. BlackBox views can be fully self-contained – that is, have their embedded model and controller (editor). For more complex views,

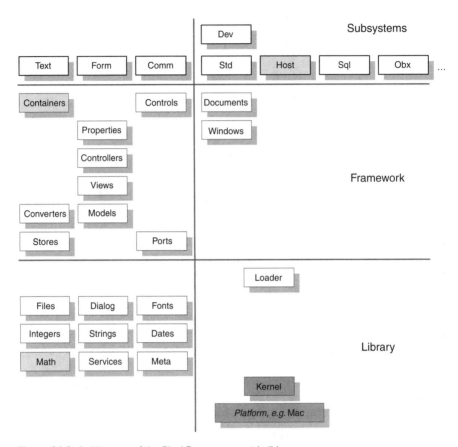

Figure 21.2 Architecture of the BlackBox component builder.

and container views in particular, a proper split into models, views, and controllers is used to enhance configurability and master complexity.

The BlackBox architecture is based on a number of novel patterns and approaches. Some of them are especially characteristic of BlackBox, namely the carrier–rider–mapper separation, directory objects, hierarchical model view separation, container modes, and cascaded message multicasting services. Each of these patterns and approaches is explained further in the following subsections.

21.3.1 Carrier–rider–mapper design pattern

This design pattern is ubiquitous in the BlackBox framework, and its uniform application greatly contributes to the understandability of the framework. The key idea is to separate data-carrying objects ("carriers"), access paths to data in these objects ("riders"), and data-formatting filters ("mappers").

A carrier maintains data that is logically accessible by position. The abstract carrier interface opens a dimension of extensibility in that many concrete implementations can implement a given carrier interface. A rider encapsulates an access path to a carrier's data at a certain position. Riders are created by their carriers and usually have privileged access to the carrier's implementation. Therefore, a rider can efficiently maintain client-specific access state to a carrier. (The separation into carriers and riders is related to the iterator pattern; Gamma *et al.*, 1995.) Clients use the combination of a carrier's direct interface and provided rider interfaces to access a carrier.

Together, the carrier and rider interfaces form a "bottleneck" interface that decouples clients from the potentially many carrier implementations. Mappers are used to provide interfaces that are more suitable for specific clients than the raw carrier and rider interfaces. Decoupled by the bottleneck interface, mappers form a dimension of extensibility that is orthogonal to that of carriers. Figure 21.3 illustrates the relationships between clients, mappers, riders, and carriers.

The list below illustrates the rich use of this design pattern in the BlackBox framework.

File system abstraction layer

mapper	Stores.Reader, Stores.Writer	internalize/externalize objects
rider	Files.Rider	random access byte read/write
carrier	Files.File	file abstraction (positional streams)

Display system abstraction layer

mapper	Ports.Frame	coordinate transformation
rider	Ports.Rider	clipping area
carrier	Ports.Port	pixelmap abstraction

Text subsystem

mapper	TextMappers.Scanner, TextMappers.Formatter
rider	TextModels.Reader, TextModels.Writer
carrier	TextModels.Model

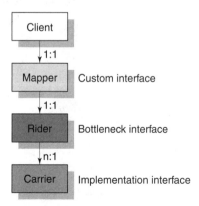

Figure 21.3 Carrier–rider–mapper separation.

Form subsystem
mapper   (no standard form mappers)
rider   FormModels.Reader, FormModels.Writer
carrier   FormModels.Model

Using the file system abstraction as an example, the following Component Pascal fragment illustrates how a specific file object and a specific mapper are combined. The file object is implemented by some file system and the mapper used is the standard object writer controlling externalization:

```
VAR f: Files.File; w: Stores.Writer; pos: INTEGER;
...
f := ...;
w.ConnectTo(f); w.SetPos(pos)
```

The writer's ConnectTo method requests a new rider from the file and attaches it to the writer. In the example, this rider is then advanced to some position in the file. The writer is then able to handle requests to externalize objects by writing a linear sequence of bytes to the file.

21.3.2 Directory objects

Blackbox abstraction in BlackBox is taken to the extreme in that not even the names of implementations of abstract interfaces are made public. As a consequence, the use of language-level NEW statements (in Java, new functions) is ruled out, as these would require the class name. Instead, new objects are created using factory objects or factory methods (Gamma *et al.*, 1995). Factory objects, which are called directory objects in BlackBox, are used where a new object is needed and no similar object is available. Such directory objects point to the currently selected default implementation in a certain context.

Each module introducing a new abstraction also provides a configurable directory object – the system-wide default for all cases for which no specific directory object is available. For example, consider the following excerpt of the file system abstraction:

```
DEFINITION Files;
  TYPE
    Locator = ...;
    Name = ...;
    File = ...;
    Directory = POINTER TO ABSTRACT RECORD
        (d: Directory) This (path: ARRAY OF CHAR): Locator, NEW, ABSTRACT;
        (d: Directory) New (loc: Locator): File, NEW, ABSTRACT;
        (d: Directory) Old (loc: Locator; name: Name): File, NEW, ABSTRACT;
        ...
    END;
  VAR dir-: Directory;   (* read-only variable *)
END Files.
```

Locators are abstract path names. A file directory object can be asked to open an existing "old" file by name or create a new one that initially has no name. (This application in the file system gave directory objects their name.) The standard file system is accessed by means of configuration variable Files.dir:

```
VAR f: Files.File;
...
f := Files.dir.Old( Files.dir.This("/dev"), "null" )
```

In many situations, an object of similar qualities to the one at hand is required. For example, when transforming an attributed data model, a buffer for temporary copies may be required. To avoid loss of specific attributions, the buffer and the data model should be instances of the same implementation. For such cases, BlackBox supports cloning of most objects, where a clone is an "empty" copy of its original. Note that this is different from copying as the source object's specific state is dropped and a freshly initialized object is returned instead.

```
VAR t, t1: TextModels.Model;
...
t := ...;
t1 := TextModels.Clone(t);
t1.InsertCopy(t, 0, 42);   (* avoid loss of attributions *)
...   (* change t1 – for example delete all lowercase characters *)
t.Replace(0, 42, t1, 0, t1.Length())   (* atomically replace with update *)
```

Consider a case where the implementation of text t adds new attributes to those defined in the standard text interface. For example, t1 might maintain an outline-level attribute. If t1 was created independently of t, support of this special attribute would not be guaranteed and the CopyStretchFrom operation would potentially have to drop this attribution. By using a clone, this loss is avoided, as t and t1 are instances of the same text model implementation.

21.3.3 Hierarchical model view separation

The original model view controller (MVC) framework (Krasner and Pope, 1988) was flat and thus unable to support compound documents. BlackBox defines a compound document model that is easily mapped to standard platforms such as OLE. (BlackBox was designed to target OLE and OpenDoc. However, OpenDoc never really materialized. This casts some doubt as to whether or not BlackBox, as it stands, would have been able to target OpenDoc.) To the programmer, BlackBox presents a hierarchical version of the original MVC framework (HMVC).

The HMVC framework is designed to accommodate very lightweight visual components as well as fully fledged heavyweight container components. For example, a view that merely displays something need only implement a single method (Restore) and is immediately usable as a first-class citizen. This is in contrast to approaches that complicate the implementation of even simple objects, such as OLE/ActiveX.

Views in BlackBox provide visual presentation of data and can be context-sensitive, active, and interactive. A view is a rectangular display object, may be transparent, and can overlap other views. Views may be embedded recursively where some views also function as containers. A BlackBox compound document itself is an outer-level view. In addition to presenting visual information directly, a view can also function as an anchor for arbitrary objects "under the hood." For example, a view can be just an icon, but refer to the results of a database search (Weck, 1996). BlackBox maps views to platform-specific abstractions – for example, to both OLE containers and servers. The framework shields view programmers from platform-specific issues, including look and feel.

A view may have a separate model, enabling multiple views to display the same model in different ways or from different perspectives. Models represent and manage data presented by views. A view can also have a separate controller, enabling the configuration of a view with a controller of the user's choice. Controllers interact with users and interpret user input. The typical interaction of models, views, and controllers has already been explained and illustrated in Chapter 9 (p. 159).

Views and also, where present, models and controllers are all modeled as persistent objects in BlackBox. Their state is stored as part of the containing document. For models, persistence is an expected property. For views and controllers, an explanation is in order. First, the actual choices of view and controller implementations matter and should be preserved. For example, one view may display a model containing a table of numbers graphically, while another may display the same model as a textual table. Likewise, one controller may support one style of editing such a view, whereas another controller may support a different style. Second, a view may be set to display a specific section of a model, such as scrolling, and may have various adjustable display properties, such as show or hide marks. These settings should also be preserved. Controllers may save the mode of a container view they belong to (see section 21.3.4).

In the HMVC approach, a model can contain nested views. This is important, as the choice of view settings of a nested view needs to be consistent across the possibly many views on to the outer model. Figure 21.4 shows a scenario in which a document is visible in two windows, one showing the document itself and the other showing, separately, an embedded view.

The document, as shown, consists of an outer text that contains several embedded game views. (By coincidence, the game is also called BlackBox. The English mathematician Dr Eric W. Solomon, whose games are distinguished by being simple but very interesting, invented it.) One of the embedded graphical game views is displayed a second time and this time enlarged in a separate window. Figure 21.5 shows how this scenario is supported by a hierarchy of an outer text view displaying a text model, which contains an embedded game view displaying a game model.

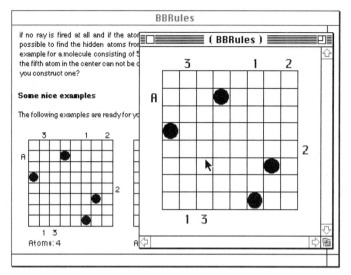

Figure 21.4 Scenario of a document displayed in two separate windows.

Documents in BlackBox are simply the root views of a model view hierarchy. A root window uniquely displays a document, but an arbitrary number of child windows may display other sections of the same document or views embedded into that document. Child windows can be opened and closed freely – they represent no persistent state. Opening and closing root windows

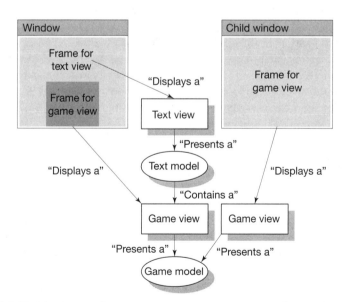

Figure 21.5 Models, view, and frames corresponding to the scenario in Figure 21.4.

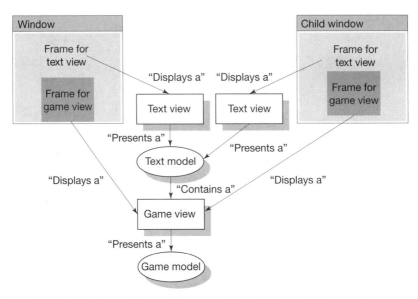

Figure 21.6 Models, view, and frames in the case of two windows onto the same document.

opens and closes documents. Closing a root window also closes all child windows on to the same document.

The root view of each window is a unique view to allow for separate scrolling, panning, and so on. The root view's models, and views embedded in this model, are shared with other windows displaying the same document. A view may be embedded in a model that is displayed by several views, possibly in several windows, and even on different display devices. A frame object represents each individual visual appearance of a view. Frames are mappers on to abstract display devices called ports. Whereas views in a document form a directed acyclic graph, frames form a tree for each window. Figure 21.6 shows how models, views, and frames are arranged when using a child window to display the original document rather than an embedded view.

21.3.4 Container modes

Traditional visual component systems distinguish the use of preassembled component instances from the assembly of component instances. An example of the former is filling in a predesigned form, while an example of the latter is designing a new form. For example, a Visual Basic form is either under construction and its controls are inactive or frozen and its controls active. The same split is advocated for JavaBeans, where a bean is either in assembly or use mode, differentiating between build- and use-time. For many applications, this split is justified as different people create and use forms.

However, compound document systems naturally unify construction and use of assemblies of visual component instances. For example, some outer levels of a compound document may be "frozen," that is turned into a fixed form, whereas at inner levels it is still possible to arrange new component instances. There is nothing wrong with filling component instances into the fields of a form if the form designer permitted this. A forms field could, besides text or numbers, easily accept pictures and other media encapsulated by instances of visual components.

Strictly separating build- and use-time is quite restrictive and rules out many advanced applications. At the same time, the strict separation also has its advantages. For instance, the user of a prefabricated form cannot accidentally damage the form while trying to fill it in.

The BlackBox container framework has a unique concept to take advantage of the unification without losing control – container modes. Using a special editor, containers on any level of a document can be set into one of several modes. The four standard modes are listed below.

- *Edit mode* The contents of the container can be selected, edited, and focused. This is the default used by a document editor where nested contents can be both edited and used, such as a text editor.
- *Layout mode* The contents of the container can be selected and edited, but not focused. This is the default used by a visual designer or component builder. Note that a BlackBox view can be active even if it is not focused – just like ActiveX objects but unlike traditional OLE objects.
- *Browser mode* The contents of the container can be selected and activated, but not edited. This is similar to standard web pages where HTML-defined text can be selected and embedded controls can be focused – a typical use is for online documentation and machine-generated reports.
- *Mask mode* The contents of the container can be activated, but neither selected nor edited; this is the default used by a predesigned form.

The other four combinations of selectable, editable, and focusable settings are also possible. For example, a container can be fully frozen by allowing none of these operations or form a palette by permitting selections but neither editing nor focusing. (Permitting editing but not selecting seems less useful.)

- no edit, no select, no focus – frozen
- no edit, no select, focus – mask
- no edit, select, no focus – palette
- no edit, select, focus – browser
- edit, no select, no focus
- edit, no select, focus
- edit, select, no focus – layout
- edit, select, focus – edit.

The modes can be individually set for each container in a document, including the outermost one. Hence, a human designer or a programmed document generator can fully determine the degree of flexibility left to the "user" of a document. Documents can thus range from fully static and immutable to freely editable templates. The mode-switching commands can be made unavailable to some users to prevent intentional misconduct.

21.3.5 Cascaded message multicasting services

BlackBox uses first-class message objects to decouple the sources of events from models, views, and display frames. Unlike ActiveX or JavaBeans, most BlackBox component instances do not need to be connected explicitly to cooperate – implicit connections are made and maintained by the framework. Essentially, change propagation is based on multicasts instead of registration of observers with subjects. The result is a lightweight and intuitive programming model, but also a potential minefield for subtle errors. Message or event multicasting raises some important problems, as pointed out in section 10.6. In particular, the relative ordering of incoming messages needs to be looked at carefully.

For example, consider a model displayed by two views. A change to the model's contents causes a notification message to be multicast to all views displaying that model. If, as a result of receiving the notification, the first view decides to change the model's contents again, then a second notification message is multicast. As depicted in Figure 10.6 (p. 188), there are two possibilities. These are that the second view receives the two notifications either in the order sent or in the reverse order. In this example, a reverse order could be devastating as the second view would receive incremental change notifications in non-causal order. If this view used these notifications to update its display incrementally, for example to avoid screen flicker, then an inconsistent display could result.

A general but very heavyweight solution to the ordering problem is to buffer all messages in queues and equip all recipients with their own threads. The messages are then delivered in causal order, where the separate threads allow for independent processing of messages. This approach is practicable in a truly distributed system with its physically separate processors. In a compound document setting, this approach would lead to a separate thread for every instance of every visual component used in any of the open documents. In addition, it would force all messages to be heap allocated.

The BlackBox component framework follows a different and more lightweight approach. Messages are normally allocated on the sender's stack frame and are delivered in natural recursive order (depth first), but the framework prohibits recursive sending of messages with overlapping semantics. When the first view in the above scenario tried to change the model's contents while a change notification was still in progress, the system would raise an exception. If the view still wanted to cause that change it would have to delay the change by registering a deferred action with the BlackBox framework. This action would be executed after the currently ongoing change notification terminated, causing nested change requests to be serialized.

If all BlackBox messages went through the same multicasting channel, the framework could not reasonably block nested message sends. To see why, consider the following typical message chain. The user pressed a key and, in reaction, the framework sent a message to the current focus view. The focus view delegated the message to its controller, which interpreted it and requested a change to the contents of its model. The model performed the change and sent a notification message to its views. Each view computed the required changes to its displayed contents and sent a message to each of the frames displaying (part of) the view on one of the display devices. Figure 21.7 illustrates how BlackBox propagates messages in a three-stage cascade.

Obviously, it would be painful to force serialization of these logically non-interfering messages. To solve this problem, the BlackBox framework provides cascaded message multicasting. For each of the three messaging levels indicated above and numbered 1 to 3 in Figure 21.7, a separate multicasting mechanism with a separate recursion barrier is provided. First, a controller message is sent along the focus path. This is a forwarded singlecast, as any container on the way to the focused view can intercept and possibly modify the message. The view consuming this message, usually the focus view, can now request a model change. This change causes a model message to be multicast to all views displaying the model. Each of these views can then multicast a view message to all frames mapping the sending view on to one of the display devices.

The rules enforced by the framework are quite simple but catch most misbehaving components just as the error occurs rather than leaving behind visual "trash" or even inconsistent document states. The first rule is that a model can send no model message while another message being sent by the same model

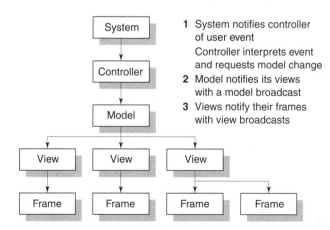

Figure 21.7 Three-stage cascaded message propagation in BlackBox.

is still on its way. The second rule is that no view message can be sent by a view while another message sent by the same view is still on its way.

By using source-addressed messages, the system can limit distribution of messages to genuinely interested recipients without maintaining explicit dependency lists. In some exceptional cases, the source of a message needs to send a message to sinks that are not even aware of the source's identity, but source addressing fails to handle such cases. Note that in these instances explicit dependency lists would not help either as the sink would not know which source to register with. Then, BlackBox also supports domaincasting of model and view messages, meaning that such messages are sent to all views and frames, respectively, that belong to a given document. Finally, omnicasting of view messages can be used to broadcast to all currently open documents. The absence of a source address forces the framework to impose very strict recursion barriers on such messages. As a result, domaincasts can only be nested if addressing different documents, and omnicasts cannot be nested at all. In addition to these restrictions, omnicasts are also less efficient than domaincasts, which are less efficient than multicasts.

21.3.6 Advanced applications based on compound documents

The BlackBox compound document model is powerful and flexible enough to support radically different application models. In particular, the standard text containers provided allow for interesting user interface variations compared with the more traditional form containers. Essentially, interfaces based on text containers are more like web pages than dialog boxes or forms, as known from Visual Basic-style applications. However, both recursive container embedding and container modes allow for interfaces that go well beyond either web-style interfaces or traditional forms. Also, as all BlackBox components have genuine programming interfaces, there is no need for separate automation or scripting interfaces. Using these programming interfaces, it is simple to synthesize on-the-fly user interfaces that exactly meet their requirements. This is similar to web pages synthesized by common gateway interface (CGI) scripts, such as reporting on the results of a search.

A first example of such novel interfaces is the BlackBox component builder's debugging support. For instance, it is possible to select a view in an open document and inspect its current state. The inspection command uses the BlackBox reflection mechanism to inspect the state of the selected view. It then generates a text displaying all fields of the view object together with the values that each field had at the time of inspection. The generated text contains controls (embedded views) to continue inspection. Link controls allow pointers (object references) to be chased and inspection of the objects to which they point. Folding controls allow expansion or collapse of parts of the inspected object to reveal or hide the state of subobjects. Figure 21.8 shows a typical screen, where a text view has been selected and state inspection

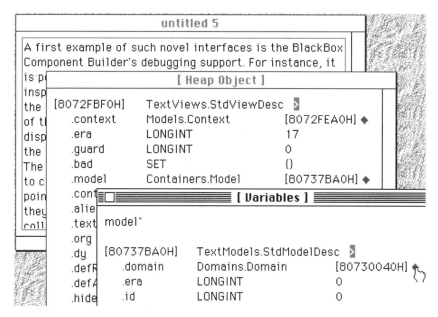

Figure 21.8 Interface generated by the BlackBox component builder's debugger.

requested. The user is then asked for the state of the view's model. As all displayed information is just regular text, the displayed material can be dragged and dropped so as to creat, for example, an eemail message to a help desk, or write a report.

A second example of the unusual interfaces that become possible when generating compound documents as user interfaces is the Debora discrete circuit simulator implemented using BlackBox (Heeb, 1993). Figure 21.9 shows a typical user interface, as synthesized by Debora. Again, the outer container is a text. This time, the actual simulation results are displayed by embedded trace views. A trace view is text context aware – if it finds that its container is a text, then it extracts the name of the signal that it should display from the surrounding text. In Figure 21.9, signal names are "Clock," "Enable," and so on. They correspond to names of signals in the simulated circuit – in this example, a cyclical 13-state counter.

21.4　BlackBox and OLE

BlackBox was designed to avoid a single language island syndrome by supporting the standard object model of the underlying platform, most prominently COM on Windows platforms. (The MacOS version of BlackBox originally aimed to support SOM and OpenDoc, but both are defunct today.)

A Direct-to-COM binding of an extended Component Pascal compiler allows for native programming of COM components. Components programmed using

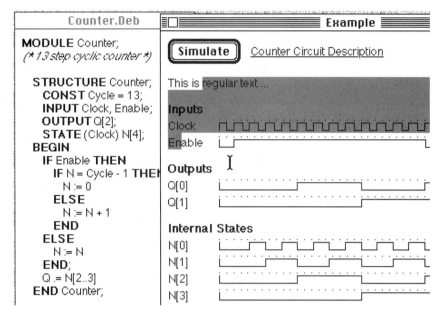

Figure 21.9 Interface generated by the Debora discrete circuit simulator.

any other language or environment can be used by BlackBox components and vice versa. On COM platforms, BlackBox is fully OLE-enabled – it is both an OLE server and an OLE container. OLE automation is fully available to the Component Pascal programmer or script author. Below is an example of a simple module that uses the Microsoft Excel spellchecker to check the spelling of the current focus text:

```
MODULE TestSpellcheck;
    IMPORT CtlExcel, TextControllers, TextMappers, TextViews;
    VAR app: CtlExcel.Application;

    PROCEDURE Next*;
        VAR c: TextControllers.Controller; s: TextMappers.Scanner;
            res, beg, pos: INTEGER; ch: CHAR;
    BEGIN
        c := TextControllers.Focus();
        IF c # NIL THEN   (* there is a focus controller and it is a text controller *)
            IF c.HasSelection() THEN
                (* there is a selection; start checking at its end *)
                c.GetSelection(beg, pos)
            ELSIF c.HasCaret() THEN
                (* there is a caret; start checking at its position *)
                pos := c.CaretPos()
```

```
    ELSE   (* else start checking from the beginning of the text *)
       pos := 0
    END;
    s.ConnectTo(c.text); s.SetPos(pos); s.Scan();
    WHILE ~s.rider.eot  &  ( (s.type # TextMappers.string)
         OR app.CheckSpelling(s.string, NIL, NIL) ) DO
       (* while there is more text and the current token either is not a
          word or is found in the dictionary, skip white space and scan
          in the next token *)
       s.Skip(ch); pos := s.Pos() - 1; s.Scan()
    END;
    IF ~s.rider.eot THEN
       (* found a word that is not in Excel's dictionary – select and show it *)
       TextViews.ShowRange(c.text, pos, s.Pos() - 1, TextViews.focusOnly);
       c.SetSelection(pos, s.Pos() - 1)
    ELSE
       c.SetCaret(c.text.Length()) (* checked entire text; remove selection *)
    END
  END
 END Next;
BEGIN
 app := CtlExcel.NewWorksheet().Application()
END TestSpellcheck.
```

This simple script module acquires a reference to an Excel application component object and stores it in a global variable. The result is efficient checking once
Excel starts up. However, the Excel server is also locked in memory for the lifetime of module TestSpellcheck. A sophisticated implementation would release
the Excel object, say, after the spellchecker had not been used for a while.

A fully functional education version of BlackBox for Windows is available
free of charge from Oberon microsystems' website (www.oberon.ch).

<table>
<tr><td>**21.5**</td><td>**Portos – a hard realtime component framework and its IDE**</td></tr>
</table>

Examples of component software outside of graphical user interfaces and compound documents are still rare. To show that there is no technical reason for
this, this section covers some technical detail of the Portos system. Since its original introduction, Portos has been superceded by JBed (www.esmertec.com).
Although rewritten to target Java, JBed still follows the overall architecture and
contributions of Portos.

Portos is a realtime operating system consisting of components (see Figure
21.10), which are all implemented in Component Pascal. New components
can be loaded at runtime if the system is connected to a server. Portos teams
up with a rapid application development tool that is built on top of BlackBox.

Integration of realtime process control components with workstation-located interactive components is possible, including full OLE integration on the workstation.

21.5.1 Structure of Portos

The Portos core is a small runtime environment for embedded or realtime systems. It includes a heap manager and a proprietary garbage collector. The garbage collector runs in the background and is designed to operate in such a way that it never interferes with other tasks. In particular, it never disables interrupts, and thus does not impede fast and predictable realtime responses.

Figure 21.10 shows the overall structure of the Portos operating system. The rectangles represent individual Component Pascal modules. Rectangles with thicker outlines are complete subsystems consisting of several modules (the Comm subsystem, for example) or open collections of component implementations (such as device drivers implementing process peripherals).

The Comm subsystem is a component framework for reliable communication via serial bytestreams. It supports extensibility in four independent dimensions, namely clients (such as the module loader), services (such as the debug server), channels (such as an Ethernet driver), and protocols (such as UDP/IP).

The process peripherals modules constitute a component framework for input/output of digital or analog data. It supports extensibility in three independent dimensions – applications (such as a process control program), device drivers (such as that for a digital–analog converter), and scales (such as a linear transformation on the analog data read or written).

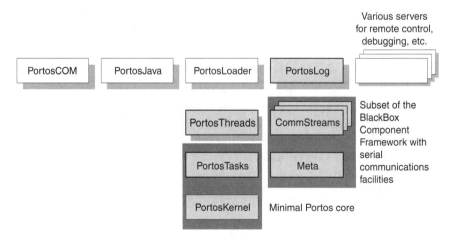

Figure 21.10 Modular structure of Portos.

Various configurations of Portos are possible. At the least, the modules PortosKernel and PortosTasks are required. PortosKernel is a private module that contains some unsafe low-level facilities and the heap manager, including the asynchronous garbage collector. Module PortosTasks is the pivotal interface for developers of hard realtime applications. It is described in further detail below. These two modules are sufficient, provided that the application contains all necessary device drivers and is linked with them. A minimal Portos application that is linked together with the core fits into a 64-kB EPROM and 128 kB of RAM. A minimal Portos application that uses TCP/IP networking and supports downloading of new components over the network starts at about 128 kB of EPROM and 256 kB of RAM.

Optionally, module PortosThreads may be added. It implements a scheduler for prioritized threads – that is, tasks that are not time-critical. Their scheduler can be plugged into module PortosTasks. If desired, PortosThreads could be replaced by other threading mechanisms.

Several modules from the BlackBox component framework are available for Portos, in particular Meta (typesafe reflection facilities) and CommStreams (reliable serial communication). Several implementation modules are available for CommStreams, in particular for communication over V24 and over Ethernet via TCP/IP and UDP/IP. PPP, FTP, and other standard internet services are provided as further options using this communication platform.

PortosLog is a simple console output service that uses the communication facilities to send output to a host computer running the Portos IDE (see next section) or a terminal program. Several optional modules implement server functionality that can be used during cross-development and for visualization purposes. In particular, a user can issue remote commands in the IDE, which are executed on Portos. New modules can be installed on Portos in this way, debug output can be fetched, and controls (in the sense of ActiveX or BlackBox controls) can display and manipulate Portos state remotely.

PortosLoader is necessary to load new modules at runtime. In particular, new code files can be downloaded from the host using the communications facilities, and then loaded into memory.

Note that the code files contain native machine code, not intermediate byte code that would have to be interpreted. Module loading and unloading is fully dynamic, allowing for field upgrades of the software without downtime. The loader is an optional service that can be left out in closed embedded systems that have no communication facilities, and thus need to be fully linked.

21.5.2 Realtime scheduler

The central module of Portos is PortosTasks. It implements the following interface (the version shown here is a slight simplification of the actual interface):

```
DEFINITION PortosTasks;
  TYPE
    (* monitor/signal synchronization primitive *)
    Synchronizer = POINTER TO EXTENSIBLE RECORD
      (s: Synchronizer) TryEnter (OUT done: BOOLEAN), NEW;
        (* non-blocking enter *)
      (s: Synchronizer) Enter, NEW;  (* lock *)
      (s: Synchronizer) Exit, NEW;  (* unlock *)
      (s: Synchronizer) Notify, NEW;  (* wake up a waiting task *)
      (s: Synchronizer) NotifyAll, NEW;  (* wake up all waiting tasks *)
      (s: Synchronizer) Awaited (): BOOLEAN, NEW;
          (* a task is waiting for notification *)
      (s: Synchronizer) Wait (usec: INTEGER), NEW
          (* await notify, with timeout *)
    END;
    (* client process controlled by a task *)
    Handler = POINTER TO ABSTRACT RECORD
      (h: Handler) Run–, NEW, ABSTRACT;(* implements the task's behavior *)
      (h: Handler) HandleException–, NEW, EMPTY
        (* optional exception handler *)
    END;
    (* tasks control the concurrent execution of handlers *)
    Task = POINTER TO LIMITED RECORD
      (t: Task) Start, NEW;  (* make task ready for scheduling *)
      (t: Task) Stop, NEW;  (* make task inactive *)
      (t: Task) Suspend, NEW;  (* wait for resumption *)
      (t: Task) Resume, NEW   (* resume after suspension *)
    END;
  VAR current–: Task;  (* the currently executing task *)
  (* factory functions for normal, periodic, and sporadic (interrupt) tasks *)
  PROCEDURE NewTask (handler: Handler;
      duration, deadline: INTEGER): Task;
  PROCEDURE NewPeriodicTask (handler: Handler;
      duration, deadline: INTEGER; period: INTEGER): Task;
  PROCEDURE NewHarmonicTask (handler: Handler;
      duration, deadline, factor: INTEGER; periodicTask: Task): Task;
  PROCEDURE NewSporadicTask (handler: Handler;
      duration, deadline, minPeriod, eventType: INTEGER): Task;
  PROCEDURE Time (): INTEGER;
  PROCEDURE Sleep (usec: INTEGER);
END PortosTasks.
```

A combination of monitor and signal is used as the synchronization construct, but its definition is compatible with the java.lang.Object class, in that it supports suitably defined Enter, Exit, Wait, Notify, and NotifyAll methods.

A task represents a concurrent process, which is implemented by a PortosTasks.Handler object. Handler objects contain an abstract method, Run, which implements the code of the process. An optional exception handler (as signified by EMPTY in the declaration) may be implemented. If it is left empty, the system's default exception handler is used, which writes symbolic debugging output to a host console if one is connected.

Tasks are inactive after they have been created with one of the NewTask factory functions. They can be started, stopped, suspended, resumed, and sent to sleep for some time. Unlike typical threads, a task may not run for an indefinite amount of time. Instead, a task (more precisely, its handler's Run method) must terminate before some deadline has passed or some amount of computation time has been consumed. If one of these constraints is violated, the handler's exception-handling method is called. This means that the hard realtime scheduler knows about time, and uses it for scheduling purposes ("Earliest Deadline First" scheduling). The interesting aspect here is that tasks can be safely composed, as long as there is sufficient computational power available. If the processor is saturated, the scheduler rejects new tasks ("admission testing"), rather than risking that some tasks may miss its deadline. This is an example of a component-oriented approach in the realtime domain, in stark contrast to the usual user-assigned priority schemes of many commercial realtime operating systems.

A Java version of Portos, called JBed (which has since superceded Portos), is largely identical to Portos, but provides Java interfaces to the kernel's services. Java objects are implemented using the Synchronizer type mentioned above. The scheduler, class loader, heap manager, and the realtime garbage collector for Component Pascal and Java are identical. Timesharing tasks, which consume the computation time left by the hard realtime tasks, implement a prioritized scheduling mechanism as defined by Java. Thus they can be used as standard Java threads. JBed is fast because the kernel directly implements the runtime environment needed for Java – there are no inefficient translations or expensive kernel calls. The Portos/JBed core is the virtual machine, except that Java byte code is translated by a cross-compiler before downloading into the embedded system. This is important to obtain systems with minimal memory footprint, and with optimal and predictable speed.

21.5.3 Cross-development environment

The Portos IDE is a cross-development environment for developing Portos applications. It is an extension of the BlackBox component builder described above. The IDE adds functionality for the transfer of code files and data to and from an embedded system running Portos, a Component Pascal cross-compiler that produces 68k or PowerPC machine code, symbolic cross-debugging support, an interpreter for remote commands, and remote (visual) controls. The IDE with BlackBox is available for Windows 98/NT/2000/XP.

Essentially, the developer opens one or several connections to an embedded processor running Portos. For simple systems, connections run over serial V24 lines. At the other extreme, several connections may be open simultaneously via TCP/IP, such as one connection to each of the processors of a multi-processor system. Typically, such connections are made over a company's intranet, but it is also possible to log into a target on another continent via the internet, say, to perform remote diagnosis.

The cross-development tools, such as the compiler and browser, work in the same way as the regular local BlackBox tools. This means that the same development environment and programming language can be used to develop local visualization software, as well as the corresponding remote Portos application.

The BlackBox forms subsystem can be used to create dialog boxes as user interfaces to a remote Portos application. For this purpose, the complete set of BlackBox controls, such as command buttons, radio buttons, text entry fields, and so on, are available also as "remote controls." Using the standard BlackBox property inspector, remote controls can be linked to program variables of a Portos module.

CHAPTER TWENTY-TWO

Component development

Component-oriented programming is a young discipline, and much work remains to be done. This chapter briefly covers the aspects of programming methodology, environments, and languages. Methodologies are needed to allow for a cohesive approach to component system partitioning, component interaction, and component construction. Environments and languages can reflect and support chosen methodologies.

22.1 The methodology – component-oriented programming

Just as object-oriented programming (OOP) addresses the fundamental aspects of programming object-oriented solutions, component-oriented programming (COP) addresses the aspects of programming components. A definition of COP in the style of typical OOP definitions is (Szyperski, 1995):

"Component-oriented programming requires support of:

– polymorphism (substitutability);
– modular encapsulation (higher-level information hiding);
– late binding and loading (independent deployability);
– safety (type and module safety)."

A proper methodology for component-oriented programming still needs to be found. Practically all existing methodologies work only within a component. The difficulties resulting from the complex interactions with other components are not adequately covered. Some issues can be addressed at the level of programming languages and approaches (Chapter 10). Connection-oriented programming in particular (see section 10.3) attracts a lot of attention in the language design communities – recent examples are ArchJava (Aldrich *et al.*, 2002) and Jiazzi (McDermid *et al.*, 2001). Yet, connection-oriented programming is only one means towards the end of component orientation.

Some significant progress towards component-oriented development methodologies has been made since the appearance of the first edition of this book, though. For instance, the Catalysis method addresses many of the specification and process issues explicitly (D'Souza and Wills, 1999). Several researchers began addressing the unique combination of top-down and bottom-up approaches that component orientation demands (for instance, Cheeseman and Daniels, 2000; Atkinson *et al.*, 2001; Hasselbring, 2002) – after all, a pure top-down approach (starting from requirements) will likely not meet existing components and a pure bottom-up approach (starting from existing components) will struggle to meet requirements.

The tiered architectural approach introduced in section 20.4 or other architectural approaches help to master complexity and guide system evolution. However, architecture alone does not suffice to guide the development of component frameworks and components. Many problems are still open. The following subsections should help to understand how extensive a "complete" component development methodology would have to be. The subsections cover selected problems at different levels and hint at possible solutions.

22.1.1   Problems of asynchrony

All current component "wiring" standards use one or another form of event propagation as one particularly flexible form of component instance assembly. The idea is simple – component instances that undergo a state change of expectedly wider interest post an event object. A separate event distribution mechanism accepts such event objects and delivers them to other component instances that have registered their interest. Component instances register their interest, because they may have to update their state to adjust to the changes indicated by the event object.

This seemingly simple mechanism introduces many subtle problems. First, the "natural" form of event distribution is multicasting – that is, delivery of an event object to more than one recipient. While a multicast is in progress, the system is in an inconsistent state. This is observable by component instances, for example by using regular method invocations to query other component instances. Second, event object recipients are themselves free to post new events. All the problems associated with relative ordering of multicasts thus need to be considered (see section 10.7). Third, the set of recipients could change while a multicast is in progress. This requires particular attention to maintain well-defined semantics. Fourth, some of the recipients might raise exceptions while handling received event objects and the multicast is in progress. Again, careful definition of the system's behavior in such a case is required.

22.1.2   Multithreading

> "Multithreading will rot your teeth."
>
> Swaine (1997, p. 93)

As Swaine explained in a subsequent publication, this and his other statements were intentionally provocative. He did not claim that they were wrong.

Multithreading is the concept of supporting multiple sequential activities concurrently over the same state space. The resulting increase in complexity over sequential programming is substantial. In particular, conflicts from concurrent writes (or reads and writes) to variables accessed by multiple threads need to be avoided. Such conflicts are also called data races as two or more threads race to make their data the winning entry. Synchronization of threads using some form of locking solves this problem but introduces a new one. Locking too conservatively or in the "wrong" order can result in deadlocks.

The main focus of multithreading is the better distribution of performance as observed by clients issuing concurrent requests. However, note that overall performance is maximized by not using threads at all and always serving the request with the shortest expected execution time first. Synchronization, even where deadlocks are avoided, can lead to substantial degradation of performance. Prolonged locking of frequently shared resources must be avoided. Also, propagation of exceptions across thread boundaries leads to the difficult problem of handling asynchronous exceptions. Finally, it is exceptionally difficult to debug code that uses multiple threads and complex interlocking patterns.

Obviously, none of these problems can be avoided where true concurrency needs to be dealt with. For example, if component instances execute on separate processors, then concurrent requests need to be handled. Complete locking of a component instance while one request is handled is possible, but may lead to deadlocks or poor response time.

A concept that would help to reduce complexity in many such cases is transactional programming. A transaction that fails to acquire all necessary locks would simply abort and could be retried later rather than deadlocking the system. However, few general-purpose programming methodologies support transactions and even fewer programming languages do. The increasing popularity of application server technologies such as COM+, EJB, and CCM, and the generic support for contextual services in CLR point in a direction of increasing availability of transactional infrastructure support for many components, though.

Non-contextual approaches to fine-grained threading tend to undermine extensibility. It is difficult (and perhaps impossible in the general case) to specify exactly how an extension and its synchronization and concurrency needs may interfere with those of the base system without causing unwanted effects. Fine-grained threading models as supported by Java or CLR are problematical and well-designed frameworks need to shield extension providers from threading issues.

22.1.3 Learning from circuit design

The problems of true concurrency, non-determinism, and synchronization are well known from other component technologies. Electronic circuit design, in particular, has a long tradition of addressing these issues. Although it is true that fully asynchronous circuits are often the best performers, they are also the most complex to design. Synchronous circuits synchronize all activities on component boundaries to clock signals. Design of component interaction can then be disentangled into phases – distinct clock cycles used to perform coordinated activities in a well-defined order. It is interesting to observe that, in general, synchronous circuits require asynchronous communications at the boundary and synchronous communication at the boundary requires asynchronous circuits. The third case – asynchronous communication among asynchronous circuits – is also feasible but clearly the most difficult design discipline.

The distinction of synchrony versus asynchrony at the levels of circuits (computation) and communication can be carried over to software. The design complexity arguments also hold as, for both computation and communication, it is actually easier to follow a synchronous approach. Unfortunately, just as in the case of communicating circuits, the two don't go together in the general case. Since the introduction of remote procedure calls (and later remote method calls) there has been a tendency to support synchronous communication, forcing the introduction of asynchronous computation, typically based on multithreading.

Combining synchronous computation with asynchronous communication is an interesting choice for software. Computing agents can be realized in a single-threaded way – or at least can be threaded in ways that are independent of communication pressure. The basic approach is simple. Instead of always directly driving computation as a result of invocation, invocations can be queued and processed in an order determined by system design rather than invocation occurrence. The resulting systems naturally use processes and asynchronous inter-process communication rather than threads with synchronous side-effects. An example of a synchronous approach from the domain of reactive hard realtime systems is Esterel (Berry and Gonthier, 1992). Another example is the popular approach of using message-oriented middleware (MOM) for enterprise-wide application integration. EJB 2.0, for instance, introduced the notion of message-driven beans.

Instead of using processes, more lightweight abstractions are also possible. For example, all computation can be split into atomic actions (Back and Kirki-Suonio, 1988). Actions are triggered by events queued by the system, but there is always at most one action executing within a single process. Availability of actions can be conditional. Ordering of activities is determined by a system-scheduling policy based on the set of enabled (available) actions. Unlike processes, actions can easily communicate via side-effects on global state, as there is no true (observable) concurrency.

22.1.4 Living without implementation inheritance

The severe problems introduced by implementation inheritance across component boundaries are justification for advocating the use of simple object composition and message forwarding instead. However, a concern frequently raised when being faced with this alternative is the resulting clumsiness when minor adaptations of available implementations are needed. It is simple to subclass a class with dozens of methods and then override just a few of them. In contrast, it is tedious to create a new wrapper class that merely forwards all but a few method invocations. In addition to the implementation overhead, plain forwarding also introduces an avoidable runtime overhead, in both execution time and code space.

Where the methods of an object are grouped into interfaces, each with only a modest number of methods, COM-style aggregation helps to avoid the performance implications of forwarding. The implementation cost can also be hidden from the programmer by using various forms of automation.

One solution is to generate the code of a forwarder's class based on the interfaces of objects to forward to. The main disadvantage is one shared by all textual code generation approaches. As the generated code needs to be edited, changes to the target object interfaces require regeneration and re-editing, or manual adjustment of the generated code.

Another solution is to use a template mechanism, such as that of C^{++}, to generate the required code at compile-time. Rather than editing generated code, templates are parametrized. Based on the template's instantiation arguments, the compiler then generates final code. This approach shares problems with all such "glorified macro" techniques. First, the template itself cannot be type checked and the compiler may report confusing errors when processing template instantiations. Second, a template cannot be compiled separately, leading to code bloat and eliminating dynamic linking of template abstractions.

22.1.5 Nutshell classes

A third solution is to use implementation inheritance... What? Recall that there is nothing wrong with implementation inheritance from whitebox classes – that is, classes that have been published in full source form and are guaranteed to be immutable. For component interfaces that are expected to be frequent targets for forwarding objects, a nutshell class that trivializes the pro gramming of forwarders can be provided (Szyperski, 1992b). A nutshell class has the same interface as the object it is forwarding to, and all methods are implemented as plain forwards to the target object. Nutshell classes are themselves abstract, although all methods are implemented as it simply makes no sense to instantiate such a class. (It is interesting that some languages, including C^{++}, have no way of expressing the fact that a class with no abstract methods is still abstract.) However, to create a useful forwarder that intercepts some of the method invocations, a nutshell class can be subclassed. The resulting overhead for the programmer is similar to that of plain implementation inheritance, except that forwarding instead of delegation semantics results.

A mechanism along these lines has recently been added to Java in the form of the Proxy class. A proxy appears to be of some given type while internally it is implemented as a subclass of Proxy. The implementation then gets an opportunity to intercept all calls as needed. CLR offers a similar mechanism via its RealProxy class.

22.1.6 Language support

A fourth, and probably preferred, solution would be language support. Where the programming language directly supports construction of a forwarder class, all disadvantages discussed so far can be avoided. The programming overhead is minimal and the runtime overhead in time and space has to be no different from that of implementation inheritance schemes. No mainstream language currently supports such a construct. For example, the C++ virtual base class mechanism does not allow for sharing of base class objects across separate objects. It also does not allow for dynamic change of base class objects, or for separate subclassing of a virtual base class. A language that does support dynamic inheritance from an object is Objective-C (Apple Computer, 2000; Pinson and Wiener, 1991).

22.1.7 Dynamic base objects with forwarding semantics

A hypothetical extension of Component Pascal would naturally introduce the required mechanism. So, where in standard Component Pascal the base type of a record is specified, a base pointer could be introduced instead. Consider the following example of a view interface:

```
TYPE
  View = POINTER TO ABSTRACT RECORD
    (v: View) Restore, NEW, ABSTRACT;
    (* many more methods *)
  END;
```

In Component Pascal, the type of text view objects that inherit interface and implementation from View would be:

```
TYPE
  TextView = POINTER TO RECORD (View)
    (v: TextView) Restore;
    (* implement other View methods *)
    (v: TextView) ThisText (): TextModel;
    (* other text view specific methods *)
  END;
```

The construction of TextView follows the traditional single implementation inheritance scheme. Using a slight modification of the base type notation, a forwarding mechanism could be introduced. For example, consider the type of objects that accept all View methods, but that intercept (at least) the Restore method. Expressed in the hypothetical extension of Component Pascal, this type is:

```
TYPE
  Decorator = POINTER TO ABSTRACT RECORD (v: View)
    (d: Decorator) Restore;
    (*other View method invocations are forwarded to base object v *)
    (d: Decorator) GetProperties ( ... ), NEW, ABSTRACT;
    (d: Decorator) SetProperties ( ... ), NEW, ABSTRACT
  END;

PROCEDURE (d: Decorator) Restore;
BEGIN
  d.v.Restore;   (* forward to base object: restore it first *)
  ...  (* draw decoration *)
END Restore;
```

A Decorator object supposedly paints its base view plus some decoration, such as a border, based on editable properties. The details of the property mechanism are of no importance here. As Decorator objects use a dynamic reference to a View object, they can be added "after the fact" to any existing view object, including ones that have already been "decorated." For example, Decorator could be used to decorate a TextView object, or any other instance of a subclass of View.

Note that, syntactically, the extension is limited to the introduction of a field name that optionally precedes the name of the base type. Semantically, if a method is left unimplemented in a wrapping object, requests are forwarded to the base object. The proposed semantics is forwarding, not delegation, to decouple the base object from the forwarder. This proposal is close to the one by Stroustrup (1987) for C++ but not adopted in the actual language (Stroustrup, 1994, section 12.7).

Note that Decorator still inherits from View and is a subtype of View. If View has fields or methods, then these are inherited into Decorator. Also, if Decorator issues a supercall, rather than a base object forward, the called method belongs to the decorator object, not the view. This inclusion of a complete base type object in the wrapper and a reference to a forwardee compatible with the base type distinguishes this proposal from that of Stroustrup. In particular, this proposal allows a Decorator object to be passed into a context expecting a View object without bypassing the decorator. In Stroustrup's proposal, the view base object would be extracted from the decorator and passed into the View context. As a result, the decorator would be out of the loop and unable to perform its function.

A subtle point is the declaration of the base object using field syntax. In Component Pascal, the export status of record fields can be individually controlled to be module private (default), read-only exported, or fully exported. The same three export modes are possible for the base object field. If the field is not exported, then clients have no way of telling that this object uses a base object – all that is visible to module-external clients is that the type has a supertype. If the field is exported read-only, then the base object can be accessed but not replaced by module-external clients. This can be used to establish stable base objects that are set at creation time, but never changed again. Finally, if the field is fully exported, then any client can replace the base object. In the example, any client could take a decorator off its current view and wrap it around some new view.

The semantics of Decorator above can be explained using rewriting into standard Component Pascal form:

```
TYPE
   DecoratorRewrite = POINTER TO ABSTRACT RECORD (View)
      v: View;
      (d: Decorator) Restore;
      (*other View method invocations are forwarded to base object v *)
      (d: Decorator) GetProperties ( ... ), NEW, ABSTRACT;
      (d: Decorator) SetProperties ( ... ), NEW, ABSTRACT
   END;

(* methods explicitly handled in Decorator are not changed: *)

PROCEDURE (d: DecoratorRewrite) Restore;
BEGIN
   d.v.Restore;   (* forward to base object: restore it first *)
   ...  (* draw decoration *)
END Restore;

(* rewrite all View methods that are not overridden in Decorator: *)

PROCEDURE (d: DecoratorRewrite) Method (...);
BEGIN
   d.v.Method(...) (* forward to base object *)
END Method;
```

Such a rewriting rule can be used to define the proposed forwarding mechanism.

22.1.8   Caller encapsulation

Another area that benefits from language support is that of interface definitions. When exposing an interface on a component boundary, two different intentions may be involved. On the one hand, component-external code may need to invoke operations of the exposed interface. On the other hand, component-internal code may need to invoke operations that implement the exposed interface. In COM terminology, this is the difference between incoming and outgoing interfaces. With the exception of Component Pascal, no languages properly support pure outgoing interfaces of components.

Consider the following example. The base class Object in Java defines a method finalize. The runtime's garbage collector calls this method before deleting objects that had become unreachable. The intention is that the object has a chance to release external resources that are out of reach of the garbage collector. For example, Java FileOutputStream objects implement the finalize method to release native file descriptors or similar resources that they may hold. Obviously, the finalize method is an "outgoing" interface exclusive to the garbage collector – no other code should ever invoke it.

To express this constraint, Java uses protected methods and Object.finalize is protected. A protected method can only be invoked by code in the introducing class, in one of its subclasses (some restrictions apply), or in the packages that contain the introducing class and the subclasses. In addition, a subclass can redeclare a protected method to be public and thus remove the protection for all direct or indirect instances of that subclass. Note that the Java package system is too weak to enforce protected-mode access fully. In the example of method finalize, the class Object is defined in package java.lang. Any new class file can claim to be part of the package java.lang and thus gain access to protected features of java.lang. Such a class can then freely call the finalize method of any object!

The properties of protected methods prevent most erroneous invocations of such methods. However, they are not strong enough to allow a base package to establish the strict invariant that no code outside this package may ever invoke such a method. The only way to achieve this in languages such as Java or C++ is to make the method private, which defeats the original purpose. To be a useful outgoing interface, it must be possible to implement such a method, but not to invoke it from outside a protected domain. (C++ has an odd construct – private virtual functions. These are methods that are not visible externally, but can nevertheless be overridden by subclasses and, if so, made public by the subclass or be called from within such a subclass.)

The need to encapsulate the caller rather than the callee, as done by most traditional encapsulation constructs, should not be surprising, once the symmetry between incoming and outgoing interfaces is accepted. However, proper caller encapsulation, suitable for the construction of components, is missing in most languages. Languages in the Simula tradition, including Beta (Lehrmann Madsen et al., 1993), support inner methods. On the level of classes, these come very close to caller encapsulation. No code outside the introducing base class can invoke the inner methods filled in by subclasses. Everyone can invoke the method itself, but execution of the base class code is guaranteed and can at least dynamically protect the base class against unwanted external callers.

A much simpler facility is available in Component Pascal. A method may be marked implement only and can then be overridden outside the defining module, like a regularly exported method. However, no code outside the defining module can invoke such a method. As the mechanism, like all

Component Pascal access protection, is at the level of modules (atomic components), calls can come from "friend" classes or procedures in the same module. For example, method FINALIZE in Component Pascal is pervasively defined as:

```
TYPE
   ANYPTR = POINTER TO ANYREC;
   ANYREC = ABSTRACT RECORD
      (a: ANYPTR) FINALIZE–, NEW, EMPTY;
   END;
```

Type ANYREC is the implicit base type of all record types in Component Pascal, in much the same way as a special class Object is the implicit base class of all classes in Java or C#. Component Pascal expresses access restrictions using export marks that follow newly defined identifiers. There are only two kinds of export marks in the language, which are * and –. An identifier marked * is exported, including its definition, from its defining module. A variable or field marked – is exported read-only – that is, it is write-protected outside its defining module. The * marks were introduced with Oberon (Reiser and Wirth, 1992); the – marks followed in Oberon-2 (Mössenböck, 1993).

In Component Pascal, the – mark has been generalized, so a method name marked – exports the method override-only – that is, it is call-protected outside its defining module. (Overriding methods remain under the override-only protection. Supercalls are legal within overriding code of call-protected methods.) The type ANYREC is defined pervasively – that is, it is part of the language and defined outside any normal module. Thus, method FINALIZE can only be called by the runtime system and the garbage collector in particular. Note that this is not a result of including FINALIZE in the language rather than in a library. Any module can export override-only methods and thus statically guarantee that no other module can contain an invocation of such a method.

Caller encapsulation is put to good use in several places in the BlackBox component framework. For example, only the framework can invoke key methods of views. If the framework has caught an exception on an earlier invocation of the same method on the same view, it stops propagating these calls. Faulty views thus degenerate without becoming fully useless or continuing to disturb the system. BlackBox is one of the few systems in which a view embedded into a compound document does not endanger the document as a whole. For example, a view with a broken Restore method will be masked by the framework, a gray raster overlaying the view's display and no further calls to Restore occurring. However, as the view's externalization may well function, the document can still be saved – and reloaded with the view intact again, once its implementing component has been repaired.

Another example of caller encapsulation from the BlackBox framework is encapsulation of an object's Externalize and Internalize methods. The framework can thus ensure that only newly allocated objects are asked to internalize themselves, protecting established objects from erroneous requests. The framework also enforces the fact that the proper environment for externalization or internalization is established before these methods are called.

22.2 The environment – selecting target frameworks

A component object cannot function outside a defined environment. Component frameworks define such environments. However, a component object can be designed to operate in multiple such environments simultaneously. Depending on the component system architecture, frameworks are separated according to various roles. For example, each framework may take care of one particular mechanism that operates across components. In this case, a distribution framework may be responsible for distribution of component instances across machines. A separate framework would be responsible for compound document integration. A component may well need to interact with both frameworks to implement objects that can be distributed and that function within a compound document.

While the first component frameworks are just appearing on the market, proper integrating component system architectures are still missing. The dangers of investing heavily in solutions based on a single framework are well understood by now. Although application frameworks are very successful, it is also known that "divorce" is almost impossible. It is already notoriously difficult to combine multiple traditional frameworks as most of them have been designed in total isolation and insist on complete control. However, it is even harder to migrate a solution from one framework to another with similar functionality. This is commonly required as providers of frameworks go out of business, no longer support all the platforms required by an evolving solution, or "better" frameworks become available. To address such problems, the first re-engineering projects for "object-oriented legacy" are already attracting funding, for example in the European Union (FAMOOS Consortium, 1996).

22.3 The tools – selecting programming languages

In principle, component programming could use almost any language – and almost any paradigm. Minimal requirements exist nevertheless. Component programming rests firmly on the polymorphic handling of other components. As interactions with other components need to be dynamic, late binding has to be supported. Safety-by-construction arguments additionally ask for support of encapsulation and safety – type and module safety (see Chapter 6) – and thus for garbage collection in most cases. In addition, component programming requires means to explicitly state dependencies and, ideally, keep such dependencies parametric. Fully parameterizing all implementation dependencies leads to connection-oriented programming (see section 10.3). At the language paradigm level, the object-oriented paradigm comes closest to expanding into the area of component-oriented programming, but other paradigms, such as the functional one, might also be suitable.

The number of programming languages that support component-oriented programming at a useful level is still quite small. Many mainstream languages, such as COBOL, Object COBOL, FORTRAN, C, C++, Pascal, Object Pascal, Modula-2, Eiffel, or Smalltalk lack the support for encapsulation, polymorphism, type safety, module safety, or any combination of these. Probably the most prominent component-oriented languages at this time are Java and C#, although Java has some defects when it comes to module safety (as explained below).

Other reasonably component-oriented languages are Modula-3, Oberon, Component Pascal, and Ada 95. None of these languages fully addresses the various language-level issues raised in the above section on component-oriented programming methodologies. Component Pascal probably comes closest, but there is room for improvement, especially in the area of support for multiple interfaces on objects. All of the languages listed fall short of supporting connection-oriented programming in a substantial way, although C# takes first steps by supporting events, event sources, and connections (called delegates) explicitly in the language. This weak support of component-oriented programming should not be surprising, given the relative youth of component software technology. Most current language technology goes back to the late 1960s, including object-oriented polymorphism!

Java, C#, and Component Pascal all support access protection on the level of packages or modules respectively. In this way, module safety can be established. Java has an open package system that is too weak in the area of module safety. Even without replacing a single compiled and possibly signed file, packages can always be augmented with new classes – and these have full access to the mechanisms protected by that package! This loophole needs to be closed by additional extralingual means. Thus, packages need to be kept in protected directories of the file system or some other repository with access control. In a context of dynamic acquisition of class files from remote servers, the situation is even more complex. Class files belonging to the same package would need to be authenticated to come from the same compiling source. To allow for more open settings, Java might benefit from a closed module construct, where each such module maps to exactly one compiled file for distribution. Nested classes in Java could help in forming true modules, but Java lacks an access protection level that spans a class and its nested classes, though nothing outside the class. Also, as the JVM does not really support nested classes, Java compilers take nested classes out of line and into separate class files.

C# is interesting in that its module-level access protection works assembly wide. Any number of constructs defined in C# (and, in fact, any other CLR-based language) can be packaged into an assembly. Once packaged, an assembly is cryptographically protected against tampering, making assembly-internal access restrictions strong and effective. This CLR notion of assembly-internal access is thus the most flexible module concept around today.

CHAPTER TWENTY-THREE

Component distribution and acquisition

By definition, software components are the units of software deployment. The only reason for their existence is to allow integration across time (versions, evolution) and space (independent vendors) of products to fulfill a shared purpose. Obviously, this requires a way of marketing components. The two technical sides of the problem are component distribution and component acquisition. Proper distribution and acquisition infrastructures are required, and these need to go far beyond pure connectivity, as provided by the internet.

23.1 Building what sells – applications not components?

Today, revenue is still predominantly generated by whole applications rather than finer-grained components. In the past, this has led to product packaging decisions in favor of applications and against components. For example, many focused helper applications, such as image viewers, would seem perfect candidates for components. Initially, the problem was a lack of business models. This is slowly changing with the growth of specialized makers of software components and successful intermediaries that match component buyers and sellers.

The Java applet role model is an example of a (so far) entirely chaotic approach. Distribution is not backed by marketing or serious cataloging efforts, acquisition being governed by browsing and random discovery. For a substantial and focused component market to develop, this needs to improve. As Java applets have been mostly free, it is not surprising that neither distribution nor acquisition strategies have yet evolved.

The situation is different for the profit-bearing market of ActiveX controls (mostly used together with Visual Basic to rapidly build applications). There are thousands of controls on the market, and traditional distributors actively market these. (With the introduction of .NET, there will eventually be a shift towards CLR-based components.) Acquisition is backed by catalogs of available controls, but, by and large, still relies on trial-and-error matching.

As soon as components package substantial domain expertise, the situation changes again. At the time of writing, the largest specialized manufacturer or software component, iLogic, specializes in components for simulation applications and sophisticated visualization. As the cost of developing such components is significant, the number of competing vendors small, and the application reasonably widespread, it is much more straightforward to create viable business models.

Finally, software services are becoming increasingly popular, especially with the arrival of web services that promise a universal substrate to mix and match such services. Services can be seen as components that are run by an operational provider. The provider is not paid for the component itself (which might never be revealed as a product), but for the service of running the component and providing its functionality as a service, possibly with guaranteed service levels. Such services enable quite traditional business models based on customer authentication and payments based on a wide spectrum of models, from flat over leveled subscription to pay-per-use.

23.2   Product cataloging and description

To get an initial handle on cataloging and abstractly comparing components, sufficiently complete descriptions of components need to be provided in a shape that is agreeable across substantial markets, if not universally.

Technically, what is required are precise specifications of what components do (and do not do) and what platform requirements they have. These specifications need to be organized into catalogs. Established component technologies in other engineering disciplines can lead the way. However, today it is not even clear how to specify a software component. Research has concentrated on how to catalog and retrieve components, but there are no methods that are proven and work with components of substantial complexity.

Microprocessors, for example, come with component specifications that effectively fill entire books. The same holds true for many other electronic, electrical, or mechanical components. Discovering components is only the main problem when focusing on components that are so lightweight and trivial that one has to expect "millions" of offerings. However, it is not productive to assemble systems out of microscopic components. Component assortments that offer a hundred different implementations of stacks or queues are not what the component market is waiting for.

Component frameworks are the next problem. Components will only interact properly if installed together with the required frameworks. In the case of the microprocessor example, the component frameworks in question would be the bus and interaction specifications that determine the embedding of the processor into compatible "motherboards." Component frameworks become products in their own right (as do motherboards). By necessity, there will be far fewer component frameworks than components, but a careful selection of frameworks is crucial to establishing a successful component-based system. Component specifications thus need to list the frameworks that are either required or could optionally be also interfaced with. More generally, component specifications need to be placed in an architectural context that includes expected or possible embedding in component frameworks, platform assumptions and requirements, and styles of composition.

A recent commercial attempt at structuring the space of component documentation is the capsule mechanism and related retrieval engine defined by IntellectMarket (no publicly accessible reference was available in early 2002). A capsule contains information and artifacts in a semi-structured form that is a compromise between machine analyzability and format simplicity. At one end of the spectrum, a capsule contains the actual component. At the other end, it contains unstructured comments, documents, and specifications. In between, a capsule contains specific information on a select number of technical and non-technical details, sorted into about a hundred properties.

23.3   Component location and selection

The location of components and component vendors based on requirement profiles is also an open problem. How can component services be described to allow for efficient retrieval with high recall and high precision? An approach that shows some potential is based on ontological approaches. An ontology is a universe of discourse covering the knowledge about entities in that universe. A basis for such an approach is a standardized way to interchange knowledge. The ANSI X3T2 committee's working draft of the knowledge interchange format (KIF), developed at Stanford, proposes such a standard (logic.stanford.edu/kif/). Essentially, KIF allows the creation of universes of discourse with predicate-logic expressions over such universes. Corinto, a consortium based in Italy, founded in 1995 and jointly run by IBM, Apple, and Selfin, has a project called Reuse Center. This is an ontology-based repository for object-oriented software components (www.corinto.it). A Stanford project specifically addresses knowledge-based CORBA component repositories (Gennari *et al.*, 1996).

A project at Stanford, the Computer Industry Project (SCIP), investigated the interaction of markets and technology that is so characteristic of components (www.stanford.edu/group/scip).

Perhaps surprisingly, it is also possible to largely "unask" the question of component location and selection. Key is the observation that component specifications need to be placed in an architectural context (previous section). Architectural reference models (how to organize systems for specific domains), referenced domain standards, component frameworks (concrete technical support for a particular architecture or subarchitecture), and platforms (abstract machines) all share one property – there are not all that many of these, especially not when focusing on a given domain of application. Therefore, if component specifications do indeed include rich references to their architectural context (including standards, component frameworks, and platforms), then it becomes much less likely that a query for a particular component simply based on primary functionality would recall a vast number of components.

More specialized component frameworks in particular could thus become rather effective selection criteria when looking for components that need to support a chosen component framework.

23.4   Superdistribution

An issue is the technical infrastructure required to establish electronic distribution channels. As components may have to be transferred as part of assemblies, there is a need to establish licensing schemes that distinguish several different forms of use. A component may be bought for purposes of unlimited use and royalty-free redistribution in assemblies. This is the common business model in today's controls market. Means that create a return proportional to the actual use of a component may be more satisfactory, both for component vendors and vendors of products using assembled components. Pay-per-use schemes (Cox, 1990) would cater for this perfectly, but they rely on a refined and tamperproof infrastructure that can verify a component's licensing status and measure a component's use. The CORBA Licensing Service is an example; the COM Licensing Service comes close.

Pay-per-use raises further technical problems. The charges per use will, in most cases, be very low. Care needs to be taken to avoid charging overheads that are higher than the actual charges. Also, service providers may want to charge their users a fixed subscription fee, but themselves pay the actual use charges to component providers. Viability of component markets could thus depend on either special hardware support in standard PCs, or on NCs (network computers), in which case servers can approximate use metering.

A flipside of the pay-per-use scheme is the problem of getting one's components to appropriate client sites. Brad Cox discussed the concept of superdistribution (1996), which is the idea that, as payments are usage-based, there is no reason to not just send a component to everyone who might at all benefit. The modern-day equivalent of carpet bombing (in the marketing sense), superdistribution works by not only allowing, but actually encouraging, satisfied users of a component to send it to their friends.

With the arrival of the Napster online music service in May 1999, one aspect of superdistribution became very real, which was the rapid distribution of digital goods to very large numbers of consumers. Founded by Shawn Fanning, then a freshman at Northeastern University, the Napster online music service promotes peer-to-peer file sharing. Napster allows users to easily trade music encoded in the MP3 format. While Napster didn't have payment or property right concepts worked out, it did spread the message that superdistribution technology works. Similar approaches followed, including Gnutella, a fully distributed peer-to-peer file-sharing network. Unlike Napster, Gnutella does not require centralized servers to back its operations.

23.5 Intermediaries

Separating organizations by areas of expertise can yield superior performance in core businesses, without dabbling in peripheral areas. Such organizational factoring also underlies many of the arguments in favor of software components. As the number of factored organizations increases linearly, the number of necessary relationships between these organizations grows quadratically. Combinatorial explosion of relationships is an old problem with such organizational (or any other) factoring. Traditional markets address this problem by favoring relationships mediated by intermediaries, such as agents, dealerships, traders, or brokers.

Intermediaries are, therefore, much more than just the proverbial redundant middlemen. Intermediaries represent bundled interests of one side to the other, with a possibility for win-win situations arising. For example, an intermediary can invest in direct-to-customer channels leveraged over the products of many manufacturers, saving the individual manufacturers from establishing and maintaining their own such channels at relatively much higher costs. Customers also benefit, despite paying a markup for the intermediary's services as the manufacturer would not be able to provide the same level of per-customer service.

In the world of software, some intermediaries are indeed redundant – warehouse operators and transport providers can be replaced by the internet. However, all other traditional intermediary services, including quality control based on careful selection of represented manufacturers, enhanced per-customer service, and integration services across products from different manufacturers all remain useful.

Another class of intermediary services also becomes possible – outsourcing of operations. So-called application service providers (ASPs) are intermediaries that provide and operate a software service to a client, instead of the traditional path of customers acquiring and installing software at their site (www.allaboutasp.org). In its first interpretation, the ASP wave emphasized remote operations. However, it is secondary to the ASP business idea whether the provided service is based on software located on ASP servers and accessed remotely or the ASP pushes some or all software on to the client's site. From this point of view, the ASP idea is also not quite as novel as it may seem. For example, Electronic Data Services (EDS), the former General Motors subsidiary and now independent provider of outsourced information technology services, has been an early leader in this business, operating since 1962.

Intermediaries focusing on cataloging, customer bundling, and sales portal functions for software components have also emerged. Two such companies are ComponentSource (www.componentsource.com) and Flashline (www.flashline.com). See sections 2.3.6 and 2.3.7 for more details of these companies' offerings.

CHAPTER TWENTY-FOUR

Component assembly

Components are units of deployment, deployable by third parties, but are never deployed in isolation. Component instances interact with each other, usually mediated by one or more component frameworks. One obvious way of assembling systems out of components is by way of traditional programming. However, the reach and viability of components are much increased by enabling simpler forms of assembly to cover most common component applications – or to avoid separate assembly altogether.

24.1 Systematic initialization and wiring

The connection-oriented programming approach described in section 10.3 can be used as the foundation of a systematic approach to explicit composition. Architecture description languages (ADLs) follow this idea: they typically have components and connectors as their core repertoire (see section 21.1.2). Composition is expressed as selecting components and interconnecting those using selected connectors. Any such composition really describes how instances of the selected components should be "wired up" using instances of the selected connectors. This detail is important as neither the components nor the connectors "used" to form a composite are themselves incorporated in the composite. For example, the same component can appear in two composites, but different instances of that component will perform in the instances of these two composites.

BML (bean markup language) is a JavaBeans composition language (Curbera *et al.*, 2000) released by the IBM alphaWorks lab in 1998 (www. alphaworks.ibm.com/formula/bml). BML is an XML-based component configuration or wiring language customized for the JavaBean component model. Using XSLT, BML can be the target of transformations from more abstract descriptions. BML itself is fairly close to the JavaBeans model and supports creating, accessing, and configuring bean instances. To enable configuration, BML supports the setting and getting of bean properties. Given such configured instances, BML can be used to bind beans as listeners to the events of other beans. BML can be either interpreted, yielding directly the executable configured subsystem, or it can be compiled into Java code. Underneath the

BML interpreter sits the bean customization framework that can be used to implement bean configuration and wiring languages different from BML.

24.2 Visual component assembly

Visual assembly of component instances is one way of simplifying the assembly process. JavaBeans components, for example, can distinguish between use and build-time of their instances. A "bean" can therefore exhibit special looks, such as building block icons; behavior, such as handles to connect instances to others; and guidance, such as dedicated online help to assist assembly personnel. During assembly, components are instantiated, and instances are connected using a uniform approach to connectable objects with outgoing and incoming interfaces. Both JavaBeans and COM support general connection paradigms for this purpose.

Where required, a scripting approach can be used to add additional behavior. A script is essentially a small program – usually a procedure – that intercepts an event on its path from source to sink and triggers special actions. The prototypical application builder supporting a dedicated scripting language is Visual Basic, although Apple's Hypercard was a precursor. (Hypercard failed to create a market for several reasons. It had a totally inadequate programming interface for new components. The set of standard properties that could be expected to be understood by all or most components was too small. Finally, the set of initial components was too small to show the full potential of the approach.) Following the assembly approach of Visual Basic, but underpinning it with a proper programming language and development environment, are Borland's Delphi, C++ Builder, and JBuilder. In all these cases, there is a sharp distinction between building and using an application and thus a continued emphasis on the concept of applications.

24.3 Compound documents to supersede visual assembly

Where component instances are naturally visual (provide a visual user interface), dedicated builders or assembly environments can be unified with environments for regular use. With compound documents, integration of build and use environments is straightforward and natural – documents are applications and document editing is component (instance) assembly. In such a system, there need not be any gap between component assembly and component use. The transition can be smooth as, using component assemblies, late assembly of further component instances or programmed generation of further assemblies can all be combined to suit application needs. To be fully useful, the assembly mechanisms need to be available at use time, if so desired. The BlackBox component builder and framework follow this approach. There is no sharp distinction between component assembly and component use, although such a line can be drawn by not deploying required builder components.

Seamless integration of build and use environments, especially in the context of compound documents, forms the strongest and most productive case yet for rapid application development (RAD). In such environments, production-quality components, prototype components, and throwaway use-once solutions can be freely combined. Requirements capturing and change request validation can be performed efficiently and effectively in this setting. Sufficiently trained end-users can continue to fine-tune their system, if that is organizationally desirable.

24.4 | Components beyond graphical user interface environments

Most early component software approaches addressed client-side front-end or standalone interactive applications. The demanding nature of modern graphical user interfaces, combined with the relative regularity of user interfaces, makes reusable components particularly valuable assets. However, other areas of computing, and server-based solutions in particular, are equally or of greater complexity and have inspired many of the current component software approaches.

For server-based components, the clear division between build- and use-time is more natural. Business objects, as proposed by Oliver Sims (1994), were one of the first proposals for "components everywhere." A next step was the development of Java "servlets," which are components designed to operate on a server but that can be assembled visually. While harmonizing well with many current models, including that favored by CORBA, assembly before use usually requires early decisions to be made as to which component instances to place where in a distributed system. Recall that, in most systems, including current CORBA implementations, there is little to no support for object migration that preserves existing object references, although migration facilities are being discussed. However, the most recent approaches around web services, based on SOAP, do not support communication of remote object references. Instead, SOAP insists on the communication of locators such as COM monikers or URLs that may resolve to a different object on a different machine every time. As remote object identity is thus not a concept in SOAP and web services, migration turns out to be a much simpler problem.

The most prominent component models for server-side solutions are Sun's EJB (part of J2EE) and Microsoft's COM+ on application servers and Sun's servlets (on JSP) and Microsoft's VB and other technologies (on ASP) on web servers. The Microsoft .NET Frameworks introduce new CLI-based components on both client and server sides.

An example of component standards for industrial embedded domains is OPC (OLE for process control), a set of interface standards for device drivers in the factory automation area (see Chapter 18).

24.5   Managed and "self-guided" component assembly

Component assembly is always about assembly of component instances. (Recall that a component instance – where the component has been implemented using object technology – is normally a web of objects.) Combining multiple components is, of course, also possible, but, in fact, closely resembles the traditional task of building higher-level libraries by using available lower-level ones. In other words, component (rather than component instance) assembly would merely be a new word for programming. Component instance assembly, however, is different. Rather than mixing the code and resources that implement components with the code that "connects" instances, the two aspects are kept separate. Lightweight programming (scripting) can be used to connect instances, while programming new instantiable components is substantially more involved – and is better not done with scripting languages and interfaces.

There is a flipside to the above observations. As assembly focuses on instances – it can operate only on instances that can be predetermined at assembly time. This is negating one of the greatest potentials of software, which is the ability to create new instances at will and in any number. Where these new instances are always to be used in the same predefined configurations, deep copying of template assemblies (prototype assemblies) can be used. A common application for this can be found in compound document systems – form templates. A form template is a document that is copied each time that a fresh form, ready to be filled in, needs to be created.

If it is necessary to work with dynamic instances of components in unforeseeable configurations, the remaining possibilities are managed and self-guided assembly. Managed assembly rests on an automated assembly component that implements the policies that govern the dynamic assembly of instances. An example would be a system that used a rule base to synthesize forms according to the current situation. Self-guided assembly is similar, but uses rules that are carried by the component instances themselves. For example, a component instance could form a "mobile agent," which is an entity that migrates from server to server and aggregates other component instances to assemble functionality based on the findings at the various servers. Obviously, this is a fairly far-fetched scenario. The point is that there is some potential beyond static assembly of component instances. Partially, this potential is tapped by contextual and data-driven composition, supported by attribute-based programming (see section 21.2).

24.6   End-user assembly

It is desirable to enable end users – who are so inclined – to assemble custom solutions when and where they need them. Implementing end-user directives leads to an interesting variation on the theme of component assembly that sits between fully self-guided assembly and static, ahead-of-time assembly. Clearly,

end users cannot be expected to perform assembly at a fully detailed technical level – hence the need for some degree of self-guidance.

Anders Mørch (1997) termed this feature end-user tailoring and distinguished three levels – customization, integration, and extension. All three levels correspond to tasks performed in component assembly. However, the focus is users that approach tailoring from their perspective of domain problems they try to address, not from the technical perspective of component assembly. Robert Slagter and Henri ter Hofte (2002) show an interesting application of this idea to computer-supported collaboration applications that enable an end user to compose groupware behavior as needed. A related concept is supported by the Groove Transceiver (www.groove.net) that enables end users to quickly assemble workspaces by selecting and configuring tools.

24.7 | Component evolution

Component technology is late assembly. The potential of components increases with the further deferral of assembly (or binding). At the same time, the fragility of the overall system increases. Components will normally undergo regular product evolution. Installation of new versions will compete with running systems that expect older versions or even with existing instances of older versions of the same component. The later a component is retrieved from a repository and instantiated against already instantiated components, the greater the potential for version conflicts.

In distributed systems, it is not realistic to shut down all current instances of a component to install a new version. Binary interoperability across clients of different versions and instances of different versions needs to be planned in (release-to-release binary compatibility). Actual upgrading of operational instances to newer versions is still an area of active research.

In realistic settings, it must be expected that various versions of the same component will have to coexist in a single system. Migration from one system generation to the next is the most important example. Besides coexistence of multiple versions, adaptation of incompatible or older software using wrapper components is required to address "legacy migration" problems. (Without solving the legacy migration problem, component technology will not be able to play a major role in the foreseeable future.)

The most robust approach to supporting version coexistence and wrapper components is that of COM. As, once published, COM interfaces are, by convention, immutable, there is no versioning problem for individual interfaces. Instead, a component offering a new service version will have to use a new interface. The key advantage is that it is possible to support simultaneously the old interface with its old semantics and the new interface with the new semantics. Obviously, old interfaces can be retired once their support is withdrawn. The absence of such an old interface will lead to a well-defined error when coming across a client still relying on this interface (QueryInterface will return an indication that the interface is not supported).

The versioning approach in CORBA is inferior in that it is still expected to merge all operations of all versions into a single interface. This does not support the notion of changing the semantics of an operation without also changing its name or signature. As a consequence, ever-new operation names need to be introduced – and there is no simple means to retire old operations without threatening binary compatibility. Even SOM's release orders cannot resolve this problem.

Another problem with version management is transitivity (Microsoft's Tony Williams brought this problem to the attention of the author). If an object creates another object, CORBA-style versioning allows verification that the server supporting the new object is of a suitable version. However, once an object has been created, references to the object can be passed around without any further version checking. This is unsound because the component originally accepting the created version may have less strict requirements than the component receiving the object reference. In other words, it is not sufficient to check versions at object creation-time only. In COM, keeping interfaces of different versions completely separate solves this problem, as a reference to a component's interface has immutable semantics. A similar solution for CORBA would be possible on the basis of CORBA 2's Repository IDs, which also uniquely identify an interface and are expected to be changed when the interface semantics change. However, the explicit use of Repository IDs in interface definitions and in client code is not yet established.

Java does not yet have a special version control mechanism. Essentially, versioning of interfaces is an unsolved problem. In particular, Java does not address the problem of coexistence of clients and providers based on different versions of the same interface. A partial solution to the problem of compatibility of persistent objects across component versions is offered by the Java Object Serialization Service (see p. 296).

However, Java does define elaborate rules on binary compatibility. Unfortunately, some of these rules are questionable. For example, many Java interfaces contain constants that are meant to be used as arguments to some of the interface's methods. When a Java client of such a class is compiled, these constants are hard coded into the generated class file and no version dependency is recorded. If the interface is then revised and constants are redefined or removed, previously compiled classes will continue to use the old constant values and pass them to methods of the new interface. This will not be discovered by the version check of the class loader and is considered a "feature." Merely recompiling such a client class then leads to potentially changed behavior. Since version tracking in Java is oblivious to such changes, hard-to-track problems can result. An incident from release J2SE 1.4 illustrates this problem. The constant java.awt.event.MouseEvent.MOUSE_LAST changed from 506 to 507. The Sun recommendation is to recompile all components that depend on this value. Although it isn't clear what impact this particular constant change has, it can lead to misbehaving user interfaces.

CHAPTER TWENTY-FIVE

On the horizon

This chapter concludes the technical coverage of component software. The following sections introduce a number of emerging approaches, selected for their potential to set new directions. Some of the approaches are still at an academic stage while others have small market shares. This section may safely be skipped, but following it through broadens the perspective for possible future developments.

25.1 Advanced object composition

Recall the important properties of object composition in a component setting. Object composition is a useful technique across component boundaries. Class composition is too static for many component applications – the class to inherit from needs to be available at compile-time. Object composition allows for the runtime extension of independently deployed components.

Object composition is usually based on message forwarding rather than delegation. Unfortunately, forwarding-based object composition introduces conceptual complexity by eliminating the identity of the whole. In contrast, when composing classes, the resulting subclass generates whole objects with a single identity. However, when composing objects using message forwarding, a web of objects represents the whole. The part objects retain separate identities.

For the programmer, this loss of identity of the whole complicates the design process. Incoming messages have to be handled by the receiving part object in a way that does not threaten the consistency of the whole. To maintain consistency, one of the part objects must be designated the "main" part. All other part objects have to be modeled as subordinates. Using delegation-based object composition can solve this problem.

25.1.1 Delegation

Class composition based on implementation inheritance introduces subtle dependencies between base class and subclass. If used across components, these dependencies lead to the fragile base class problem. Object composition based on message forwarding does not suffer from this problem. However, if delegation is used, object composition is just as problematical as class composition.

Much research has been undertaken over the past many years to develop a firm handle on the complex semantics of implementation inheritance. It is not yet clear if this research effort will eventually succeed in producing a practicable method of harnessing implementation inheritance while preserving most of its flexibility. If such a method can be devised, then it will simultaneously solve the equivalent problem of delegation-based object composition. A restriction to selection of delegates at object creation-time, with no dynamic changes allowed, may then become necessary to harness delegation.

Solving the problems of delegation across component boundaries is equivalent to solving the semantic fragile base class problem. Once solved, delegation-based object composition can be used to form composites at runtime that, as a whole, have a single identity. The language-level mechanisms have been around for a while (Ungar and Smith, 1987). Systems using delegation-based object composition with fine-grained objects initially performed poorly, but it has been demonstrated that good performance is achievable (Hölzle, 1995). There has also been some work on integrating delegation into statically typed languages (Kniesel, 1999). However, none of these mechanisms avoids the issues of the semantic fragile base class problem, which thus remains in the way of plausible adoption of delegation (or inheritance) across component boundaries.

25.1.2 Split objects

A web of objects with a common identity established by means of delegation is sometimes called a split object (for example, Astudillo, 1996; Bardou and Dony, 1996). The idea is to treat the split object as a whole and maintain encapsulation for the whole. A fragment of a split object individually does not have object status as it shares its identity with all other fragments of the same split object. Delegation across split objects is excluded in this model, and delegation is thus disciplined to allow for system structure.

A possible direction for future research is hierarchical split objects. Each fragment of a split object could have private parts that are organized internally as split objects. This generalized model could form an interesting basis for recursive composition of objects out of fragments.

Another problem with split objects is reorganization (Astudillo, 1996). The fragments of a split object are exposed to clients to enable viewpoint-specific selection of features. Evolution of individual fragments is thus much easier than evolution of the fragmentation itself. Merging or splitting of fragments breaks existing clients.

Finally, the question of type arises with split objects as they would seem to require a particularly dynamic notion of type. The clover approach (Stein and Zdonik, 1998) is one example of an attempt to close this gap. Objects are represented as sets of "chunks," where each type that the object adheres to corresponds to a subset of chunks. These subsets can overlap, leading to clover-shaped Venn diagrams, hence the name.

25.1.3 **Environmental acquisition**

Closely related to delegation in split objects is the concept of objects that form parts of aggregates and acquire properties from their enclosing objects (Gil and Lorenz, 1996). Instead of forming a flat web of parts, as in the case of split objects, objects are embedded in a containment hierarchy. Delegation or forwarding requests that cannot be handled by a part are sent up the containment hierarchy. The innermost enclosing container that can handle a request will do so.

Like split objects, environmental acquisition is a form of disciplined delegation.

25.1.4 **Dynamic inheritance**

Instead of strengthening the static properties of delegation, it is also possible to loosen those of implementation inheritance. The idea is to generalize the concept of a base class to that of a base object selected at object construction time. This is called dynamic inheritance or configurable inheritance. Stroustrup had proposed a scheme along these lines for C++ (Stroustrup, 1994; section 12.7).

Usually, proposals for dynamic inheritance try to preserve the self-recursion semantics of inheritance and, hence, rely on delegation semantics between an object and its base object(s). An unusually lightweight proposal based on single inheritance and forwarding semantics can be found in Chapter 22.

25.2　New forms of object and component abstraction

A fundamental property of objects is their uniform presentation of features irrespective of the actual client. Subtyping allows for objects that have more features than are statically known. However, for a traditional inheritance approach, all these features need to be grouped into classes, which then form a static inheritance graph. The number of different perspectives or viewpoints on an object is thus statically fixed.

Traditional inheritance only allows for the addition of subtypes. However, it may be necessary to present a viewpoint that is effectively a supertype of existing types. Most approaches would require refactoring of the class graph to introduce a new superclass. Few languages support the explicit construction of supertypes, but Sather is one such language (Szyperski *et al.*, 1994; Omohundro and Stoutamire, 1996).

25.2.1 **Subject-oriented programming**

In 1993, Harrison and Ossher proposed the concept of subject-oriented programming. The idea is that a subject can associate state and behavior with an object identifier as required by that subject. Different subjects can then see the same "object," by referring to the same object identifier, as having different properties and behavior. Composition of subjects – that is, composition of associations of state and behavior with object identifiers – has also been studied (Ossher *et al.*, 1995).

An approach similar to subject orientation, but much older, is the association of property lists with objects. Associated properties are only meaningful to those knowing certain property types, whereas objects abstractly maintain the union of associated properties. The concept of associated property lists goes back to early Lisp systems. However, object-oriented models do not normally support the generic association of properties with objects.

Subject-oriented programming has evolved into the generalized concept of separation of concerns along hyperplanes.

25.2.2 Aspect-oriented programming

Promoted by Gregor Kiczales (1994), aspect-oriented programming is about explicitly slicing programs according to the various aspects they address. By analogy, the engineering of a building is split into aspects of statics, safety, plumbing, electricity, ventilation, and so on. Instead of creating "modules" for each section of the building that specify solutions to all these aspects, typical building plans are fully separated according to aspect. The binding concept is the physical coordinates of the building's shell.

Aspect-oriented programming (AOP) aims to follow the lead of other engineering disciplines by supporting the individual programming of separate aspects. Obviously, as in the building example, the various aspects are separate but not independent. Kiczales thus proposes a weaver tool that merges the aspect-oriented fragments into a whole. Weaving is a complex task, as mutual dependencies among the fragments need to be respected. With AspectJ (aspectj.org) and Hyper/J (www.research.ibm.com/hyperspace/) weaving tools are now available for Java programmers.

As aspect weaving is essentially a compilation step, it leads to a tight bond between the woven fragments. Even if individual fragments would have qualified as software components, they lose that status if subjected to a weaving step. To preserve the property that a component is a unit of deployment, weaving has to take place either within a component before deployment or across component boundaries after deployment. The former is what current AOP weavers can be used for – as a corollary, such weavers can be used to construct individual components and, if aspect separation is taken too far, will lead to large monolithic components. (See section 21.1.4 for a discussion of how AOP relates to component frameworks.)

The alternative – post-deployment weaving – would be somewhat similar to what JIT compilers do when optimizing across component boundaries – not just after deployment, but, in this case, even after loading. In the future, aspect weaving technology could migrate into the install-/deploy-time mechanisms or even the JIT mechanisms of virtualizing platforms such as JVM and CLR.

To retain the property of components as units of versioning (including concepts of side-by-side installation and replacement), post-deployment weaving must remain effectively undoable. If a component woven into the installed system needs to be replaced, the weaving infrastructure needs to know how to "unweave" that component. Again, there is a strong analogy in the world of optimizing JIT compilers. If a JIT compiler, for instance, observed that a particular type is actually not subtyped, all variables of that type become monomorphic, allowing the JIT compiler to eliminate dynamic dispatch on these variables. However, if loading of another component introduces a subtype of that type, then all these variables suddenly turn polymorphic and the JIT compiler must be capable of undoing these optimizations again.

25.2.3 XML components

The world of XML is mostly declarative in nature. However, XML-related languages such as XPath, XQuery, and XSLT are applicative (functional) languages that extract information from XML documents and, in the case of XQuery and XSLT, lead to results that are again in XML form (see section 12.4 for an overview of these and related XML standards.)

A circle that is now forming, but hasn't yet been closed at the time of writing, introduces a particular world of programming into XML. As long as the involved program fragments stay small and remain tightly coupled to their specific application, not much more is needed. However, XPath and XQuery support user-definable functions. That suggests the emergence of XPath/XQuery function libraries. In XSLT, there is a further opportunity to factor matching patterns. The use of XPath/XQuery/XSLT to describe transformations performed by integration servers suggests that libraries of "reusable" query fragments, matching patterns, and functions are likely to emerge. The next step would be to establish an appropriate component concept. However, perhaps surprisingly, functional languages have had an historic lag in picking up component support, probably because the side-effect-free nature of purely applicative functions naturally eases composition. So, it may be a while before componentization hits the space of XML at this level.

At another level, XML web services are quickly evolving to establish grounds for a new component universe. Since XML web services are only about boundaries of systems and interaction between systems, they will not prescribe anything about how such components will be delineated or realized inside those systems. However, much like CORBA, there is an opportunity for a new level of integration and interoperation. The .NET Framework was designed to take advantage of this opportunity and J2EE has been augmented to support the web services standards. Though not about XML components in the literal sense, these efforts establish a space for XML-enabled and XML-composable components.

PART FIVE

Markets and components

This part, which is of a non-technical nature, closes the circle and links up with Part One. The technical essence of Part Four is briefly rehashed where necessary to derive market- and profession-oriented consequences. Chapter 26 develops arguments for the markets that are likely to develop around component software in the future. Chapter 27 presents a similar analysis for some important new professions and their job profiles. Finally, Chapter 28 addresses the seemingly paradoxical situation that software component development obviously costs and therefore needs to be amortized. People have the tendency not to pay for widely accessible information (and do not perceive software as "hard" products).

See Messerschmitt and Szyperski (2002) for a comprehensive discussion of the many issues surrounding the interaction of the software industry and its environment.

CHAPTER TWENTY-SIX

Gamut of markets

A variety of market segments is directly motivated by the emergence of software components, with segments both in product and in service areas. In particular, product markets focus on components themselves, component infrastructure (such as application servers) and componet-related tools (such as assembly tools). Service markets have a broader nature and range from per-component value adds, such as component certification (third-party quality assurance) or price/performance rankings, to the assembly of custom applications from components. Whereas software component products on their own may be difficult to market, a combination with services strengthens the offering. Service markets specialize on customer and domain specifics and therefore have a tendency to strongly increase the number of organizations active in the market at large, including the introduction of mediating itermediaries. The introduction of services thus improves the overall market momentum and accelerates diversification and customer reach. The following brief discussion of markets thus distinguishes component, component infrastructure, component tool, and component service markets.

26.1　Components

The obvious market is the one for components targeting horizontal or vertical domains. To be more precise, each of these domains is likely to create its own market, as competition across domains is not likely to be strong.

Marketing components to recover the cost of their development (and make a profit) is a challenging problem of its own. Whereas the infrastructure, tools, and services markets described in the following sections are fairly well understood, marketing of software components falls into unknown territory. There seems to be little that can be learned from traditional component markets in other engineering disciplines. Software components are too "soft" to have direct analogies to warehouses and distributor chains. Nevertheless, there are some successful companies that play the role of intermediaries so essential for functioning markets. Examples are ComponentSource and Flashline. For a detailed discussion, see Chapter 28.

26.2 Component platforms and infrastructure

The value of appropriate component platforms and infrastructure can exceed that of the used components. This is the case if individual components are sufficiently specialized that they tend to not find a market. In such a case it would seem that the value proposition of using components in the first place is in jeopardy. However, that is not so. As components can be recomposed and flexibly realigned after replacing, upgrading, or adding only a subset of components, the cost of keeping a solution current is reduced. The most common case for this scenario is components implementing business concepts that are used as part of enterprise applications.

The construction of components for such specialized applications can be too expensive to deliver on the recomposition argument. There are two ways to reduce the cost of component construction in such a case, both starting from the idea that a component can be made cheaper if its implementation focuses on the value added by that component. The first approach is to generate components from some form of "higher-level" specification, mixing in the implementation of standard "aspects," such as transaction or error handling. This is essentially using aspect-oriented programming to synthesize individual components (see section 21.1.4) and related products would fall into the component tools category discussed below. The second approach factors such standard implementations into a separate container or context (section 21.1.3).

There are many products conceivable in this category. The most successful at the time of writing are application and web servers. However, integration servers, database servers, management servers, and so on, all have the potential to create frameworks for contextual composition (that is, provide container services). For instance, database servers are beginning to support components where they used to support so-called stored procedures only.

By focusing on the component framework and underlying major server functionality, the marketing situation shifts from the marketing of vertical components to the marketing of horizontal infrastructure that enables cost-effective production of vertical components.

26.3 Tools

Software component development and use are far more demanding on developers than traditional software development was. It can therefore be expected that component technology will raise the level of expectations on supporting tools. Most of the traditional tools of the software engineer will continue to be useful. In addition, a considerable number of new tools will be needed.

26.3.1 Component design and implementation tools

Component design rests on the environmental specifications – usually given by a component framework and an underlying component (or object) model.

Ideally, component development should use rapid application development (RAD) methods to capture requirements quickly within a working component system. The same environment is used to prototype a component, within a characteristic environment, and implement the component.

Support for the construction of models (typically in UML) and supporting further metadata can help guide the component construction process. At a minimum, such models help in documenting an effort. In practically relevant cases – such as components representing relatively straightforward business concepts in the presence of evolved application servers (see section 26.2) – components can actually be generated from their models with little further input from developers. Where this approach succeeds, modeling and generator tools can take the marketing position of RAD tools.

26.3.2 Component testing tools

Testing of components is possibly the single most demanding aspect of component technology. By definition, components can only be tested in a few, hopefully representative, configurations. Systematic approaches to testing of components are needed, and intense tool support for this purpose is likely to be required.

Faced with the extreme difficulties of component testing, two strategies seem advisable. The first strategy is to avoid errors statically wherever possible. For example, a safe and expressive language can allow a compiler or analyzing tool to catch substantial errors statically. Even better, a carefully crafted language can rule out entire classes of errors. Prominent examples are languages that have no explicit notion of memory deallocation – dangling references and memory leaks are simply eliminated. More subtle examples are language-enforced access modes and visibility rules eliminating programmed side-effects that break encapsulation and, thus, invariants.

■ A rule of thumb is that most errors that can be caught using automated runtime debugging aids could be statically avoided, had a "better" language been chosen for the implementation.

The second strategy is to make sure that components are deployed in such a way that faults leave logged traces. In this way, a failure in a production component system can at least be traced.

26.3.3 Component assembly tools

Components are assembled by instantiating and connecting component instances and customizing component resources. While component instances at runtime may or may not correspond to visual entities, it is useful to assume that all component instances have a visual representation at assembly-time. It is then possible to use powerful document-centric builder tools to assemble components, even if the runtime environment is a server or batch one. JavaBeans is a component standard that explicitly distinguishes between assembly time and runtime and that allows component instances to look and behave differently during assembly-time and runtime.

An important aspect often overlooked by current "builder tools" is that assembly itself needs to be automated. Software assembly is different from hardware assembly in that it is not necessary to assemble individual instances repeatedly – the entire assembled product can instead be cloned. However, a different aspect of assembly processes also still holds for software assembly. If future versions of components become available, then it is important that the assembly process can be repeated – only modified where necessary to live with or take advantage of the new component versions.

26.3.4 Component system diagnosis and maintenance

Related to component testing, it is important that an entire component system in the field can be diagnosed. Diagnosis is tricky, as the system is likely to consist of components from many different and independent vendors. Either a diagnosis tool has to concentrate selectively on the contributions made by those components from a selected set of vendors or, preferably, a diagnosis standard should be established and component vendors should provide diagnosis components that can be configured into the diagnosis tools.

Once diagnosis is possible, maintenance follows. It may be necessary to replace components and their instances and resources in a running system. To make diagnosis and maintenance at all feasible, a component system needs to be architected with these requirements in mind. The CORBA system management common facility is an example in this direction. Diagnosis and maintenance would normally be performed remotely. As these tasks require special clearances, overall security policies need to consider them.

26.4   Professional services

The overall complexities of component-based software development and the varierty of skills required lend themselves to specialization and outsourcing opportunities. This section briefly covers some of these opportunities.

26.4.1 Component system and framework architects

As described in detail in the next chapter, the tasks of architecting component systems or component frameworks are extremely demanding. It is likely that most organizations will not develop the in-house expertise required to do so successfully. Independent architecture firms can concentrate the expertise and amortize it over projects for many customers.

Component system architects are likely to work with a few clients in a tight consultancy relationship. Component framework architects, on the other hand, may well aim at open markets.

26.4.2 Component assembly consultants

Component assembly is supposedly simple enough to re-enable the use of customized software even by small organizations. Obviously, this is relative. The more demanding components are, the less obvious it is which ones to select from a large palette of possibilities. Consultants specializing in the mere assembly of components can find a broad market. Some may go further and offer custom production of the "missing" components to create true custom solutions.

Categories such as COTS (commercial off the shelf) have been formed to indicate the nature of components (and other building blocks, such as entire servers) that target a broad market. Typically, such components cover a large percentage of the requirements of many, but tend not not meet all requirements of any individual customer. Also, COTS components today have a tendency to attract relatively short-lived support by their manufacturers (of, say, around five years). Assembly consultants can specialize in knowing the potential and limitations of such products and help gauge the risks and benefits.

26.4.3 Component configuration management

With complex remote diagnosis and maintenance mechanisms in place, these tasks are a good opportunity for outsourcing. Part of a management contract could be the monitoring of component markets for the arrival of more suitable components. Other parts could be the development of gradual migration plans and the integration of new components into existing systems.

A particularly daunting task is the migration from monolithic solutions to component-based ones. Too many assumptions can pass undocumented in a monolithic solution. Reverse engineering can answer some of the questions. The parallel operation of the old and a proposed new system over an extended period is often the only way to convince everyone involved that the new system is capable of taking over. A practical example is the use of COM to support system services from different generations simultaneously.

For the parallel operation of systems from different generations and the extraction and analysis of observed differences, substantial expertise is required. It may even be necessary to emulate older hardware or software that itself is no longer available. The relevant detailed information could well be a critical trade secret. Likewise, the successful transition can be of vital importance for an entire business.

26.4.4 **Component warehouses, marketing, and consulting**

A traditional aspect of components is the necessary mediation between component providers and component users. Component warehouses, distributors, and marketing and consultancy firms all have their place. However, with software components all activities are likely to be fully electronic, such as via the internet. It is not clear to what extent traditional component businesses find analogies in the software component markets. For a discussion of remaining and new functions, see Chapter 23.

Note that the internet scenario assumes that the legal and practical protection offered by physical packaging becomes unnecessary. Today, software is cast on physical media, burdened with piles of printed material, and the resulting "bricks" are shrink-wrapped.

26.4.5 **Component operators, web services, application service providers**

For expensive machinery, it has always been an interesting business model to outsource operations to a specialist. The same can hold for software in general and software components in particular. As discussed in Chapter 23, a component paired with a service provider forms a marketable service. Whether application service providers or web service providers, the idea is the same. The business model rests more on the provisioning service combined with availability and help desk services, to name but two, than on the technicalities of the component used. In a functioning market, the granularity of services offered by such service providers adjusts automatically to meet the demand, providing strong and interpretable feedback to the makers of software components.

CHAPTER TWENTY-SEVEN

New professions

This chapter is somewhat speculative in nature. It is not intended to present polished job profiles. Instead, the goal is to point out the variety and complexity of the tasks involved and suggest the creation of specialist areas. The following descriptions can be compared with traditional task descriptions, including those of system analysts and programmers. One of the most interesting phenomena that can be observed when performing such a comparison is the emphasis on independence in the component case.

Component technology does not make sense when it is addressed in a traditional top-down fashion. This needs to be reflected in the organizational structure. For example, while a component systems architect creates the foundations for a component framework architect to begin working, the two jobs are not in a traditional hierarchical order. It has to be expected that the two tasks be performed by independent organizations, mediated by market and standardization effects.

The independence of the various levels is emphasized further when realizing that a component can be made to function within multiple component frameworks. Likewise, a component framework can be made to function within multiple component systems. Component systems and component frameworks are likely candidates for (partial) standardization, whereas components are likely to remain "free" and bound only by the standardized frameworks on which they depend.

Independence leads to independent evolution and, necessarily, (technical) conflicts. There is no simple answer to this problem – weakly coordinated co-evolution in an industrial environment is probably the only way. However, an emphasis on architecture is crucial if independently developed interoperable components are to become reality.

27.1 Component system architect

The architecture of a component system is the single most important and, at the same time, by far the most demanding, aspect. Components can only function when embedded in a component framework. A component system typically consists of many component frameworks. Each framework needs to obtain enough resources and control to enable and, where possible, enforce a smooth interoperation of the components it integrates. Component frameworks are therefore at a much greater risk of mutual exclusion than are individual components. Correct interoperation of the component frameworks in a system is a prime objective of a component system architecture. A possible but not yet fully understood approach is to create system frameworks that integrate all component frameworks in a system.

The role of a component system architect would be to analyze system requirements, both of the existing systems and those that it is planned will be introduced. A main goal is to devise a system partitioning into component frameworks that combines interoperability of the frameworks with sufficient room for independent operation and evolution of the frameworks. For each of the component frameworks, the basis needs to be created for largely independent detailed work of a component framework architect.

A component system architect provides architecture for the architects – the architects of component frameworks. It is what city master planning is to the architects of individual buildings.

27.2   Component framework architect

A component framework accepts the plugging in of components. It facilitates the interoperation of these components and partially enforces their organized interaction. The rules by which components have to "play" to be acceptable for the framework need to be precise enough to allow largely independent creation and evolution of components.

A component framework architect needs to understand fully the horizontal or vertical domain that the framework in question should address. Both creation of new frameworks and evolution of established ones are required. Framework evolution has to respect two issues – preservation of compatibility with (most) existing components and preservation of interoperability rules established by (most) component systems using the framework.

A component framework is not just a design, but may itself contain substantial implementation parts. The framework implementation is the basis for the interoperation with other frameworks, rules of component interaction, and provision of component default behavior where applicable. Depending on the project size, separate programmers may be required to take the framework design and implement it.

For the component programmer, a component framework architect has to specify very precisely what the framework expects from and provides to a component. In the absence or impracticability of fully formal specifications of all aspects, it is particularly important to provide documents that help a component programmer form the right intuition about the concepts of the framework.

Component frameworks are complex and difficult to get "right." Iterative design of a component framework is unavoidable. It is likely that a framework design stabilizes only after different people in multiple projects have used the framework. It is difficult, but crucial, that the experience condensed in a successful framework design is properly documented.

27.3   Component developer

Components are the "leaves" of a component system. As such, they are the parts of greatest replaceability and cross-organizational exchange. Components do not have a bounded size. However, given that they form the units of configuration and assembly, it makes sense to concentrate on components with well-defined and bounded functionality.

A component developer takes component framework specifications and specific component requirements and develops, by means of analysis and design, these ideas into implementable components. Traditional factoring into teams may be required for very large components. However, normally, individual components remain in the bounds of what a single person can manage (backup strategies may still ask for teams, though).

27.4   Component assembler

Component systems with their frameworks and components do not perform any useful function unless customized to do so. The concept of traditional applications disappears with many component systems, being replaced, for example, by document-centric, data- or workflow-driven computing. Nevertheless, the majority of users will continue to look for "applications" – that is, solutions to concrete problems in their routine. Obviously, where a layperson's component assembly can yield a good solution, this will be done. Highly specialized niches will find workable solutions where current technology has fallen short of offering the required flexibility-per-dollar ratio.

As "end users" become component assemblers, the state-of-the-art rises. Ad hoc crafted solutions are acceptable where they solve a problem and where the problem and its solution do not form part of the core business of the organization. To maintain a competitive edge, a business needs to do better in its core areas. Professional experienced component assembly staff members fill this gap.

A component assembler (or composer) takes application requirements, selects appropriate components – and perhaps component frameworks – and assembles these. Component assembly may be largely automated by an available builder tool, or it may require substantial programming (or scripting) to provide the "glue." Which end of the scale a particular assembly task will end up at depends on the inherent complexity of the application domain and the number of sufficiently similar demands being met in the market. If, despite substantial complexity, the market is large enough, it is likely that components and builder tools that reduce the burden on the component assembler will be found.

The more individual the task, the more creativity and programming effort are required of the component assembler to create solutions based on components – and perhaps component frameworks – on the market. Free selection of component frameworks is not normally possible, however. Higher-level organizational requirements often prescribe the use of a specific component framework. This may be done to optimize interoperability, minimize training costs, or reduce overall project costs.

An important role of a component assembler is to provide feedback on the feasibility and practicability of currently used frameworks and components. Unless already discovered during analysis, it is to be expected that the component assembler makes the final decision as to whether or not a solution can be based on available components. If not, a new component would need to be programmed. The decision as to whether or not to pursue such individual component development efforts or loosen the requirements can have dramatic effects on the viability of the project and is, thus, left to management.

A component marketing paradox

Software, as its name suggests, is not a tangible product. In the literal sense, as the opposite of hardware, there is nothing physical or unique about a particular copy of a software artifact. Two copies of the same software artifact are indistinguishable.

When software is sold in bulky, shrink-wrapped boxes that contain thousands of pages of printed documentation and enormous piles of software on media, customers seem to get something for their money. If the same functionality and documentation are made accessible via electronic distribution channels, the true "softness" of the traded goods becomes obvious. Are people willing to pay for bits as they come in over the network link?

A significant trend in recent years has been the total collapse of access charges to the internet. Essentially, the internet is now increasingly available at low and flat access rates, independent of the actual access pattern. This has a dramatic consequence – the internet becomes so cheap that it will grow faster than ever before. The internet already threatens other carriers. Telephony and fax, video conferencing, distributed groupware – everything will find its place on the internet to make it the one and only total communication interconnection point.

Software distribution is bound to move from stores to virtual stores. The appeal of printed and neatly bound documentation will, for some time, continue to create a "physical" market. However, as devices become smaller, display technology improves, and browsing metaphors leave "thumbing of pages" behind, this may also change. (With the introduction of CDs, many believed traditional LPs would continue to hold their appeal. With the exception of DJs and a relatively small collectors' market, LPs have almost vanished.)

What would be the good of almost free internet access if the contents provided were expensive? Alternative vendors will always try to steal the show of established content providers, by making the same functionality available for less. If a component is useful to many or all, then its availability merely raises the standard for what is thought of as being state of the art. Everyone willing to remain competitive will have to get this component eventually. Early adopters may still be willing to pay and perhaps pay well. As the mainstream catches on, the market volume explodes, but the willingness to pay anything diminishes.

People have a tendency not to pay for information of common value. They are willing to pay, though, for services where they are obviously tailored to their needs. An attempt to charge for services, or soft products, that are mass marketed will fail in the absence of monopolies or cartels. The internet creates a worldwide market, bridging all nations and local markets. Its physical infrastructure is increasingly distributed and redundant. For horizontal markets, upholding of monopolies or cartels in this environment is difficult, if not impossible.

If customers do not want to pay for software components they download from the internet, how should the investment in producing the components be amortized? This is the central paradox of component marketing and its resolution is at the heart of success or failure of the software component approach. It is not likely that people will ever be willing to pay significant amounts for electronically acquired "generalware" – components of widespread usefulness. Other profit-generating models have thus to be evaluated by developers and distributors of such generally useful components. The diversity and usefulness of the entire component "market" are at stake.

28.1 Branding

The problem of a need to control quality and prices has been known for some time in most established commodity markets. How can vendors of bananas distinguish themselves from others? Are not all bananas equal? The answer is branding. Using focused marketing, a brand is carefully associated with hallmarks of quality, performance, affordability, and so on.

Establishing powerful brands will become important for software components as well. In a world in which access to many components will have to be inexpensive, it can become prohibitive to market individual components. Instead, users are encouraged to browse the catalogs carrying the "right" brand. Rather than component manufacturers, wholesalers, brokers, or other intermediate agents may well establish such brands.

An interesting effect of branding is the possible creation of cross-product brand loyalty. Successful examples are IBM's WebSphere and Microsoft's .NET brands. Both unite a broad collection of products of varying levels of interoperability and technical alignment. Weaker products under such a brand benefit from the market pull caused by their stronger peers under the same brand.

28.2 Pay per use

Brad Cox proposed models of pay per use (1990, 1996). The infrastructure should guarantee that every use of a component is tracked and billed. This is an obvious model, and support in the form of licensing services has been built into both COM and CORBA. Java so far lacks a licensing service.

On second thoughts, the pay-per-use approach is flawed. Software components are not necessarily at a level of granularity that makes any sense to end

users. If a bill lists zillions of uses of ridiculous numbers of components, then customers will (rightfully) object and the service will collapse. Transparency of cost is essential. For example, just by browsing through web pages, a user may receive and temporarily use an enormous number of applets (or ActiveX objects or...). Billing per use would be unacceptable unless the user were made aware of the cost before using an object. Normally, that would require prompting before entering a web page. This model works as long as it is used sparingly and only for services that are of obvious and immediate value to the customer. It can be expected that users will simply ignore services that announce billing – and they will rightly refuse to pay unannounced bills.

A property of component software that makes pay per use particularly inadequate is the concept of late composition. Anyone and even automated services can combine components to form a new whole. Sub-billing of the part components involved is out of the question as that would not be transparent. Licensing of subcomponents by the assembling organization will work only where the composition (assembly) is not delayed until the last moment. However, it is just this possibility of delaying assembly until a concrete request comes in that makes software components particularly flexible. A solution would be a billing hierarchy. As a result, the end user is billed only for the top-level components used directly, but the price will vary potentially from use to use as the subcomponent prices change. It is not clear whether customers would generally accept such a bazaar-like situation or not.

Pay per use has an advantage, however. If combined with a billing hierarchy to maintain billing transparency, income can be fairly distributed to all involved component vendors. Small component shops can exist even without massive marketing efforts. To some extent, this would be a developer's paradise. Although the above arguments make pay per use a not so obvious winner in the current component marketing strategy "wars," it should be noted that the required billing technology is at least almost ready.

Brad Cox proposes transitive payment contracts between components (1996). A component then can have a budget it has to live with – the maximum amount it is allowed to bill itself. Such a budget drives the selection of services from other components without divulging such hierarchical payments to the end user.

Smartcard systems can be used conveniently to authenticate the principal, who is the real user willing to pay. The same cards can also hold the electronic cash for direct debit, or the credit information for later collective billing. The problems of local tampering with endpoints (PCs) largely disappear with the introduction of pure network computing. A network computer (NC) does not function autonomously and all customization is reduced to "user profiles" kept in the network. On NCs, the network can perform accounting and billing in a highly reliable way. However, such NCs are effectively glorified terminals and do not serve the needs of rich client-side integration across multiple service providers. A different approach is to "harden" PCs. By introducing special hardware support, a PC can remain as flexible as it is and yet offer strong digital rights management (DRM). In such a system, hardware similar to a sealed smartcard protects a secret code unique to the particular PC. Protected contents are kept encrypted at almost all times except when needed for actual processing or presentation. All channels, in hardware and software, that see decrypted protected contents are themselves protected and require authorization based on a trust management scheme. (The management of rights is an interesting subproblem, but the XrML 2.0 rights management language is emerging as a standard in this space; www.xrml.org.)

Finally, service providers addressing end users may decide to accept flat fee subscriptions and deal with pay-per-use issues in internal agreements with component vendors. This model is particularly attractive where end users merely use NCs that cannot locally retain copies of components. However, it can be easily extended to cases where end users use full computers (PCs and other fully programmable and configurable devices such as palm-sized ones). The growing industry of application service providers (ASPs) focuses on the use of subscription models to provide continuously maintained and updated application-level services to end users via the network.

An interesting downside of pay per use has been proposed in an IDC white paper (Steel, 1996). It is that suppliers may have no interest in pay-per-use systems revealing the actual use profiles of the software they sell. The report claims that most companies currently have no clue how the software they have acquired is actually used – if at all. Pay-per-use systems offer an unparalleled degree of scrutiny in that components not used will not be requested and will not be paid for. The percentage of mostly unused components in a best-selling mainstream application will become obvious.

On second thoughts, however, it seems questionable that this observation would affect the bottom line of software vendors. It seems reasonable to assume that the pricing models are set to produce similar or better returns when compared to the traditional sale of shrink-wrapped software. If that is the case, then pay-per-use modes may lead to the actual installation and use of potentially fewer components, but should lead to comparable revenues. Competition can affect pricing in either case, but the number of components used (from a single vendor) only affects pricing to the degree that the vendor wishes to use value pricing and differentiation strategies, none of which are fundamentally different in a subscription/pay-per-use setting. (Any such observation needs to be taken with a grain of salt, as law and regulation can make a difference that varies from market to market and region to region.)

Changing the perspective of paying customers from a focus on a relatively small number of applications and suites to task-oriented services can also have the opposite effect – the number of components effectively used might go up as users discover more and more services they find useful for their various tasks. This would be quite closely related to the discovery of features over time as users explore complex office application suites.

28.3   Co-placement of advertisements

Instead of centering in on pay per use, it is instructive to compare the cost recovery methods used by other "soft" media. Print media reached the point a long time ago when the price tag at the local kiosk was lower than the actual production cost. "Free to air" television networks are even more extreme – as their name suggests, their services are free. In both cases, costs are recovered by advertising. Advertising has already become a major source of income on the web, although it seems that a plateau had been reached by early 2000.

Advertising ruins the quality of television offerings, but does so to a much lesser degree for print media. The reason is simple. Print media do not force the consumer into a sequential consumption mode. Content and advertisements compete for the reader's attention. Reading is a selective process. The same is true on the web – advertisements there are better compared to those in print media than to the irritating interceptions on free television. Furthermore, advertising on the web can be "subject-oriented" ("targeted" in marketing-speak). Unlike print media, web servers can attempt to build user profiles and make advertisements available in a more selective fashion. For example, the home page of an organization might display specific technical advertisements only to those users who, in their (provided or generated) profiles, indicate interest in technical matters. Although intelligent and targeted advertising is useful to both vendors and consumers, it collides with a major issue – privacy. The collection and use of user-related profile information is easily at odds with the right for privacy. An example of a well-balanced form of targeted marketing is the sponsored links on search engines such as Google (www.google.com). There is no need to build up deep consumer profiles as consumers indicate their interestes in the searches they perform. Sponsored links – if placed carefully – have a good chance of attracting customer attention. This phenomenon is similar to traditional advertising in the Yellow Pages.

There is a second-order component-marketing paradox when relying on returns from advertisements. Such advertisements obviously cannot advertise software components as their vendors would not normally be willing or able to pay for advertisements – after all, they rely on advertisements to generate income. Hence, to break a seemingly vicious circle, advertisements for "hard" products and individualized services are required. (As long as people are willing to pay high prices for carbonated, sugared, and colored water, or even just water, a steady income stream from advertisements can be guaranteed.) An interesting example of a service industry based on a freeware product developed around the Linux operating system. Consultants charge for installing and maintaining Linux systems, although Linux itself and all its documentation is available free of charge.

In the long run, it seems most likely that co-placement of advertisements will become only one of several means of generating revenue. An interesting extension of this model, integrating with other revenue-generating approaches, would link advertisements, information search and retrieval, and service discovery and provisioning. Once again, besides suitable pricing and billing infrastructures, it is protection of privacy and the intelligent integration of offerings that remains the biggest challenge in this area.

28.4 Leveraging on newly created markets

Creators and providers of a domain-specific component system architecture or component framework can create new markets if the initially available infrastructure and functionality has critical mass. The latter is required for initial sufficiently broad user acceptance.

The first company to introduce a component approach to a domain traditionally dominated by monolithic solutions will initially be able to capture a large fraction of the new but still small market. During market formation, clients will be willing to pay for the new infrastructure and the first components – the approach offers a competitive edge. As further vendors enter the new market, the situation gradually changes to the one of established component markets as described above.

Companies with highly specialized domain expertise are required to break the initial ice. However, the market startup effect that does allow for initial and substantial charges makes the effort worthwhile (Szyperski, 1997). Substantial initial capital is required to accumulate the critical mass before the new market can take off. The critical mass required is simple to estimate. The first successful component infrastructure must already come with sufficient quality components to provide an edge for early adopters.

The case must be convincing as an early adopter is likely to be willing to invest in the development of a few highly specialized components, but the bulk must already be there. As the new component approach has to compete with established monolithic software in the target market, the flexibility of component approaches needs to be fully leveraged. A good starting point is to analyze where current clients of the monolithic solutions compromise their internal business processes to live with the inflexible solutions. Only where such compromises can be expressed as costs that could be saved or productivity losses that could be removed will a more flexible approach based on component technology be competitive. Two important advantages of component technology that contribute to such savings are the reduction in time to market and the more flexible response to rapidly changing business conditions. Generally speaking, it is more important to adapt quickly than reduce costs.

One of the biggest success stories for component-based approaches in an area traditionally dominated by monolithic approaches has been contextual composition frameworks for transactional applications – MTS, EJB, COM+, J2EE, and CLR. The significant demand for line-of-business (LOB) applications, incentives for cutting costs, and substantial head start offered by these frameworks made the transition possible. Interestingly enough, significant markets for components have yet to develop in this area, although this might be a matter of time. In particular, such markets may unfold as the current efforts to standardize schemas and protocols around XML solidify.

28.5 Leverage of integrative forces

Even where direct competitiveness of a component approach over established monolithic approaches is hard to establish, introduction of component technology can be worthwhile. The benefits are the software engineering advantages of component technology. Solutions that are well modularized into components are easier to maintain, evolve, and refactor. Careful selection of component frameworks and component system architecture allows for the integration of previously separate business processes. With components from independent vendors, integration is an implicit outcome of the underlying approach. With monolithic solutions from independent vendors, integration is difficult to achieve unless an industry leader sets standards that at least serve as a lowest common denominator. This is not likely when attempting to integrate across different domains and organizations.

Thus, where the target market covers sufficiently large organizations with investments in several domains, a joint effort to introduce component technology-based integration across some of these domains could pay off. Initial investments are even larger than in the case of creating a component market for an individual domain. Formation of common interest groups is likely to be required. The market startup effect can again be expected to produce initial direct returns before a transition to an established market occurs.

A final note: in some cases, a component market will remain small and therefore never reach the "established market" effects. Then, the group of vendors and clients of components remains small, so the business remains a matter of mutual agreements rather than open markets. This is where small, highly specialized vendors are likely to blossom.

Epilogue

"Is this the end?"

The Doors

Unlike technologies, markets do have a tendency to function even when left unattended. Market forces do not automatically thrive on technical excellence. However, in a situation in which everything else is equal, technology can be the deciding competitive edge. Technological superiority of an approach needs to be established on a broad basis. It is difficult to evaluate all tradeoffs before a technology is put to use.

Software component technology, like all component technologies, can exist only in the combined "forcefields" of technology and markets. Understanding the technical factors, but also what is "good enough" to hit the markets, is important. Time to market is crucial – the quality of an approach cannot be measured on the basis of technical merit alone.

This book has presented an attempt at a unique merger of technology and market aspects driving component software. In an area evolving as quickly and dramatically as this, much had to be left unsaid. Where approaches come and go, fundamental problems and principles stay. Fundamental aspects are therefore at the heart of this book. To make such aspects accessible and meaningful, strong links to current approaches have also been drawn. It is the tension between what could be done and what can be done that leads to deeper insight – a tension that, in the area of component software, is not likely to be resolved soon.

Java versus C# versus Component Pascal

Despite the declared independence of components from programming languages (Component Liberation Act, 1997), components still need to be constructed somehow. Component construction itself can be performed using almost arbitrary programming languages, as long as the language and its implementation support the particular component standard's interface, type, and metadata conventions. These conventions usually include notions of object or interface references. However, as argued in Chapters 5–7, there are obligations left with the component implementer that may ask for proper language support. Issues of primary concern are performance, component safety, and component framework safety.

This appendix compares three of today's few component-oriented programming languages. One – Java – is very well known, while the other – Component Pascal – is less so, and the third, C#, arrived only recently. The first two languages evolved independently and have their roots in the two major language strands found today, which are C and Pascal respectively. (One might argue that Java really is rather more in line with the Pascal language family, inheriting many of its strengths from Oberon or Modula-3. The "C touch" of Java can indeed be seen as a clever camouflage.) C# incorporates many of the features of Java, a few of the features of Component Pascal, adds many interesting features of its own, and also corrects a few design mistakes found in most other languages. The following is a compact rehash of material discussed in more detail throughout this book.

The Component Pascal language report and further documents can be found on the web (www.oberon.ch) and there is also information on ports to JVM and CLR (www.plasrc.qut.edu.au).

Component Pascal and its more academic root, Oberon, rest on 15 years of experience – 35 years since the introduction of Pascal. The language has been used for a wide spectrum of tasks:

- low-level systems programming, including hard realtime programming – device drivers, embedded systems, realtime programming, garbage collectors, operating system kernels, interrupt handlers;

- complex graphical user interfaces, compound document systems (OLE-compliant on Windows; close to the original OpenDoc user interface guidelines on MacOS), the BlackBox component framework;
- high-level scripting.

Component Pascal can be implemented efficiently. For example, the entire BlackBox component developer, including the garbage collector, is implemented in Component Pascal. At the same time, Component Pascal is a safe language. A simple proof of concept is that Component Pascal can be compiled to Java bytecode (however, some improvements to the Java virtual machine would enable more efficient mappings). Component Pascal can be compiled also to CLR IL (and, with a few exceptions, can be mapped efficiently in this case). There are few languages that are sufficiently safe to enable compilation to Java bytecode or safe CLR IL. Another example is Ada 95, and the first "Ada 95 applets" appeared in early 1997. A further example is Jython – a full implementation of Python for the Java platform. A compilation to Java bytecode is not possible for languages in the C family, including C itself, C++, and Objective C. It is also impossible for most languages in the Pascal family, including Pascal itself, Object Pascal, and Modula-2. A compilation of these languages to CLR IL is possible, but only when including the unsafe IL subset.

Why is compilability to bytecode or IL relevant? Because the Java virtual machine's verifier and the CLR target compilers perform safety checks as part of the loading process that establish minimal safety properties of a loaded class. These checks redundantly recheck what compilers for Java and safe CLR languages check already. By doing so, these systems safeguard against bytecode or IL sequences that have been tampered with or aren't demonstrably safe. The above languages are all ruled out, because they cannot be mapped into the safe world of the Java virtual machine or the safe subset of CLR IL. Of course, crippled subsets of these languages could, but it is fair to say that such subsets really represent different languages. (Recall that Java is sometimes sold as a safe subset of C++.)

Statically established and, at load-time, enforced safety properties allow a component infrastructure to execute multiple components efficiently within the same protection domain (see Chapter 6).

The following comparison combines language-level features with features really provided by the underlying runtime infrastructure. In the case of Component Pascal and Java, there is no need to refer to these by separate names. In the case of C#, the CLR establishes its properties beyond C# or any other single language supported by the CLR. The comparison therefore, where useful, explicitly distinguishes C# and CLR.

Here are the areas where Component Pascal (CP), Java, and C#/CLR use essentially identical approaches:

- smallest unit of deployment (smallest component) – CP, compiled module; Java, compilation unit (part of a package)/class file; CLR, assembly;
- support for object-oriented programming – CP, Java, CLR, yes;
- support for type-safe separate compilation – CP, Java, and CLR, yes;
- implementation inheritance – CP, Java, and CLR, single;
- open packages – CP, open packages, called subsystems, supported by environment rather than language; Java, open package system in language; C#, open packages called namespaces at language level (at CLR level, namespaces are a mere convention);
- cross-class protection (replacement for "friend" mechanisms *à la* C++) – CP, module; Java, package-private mode; CLR: assembly-internal mode;
- runtime type system – CP, type test and type guard; Java, instanceof test and checked type cast; CLR, type test, null-returning checked type cast, exception-throwing checked type cast;
- metaprogramming – CP and Java, reflection library; CLR, extensible meta-attribution, reflection library, dynamic code generation library;
- basic types – CP, Java, and CLR, platform-independent, fixed ranges, Unicode; pointers, references: CP and Java, no C pointers, safe references only (called pointers in CP); CLR safe references and unsafe pointers (in contained unsafe code only);
- memory management – CP, Java, and CLR, no explicit destruction, fully garbage collected;
- I/O – CP, Java, and C#, libraries, no language-level features;
- interfacing with native platform – CP, yes, can directly interface with native APIs and DLLs; Java, yes via JNI, but needs wrapper classes; C#/CLR, yes, full interoperability with COM and full support of direct platform invocation;
- assertions – CP, simple assert statement that traps if a Boolean assertion does not hold, optional string message; Java (as of 1.4), assert statement throws an exception if a Boolean assertion does not hold, optional string message; C# (planned), assert statement;
- generics (parametric polymorphism) – CP, simple design (Roe and Szyperski, 1997), implementation planned in gpcp (Gough, 2001); Java (planned for 1.5); C# (planned; Kennedy and Syme, 2001);
- platform-independent "executables" – CP, encoded parse tree + native compiler on first load (although this was only implemented in the Gazelle project – Paznesh, 1997; there is also a CP compiler for the CLR that generates CIL); Java, bytecode + interpreter, optional native just-in-time compiler; CLR, common intermediate language (CIL) + native target compiler on install or load.

Here are areas where Component Pascal, Java, and C#/CLR differ:

- closed modules – CP, closed modules in language; Java, no closed modules (available since Java 1.1, outer classes could almost serve as closed modules, but the definition of "protected" still grants package- rather than module-level access to protected features and subclasses can change attribution from protected to public access); C#/CLR, closed modules in CLR (assemblies) with access protection support in C# (internal);
- expressiveness of protection system ("module safety") – CP, field access protection (no access, read-only, read/write), instantiation protection (not exported, abstract, module limited, public), caller encapsulation (not exported, override only, override or call, call), extension protection (not exported, not extensible, extensible); Java, field access protection (no access, read/write), instantiation protection (abstract, private, package, protected, public), caller encapsulation (private, package, protected, public), extension protection (private, final, extensible); C#/CLR, field access protection (no access, read-only, read/write), instantiation protection (abstract, private, internal, protected, public); caller encapsulation (private, internal, protected, public), extension protection (private, sealed, internal, public);
- runtime checks on integer arithmetic – CP and Java, division by zero check only, otherwise modulo semantics of overflowing computations (C style); C#/CLR, optionally either checked (Pascal style) or unchecked (C style), selectable at statement or compilation unit level.
- exception handling – CP, left to libraries; Java, language-level support for declaring new and throwable exceptions, throwing and catching exceptions, as well as "unchecked exceptions" against which only catch-all handlers offer protection, much the same as CP's library-based exception handling; C#/CLR, language support for declaring new, throwing, and catching exceptions, but not for declaration of throwable exceptions (all CLR exceptions are "unchecked" in the Java sense);
- multithreading and synchronization – CP, left to libraries; Java, language level plus libraries; C#, minimal language-level support (locking statement) plus libraries plus context infrastructure to custom build containers;
- interface inheritance – CP, not separate, multiple interfaces per object supported by COM-like design pattern ("record riders"); Java, separate and multiple, but folds methods with matching signatures into a single method; C#/CLR, separate and multiple, allows for separate implementation of methods, even if signatures match, across multiple interfaces on a class;
- circular imports – CP, illegal; Java, legal, arbitrarily across packages; C#, legal, arbitrarily among definitions within a module (a single compilation step – can compile any number of C# source files in a single

step), illegal across module boundaries and, thus, CLR assembly boundaries (an assembly contains one or more modules);

- statically allocated objects and arrays – CP, fully supported, safe, efficient; Java, not supported, non-basic types are always heap allocated; C#/CLR, fully supported (value types), safe, efficient, automatic boxing and unboxing to allow all types under type Object; C# supports both rectangular multidimensional arrays (such as CP) and jagged arrays (such as Java);
- procedural programming – CP, fully supported, including procedure types and variables; Java, partially supported, camouflaged under static classes, static attributes, and static methods; no support of procedure types or variables; interfaces with single methods in conjunction with anonymous inner classes, since Java 1.1, are more general, but also more heavyweight than procedure types and variables; C#/CLR, static classes/attributes/methods plus delegate types and variables (a CLR delegate is a "method pointer" that works on static and instance methods);
- explicit support for low-level programming – CP, fully supported, safely contained; Java, none (must exit to native code implemented in different language); C#/CLR, fully supported, safely contained;
- explicit support for interoperability – CP, some support for COM interop, safely contained; Java, none (via JNI, must exit to native code implemented in a different language), but library-level support for CORBA interop; C#/CLR, fully supported COM interop as well as platform invocations (DLL entry points), safely contained;
- full language and runtime system implementation using same language – CP, yes, everything implemented in CP; language-level strict and static separation of safe and unsafe modules; Java, no, needs to rely on "native" libraries, implemented using a different language (usually C or C++), although such libraries can be kept at a minimum; C#/CLR, possible, language-level static and runtime-level enforced strict separation of safe and unsafe code, current full CLR is implemented in C/C++/C#.

Component Pascal is a small language – much smaller than most other commercial languages, including Java and C#. Libraries handle the features left out in Component Pascal. Component Pascal is easy to teach and learn incrementally, whereas feature interaction in Java requires an almost complete understanding of the language before developing even small working examples. (For instance, the use of checked exceptions in the interfaces of basic input libraries requires the early introduction of exceptions and exception handling.) Component Pascal, Java, and C# code are about equally readable "in-the-large." The syntax for statements, typed declarations, and expressions differs significantly, following the Pascal and C heritage respectively. Java is somewhat smaller than C#, but C# provides support for concepts not available in Java, including value types and custom meta-attributes. C# also includes direct support for a connectable objects model based on properties, events, and delegates. The equivalent Java model is JavaBeans, but the Java language does not support it explicitly. Java and C#, but not Component Pascal, support the nesting of classes, interfaces, and (in the case of C#) other types inside classes. Only Java supports the nesting of classes inside expressions and only Java explicitly supports nested instances (instances of nested element classes).

Useful addresses and bibliography

Addresses and websites

The following non-exhaustive list of points of contact is meant to simplify the reader's task. No responsibility is accepted for completeness, correctness, or accuracy of the information provided.

Apple Computer, Inc. (Objective C, Mac OS X)

Mail: Microsoft Way, Redmond, WA 98053, USA
Tel: (+1) 425 882 8080; Fax (+1) 425 936 7329
Website: www.apple.com

Corinto (ontology-based component repositories)

Website: www.corinto.it

DMTF – Distributed Management Task Force

Mail: c/o MacKenzie Kesselring, Inc., 200 SW Market Street, Suite 450, Portland, OR 97201, USA
Tel: (+1) 503 416 2116; Fax: (+1) 503 225 0765
E-mail: dmtf-info@dmtf.org
Website: www.dmtf.org

ECMA – Standardizing Information and Communication Systems

Mail: 114 Rue du Rhône, CH-1204 Geneva, Switzerland
Website: www.ecma.ch

esmertec ag (JBed)

Mail: Lagerstrasse 14, CH-8600 Dübendorf, Switzerland
Tel: (+41) 1 823 8900; Fax: (+41) 1 823 8999
E-mail: info@esmertec.com
Website: www.esmertec.com

Forrester Research, Inc.

Mail: 400 Technology Square, Cambridge, MA 02139, USA
Tel: (+1) 617/613 6000; Fax: (+1) 617/613 5000
E-mail: forrester@forrester.com
Website: www.forrester.com

IBM (WebSphere, Visual Age, ComponentBroker)

Mail: 1133 Westchester Avenue, White Plains, NY 10604, USA
Tel: (+1) 800 426 4968
E-mail: askibm@vnet.ibm.com
Website: www.ibm.com   www.software.ibm.com   www.alphaworks.ibm.com

International Data Corporation (IDC)

Mail: 5 Speen Street, Framingham, MA 01701, USA
Tel: (+1) 508 872 8200
Website: www.idcresearch.com

IONA (Orbix)

Mail: The IONA Building, Shelbourne Road, Ballsbridge, Dublin 4, Ireland
Tel: (+353) 1 637 2000; Fax: (+353) 1 637 2888
E-mail: info@iona.com
Website: www.iona.com

Meta Group, Inc.

Mail: 208 Harbor Drive, PO Box 120061, Stamford, CT 06912 0061, USA
Tel: (+1) 203 973 6700; Fax: (+1) 203 359 8066
Website: www.metagroup.com

Microsoft Corporation (COM, DCOM, ActiveX, OLE, ASP, CLR, .NET)

Mail: Civica Office Bilding, 205 108th Avenue, North East, Suite 400,
Bellevue, WA 98004, USA
Tel: (+1) 425 705 1900; Fax: (+1) 425 936 7329
Website: www.microsoft.com   www.microsoft.com/com/
www.microsoft. com/net/   www.gotdotnet.com

OASIS – Organization for the Advancement of Structured Information Standards

Mail: PO Box 455, Billerica, MA 01821, USA
Tel. (+1) 978 667 5115; Fax : (+1) 978 667 5114
E-mail: info@oasis-open.org
Website: www.oasis-open.org

Oberon microsystems, Inc. (Component Pascal, BlackBox)

Mail: Technoparkstrasse 1, CH-8005 Zurich, Switzerland
Tel: (+41) 1 445 1751; Fax: (+41) 1 445 1752
E-mail: info@oberon.ch
Website: www.oberon.ch

Object Management Group, Inc. (OMA, CORBA, IIOP, CCM)

Mail: 250 First Avenue, Needham, MA 02494, USA
Tel: (+1) 781 444 0404; Fax: (+1) 781 4444 0320
E-mail: info@omg.org
Website: www.omg.org

OPC Foundation (OLE for process control)

Mail: 16101 North 82nd Street, Suite 3B, Scottsdale, AZ 85260 1830, USA
Tel: (+1) 480 483 6644; Fax: (+1) 480 483 702
E-mail: mj.bryant@mindspring.com
Website: www.opcfoundation.org

Open Applications Group, Inc. (business transaction APIs)

Mail: 1950 Spectrum Circle, Suite 400, Marietta, GA 30067, USA
Tel: (+1) 770 980 3418; Fax: (+1) 770 234 6036
E-mail: info@openapplications.org
Website: www.openapplications.org

The Open Group (x/Open, OSF)

Mail: 298 Montvale Avenue, Woburn, MA 01801, USA
Tel: (+1) 781 376 8200; Fax: (+1) 781 376 9358
Web: www.opengroup.org

Ovum, Inc.

Mail: 301 Edgewater Drive, Suite 220, Wakefield, MA 01880, USA
Tel: (+1) 781 246 3773
E-mail: webinfo@ovum.com
Website: www.ovum.com

Patricia Seybold Group

Mail: 85 Devonshire Street, 5th Floor, Boston, MA 02109-3504, USA
Tel: (+1) 617 742 5200; Fax: (+1) 617 742 1028
E-mail: feedback@psgroup.com
Website: www.psgroup.com

SAP AG (R/3 with components via COM)

Mail: SAP AG, Neurottstrasse 16, 69190 Walldorf, Germany
Tel: (+49) 6227 7 47474; Fax: (+49) 6227 7 57575
Website: www.sap.com

Software AG (EntireX)

Mail: Uhlandstrasse 12, 64297 Darmstadt, Germany
Tel: (+49) 6151 920; Fax: (+49) 6151 92 1191
E-mail: webinfo@softwareag.com
Website: www.softwareag.com

Software Engineering Institute (software architecture)

Mail: Carnegie Mellon University, Pittsburgh, PA 15213 3890, USA
Tel: (+1) 412 268 5800; Fax: (+1) 412 268 5758
E-mail: customer-relations@sei.cmu.edu
Websites: www.sei.cmu.edu   www.sei.cmu.edu/ata/

Strategic Focus

Mail: 500 East Calaveras Boulevard, #321, Milpitas, CA 95035, USA
Tel: (+1) 408 942 1500; Fax: (+1) 408 262 1786
E-mail: jay@strategicfocus.com
Website: www.strategicfocus.com

Sun (Java, JavaBeans, Enterprise JavaBeans, J2EE, ONE)

Mail: Sun Microsystems, Inc., 4150 Network Circle, Santa Clara, CA 95054, USA
Tel: (+1) 650 960 1300
Website: java.sun.com java.sun.com/beans java.sun.com/j2se/ java.sun.com/j2ee/

Books

Below is a non-exhaustive list of books that complement the material presented in this book. The full bibliographical details can be found in the References section.

Grady Booch, *Object-Oriented Analysis and Design* (Booch, 1994)

> Classic reading. Before the arrival of today's component technology.

Don Box, *Essential COM* (Box, 1998)

> Practical programming of components implemented in C^{++} and utilizing COM.

Kraig Brockschmidt, *Inside OLE* (Brockschmidt, 1995).

> Thorough and in-depth coverage of OLE and COM just before DCOM.

David Chappell, *Understanding ActiveX and OLE – A Guide for Developers & Managers* (Chappel, 1996).

> For those looking for overall understanding rather than endless detail, this is the best current account of Microsoft's COM-based technologies with just enough technical detail to enable a thorough understanding of all essential aspects.

Adam Denning, *ActiveX Controls Inside Out* (Denning, 1997)

> Standard text on ActiveX control programming.

Erich Gamma, Richard Helm, Ralph Johnson, John Vlissides, *Design Patterns: Elements of Reusable Object-Oriented Software* (Gamma *et al.*, 1995).

> A very well-written and presented catalog of fundamental design patterns for object-oriented programming. Also an excellent introduction to the subject of patterns in programming.

Adele Goldberg and Kenneth S. Rubin, *Succeeding with Objects: Design Frameworks for Project Management* (Goldberg and Rubin, 1995).

> A high-level introduction to all aspects of object-oriented software development. Targeted at project managers, this book combines technically shallow (but informative) material with the process and market underpinning required to facilitate managerial decision making. Also a rich source of case studies and quantitative breakdowns.

Richard Monson-Haefel, *Enterprise JavaBeans*, 3rd edition (Monson-Haefel, 2001).

> Excellent overview, technical introduction, and development guidelines. The third edition covers EJB 1.1 and EJB 2.0 in a comparative style.

Oscar Nierstrasz and Dennis Tsichritzis (eds), *Object-Oriented Software Composition* (Nierstrasz and Tsichritzis, 1995).

> A collection of papers.

David S. Platt, *Understanding COM+* (Platt, 1999).

> A high-level overview of the COM+ architecture.

Jeffery Richter, *Applied Microsoft .NET Framework Programming* (Richter, 2002).

> An in-depth and comprehensive description of how to use the .NET Framework most effectively.

Dale Rogerson, *Inside COM* (Rogerson, 1997).

> An excellent introduction to COM programming. For the beginning developer.

Kennard Scribner, *Understanding SOAP: Simple Object Access Protocol* (Scribner, 2000).

> A description of the SOAP standard and its use in the context of COM, effectively replacing DCOM to achieve scalability and interoperability. Also contains a description of the Microsoft BizTalk initiative.

Jon Siegel, *CORBA 3: Fundamentals and Programming* (Siegel, 2000).

> A comprehensive and readable overview of all of CORBA 3, the OMA, services, facilities, domain efforts, and the CORBA Component Model. Technical details are almost completely elided, even at a level such as listing the interface names that make up particular services. However, much of the rationale is provided, explaining the origins of and forces behind the CORBA 3 constellation.

Brian E. Travis, *XML and SOAP Programming for BizTalk Servers* (Travis, 2000).

> Good introduction to XML, SOAP, and the Microsoft BizTalk initiative.

Mark Wutka, *Special Edition: Using Java 2 Enterprise Edition* (Wutka, 2001).

> Excellent and detailed coverage of all aspects of J2EE and related material, such as SQL and XML.

References and further reading

This list contains the bibliographical details of all the publications referred to in this book. Most of the references point to articles of interest to those readers with the academic nerve and patience to follow up on some of the loose ends and unresolved problems mentioned in this book.

(OOPSLA is the ACM Conference on Object-Oriented Programming Systems, Languages, and Applications. Its proceedings appear as issues of *ACM SIGPLAN Notices* and, unless stated otherwise, are jointly published by ACM Press, New York, NY, and Addison-Wesley, Reading, MA. ECOOP is the European Conference on Object-Oriented Programming. IETF is the Internet Engineering Task Force. LNCS is the Lecture Notes in Computer Science series, published by Springer-Verlag, Berlin. ISO is the International Organization for Standardization. OMG is the Object Management Group. W3C is the World Wide Web Consortium.)

Abadi, M., and Cardelli, L. (1996) *A Theory of Objects.* Springer-Verlag, Berlin.

Abelson, H., Dybvig, R. K., Haynes, C. T., Rozas G. J., Adams IV, N. I., Friedman D. P., Kohlbecker E., Steele Jr, G. L., Bartley, D. H., Halstead, R., Oxley, D., Sussman, G. J., Brooks, G., Hanson, C., Pitman, K. M., and Wand, M. (1998) *The Revised(5) Report on the Algorithmic Language Scheme.* (Kelsey, R., Clinger, W. and Rees, J., eds), MIT, Boston, Mass. (www.scheme.org)

Accetta, M., Baron, R., Bolosky, W., Golub, D., Rashid, R., Tevanlan, A., and Young, M. (1986) Mach: a new kernel foundation for UNIX development. *Proceedings, Summer USENIX Conference,* Atlanta, Georgia, July.

Acly, E. (1999) *Middleware and Businessware: 1999 Worldwide Markets and Trends,* Doc No 19164, June, International Data Corporation (IDC), Framingham, MA.

Agha, G., and Hewitt, C. (1987) Actors: a conceptual foundation for concurrent object-oriented programming. In Shriver, B., and Wegner, P. (eds), *Research Directions in Object-Oriented Programming,* pp. 49–74. MIT Press, Cambridge, MA.

Aksit, M., Wakita, K., Bosch, J., Bergmans, L., and Yonezawa, A. (1994) Abstracting object interactions using composition filters. In Guerraoui, R., Nierstrasz, O., and Riveill, M. (eds.) *Proceedings, ECOOP '93 Workshop on Object-Based Distributed Programming, LNCS* 791, pp. 152–184.

Aldrich, J., Chambers, C., and Notkin, D. (2002) ArchJava: Connecting Software Architecture to Implementation. *Proceedings, ICSE 2002.* IEEE Computer Society, Los Alamitos, CA.

Alexander, C., Ishikawa, S., Silverstein, M., Jacobson, M., Fiksdahl-King, I., and Angel, S. (1977) *A Pattern Language: Towns, Buildings, Construction.* Oxford University Press, Oxford, England.

Allen, P. (2000) *Realizing e-Business with Components,* Component Software Series, Addison-Wesley, Harlow, England.

Allen, P., and Frost, S. (2001) Planning team roles for CBD. In (Heinemann, G. T., and Councill W.T., 2001) pp. 113–129.

Almeida, P. S. (1997) Balloon Types: controlling sharing of state in data types. In Aksit, M., and Matsuoka, S. (eds.) *Proceedings, ECOOP '97, LNCS* 1241, pp. 32–59.

America, P. (1991) Designing an object-oriented programming language with behavioral subtyping. In de Bakker, J. W., de Roever, W. P., and Rozenberg, G. (eds) *Foundations of Object-Oriented Languages*, REX School/Workshop, Noordwijkerhout, The Netherlands. *LNCS* 489, pp. 60–90.

Anderson, B., Shaw, M., Best, L., and Beck, K. (1993) Software architecture: the next step for object technology (panel). *Proceedings, OOPSLA '93*, ACM SIGPLAN Notices **28**(10) 356–359.

Atkinson, C., Bayer, J., Bunse, C., Kamsties, E., Laitenberger, O., Laqua, R., Muthig, D., Paech, B., Wust, J., and Zettel, J. (2001) *Component-Based Product Line Engineering with UML*. Addison-Wesley, Reading, MA.

Apple Computer (1992) *Dylan – An Object-Oriented Dynamic Language*. Apple Computer Eastern Research and Technology Center, Cambridge.

Apple Computer (2000) *Inside Cocoa: Object-Oriented Programming and the Objective-C Language*. Apple Computer, Cupertino, CA. (developer.apple.com/techpubs/macosx/Cocoa/ObjectiveC/index.html).

Arnold, K., and Gosling, J. (1996) *The Java Programming Language*, Addison-Wesley, Reading, MA.

Arnold, K., O'Sullivan, B., Scheifler, R., Waldo, J., and Woolrath, A. (1999) *The Jini Specification*. Addison-Wesley, Reading, MA.

Astudillo, H. (1996) Reorganizing split objects. *Proceedings, OOPSLA '96*, ACM SIGPLAN Notices **31**(10), 138–149.

Back, R. J. R., and Kurki-Suonio, R. (1988) Distributed co-operation with action systems. *ACM Transactions on Program Languages and Systems (TOPLAS)*, **10**, 513–554.

Bardou, D., and Dony, C. (1996) Split objects: a disciplined use of delegation within objects. *Proceedings, OOPSLA '96*, ACM SIGPLAN Notices **31**(10) 122–137.

Bass, L., Clements, P., and Kazman, R. (1998) *Software Architecture in Practice*. Addison-Wesley, Reading, MA.

Batory, D., and O'Malley, S. (1992) The design and implementation of hierarchical software systems with reusable components. *IEEE Transactions on Software Engineering and Methodology (TOSEM)* **1**(4) 355–398.

Berry, G., and Gonthier, G. (1992) The Estrel programming language: design, semantics, and implementation. *Science of Computer Programming*, **19**(2) 87–152.

Biggerstaff, T. J. (1998) A Perspective of Generative Reuse. *Annals of Software Engineering* **5** pp. 169–226, Baltzer Science Publishers, AE Bussum, The Netherlands.

Birkhoff, G. (1940) *Lattice Theory*. American Mathematical Society.

Birman, K. P. (1985) Replication and fault-tolerance in the ISIS system. *Proceedings, 10th ACM Symposium on Operating System Principles (SOSP). ACM Operating System Review*, **19**(5), 79–86.

Birrel, A. D., and Nelson, B. J. (1984) Implementing remote procedure calls. *ACM Transactions on Computer Systems (TOCS)*, **2**(1), 39–59.

Birrel, A., Evers, D., Nelson, G., Owicki, S., and Wobber, E. (1993) Distributed garbage collection for network objects. *Technical Report* 116, Compaq Systems Research Center, Palo Alto.

Birrel, A., Nelson, G., and Owicki, S. (1994) Network objects. *Technical Report* 115. Compaq Systems Research Center, Palo Alto.

Blackman, K. R. (1998) IMS celebrates thirty years as an IBM product. Technical Note. *IBM System Journal* **37**(4).

Blaschek, G. (1994) *Object-Oriented Programming with Prototypes*. Springer-Verlag, Berlin.

Bokowski, B., and Vitek, J. (1999) Confined Types. *Proceedings, OOPSLA '99*. ACM SIGPLAN Notices **34**(10) 82–96.

Boehm, B. (1981) *Software Engineering Economics*. Prentice Hall, Englewood Cliffs, NJ.

Boehm, B., and Sullivan, K. (2000) Software economics: a roadmap. In Finkelstein, A. (ed.) *The Future of Software Engineering*, ACM Press, New York, pp. 319–44.

Boling, D. (2001) *Programming Microsoft Windows CE (2nd edn)*. Microsoft Press, Redmond, WA.

Booch, G. (1987) *Software Components with Ada: Structures, Tools, and Subsystems*. Benjamin-Cummings, Redwood City, CA.

Booch, G. (1994) *Object-Oriented Analysis and Design*, 2nd edn. Benjamin-Cummings, Redwood City, CA.

Bosch, J. (1996) Language Support for Design Patterns. *Proceedings, TOOLS Europe '96*. Prentice Hall, Englewood Cliffs, NJ.

Box, D. (1998) *Essential COM*. Addison-Wesley, Reading, MA.

Bracha, G., and Cook, W. (1990) Mixin-based inheritance. In Meyrowitz, N. (ed.) *Proceedings, OOPSLA/ECOOP '90*, ACM SIGPLAN Notices **25**(10) 303–311.

Bracha, G., and Griswold, D. (1993) Strongtalk: typechecking Smalltalk in a production environment. *Proceedings, OOPSLA '93*, ACM SIGPLAN Notices **28**(10) 215–230.

Bracha, G., Odersky, M., Stoutamire, D., and Wadler, P. (1998) Making the future safe for the past: Adding genericity to the Java programming language. *Proceedings, OOPSLA '98*. ACM SIGPLAN Notices **33**(10) 183–200.

Brockschmidt, K. (1995) *Inside OLE*, 2nd edn. Microsoft Press, Redmond, WA.

Brodie, L. (1984) *Thinking FORTH*. Prentice Hall, Englewood Cliffs, NJ.

Brodie, M. L. (1996) Putting objects to work on a massive scale. *Proceedings, 9th International Symposium on Methodologies for Intelligent Systems* (ISMIS), Zakopane, Poland, *LNCS* 1079, pp. 1–18.

Brodie, M. L., and Stonebreaker, M. (1995) *Migrating Legacy Systems: Gateways, Interfaces, and the Incremental Approach*. Morgan Kaufmann Publishers, Palo Alto, CA.

Brookshier, D., Govoni, D., Krishnan, N., Soto, J. C. (2002) *JXTA: Java P2P Programming*. SAMS Publishing, Indianapolis, IN.

Brown, A. W. (ed.) (1996) *Component-based Software Engineering: Selected Papers from the Software Engineering Institute.* IEEE Computer Society Press, Los Alamitos, CA.

Brown, C. L. (1994) NATO standard for the development of reusable software components, three documents, Public Ada Library (wuarchive.wustl.edu/languages/ada/docs/nato_ru/).

Brown, K., and Whitenack, B. (1995) *A Pattern Language for Relational Databases and Smalltalk.* www.ksc.com/article2.htm.

Broy, M., and Stølen, K. (2001) *Specification and Development of Interactive Systems – Focus on Streams, Interfaces, and Refinement,* Springer-Verlag, Berlin.

Bruce, K. B., Fiech, A., and Petersen, L. (1997) Subtyping is not a good match for object-oriented languages. *Proceedings, ECOOP '97, LNCS* 1241, pp. 104–127.

Büchi, M., and Weck, W. (1997) A plea for graybox components. Workshop on Foundations of Component-Based Systems, Zürich. *Technical Report No. 122,* Turku Centre for Computer Science, Turku, Finland.

Büchi, M., and Weck, W. (1998) Compound Types for Java. *Proceedings, OOPSLA '98.* ACM SIGPLAN Notices **33**(10) 362–373.

Büchi, M., and Weck, W. (1999) The Greybox Approach: When Blackbox Specifications Hide Too Much. (Revised) *Technical Report No. 297a,* Turku Centre for Computer Science, Turku, Finland.

Buschmann, F., Meunier, R., Rohnert, H., Sommerlad, P., and Stal, M. (1996) *Pattern-Oriented Software Architecture: A System of Patterns,* John Wiley & Sons, New York.

Campagnoni F. R. (1995) IBM's System Object Model, *Dr. Dobbs Journal,* pp. 24, Special Report, Winter 1994/95

Cardelli, L. (1989) Typeful programming. *Technical Report* 45, Compaq Systems Research Center, Palo Alto.

Cardelli, L. (1994) Obliq – A language with distributed scope. *Technical Report* 122, Compaq Systems Research Center, Palo Alto.

Cardelli, L. (1997) Program fragments, linking, and modularization. *Proceedings, 24th ACM SIGPLAN-SIGACT Symposium on Principles of Programming Languages (POPL),* pp. 266–277 (also available as *Technical Report* 144, Compaq Systems Research Center, Palo Alto).

Carriero, N., and Gelernter, D. (1988) How to Write Parallel Programs: A Guide to the Perplexed. *Technical Report* 628, Department of Computer Science, Yale University, New Haven, CT.

Cartwright, R., and Steele Jr, G. L. (1998) Compatible genericity with runtime types for the Java programming language. *Proceedings, OOPSLA '98.* ACM SIGPLAN Notices **33**(10) 201–215.

Casais, E., Taivalsaari, A., and Trauter, R. (organizers) (1996) *Workshop on Object-Oriented Software Evolution and Reengineering* at OOPSLA '96 (www.nokia.com/oopsla96ws18/).

Chandy, K. M., and Misra, J. (1988) *Parallel Program Design – A Foundation.* Addison-Wesley, Reading, MA.

Chappell, D. (1996) *Understanding ActiveX and OLE – A Guide for Developers & Managers.* Microsoft Press, Redmond, WA.

Chappel, D. (1997) The next wave: component software enters the mainstream. Chappel & Associates, Minneapolis, MN
(www.rational.com/support/techpapers/nextwave/index.html).

Chappel, D. (1998) COM+: the future of Microsoft's Component Object Model. *Notes on Information Technology,* November, Patricia Seybold Group, Boston, MA.

Cheeseman, J., and Daniels, J. (2000) *UML Components: A simple process for specifying Component-Based Software.* Component Software Series, Addison-Wesley, Harlow, UK.

Cheung, D. (1996) ATM software analysis and design. *Dr Dobb's Journal* #252, **21**(10) 70–76.

Clark, D. D. (1985) Structuring a system using upcalls. *Proceedings, 10th ACM Symposium on Operating System Principles (SOSP). ACM Operating System Review* **19**(5) 171–180.

Coleman, D., Arnold, P., Bodoff, S., Dollin, C., Gilchrist, H. (1993) *Object-Oriented Development: The Fusion Method.* Prentice Hall, Englewood Cliffs, NJ.

Coplien, J. O., Hoffman, D., and Weiss, D. (1998) Commonality and variability in software engineering. *IEEE Software* **15**(6) 37–45.

Coplien, J. O., and Schmidt, D. C. (eds) (1995) *Pattern Languages of Program Design.* Addison-Wesley, Reading, MA.

Cox, B. J. (1990) Planning the software industrial revolution. *IEEE Software* 7(6).

Cox, B. J. (1996) *Superdistribution: Objects as Property on the Electronic Frontier.* Addison-Wesley, Reading, MA.

Crelier, R. (1994) *Separate Compilation and Module Extension,* PhD Thesis No. 10650, Swiss Federal Institute of Technology Zurich.

Curbera, F., Weerawarana, S., and Duftler, M. J. (2000) On Component Composition Languages. *Proceedings, 5th International Workshop on Component-Oriented Programming* (WCOP 2000), with ECOOP 2000.
(www.ipd.hk-r.se/bosch/WCOP2000/submissions/Weerawarana.pdf).

Cutler, D. N. (1993) *Inside Windows NT.* Microsoft Press, Redmond, WA.

Czarnecki, K., and Eisenecker, U. (2000) *Generative Programming: Methods, Tools, and Applications,* Addison-Wesley, Boston, MA.

Dahl, O.-J., and Nygaard, K. (1970) *Simula-67 Common Base Language,* Publication S-22, Norwegian Computing Centre, Oslo 1970, 1972, 1984; current version: *Data Processing – Programming Languages – SIMULA,* Swedish Standard SS.63.61.14, SIS.

DeMichiel, L. G., and Gabriel, R. P. (1987) The Common Lisp Object System: an overview. In Béziwin, J., *et al.* (eds) *Proceedings, ECOOP '87, LNCS* 276, pp. 151–170.

DePalma, D. A., Dolberg, S., Mavretic, M., and Jonson, J. (1996) Objects on the net. *Software Strategy Report.* Forrester Research, Inc., Cambridge, MA.

DeRemer, F., and Kron, H. (1976) Programming-in-the-large versus programming-in-the-small. *IEEE Transactions on Software Engineering* 2(2) 80–87, June.

De Volder, K., and D'Hondt, T. (1999) Aspect-Oriented Logic Meta Programming. *Proceedings, 2nd International Conference on Meta-Level Architectures and Reflection (Reflection '99). LNCS* 1616, pp. 250–272.

Denning, A. (1997) *ActiveX Controls Inside Out – Harness the power of ActiveX controls*, 2nd edn, Microsoft Press, Redmond, Washington.

Deutsch, P. (1989) Design reuse and frameworks in the Smalltalk-80 system. In Biggerstaff, T. J., and Perlis, A. J. (eds) *Software Reusability*, Vol. 2. ACM Press, New York.

Dijkstra, E. W. (1968) The structure of the THE multiprogramming system. *Communications of the ACM* 11(5) 341–346.

Dijkstra, E. W. (1972) *Notes on Structured Programming*. Academic Press, London.

Dijkstra, E. W. (1976) *A Discipline of Programming*. Prentice Hall, Englewood Cliffs, NJ.

Dodds, L. (2001) Intuition and binary XML. O'Reilly's xml.com, April. (www.xml.com/pub/a/2001/04/18/binaryXML.html)

Dony, C., Malenfant, J., and Cointe, P. (1992) Prototype-based languages: From a new taxonomy to constructive proposals and their validation, *Proceedings, OOPSLA '92*, ACM SIGPLAN Notices 27(10) 201–217.

D'Souza, D. F., and Wills, A. C. (1999) *Objects, Components, and Frameworks – The Catalysis Approach*, Addison-Wesley, Reading, MA.

Dutoit, A., Levy, S., Cunningham, D., and Patrick, R. (1996) The Basic object system: supporting a spectrum from prototypes to hardened code. *Proceedings, OOPSLA '96, ACM SIGPLAN Notices* 31(10) 104–121.

Dyer, M. (1992) *The Cleanroom Approach to Quality Software Development*, John Wiley & Sons, New York.

Eichner, B., Kamber, D., and Murer, S. (1997) CORBA: Principles and practical experiences. *Informatik/Informatique*, February.

ebXML (2001) ebXML Requirements Specification (Version 1.06 6). OASIS and UN/CEFACT. (www.ebxml.org/specs/ebREQ.pdf)

ECMA (2001a) *ECMA-334: C# (C sharp) Language Specification*. ECMA, Geneva, Switzerland. (www.ecma.ch/ecma1/STAND/ecma-334.htm)

ECMA (2001b) *ECMA-335: Common Language Infrastructure*. ECMA, Geneva, Switzerland. (www.ecma.ch/ecma1/STAND/ecma-335.htm) Additional informational material in ECMA Technical Report TR/84. (www.ecma.ch/ecma1/TECHREP/E-tr-084.htm)

Edwards, S. H. (1996) Representation inheritance: a safe form of "whitebox" code inheritance, *Proceedings, 4th International Conference on Software Reuse*, 195–204, IEEE Computer Society Press. Also in: *IEEE Transactions on Software Engineering* 23(2) 83–92, 1997.

Ellis, A., and Stroustrup, B. (1994) *The Annotated C++ Reference Manual* (corrected reprint). Addison-Wesley, Reading, MA.

FAMOOS Consortium (1996) *Framework-based Approach for Mastering Object-Oriented Software Evolution*, ESPRIT Project 21975, www.sema.es/projects/FAMOOS/.

Fayad, M. (2002) How to deal with software stability. *Comm. ACM* **45**(4) 109–112.

Fenton, N., Pfleger, S. L., Glass, R. (1974) Science and substance: a challenge to software engineers. *IEEE Software*, July, pp. 86–95.

Findler, R. B., and Felleisen, M. (2001) Contract soundness for object-oriented languages. *Proceedings, OOPSLA 2001*, ACM SIGPLAN Notices **36**(11) 1–15.

Flatt, M., and Felleisen, M. (1998) Units: Cool modules for HOT languages. *Proceedings, ACM Conference on Programming Language Design and Implementation (PLDI '98)*. ACM SIGPLAN Notices **33**(5) 236–248.

Forman, I. R., Conner, M. H., Danforth, S. H., and Raper, L. K. (1995) Release-to-release binary compatibility in SOM. *Proceedings, OOPSLA '95, ACM SIGPLAN Notices* **30**(10) 426–438.

Fowler, M. (1999) *Refactoring: Improving the Design of Existing Code*. Addison-Wesley, Reading, MA.

Franz, M. (1994) *Code-Generation On-the-Fly: A Key to Portable Software*, PhD thesis, ETH Zurich, Verlag der Fachvereine, Zurich.

Frieder, O., and Segal, M. E. (1991) On dynamically updating a computer program: from concept to prototype. *Journal on Systems Software* **14**, 111–128.

Furber, S. (1996) *ARM System Architecture*. Addison-Wesley, Reading, MA.

Gabriel, R. P., White, J. L., and Bobrow, D. G. (1991) CLOS: integrating object-oriented and functional programming. *Communications of the ACM* **34**, 942–960.

Gamma, E. (1992) *Object-Oriented Software Development based on ET++: Design Patterns, Class Library, Tools* (in German). Springer-Verlag, Berlin.

Gamma, E., Helm, R., Johnson, R., and Vlissides, J. (1995) *Design Patterns: Elements of Reusable Object-Oriented Software*. Addison-Wesley, Reading, MA.

Ganter, B., and Wille, R. (1999) *Formal Concept Analysis – Mathematical Foundations*. Springer-Verlag, Berlin.

Garlan, D., Allen, R., and Ockerbloom, J. (1995) Architectural mismatch or why it's hard to build systems out of existing parts. *IEEE Software* **12**(6) 17–26, November.

Garlan, D., Monroe, R., and Wile, D. (1997) Acme: An Architecture Description Interchange Language. *Proceedings, Centre for Advanced Studies Conference (CASCON '97)*, Toronto, Ontario, November, pp. 169–183.

Garlan, D., and Shaw, M. (1993) An introduction to software architecture. In *Advanced in Software Engineering and Knowledge Engineering*, Vol. 1, World Scientific Publishing.

Garone, S., and Cusack, S. (1999) *Components, Objects, and Development Environments: 1999 Worldwide Markets and Trends*, Doc No 19112, June, International Data Corporation (IDC), Framingham, MA.

Gennari, J. H., Stein, A. R., and Musen, M. A. (1996) Reuse for knowledge-based systems and CORBA components, *Proceedings, 10th Knowledge Acquisition for Knowledge-Based Systems Workshop*, Banff, Alberta, Canada. (ksi.cpsc.ucalgary.ca/KAW/KAW96/gennari/)

Gil, J., and Lorenz, D. H. (1996) Environmental Acquisition: A new inheritance-like abstraction mechanism. *Proceedings, OOPSLA '96*. ACM SIGPLAN Notices **31**(10) 214–231.

Goldberg, A., and Robson, D. (1983) *Smalltalk-80: The Language and its Implementation*. Addison-Wesley, Reading, MA.

Goldberg, A., and Robson, D. (1989) *Smalltalk-80: The Language*, revised edition. Addison-Wesley, Reading, MA.

Goldberg, A., and Rubin, K. S. (1995) *Succeeding with Objects: Design Frameworks for Project Management*, Corrected Reprint. Addison-Wesley, Reading, MA.

Gong, L. (2001) Project JXTA: A Technology Overview. Sun Microsystems, Palo Alto, CA. (www.jxta.org/project/www/docs/TechOverview.pdf)

Gough, K. J., Cifuentes, C., Corney, D., Hynd, J., and Kolb, P. (1992) An experiment in mixed compilation/interpretation. *Proceedings, 14th Australasian Computer Science Conference (Hobart, Australia)*, Australian Computer Science Communications, **15**(1).

Gough, K. J. (2001) *Compiling for the .NET Common Language Runtime (CLR)*. Prentice Hall, Englewood Cliffs, NJ.

Gosling, A., Joy, B., and Steele, G. (1996) *The Java Language Specification*. Addison-Wesley, Reading, MA.

Griffel, F. (1997) *Konzepte und Techniken eines Softwareparadigmas* (in German). dpunkt Verlag, Heidelberg.

Grosu, R., Broy M., Selic, B., and Stefanescu, G. (1999) What is Behind UML-RT? In *Behavioral Specifications of Businesses and Systems*, pp. 74–88. Kluwer Academic Publishers, Dordrecht, The Netherlands.

Gunnerson, E. (2000) *A Programmer's Introduction to C#*. Apress, Berkeley, CA.

Harel, D. (1987) Statecharts: a visual formalism for complex systems. *Science of Computer Programming* **8** pp. 231–274.

Harrison, N., Foote, B., and Rohnert, H. (1999) *Pattern Languages of Program Design 4*. Addison-Wesley, Reading, MA.

Harrison, W., and Ossher, H. (1993) Subject-oriented programming (a critique of pure objects). *Proceedings, OOPSLA '93*, ACM SIGPLAN Notices **28**(10) 411–428.

Hasselbring, W. (2002) Web data integration for e-commerce applications. *IEEE Multimedia* **9**(1) 16–25.

Hauck, F. J. (1993) Inheritance modeled with explicit bindings: an approach to typed inheritance. *Proceedings, OOPSLA '93*, ACM SIGPLAN Notices **28**(10) 231–239.

Heeb, B. U. *Debora: A System for the Development of Field Programmable Hardware and its Application to a Reconfigurable Computer*, PhD Thesis No. 10049, Verlag der Fachvereine, Zurich.

Heinemann, G. T., and Councill, W. T. (2001) *Component-Based Software Engineering: Putting the Pieces Together*. Addison-Wesley, Reading, MA.

Helm, R., Holland, I. M., and Gangopadhyay, D. (1990) Contracts: specifying behavioral compositions in object-oriented systems. In Meyrowitz, N. (ed.) *Proceedings, OOPSLA/ECOOP '90*, ACM SIGPLAN Notices **25**(10) 169–180.

Herzum, P., and Sims, O. (2000) *Business Component Factory*, OMG Press series, John Wiley & Sons, New York.

Hoare, C. A. R. (1961) Algorithm 63: Partition; Algorithm 64: Quicksort; Algorithm 65: Find. *Communications of the ACM* **4**, 321–322.

Hoare, C. A. R. (1969) An axiomatic basis for computer programming. *Communications of the ACM* **12**, 576–580, 583.

Hogg, J. (1991) Islands: aliasing protection in object-oriented languages. *Proceedings, OOPSLA '91*, ACM SIGPLAN Notices **26**(10) 271–285.

Holland, I. M. (1992) Specifying reusable components using contracts. In Lehrmann Madsen, O. (ed.) *Proceedings, ECOOP '92, LNCS* 615, pp. 287–308.

Hölzle, U. (1995) *Adaptive optimization for Self: Reconciling High Performance with Exploratory Programming*, PhD thesis, Stanford University. (Available as Technical Report SMLI TR-95–35, Sun Laboratories, Mountain View, CA.)

Humphrey, W. (1996) *Introduction to the Personal Software Process*. Addison-Wesley, Reading, MA.

Hürsch, W. L. (1994) Should superclasses be abstract? In Tokoro, M., and Pareschi, R. (eds.) *Proceedings, ECOOP '94, LNCS* 821, pp. 12–31.

Hutchinson, N. C., Raj, R. K., Black, A. P., Levy, H. M., and Jul, E. (1987) The Emerald Programming Language Report. Technical Report UWCS 87-10-07, Department. of Computer Science, University of Washington, Seattle, Washington. Also available as DIKU Report no. 87/22, Department of Computer Science, University of Copenhagen, Denmark and as TR no. 87-29, Department of Computer Science, University of Arizona, Tucson, Arizona. (Revised August 1988.)

Hüttel, H. (1991) *Decidability, Behavioural Equivalences and Infinite Transition Graphs*, PhD thesis, ECS-LFCS-91–181, Computer Science Department, University of Edinburgh.

IBM (1994) The System Object Model (SOM) and the Component Object Model (COM): A comparison of technologies from a developer's perspective. White Paper. IBM Corporation, Object Technology Products Group, Austin. (www.ibm.com/software/ad/som/library/somvscom.html)

IBM (1997) NetRexx 1.0, www2.hurley.ibm.com/netrexx/, May.

IETF (1998) Uniform Resource Identifiers (URI): generic syntax (T. Berners-Lee, R. Fielding and L. Masinter). IETF RFC 2396. (www.ietf.org/rfc/rfc2396.txt)

IETF (1999) Hypertext Transfer Protocol – HTTP/1.1 (R. Fielding, J. Gettys, J. Mogul, H. Frystyk, L. Masinter, P. Leach and T. Berners-Lee). IETF RFC 2616. (www.ietf.org/rfc/rfc2616.txt)

IETF (2000) An HTTP extension framework (H. Nielsen, P. Leach and S. Lawrence). IETF
RFC 2774. (www.ietf.org/rfc/rfc2774.txt)

IETF (2001) Tags for the identification of languages (H. Alvestrand). IETF RFC 3066.
(www.ietf.org/rfc/rfc3066.txt)

Intermetrics (1997) AppletMagic Ada '95 to Java bytecode translator, Intermetrics,
www.appletmagic.com/, February.

IONA (1996) Orbix Desktop for Windows. White Paper. IONA Technologies,
www.iona.com, July.

ISO (1986) Information processing – Text and office systems – Standard Generalized
Markup Language (SGML) ISO 8879:1986. (www.iso.ch)

ISO/IEC and ITU (1995a) Recommendation X.902, Open Distributed Processing –
Reference Model – Part 1: Overview. ISO/IEC and ITU. (www.iso.ch)

ISO/IEC and ITU (1995b) Recommendation X.902, Open Distributed Processing –
Reference Model – Part 2: Foundations. ISO/IEC and ITU. (www.iso.ch)

Jacobson, I. (1993) *Object-Oriented Software Engineering*, Revised Printing. Addison-
Wesley, Reading, MA.

Jacobson, I., Ericson, M., and Jacobson, A. (1994) *The Object Advantage – Business Process
Re-engineering with Object Technology*. Addison-Wesley, Reading, MA.

Jacobson, I., Griss, M., and Jonsson, P. (1997) *Software Reuse: Architecture, Process and
Organization for Business Success*. Addison-Wesley, Reading, MA.

JCP (2001) JSR 14: Add Generic Types To The Java Programming Language. Public
Review, August. *Java Community Process*. (jcp.org/jsr/detail/14.jsp)

Johnson, R. (1992) Documenting frameworks using patterns. *Proceedings, OOPSLA '92*,
ACM SIGPLAN Notices **27**(10) 63–76.

Johnson, R. (1994) How to design frameworks. In: *Object-Technology at Work*, Tutorial
Notes, University of Zurich.

Jonkers, H. (2001) Interface-centric Architecture Descriptions. *Proceedings, The Working
IEEE/IFIP Conference on Software Architecture* (WICSA), IEEE Computer Society, Los
Alamitos, CA.

Jordan, M., and Van de Vanter, M. (1997) Modular system building with Java packages,
Proceedings, 8th Conference on Software Engineering Environments (SEE97), April.

Kang, K., Cohen, S., Hess, J., Novak, R., and Peterson, S. (1990) Feature-Oriented Domain
Analysis feasibility study: interim report. *Technical Report* CMU/SEI-90-TR-21, August.
(www.sei.cmu.edu/publications/documents/90.reports/90.tr.021.html)

Kennedy, A. and Syme, D. (2001) Design and implementation of generics for the .NET
common language runtime, *Proceedings, ACM SIGPLAN Conference on Programming
Language Design and Implementation (PLDI 2001)*, ACM SIGPLAN Notices **36**(5)
1–12.

Kernighan, B. W., and Ritchie, D. M. (1978) *The C Programming Language*, 2nd edn
1989. Prentice Hall, Englewood Cliffs, NJ.

Kiczales, G. (1994) Why are blackboxes so hard to reuse? Toward a new model of abstraction in the engineering of software, Invited Talk, *OOPSLA '94.* (www.uvc.com/kiczales/transscript.html)

Kiczales, G., and Lamping, J. (1992) Issues in the design and specification of class libraries, *Proceedings, OOPSLA '92,* ACM SIGPLAN Notices **27**(10) 435–451.

Kiczales, G., de Riviere, J., and Bobrow, D. G. (1991) *The Art of the Metaobject Protocol.* MIT Press, Cambridge, MA.

Kleindienst, J., Plasil, F., and Tuma, P. (1996) Lessons learned from implementing the CORBA Persistent Object Service, *Proceedings, OOPSLA '96,* ACM SIGPLAN Notives **31**(10) 150–167.

Kniesel, G. (1999) Type-safe Delegation for Runtime Component Adaptation. In Guerraoui, R. (ed.): *Proceedings, ECOOP '99. LNCS* 1628, pp. 351–366.

Krasner, G. (ed.) (1983) *Smalltalk-80 Bits of History, Words of Advice,* Addison-Wesley, Reading, MA.

Krasner, G. E., and Pope, S. T. (1988) A cookbook for using the Model-View-Controller user interface paradigm in Smalltalk-80. *Journal of Object-Oriented Programming* **1**(3), 26–49.

Krol, N., and Yockelson, D. (1994) *Component Software.* White Paper Program – The Meta Group, Stanfort, CT, December.

Krogdahl, S. (1984) Multiple inheritance in Simula-like languages. *BIT,* **25,** 318–326.

Kruchten, P. (1995) The 4+1 view model of architecture. *IEEE Software* **12**(6) 42–50, November.

Kruchten, P. (1998) *The Rational Unified Process – An Introduction.* (2nd edn.) Addison-Wesley, Reading, MA.

Lakos, J. (1996) *Large-Scale C++ Software Design.* Addison-Wesley, Reading, MA.

Lamping, J. (1993) Typing the specialization interface. *Proceedings, OOPSLA '93,* ACM SIGPLAN Notices **28**(10) 201–215.

Lamport, L. (1997) Composition: A Way to Make Proofs Harder. *Technical Report* 30a, Compaq Systems Research Center, Palo Alto.

Lange, D. B., and Chang, D. T. (1996) *IBM Aglets Workbench: Programming Mobile Agents in Java,* White Paper (www.tri.ibm.co.jp/aglets/whitepaper.htm), IBM Japan.

Larcie, D. (1993) *Component Software: A Market Perspective on the Coming Revolution in Software Development. In-depth Report.* Patricia Seybold Group, Boston.

Lau, Ch. (1994) *Object-Oriented Programming Using SOM and DSOM.* Van Nostrand Reinhold, New York.

Leach, N., and Moeller, M. (1997) ActiveX lags in Web race. *PC Week,* 9 June 1997.

Ledru, P. (2002) Smart proxies for Jini services. *ACM SIGPLAN Notices* **37**(4) 57–59.

Lehrmann Madsen, O., Magnusson, B., and Møller-Pedersen, B. (1990) Strong typing of object-oriented languages revisited. In Meyrowitz, N. (ed.) *Proceedings, OOPSLA/ECOOP '90,* ACM SIGPLAN Notices **25**(10) 140–150.

Lehrmann Madsen, O., Møller-Pedersen, B., and Nygaard, K. (1993) *Object-Oriented Programming in the Beta Programming Language.* Addison-Wesley, Wokingham, England.

Leino, K. R. M. (1995) *Toward Reliable Modular Programs,* PhD thesis, California Institute of Technology. (Available as Caltech-CS-TR-95-03.)

Leino, K. R. M. (1998) Data groups: specifying the modification of extended state. *Proceedings, OOPSLA '98,* ACM SIGPLAN Notices **33**(10) 144–153.

Leveson, N. G. (1995) *Safeware: System Safety and Computers,* Addison-Wesley, Reading, MA.

Lewis, T. G. (1995) *Object-Oriented Application Frameworks.* Manning/Prentice Hall, New York.

Leymann, F. (2001) Web Services Flow Language (WSFL 1.0), IBM Software Communications Department, Somers, NY. (www-4.ibm.com/software/solutions/webservices/pdf/WSFL.pdf)

Lieberman, H. (1986) Using prototypical objects to implement shared behavior in object-oriented systems. In Meyrowitz, N. (ed.) *Proceedings, OOPSL '86,* ACM SIGPLAN Notices **21**(11) 214–223.

Lins, C. (1988) *The Modula-2 Software Component Library* (four volumes), Springer-Verlag, New York.

Liskov, B., and Wing, J. M. (1994) A behavioral notion of subtyping. *ACM Transactions on Programming Languages and Systems (TOPLAS),* **16**(6) 11–41.

Lorenz, D. H., and Vlissides, J. (2001) Designing components versus objects: a transformational approach. *Proceedings, ICSE 2001.* IEEE Computer Society, Los Alamitos, CA.

Luckham, D. C., Kenney, J. J., Augustin, L. M., Vera, J., Bryan, D., and Mann, W. (1995) Specification and Analysis of System Architecture Using Rapide. *IEEE Transactions on Software Engineering,* Special Issue on Software Architecture, **21**(4) 336-355, April.

Magee, J., Dulay, N., Eisenbach, S., and Kramer, J. (1995) Specifying Distributed Software Architectures. In Schäfer, W., and Botella, P. (eds.) *Proceedings of 5th European Software Engineering Conference (ESEC '95),* LNCS 989, pp. 137–153.

McCarthy, J. (1979) History of Lisp. Artificial Intelligence Laboratory, Stanford University. (www.formal.stanford.edu/jmc/history/lisp/lisp.html)

McDirmid, S., Flatt, M., and Hsieh, W. (2001) Jiazzi: New Age Components for Old-fashioned Java. *Proceedings, OOPSLA 2001,* ACM SIGPLAN Notices **36**(11) 211–222.

McGraw, G., and Felten, E. (1997) *Java Security: Hostile Applets, Holes, and Antidotes.* John Wiley & Sons, New York.

McIlroy, M. D. (1968) Mass-produced software components. In (Naur *et al.,* 1969), pp. 88–98.

Magnusson, B. (1991) Code reuse considered harmful (guest editorial). *Journal of Object-Oriented Programming* **4**(3) 8.

Malenfant, J. (1995) On the semantic diversity of delegation-based programming languages. *Proceedings, OOPSLA '95,* ACM SIGPLAN Notices **30**(10) 215–230.

Martin, R. C., Riehle, D., Buschmann, F., Vlissides, J. (1997) *Pattern Languages of Program Design 3.* Addison-Wesley, Reading, MA.

Mauro, J., McDougall, R. (2001) *Solaris Internals: Core Kernel Architecture.* Sun Microsystems Press, Prentice Hall, Upper Saddle River, NJ.

Meijer, E. and Szyperski, C. (2002) Overcoming independent extensiblity challenges, *Communications of the ACM*, to appear.

Messerschmitt, D., and Szyperski, C. (2000) The economic and industrial properties of software. *Technical Report UCB//CSD-01-1130*, University of California at Berkeley Computer Science Division, CA. *Technical Report MSR-TR-2001-11*, Microsoft Corporation, Redmond, WA.

Messerschmitt, D., and Szyperski, C. (2002) *Software Ecosystem: Understanding an Indispensable Technology and Industry.* MIT Press, Cambridge, MA.

Meyer, B. (1988) *Object-Oriented Software Construction*, 2nd edn 1997, Series in Computer Science. Prentice Hall, Englewood Cliffs, NJ.

Meyer, B. (1990) *Eiffel – The Language*, Series in Computer Science, Prentice Hall, Englewood Cliffs, NJ.

Meyer, B. (1994) *Reusable Software: The Base Object-Oriented Component Libraries.* Prentice Hall, Englewood Cliffs, NJ.

Meyer, B. (1996) Static typing and other mysteries of life. *Object Currents* 1(1), www.sigs.com/objectcurrents.

Mezini, M. (1997) Maintaining the consistency and behavior of class libraries during their evolution. *Proceedings, OOPSLA '97*, ACM SIGPLAN Notices **32**(10) 1–21.

Microsoft (2000) *BizTalk Framework 2.0: Document and Message Specification.* Microsoft, Redmond, WA. (www.microsoft.com/biztalk/techinfo/BizTalkFramework20.doc)

Miller, G. A. (1956) The magical number seven, plus or minus two: some limits on our capacity for processing information. *The Psychological Review*, vol. 63, pp. 81–97. (psychclassics.yorku.ca/Miller/)

Mikhajlov, L. (1999) *Ensuring Correctness of Object and Component Systems.* TUCS Dissertations No. 18, Turku Centre for Computer Science, Turku, Finland.

Mikhajlov, L., and Sekerinski, E. (1998) A study of the fragile base class problem. In Jul, E. (ed.) *Proceedings, ECOOP '98, LNCS* 1445, pp. 355–382.

Mitchell, J. G., Maybury, W., and Sweet, R. (1979) Mesa language manual, version 5.0. *Technical Report CSL-79-3*, Xerox Palo Alto Research Center, Palo Alto, CA.

Moon, D. A. (1986) Object-oriented programming with flavors. In Meyrowitz, N. (ed.) *Proceedings, OOPSLA '86*, ACM SIGPLAN Notices **21**(11) 1–8.

Monson-Haefel, R. (2001) *Enterprise JavaBeans*, 3rd edn 2001. O'Reilly & Associates, Sebastopol, CA.

Mørch, A. I. (1997) Three levels of end user tailoring: customization, integration, and extension. In Kyng, M., and Mathiassen, L. (eds.) *Computers and design in context*, pp. 51–76. The MIT Press, Cambridge, MA.

Morgan, C. (1990) *Programming from Specifications*, 2nd edn 1994, Prentice Hall, Englewood Cliffs, NJ.

Morris, C. R., Ferguson, C. H. (1993) How architecture wins technology wars. *Harvard Business Review* 71(2) 86–96, March/April.

Morrison, J. P. (1994) *Flow-based Programming: A New Approach to Application Development*. Van Nostrand Reinhold, New York.

Mössenböck, H. (1993) *Object-Oriented Programming in Oberon-2*. Springer-Verlag, Berlin.

Mühlhäuser, M. (ed.) (1997) *Special Issues in Object-Oriented Programming – ECOOP '96 Workshop Reader*. dpunkt Verlag, Heidleberg.

Mullender, S. (1993) *Distributed Systems*, 2nd edn. Addison-Wesley, Reading, MA.

Musser, D. R., and Saini, A. (1996) *STL Tutorial and Reference Guide*. Addison-Wesley, Reading, MA.

Myers, A. C., Bank, J. A., and Liskov, B. (1997) Parameterized Types for Java. *Proceedings, 24th ACM Symposium on Principles of Programming Languages (POPL '97)*, pp. 132–145. ACM Press, New York.

Naur, P., and Randell, B. (eds) (1969) *Proceedings, NATO Conference on Software Engineering*, Garmisch, Germany, October 1968, NATO Science Committee, Brussels (published as a book in 1976).

Necula, G. C., and Lee, P. (1996) Safe Kernel Extensions Without Runtime Checking. *Proceedings, 2nd Symposium on Operating Systems Design and Implementation (OSDI '96)*, 229–243, October.

Necula, G. C. (1997) Proof-Carrying Code, *Proceedings, 24th Annual ACM Symposium on Principles of Programming Languages (POPL97)*, 106–119, January.

Nelson, G. (ed.) (1991) *Systems Programming with Modula-3*. Prentice Hall, Englewood Cliffs, NJ.

Netscape (1996) *Netscape ONE – Open Networking Environment*, White Paper Version 1.0, Netscape Communications Corporation, July.

Nierstrasz, O. (1991) The next 700 concurrent object-oriented languages – reflections on the future of object-based concurrency. In Tsichritzis, D. (ed.) *Object Composition*. Centre Universitaire d'Informatique, University of Geneva.

Nierstrasz, O. (1993) Regular types for active objects. *Proceedings, OOPSL '93*, ACM SIGPLAN Notices **28**(10) 1–15.

Nierstrasz, O., and Dami, L. (1995) Component-oriented software technology. In Nierstrasz, O., and Tsichritzis, D. (eds) *Object-Oriented Software Composition*. Prentice Hall, Englewood Cliffs, NJ.

Nierstrasz, O., and Tsichritzis, D. (eds) (1995) *Object-Oriented Software Composition*. Prentice Hall, Englewood Cliffs, NJ.

Nierstrasz, O., Gibbs, S., and Tsichritzis, D. (1992) Component-oriented software development. *Communications of the ACM*, **35**(9), 160–165.

Nori, K. V., Amman, U., Jensen, K., Nägeli, H. H., and Jacobi, C. (1991) Pascal-P implementation notes. In Barron, D. W. (ed.) *Pascal: The Language and its Implementation*. John Wiley & Sons, New York.

Oberon microsystems, Inc. (1994) *Oberon/F Users Guide*, Oberon microsystems (www.oberon.ch).

Oberon microsystems, Inc. (1997a) *Portos Realtime Operating System and Integrated Development Environment for Portos*. Oberon microsystems (www.oberon.ch).

Oberon microsystems, Inc. (1997b) *BlackBox Developer and BlackBox Component Framework*. Oberon microsystems (www.oberon.ch).

Odersky, M., and Wadler, P. L. (1997) Pizza into Java: translating theory into practice. *Proceedings, ACM Symposium on Principles of Programming. Languages. (POPL '97)*, pp. 146–159. ACM Press, New York.

Olafsson, A., and Bryan, D. (1997) On the need for required interfaces of components. In Mühlhäuser, M. (ed.) *Special Issues in Object-Oriented Programming – ECOOP '96 Workshop Reader*, pp. 159–171. dpunkt Verlag, Heidelberg.

OMG (1997a) *The Common Object Request Broker: Architecture and Specification*, Revision 2.0 July 1995, Update July 1996, Object Management Group, formal document 97–02–25 (www.omg.org).

OMG (1997b) *The Object Management Architecture Guide*. Object Management Group (www.omg.org).

OMG (1997c) *CORBAservices: Common Object Services Specification*, Object Management Group, formal document 97–02–04 (www.omg.org).

OMG (1999) *Unified Modeling Language (UML), version 1.3*. Object Management Group (www.omg.org).

OMG (2000) *Meta-object Facility (MOF), version 1.3*. Object Management Group (www.omg.org).

OMG (2001) *Model-driven Architecture (MDA)*. Object Management Group (www.omg.org/mda).

OMG (2002) *UML Profile for Schedulability, Performance, and Time Specification*. Object Management Group (www.omg.org).

Orfali, R., and Harkey, D. (1995) Object component suites: the whole is greater than the parts. *Datamation*, February 15.

Orfali, R., Harkey, D., and Edwards, J. (1996) *The Essential Distributed Objects Survival Guide*. John Wiley & Sons, New York.

Omohundro, S., and Stoutamire, D. (1996) *Sather 1.1 Language Specification, Technical Report* TR-96-012, International Computer Science Institute, Berkeley, CA. (www.icsi.berkeley.edu/~sather/)

Ossher, H., and Harrison, W. (1992) Combination of inheritance hierarchies. *Proceedings, OOPSLA '92*, ACM SIGPLAN Notices **27**(10) 25–40.

Ossher, H., Kaplan, M., Harrison, W., Katz, A., and Kruskal, V. (1995) Subject-oriented composition rules. *Proceedings, OOPSLA '95*, ACM SIGPLAN Notices **30**(10) 235–250.

Palsberg, J., and Schwartzbach, M. I. (1991) Object-oriented type inference. *Proceedings, OOPSLA '91*, ACM SIGPLAN Notices **26**(10) 146–161.

Parnas, D. L. (1972a) A technique for software module specification with examples. *Communications of the ACM* **15**(5) 330–336, May.

Parnas, D. L. (1972b) On the criteria to be used in decomposing systems into modules. *Communications of the ACM* **15**(12) 1053–1058, December.

Parnas, D. L. (1976) On the design and development of program families. *IEEE Transactions on Software Engineering* **SE-2**, 1–9, March.

Paznesh, E. (1997) Gazelle: An Oberon/F based Internet development framework. *The Oberon Tribune*, **2**(1), 23–24. Oberon microsystems, Inc., Zurich (www.oberon.ch).

Perry, D. E., and Wolf, A. L. (1992) Foundations for the study of software architecture. *ACM SIGSOFT Software Engineering Notes* **17**(4) 40–52, October.

Pinson, L. J., and Wiener, R. S. (1991) *Objective-C: Object-Oriented Programming Techniques*. Addison-Wesley, Reading, MA.

Platt, D. S. (1999) *Understanding COM+*. Microsoft Press, Redmond, WA.

Potel, M., with Cotter, S. (1995) *Inside Taligent Technology*. Addison-Wesley, Reading, MA.

Pritchard, J. (1999) *COM and CORBA Side by Side*. Addison-Wesley, Reading, MA.

Ran, A. (1999) Software Isn't Built From Lego Blocks. *Proceedings, ACM Symposium On Software Reusability* (SSR), 164–169. ACM Press, New York.

Rappin, N., and Pedroni, S. (2002) *Jython Essentials*. O'Reilly & Associates, Sebastopol, CA.

Reid, A., Flatt, M., Stoller, L., Lepreau, J., and Eide, E. (2000) Knit: Component Composition for Systems Software. *Proceedings, 4th Symposium on Operating Systems Design and Implementation (OSDI 2000)*, pp. 347–360, October.

Reiser, M., and Wirth, N. (1992) *Programming in Oberon*. Addison-Wesley, Reading, MA.

Richter, J. (2002) *Applied Microsoft .NET Framework Programming*. Microsoft Press, Redmond, WA.

Ring, K., and Carnelly, P. (1995) *Distributed Objects – Creating the Virtual Mainframe*. Ovum, London.

Roe, P., and Szyperski, C. (1997) Lightweight parametric polymorphism for Oberon. In Mössenböck, H. (ed.) *Proceedings, 4th Joint Modular Languages Conference (JMLC97)*, Lecture Notes in Computing Science 1204, pp. 140–154.

Roe, P., and Szyperski, C. (2000) Mianjin: A Parallel Language with a Type System that Governs Global System Behaviour. In Gutknecht, J., and Weck, W. (eds.) *Proceedings, 5th Joint Modular Languages Conference (JMLC 2000), Lecture Notes in Computing Science* 1897, pp. 38–50.

Rogerson, D. (1997) *Inside COM*. Microsoft Press, Redmond, WA.

Rossie Jr, J. G., and Friedman, D. P. (1995) An algebraic semantics of subobjects. *Proceedings, OOPSLA '95*, ACM SIGPLAN Notices **30**(10) 187–199.

Rumbaugh, J. (1994) The life of an object model: How the object model changes during development. *Journal of Object-Oriented Programming*, 7(1), 24–32.

Rumbaugh, J., Blaha, M., Lorenson, W., Eddy, F., and Premerlani, W. (1991) *Object-Oriented Modelling and Design*. Prentice Hall, Englewood Cliffs, NJ.

Rumbaugh, J., Jacobson, I., and Booch, G. (1997) *Unified Modeling Language Reference Manual*. Addison-Wesley, Reading, MA.

Sametinger, J. (1997) *Software Engineering with Reusable Components*. Springer-Verlag, Berlin.

Sanchez, E., Patel, K., and Fenner, J. (2001) Part 1: Integration Powered, May 28. Part 2: Integration Platforms For E-Business, June 4. *Information Week*. (www.informationweek.com/839/integration.htm and www.informationweek.com/840/integration.htm)

Schmid, H. A. (1995) Creating the architecture of a manufacturing framework by design patterns. *Proceedings, OOPSLA '95*, ACM SIGPLAN Notices **30**(10) 370–384.

Schmidt, D. C., Stal, M., Rohnert, H., and Buschmann, F. (2000) *Pattern-Oriented Software Architecture: Patterns for Concurrent and Networked Objects*. John Wiley & Sons, New York.

Schmidt, H. W., and Chen, J. (1995) Reasoning About Concurrent Objects. *Proceedings, Asia-Pacific Software Engineering Conference* (APSEC '95), Brisbane, pp. 86–95. IEEE Computer Society, Los Alamitos, CA.

Scribner, K. (2000) *Understanding SOAP: Simple Object Access Protocol*. Sams Publishing, Indianapolis, IN.

Scullin, W. (1998) Modularization Techniques, The Mozilla Organization. (www.mozilla.org/docs/modunote.htm)

Selic, B., Gullekson, G., Ward, P., and McGee, J. (1994) *Realtime Object-Oriented Modeling*. John Wiley & Sons, New York.

Sessions, R. (2001a) Java 2 Enterprise Edition (J2EE) versus the .NET Platform: two visions for eBusiness. (March) ObjectWatch, Austin, Texas. (www.objectwatch.com/FinalJ2EEandDotNet.doc)

Sessions, R. (2001b) Is Java language neutral? *ObjectWatch Newsletter* 33 (June), ObjectWatch, Austin, Texas. (www.objectwatch.com/issue_33.htm)

Shapiro, M. (1989) Structure and encapsulation in distributed systems: the proxy principle. *Proceedings, 6th International Conference on Distributed Computer Systems (ICDCS86)*, IEEE Press, May 1986.

Shaw, M., and Garlan, D. (1996) *Software Architecture: Perspectives on an Emerging Discipline*. Prentice Hall, Englewood Cliffs, NJ.

Siegel, J. (2000) *CORBA 3: Fundamentals and Programming*, 2nd edn. John Wiley & Sons, New York.

Sims, O. (1994) *Business Objects: Delivering Cooperative Objects for Client–Server.* McGraw-Hill, New York.

Slagter, R. J., and Ter Hofte, G. H. (2002) End-user composition of groupware behaviour: The CoCoWare .NET architecture. In Neuwirth, C. M., and Rodden, T. (eds.) *Proceedings, ACM Conference on Computer Supported Cooperative Work* (CSCW 2002), New Orleans. (in press). ACM Press, New York.

Smaragdakis, Y. (1999) *Implementing Large-scale Object-Oriented Components.* Ph.D. Dissertation, Department of Computer Sciences, University of Texas at Austin.

Smaragdakis, Y., and Batory, D. (1998) Implementing Layered Design with Mixin Layers. In Jul, E. (ed.) *Proceedings, ECOOP '98. LNCS* 1445 pp. 550–570.

Smith, G., Gough, J., and Szyperski, C. (1998) Conciliation: The Adaption of Independently Developed Components. In Gupta, G., Pritchard, P., and Shen, H. (eds) *Proceedings, 2nd International Conference on Parallel and Distributed Computing and Networks* (PDCN), pp. 31–38, Acta Press, Calgary, AB, Canada.

Smith, R. B., and Ungar, D. (1995) Programming as an experience: the inspiration for Self. In Olthoff, W. (ed.) *Proceedings, ECOOP '95, LNCS* 952, pp. 303–330.

Snyder, A. (1986) Encapsulation and inheritance in object-oriented programming languages. In Meyrowitz, N. (ed.) *Proceedings, OOPSLA '86,* ACM SIGPLAN Notices **21**(11) 38–45.

Snyder, A. (1987) Inheritance and the development of encapsulated software components. In Shriver, B., and Wegner, P. (eds) *Research Directions in Object-Oriented Programming,* pp. 165–188. MIT Press.

Stata, R., and Guttag, J. (1995) Modular reasoning in the presence of subclassing. *Proceedings, OOPSLA '95,* ACM SIGPLAN Notices **30**(10) 200–214.

Stata, R. (1997) Modularity in the presence of subclassing. *Technical Report* 145, Compaq Systems Research Center, Palo Alto, CA, April.

Steel, J. (1996) *Component Technology,* IDC White Paper (part one), International Data Corporation, London.

Stein, L. A. (1987) Delegation is inheritance. *Proceedings, OOPSLA '87,* ACM SIGPLAN Notices **22**(12) 138–146.

Stein, L. A., and Zdonik, S. B. (1998) Clovers: the dynamic behavior of types and instances. *International Journal of Computer Science and Information Management* **1**(3).

Steyaert, P., Lucas, C., Mens, K., and D'Hondt, T. (1996) Reuse contracts: managing the evolution of reusable assets. *Proceedings, OOPSLA '96,* ACM SIGPLAN Notices **31**(10) 268–285.

Stroustrup, B. (1987) Multiple inheritance for C^{++}. *Proceedings, EUUG Spring Conference,* May (also in: *Computing Systems,* **2**(4), 1989; for a discussion, see Stroustrup, 1994).

Stroustrup, B. (1994) *The Design and Evolution of C^{++}* (corrected reprint 1995). Addison-Wesley, Reading, MA.

Sun (1996) *JavaBeans*, Version 1.00, java.sun.com/beans, October. Update 1.00-A, December. Sun Microsystems, Palo Alto, CA.

Sun (1997) *Java Electronic Commerce Framework (JEFC)*, java.sun.com/products/commerce/, Version 0.6 alpha, May. Sun Microsystems, Palo Alto, CA.

Sun (2001) *Java 2 Platform Enterprise Edition Specification, v1.3*. Sun Microsystems, Palo Alto, CA.

Swaine, M. (1997) Some observations on Apple and Java. *Dr. Dobb's Journal*, #262, **22**(2), 91–93.

Sime, D., and Kennedy, A. (2001) Design and implementation of generics for the .NET Common Language Runtime. *Proceedings, ACM SIGPLAN Conference. on Programming Language Design and Implementation (PLDI 2001)*. ACM SIGPLAN Notices **36**(5) 1–12.

Szyperski, C. (1992a) Import is not inheritance – why we need both: modules and classes. In Lehrmann Madsen, O. (ed.) *Proceedings, ECOOP 92, LNCS* 615, pp. 19–32.

Szyperski, C. (1992b) *Insight Ethos: On Object-Orientation in Operating Systems*, PhD thesis, ETH Zurich, No. 9884. Informatik Dissertationen der ETH Zürich, No. 40, Verlag der Fachvereine, Zurich.

Szyperski, C. (1995) Component-oriented programming: a refined variation on object-oriented programming. *The Oberon Tribune*, **1**(2), Oberon microsystems, Inc., Zurich (www.oberon.ch), December.

Szyperski, C. (1996) Independently extensible systems – software engineering potential and challenges. *Proceedings, 19th Australasian Computer Science Conference. Australian Computer Science Communications* **18**(1) 203–212.

Szyperski, C. (2000) Modules and components – Rivals or partners. In Böszörményi, L., Gutknecht, J., and Pomberger, G. (eds.) *The School of Niklaus Wirth – The Art of Simplicity*, dpunkt Verlag, Heidelberg and Morgan Kaufmann Publishers, San Francisco.

Szyperski, N. (1997) Component software: A market on the verge of success. *The Oberon Tribune* **2**(1) 1–4, Oberon microsystems, Inc., Zürich (www.oberon.ch), January.

Szyperski, C., and Gough, J. (1995) The role of programming languages in the lifecycle of safe systems. *Proceedings, International Conference on Safety through Quality (STQ95, Kennedy Space Center, Cape Canaveral, Florida)*, pp. 99–114. Alpha Books, Bristol, UK.

Szyperski, C., Omohundro, St., and Murer, St. (1994) Engineering a programming language – the type and class system of Sather. In Gutknecht, J. (ed.) *Proceedings, First International Conference on Programming Languages and System Architecture, LNCS* 782.

Szyperski, C., and Pfister, C. (1997) Workshop on Component-Oriented Programming, Summary. In Mühlhäuser, M. (ed.) *Special Issues in Object-Oriented Programming – ECOOP '96 Workshop Reader*. dpunkt Verlag, Heidelberg.

Szyperski, C., and Pfister, C. (1999) BlackBox: a component framework for compound user interfaces. In Fayad, M., Schmidt, D., and Johnson, R. (eds.) *Implementing Application Frameworks: Object-Oriented Application Frameworks at Work*, John Wiley & Sons, New York.

Szabo, M. E. (1969) *The Collected Papers of Gerhard Gentzen*. North-Holland, Amsterdam.

Taligent (1994) *Taligent's Guide to Designing Programs: Well-mannered Object-Oriented Design in C++*. Addison-Wesley, Reading, MA. (pcroot.cern.ch/TaligentDocs/TaligentOnline/DocumentRoot/1.0/Docs)

Thatte, S. (2001) XLANG: Web services for business process design. Microsoft, Redmond, WA. (www.gotdotnet.com/team/xml_wsspecs/xlang-c/default.htm)

Thomas, A. (1999) Comparing EJB and MTS: Server component models. *Notes on Information Technology*, February, Patricia Seybold Group, Boston, MA.

Thomas, A. (1999) EJB Roadmap: Updates on the EJB specification. *Notes on Information Technology*, March, Patricia Seybold Group, Boston, MA.

Thomas, A. (1999) Regular versus Enterprise JavaBeans – What's the difference? *Notes on Information Technology*, April, Patricia Seybold Group, Boston, MA.

Travis, B. E. (2000) *XML and SOAP Programming for BizTalk Servers*. Microsoft Press International, Redmond, WA.

Udell, J. (1994) ComponentWare. *BYTE Magazine*, **19**(5), 46–56.

Udell, J. (2000) JVM and CLR. *BYTE Magazine*, 18 December. (www.byte.com/documents/s=505/byt20001214s0006/index.htm.)

Ungar, D. (1995) Annotating objects for transport to other worlds, *Proceedings, OOPSLA '95*, ACM SIGPLAN Notices **30**(10) 73–87.

Ungar, D., and Smith, R. B. (1987) Self: the power of simplicity. *Proceedings, OOPSLA '87*, ACM SIGPLAN Notices **22**(12) 227–241 (a revised version appeared in *Lisp and Symbolic Computation* **4**(3) 187–205, 1991).

Valdés, R. (1994) Introducing interoperable objects. *Dr. Dobb's Journal* #225, **19**(16) 4–6, special issue, Winter 1994/95.

Visual Basic (1992) *Visual Basic*. Microsoft Press, Redmond, WA.

Vlissides, J. M., Coplien, J. O., and Kerth, N. L. (1996) *Pattern Languages of Program Design 2*. Addison-Wesley, Reading, MA.

W3C (1999a) *Namespaces in XML*. W3C Recommendation 14 January 1999. (Latest version: www.w3.org/TR/REC-xml-names)

W3C (1999b) *Resource Description Framework (RDF) Model and Syntax Specification*. W3C Recommendation 22 February 1999. (Latest version: www.w3.org/TR/REC-rdf-syntax)

W3C (1999c) *WAP Binary XML Content Format*. W3C Note 24 June 1999. (Latest version: www.w3.org/TR/wbxml)

W3C (1999d) *XML Path Language (XPath) Version 1.0*. W3C Recommendation 16 November 1999. (Latest version: www.w3.org/TR/xpath)

W3C (2000a) *Simple Object Access Protocol (SOAP) 1.1*. W3C Note 08 May 2000. (Latest version: www.w3.org/TR/SOAP)

W3C (2000b) *Extensible Markup Language (XML) 1.0 (Second Edition)*. W3C Recommendation 6 October 2000. (Latest version: www.w3.org/TR/REC-xml)

W3C (2000c) *Document Object Model (DOM) Level 2 [Core/Views/Events/Style/Traversal and Range] Specification Version 1.0.* W3C Recommendation 13 November 2000. (Latest version: www.w3.org/TR/DOM-Level-2-xxx/ with *xxx*=Core, Views, Events, Style, or Traversal-Range)

W3C (2000d) *SOAP Messages with Attachments.* W3C Note 11 December 2000. (Latest version: www.w3.org/TR/SOAP-attachments)

W3C (2001a) *Web Services Description Language (WSDL) 1.1.* W3C Note 15 March 2001. (Latest version: www.w3.org/TR/wsdl)

W3C (2001b) *XML Schema Part 1: Structures.* W3C Recommendation 02 May 2001. (Latest version: www.w3.org/TR/xmlschema-1)

W3C (2001c) *XML Schema Part 2: Datatypes.* W3C Recommendation 02 May 2001. (Latest version: www.w3.org/TR/xmlschema-2)

W3C (2001d) *XHTML 1.1 – Module-based XHTML.* W3C Recommendation 31 May 2001. (Latest version: www.w3.org/TR/xhtml11)

W3C (2001e) *XML Linking Language (XLink) Version 1.0.* W3C Recommendation 27 June 2001. (Latest version: www.w3.org/TR/xlink)

W3C (2001f) *XML Pointer Language (XPointer) Version 1.0.* W3C Candidate Recommendation 11 September 2001. (Latest version: www.w3.org/TR/xptr)

Wahbe, R., Lucco, S., Anderson, T., and Graham, S. (1993) Efficient software-based fault isolation. *Proceedings, 14th ACM Symposium on Operating System Principles (SOSP93),* pp. 203–216, December.

Wallace, E., and Wallnau, K. C. (1996) A situated evaluation of the Object Management Group's Object Management Architecture (OMA). *Proceedings, OOPSLA '96,* ACM SIGPLAN Notives **31**(10) 168–178.

Weck, W. (1996) *On Document-centered Mathematical Component Software,* PhD Dissertation, ETH Zurich, No. 11817.

Weck, W. (1997) Independently extensible component frameworks, *Proceedings, International Workshop on Component-Oriented Programming (WCOP '96)* at ECOOP '96, Linz, Austria. In Mühlhäuser, M. (ed.) *Special Issues in Object-Oriented Programming – ECOOP '96 Workshop Reader.* dpunkt Verlag, Heidelberg.

Wegner, P. (1987) Dimensions of object-based language design. *Proceedings, OOPSLA '87,* ACM SIGPLAN Notices **22**(12) 168–182. Also appeared in *Journal of Object-Oriented Programming,* 1(1).

Whitehead, K. (2002) *Component-based Development – Principles and Planning for Business Systems.* Component Software Series, Addison-Wesley, Harlow, UK.

Wiederhold, C., Wegner, P., and Ceri, S. (1992) Toward megaprogramming. *Communications of the ACM* **35**(11) 89–99.

Williams, J. W. J. (1964) Algorithm 232: Heapsort. *Communications of the ACM* 7(6) 347–348.

Williams, S., and Kindel, C. (1995) The Component Object Model. *Dr. Dobbs Journal*, pp. 24, Special Report, Winter 1994/95.

Williams, T. (1988) Dealing with the Unknown – or – Type safety in a dynamically extensible class library. research.microsoft.com/comapps/docs/Unknown.doc

Williams, T. (1990) On inheritance: what it means and how to use it. research.microsoft.com/comapps/docs/Inherit.doc

Wills, A. (1991) Capsules and types in Fresco – program verification in Smalltalk. In America, P. (ed.) *Proceedings, ECOOP '91, LNCS* 512, pp. 59–76.

Wilson, J. Y. and Havewala, A. (2001) *Building Powerful Platforms with Windows CE.* Addison-Wesley, Reading, MA.

Wirth, N. (1971) The programming language PASCAL. *Acta Informatica*, 1, 35–63.

Wirth, N. (1977) Modula: a programming language for modular multiprogramming. *Software – Practice and Experience* 7(1) 37–52.

Wirth, N. (1982) *Programming in Modula-2.* 4th edn 1989. Springer-Verlag, Berlin.

Wirth, N., and Gutknecht, J. (1992) *Project Oberon – The Design of an Operating System and Compiler.* Addison-Wesley, Reading, MA.

Wirthman, L. (1997) SunSoft Plan: OS Modularity. *PC Week*, 21 April.

Wutka, M. (2001) *Special Edition: Java 2 Enterprise Edition.* Que Publishing, Indianapolis, IN.

Yang, B. (2001) E++: A pattern language for J2EE applications (two parts). *Java World,* April and August. www.javaworld.com/javaworld/jw-04-2001/jw-0420-eplus.html (part 1) and www.javaworld.com/javaworld/jw-08-2001/jw-0810-eplus2.html (part 2).

Zweben, S., Edwards, S., Weide, B., and Hollingsworth, J. (1995) The effects of layering and encapsulation on software development cost and quality. *IEEE Transactions on Software Engineering*, 21(3), 200–208 (IEEE 0098-5589/95).

Glossary

The following glossary provides a brief introduction to the terminology used in this book, including a definition of most of the acronyms. Most entries refer to larger entries, which are meant to be read as compact summaries that bring together several terms and concepts. More thorough definitions and comments can be found in the body of this book. Please also refer to the index.

Abstract class
A *class* that cannot be instantiated – that is, no object can be a direct instance of an abstract class. An abstract class can have unimplemented *methods* (abstract methods). Non-abstract classes inheriting from an abstract class have to implement all such abstract methods.

ActiveX
A Microsoft standard for controls that reside in documents in the widest sense, including web pages. Controls are visual objects ranging from push buttons to complex mini-applications, such as spreadsheets. ActiveX controls are a generalization of the older OLE custom extensions (OCXs). These again developed out of the original Visual Basic Extensions (VBXs). Unlike OCXs, ActiveX controls can be *containers* themselves, allowing for the nesting of controls. Also, unlike OCXs, ActiveX controls can have non-rectangular shape.

Adapter
A *component* that mediates between clients and providers that use different sets of *interfaces*.

Applet
Java terminology for a visual object embedded in a web page. Applets can be compared to *ActiveX* controls, but today cannot be containers and therefore do not support nesting.

Application framework
See *Class framework*.

Architecture
Overall design of a system. An architecture integrates separate but interfering issues of a system, such as provisions for independent evolution and openness combined with overall reliability and performance requirements. An architecture defines guidelines that, together, help to achieve the overall targets without having to invent ad hoc compromises during system composition. An architecture provides guidelines for safe system evolution. However, an architecture itself must be carefully evolved to avoid deterioration as the system

itself evolves and the requirements change. The right architectures and properly managed architecture evolution are probably the most important and challenging aspects of component software engineering.

ASP (active server pages)
A Microsoft web server technology that supports the embedding of code fragments in text pages that typically follow *HTML* or *XML* formats. Superseded by *ASP.NET*.

ASP.NET (active server pages for .NET)
A Microsoft *.NET* web server technology that supports the embedding of code fragments in text pages that typically follow *HTML* or *XML* formats. ASP.NET replaces the older *ASP*. Unlike ASP, pages are used to generate source code that is then compiled (similar to *JSP*). All *CLR*-hosted languages can be used, provided an ASP.NET helper plugin is available.

Assembly
The unit of deployment, installation, versioning, and management in the *.NET Framework*.

Attribute
Also called field. A feature of a *class*.

Behavioral subtyping
Regular *subtyping* refers only to the availability of operations as far as their signatures are concerned. Behavioral subtyping restricts this further by also requiring behavioral consistency. An object of a subtype, if seen as a member of its base type, may only exhibit behavior (state transitions and answers to queries) that is explicable on the basis of the *specification* of the base type alone. Objects of behavioral subtypes are always *substitutable* for the base type objects.

BlackBox component framework and builder
The BlackBox family of products from Oberon microsystems focuses on the construction of components for compound document and compound user interface-based applications. BlackBox is available for a number of platforms and integrates with the platform's native object and compound document models. For example, the Windows version integrates with COM, OLE, and ActiveX. BlackBox is fully implemented in *Component Pascal*, and the BlackBox component builder uses Component Pascal as an all-purpose component-oriented programming language, from scripting, to component construction, to component framework construction. Direct support of standard object models enables seamless integration with components developed using other languages or tools.

Blackbox reuse
Reusing a component solely on the basis of its interfaces and their contractual specification. Reusability of a blackbox component thus fully depends on the quality of the interfaces and their specification. In contrast, glassbox reuse

allows for inspection of the implementation of a component (but not its modification). The implementation thus serves as the most specific specification of the component, effectively preventing any further evolution of the component without the risk of breaking clients (*semantic fragile base class problem*). Whitebox reuse also allows modification of the implementation of a reused component. If used without restricting conventions (discipline), implementation inheritance is a technique to apply arbitrary modifications to an implementation that is inherited from. In a true component setting, such intrusive modifications cannot be allowed, as they eliminate the potential for independent evolution. Finally, graybox reuse is a term sometimes used to refer to the case where part of a component's implementation is opened for inspection and modification (via inheritance). Many blackbox abstractions in current practice are actually gray.

Boxing
Process of converting a *value type* into a *reference type*. Typically, a cell (the "box") is allocated on a heap and the value is copied from a given variable into that cell. The reference to the cell is then of reference type. The reverse process is called unboxing. It typically involves copying the value out of a referenced heap cell into some variable.

C++
A hybrid object-oriented programming language. C++ is typed but not *type-safe*. C++ does not have a *module* system. C++ does not have *automatic memory management*. Implementing *components* in C++ requires *hardware protection* or software *sandboxing*.

C#
A *pure object-oriented programming language*. C# objects are either instances of classes (passed by reference) or of structs (passed by value). A class inherits implementation from exactly one superclass; the default is class Object. Every C# class and struct can, in addition, implement any number of interfaces. An interface is equivalent to a fully *abstract class*. C# is *type-safe*, but contains a C-like language subset available in "unsafe" methods to enable, yet contain, low-level programming. In the *.NET Framework*, C# is compiled to *assemblies*. Declarations declared as "internal" are accessible only within their containing assembly. Assemblies are closed units of deployment that make C# *module-safe*.

CCM (CORBA component model)
See *OMA*

CIL (common intermediate language)
See *.NET Framework.*

Class
A static description specifying the state (fields) and behavior (methods) shared by all objects that are instances of that class. A class can use *interface inheritance*

and *implementation inheritance* to inherit fields and methods from other classes, its superclasses. Also, other classes, called subclasses, may inherit from a class. The inheritance graph has to be acyclical. It may or may not have a single root. It may or may not allow for multiple superclasses of a class (multiple versus single inheritance). An object is said to be a direct instance of a class if that class is the most refined class that the object is an instance of. The object is said to be an indirect instance of all superclasses of that class. Fields introduce instance variables, unique to each instance of a class, or class variables, shared by all instances of a class. Methods introduce named operations that accept arguments and have an implementation. Class methods operate only on the shared state of that class, its class variables. Instance methods operate on the specific state of an object, its instance variables. Instance methods are invoked by dynamically determining the direct class of the object that the method is invoked on (method dispatch). This is sometimes called sending a message to an object; a method is then said to handle such a method. Classes interact with *types*.

Class framework
A framework that defines a set of classes and the part of their interaction that is common to multiple applications in the domain of the framework. Applications are created by subclassing some of the framework's classes (cf. *whitebox reuse*).

Cleanroom
A component development method based on rigorous formal methods. All provided and required interfaces of the component need to be fully specified (*contract*). Testing is not used except for final statistical quality measurement.

CLI (common language infrastructure)
ECMA standard. See *.NET Framework*.

Cloning
Creation of a new object by copying an existing object, sometimes called a prototype (object). Depending on the system, the clone is either initialized to the state of the prototype or initialized to a normal initial state, possibly based on arguments to the clone operation.

CLR (common language runtime)
See *.NET Framework*.

CLS (common language specification)
See *CTS*.

Co/contra/invariance under subtyping
The objects of a *subtype* must accept all operations defined over their base type. However, they can refine these operations by weakening *preconditions* (expecting less) or strengthening *postconditions* (guaranteeing more). In particular, types of input parameters can be widened to supertypes (contravariance), types of output parameters can be narrowed to subtypes (covariance), and types

of in/out parameters must be left unchanged (invariance). An interesting exception is those parameters that are used to select an operation's implementation. These can be modified covariantly regardless of mode (in, out, or in/out). In traditional object-oriented languages, only one such dispatch parameter exists – the receiver object.

Code inheritance
See *Inheritance*.

COM (component object model)
Microsoft's initial component object model. A binary standard for the efficient interoperation across *component* boundaries. A COM component can implement several COM classes, each uniquely identified by a class ID (CLSID). Each COM class can implement several *COM interfaces*. A COM interface provides a set of operations and is uniquely identified by an interface ID (IID). A COM object is an instance of a COM class, but does not necessarily constitute a single object (*split object*). Clients use COM objects solely via the interfaces provided by that object. Each interface has a QueryInterface operation that can be used to ask for any of the other interfaces of the COM object based on IIDs. COM *object servers* execute in processes that can be partitioned into *COM apartments*.

COM+
COM+ is an integration of previously separate *COM*-based services that first shipped with Windows 2000. The two most prominent services that were blended into COM+ are *MTS* and *MSMQ*.

COM apartment
A COM apartment provides a space for objects to execute under a guaranteed threading model. Per apartment, COM supports single threading (always the same thread), rental threading (one thread at a time), and free threading (any number of concurrent threads). Apartments thus provide synchronization domains, which are classes that can be attributed with threading constraints and objects of such classes are then placed in apartments that respect their classes' constraints. For example, several single-threaded apartments can coexist with a multithreaded apartment in a single process. Apartments are the earliest commercial form of *contextual composition*, a key means to establishing system-wide properties in the presence of component composition.

COM interface
A *COM* interface is uniquely identified by an interface ID (IID). Once published, a COM interface is considered *immutable*. New versions of the interface or its specification require allocation of a new IID, effectively forcing the introduction of a new interface. Multiple versions can thus be supported simultaneously. Old versions can be phased out by no longer supporting them in a COM class.

Common Object Request Broker Architecture (CORBA)
See *OMA*.

Complexity
Notion of inherent difficulty of a problem, a solution, or an approach. If difficulties would be avoidable, then the related notion of complication applies. In the theory of algorithms and data structures, complexity measures indicate lower and average bounds on time and space requirements. In the space of architecture and design, complexity measures indicate degrees of abstraction (ratio of surface area to volume – detail ratio of interface to implementation) and degrees of modularity (strong cohesion and weak coupling). Unnecessary complication is often a consequence of inappropriate engineering or of design degeneration over a longer cycle of evolutionary revisions. Unnecessary complexity is usually a consequence of unnecessary requirement statements. For instance, given the requirement to have a highly accurate clock, a grand mechanical chronometer is complicated, but its complication can be avoided using electronics. (If there was a requirement to solely use mechanical means, then the chronometer design is complex.)

Complication
See *Complexity*.

Component
In the context of this book, always a software component. A component is a unit of composition with contractually specified interfaces and explicit context dependencies only. Context dependencies are specified by stating the required *interfaces* and the acceptable execution platform(s). A component can be deployed independently and is subject to composition by third parties. For the purposes of independent deployment, a component needs to be an executable unit. To distinguish between the deployable unit and the instances it supports, a component is defined to have no observable state. Technically, a component is a set of atomic components, each of which is a module plus resources. A component targets a particular component platform. The composition of components follows one or more composition schemes that are mandated by that component platform.

Component framework
A collection of rules and interfaces (*contracts*) that govern the interaction of *components* plugged into the framework. A component framework typically enforces some of the more vital rules of interaction by encapsulating the required interaction mechanisms. The concept can be applied hierarchically, such that component frameworks are themselves components plugging into higher-tier component frameworks. Examples at tier one are container frameworks such as EJB containers, COM+ contexts, or CLR contexts. Tier-two examples are work flow and integration servers, such as Flowmark or BizTalk. Tier-three examples are emerging federated flow control models at the interorganizational level, such as *B2B*.

Component instance

A simplifying notion. *Components* as such do not normally have direct *instances*. However, typical components provide a number of instantiable abstractions, such as *classes*. Where a web of instances created by a component forms a conceptual whole, this whole is sometimes called a component instance. For example, a component may provide three classes and every useful interaction with the component is an interaction with a triple of objects, one instance from each of the classes. Such an object triple would then be called a component instance.

Component-oriented programming (COP)

Programming that focuses on the design and implementation of *components* – in particular, on the concepts of encapsulation, polymorphism, late binding and safety. Contrast this with the key concepts underpinning *object-oriented programming*.

Component Pascal

A *hybrid object-oriented programming language* that is particularly suitable for *component-oriented programming*. Component Pascal is *type-safe*, *module-safe*, and provides *automatic memory management*. A bit of (incomplete) history: Component Pascal evolved out of Oberon-2, an object-oriented extension of Oberon. Oberon is the descendant of Modula-2, which itself followed Pascal. Pascal, Modula-2, Oberon, and Oberon-2 were developed at the Swiss Federal Institute of Technology (ETH Zurich). Component Pascal is a development of Oberon microsystems, Zurich. Modula-3 is an independent offspring developed at the Compaq System Research Center, Palo Alto. Modula-3 evolved out of Modula-2+ (Olivetti Research), which had its roots in Modula-2. Modula-3 notably influenced the design of Java.

Component platform

The foundation for components to be installed and execute on. A platform includes at least an execution environment, but typically adds a collection of services. Unlike a *component framework*, a component platform is itself not a component in the world of components that it supports. Platforms may layer on top of other platforms and may thus be components of a different component world. For example, a *JRE* (*JVM* and core Java libraries) is a sufficient platform for JavaBeans components. A JRE typically rests on top of an operating system. To host EJB components, an *EJB* container/server is required: a much more demanding platform that nevertheless is layered on top of the basic JRE platform. A similar hierarchy exists in *.NET*, where *ASP.NET* rests on the *CLR*, which rests on Windows.

Component system

A composition of *components*, possibly structured into a number of *component frameworks*, which themselves may be arranged in layers and tiers. A component system targets at least one component platform, but may leverage interoperability services (possibly encapsulated by component frameworks) to spread across multiple component platforms.

Composite
See *composition*.

Composition
Assembly of parts (*components*) into a whole (a composite) without modifying the parts. Parts have compositional properties if the semantics of the composite can be derived from those of the components.

Composition filters
Approach to layer interception filters around an object to perform *aspect* processing. For example, a synchronization filter can add synchronization properties to an object.

Context
General: see *composition*. Special: see *contextual composition*.

Contextual composition
A context is a set of properties that characterize constraints equally adopted by all objects inside the context. If objects in separate contexts agree on a particular property, they are said to be in the same domain (with respect to that property). For example, a context may have synchronization and transactional properties, where it shares the transactional property with another context, but not the synchronization property. Then, two objects in these two contexts would be in the same transaction domain, but not in the same synchronization domain (and could thus execute concurrently). Contextual composition extends the notion of *composition filters* by supporting multiple objects in a single context. Contextual composition was first supported with *COM* apartments for purposes of synchronization, and then extended to transactional and several other contextual properties in *MTS*, adopted partially in *EJB*, generalized further in *COM+*, and opened up as an extensible and generic infrastructure in *CLR*. While original COM and again CLR are open for wide classes of components, MTS, COM+, and EJB emphasize server-based transactional components that typically reside in some middle tier between clients and databases.

Container
In general, an object that contains other objects, in particular a visual object that can contain other visual objects. For example, *ActiveX* controls can be container controls.

Contract
Specification attached to an interface that mutually binds the clients and providers (implementers) of that interface. Contracts can cover functional and extra-functional aspects. Functional aspects include the syntax and semantics of an interface. Extra-functional aspects relate to quality-of-service guarantees.

Contravariance
See *co/contra/invariance* under *subtyping*.

Control
See *ActiveX*.

CORBA (common object request broker architecture)
See *OMA*.

Covariance
See *co/contra/invariance* under *subtyping*.

COTS (commercial off the shelf)
Category of products, including software components, that are commercially available in pre-packaged form. (Most current software products in this category are applications, operating systems, server products, and middleware products, all of which can be used to build solutions by integration.) Other categories are occasionally formed by following this pattern; for example, GOTS for government off the shelf.

CTS (common type system)
The unifying type system underlying the *.NET Framework*. CLR supports full reflection and other type-based concepts for all types expressible within CTS. CTS is a superset of concepts found in many different languages of object-oriented, procedual, and functional nature. Interoperation between languages is established by means of three hierarchical CTS subsets. This system of CTS subsets is called CLS (common language specification). In increasing order of complexity, CLS defines CLS consumer, CLS producer, and CLS extender languages. A CLS consumer can use all CLS types, but not define new ones. A CLS producer can also define new types, but not extend existing ones. A CLS extender can extend existing types (using multiple interface or single class inheritance).

DCE (distributed computing environment)
A set of standards, now called OSF DCE, originally maintained by OSF (open software foundation), which has been incorporated into the Open Group. *CORBA* defines some inter-ORB protocols based on DCE standards; GUIDs have their roots in DCE UUIDs; and both COM IDL and DCOM build on a number of DCE standards, including DCE IDL. Superseded by CORBA, DCOM, Java RMI, .NET remoting, and web services, DCE is primarily of importance in the context of legacy systems. Nevertheless, there are still a large number of sites that use DCE.

Decomposition
See *Partitioning*.

Deployment
In the context of this book, installation of a *component* into a *component system* without modification of the component. The deployed component is typically acquired from an independent source or developed in-house. The component system combines components from independent sources (principle of *independent extensibility*).

Deserialization
See *Externalization*.

Dispatch
Synonym for dynamic binding.

Dispatch interfaces
Special COM interfaces that allow for dynamic binding.

Effectiveness
See *Efficiency*.

Efficacy
See *Efficiency*.

Efficiency
Degree of resource consumption of an approach or a solution in achieving a desired outcome. Resources in this sense include energy, effort, space, and time. An approach is efficient if it uses minimal resources; an approach is effective if it achieves a desired outcome. Effective approaches can be inefficient, but not vice versa. Effectiveness is also called efficacy. In the space of algorithms and data structures, low complexity yields high efficiency. In the space of architecture and design, high complexity levels can be necessary to yield required levels of efficiency of compliant implementations.

EJB (Enterprise JavaBeans)
The *Java* approach to *contextual composition* in the area of transactional, server-based components. A specification for containers, the services they offer, for EJB components (EJBs) that are hosted by such containers, and for how such EJBs and containers interact. Despite the name, EJBs are unrelated to *JavaBeans* (that is, an EJB is not automatically a JB, nor vice versa).

Encapsulation
Enclosure of a part of the state space of a system, such that only operations enclosed together with that part can effect state changes on that part. Typical units of encapsulation are *objects, classes, modules,* and *packages.*

Ethos
An experimental operating system that supported *independent extensibility* on all levels – from device drivers over schedulers, memory management, file systems, to compound document frameworks, applications, and scripts. The conceptual root of the *BlackBox component framework and builder.*

Events

If a part of a system detects a state change that it expects other parts to be interested in, it can raise an event. Events are propagated using descriptors, called messages or event objects. These descriptors travel from the event source to the interested event sinks. The transport mechanism can be direct as sinks register with sources. Alternatively, it can be indirect and events are sent to a distribution service. Either sinks register with such a service or the service uses a multicasting or broadcasting strategy to locate potentially interested sinks.

Externalization

The mapping of an object's identity and state, including references to other objects, to a serial stream. Also called serialization. The inverse mechanism that maps a stream back to webs of objects is called internalization or deserialization. Fundamental problems of externalization and internalization are support of evolving object implementations without breaking previously externalized files; proper re-establishment of the sharing structure occurring when multiple objects refer to the same third object; protection of an object's encapsulation barrier; partial internalization in the absence of some of the objects' classes (not installed, version clash, and so on).

Factory

An abstraction that creates instances of other abstractions. Examples are factory *methods* and factory *objects*. The *indirection* introduced by factory abstractions allows for late configuration of running systems.

Field

A feature of a *class*.

Fragile base class problem

A problem occurring when a *class* and its subclasses can evolve independently. This is a significant problem when using implementation inheritance across *component* boundaries.

Framework

A partial architecture for a system.

Function

An operation that deterministically returns results solely based on its arguments. A function does not have any effect on state.

Glassbox reuse

See *Blackbox reuse*.

Graybox reuse

See *Blackbox reuse*.

Hardware protection

Isolation of processes or other computing resources using strict hardware protection barriers.

"Has a" relationship

Relationship between an object and one of its conceptually contained objects. Containment is not normally directly expressible in object-oriented languages. Instead, a regular reference to the contained object is used to represent the containment relation (cf. *"is a" relationship*).

History

The conceptual trace of states that would be recorded when tracking all state changes affected by a system under observation. Formal specifications can be formulated in terms of permissible histories. For example, algebraic specifications describe all legal state changes given an established legal (well-formed) history. Such specifications therefore precisely describe all legal ways to reach a valid state from a valid initial state.

HTML (hypertext markup language)

A *W3C* standard that is used to describe the contents and presentation format of web pages.

HTTP (hypertext transfer protocol)

An *IETF* standard enabling generic transport of documents – initially introduced to support transport of HTML-encoded documents. Typically implemented on top of TCP/IP, two further IETF standards.

Hybrid object-oriented programming language

A programming language that supports other programming paradigms besides that of object-oriented programming. Typical hybrid OOPLs add procedural programming. Examples are: C⁺⁺ and Component Pascal.

Identity

A property of *objects*.

IDL (interface definition language)

Used to define an *interface* according to a certain model (usually an *object* model) in a programming language-neutral form. Two prominent examples are *OMG* IDL and *COM* IDL. OMG IDL is based on a traditional object model, where an object has a single interface that can be composed out of other interfaces using multiple interface *inheritance*. The methods of an OMG IDL-described interface are called operations. OMG IDL also supports a set of primitive (non-object) types, such as basic types and a selection of constructed types, including structures, arrays, and sequences. COM IDL is based on the COM object model and is a derivative of the older *DCE* IDL. It does not at all refer to objects or classes, but merely specifies interfaces. A COM object can implement any number of such interfaces. COM IDL supports single interface inheritance as a convenience feature. In both IDLs, *polymorphism* is achieved by separating implementations from interfaces. In OMG IDL, additional polymorphism is achieved via multiple interface inheritance. In COM IDL, additional polymorphism is achieved via subsets of interface sets implemented by objects.

IETF (Internet Engineering Task Force)
A standardization body looking after the bulk of the standards enabling the operation of the internet. Important IETF standards include IP (internet package protocol), TCP (transport control protocol), *HTTP* (hypertext transfer protocol), and SNMP (simple network management protocol).

Indirection
"There is no problem in computer programming that cannot be solved by an added level of indirection" (Maurice Wilkes). The corollary: "There is no performance problem that cannot be solved by eliminating a level of indirection" (Jim Gray). (As quoted in Orfali *et al.*, 1996.)

Immutability
The property that an item does not change over time.

Immutability of components
See *Component*.

Immutability of interfaces
The concept that an *interface* and its specification must no longer be changed once published.

Implementation
A software fragment that implements the operations defined in an *interface*. The implementation has to satisfy its side of the *contract* serving as the interface's specification.

Implementation inheritance
See *Inheritance*.

Inclusion polymorphism
See *Polymorphism*.

Independent extensibility
A key property of *component systems*. As *components* can be independently developed, acquired and deployed, the system is open and cannot be subjected to global analysis. Proper functioning of the whole must be derivable from the parts. Components need to be analyzed (and tested!) individually against the contracts attached as specifications to the interfaces they provide and the interfaces they require. An extreme approach to developing components is *Cleanroom*.

Inheritance
Incorporation of aspects of one abstraction into another, in particular inheritance of interfaces or implementation or both. Inheritance of interfaces under observation of certain rules (*co/contravariance*) leads to formation of *subtypes*. Typical subclassing involves interface and implementation inheritance.

Instance
Abstractions fall into three categories. They are either state-less, operate on a fixed state, or support multiple instances (copies) of the state space. *Functions*

are an example in the first category, abstract data structures one in the second, and abstract data types or *classes* are an example of the third. The instances of classes are called *objects*.

Interface
Abstraction of a service that only defines the operations supported by that service (publicly accessible variables, procedures, or *methods*), but not their *implementation*.

Interface definition language
See *IDL*.

Interface inheritance
See *Inheritance*.

Internalization
See *Externalization*.

Invariant
Formal property expressed over a confined state space and guaranteed to hold at certain static points of a program that can observe (part of) the state space. Important examples are loop, class, and module invariants. A loop invariant is a property over variables modified by a loop that holds on entry into a loop and is either left intact or is re-established by every branch of the loop and, hence, also holds on exit from the loop. A class invariant is a property over fields that always holds on calls to public methods of that class. A module invariant is a property over (part of) the state space introduced by that module, including global variables and fields of classes nested in that module.

"Is a" relationship
See *Substitutability*. Compare with *"has a" relationship*.

J2EE (Java 2 Enterprise Edition)
A collection of specifications, a superset of *J2SE*. J2EE includes *EJB, JMS, JNDI, JSP,* and *Servlets*.

J2ME (Java 2 Micro Edition)
A collection of *Java* specifications targeting small and embedded devices. Not a proper subset of *J2SE*.

J2SE (Java 2 Standard Edition)
A large collection of *Java* specifications. Also includes the Java runtime environment (JRE).

Java
A large set of specifications driven by JavaSoft (Sun) for a language (called Java), many frameworks (Java packages), and infrastructure specifications (such as *EJB*). The specifications are packaged into editions called *J2ME, J2SE,* and *J2EE*. Reference implementations are provided as SDKs (software develop-

ment kits) and platform implementations are provided as JREs (Java runtime environments), which include an implementation of the JVM (Java virtual machine). Java, the language, is a *pure object-oriented programming language*. Java objects are instances of classes. A class inherits implementation from exactly one superclass; the default is class Object. Every Java class can, in addition, implement any number of interfaces. An interface is equivalent to a fully *abstract class*. Java is *type-safe*. A Java package consists of an open set of class files. As Java packages are open constructs, Java is not inherently *module-safe*. Package-level access protection can be subverted by adding a new class file to an existing package and is, in fact, not enforced by the Java verifier. However, module safety can be enforced by simple checks on configurations – the addition of new class files from untrusted sources to existing packages needs to be prevented. Java, therefore, assumes that classes within packages are mutually well-behaved and therefore from a single controlling provider. Java software components are JAR (Java archive) files. A JAR file contains a manifest describing its contents, deployment information, resources, and Java class files, which are compiled Java classes. A Java virtual machine loads and executes such class files.

JavaBeans
A simple component model for Java that aims at *connectable objects* that communicate by events. Multicasts and veto mechanisms are supported. JBs distinguish design-time from runtime, enabling special visual support to be provided by JBs at design-time, collaborating with wiring/assembly tools.

JMS (Java Message Service)
A set of *Java* specifications, part of *J2EE*, that provide access to messaging services.

JNDI (Java Naming and Directory Interface)
A set of *Java* specifications, part of *J2SE*, that provide access to name and directory services. As of version 1.3, JNDI includes support for *LDAP* version 3, *NIS*, and the *CORBA* naming service.

JScript (ECMAScript, JavaScript)
A scripting language introduced by Netscape. Originally called LiveScript, then JavaScript, but bearing only a superficial resemblance to Java. Later standardized by ECMA and, thus, occasionally referred to as ECMAScript. Untyped and not capable of introducing new classes. Includes a powerful eval function that interprets a string as JScript source and evaluates that source in the current context (including local variables). Safety is guaranteed by the execution environment (normally an interpreter).

JSP (Java server pages)
A set of *Java* specifications. JSP defines a textual format for so-called JSP pages and means of processing such pages. A JSP page embeds *Java* code in other

textual formats, typically *HTML*, *XHTML*, or *XML*. A JSP server transforms such a page into a *servlet*, which can then be loaded by a servlet engine to handle requests and send back responses. The most prominent use of JSP today is the creation of HTML pages that contain mutable data.

Juice
Technology developed at the University of California at Irvine that supports platform-independent delivery of Oberon components (*Gazelle*).

JVM (Java virtual machine)
See *Java*.

Late binding
Generally, an approach to defer decisions about the association of parts of a system. Early binding refers to a more static decision, the earliest being at compile-time. Late binding refers to decisions after compile-time, for example at link-time, load-time, or runtime. For example, late binding in the context of *method invocations* refers to the dynamic determination of the *method* implementation to be invoked. The implementation is determined based on the *class* to which the *object* that should handle the method invocation belongs. As variables are dynamically bound to objects of different classes (unless the variable has monomorphic type), the method dispatched on a variable cannot normally be statically resolved. Even later binding occurs when a call to a method of computed name is performed.

LDAP (lightweight directory access protocol)
A family of *IETF* standards. The most widely supported vendor-neutral protocol for accessing naming and directory services.

Memory safety
Property of a system that certain invariants over memory areas are always upheld. The most basic example is address space-based protection in operating systems. Processes are mutually memory safe – that is, cannot directly modify each other's memory areas. (Explicitly shared memory segments are an extension to such models, rather than an exception, because they support more refined invariants.) More elaborate examples aim to protect the memory areas covered by units of encapsulation, such as objects or modules. For example, the Java verifier and the CLR target compilers ensure that no code can be executed that might violate the static type invariants of basic types (such as integers or references) or that might violate the encapsulation boundaries of packages (Java) or assemblies (CLR). (Compare *module safety*, *type safety*, and *type soundness*.)

Message
A unit of data produced by a sender and addressing either a specific receiver or set of receivers or a distribution medium to which receivers can subscribe. Messages can form part of a communication protocol, such as a *method invocation*. A message can also be correlated with an *event*. (Compare *middleware*.)

Message-oriented middleware

See *middleware*.

Metaprogramming

The acting of a system on its own representation using *reflection* of its own structure and effecting changes on this structure. For example, metaprogramming can be used to dynamically create new *classes*, insert them into an existing *inheritance* graph, and then instantiate them.

Method

A feature of a *class*.

Method dispatch

See *Late binding*.

Middleware

Category of software that is neither dedicated to the operation of a specific system (handled by operating systems) nor to the functionality of specific applications. Middleware typically addresses cross-system concerns, such as communication, synchronization, and coordination, that are of importance to multiple applications. Middleware that centers on the disciplined distribution of messages is called message-oriented middleware (MOM). Examples include products by TIBCO and Vitria, IBM's MQ Series, and Microsoft's message queuing services (part of COM+). Middleware that centers on object abstraction and method invocations is called object-oriented middleware (OOM). Examples include *CORBA, DCOM, Java RMI*, and .NET remoting.

Modula-2, Modula-3

See *Component Pascal*.

Module

A closed static unit that *encapsulates* embedded abstractions. Such abstractions include *types*, variables, functions, procedures, or *classes*. As a module is a closed unit, its encapsulated domain is fixed and can be fully analyzed. In a *module-safe* approach, such modules can be used to establish strong invariants that cannot be invalidated by other modules in the same system. Compare with *package*. In many object-oriented languages, a *class* is the largest expressible module. Some languages, such as C++, support the encapsulation of nested classes, thus forming a richer module system.

Module safety

A module-safe programming language enables the programming of *modules* that can establish module *invariants* irrespective of other modules in the system. To be module-safe, a language needs to strictly enforce memory invariants (see *memory safety*) and enable modules to erect static access protection barriers that limit access from external importing modules to certain exported parts of the module. (Compare *type safety* and *type soundness*.)

MOM (message-oriented middleware)
See *Middleware*.

Monomorphic
Opposite of *polymorphic*. The property that a view on entities in a given context always refers to the same kind of entities. For example, a monomorphic variable can only be bound to *objects* of exactly the variable's type, but not to objects of a *subtype*.

MTS (Microsoft transaction server)
Introduced the concept of *contextual composition* to transactional processing. *EJB* containers follow some of the MTS context design. Originally a separate service, MTS later got blended into *COM+*.

MSMQ (Microsoft message queue)
First Microsoft implementation of messaging middleware. Originally a separate service, MSMQ was later blended into *COM+*.

Multiple subtyping
A term coined after *multiple inheritance*, but somewhat misnaming the important property. Creation of multiple subtypes of a type is the normal case. However, multiple subtyping is about types that can have multiple supertypes. On the basis of the definition of types as sets of values, multiple supertypes are easily explained as multiple supersets that all fully include the set defined by the common subtype.

.NET Framework
The Microsoft .NET Framework comprises the common language runtime (CLR), a large number of partially interface, partially class-based frameworks, packaged into *assemblies*, and a number of tools. CLR is an implementation of the common language infrastructure (*CLI*) specification, adding COM+ interoperation and Windows platform access services. In particular, CLR offers dynamic loading and unloading, garbage collection, context interception, metadata reflection, remoting, persistence, and other runtime services that are fully language independent. Presently, Microsoft supports four languages on CLR – $C^{\#}$, *JScript*, Managed C^{++}, and Visual Basic.NET. Assemblies are the units of deployment, versioning, and management in .NET – that is, they are the .NET software components. Side-by-side use of the same assembly in multiple versions is fully supported. Assemblies contain metadata, modules, and resources, all of which are expressed in a platform-independent way. Code in modules is expressed in *CIL* (common intermediate language) that roughly resembles Java, Smalltalk, or Pascal-P bytecode. Unlike these earlier bytecode formats, the one used in assemblies is unsuitable for interpretation. CLR either compiles at install- or load-time, always executing native code. CLR reflection and other type-based concepts cover a large type system space called *CTS* (common type system).

NIS (network information service)

Originally known as Yellow Pages, NIS was introduced by Sun microsystems to make password files and similar information available across a network. The latest version of this service is called NIS+, which improves on NIS's security, speed, availability, and scalability to provide generalized directory and naming services. NIS is one of the services accessible via *JNDI*.

Oberon, Oberon-2

See *Component Pascal*.

Object

An entity that combines state (*fields*) and behavior (*methods*) and has a unique identity – that is, can be consistently distinguished from all other objects of overlapping lifetime and access domain, irrespective of changes to its or other objects' state.

Object linking and embedding

See *OLE*.

Object management architecture

See *OMA*.

Object modeling technique

See *OMT*.

Object Management Group

See *OMG*.

Object-oriented middleware (OOM)

See *Middleware*.

Object-oriented programming (OOP)

Programming that focuses on the design and implementation of *objects*. In particular, OOP builds on the concepts of encapsulation, polymorphism, and implementation inheritance. Contrast this with the key concepts underpinning *component-oriented programming*.

Object server

A process that executes the *component* implementing an *object*.

Object type

A specific kind of *type*.

OCX (OLE custom extension)

See *ActiveX*.

ODBC

OLE database connectivity. Microsoft interfacing standard to connect data consumers to data providers. ODBC found wide multivendor support – almost all database products provide ODBC connectors.

OLE
Microsoft collection of *COM* interfaces supporting compound documents. (Originally, OLE stood for object linking and embedding, but today it is used as a word rather than as an acronym.)

OLE custom extension
See *ActiveX*.

OLEDB
Microsoft collection of *COM* interfaces to facilitate data access to a wide spectrum of data providers, from simple files to full-scale databases. OLEDB replaces the older *ODBC* design For example, OLEDB is used between the query processor and the storage engine of Microsoft SQL Server 2000.

OMA (object management architecture)
The OMA organizes the wide spectrum of standards that the *OMG* is working on. The heart of the OMA is CORBA, the common object request broker architecture. First and foremost, CORBA covers the specification of the interfaces of object request brokers (ORBs). An ORB accepts requests for method invocations and relays them to the addressed object, bridging platform and language gaps. An ORB also provides interface and implementation repositories that make the system fully self-describing (*reflection*). CORBA also covers the binding of programming languages to ORB-understood interfaces. Such interfaces are described in a standardized interface definition language (*IDL*). Today, bindings for Ada, C, COBOL, C++, and Smalltalk exist. A binding for *Java* is about to be finalized (although still based on Java 1.0.2). Further OMA standards are grouped into two areas – general object services (CORBAservices) and general horizontal and vertical (domain-specific) facilities (CORBAfacilities). Important general services include transaction and naming services. Domain-specific standards are under preparation in many areas – banking is an example. CORBA 3 added the CORBA component model (CCM), which is designed to be a superset of *EJB*.

OMG (Object Management Group)
The OMG is a large international standardization body working on a wide range of standards based on the object management architecture (*OMA*). The OMG has around 800 member companies.

OMT (object modeling technique)
A technique to describe object designs graphically. Superseded by *UML*.

Operation
General: collective name for *functions, procedures*, and *methods*. Particular use is as a synonym for method, such as in *OMG IDL* terminology.

Open Group
Member-driven standardization body with around 175 members. Incorporated the Open Software Foundation and with it the OSF *DCE* standard.

Orthogonality

Two features or aspects of a system are orthogonal with respect to some set of properties if choices in their respective domains are independent. For instance, the choice of syntax and semantics for a language with a given abstract syntax is independent, making syntax and semantics orthogonal aspects of that language. As another example, security and messaging services usually do display interdependencies, rendering security and messaging services non-orthogonal in most architectures. (For engineering purposes, it is useful to base orthogonality criteria on a notion of statistical rather than causal independence. For example, adding practical amounts of coloring to two distant parts of an ocean will not cause statistically observable interference – yet, there is a demonstrable causal link at the physical level.)

Package

A package is either closed – that is, a *module* (for example, Ada) – or open (for example, *Java*). An open package can be joined by new abstractions and implementation fragments at any time. Open packages themselves cannot establish strong invariants based on package encapsulation, as, by definition, new parts can join the package at any time. A package needs to be closed before it can be fully analyzed to verify that a given invariant holds. Statically closing a package creates a module. Dynamically closing a package can be used to erect protection barriers in a system with partially open access, for example a web browser combining locally installed Java packages and remotely downloaded packages.

Parametric polymorphism

See *Polymorphism*.

Partitioning

Splitting a system into non-overlapping parts, such that the sum of the parts covers the whole system. In conjunction with *components*, the term decomposition of a composite is also used.

Pattern

A structure that occurs repeatedly in similar form. The pattern description captures the similarity and its typical variations (pattern applications). A prominent example is program design patterns.

Persistence

An object is said to have persistent state if that state survives the particular instantiation of the object. The object itself is said to be persistent if it survives the context in which it was created without losing its identity. Identity preservation requires preservation of references between persistent objects.

Polymorphism

The ability to view different kinds of entities by means of a common projection. For example, various objects of different classes may be compatible with a certain variable type. Then this variable is polymorphically typed, as its bindings can be of varying most specific type. Another example is a polymorphic operation – one that has parameters of polymorphic type. Two main forms of polymorphism are parametric and inclusion polymorphism. Parametric polymorphism assigns a fixed monomorphic type to any instance of a variable, but allows for different type assignments from one instance to the next. Parametric polymorphism is particularly useful for assigning the same type to instances of multiple variables, ensuring mutual compatibility of these variables. Inclusion polymorphism (also called *subtyping*) allows a polymorphic variable of a certain type to be bound to objects of any subtype of the variable's type.

Postcondition
A formal condition that is expected to hold just after completion of an *operation*.

Precondition
A formal condition that is expected to hold just before execution of an *operation*.

Procedure
A self-standing operation that can have effects – that is, modify *state*. Compare with *function* and *method*.

Prototype object
See *Cloning*.

Quality of service
The extra-functional aspects guaranteed under a *contract*. Examples are guaranteed levels of performance, reliability, or security.

Reference type
A specific kind of *type*.

Release-to-release binary compatibility
See *syntactic fragile base class problem*.

Resources of a component
As *components* are units of deployment, they have to come with all resources that are not listed as context dependencies. Such resources may include images or other frozen media used by the component for presentation and user interface purposes. Mutable resources are not included, as they are conceptually associated with concrete instances supported by a component. Thus, a database is not part of a database component, but part of the state maintained by a database object supported by the database component. (A typical database component would contain implementations, classes, for many other objects.) This separation of mutable from immutable persistent state eliminates the management problems resulting from a proliferation of components' versions.

RM-ODP (reference model for open distributed processing)

Joint ISO/IEC and ITU recommendation (X.902) for a reference model for the high-level description of open distributed processing systems (ISO/IEC and ITU, 1995a/b). RM-ODP introduced five viewpoints, each providing sets of concepts, structures, and rules to describe a system from the particular viewpoint's perspective. The viewpoints are enterprise (purpose, scope, policies), information (semantics of information, information processing), computational (functional decomposition), engineering (infrastructure), technology (technology choices for implementation, testing).

Safe language

A programming language is called safe if the artifacts produced using that language achieve certain *safety* levels, provided the language implementation and runtime system are correct. Safety levels include *memory safety*, *type safety*, and *module safety*. For example, Smalltalk is memory-safe, Sather is also type-safe, and Component Pascal is, in addition, module-safe.

Safety

The property of a system to prevent certain failures either by statically eliminating classes of errors or by dynamically detecting errors and handling them to avoid failures.

Safety of a component system

Components are either strictly separated from each other, such as when using *hardware protection*, or need to be individually safe. The principle of *independent extensibility* of component systems excludes global analysis as a means of verifying that the composite is safe, while each of the components would have the potential to be unsafe.

Sandboxing

Exclusion of unwanted side-effects caused by the execution of a component's implementation. Such side-effects can occur if a component has been constructed using a language supporting unsafe access to a low-level memory model. Accidental or malicious interference with memory allocated to a different component endangers the integrity of a component system. Software sandboxing uses conservative checking of code at compile-time, link-time, loadtime, or runtime. To facilitate the last-mentioned, code may need to be interpreted or rewritten at loadtime to incorporate checks. Alternatives to sandboxing are *hardware protection* or the use of *type-safe* and *module-safe* languages.

Script

A program fragment that, on its own, does not introduce any abstractions based on persistent state (cf. *script component*).

Script component

A script component is a degenerated component that merely packages *scripts*.

Semantic fragile base class problem
The subproblem of the general *fragile base class problem* that covers the aspects of semantic incompatibility between different releases.

Serialization
See *Externalization*.

Server
See *Object server*.

Servlets
A *Java* specification. Servlets are components deployable in servlet engines, either standalone (as in the Apache Tomcat implementation) or as part of a *J2EE* server. Servlets are either explicitly programmed in Java or generated by a *JSP* engine.

SOAP (simple object access protocol)
An *XML*-based protocol for requesting services. Essentially, SOAP defines how to marshal arguments to a service invocation as well as results of such an invocation into XML documents that also include envelope information, such as addresses and other protocol-level information, such as authentication or routing information.

SOM (system object model)
IBM technology that evolved out of the OS/2 Workplace Shell into a *CORBA*-compliant *object request broker*. Had unique support for *metaprogramming*. Established release-to-release binary compatibility by maintaining a release order – features are added to classes in a way that preserves offsets and indices assigned to features already present in earlier releases. Clients continue to be able to access such features, even if compiled against an old release, but then (dynamically) linked against a new release. Thus, SOM solved the *syntactic fragile base class problem*.

State
The binding of values to mutable variables at any given point in time.

Static method
See *Procedure*.

Subclassing
See *Inheritance*.

Substitutability
The property that one object can be substituted for another, normally of different type, without breaking the clients of that other object. An object can thus be substituted for another if it respects the *contract* between that other object and its clients. The relationship between an object and another that it can be substituted for is called an *"is a" relation*.

Subtyping

Formation of subtypes of a *type*. As a type is a set of objects and a subtype is a subset of such a set, subtyping can only reduce (narrow) the set of objects. In particular, all operations valid on any object of a certain type are also valid on objects of a subtype. Subtyping is therefore also called interface inheritance. Subtyping is fundamental to inclusion polymorphism, which is the ability to refer to a family of types by statically referring only to the supertype of this family while dynamically retaining the precise types. In strongly typed languages, variables are for their lifetime of a certain type. With subtyping, such variables can actually refer to objects of subtypes of the variables type and this fact can be discovered dynamically.

Subtyping and type matching

Type matching is a relationship between types that is similar to, but different from, subtyping. Type matching effectively distinguishes between monomorphic contexts – when a typed variable can only refer to objects of exactly that type – and polymorphic contexts – when a variable can also refer to objects of subtypes. In monomorphic contexts, the strict co/contravariance requirements of subtyping can be relaxed. For example, if the exact type of two objects is statically known, it is safe to invoke an operation that works for two objects of this type, but not for two objects of (possibly different) subtypes.

Syntactic fragile base class problem

The subproblem of the general *fragile base class problem* that covers the aspects of binary release-to-release compatibility. For example, if method indices for the same methods are not preserved across releases, then clients compiled on the basis of such indices will break.

Trace

See *History*.

Type

A type is a set of values. Subsets of values are characterized by *subtypes* and supersets by supertypes. Operations are said to have a signature that specifies the types of values they operate on. For example, a method specifies, as part of its signature, the type of the receiver (the object the method is dispatched on), the type of all parameters, the return type (if present), and the types of declared (checked) exceptions (if present). The type of an object may require the object to support a certain set of *methods* or *fields*. Object types are typically sets of object references, that is, variables of object type typically contain a reference to an object and not the object itself. Such types are called reference types and equality over reference types is usually expressed as equality of reference values. In contrast, value types are sets of values, where these values are of immediate interest. Equality is typically defined as equality of these values. The process of converting from value to reference types and back is called *boxing* and unboxing, respectively.

Type matching
See *Subtyping*.

Type safety
Property of a language that operations defined over certain types can only be applied to values of these or compatible types. A language is said to be strongly typed if all operations and their arguments are type-safe. It is statically typed if type safety is fully established at compile-time. It is dynamically typed if type safety is established on the basis of runtime checks. Modern object-oriented languages combine aspects of static and dynamic type safety. For example, invoking an operation of computed name and arguments on an arbitrary object is a powerful operation, but it cannot be statically type-checked. (Compare *memory safety* and *type soundness*.)

Type soundness
Property of a language that operations defined over certain types, when applied to values of such acceptable types, can only yield values of the type predicted by the operation's signature. Type soundness implies *type safety*, but not vice versa. For example, both the Java verifier and CLR target compilers ensure that code that is not type-safe will not do any harm. However, neither guarantees type soundness as, under certain circumstances, values (such as object references) are allowed to violate their static type, but code that could use this to do harm is never allowed to execute. (The technical details here are complicated. One class of examples in Java is caused by release-to-release binary compatibility, which allows methods promised by the static type to actually not be supported in an implementation. Attempts to call such missing methods lead to the throwing of an exception.)

UML (unified modeling language)
A merger and refinement of several popular object design notations, including the *OMT*.

Unboxing
Inverse of *boxing*.

Units of <property>
In this book, software fragments are categorized on the basis of properties that hold for an entire fragment. Important properties include those that support separate development, separate static analysis, separate compilability, separate delivery and deployment, and so on. A fragment that satisfies such requirements is called a unit of analysis, a unit of compilation, and so on. See Chapter 8 for a detailed discussion. *Components* are at least units of independent deployment.

Unified modeling language
See *UML*.

URI (universal resource identifier)

An IETF standard (RFC 2396). A URI can be a *URN*, a *URL*, or both. A URI is formed as a pair of a scheme name and an identifier formed according to conventions of that scheme.

URN (universal resource name)

An IETF standard (RFC 2396). A family of formats to textually form names that are required to be globally unique and persistent, even if the named resource ceases to exist. A *GUID* is one valid kind of URN (if preceeded by the scheme "guid:").

URL (universal resource locator)

An IETF standard (RFC 2396). A URL identifies a resource via a representation of its primary access mechanism (such as, its network "location"), rather than identifying the resource by name or by some other attribute(s) of that resource. The most prominent example is *HTTP* URLs used to locate websites. The HTTP scheme requires the locator to be a pair of a domain name and a local resource locator. In http://example.com/overview/default.html, http is the scheme name, example.com the domain name, and overview/default.html the resource locator local to the named domain.

Value type

A specific kind of *type*.

VBX (Visual Basic extension)

See *ActiveX*.

Visual Basic extension

See *ActiveX*.

W3C (Worldwide Web Consortium)

The standardization body looking after standards such as *HTML*, *XML*, and emerging standards such as SVG (scalable vector graphics).

Whitebox reuse

See *Blackbox reuse*.

Wrapper

An *adapter* that fully encapsulates one party. A common approach is to wrap legacy systems to make them comply with some more advanced technology, typically object- or component-oriented.

XHTML

See *XML*.

XLink

See *XML*.

XML (extensible markup language)

XML is a relatively simple concrete, textual syntax representing "forest-structured" documents (where a forest is a sequence of trees). Trees are represented as elements – a pair of tags that enclose the tree's root node and all its subtrees, so tags are always balanced. The opening tag of an element can carry attributes – simple name/value-pairs where all values are expressed as strings. An element can contain nested elements and nested raw data (text). For example, *HTML* can be reformulated to follow stricter rules and then be seen as describing one particular kind of XML documents – the result is called XHTML. There is a large number of backing and affiliated standards and emerging standards around XML. For example, XML documents that describe the structural and type constrains for other XML documents, called schemas, are captured using XML Schema. References to particular elements inside XML documents are expressed using XML Path (XPath) or XML Pointer (XPointer). Links among XML documents can be expressed using XML Linking (XLink). Presentation information, which is not normally embedded in XML documents (unlike HTML), can be captured using XML stylesheet language (XSL). Certain transformations of XML documents can be described using XSLT (XSL transforms) – an approach originally introduced to apply XSL sheets to XML documents, but that is actually much more general.

XML Schema

See *XML*.

XPath

See *XML*.

XPointer

See *XML*.

XSL (XML stylesheet language)

See *XML*.

XSLT (XSL transforms)

See *XML*.

Index

Realizing eBusiness with Components

Paul Allen

Unfortunately, there is a great deal of hype and over-expectation surrounding e-business. Many organizations are jumping on the e-business bandwagon without understanding what they are getting into. Lack of planning and analysis, resulting in inflexible solutions that are unable to integrate with existing systems, are all too common. At the same time, e-business calls for a closer relationship between those involved in business development and those required to support these initiatives within the company's information technology infrastructure.

This book is designed to provide practical advice for planning, analysis and design of e-business systems using component-based development (CBD). Just as e-business is more than a series of web pages, so CBD is not just an approach to problem-solving using software building blocks. It includes architectures, processes, modeling techniques, economic models and organizational guidelines, all of which are well placed to ease migration of large organizations to e-business.

The author defines the key concepts relating to CBD, and introduces component standards, component frameworks, middleware and all the relevant internet technologies. The book also deals with issues such as the business case for adopting CBD, pragmatic approaches to modeling business requirements, putting CBD to work using the Catalysis process, migrating to CBD from legacy systems, and the issues associated with sourcing components from off-the-shelf purchasing to bespoke design.

This book shows you:

- how to obtain commitment for a CBD strategy at board level
- how to deploy catalysis modeling techniques and other commercial approaches
- how to use component modeling techniques to create innovative eBusiness solutions
- how to gain competitive advantage with TNBT and Collaborative Commerce

The core of the book is an extensive example that tracks the experiences of a typical company, with a traditional set of business processes and supporting software systems, through various stages along the road to e-business.

ISBN 0 201 67520 X

Visit us on the world wide web at
www.it-minds.com
www.awprofessional.com

Find more information about the **Component Software Series** at
www.awprofessional.com/series/index.asp